THE PAST BEFORE US: HISTORICAL TRADITIONS OF EARLY NORTH INDIA

ROMILA THAPAR

The Past Before Us: Historical Traditions of Early North India

Harvard University Press
Cambridge, Massachusetts
London, England
2013

Printed in the United States of America

First published in India by Permanent Black, 2013

First Harvard University Press edition, 2013

Typeset in Gandhari by Guru Typograph Technology, Dwarka, New Delhi

Library of Congress Cataloging-in-Publication Data

Thapar, Romila.
The past before us : historical traditions of early north India / Romila Thapar. — First Harvard University Press edition.
pages cm
Includes bibliographical references and index.
ISBN 978-0-674-72523-2 (cloth : alk. paper)
1. India, Northeastern—Historiography. 2. India, Northeastern—History—To 1500. 3. Literature and history—India, Northeastern. 4. Collective memory—India, North. I. Title.
DS483.65.T53 2013
934.0072—dc23 2013013539

In memoriam

D. D. Kosambi
Arnaldo Momigliano

friends and mentors

Contents

MAPS AND TABLES

*Maps of Locations of the More Important Places, Clans,
and Dynasties*

Tables

Preface

This book has been many years in the making, for it simmered whilst other ideas took shape and form in various publications. Inevitably therefore I have many people to thank and much to acknowledge.

My interest in historiography began in the 1960s but remained without focus. This was largely because historians in India at that time, with a couple of exceptions, were dismissive of the subject, although my earlier conversations with D.D. Kosambi and reading his writings had made me realize the centrality of historiography.

The Mary Talbot Fellowship at Lady Margaret Hall (LMH), Oxford, in 1967 initiated the process more purposefully. My interest became better defined that year through discussions with Professor Arnaldo Momigliano, who ran a seminar on the theme at University College, London. He introduced me to *History and Theory* and other studies of the historiographies of early societies and encouraged my interest in historiography. Further explorations resulted from conversations with Eric Hobsbawm, whom I first met as an undergraduate when I attended his lectures at Birkbeck College, London. I returned frequently to LMH and especially enjoyed my conversations, as I still do, with Susan Reynolds, and I am sorry that Anne Whiteman and Rosalie Collie are no longer around to discuss the contents of this book.

I gradually began reading texts of the ancient period from the perspective of historiographical analysis. The reading has continued over the last four decades with the discovery on each reading that there were many further genres of writing that could be examined. There were of course ventures into other themes during this time. Nevertheless this reading remained constant, with the publication of some occasional papers on historiography.

A period at Cornell in 1974 where I gave some seminars on the theme added other dimensions, particularly from the comments of Leighton Hazlehurst and Oliver Wolters. A Nehru Fellowship during 1976 and 1977 provided the opportunity for some tangential research which was published in 1984 as *From Lineage to State*. The thesis of this earlier book is seminal for the first part of the present one. A semester at Peradeniya University in Sri Lanka in 1978 led to discussions on Buddhist historiography with Sirima Kiribamune and the late Leslie Gunawardana. These discussions evoked earlier conversations with Lakshman Pereira. I have also had the benefit over the years of conversations on the subject with the late Frits Staal, and with Thomas Trautmann, Herman Kulke, Daud Ali, and Robert and Sally Goldman.

An earlier version of this theme was given as the Radhakrishnan Lectures at Oxford in 1987 and as a series of lectures at the College de France in Paris in the same year. I also enjoyed trying out my ideas on various colleagues in the Centre for Historical Studies of the Jawaharlal Nehru University, which I hope they did not regard as a terrible imposition. More recently, Kumkum Roy and Kunal Chakrabarti have gallantly read and commented on lengthy chapters, as has Naina Dayal, comments that have helped me in organizing data and arguments. I would also like to thank Nivita Kakria, who helped to prepare the Bibliography and the Index. And special thanks to Rukun Advani, for his meticulous editing, for the questions he asked which helped me clarify what I was saying, as also for his patience and accommodation with my ineptitude in handling the many problems I had with the computer.

Work on other categories of texts as part of this project was carried out later on an ICSSR Fellowship in 1988–9 and a Bhabha Senior Research Fellowship in 1992–3. My ideas on this subject then hibernated for a while whilst I published on other themes. But the period of hibernation led to reformulations and new ways of looking at the subject. The most recent period of intensive reading and writing on early Indian historiography, which helped me formulate many thoughts included here, was as a Fellow of the Nehru Memorial Museum and Library, and at the Library of Congress during 2003–4, and also when I held an Indian Council for Historical Research (ICHR) National Fellowship, 2007–9.

I would like to apologize for the length of this book, but to some extent this was required, given the widespread denial that early India can provide evidence of a sense of history. This statement, in fact, is what I came to see as largely irrelevant with the realization that every society sees its past in a particular way, which it may refer to as history or not, but which is relevant to understanding that society. The enjoyment in discovering nuances in the texts that were new to me, and trying to follow up some of the questions I was beginning to formulate, made me return again and again to the theme.

I have not compared the various recensions of the texts, although such comparisons have considerable historiographical value, as it would have made the reading for and the writing of this book impossibly long. It can in any case be better done by examining the historiographical context of each text in greater detail.

Given the length of the book it would doubtless help if I explained how the argument proceeds, although I can only do so briefly at this stage. In the first chapter I have discussed the reasons for it being said that there was no historical writing in early India. The second chapter indicates what made it possible to question this view and what I believe were the main historical traditions. I thought it appropriate at this point to provide the direction of my argument so as to facilitate the reading of my perspective on the chosen texts. The remaining fifteen chapters discuss various categories of texts, moving from embedded history to historical texts, and which hopefully illustrate my argument. The concluding chapter is an attempt to set out briefly what I understand of the early Indian historical tradition.

The subject considered here has immense variations because of the variety of genres in which the texts are written. This complicates the argument since each genre has it own characteristic way of recording the past. I have tried to draw out a series of propositions which I hope will hold. Whether or not these propositions will be largely acceptable is perhaps not as important as the real purpose of the book, namely, to create an interest in looking at these questions and relating them to the texts of early India since they provide new facets in its study.

ROMILA THAPAR
SEPTEMBER 2012

Acknowledgements

Given the length of time it has taken to research and write this book, some chapters inevitably draw on material from earlier papers, and material from some parts of other chapters has been used in writing papers on the subject.

The latter consist of a paper, "The *Dāna-stuti* Hymns of the *Ṛgveda*", in S. Pollock (ed.), *Epic and Argument in Sanskrit Literary History*, Delhi, 2010, 235–54, which draws on material from Chapter 3; and "Chiefdoms and Early Kingdoms in the Mahabharata" (forthcoming), which draws on material from Chapter 4.

Earlier versions of the theme of Chapter 5 have been published in "The Ramayana: Theme and Variation", in S.N. Mukherjee (ed.), *India: History and Thought*, Calcutta, 1982, 221-53. This was republished in Romila Thapar, *Cultural Pasts*, Delhi, 2000, 647–579; it also borrows from my lecture *Exile and the Kingdom,* Bangalore, 1978, and is partially reflected in "Epic and History: Tradition, Dissent and Politics in India", *Past and Present*, 1989, 125, 3-26. It was developed further in "Variants as Historical Statements: The Rama-katha in Early India", in H.L. Seneviratne (ed.), *The Anthropologist and the Native: Essays for Gananath Obeyesekere*, Florence, 2009, 349-94.

An earlier version of Chapter 6 was published as "Genealogical Patterns as Perceptions of the Past", *Studies in History*, January–June 1991, 7, 1, 1-36.

A paper published as "A *Vaṃśāvalī* from Chamba: Reflections on a Historical Tradition", in *India and Indology: Past, Present and Future*", Kolkata, 2000, 581-92, draws on material used in Chapter 16.

Chapter 7 is a revised and expanded version of a paper on the same subject entitled "Inscriptions as Historical Writing in Early India: Third Century BC to Sixth Century AD", in A. Feldherr and G. Hardy (eds), *The Oxford History of Historical Writing*, vol. I: Beginnings to AD 600, Oxford, 2011, 577-600.

Footnotes provide the minimum necessary information. Publication details of the sources cited are given in the Bibliography, which is divided into two sections—primary sources and secondary sources. Footnoted citations of primary sources provide the source name, the editor's name where required, the volume number, and the pages or folios—e.g. *Dasaratha-rājaputta*, in V. Fausboll, *The Jātaka*, vol. VI, 558; citations of secondary sources show the name of the author or editor, the book or essay title, the volume number where required, and the page numbers—e.g. E.J. Rapson (ed.), *The Cambridge History of India*, vol. I, 57; H.H. Wilson, "Analysis of the Puranas", *JRAS*, V, 61ff. In cases where a source does not include the author's name (making it impossible to trace the item in the Bibliography), the footnote provides the required bibliographical information—e.g. Nanyaura Plate A of Dhaṅga, *Ind. Ant.*, 1887, XVI, 201-4. Full names of journals cited in abbreviated form in the footnotes and Bibliography can be found in the list of abbreviations below.

Sanskrit, Pāli, and Prākrit words, whether familiar or not, have been transliterated using the standard forms of diacritical marks and spellings—e.g. *brāhmaṇa* instead of brahmin. Place names in current use do not have diacritics—e.g. Varanasi. Where nouns are used as qualifiers—e.g. Puranic—they do not have diacritics.

Abbreviations

ABORI	*Annals of the Bhandarkar Oriental Research Institute*
AHR	*American Historical Review*
AJIAI	*African Journal of the International African Institute*
Anth. SI	*Anthropological Survey of India*
ARE	*Annual Report on Epigraphy*
ASI	*Archaeological Survey of India*
ASIAR	*Archaeological Survey of India—Annual Reports*
ASR	*Archaeological Survey Reports*
ASS	Anandasram Sanskrit Series
ASWI	*Archaeological Survey of Western India*
BEFEO	*Bulletin de l'École Francaise d'Extreme-Orient*
BEI	*Bulletin des Études Indiennes*
BSOAS	*Bulletin of the School of Oriental and African Studies*
CII	*Corpus Inscriptionum Indicarum*
Contributions	*Contributions to Indian Sociology*
CSSH	*Comparative Studies in Society and History*
DED	*Dravidian Etymological Dictionary*
EJVS	*Electronic Journal of Vedic Sudies*

Ep. Ind.	*Epigraphia Indica*
EPW	*Economic and Political Weekly*
EW	*East and West*
FEQ	*Far Eastern Quarterly*
HR	*History of Religions*
HT	*History and Theory*
IAR	*Indian Archaeology—A Review*
IESHR	*Indian Economic and Social History Review*
IHQ	*Indian Historical Quarterly*
IHR	*Indian Historical Review*
IIJ	*Indo-Iranian Journal*
Ind. Ant.	*Indian Antiquary*
JAH	*Journal of African History*
JAOS	*Journal of the American Oriental Society*
JAS	*Journal of Asian Studies*
JASB	*Journal of the Asiatic Society of Bengal*
JBBRAS	*Journal of the Bombay Branch of the Royal Asiatic Society*
JESHO	*Journal of the Economic and Social History of the Orient*
JESI	*Journal of the Epigraphical Society of India*
JIH	*Journal of Indian History*
JIP	*Journal of Indian Philosophy*
JOI	*Journal of the Oriental Institute (Baroda)*
JRAIGBI	*Journal of the Royal Anthropological Institute of Great Britain and Ireland*
JRAS	*Journal of the Royal Asiatic Society*
JUB	*Journal of the University of Bombay*
MAS	*Modern Asian Studies*

MASI	*Memoirs of the Archaeological Survey of India*
P and P	*Past and Present*
PTS	Pāli Text Society
SLJH	*Sri Lanka Journal of the Humanities*
ZDMG	*Zeitschrift der Deutschen Morgenländischen Gesellschaft*

PART I

The Search for a Historical Tradition

1

Searching for Early Indian Historical Writing

1. The Diversity of Historical Traditions

Generalizations about the nature of a society or civilization, when they take root, spread adventitiously. A couple of hundred years ago it was stated that Indian civilization was unique in that it lacked historical writing and, implicitly therefore, a sense of history. With rare exceptions, there has been little attempt since to examine this generalization. So entrenched is the idea now that one almost hesitates to argue for a denial of this denial of history. I would like to suggest that while there may not in the early past have been historical writing in the forms currently regarded as belonging properly to the established genres of history, many texts of that period reflect a consciousness of history. Subsequently, there come into existence recognizable forms of historical writing. Both varieties of texts—those which reflect a consciousness of history and those which reveal forms of historical writing—were used in early times to reconstruct the past, and were drawn upon as a cultural, political, religious, or other such resource at various times, in various situations, and for a variety of reasons. To determine what makes for this historical consciousness is not just an attempt to provide Indian civilization with a sense of history, nor is it an exercise in abstract research. My intention is to argue that, irrespective of the question of the presence or absence of historical writing as such, an understanding of the way in which the past is perceived, recorded, and used affords insights into early Indian society, as it does for that matter into other early societies.

Historical consciousness begins when a society shows consciousness of both past and future, and does so by starting to record the past. "There is no more significant pointer to the character of a society than the kind of history it writes or fails to write."[1] To argue over whether a particular society had a sense of history or not on the basis of our recognition of the presence or absence of a particular kind of historical tradition—one which has been predetermined as being properly historical in perpetuity—seems somewhat beside the point. It is more purposeful to try and ascertain what each culture regards as its historical tradition and why it does so; and to analyse its constituents and functions as well as assess how it contends with competing or parallel traditions.

Historical traditions emanate from a sense of the past and include three aspects: first, a consciousness of past events relevant to or thought of as significant by a particular society, the reasons for the choice of such events being implicit; second, the placing of these events in an approximately chronological framework, which would tend to reflect elements of the idea of causality; and third, the recording of these events in a form which meets the requirements of that society.

Such a definition does not necessarily assume that political events are more relevant than other sorts of events, although as issues of power they tend to be treated as such. If the above definition is acceptable, then it can in fact be said that every society has a concept of the past and that no society is a-historical. What needs to be understood about a historical tradition is why certain events are presumed to have happened and receive emphasis, and why a particular type of record is maintained by the tradition.

A distinction may therefore be made between the existence of a historical tradition and a philosophy of history. The latter may follow the former. An awareness or confirmation of a philosophy of history may make a historical narrative more purposeful. But such a narrative does not thereby necessarily express greater

[1] E.H. Carr, *What is History?*, 43.

historical veracity: narratives based on the theory that history is determined by divine intervention are fired by purpose rather than by the sifting of evidence. On the other hand, a historical tradition may not concern itself with either divine purpose in history or any other philosophical notion of history and yet be an authentic record—if not of actual events, certainly of believed assumptions about the past.

A historical tradition is created from the intellectual and social assumptions of a society. Consciously selected events are enveloped in a deliberately created tradition which may only be partially factual. An attempt to understand the tradition has to begin by relating it to its social function, to ask the question: "What purpose was served by creating and preserving this tradition?" And, flowing from this, to see how a changing society made use of the tradition.

Historical traditions emerge from and reflect their social context, and the context may produce and extend to a broad range of social forms. Within these forms, history is generally the record of recognizable socio-political groups. Historical writing in such cases tends to incorporate a teleological view, even if it seems to be only a narrative of events. So, cultural symbols and stereotypes have a role in delineating the past.

Studying a tradition involves looking at a number of indices: first, the point in history at which the need to create and keep a tradition becomes imperative; second, the social status of the keepers of a tradition; third, whether the tradition was embedded in sacred literature to ensure its continuity; fourth, the genres that emerged in order to record the tradition independent of other literary forms; fifth, the social context in which the historical tradition was composed and the changes that it underwent when society itself changed; sixth, the audience for which any specific text of that tradition was intended; seventh, the social groups which used or manipulated the tradition, and their reasons for doing so; for, above all, such a tradition legitimizes the present and gives it sanction.

Together, these constitute the broad framework of analysis for the texts and traditions that I examine in the book. Flowing from the framework, certain key questions recur or are implicit during the examination of a text or tradition: does it provide an instance of a past authorship looking further back into a more distant past in order to record or interpret that past? Can it be seen as outlining a sense of time and/or a fresh chronology of past and sometimes a future time? Can we detect in the material the deployment of historical events or the construction of narratives that are at bottom historical for hegemonic purposes or for cultural and political legitimation?

The precise point at which a historical tradition emerges is often difficult to determine. Initially, it may take an oral form. When, with increased literacy, it comes to be written, its form may change. Each generation prunes its historical tradition in accordance with what it believes to be most worthy of preservation, thus making it virtually impossible to locate the tradition's starting point. Examining the process of reformulation and pruning is, of course, of interest in its own right. Every explanation of the past is coloured by values existing at the time of the explanation. Periodic explanations of the same event introduce new interpretations, and these become the basis of historiography. The interpretations are conditioned by the social and intellectual background of the compiler of the tradition. Historical tradition, therefore, refers to those aspects of the past, recorded orally or in texts, which are consciously transmitted from generation to generation carrying the sanction of antiquity and a believed historicity. Historical writing, when it emerges, can question that believed historicity. But it need not always, and does not if it is building on such foundations of belief.

The existence of historical traditions then relates less to historical writing and more to historical consciousness. Such consciousness implies the need to refer to a past, perhaps even to construct a past, for the past has a social function.[2] Societies are

[2] Freud argues that to construct is to make out what has been forgotten from the traces left behind. He also raises the question of whether this is construction

aware of their past, or, more correctly, of their many pasts, and communities have constantly to situate themselves in relation to the past.[3] The past is therefore a permanent dimension of human identity, although its constructions and contents can change with new definitions of identity. This is sometimes demonstrated by the existence or appearance of variant readings of the past; it becomes particularly apparent when there is an official version which differs from other versions. The meaning of such constructions is not always apparent, requiring historians to reach behind the symbols. Because the past is often constructed from the perspective of the present it can become an attempt, sometimes subconsciously, to intertwine the present with past society.

To ask why a society records an event, and in what form, involves understanding some of the ideological debates of the past. A tradition is created and taken forward, but it often needs reformulation in accordance with later requirements. This process then constitutes a historical tradition—although not necessarily history. The narrative is given a chronological framework, and the explanations of events assume some causal connections. Proving the veracity of the record is at this point less crucial than examining the nature of its construction. History, or historical writing in the forms that we now acknowledge as history, emerges from such historical traditions.

A historical tradition has to claim that what it narrates are events that happened in the past, a claim which differentiates it from fiction. Such constructions of the past draw either on a transmission which is said to have been handed down, or on witnesses who, while writing about contemporary events, are also aware of posterity as an audience. The tradition seeks to provide origins, and it claims that its explanations are valid for all time. But, as noted earlier, the tradition can change over time, partly on account of the many ways in which the past is used in the present. Historical consciousness is not therefore reflected whimsically

---

or reconstruction by making a comparison with archaeologists who reconstruct from excavated evidence. S. Freud, "Constructions in Analysis", 255–70.

[3] E.J. Hobsbawm, "The Social Function of the Past: Some Questions", 3–18.

via just any sort of construction of past times. The construction has a function, it claims historicity, and it implies some degree of causation.

Our reading of the nature of historical perceptions manifest within a tradition also has to relate to a range of evidence on the society contemporary with the period of the perceptions: else our reading will be arbitrary. The perspectives and perceptions that constitute a historical tradition can be juxtaposed to observe how some either conflict with others, or possibly incorporate and reformulate them.

To reiterate: it is not my intention to prove the historical authenticity of what is being narrated about the past in early Indian texts. Therefore, whether or not early Indian society produced historical writing of a kind that we are now familiar with is not my question. My concern is with trying to read some of the perceptions of historical consciousness in the texts from early Indian society. These, I suggest, can provide clues to how that society viewed its past and why it did so. Such a project can enlarge our understanding of how their historical perceptions reflect the societies of that time.

This kind of inquiry may also help us understand the texts that purport to represent the past, why they took the form they did, and what within the past was of central importance to their authors. I would like to explain why the supposed absence of a sense of history in these texts is not a significant question.

Three kinds of enquiries may seem appropriate at this point. One is that since historical traditions emanating from diverse cultures will inevitably differ, comparisons between traditions have to be made more precisely than they have tended to be. Historical writing is in fact better viewed initially within its historiographical context, for it varies from one society to another ranging from being either apparent or minimal. Another aspect pertains to why it was necessary for historians to argue, in the last couple of centuries, that Indian civilization lacked a sense of history. Even more important, and what is in effect the most substantial, has to do with the nature of representations of the past in the texts of the early Indian historical tradition.

2. Recent Evaluations of Early European Historical Traditions

The obsession in the nineteenth century with history as central to civilization was derived from the conviction that every branch of knowledge had to have a history. History was the path into that knowledge, whether it was geology or botany or astronomy or any other. Therefore, a people without history were a people without knowledge. Notions of the history of a civilization also derived from humanist traditions which maintained that there was a unified European identity central to European thought. This identity was said to show continuity from the Greeks to modern Europe, and was meant to be accessible in European literature, especially in texts that pertained to the past.[4] Similar notions of identity, supposedly unifying all societies, were sought in the historical writing of other civilizations. Such views have undergone some reconsiderations in recent times. The views as well as the reconsiderations are pertinent to the history of historical writing.

The discussion of historical writing in ancient societies begins by convention with the Greeks. In effect, there are earlier traditions in Mesopotamia. In China, such writing was based on the records of scribes and culminated in the work of Sima Qian, who in the second century AD records events that he considers important and includes biographies of persons on whom he bestows fame whenever he thinks fit. As with the Greeks and Indians, cosmological time in his work is cyclical. Records of the past are treated as a major source of knowledge and were essential to the training of bureaucrats and civil servants. The editing of various annals was a way of pruning history. Characterized by concrete analogical thinking, Sima Qian's work draws on questions of ethics and causation.[5] Another view maintains that China had historical writing

[4] A. Ahmad, "Orientalism and After", 98–116; idem, *In Theory: Classes, Nations, Literatures*.

[5] C.C. Huang, "The Defining Characteristics of Chinese Historical Thinking", 180–8.

but was preoccupied with didacticism, and therefore less with a critical spirit and historical consciousness. The argument is that the difference between the "past" and "history" is not apparent.[6]

The Greco-Roman tradition was viewed as quite independent of antecedents, although more recent scholarship suggests possible traces of Mesopotamian ideas in the formulation of the early Greek tradition. Mesopotamian king-lists and chronicles of a later period are sometimes viewed as precursors of Greek writing. The authenticity of the king-lists, or for that matter the epic of Gilgamesh, has been under scrutiny. The Sumerian historical tradition has some roots in "omen literature", with divination based on the entrails of sacrificed animals, the reading of which was said to be linked to historical events. Parallels can be seen in the Chinese reading omens from "oracle bones".

Greco-Roman writing on the past, and to some degree on contemporary times, was said to be historical because it was believed to be factual and drew on rational explanations. Recent analytical studies of Greek and Roman historiography suggest that, in their representations of the past, history and fiction were interwoven. The term *historia* in Greek referred originally to an enquiry into a matter, perhaps controversial or emotionally charged.[7] Gradually, this grew into a literary genre, showing the predominance within it of narrative. It has been said that "history was not a philosophical problem to the Greeks and the Romans", and that "the idea of history then, was not understood as being dependent upon or derivative from the idea of time. Moreover there was not a universal Greek view of time as a link . . ."[8] It has also been argued that "if one starts by distinguishing between Oriental or mythical or mythologizing historiography and a rational and scientific historiography which strictly sticks to sources and facts, it is questionable whether Thucydides can be counted among the latter."[9] This may be a somewhat harsh judgement, but it is all

[6] Q.E. Wang, "Is There a Chinese Mode of Historical Thinking? A Cross-Cultural Analysis", 201–9.

[7] F.M. Cornford, *Thucydides Mythhistoricus*.

[8] G.A. Press, "History of the Development of the Idea of History in Antiquity", 280–96.

[9] W. den Boer, "Greco-Roman Historiography in its Relation to Biblical and Modern Thinking", 60–75.

the same worth considering. Herodotus, for example, did not sift fact from myth in his comments about Persia and India. It is often forgotten that Herodotus was frequently accused of lying, in part because he used the oral tradition quite extensively. This was not unusual, there being no precise test of factuality at that time.[10] As Momigliano has pointed out, later writers such as Manetho and Plutarch did not accept Herodotus's statements.[11] This is an early example of inconsistencies between oral and textual data which are now recognized as inconsistencies of both genre and content.

Paul Veyne makes the point that the Greeks did not differentiate between primary and secondary sources,[12] and this would apply to many writings from early societies. History here is born as tradition and not as having to be built up from source material. Herodotus did not know the Persian of the sources that he refers to. Nor were histories of ancient times interested in theories of explanation. These were part of a general notion of causes, even if a rather subconscious part. History involved collating information, and events were judged by internal criteria. The citing of sources at this time was, ironically, more important to theology.

Texts of these ancient traditions tend to focus on recent events which were treated from the perspective of contemporary concerns. Collingwood's statement bears reflection not only with reference to Greek writing but also to the historical perceptions of many past cultures: "One might almost say that in ancient Greece there were no historians in the sense in which there were artists and philosophers; there were no people who devoted their lives to the study of history; the historian was only the autobiographer of his generation and autobiography is not a profession."[13] Thucydides did at least emphasize the significance of political events and evaluate premises as the basis for information.

Records from the ancient European world gave attention to genealogy, causality, sequential narrative, and time-reckoning.

[10] A. Momigliano, "Greek Historiography", 1–23.

[11] A. Momigliano, "The Place of Herodotus in the History of Historiography", 1–13.

[12] P. Veyne, *Did the Greeks Believe in their Myths?*

[13] R.G. Collingwood, *The Idea of History*, 26.

The Greek perception of their own past and identity was tied to the projection of the "Other"—the non-Greek-speaking barbarian, living in a different territory with a different ethnicity and culture. This made the consciousness of claiming a historical past more acute.

Polybius and other Roman historians were concerned with rhetorical preoccupations and political motives. The latter took the form of imperial history in later writing. In recounting the past, Roman writing was more closely tied to the requirements of the state and reflects the perception of the upper echelons of society because of the nature of what it selects from the past.[14]

3. Europe and its Christian Historical Traditions

Some have argued that to the Greek mind, as against the Jewish and Christian, history was of minor interest. Jewish writing was contemporary with the Roman and there was occasionally an appropriation of the earlier tradition into the Jewish format.[15] With the coming of history infused by Judaism and Christianity, beginning with Eusebius and Jerome and culminating with Augustine, over the third to the fifth centuries AD, the notion of history from European antiquity shaping the present was virtually set aside. The fallout effect of this can be seen in histories of medieval European times, such as that of Bede in the eighth century. History was now a record of the power of God and of the actions of God in human affairs, with divinity guiding destiny and the reflection of both being presumably through the Christian Church. Based on the Bible, eschatology was an essential feature, providing teleology from the Garden of Eden to Judgement Day, and incorporating the latter as the ultimate end of history. A distinctive historical tradition also emerges when there is a contestation with the views of the Other, and in the case of Church histories there were many Others, the

[14] A. Momigliano, "Polybius and Posidonius", in idem, *Alien Wisdom: The Limits to Hellenism.*

[15] A. Momigliano, *The Classical Foundations of Modern Historiography*, 29.

Jewish historical tradition being among these. Competing histories represent an indirect way of staking a claim to the resources of society.[16] A new narrative of the past which competes with the one that is dominant is usually a discursive strategy by a social group to lay claim to power.

Ecclesiastical history was different from the Greco-Roman as it presupposed revelation, and history was made subservient to revelation. The destiny of man now lay in the actions of the Church. Eusebius made a distinction between the history of the state and of the Church. The latter drew from aspects of earlier Jewish historical writing, such as that of Josephus of the first century AD, where revelation and the command of God were intrinsic to recording the past. Given that the God was a single jealous God, revelation was in essence an unquestionable statement. Church history was supported by the patronage of the aristocracy and of those of learning, and by monasteries which had become powerful institutions. When monasteries emerged as centres of authority, they tended to undermine secular authority.[17] Chronicles of regions fed the importance of political history, but in them power was often seen through the prism of the Church. These also referred themselves to certain concepts of succession—both of kings and bishops; of orthodoxy and deviations; and of quoting sources as testimony to a statement. But above all, history was intended to support dogma.

Apart from ecclesiastical history in medieval Europe, there were texts on the histories of aristocratic families. These narrated the antecedents of elite groups. Geoffrey of Monmouth in the twelfth century traced ruling families back to the heroes of the Roman epics such as Aeneas. Joachim of Fiore of the same period emphasized chronological placements and discussed events pertaining to the theory of the six ages, or time periods, as envisaged at that point, sometimes given a theological dimension. Chronologies and concepts of time had been important to both Augustine in *De Civitate Dei* (fourth century) and to Bede's *History of the English Church and People* (ninth century). Although not divorced from

[16] F. Furedi, *Mythical Past, Elusive Future*.

[17] A. Momigliano, "Christianity and the Decline of the Roman Empire".

theology, there was nevertheless by the twelfth century a gradual breaking away from it.[18] Chronicles and biographies moved in a more secular direction.

Historiography now becomes important to Europe because the Judeo-Christian religions required the authenticating of certain traditions. This made history decisive. Subsequently, this pattern of history was to influence the provision of a community identity to the nations of Europe as they emerged. Notions of physical and biological evolution as explanations simultaneously sought parallels in historical data.[19]

A departure from involving only the Church in history writing was introduced in Renaissance writing, which shows an initial focus on Greek and Latin texts encouraging the possibility of reconnecting with this past. The Renaissance view of history from the fifteenth century results in attempts at a continuous narrative from Greek times. Antiquarianism, as well as the visibility of Greco-Roman remains, strengthened the ideas of continuity and connectedness. It took a more secular form with the Enlightenment a couple of centuries later, rational analysis and human activity being seen as the pivot of the universe. Every human activity had a history. The intellectuals of the Renaissance and Enlightenment—Bodin, Bacon, Descartes, and Vico—were dismissive of earlier Classical history, instead emphasizing empirical evidence and rational explanation. A new periodization was sought, historical veracity underlined, and the earlier insistence on revealed truth subordinated to reason. This encouraged the primacy of the idea of progress wherein Judeo-Christian teleology was converted to a secular one. These changes allowed for what was to follow, with explanations of how and why events occurred in the past becoming the major enterprise of historians.

What needs underlining is the change in European historiography at the point where history, as constituted in the Greco-Roman tradition, was substantially diverted to other functions in Christian Europe. Generalizations can hardly be made about a single, unified sense of history in the West. Furthermore, the understanding

[18] R.W. Southern, "Aspects of the European Tradition of Historical Writing", 159–79.

[19] A. Momigliano, "History and Biography", 155–84.

among historians of what constitutes a historical consciousness is different now, as compared to what it was a century ago. This change is also of significance when we look at Indian texts. The same evidence can be read differently, depending on the nature of the enquiry, and the question then is of evaluating the reading.

4. The Islamic Traditions

In Europe the change was from the Greco-Roman, to medieval Christianity, to the Enlightenment. Each of these historiographies had many strands. What is often referred to as "Islamic historiography" also had diverse strands, of which at least three can be recognized. Historical writing in Arabic drew on Islamic thought, although again not barring the imprint of other prior ways of looking at the past—such as the Hebraic and Christian—which were incorporated into the Islamic. Statements supposedly emanating from divine sources were taken as true and therefore treated as authoritative, and there had to be a clear chain of transmission. Persian historical writing carried a different legacy, that of the Zoroastrian and Manichaean prior to the Islamic. It hinted at a more secular history, with enquiry holding a respectable position in readings of the past. The Turks and the Afghans, as the third component, inherited Shamanism and Buddhism before incorporating Islam into their cultural legacy. Such diversity produced history with variable nuances, and these were important, for example, to the internalizing of Islamic historiography in India.

The better-known texts of Islamic historiography are contemporary with the later Church histories of Europe, but they emerged independently. Among the Persian histories the most familiar is the *Shahnameh* of Firdausi, written in the eleventh century and narrating the history of Persia. There is much in this tradition taken from oral sources, as well as those of Zoroastrianism, to reconstruct pre-Islamic history, and the heroes here are those well known from other sources.[20] There is a relatively smooth transition to Islamic times, the narrative continuing unbroken. Firdausi sought the

[20] J.S. Meisami, *Persian Historiography to the End of the Twelfth Century*, 107ff.; K. Yamamoto, *The Oral Background of Persian Epics: Story-telling and Poetry*.

patronage of Mahmud of Ghazni in the early eleventh century. But Mahmud was not a generous patron, so Firdausi left the Ghazni court and his glorification of pre-Islamic heroes was not objected to. His close contemporary was the scribe Abu'l Fazl-i-Bayhaqi, whose account, the *Ta'rikh-i-Bayhaqi*, includes references to sources and judgements on morality and good government. The role of the king is idealized, especially when he consults advisors. A major aspect of kingship is seen as the transference of power through dynastic succession. Unlike Firdausi, but not surprising in a scribe of that time, Bayhaqi's language carries the imprint of Arabic learning.[21]

Associated with this period and with India is the *Tahqiq-i-Hind* of Al-Biruni, a study of the culture of India. Al-Biruni, visiting India in the eleventh century, writes that Hindus do not pay much attention to the historical order of things and are careless in narrating the historical succession of their rulers.[22] He was unaware of the historiographies of Indian society and was seeking a parallel to the Islamic: his comments follow from a partial knowledge of the texts available. Al-Biruni came from a society in Central Asia that had a strong pre-Islamic Buddhist culture: he mentions the *śramaṇas/shamaniyyas* as important to the religion of India and hostile to the *brāhmaṇas*. Yet his conversations seem to have been limited to *brāhmaṇa* ritual specialists and a few others knowledgeable about astronomy and the calendar. This knowledge was not a source of history. He distinguishes between chronology as given in the *Purāṇas*, which was more fantasy than astronomical calculation, and texts on astronomy based on mathematics. But the distinction is not maintained in his discussion of chronology. Had he conversed with scribes at the royal courts he might have come to know about inscriptions as royal annals, and their focus on dynastic succession as well as their careful calculation of chronology. Had he looked into the *śramaṇa* tradition—that of the Buddhists and Jainas—he would have found narratives different from the *Purāṇas*, with a stronger flavour of the historical.

Al-Biruni's insufficient awareness of the writing of history in

[21] M.R. Waldman, *Towards a Theory of Historical Narrative*, 109–20.
[22] *Alberuni's India*, II.10–11.

forms other than the ones he was familiar with is a problem which also lay at the root of other commentators who commented on the lack of histories. Much the same can be said of the seventeenth-century writer Ferishtah's comments on Indian history. He based himself largely on writings from the courts of the sultans ruling in India and did not care to acquaint himself with the earlier tradition. In a sense, a tradition of ignorance or limited understanding had come into being in relation to historiography in the Indian context, and writers within it such as Al-Biruni and Ferishtah were the forerunners of a similar position later taken by European commentators. What seems interesting is not that they both say the same thing about a lack of history, but that they both limit themselves to consulting only the *brāhmaṇas*—and, moreover, largely only ritual specialists.

The best-known historian associated with Islam was a Tunisian, Ibn Khaldun, who wrote the *Kitabal'ibar* in the fourteenth century, in Arabic. The introduction to this book, the *Muqaddimah*, is what is generally quoted.[23] The work is different from most Persian histories. For Ibn Khaldun, history is about social organization, of which the best form is civilization, which envelops the community and royal authority, and which has to contradict varieties of untruths. He concedes that social factors may underlie some historical changes.

Given this diversity, when we consider Sultanate and Mughal historiographies in India we cannot assume they emerge from a single source conveniently labelled "Islamic history", since in fact they combine elements of the Islamic and broader Indian heritage.

The historiographies most frequently taken as a measure of historical writing proper are the Judaeo-Christian and Islamic. These have a clear eschatology of the beginning and end of the human story with a teleology built in it, and both view time as largely linear. The others, in which this is not so clearly evident, are the Greco-Roman, the Chinese, and the Indian. In these there

[23] F. Rosenthal, *Ibn Khaldun: The Muqaddimah.*

is eschatology, but not as well defined, and time takes various forms—linear, spiral, cyclic. The Greco-Roman, which is seen as foundational to European historiography, has little in common with the Judaeo-Christian. Given this variegated background of historiographies, the colonial judgement on history in India seems either simplistic or devious.

5. Colonialism and Early Indian History

In the foregoing discussion on historical writing in early India, the imprint of colonial formulations was the bedrock of the argument, as it was of other aspects of reconstructing the past. It would be useful to consider how these formulations were arrived at, and how historians today would reformulate the questions when analysing the data.

The search for indigenous histories of early India began in the eighteenth century. European scholars, viewing historical literature as a distinct category recording the past, looked in vain for recognizable histories from the Sanskrit tradition. Indian culture, and particularly the Sanskrit articulation of what came to be called Hindu culture, was defined therefore as a-historical. William Jones, the leading Indologist of the late eighteenth century, working at Calcutta suspected that some texts, even when they included the myths and legends of the Hindus, probably contained the core of a history:

> That no Hindu nation but the Cashmerian, have [*sic*] left us regular histories in their ancient language, we must ever lament; but from the Sanskrit literature, which our country has the honour of having unveiled, we may still collect some rays of historical truth . . . The numerous Puranas, Itihasas, or poems mythological and heroic are completely in our power; and from them we may recover some disfigured but valuable pictures of ancient manners and governments; while the popular tales of the Hindus, in prose and verse, contain fragments of history . . .[24]

Attempts were made to compare these texts with others from the ancient world as it was assumed that links would give credence

[24] W. Jones, "On the Mystical Poetry of the Persians and Hindus", 165ff.

to their historical authenticity.[25] Most scholars, however, tended to dismiss these narratives as entirely fanciful and pointed out that the texts showed little concern for an accurate record of the past. It was agreed that the only exception was the *Rājataraṅgiṇī* of Kalhaṇa, a twelfth-century history of Kashmir. This work was regarded as atypical among Sanskrit texts because it was a history in the conventional sense, and for that reason much acclaimed by those searching for such ancient histories.

It might be worth keeping in mind that the word "myth" was used casually in these writings, with little attempt to define it or distinguish it from history. Myth relates the world of deities to that of humans, and some divine interventions as incarnations are occasionally introduced into the narrative. The claim that some kings were incarnations of particular deities was probably more for emphasis and was doubtless not universally accepted. Myth also refers to a remote past, although it is relevant to the present in terms of the message that it carries. Mythical time therefore can be vast, even unending. Myths are allegories and riddles whereas narrations claiming to be historical tend to keep such matters to a minimum.

A century later MacDonell's searing remark, "early India wrote no history because it never made any",[26] was modified by Rapson, who subscribed to the general view: "In all the large and varied literatures of the Brahmans, Jains and Buddhists there is not to be found a single work which can be compared to the *Histories* in which Herodotus recounts the struggle between the Greeks and the Persians or to the *Annals* in which Livy traces the growth and progress of Roman power."[27] However, Rapson goes on to add, "But this is not because the people of India had no history . . . We know from other sources that the ages were filled with stirring events; but these events found no systematic record." Comparisons with the Chinese chronicles of Sima Qian and the Arabic writings of Ibn Khaldun or even the Biblical genealogies, not to mention

[25] W. Jones, "On the Chronology of the Hindus", 111ff.; idem, "On the Gods of Greece, Italy and India"; idem, "Third Anniversary Discourse", 221ff.

[26] A.A. MacDonell, *History of Sanskrit Literature*, 11.

[27] E.J. Rapson (ed.), *The Cambridge History of India*, vol. I, 57.

Greco-Roman texts, strengthened, if only by contrast, the axiom that Indian society denied history.

In the supposed absence of a systematic record, the intellectual premises for the reconstruction of early Indian history by European scholars were drawn from contemporary European historiography. Awareness of evidence, interest in causation, and a premium on chronology together with sequential narrative were features of the Renaissance sense of the past; together these represented a departure from the historiography of medieval times with its focus on the activities of the Christian Church.[28] The colonial perception of the Indian past represented a break, therefore, with the indigenous traditions of earlier times. These included not only the Puranic and the Sramanic but also the Islamic historical traditions. The last had sought to link local dynasties of the Sultanates and Mughals with the wider framework of Islamic historiography, but had also, on occasion, included mention of elements of the past as given in Puranic texts. Some of this hybrid history had seeped into the origin myths of ruling families which, in fact, had no links with the Turks or the Arabs, as is evident from some of the myths of Rajput clans recorded by Tod. Even more remote to colonial views was the possible link between a sense of history in Sanskrit sources with the new colonial reconstruction of Indian history, for presuppositions among colonial historians about the relevance of the past to the present were, as I hope to show, far too different.

Attempts were made to reconstruct early Indian history by focusing on chronology and sequential narrative. The acclamation given to the identification by William Jones of Sandracottos with Candragupta, the Mauryan king, thus linking him with Alexander, shows the kind of concern with chronology among those who were probing the Indian past.[29] This became the bedrock of Indian chronology for those times (it has been superseded by the more precise reference to the contemporary Hellenistic kings in an

[28] P. Burke, *The Renaissance Sense of the Past.*

[29] S.N. Mukherjee, *Sir William Jones: A Study in Eighteenth Century British Attitudes to India*, 80–90; O.P. Kejariwal, *The Asiatic Society of Bengal and the Discovery of India's Past.*

inscription of Aśoka). It was also additional evidence for the theory that Greek and Sanskrit were cognate languages. Greek writers such as Megasthenes confirming the centrality of genealogies as a record of the past seemed less significant, because chronology in Indian sources was said to have been so disguised by the fantasies of the *brāhmaṇas* that it was almost impossible to unravel it.

Yet, on the other hand, much effort went into endless attempts at correlating Indian data with Biblical and Mesopotamian chronology. The figures quoted for the enormous time periods of the *yugas* and the *kalpas* were tested for factuality and naturally found wanting in comparison with modern calculations. So enthusiastic was this effort that forgeries by local pandits, obviously produced to please the new masters, were the basis of an equally enthusiastic investigation.[30] But the attempted correlations with Biblical genealogies had turned out even more fanciful than the theories of the *brāhmaṇas*.[31] Some went further afield and quoted Arab sources in an attempt to rationalize early Indian chronology.[32] Parallels between Old Testament chronology and Hindu traditions were pointed out, but these did not constitute a history.

The search, therefore, was for a history of India devised along the lines drawn by the humanist version of Enlightenment historiography which would reveal the identity of Indian civilization. Officers of the East India Company constituted the largest proportion of scholars working on India at the time. Their informants were learned *brāhmaṇas* whom they tapped for information on law and religion. It has been said that Jones' attempt was to domesticate the Orient through control over its knowledge. Thus, proposing the difference between the Orient and the Occident would establish the superiority of the latter.[33] His informants

[30] F. Wilford, "An Essay on the Sacred Isles in the West, with Other Essays Connected with That Work", 245ff.

[31] F. Wilford, "On the Chronology of the Hindus", 241–95; J. Bentley, "Remarks on the Principal Eras and Dates of the Ancient Hindus", 315–93; idem, "On the Hindu System of Astronomy", 195–249; W. Jones, "On the Chronology of the Hindus", 111ff.; S. Davis, "On the Indian Cycle of Sixty Years", 289ff.

[32] M. Anquetil du Perron, *Recherches Historiques et Geographiques sur l'Inde*, vol. II.

[33] E. Said, *Orientalism*, 77.

emphasized the centrality of the texts important to Brahmanism, such as the *Dharmaśāstras* and *Vedas*, and to a lesser extent the *Purāṇas*, the latter regarded as second-order knowledge. For example, Colebrooke worked primarily with Maithil *brāhmaṇas*, reputed to be among the most orthodox, who would have urged their foreign rulers to concentrate only on ritually important brahmanical texts.

Other systems of knowledge emanating from non-*brāhmaṇa* sources, including the Buddhist and Jaina, were initially not given much importance. This was partly because the early Orientalists lacked familiarity with these texts, there being no Buddhist monks or lay persons in India to introduce Buddhistic texts, and also because these, being regarded as inferior branches of Hinduism, were not thought to be a mainstream of information. Buddhism was barely recognized as important to India since it was no longer a formal religion of significance in the land of its origin. Together with Jainism, it was at best treated as a variant belief system within the larger fold of what came to be called Hinduism. That these could earlier have been independent but interacting systems of knowledge, let alone alternative systems, was hardly conceded.

The work of Jones, and similar studies recorded in the *Asiatic Researches,* were later to encourage the discipline of comparative philology, especially in European universities. H.H. Wilson who later held the Chair in Sanskrit at Oxford, was also part of this tradition and ventured further in his studies, as for example in the work which he did on the *Viṣṇu Purāṇa*. The attempt was to give order to the multiplicity of beliefs that were being described as "Hinduism".

Giving primacy to Hinduism had many reasons. European attitudes to Indian Islam as a major non-Hindu culture were mediated by the perspective of it being a Semitic religion with a heritage in part common to Christianity (though alien nevertheless). This was reinforced by Europe's experience of confronting Islam in the second millennium AD, going back to the Crusades. Islam in India was seen once again as a political rival. But, from the point of view of the Christian missions, the major competition came from what was perceived as the even more alien religion of Hinduism. Doubtless the exotica and the incomprehension of a religion so different from the Semitic must also have been intriguing and challenging—as it still is. This seems one reason why attempts were made to try and induct it into a recognizable framework, and to provide it with the kind of history that would make it less alien, and therefore easier to comprehend as well as confront.[34]

The initial reading was mainly of texts that provided information on Hindu law and religion, the latter defined by deities, cults, sects, and philosophical schools. What this scholarship brought into prominence was largely a limited, upper-caste Hinduism. The more essential features of its history, namely, the tension or the changes implicit in the evolution of sects, or their relations with particular castes, was of less interest. The concern with religion encouraged the reading of texts for whatever may have been their theological approach, rather than for discovering the relationship between sects and society—which would have involved some recognition of how these texts recorded the past.

At the same time, William Jones referred to the three great nations of Asia as the Hindus, the Arabs, and the Tartars.[35] It is significant that he used the term "nation", for nations require a history. Jones was using the word more in its contemporary sense, as a synonym for "people", rather than in its current association with a state. Did the concept of a Hindu "nation" influence the search for a particular kind of Hindu history? Perhaps Hindu identity was of interest because it was non-Semitic and represented, numerically, the larger segment of the Indian people. Jones' emphasis on the study of non-Semitic cultures was important to his theories of the monogenesis of cultures and languages. Thus, the study of Indian history in itself also became a search for the empirical "Truth", and attempts were made to unravel the legends. The definition of a Hindu identity was significant to these considerations, even if such an identity was difficult to isolate from the sources, and despite this identity being constructed almost entirely from a brahmanical perspective. The very idea of seeking a subcontinental

[34] R. Thapar, "Imagined Religious Communities: Ancient History and the Modern Search for a Hindu Identity", in idem, *Interpreting Early India*, 60–88.

[35] W. Jones, "On the Gods of Greece, Italy and India", 221ff.

history limited to Sanskrit sources, and expecting such sources to hold a view of the past similar to the current European, does seem somewhat meaningless.

6. The View of the English Utilitarians

A different reconstruction of early Indian history, based on a new set of premises, arose from Utilitarian thought, also in the nineteenth century. Utilitarian views of historical origins and explanations referring to India set aside the need for a tradition of historical writing, or, for that matter, even a concern for the past in the indigenous tradition. The new scholarship again drew its inspiration from European ideological debates and perceptions. Thus, a familiarity with the intellectual history of Europe in the nineteenth century became a precondition for understanding these new interpretations of Indian history. The supposed non-existence of historical writing was explained as an outcome of the nature of Indian society. Both the theory and the explanations became an imperative of colonial policy in a changing relationship between the colonial power and the colony.[36]

The denial of a sense of history in the colony was also implicit in the attempt to explain the Indian past as one conforming to the theory of Oriental Despotism. This is evident in what has been referred to as the hegemonic text on Indian history, James Mill's *The History of British India*, published between 1818 and 1823.[37] This was the first attempt to survey the past, encompassing what was known and written in English of the history of British India as a continuous narrative. Mill's view became seminal to interpreting Indian history, in particular his tripartite division of Indian history into Hindu and Muslim civilizations, and the period of British rule. Hindu civilization was for Mill not only irrational, backward, and stagnant, but registered no change at all,[38] a view which reached

[36] R. Thapar, "Ideology and the Interpretation of Early Indian History", in idem, *Interpreting Early India*, 1–22.

[37] R. Inden, "Orientalist Construction of India", 401–46; idem, *Imagining India*.

[38] J. Mill, *The History of British India*, vol. I, 33ff.

the more abstract levels of historical generalization in Hegel's comments on Indian history.

The despotic state was thought to be the characteristic political form in India since the beginning. For Mill, change was only meaningful if it was compatible with his definition of progress, a teleological movement with history as its narrative. The static character of Indian society, as in all oriental despotisms, needed to be broken by introducing change. British administration could bring in change through legislation. These views were in part the reflection of a colonial policy that sought an interpretation of the Indian past which would serve to back its political agenda. Mill's *History* was also an attempt to present a pan-Indian view, even though what he knew was limited to British India.

Mill's *History* critiqued earlier British Orientalist views sympathetic to Indian civilization, more so those associated with the Asiatic Society at Calcutta. It has been argued that Mill saw Jones' view of the Orient as the product of undisciplined imagination, dangerous on epistemological and political grounds.[39] Mill's *History* was an attempt at defining a new idiom for the empire. His project was different from that of the Orientalists, who were seeking parallels in India to European ideas of the past and insisting on understanding the indigenous law and the social articulation of India. Mill's notion of empire was, of course, modelled on the Roman. But because the British empire required a particular kind of economic link with its colonies, his emphasis, and that of those who thought like him, was gradually less on campaigns to acquire land and revenue and more on restructuring the colonial economy to enhance the wealth of the colonial power. Mill also realized that support for what was viewed as indigenous law could result in the endorsement of a position far more conservative in India than was practised all the time.

Mill rejected Jones' contention that historical material could be culled from the epics and other Indian sources. The Orientalists were accused of legitimizing themselves by deploying indigenous idioms. It was not seen that they were doing so through their own interpretation of the indigenous idiom, which resulted in their

[39] J. Majeed, *Ungoverned Imaginings*, 4ff.

arriving at a version not necessarily indigenous. Mill's views on India also ran parallel at some points with those of contemporary British missionaries who proposed radical change, except that the missionaries believed that the more effective solution to Indian backwardness was conversion to Christianity.[40]

As a historian Mill saw himself in the role of a judge, familiarizing himself with the pros and cons of the argument and pronouncing judgement while keeping a distance. This legal perspective not only validated the distance from Indian society evident in his history, but also excused his lack of first-hand knowledge about the country. As a metaphor, this legalistic distancing of the historian from his subject came to be widely upheld by other historians writing on India, both British and Indian. It is curious that the two nineteenth-century protagonists in the debate on the interpretation of India's past, James Mill and later Max Müller, each supporting opposed theories and adhering to different political loyalties, declined to visit India and never experienced its lived reality.

In 1840 H.H. Wilson annotated Mill's *History*, and in doing so made a spirited defence of Jones. Strangely, he did not attempt an alternative history but was content to incorporate his defence of Jones in the annotations. The Orientalists of the nineteenth century, as against those of the eighteenth, despite their meticulous research into texts of the ancient period, did not feel the need to effectively criticize the views on early Indian society held by Utilitarians and others who supported imperialist interpretations.[41] It looks as though by about 1840 there had come about a reconsideration in imperial attitudes as to how India was to be governed. This change resulted in greater sympathy for Mill's view than could be openly expressed among those concerned with the study of India.

Mill believed in legislating change, and therefore any society which did not conform at least minimally to the laws governing contemporary European society—which for him were potentially the criterion of progress—would have to be forced to change through new laws. These would convert barbarism into

[40] A. Embree, *Charles Grant and the Evangelicals.*

[41] D.N. Lorenzen, "Imperialism and the Historiography of Ancient India", 84–102.

civilization and progress. If the Greeks cultivated history and the Hindus had failed to, then the latter failed the test of civilization. Some Orientalist scholars, such as Max Müller, were projecting utopias in their description of the nineteenth-century village community in India. This was not, however, the case with those who drew their intellectual sustenance from Utilitarianism. For those who thought like Mill, India provided no alternative to the bewildering changes of industrializing Europe.

The insistence on Indian society being static eliminated the need to look for points of change and, to that extent, for records which may have registered this change. One of the functions of using the past is to legitimize changes in the present. This becomes irrelevant if there is no change and no record of change. From Mill's perspective, the idea of a lack of history and thereby the elimination of a past lends support to the idea of despotic power. Any changes implemented cannot then be accused of violating tradition, nor can any appeal be made to thwart despotism in the name of the past. For Mill, therefore, the legends which accrued in Hindu texts were fantasies, and he was opposed to Jones' view that historical events could be gleaned from such legends.

Such theories were current in much European thought about India. "Oriental Despotism" had its own history in Europe and had been much debated in the eighteenth century, focusing on the question of whether or not there was an absence of private property in land, pertinent to the current European debate on how private property impacted society.[42] Tracing its roots to Aristotle and Greek views on the Persian empire, it was revived in Europe after the Renaissance. During the Enlightenment debates, it came to the fore in a controversy between Montesquieu and Voltaire. The former supported the idea that there could be no private property in a system

[42] P. Anderson, *Lineages of the Absolutist State*, 462–549; D. Thorner, "Marx on India and the Asiatic Mode of Production", 33ff.; B. Hindess and P.Q. Hirst, *Pre-Capitalist Modes of Production*; B. O'Leary, *The Asiatic Mode of Production*; L. Krader, *The Asiatic Mode of Production*.

of Oriental Despotism: this was also the view of Adam Smith, David Ricardo, and G.W.F. Hegel. But Voltaire and the Physiocrats felt that the absence of private property in land in Asia was not feasible.

As a theory of explanation, Oriental Despotism was useful to the British administrator arguing for the termination of existing systems and the introduction of new institutions. The change would also allow the state to control the new system, a control to which Asian societies would acquiesce because they had not known better. These ideas filtered through to colonial administrators trained in Haileybury College and Fort William. A parallel to this was discovering and interpreting a history for the early Indian past. That views of Indian society were not all entirely bleak is suggested by the debate on the village community, where opinion was divided as to whether the village communities were subordinated to the despot or whether they were autarchic and constituted a collection of republics. These views grew out of investigating the revenue systems of pre-colonial India, a study which could have deflected the investigation into more empirical avenues had there not been the imprint of theories such as Oriental Despotism.

7. The German Romantic Movement and India

New theories of a different kind emerged from the European excitement at discovering what many believed was the cradle of world culture. This was in part fuelled by the thought that there might be found an Oriental Renaissance in the texts of Asia, propelling innovative knowledge similar to the earlier revival of Classical European learning.[43] Adding to this anticipation was the slowly increasing study of comparative philology, which underlined the closeness of some Oriental languages, Sanskrit in particular, to classical European languages. Some among German philosophers and linguists, such as F. Schlegel, constructed an ancient past for Indians as people enveloped in a childlike innocence and purity. This involved studying the roots of ancient languages such as Indo-Aryan and Dravidian. This then meant coping with

[43] R. Schwab, *La Renaissance Orientale*.

a degree of competition and tension between those arguing for the priority of each language.[44] Indo-Aryan soon assumed greater importance, initially due to the dominant status of the *Vedas* as part of brahmanical learning and on account of it being a cognate of Old Iranian and Greek.

The earlier emphasis on religion and mysticism being characteristic of Indian culture, to the virtual exclusion of rational ways of systematizing knowledge, was reinforced by some aspects of German Romanticism. The discovery of India was as if Europe had come upon a pristine civilization with which it had once, in the distant past, had links. Such ideas tended to divide views on India and even led to accusations of Indo-mania.[45] Among those joining issue was G.W.F. Hegel, who was especially critical of the absence of individual freedom in Indian society. To this was linked his insistence that India was a land without recorded history and given to fantasies about the past.[46] Added to this was the argument that in India caste, viewed as civil society, had overwhelmed the state, and without a state there could be no history. The debate continued in the writings of Friedrich Schelling and Arthur Schopenhauer. But much of this remained in the form of sporadic views. Systemizing these ideas into theories applicable to Indian texts came from others.

A different analysis grew out of the interest of German writers linked to Romanticism in literature. Sanskrit literature was said to embody the oldest yet the most developed human language, and so whether or not there were texts that were histories was of little consequence. Literature in Sanskrit was said to articulate an intense closeness between nature and culture, a subject of immense interest to German Romanticism. Although Hegel was critical of Indological studies, Johan Herder and August Wilhelm Schlegel were deeply interested in these themes. Such views fed into what was emerging in the latter part of the nineteenth century as a major theory of the origins of language and culture, and it was inevitably tied to how the beginnings of Indian history came to be viewed.

[44] T. Trautmann, *Aryans and British India*.

[45] W. Halbfass, *India and Europe*.

[46] G.W.F. Hegel, *Lectures on the Philosophy of History*, 140–1, 162–4.

The most influential theory of origins in the interpretation of early Indian history was the theory of an Aryan race. This made an impact and became popular. It postulated an invasion of northern India by a racial group identified as the Aryans, a people who spoke an Indo-European language which was differentiated from other Indo-European languages by being labelled "Indo-Aryan". The argument for the existence of an Aryan race drew on comparative philology, the affinities between Indo-European languages, and the mythology and social institutions of those who spoke these languages.[47] The idea of an Aryan invasion was based on references in the *Ṛgveda* to hostilities against the *dāsas*, or those already settled on the land, and where the victorious *āryas* were the authors of the texts.[48] (The *Ṛgveda* was viewed in the nineteenth century as the earliest historical record in India, a view which has had to be radically altered by the uncovering of archaeological evidence, especially that of the Harappan cities.) The entirely different Puranic version of historical beginnings was ignored on the ground that these texts were of less importance and compiled at a later date.

The upper castes, and particularly the *brāhmaṇas*, were seen as lineal descendants of the Aryan race, while the lower castes and untouchables were regarded as the indigenous non-Aryans. Caste as a social system was traced back to the notion of racial segregation and differences of skin colour. References to *ārya* and *dāsa varṇa*, where *varṇa* means colour largely as a classifier, were read literally as distinguishing fair-skinned *āryas* from dark-skinned *dāsas*, with little concession to other possible readings. Caste as *varṇa* came to be seen as a rigid system of social organization, essentially unchanging since early times.

This theory has also to be seen against the wider application of these ideas to European racial identities popularized through the much-discussed writings of Comte de Gobineau and others. The social origins of Europe were explained by identifying Aryan and non-Aryan elements in which the former were, inevitably, associated with the aristocracy.[49] The white race was said to be

[47] L. Poliokov, *The Aryan Myth*.

[48] R. Thapar, *The Aryan: Recasting Constructs*.

[49] J.A. Comte de Gobineau, *Essai sur l'inégalite des races humaines*, 1–4.

blessed with the two main elements of civilization, a religion and a history.[50] The scholarship of Orientalism was not immune to these ideas, particularly in relation to German Romanticism, which had turned its attention to the study of primitive origins and the purity of peoples as embodied in myth, saga, and legend.[51] There was an insistence on the pristine purity of Sanskrit as an ur-language. Those associated with the language—the Aryan Hindus—were seen as the founders of civilization. The ideas of Gobineau were propagated by Ernest Renan, also a friend of Max Müller.[52] The wish to classify humankind was reinforced by the intellectual ascendancy of the theories of Social Darwinism, which were applied to societies and peoples in determining their status. References to the *āryas* in the *Ṛgveda* seemed to fall propitiously into place in a theory which counterposed Aryans with non-Aryans.

The initial identification of language with race was rapidly accepted; few paused to make a demarcation. Although later it was cautioned against even by scholars such as Max Müller, both he and others tended to use the terms interchangeably. By the end of the nineteenth century it was generally assumed that the early history of India was to be viewed as the spread of the Aryan race over the subcontinent, with the Aryan-derived languages being used to gauge this expansion. History therefore lay in starting with the foundations of Aryan culture in the Vedic texts, and its development and establishment in northern India, and later elsewhere. This explanation of origins presupposed that Vedic Brahmanism was to be equated with Aryan culture, and since Vedic Brahmanism showed little concern for history, there was in the civilization a general absence of a sense of history.

Furthermore, the notion of an invasion by "the Aryans"—their conquest of northern India and the attribution of having brought civilization to India—came to be seen as an earlier parallel to British conquest and imperialism in the present.[53] Everything seemed to fall neatly into place: that the history of a language is distinct, and that linguistic changes in themselves provide

[50] L. Poliokov, *The Aryan Myth*, 214ff.

[51] W. Halbfass, *India and Europe*, 69ff.

[52] E. Renan, "L'avenir de la Science", 728ff.

[53] E. Leach, "Aryan Invasions over Four Millennia".

historical evidence, was not investigated. Doubts about the Aryan race as applied to India arose both from new evidence, particularly from archaeology and linguistics, as well as altered perspectives on the history and cultures of this period.

There is much in this theory open to question. "Aryan" is a label used for a language, whereas race has a biological origin. The two cannot be confused. The notion of rigorous racial segregation defined by language is untenable. People of varying ethnic origins can use the same language; or, alternatively, people of the same ethnic origin can use different languages. Where those settled in the same area use different languages and yet intermingle, there the cultural and ideological idioms are bound to overlap. The texts from such cultures do not represent a single cultural articulation but evolve out of the relations between multiple cultural groups, with some limited continuities from earlier times.[54]

8. Attempts to Explain Indian Society: Marx, Weber, and Others

The debate on the nature of Indian society and history was in many ways an exercise in theory, drawing upon existing European controversies. In this debate the Oriental culture being examined seems largely to have become an arena for trying out the validity of these ideas. The diversity in ways of perceiving the Indian past can be seen in the theories. Even in the rubric of Orientalism, variations can be recognized.[55] The premises of these theories also yielded a hierarchy in which to position texts. The *Vedas*, *Purāṇas*, and *Dharmaśāstras* were given precedence over *caritas* and other literature, whereas any genuine search for a historical tradition would have given priority to these other texts. If current European theory privileged the validity of European historical writing, the application of this notion to a society which supposedly had none became an exercise in testing that theory. Arriving at this conclusion was distinct from its practical advantage: such a

[54] D.D. Kosambi, *An Introduction to the Study of Indian History*, 93–101; R. Thapar, *The Aryan: Recasting Constructs*, 53ff.

[55] P. Heehs, "Shades of Orientalism: Paradoxes and Problems in Indian Historiography", 169–95.

reading provided the opportunity for formulating a history for the colony that would underpin colonial policy. The present of India was thus viewed as the past of Europe within the general format of social evolutionism.[56]

These theorists were not much concerned with the empirical details of the society being studied. For some of these scholars, Asian societies provided a form of exotica and permitted a play of fantasy. There were curious anomalies in these attitudes. There was, for instance, little attempt, on the part of those learning from their informants, to use the information for a discourse on the wider context of the texts and the worldview of their authors. Although the Asiatic Society was founded in 1784 as a forum for Indological research, it remained closed to Indian participation until 1829, almost half a century later. Then, too, the Society's interest seems to have lain largely in encouraging wealthy Indians to provide donations, which the latter gladly did, seeing it as a means of acquiring status.[57]

Colonial attitudes to knowledge pertaining to their colonies assumed that such knowledge was a form of control.[58] Thus, William Jones wrote of the *itihāsas* and *Purāṇas* being "in our power", and a century or so later Lord Curzon saw the intellectual discovery of the Orient as the necessary furniture of empire. History was the portal to knowledge about the colony and every aspect of colonial activity was formulated as a history of knowledge-gathering. This control would be enhanced if it could be maintained that the colonial society had no awareness of its past, and, even such awareness as it had, had been procured by the colonial power. Thus, if Indian civilization could be shown to be a-historical, the European discovery of Indian history would constitute an additional aspect of power articulated as knowledge, and become an aspect of domination.

Assisting this process was the almost obsessive concern with seeing the Orient necessarily as "the Other" of western Europe.

[56] B. Cohn, *An Anthropologist among the Historians and Other Essays*, 50ff.

[57] O.P. Kejariwal, *The Asiatic Society of Bengal*, 153.

[58] E. Said, *Orientalism*.

The two most influential statements on "Otherness" are to be found in Karl Marx and Max Weber. The starting point was the question why Asian societies did not develop capitalism and were therefore a contrast to Europe. This exploration was conditioned by the rather fragmentary historical knowledge gathered up to that point, and by the centrality given to theories about Asian societies even when these conflicted with empirical data (a predilection which has not been altogether discarded even now).

The construction of "the Other" was derived not from trying to understand a different world's perception of itself but from the absence of European characteristics. Marx emphasized the lack of change in India, and therefore of dialectics and history.[59] He says: "India then could not escape the fate of being conquered and the whole of her past history if it be anything is the history of successive conquests she has undergone. Indian society has no history at all, at least no known history. What we call its history is but the history of the successive intruders who founded their empires on the passive basis of that unresisting and unchanging society."[60] His historical treatment of Asian societies in his Asiatic Mode of Production again emphasized the static nature of such societies, and the inevitability therefore of their not having either a history or historical writing.

Weber's emphasis on what has been called the "*karma* theodicy"—the tying in of one's actions with birth into a specific caste—precludes the possibility of both innovations and the defiance of caste rules.[61] Added to this was his view, now regarded as controversial, that caste was a significant factor in the failure of economic rationalism.[62] India, according to him, registered an

[59] B. Hindess and P.Q. Hirst, *Pre-capitalist Modes of Production*; B. O'Leary, *The Asiatic Mode of Production*; L. Krader, *The Asiatic Mode of Production*; R.A.L.H. Gunawardana, "The Analysis of Pre-colonial Social Formations in Asia in the Writings of Karl Marx", 365–88.

[60] S. Avineri (ed.), *Karl Marx on Colonialism and Modernisation*, 132–3; Karl Marx, "The Future Results of British Rule in India", 217–22.

[61] J. Heesterman, "Caste and Karma", in idem, *The Inner Conflict of Tradition*, 194ff.

[62] D. Kantowsky, "Max Weber on India and Indian Interpretations of Weber", 141–74; idem, "Max Weber's Contributions to Indian Sociology", 307–17; idem (ed.), *Recent Research on Max Weber's Studies on Hinduism*; S. Munshi, "Max

absence of the economic rationalism necessary to capitalism, as also the rational ethic of ascetic Puritanism. This would doubtless also support the notion of an absence of the articulation of history as a rational narrative. In a larger sense, how the Other was constructed is a question that came to be asked only relatively recently, pioneered by Edward Said's *Orientalism*.

Interest in caste had by now come to take a central position in the definition of the Other, as well as in trying to understand Indian society. Whereas in the eighteenth century relatively little was written on caste, by the end of the nineteenth century it had become the focus of explaining social functioning.[63] Given the premise in much of Indological studies that the individual was not a fundamental entity in Indian society, caste in a sense stood in for the functions normally associated with individual interests. Hegel had also argued that caste appropriated the state, thereby negating a fundamental characteristic of a civilization, namely the balance between state and society.[64] There was now a seeming replacement of the textual base of Orientalist scholarship by an empirical examination of the functioning of caste. Yet, within the explanations offered, earlier theories conditioned many of the views on caste. Thus, Herbert Risley accepted racial segregation as the basis of caste.[65] Although others rejected this in favour of occupation or kinship relations or ritual status, the combination of the theory of an Aryan race and the nineteenth-century reading of caste came to stay. Into this there entered the priority given to the *Dharmaśāstra* texts as guides to caste functioning.

Weber's views on caste reflect the theories then current in addition to his own reading of the texts.[66] Weber saw caste as a status group with rigid rules of marriage and with pollution acting as

---

Weber on India: An Introductory Critique", 1–30; R. Thapar, "Durkheim and Weber on Theories of Society and Race Relations Relating to Pre-colonial India", in idem, *Cultural Pasts*, 21–51.

63 N.B. Dirks, *Castes of Mind: Colonialism and the Making of Modern India*.

64 G.W.F. Hegel, *Lectures on the Philosophy of History*, 160ff.

65 H. Risley, *The People of India*.

66 M. Weber, *The Religion of India: The Sociology of Hinduism and Buddhism*.

a discriminating factor in social relations. The spread of caste society was brought about by three agencies: conquest, the conversion of tribes (clans) into castes, and the subdivision of castes. The juxtaposition of racial differences was significant, but he did not see race as the basis of caste. Conquerors claimed rights in land, and the conquered became subservient and lost their rights. The levels at which tribes were converted to castes varied. Ruling families were often given *kṣatriya* status, and an entire tribe could be converted to a single caste. The subdivision of castes meant that a new caste could branch off from an existing one by migration, a change in ritual duties, entry into a new religious sect, a change of occupation, and differences in the inheritance of property where the better-off would imitate high-caste behaviour. A new caste was established when there was a denial of connubial rights and commensality from the existing caste, and the adoption of new rituals by the new caste. The formation of castes was fundamental to the Indian social order.

Yet the possibilities of castes maintaining their own histories, although known to exist, received little attention as a variation on potential historical records. Such views, coming out of European sociological interests and empirical ethnographic data, did lead to Indian historians and sociologists giving more attention to the evidence on society in the past; but the questioning of the stereotypes inherited from the nineteenth century was yet to come. What was missed out was the fact that changing the status of a caste, such as that of the scribes, was an aspect of social change. The establishing of social change requires records of previous and current statuses, and these are an aspect of historical traditions.

9. The Imperial View and Nationalist Reactions

Meanwhile, throughout the nineteenth century, the discovery of data for the reconstruction of Indian history had continued apace, with the early attempts of the Asiatic Society being pursued by officers involved in the administration of India. The Asiatic Society was the base both for explorers and surveyors such as James Rennell, Francis Buchanan, and Colin Mackenzie, as well as for scholars who, subsequent to William Jones, were intent on linking the history of India to other centres of civilization, more so those associated with the Biblical theory of creation or with Greco-Roman parallels.[67] Colin Mackenzie collected a vast number of manuscripts relating to local history of various kinds.[68] The collection had been made primarily by *brāhmaṇas*, and thus the choice was selective; and, naturally, a *brāhmaṇa* discourse mediated between the text and its reading. Mackenzie's interest was in data relating to the history of places. Interest in the history of peoples and castes was to develop later. The Asiatic Society did not permit Mackenzie's Indian assistants to work on his archive, and so once again the social context of knowledge was separated from the information gathered.[69]

Gradually, however, the main concern shifted to obtaining hard evidence on the Indian past, even if mostly in relation to other civilizations. This was done through work in epigraphy, archaeology, and numismatics. Painstaking scholarship yielded rich results. James Prinsep deciphered inscriptions in the *brāhmī* script, the major breakthrough being what were later identified as those of the Mauryan king Aśoka. Alexander Cunningham followed the itinerary of the seventh-century Chinese Buddhist pilgrim Xuanzang and located a number of Buddhist sites mentioned in his text.[70] Buddhist monuments made it incumbent to study Buddhist texts, and a new area of interest emerged with these studies, although these texts were never at that time given the centrality associated with brahmanical literature. Numismatics helped in deciphering scripts where the coins were bilingual—such as those of the Indo-Bactrian Greeks with names in Greek and *brāhmī*—thus also linking Indian and Hellenistic history. Temple architecture and Hindu icons attracted attention, though even in the study of these the familiarity of the Greek aesthetic was sought and the imprint of "the Greek miracle" could never quite be sloughed off.

This was largely a continuation of Orientalist scholarship. At

[67] See also O.P. Kejariwal, *The Asiatic Society of Bengal and the Discovery of India's Past.*

[68] H.H. Wilson, *MacKenzie Collection: A Descriptive Catalogue*, 2 vols.

[69] N.B. Dirks, *The Hollow Crown.*

[70] Abu Imam, *Alexander Cunningham and the Beginnings of Indian Archaeology.*

the level of the technique of discovery, it remains impressive. But over its reconstruction and interpretation of the larger flow of history European models hovered, and comparisons with Europe loomed large. The knowledge that surfaced came from elite and upper-caste sources and informants who had configured a specific reconstruction of the past in ways conducive to their self-interest. This "subject positioning" was not taken into account. Admittedly, data for lower social groups were not so forthcoming; nor, however, were they sought. Underlying all this activity was the conviction that the Indian past had to be wholly reconstructed through contemporary scholarship, and that this scholarship had to do with testing textual data for authenticity determined by current concepts.

An adjunct to this scholarship was the interest in the largely oral compositions of the bards (although some by now had been recorded as texts). James Tod had a romantic vision of Rajput clans and argued that his sources, collected from bards and Jaina monks, constituted historical records.[71] He also attempted to link the European to the Indian past and suggested that the Rajputs were of Scythian or even Scandinavian origin. In the early twentieth century L.P. Tessitori made a systematic attempt to collect bardic material in the form of prose chronicles, poems, and genealogies from Rajasthan and Central India, and tried to correlate them with inscriptions.[72] But there was little dialogue between those who were interested in such documents on the one hand, and those who on the other were reconstructing what they perceived as an impersonal narrative of the early history of India, using what they regarded as the more reliable brahmanical textual sources. Whereas material from bards and similar sources was allowed within limits as data for local history, it was largely ignored when discussing the wider concerns of history.

By and large, the bardic data was treated essentially as folk literature, more the art of the storyteller than even of the chronicler.

[71] J. Tod, *Annals and Antiquities of Rajasthan*.

[72] L.P. Tessitori, "A Scheme for the Bardic and Historical Survey of Rajputana", vol. 10, 373–86; idem, vol. 15, 5–79; idem, vol. 16, 251–79; idem, "Bardic and Historical Survey of Rajputana: A Descriptive Catalogue of Bardic and Historical Manuscripts".

With linear chronology and politics in an elementary sense seen as the ingredients of history, the bardic records, dependent on a long oral tradition, were often set aside as unreliable. There was not as yet a sufficient understanding of the status of the bard in Indian society, a status that was special yet separate—even as the *brāhmaṇa* took over the compositions of the bard. The records with which the latter had been associated, the account of a family, a clan, or a caste—forms of which continue to this day in the hands of both bards and of some categories of *brāhmaṇas*,[73] were considered low in the hierarchy of historical sources. That the recording of the past could be a separate occupational function within the parameters of a caste society was not fully recognized. Even now, recognition of the bardic tradition, both oral and literate, is different from the textual records. The oral tradition is met with in Central India, among many clans and tribes, such as the Pradhans, and at places of pilgrimage.[74] Written texts are more extensive in some areas, and these correlate information on what was regarded as central to society, namely, consanguinity, marriage alliances, and property.[75] This tradition is still in practice since genealogies of high-status families continue to be maintained at centres of pilgrimage.

There was a gulf between these keepers of a historical tradition and historians, perhaps best demonstrated in the rather literal fashion in which genealogical data was used by some historians. Genealogical lists from the epics and *Purāṇas* were taken as factual records and attempts were made to identify them with various racial groups;[76] or else attempts were made to use genealogies for the reconstruction of the chronology of earliest Indian history.[77]

[73] S. Havale, *The Pradhans of the Upper Narbada Valley*; N. Zeigler, "Mewari Historical Chronicles", 219ff.

[74] The category of *brāhmaṇas* known as the *pāṇḍās* maintain the genealogies of dominant castes. They are located in centres of pilgrimage where their status is lower than that of the *brāhmaṇas* who are ritual specialists.

[75] C. von Fürer-Haimendorf, "The Historical Value of Indian Bardic Literature", 87–93.

[76] F.E. Pargiter, "Earliest Indian Traditional History", 265–95 and 741–5; idem, *Ancient Indian Historical Tradition*.

[77] S.N. Pradhan, *Chronology of Ancient India*; A.D. Pusalker, *Studies in the Epics and Purāṇas*; R. Morton-Smith, *Dates and Dynasties in Earliest India*.

Much effort has gone into trying to unravel the genealogical lists and arrange them in some chronological order which might be backed by other historical evidence, but so far the earlier sections of such lists have defied such order.

Oral traditions have now been examined as sources of history, particularly as in some societies the oral tradition can be the sole source of any sort of record of the past. There is an interest in the oral traditions of societies without literacy, societies which by the earlier definition were said to be without history.[78] Oral traditions claim to draw from memory. The contention between history and memory is not recent. It has existed in records; these often contest what is claimed to have happened on the one hand, and on the other the perceptions of those happenings among various people. The two have been in dialogue, but to go back to the texts and try to unravel the dialogue is difficult. Pierre Nora suggests a difference: that history in our times is intellectual and secular, calling for analysis and criticism; and memory can install remembrance in what is sacred. The latter presumably cannot be analysed in the same way and has to be drawn out by history.

The demarcation between history and the bardic tradition was such that even the earlier Indian historians did not feel the need to speak to bards about their records. Historians working on pre-Islamic India initially subscribed to the colonial view on the question of a historical tradition, with most accepting the view that Indian society was a-historical. Their interest was largely antiquarian and focused on collecting data. These historians were more often themselves from the upper castes—*brāhmaṇa* and *kāyastha* or its equivalent. Interestingly, they were the castes that kept the records in the past, more particularly official records, and so were naturally not given to questioning the premises of the colonial interpretations, at least not until the impact of a nationalist ideology began to become effective from the early twentieth

[78] J. Vansina, *The Oral Tradition*; idem, *Oral Tradition as History*; D.P. Henige, *The Chronology of Oral Tradition*; idem, *Oral Historiography*; A.M. Shah and R.G. Shroff, "The Vahivanca Barots of Gujarat: A Caste of Genealogists and Mythographers", 40–70; N.P. Ziegler, "The Seventeenth Century Chronicles of Marvara: A Study in the Evolution and Use of Oral Tradition in Western India", 127–53.

century. A possible Aryan race, for example, was a notion attractive to such Indian historians because, among other things, it linked early India with the roots of European culture and endorsed the special status of the upper castes claiming Aryan descent. Common roots were postulated when Max Müller, speaking to British probationers of the Indian Civil Service in 1882, told them that in going out to India they were going to their original home, a place full of memories which only scholars like him could read. Complementing this, Keshab Chandra Sen spoke of the coming of the British to India as the meeting of parted cousins.[79] Nationalist historiography also incorporated the views of those such as B.G. Tilak who fully supported the Aryan theory, ignoring the views of Jyotiba Phule, for example, who turned the theory on its head, as it were, by arguing that the Aryans and therefore their descendants were foreign to India.[80]

Although the concept of Oriental Despotism was rejected, Mill's periodization of Indian history was not questioned. A century later the nomenclature was changed from Hindu, Muslim, and British to Ancient, Medieval, and Modern, in an attempt to secularize it and make it happily coincide with the periodization of European history. In late imperial and early nationalist histories, the Hindu/Ancient period was projected as one of sustained prosperity, an argument which subconsciously conceded the early argument for the absence of major historical change in that period. Current reconstructions became so much a part of the definition of history that Indian historians, at this point in time, tended to regard as peripheral the views of the past that were given in early sources. There was little attempt to analyse these sources, in terms either of what they were propagating or the nature of their biases. The colonial construction of the past, followed by nationalist

[79] M. Müller, *India: What Can it Teach Us?*, 20; K.C. Sen, *Keshab Chandra Sen's Lectures in India*, 323.

[80] The theory of an Aryan invasion is axiomatic to those who claim to be the first inhabitants of India—and thus the inheritors of the land—and is therefore popular among some Dalits. The Hindutva view, which claims India as the cradle of the Aryans, is equally opposed to the notions of both invasion and the migration of the Indo-Aryan language from West Asia: R. Thapar, *The Aryan: Recasting Constructs*, 65–88.

historians, was methodologically therefore a departure from the early Indian tradition.

Indian historians writing in the early twentieth century questioned some of the generalizations generated by colonial interpretations of early Indian history. But on the question of historical writing in ancient Indian there was ambivalence, the prevalent view being summed by in the statement of R.C. Majumdar: "It is a well-known fact that with the single exception of the *Rājataraṅgiṇī* (History of Kashmir) there is no historical text in Sanskrit dealing with the whole or even parts of India. But ideas of history and historical literature were not altogether lacking."[81] To assume that there could have been a history of India as a single entity is to assume the impossible for those times. Majumdar mentions various categories of data that could be associated with the writing of history, but none of which constituted historical writing. He does however dismiss the popular argument that there was historical writing in the past, the texts having since been lost.

10. Shifting the Paradigm: Recent Views

The 1960s saw a turning point in the idea that it might be feasible to search for history in the early period. Even though a historical tradition seemed debatable, there was the possibility of looking afresh at the subject. The recognition that Indian society was not static and did undergo change, and that the nature of such change was not uniform in time and space, constituted a radically different view of the Indian past from the one held earlier. The so-called Hindu period, stretching from the Harappan civilization in the third millennium BC to the establishment of the Delhi Sultanate in the thirteenth century AD, is now seen not as an unbroken continuity but as registering periods of major change within this timespan. Recognition of change is always a nodal point in history, enabling the emergence of new identities as well as reformulations of the past for the purposes of the present.

Alternative theories of explanation pointing to varieties of historical change came with a later generation of scholars, using

[81] R.C. Majumdar, "Ideas of History in Sanskrit Literature", 13–28.

both data and methods drawing on a number of disciplines and new theories of analyses, some initially drawn from Marxism. The work of D.D. Kosambi attempted a creative use of Marxist methodology even while distancing itself from many of Marx's specific views on Asian society.[82] This was a paradigm shift. In the last few decades it has acted as a point of departure for a number of analyses of Indian social reality, some of which have drawn more widely from theories of social change as well as theories from related disciplines. These have resulted in a considerable interest in economic history, and the degree to which economic change affected a broader historical change or was part of such a change; and in social history, towards understanding social hierarchies and caste historically; and in the links between social forms and ideological expressions, including changes in religion.

Kosambi argued that history was not the recital of kings in chronological order—which was a weakness in the early writing of Indian history—but rather of the events and organization of a society on which information was forthcoming. Although Kosambi did not argue directly for the existence of historical traditions, his analysis of early Indian society made the recognition of such traditions a probability. Such analyses also have a bearing on the question of how a society views its own past. Early records of such views may not conform to modern definitions of historical writing, but their perspective on the past nevertheless remains a matter for study.

Historical change was also central to the research of R.S. Sharma, whose work, primarily on social and economic history, came to focus on the mutation to feudalism in post-Gupta India.[83] Sharma argued for feudal society marking a crucial difference from earlier times. The debate that ensued on whether or not there was feudalism was extensive and vigorous, and triggered many perceptive discussions on the various societies of the subcontinent in that

[82] See, in particular, D.D. Kosambi, *An Introduction to the Study of Indian History*; idem, *Myth and Reality*; idem, *The Culture and Civilisation of Ancient India in Historical Outline*; and Kosambi's papers from various journals, collected and republished in B.D. Chattopadhyaya (ed.), *D.D. Kosambi: Combined Methods in Indology and Other Writings*.

[83] R.S. Sharma, *Indian Feudalism*; idem, *Early Medieval Indian Society*.

period. These in turn have encouraged investigation into regional history. The recognition of these historical processes by various historians, whilst not directly concerned with historiography, has neverthless made the exploration of historical ideas more feasible. When historical change was conceded, there was a searching yet again for historical traditions. However, the initial foray tended to endorse the notion of the a-historicity of Indian civilization. Some studies of this theme have been made, but they remain sporadic. These include a collection of essays in which a few fresh ideas were thrown up, though by and large the older thesis of an absence of historical writing tended to be repeated.[84] Nevertheless, that historiographical possibilities for pre-Islamic India were considered was in itself a major departure. An attempt was made later to introduce a category of texts as distinctively historical, though yet again without much discussion to support this claim and with only a brief résumé of some of these texts.[85] A more detailed exploration of the texts which claim to incorporate historical perspectives is necessary before they can be described as histories.

There has been some limited discussion since then on the early Indian historical tradition. Historians have argued that a historical tradition in early India did exist, but that it was a weak tradition and much of the discussion therefore focuses on why, given the intellection evident within sections of early Indian society, it never developed into a major tradition. This has been in part attributed to the decentralized nature of political institutions, whereas by contrast a centralized state asserts its legitimacy with greater emphasis. However, even in a condition of political decentralization, competition for power among a range of contenders, each drawing on the past, can equally encourage strong claims. The absence has also been attributed to the role of the priestly elite in fabricating genealogies for rulers of low caste whose status could not be openly disclosed, and to the exclusive control of *brāhmaṇas* over the transmission of the tradition.[86]

[84] C.H. Philips (ed.), *Historians of India, Pakistan and Ceylon.*

[85] A.K. Warder, *An Introduction to Indian Historiography.*

[86] B. Stein, "Early Indian Historiography: A Conspiracy Hypothesis", 41–60.

Another explanation points to the bifurcation between the keepers of state records, largely the scribal castes, and the *brāhmaṇas* from whom a critical intellectual assessment might have been expected.[87] But the records of these two castes have not been collected and analysed for historical ideas. Where there are state records, there would not be too much difference between them since both emanated from administrators. It is not that either category was incapable of intellectual assessments, but the fact that the emergence of historical traditions requires more than just the keepers of traditions.

A further explanation argues that Mīmāṃsā philosophy underplayed the centrality of history, especially in relation to the *Vedas*.[88] The point, however, is that the Vedic corpus was the least important as historical writing, as indeed there were other ways of thinking, such as the Buddhist and the Jaina, as also their participation in debates with Nyāya philosophers, which were more attuned to historical perspectives.

A more defensive view takes the position that history is a Western invention and that Indian society's record of itself was differently done. Since historical writing of the Western variety (whichever that might be) was not important, there were no histories.[89] Along similar lines it is said that historiography was replaced by a wilful amnesia that allowed Indians to forget their subjection to foreign rulers.[90] There is here a failure to recognize that much of Indian history was not centrally involved with foreign rule, nor was what we today may call foreign rule necessarily seen as such. Such views have encouraged the generalization about the absence of history in India even among historians not working on Indian data.[91]

It has also been argued that in fact there was a historical

[87] H. Kulke, "Geschichteschreibung und Geschichtesbild in Hinduistechen Mittelalter", 100–13; idem, "Historiography in Early Medieval India", 71–83.

[88] S. Pollock, "Mīmāṃsā and the Problem of History in Traditional India", 603–10.

[89] A. Nandy, "History's Forgotten Doubles", 44–66.

[90] V. Lal, *The History of History: Politics and Scholarship in Modern India*, 14–16, 58–60.

[91] P. Veyne, *Writing History*, 80ff.; M. de Certeau, *The Writing of History*.

tradition—although it is not described as such—but that, despite its existence the colonial power insisted that the colonized had refused to reveal their past. It was also an attempt to cut off the newly educated from their traditional past, which was "the generic discourse by which our culture had constructed and cyclically reproduced the past in sacred and ancestral time."[92] Statements such as this are rather confusing. Are we to understand that the cyclic reproduction of the past in sacred and ancestral time (possibly the reference here is to the *Purāṇas*) represents history as we know it now, or that it is opposed to present-day history and therefore has a validity of its own as history. If it is the latter, then this has to be explained with reference to pre-colonial texts incorporating historical traditions, else such statements read merely like celebrations of altruistic "native" traditions.

It has been stated more than once that the specific ways of ordering the past differ from culture to culture. Such an ordering or historiography would not be obvious from the Indian tradition to those familiar largely with the European. This, having been problematic to the colonial perspective on Indian historiography, continued as a given into later times.

Historical writing in the Indian regional languages from the mid-second millennium AD could seem familiar, up to a point, to a history emphasizing chronology and sequential narrative. But this may well have had elements of a continuity from earlier times and been influenced by the chronicles maintained at the courts of the Sultans. Court languages have always had a dialogue with regional languages and with their traditions, and even more so in the records of the second millennium AD, prior to the colonial period.

An exception to the above views was an important discussion of one specific genre, which was a study of substance relating to a particular category of early Indian historical traditions—*carita* (biographical) literature.[93] An attempt was made to draw from them current views about the past. Equally significant is the

[92] R. Guha, *History at the Limit of World History*; idem, *An Indian Historiography of India*, 33.

[93] V.S. Pathak, *Ancient Historians of India*.

statement that not enough attention has been given to texts that support the existence of a historical tradition, even, for example, the *vaṃśāvalīs* (chronicles).[94] More recently, attention has turned to texts from medieval times in regional languages, as in Telugu, Marathi, and Tamil, which have been discussed as constituting a historical tradition even if not premised on modern historical thinking.[95] Such writings are linked to earlier forms.

Textures of Time has been widely discussed. The texts analysed are in part similar to some that I shall refer to, but there is a considerable difference in historical background since they are later than the ones I have chosen, and their location is in peninsular India. The expectation of history is somewhat different. The book raises the important question of how societies of those times defined history. Even where a text is described as *kāvya* (literary composition), a distinction has to be made between texts intended as history and those with a broader literary interest. This distinction is important to ascertaining what constitutes a historical tradition. It would not be valid to deny the distinction and treat all texts relating to the past as history, and of equal value. As stated by the authors, the genres recording history are not identical with those of the Western tradition and there is no single genre of history carrying a specific name. Since history is culturally formed, much depends on the purpose of the record and the interaction of the author with the audience. In the absence of a single term for the genre, the categorization of texts would indicate intention. This study also shows a degree of continuity in historical forms and perspectives, not unconnected to questions about the nature and function of history.

A close knowledge of pre-Islamic historiography throws light on how the past was continually reformulated even before history-writing came to be practised at the Sultanate and Mughal courts.

[94] M. Witzel, "On Indian Historical Writing", 1–57.

[95] D. Ali, "Royal Eulogy as World History"; S. Guha, "Speaking Historically: The Changing Voices of Historical Narratives in Western India 1400–1900", 1084–1103; V. Narayana Rao, *et al., Textures of Time: Writing History in South India 1600–1800*; P. Deshpande, *Creative Pasts*; R. Aquil and P. Chatterjee (eds), *History in the Vernacular*. See also the debate on *Textures of Time* in *History and Theory*, 2007, 46, 364–426.

It seems evident that the past was not treated as an undifferentiated past, for several forms of earlier writing show awareness of historical change. What we call historical traditions were evolved forms sieved through many of these points of change where, at each new point, the past was reformulated from the repertoire of earlier texts and from current concerns.

2

Towards Historical Traditions

1. Early Historiographies

Colonial constructions of the early history of India are different from those of more recent times. This is in part because of the additional evidence that we now have, but more because of new ways of interpreting the evidence. These new interpretive methods make it possible to illumine the reading of historical views of earlier periods. When trying to arrive at an understanding of the idea of history in an earlier period, a distinction has to be maintained between how the past is understood and represented, and a perception of the past as specifically historical. These are interconnected and involve questions of historiographical frameworks.

Societies represent their past in various ways. A distinction may be made between on the one hand "the past"—the reality of which can only be known in an abstract sense but can be understood; and on the other the nature of its representation, which is in part what is intended by the writing of history. In early periods, this representation took the form of a narrative that related what was believed to have happened in periods prior to the present. This could involve some attempts to explain the events of the past, and in turn required establishing a causal connection between the events and whatever was viewed as the agency determining their form. Historicity comes to the fore when the past is used more purposefully—to legitimize the present—and when causation becomes an important aspect of the philosophy underlying that history. Historical traditions in turn create a historiographical context that includes changing ideologies. Societies, in giving a structure to their past through the process of writing history, draw on this context or framework.

The Indian historical tradition has two distinct historiographies. One emerges from what might be called a Puranic framework, and the other from that of the Sramanic ideologies, particularly the Buddhist and Jaina. These two forms give divergent interpretations, highlighting or suppressing events and persons from the past. They are evidently aware of the alternative position, although this is not always stated, being reflected in mutual borrowings or exclusion. In both, the creation of an identity for the Self involves measuring oneself against the identity of the Other.

There is a third tradition, less clearly differentiated from the other two. This tradition, maintained by bards, goes back to the early epic compositions where, in whatever manner the subsequent authors (who contributed later additions to the epics) happen to be projected, the earlier association with bards cannot be erased. The bardic tradition continues as a substratum into later times as well, even when historical writing was the preserve of scribes and *brāhmaṇas*. The bards claimed that they were maintaining the genealogies of families that were of high status and had the authority that could mutate into dynasties. In the second millennium AD these compositions acquired importance as historical sources. It remains for them to be analysed as essentially oral traditions, and to be put through the investigations that are being made of oral traditions as forms of history.

Both Puranic and Sramanic historiographies contain narratives relating the past. The way the narrative is formulated has to do with the historiography that it represents. The ideologies that influence the historiography draw from both existing political economies and religious concerns, and the historiography changes when these change. Therefore, more than one genre is deployed in generating texts. An essential interest running through them all is, of course, a curiosity about the past and its function in the present.

Where history is tied to the aspirations of a particular community, it takes the form of a single narrative which seeks to make acceptable a particular view of the past. But historical changes led to other alternative narratives of the same past. This then introduced the notion of explaining why some narratives were more accurate than others, although the definition of accuracy could be subordinated to the prejudices of ideology. This reminds us that the reconstruction of the past as history is always a representation and cannot be the "complete truth". The past cannot be resurrected, it can only be comprehended and explained. An awareness of the reasons for accepting particular claims to knowledge, and an insistence on evidence, help to separate fact from fiction. In the words of Jan Huizinga, "History is the intellectual form in which a civilization renders account to itself of its past."[1] History as the narrative of a single voice also became problematic because each such text is also an articulation of its context: the historian has to be aware of both, and this was seldom recognized in premodern times.

The context is what allows us today to observe the complexities of the past looking at its own earlier past. We need to be aware of what is selected and what is left out; of the audience directly addressed and the audience presumed; of the awareness within the narrative of political organization and its possible collaboration with the author; and, finally, we must know whose culture is being discussed.[2]

Narratives about the past go into the making of historical consciousness and become the basis for collective identity. Social memory is said to be reclaimed by what remains of the past, whether in texts or artefacts. A claim is then made for the existence of collective memory. But does such a social memory exist, or does it have to be created? Memory is individual; therefore, what is the process by which it is made "social"? Historical consciousness is rooted in what is believed to be historical memory. This is the turning point to past experience.[3] But historical memory is in itself a creation of the interplay of the past with the present.

[1] J. Huizinga, "A Definition of the Concept of History", 8–9.

[2] A. Momigliano, "Polybius and Posidonius", in idem, *Alien Wisdom: The Limits of Hellenisation*; idem, *Historicism Revisited,* 63–70.

[3] J. Ruesen, *Western Historical Thinking*.

The past can be recast so as to be used as a source of authority and legitimacy in the present. Memories change because aspects of the past can be refitted to the present, which involves some highlighting and some suppression. But this construction, a hybrid made out of the interplay of past and present, cannot be ignored and can even achieve the status of historical tradition.

Essential to history is the shape and accounting of time. A distinction can be made between the past and the present, which is initially often made through symbols, but gradually comes to incorporate measurements of time. Much has been made of the lack of history in India being tied to a cyclic concept of time, an insistence which continues despite research to the contrary.[4] This is contrasted with the linear time of the Judeo-Christian tradition, which is said to provide a necessary factor for historical thinking.

A sharp dichotomy between linear and cyclic time is not feasible since elements of each overlap. The Greeks observed some categories of time in cycles, as did the Indians, and the form of time varied according to its function. Cyclic time is often viewed as cosmological time, whereas the more measured time, in human terms, is linear, recording generations and individual chronologies. Where cyclic time takes a spiral form, it can be seen as almost linear when stretched. This variation can be demonstrated with reference to Indian time calculation.

Even in cyclic time, the present is not a repetition of the past, as has been maintained. Each cycle records change. This too has to be represented, which is done in various ways. Time cycles are constructed through conjuring up figures from a variety of sources—magical numbers and their multiples, or the more precise numbers used by astronomers in their calculations. The measures of linear time are more realistic, generally concerned with life-spans or the period of a dynasty. The notion of a past that is different from the present also assumes a future that is different from both.

[4] M. Eliade, *Cosmos and History: The Myth of the Eternal Return*; idem, *Images and Symbols: Studies in Religious Symbolism*; R. Thapar, *Time as a Metaphor of History*.

2. The Historical Traditions of Early India

I would like to turn the focus away from the now dog-eared arguments about the absence of historical writing and consider more apposite questions of how the past was perceived and recorded in early India. Throughout the book, in each of the ensuing chapters, these are among the basic questions I try to answer, and they form key parts of its framework: Did perceptions in early India encourage notions of historiography? How do we explain the historiographical variants apparent from different perceptions? Answers to these questions, even if partial, provide insights.

My interest in looking at the relevant texts afresh has also arisen because historians are now turning to themes which had earlier been precluded from history.[5] There is now a clear recognition that groups in society have their own versions of history which, however fanciful, reflect their particular perception of the past. These versions can remain discrete or get amalgamated, depending on the intention of the authors. Even a fabricated version claiming to be historical tells us much about its authors and their society. Fabrication may be used as the rhetoric of an ideology, and the reason for the fabrication has to be sought.[6] It does, however, require the recognition that it is a fabrication.

The historian of early periods is now sensitive to spotting change; therefore, the consciousness of the past, and its function within the society showing such consciousness, become relevant questions when studying early societies. To look for similarities with Greco-Roman, Chinese, or Arab models of historical writing is not required when studying the Indian past. It is more pertinent to analyse the forms in which Indian society has chosen to record its past. Similarities between these and forms forged in other civilizations will be self-evident. The more relevant fact is that historical traditions of the early past differ, for each relates to a specific society and sometimes even a specific community.

[5] J. LeGoff and P. Nora (eds), *Constructing the Past*.

[6] E.J. Hobsbawm, "The Social Function of the Past: Some Questions", 3–18; S. Errington, "Style in the Meaning of the Past", 231–44; J. Siegal, *Shadow and Sound: The Historical Thought of a Sumatran People*; M.D. Sahlins, *Islands of History*.

Exploring a particular historical tradition shows its links with that society and might explain why it takes the particular form that it does. Furthermore, every society has many pasts, and this is especially so in a society constituted of multiple social and cultural segments. The records of these many pasts are bound to vary in form. As regards their content, there are again bound to be occasions when assertions conflict, and others where they cohere. A comparison of the variants of a narrative recalling the past can provide insights into the narrative.

Such a shift of emphasis implies raising a number of fresh questions. A view of the past becomes particularly important at times of transition and points of change, for this is when the past can either be rejected, or become a model, or be used to legitimize the changing present. Because a significant function of history has been to legitimize those in power, much of the historical writing which survives from early periods is in the form of statements of the ruling class and the elite. What others had to say has largely to be extrapolated from these statements, or from alternative sources, if any. Attempts at legitimation need not be seen as fraudulent even if recognized as such. The rules of the game were known and the texts have to be decoded accordingly. This also requires that historical traditions be comprehended in terms of the social and political identities from which they emanate.

Perceptions of major historical change are provided in specific and varying images of their past within the historical traditions of particular communities. Underlying the variety, however, what is significant is the notion of change. Also significant is the idea that history means viewing the past from a particular perspective, from a point in time, and that this often also means privileging the present. Therefore, texts which purport to relate to the past have also to be placed in their contemporary context. This implies a relation between the past, the text, and its audience—a relation in effect between the author, even if anonymous, and the community. The form in which time is projected is another way of making a statement. Time is characterized by putting events which are culturally and socially important into a specific chronology, so the perspective of those recording these events is inescapable.

3. The Many Facets of *Itihāsa*

My focus in this book is on why the past was constructed, reconstructed, and represented in particular ways, and on whether these provide evidence of a consciousness of history. I am therefore concerned with trying to analyse awareness of the past in terms of historical processes. Is there a sense of change over time, and how is this recorded? This, in turn, relates to the question of how the past was used in later times, and the self-perception of certain segments of society as part of this continuum. Where there are contending views of the same past, these sharpen the particularities of the perceptions. I will therefore look at the structuring of this consciousness of the past, and the uses made of the construct.

A fine knowledgeable introduction to the subject that differs from earlier attempts is to be found in the opening chapter of the book by Pathak. He scans the *Vedas* and the *Purāṇas* and then focuses on the *caritas* (historical biographies) of the first millennium AD, suggesting the trajectory in the creation of the historical tradition. The hero-lauds of the *Vedas* were not regarded as the revealed literature of the gods but were nevertheless located in the collection of hymns. The authors of the narratives were the Vasiṣṭha priests but the concentration soon moved into the hands of the Bhṛgvāṅgirasa priests, and they seem to have given direction to the tradition. The earlier authorship had been that of the *sūtas* (bards and genealogists), but they were gradually set aside and their compositions appropriated as part of the *itihāsa-purāṇa* tradition.[7]

The two terms associated either separately or conjointly with traditions relating to the past are *itihāsa* and *purāṇa*. *Itihāsa* literally means "thus indeed it was" and has come to be used now to mean history, but earlier it was not history in any modern sense of the term. Mention is also made of *aitihāsikas*, people who comment on a believed history, but these are sparse.[8] *Purāṇa* means that which is old and includes events and stories believed to go

[7] V.S. Pathak, *Ancient Historians of India.*

[8] *Nighantu tathā Nirukta*; *Nirukta* of Yāska, 2.10, 3.19, 4.6.

back to ancient times. Later, by the first millennium AD, this term was applied to a specific body of texts, the *Purāṇas,* which are primarily focused on particular deities. They become religious sectarian texts by providing information on myths and rituals associated with the deity. But some of the *Purāṇas* have distinctive sections that are claimed as historical records.

The *Atharvaveda* and the *Śatapatha Brāhmaṇa* refer to *itihāsa* and *purāṇa*.[9] The conjoint term, *itihāsa-purāṇa*, referring to that which was believed to have happened in the past, is mentioned in the *Brāhmaṇas* and the *Upaniṣads* of the early to mid-first millennium BC.[10] It is described as the fifth *Veda*, which makes it an important but separate branch of knowledge, although the term included the more esoteric kinds of knowledge, such as *sarpavidyā* (serpent lore) and *asuravidyā* (demonology). Promotion to the status of a fifth *Veda* was sometimes given to texts whose subject matter was initially outside the interests of Vedic Brahmanism but which had a specific importance of their own. Bharata's *Nāṭyaśāstra* and the *Mahābhārata* are also described as such. The notion of a fifth *Veda* could suggest a claim to divine sanction but not divine revelation. From the perspective of Vedic Brahmanism it tended to be seen as second-order knowledge. This might have given the impression that Indian civilization—seen as brahmanic—was unconcerned with the past as history.

The *itihāsa-purāṇa* was central to the *kṣatriya* tradition—the tradition of the ruling clans—and the *Upaniṣads* incorporate the concerns of the *kṣatriyas* as well as those of some *brāhmaṇas* proficient in the *Vedas*.[11] This might also have led to it being called the fifth *Veda*. The *Vedas* make a point of including the *gāthās* (hymns) and *nārāśaṃsīs* (poems in praise of heroes) as part of *itihāsa*. The recitation of the *itihāsaveda* and the *purāṇaveda* is recommended during the *aśvamedha* sacrifice.[12] The *Nirukta* of

[9] *Atharvaveda*, 15.6.4, 11.7.24; *Śatapatha Brāhmaṇa* 13.4.3.12–13.

[10] S. Radhakrishnan, *The Principal Upanishads*; *Bṛhadāraṇyaka Upaniṣad*, 2.4.10; *Chāndogya Upaniṣad*, 7.1.2, 7.7.1ff.

[11] R. Thapar, "Sacrifice, Surplus and the Soul", in idem, *Cultural Pasts*, 809–31.

[12] *Aśvalāyana Śrautasūtra*, 10.7; *Gopatha Brāhmaṇa*, 1.10.

Yāska, an etymological text, explains the term *aitihāsika* as one who uses *itihāsa* to explain the *mantras* through narratives relating the past. (The meaning of *mantra* was problematic.[13]) It is also said that a newborn child should be ritually introduced to the three *Vedas* and the *itihāsa-purāṇa*, or that at the funeral of a guru the bereaved should stay up all night hearing *itihāsa-purāṇa*.[14]

The widest definition of *itihāsa* is in the *Arthaśāstra*,[15] where it is associated with a number of more secular forms such as *purāṇa itivṛtta* (past events), *ākhyāyikā* (narrative), *udāharaṇa* (example), as well as *dharmaśāstra* and *arthaśāstra* (ideas on, respectively, social and sacred duty, and political economy).[16] According to some, the idea that instruction in the three human values of *dharma* (sacred duty), *artha* (livelihood), *kāma* (fulfilment of desires), leading to *mokṣa* (release from rebirth), was implicit in the narration of the past described as *itihāsa*.[17] Kings who failed to be familiar with *itihāsa* came to grief, but those that knew it succeeded.[18]

The Buddhist tradition gives the conventional meaning to *itihāsa* but recognizes its association with brahmanical sources.[19] *Purāṇa* is anything which is old, but *porana* in Pāli is closer in meaning to *purāṇa*, implying a written authority. Others are more particular and Jinasena, the ninth-century Jaina author of the *Ādipurāṇa*, defines *itihāsa* as relating that which actually happened: he describes it as synonymous with *itivṛtta* and *amnaya* (authentic tradition).

I would like to examine the reconstruction of the past in the body of literature which is linked to the *itihāsa-purāṇa* tradition in order to ascertain whether, in its view of the past, it reflects

[13] L. Renou, *Études Vediques et Paninéennes*, vol. VI, 62ff.

[14] *Śāṇkhāyana Gṛhyasūtra*, 1.24.8; *Āśvalāyana Gṛhyasūtra*, 4.6.6.

[15] The existing text is dated to the early Christian era but incorporates still earlier sections, some of which may well go back to the Mauryan period.

[16] *Arthaśāstra,* 1.5.

[17] Apte, *Sanskrit–English Dictionary*, 245.

[18] *Manu's Code of Law*, 7.40–3; *Arthaśāstra*, 1.5.12, 1.2.6.

[19] *Pali–English Dictionary*, 119; *Dialogues of the Buddha: Dīgha Nikāya,* 1.88; F.W. Woodward and E.M. Hare (trans.), *The Book of Gradual Sayings*: *Aṅguttara Nikāya,* 1.163; *Mahāvastu*, ed. E. Senart, 1.556.

socio-political changes and emphasizes what the authors of this tradition took to be significant. Where the tradition takes variant forms, it would be worth investigating whether there is a resonance with actual historical change. The change in the genres of texts associated with *itihāsa* is not incidental. It is linked to the major historical changes that have been examined for the long period from *c.* 1000 BC to *c.* AD 1300, but seen more effectively as substantially two periods registering difference: one from *c.* 1000 BC to *c.* AD 500 and the second from *c.* AD 500 to *c.* AD 1300, with a gradual change from one to the other in various parts of the subcontinent.

The categories of texts considered here come from diverse areas. My purpose is not to offer a comprehensive list of texts and their analyses. I intend to take a few representative examples to show the nature of the records as well as what they suggest in terms of encapsulating a historical tradition. I shall, further, confine myself to the areas I know best, which are parts of northern India. The time period by definition peters out in the early second millennium AD. Although historical genres of the late first millennium AD continue into the second, modern historians tend to overlook the continuity. The writings of the latter are viewed generally as being under the influence of Islamic historiography, rather than as an aspect of the continuity of the pre-Islamic, at least in some part. The disjunctures of the periodization of Mill disallow continuities and mutations.

In the absence of deciphered Harappan texts, we have perforce to begin with the early compositions of the *Vedas* such as the *Ṛgveda* and the *Brāhmaṇas*, and their hymns and narratives about heroes. Some segments within larger texts are referred to as *itihāsa,* but even a voluminous text such as the *Mahābhārata* is classified as such. The *purāṇa* emerges by the mid-first millennium AD as a distinct category, although what can be broadly described as historical constitutes only a part of some *Purāṇas*. I have, therefore, selected from among those texts that are either referred to as *itihāsa*; or those that are distinctly concerned with a past which is projected as a statement of events and personalities believed to be historical.

In the early texts, historical consciousness is to be found in an embedded form—veins within the larger structure of texts—and therefore has to be prised out.[20] These are statements that recall the past, or in referring to the present are aware that the past may be recalled in the future. They recur primarily in ritual texts, or in those that may not have been such to begin with but were gradually converted into sacred texts, such as those discussed below in Part II. The text itself is not history and retains its function as a ritual text, or its association with the sacred, but fragments of the historical tradition grow into the text. These embedded forms are often origin myths, compositions in praise of heroes, or genealogies of ancient descent groups. Inasmuch as such forms encapsulate social assumptions and are used to prescribe conduct for the present, they are significant as a specific recollection of the past. Subsequent to this, the genres are more evidently autonomous and historical, or what I have called "externalized". Later historical traditions are articulated in a variety of ways, in forms created specifically to record history, and more centrally structured around author, audience, patron, and occasion. It is these changing forms, in many genres, that I shall be discussing.

The first part of the book looks at the embedded forms up to the point where they are gradually released from ritual texts. A gradual emergence of historical consciousness from ritual texts moves it towards forms that have or claim to have a representation of the past, such as sections of the *Purāṇas*, the early inscriptions, and some creative literature—as discussed in Part III. The alternative Buddhist historical tradition was expressed in a distinctively different body of texts, more centrally historical. This is evident in the Buddhist Pāli Canon encapsulating the early history of Theravāda Buddhism, in the chronicles of the Mahāvihāra monastery, and in the biographies of the Buddha associated with northern Buddhism—all considered in Part IV. The texts that are specifically intended as historical—the royal biographies, inscriptions, and chronicles—are viewed as independent new historical genres in Part V. It seems to me, therefore, that there is within the various historical traditions a gradual change from fragments of

[20] R. Thapar, "Society and Historical Consciousness: The *Itihāsa-purāṇa* Tradition", 353–83.

believed history to the setting out of narratives focused on a more clearly defined history.

Since the notion of embedded history is somewhat unfamiliar, let me explain it in a little more detail. The origins of the *itihāsa-purāṇa* tradition go back to forms that are embedded in ritual texts, and, as accounts of activities of heroes and chiefs, tend to be scattered. Some categories are familiar, such as the *dāna-stuti* hymns of the *Ṛgveda* in praise of generous patrons; or the *nārāśaṃsīs* and the *ākhyānas* (narratives). The inclusion of the narrative as part of the sacrificial ritual perhaps gave it greater credence in referring to contemporary heroes, but certainly ensured its continuity since it would be recalled with each performance of the ritual. Some of these narratives are called *itihāsa.*

Variant versions in later texts introduce new features into these narratives, for the appeal to the past can be to fix a precedent for action in the present. The *Mahābhārata* as *itihāsa* was used on occasion for this purpose. Although rooted in clan society, it demonstrates the transition to kinship largely through the interpretation of the later Śānti and Anuśāsana *parvans* endorsing kingship. In terms of the polity it represents, the Vālmīki *Rāmāyaṇa* narrates the victory of kingship over the clan societies of the *rākṣasas*.

This was all part of the raw material of what was incorporated into the later compilation of the *itihāsa-purāṇa* tradition. The incorporation changed the form. Genealogies went into greater depth in the epics than in the Vedic hymns. In the genealogical section of the early *Purāṇas*—the *vaṃśānucarita*—these were expanded into patterns of *vaṁśas*, or succession lists, and put together in a written form in the early centuries AD, thus representing a construction of the past referring back to earlier times and based on earlier material.

Such a construction of genealogical patterns, reflecting perceptions of the past, evolves out of the embedded form and comes to be used in the more evidently historical texts, such as the *caritas* (biographies) and the *vaṃśāvalīs* (chronicles) of the period subsequent to the seventh century AD. The evolution of these constructions therefore assumes importance and has to be examined. I shall initially consider the embedded forms found in the Vedic corpus, the epics—the *Mahābhārata*, and the *Rāmāyaṇa*—and in the genealogical sections of the *Purāṇas*, as the sources of many concepts which become more central later in the rather different, externalized, embodied forms of the tradition.

This more externalized historical form, embodied in specific texts distinct from earlier ones, comprises biographies of rulers or those in authority, set in a conventionally recognizable form; and chronicles which come either in a literary format, or more concisely in inscriptions. The reading of inscriptions in recent times has focused on information relating to chronology, dynastic history, and economic change, and has tended to overlook the fact that a few are a literal embodiment of historical consciousness.[21] Free-standing inscriptions, as on pillars, were re-used from earliest times.[22] Similarly, the re-use of architectural fragments may have been because of their historical identity, although there are other explanations. Styles can be borrowed, as in the Gupta period emulation of the capitals of Aśokan pillars. Such re-use and imitations make many statements and lead to many questions. Why were particular objects selected, and what meaning did they convey? Re-use is both an act of inheriting the past and translating it. It is one of the ways of making the past visible, both as an object and in its symbolic meaning.

Any codification of the past tends to be selective, and the reasons for making a particular selection are significant to the actual selection. The *itihāsa-purāṇa* tradition, as I hope to show, came to constitute the core of what may be described as one kind of historical thinking. This includes variations in the working over of the tradition, which moved from a heroic to a courtly phase, and from clan societies to kingdoms, although elements of the first

[21] As for example the reading by various historians of inscriptions, such as these: "The Junagadh Rock Inscription of Skandagupta", J.F. Fleet, *Corpus Inscriptionum Indicarum*, vol. III, 56ff.; "Junagadh Rock Inscription of Rudradāman", *Ep. Ind.*, 8, 36ff.; The Allahabad Posthumous Stone Pillar Inscription of Samudragupta, in J.F. Fleet, *Corpus Inscriptionum Indicarum,* 1ff.

[22] F.B. Flood, "Pillars, Palimpsests and Princely Practices", 95–116.

continued into the second. There were, of course, other parallel traditions, equally important in their own right, incorporating a historical consciousness but taking variant forms. The bardic tradition was among these, and the tension between the courtly and the bardic remains an undercurrent. The retrieval of the oral bardic tradition for the early period is problematic since the oral compositions were given a literary form overriding the oral. In addition, there were interpolations from a literary authorship which further smothered the oral. The Buddhist and Jaina traditions were important in recording other persons and events in a different framework.

Texts within the rubric of the *itihāsa-purāṇa* tradition were not examined carefully as representing history because they recorded events that, as noted earlier, were not of central importance to colonial historians. But there was in them a concern with legitimacy as part of origins and status; they show that political power was open and contested; they refer to relations between the state and other important institutions; from them it is evident there was no state religion, although the establishing of a state was often accompanied by both royal patronage to those organized religious sects which had a substantial following, as well as the building of temples, and in some instance *stūpas*, as political statements.

The establishing of a state encouraged the writing of official versions of its history. This was articulated in a somewhat scattered and fragmentary form in Prākrit and early Sanskrit inscriptions (*c.* third century BC to second century AD). These were the precursors to a more systematic coverage of dynasties through inscriptions issued after the mid-first millennium AD.

Attempts at invoking history were made by the dramatist Viśākhadatta, in about the fifth–sixth century AD. He chose to reconstruct historical moments, as in the shift in power from the Nandas to the Mauryas, or a narrative about Cāndra Gupta II. Viśākhadatta's plays remain virtually the only examples of a focused historical drama. These were forays in the Gupta period, and, soon after, at releasing history from ritual texts by providing it with new genres.

This may have been encouraged through some dialogue with the Sramanic historical traditions, although such a dialogue is not mentioned. The latter were not divorced from religious intent; nevertheless they did attempt to give centrality to history—as they viewed it.

Other influential views came from various Sramanic sects and were expressed primarily in the literature of the Buddhists and Jainas. Monasteries, as the institutional centres for preserving the Buddhist and Jaina historical tradition, maintained chronicles of monastic and sectarian activities, not to mention the other literature of such religious sects which referred to the past. A range of reasons could be suggested for this different perspective, among them the historicity of the founders, the breaking away from what has been regarded as orthodoxy or orthopraxy, the importance of eschatology, the social background of the patrons of these sects, the initial urban and literate milieu of the teaching, the institutionalization of sects as orders, the need to maintain versions of sectarian conflicts among these orders as well as their property relations, and the interplay between the religious order and political power.

The dialogue between the Brahmanic and Sramanic views of the past is implicit in a few genealogies and biographies but is not directly referred to. Nevertheless, the awareness of alternative views and traditions is apparent. The choice of royal patrons from history differs: the patrons of each are projected as separate and distinct subjects of the history as recorded by the various sects. The Buddhist monastic chronicles of Sri Lanka, such as the *Dīpavaṃsa* and the *Mahāvaṃsa* of the mid-first millennium AD, reveal much early history by drawing on the history of India associated with the coming of Buddhism to Sri Lanka, in which Aśoka is made to play a major role. In the Mahāyāna of Northern Buddhism, the representation of Indian history is more evident in the *Avadāna* texts and in the biographies of rulers and teachers. Of these, the *Aśokāvadāna* attempts to give an interpretation of the activities of Aśoka Maurya, and clearly from a Northern Buddhist perspective.

Historical writing of a recognizable kind—no longer embedded in ritual texts—emerged in post-Gupta times. It takes three distinct forms: *caritas*, *praśastis*, and *vaṃśāvalīs*. *Caritas*, or historical biographies, were written primarily as *kāvyas* but inevitably incorporated historical views. The earliest and most successful was Bāṇabhaṭṭa's *Harṣacarita*, which captures the historical ambience of the early seventh century and the attempt by Harṣa to acquire sovereignty. The second is Sandhyākaranandin's *Rāmacarita*, later in date, and which provides a perspective on a rebellion by landowning intermediaries.

Many inscriptions subsequent to the seventh century AD can be read additionally as dynastic annals, listing the dynasty chronologically and providing some information on events. I shall be illustrating this by examining the inscriptions of the Candellas, a dynasty chosen at random, but representative of the kingdoms of those times. These inscriptions follow a fairly uniform pattern, since the administration and economy of northern India of this period tend to be similar. The section of the inscription that carries historical information about the dynasty is the *praśasti*, which is in effect a eulogy on the kings and their achievements. The inscriptions of individual kings when read seriatim, read like a chronicle.

Historical traditions of a more elaborate kind, where historical events are central, are found in the *vaṃśāvalīs*, the chronicles maintained in some kingdoms where it was felt that their status required it. The most impressive example is, of course, Kalhaṇa's *Rājataraṅgiṇī*, long recognized as such. I shall be juxtaposing the *vaṃśāvalī* from Chamba with the *Rājataraṅgiṇī* because it comes from the adjoining state, and, although inferior by comparison with Kalhaṇa's work, nevertheless has some characteristics of the genre. Similar to these but from a contrasting ideological position is the *Prabandha-cintāmaṇi* of Merutuṅga, composed in the fourteenth century AD. This is a history of the dynasties of Gujarat with a focus on the Caulukyas. Merutuṅga, as a Jaina author, has concerns rather different from those of Kalhaṇa.

4. Historical Change and the Emergence of Historical Traditions

In an analysis of early historical traditions, a familiarity with the historical background that forms the social, political, and economic context to the traditions is helpful, since these traditions are shaped by the requirements of their contexts. If Indian historical traditions are to be read in the way that I think they were intended, then we have to relate them to the dialectic of their history.

There were obvious processes of change in the institutionalizing of power and resources, from the early societies to the later, more complex, forms. This would also have affected the manner in which the changes were legitimized. These changes are fundamental to understanding why historical traditions mattered, and the form they took. I am arguing that there were changes in historiographical perceptions and genres of writing in the period subsequent to the mid-first millennium AD; therefore, historical change needs to be probed to see if the historical perceptions coincide with this change.

The basic premise of colonial writing on early history was, as we saw, that Indian society was static and registered no change, which argument in large part accounted for an absence of historical consciousness. Although this statement was not seriously questioned by nationalist historical writing, it has been disproved by investigations into history during the last six decades. The recognition of historical change is in part what has encouraged the search for historical traditions, even if only marginally so far. Since my discussion of these traditions derives from the fact of change, and their ways of reflecting the change, I would like to briefly indicate the background that I have in mind when I write about the historical context.

At the level of a broad generalization, I would like to propose that there is evidence for two recognizable forms of organizing societies in early India. The earlier form was that of clan societies. This was followed later by kingdoms, although in some situations and periods of time the two could and did coexist. This observation about the context might also explain why the functions and forms of the historical traditions changed from earlier to later periods. The two forms, clans and kingdoms, were not always exclusively demarcated: there were overlaps and some continuities; and although on occasion they coexisted, one of the two would be prominent at a particular time and place. Since reference will frequently be made in this book to clan societies and kingdoms, the two basic forms, it would be best to define these terms at the start.[23]

A beginning can be made with the definition of a lineage-based society.[24] Identity in such a society derived from the clan—a corporate group of unilineal kin united by an actual or fictive genealogical bond. Persons within the same lineage would trace themselves to the same ancestor.[25] The extended family was the smallest effective social cell. Kinship recognized social ties and controlled a variety of functions within the society. The relationship among members was stated in kinship terms and involved claims and obligations. This explains the insistence on genealogies, fictive or actual, an insistence that was carried over in records of royal descent.

Genealogies became records of identity, both of the past and the present. They are important to two processes in clan societies: one is fission, which is when a large clan can break up and establish smaller ones, some of whom might migrate; and the other is fusion, which is when a few clans come together to form a large lineage group, or induct new clans and form a confederacy. Genealogies, combined with clan myths, can help keep track of these processes. A cluster of clans, dwelling in proximity and claiming to be connected, could constitute the largest unit, the *jana*, sometimes translated as the tribe.[26] Groups descended from a particular ancestor could be recorded as segments, and social organization would be seen as a network of segments, some connected through kinship.

A person was identified through his or her clan as a consequence of being born into it or claiming so. Marriage alliances involving the exchange of women were significant within this. There were

[23] R. Thapar, *From Lineage to State*.

[24] The word "lineage" has varied interpretations in anthropological literature, not all of which are in agreement. My use of the word derives from its basic meaning, namely, that a lineage consists of those who trace their origin to a common ancestor, actual or fictitious, and who claim to have connections in the same descent group.

[25] E. Evans-Pritchard, *The Nuer*.

[26] However, the word "tribe" has been used for such varied situations in the Indian context that it has almost become meaningless. Many scholars prefer to substitute it by lengthier descriptions, as I am trying to do.

rules of endogamy and exogamy which, in effect, stipulated the clans within which a person could and could not marry. These rules underlined the importance of identity as well as the pattern through which women were exchanged. Each clan was relatively egalitarian, although the families of chiefs had a higher status and greater wealth. Considerations of power were expressed through authority vested in seniority, with age as a social marker and the focus of respect. Lineages were ordered hierarchically, and this ordering, if so required, could be recorded or reformulated in genealogical or other forms even at a stage subsequent to that ordering. Because of this hierarchy, some lineages were better placed than others for access to resources. The initial stratification was in terms of a ruling lineage or senior line, and lesser lineages or cadet lines. Lineage-based societies generally maintained some record of their past heroes and events.

Where agro-pastoralism was the main activity, as was the case in early India, herding was the source of wealth. The more effective method of increasing livestock was through raids conducted by the clans, as is evident not only from the *Vedas* but also the many hero-stones of later times, memorializing heroes who died defending the village cattle. Cattle were valuable items of wealth and consequently were given and received as gifts. Pastoralism did not exclude agriculture, undertaken largely by the cadet lines, the produce being offered ritually to the ruling families. The livelihood of such societies would have permitted them to live only in huts, though of course poetic description could convert the huts into fantasy palaces. Wealth was in the form of prestations, offerings, and gifts to the chief. Some would be distributed among clansmen, depending on their function, but the more substantial amount was both consumed in the ritual and given to those performing the ritual. As a form of exchange, the priest legitimized the status of the chief and invoked the blessings of the gods—an intangible gift; in return the priest received the tangible gift of material wealth from the chief.

Such distributions were not arbitrary. Rights of usage extended to land, both pasture land and arable land. In such conditions, land tended to be treated as patrimony rather than commodity. It was not private property, but jointly owned by the clan and, like the lineage name, constituted another form of identity for the clan. A degree of migration is inherent in such societies: pastoralists need new grazing grounds and accessible water resources, and shifting cultivators have to clear new land every few years.

Two categories of persons existed outside the lineage: the men of religion and ritual; and those outside the cadet lines who laboured for the clan. The latter did not share the identity of the clan and were segregated. Possibly, in this process, some were reduced to a status equivalent to that of slaves. Both these categories observed their own social codes. The former organized the rituals, with the more effective ceremonial gatherings tending to become clan assemblies. Some among these ritual specialists were shamans, but, in tandem with a clan's increasing importance, a regular category of priests came to perform rituals. Worship ranged from animism to deities of various kinds. Places of worship were selected when and where required. Ritual specialists were also associated with clan polity. There were among them those who memorized traditions about the past and narrated these on special occasions, an activity also linked to bards and poets.

The chief had to be the hero, and it was the function of the poet-priest to make him one: hence the significance of hero-lauds and ballads. Such poems were generally not very long, but they imbued the chief with the qualities that made him seem exceptional. The recitations of these were when the clan assembled and reiterated, as it were, its identity. Thus the songs in praise of the chief were important both to the chief and to the clan. If the priest had a special role in bestowing on the hero power drawn from the gods, the poet had a special role in marking out the hero as extraordinary. What made him special were both his actions in protecting the clan and his generosity in distributing the offerings that he had acquired. Clan societies had little hesitation in declaring their material needs. The prayer for wealth runs like a chorus through their literature, probably reflecting the need to cope with difficult environments.

This was the bare structure of a clan system. There were variants within this system, with different emphases. The texts mention at least three kinds of clans. One comprised forest-dwelling clans living away from settlements, referred to as *aṭavikas*. The difference of environment between forest-dwellers and cultivators is encapsulated in the two terms commonly contrasted: the *araṇya* or the *vana* was the wilderness or the forest, the unpredictable unknown; and the *grāma* or the *kṣetra* was the settlement, orderly and familiar. Gradually, the former was encroached upon by the latter, most frequently by clearing parts of the forest for cultivation. Slowly, over the centuries, the *vana* was domesticated and became the romantic backdrop to many narratives.

The clan system is also reflected in a second category, that of the *viś* (clan) of Vedic society, comprising agro-pastoralists settled in villages (*grāmas*), as were similar clans described in the *Mahābhārata*. The forest was still the unknown, but since the settlement was more secure the forest was becoming familiar.

The third category of clans was made up of powerful clan societies of long-established cultivators and where social hierarchies were not absent. These were the *gaṇa-saṅghas/gaṇa-rājyas*—clans or assemblies of clans—which formed the earlier stratum in northern Indian society. These are perhaps better described as oligarchies and chiefships. They were more complex than the clans of the *Vedas* and the *Mahābhārata*, boasting of urban centres that were not only the seats of government, handling revenue and administration, but also centres for the exchange of goods. Such centres provided the context to the sophisticated thinking of Mahāvīra and the Buddha. The Pāli Buddhist Canon depicts these societies in greater detail, the Buddha having belonged to the *gaṇa-saṅgha* of the Śākyas and much admired the system. Inscriptions and coins establish their continuity to the early centuries AD in other areas, existing conjointly with kingdoms.

Some among these categories were firmly committed to the clan system, but a few were beginning to hover on the edges of kingship. This ambiguity is reflected in the tensions depicted in the *Mahābhārata* and *Rāmāyaṇa* over forms of control, authority, and power.

Kingship emerged in the middle Ganges plain in about the mid-first millennium BC. It is associated with a number of significant changes. The increasing tendency to invest greater authority in the person of the family of the chief is a reflection of one such mutation. This was expressed through a range of rituals. But in effect it was dependent on the accumulation of wealth by the chief which, unlike earlier times, was not gifted or destroyed through the ritual of sacrifices but was retained by the chief aspiring to kingship. Together with this came the intensification of agriculture, providing greater wealth, assisted by the introduction of a more extensive iron technology by the mid-first millennium BC in both agricultural and artisanal production. The latter led to the creation of centres of exchange, and some of these grew into urban centres, initiating a new urban culture. Basic to this change was greater hierarchy in society, now regulated through caste, and the use of *śūdras* and untouchables as labour. The complexity of social organization, which became greater over time, required governance by a central figure with more individual rights than had been known in clan societies. Kingship slowly emerged and eventually became the norm.

The shift towards kingship was strengthened by the idea of a state, since the office of the king was an accrual of power and was viewed as symbolizing the state. The state was effective in a society divided into hierarchical groups, and in this case the stratification was by caste. This was visualized as the *varṇāśrama-dharma* in the brahmanical *Dharmaśāstras*.The emergence of kingdoms was coterminous with the gradual marginalization of clan society. Groups that claimed control in kingdoms did so not through kinship but through coercive agencies, drawing legitimacy for themselves by appropriating resources and technologies, maintaining however that they had divine sanction.

Gradually, kinship became less important and the functional roles of non-kin persons at the upper levels of society replaced the network of kinship. The political authority of the chief of the clan increased, not only via claims to divine sanction, but also as a consequence of his being accepted as the protector of people, law, and order. His claim to wages in return for this function took the form of a stipulated share of the revenue collected from all that was produced. Those dependent on his authority were no longer kinsmen but non-kin subjects. An echo of the previous system lay in their being referred to as *prajā* (literally "children"), or *prakṛti* (literally "nature"). Appropriations of various kinds also encouraged the demarcation of territory into kingdoms.

The term *rājā* has been translated as "king" quite consistently, without much thought given to the political system within which the word is used. It is possible to argue that *rājā* was initially the word used for the chief of the clan, and that its etymology came from *raj, meaning one who shines or is at the forefront. The frequency of *rājan*, and then of *rājanya*, in the Vedic corpus would tend to support this reading. The context is not that of a king at the head of a state or a kingdom. Although the term *mahārāja* does occur sporadically in the Vedic corpus, it is more in the sense of a great chief rather than the altogether different office of king.[27] As a title *mahārāja* is adopted quite late in the post-Mauryan period by the Indo-Bactrian Greeks, and by Khāravela of Kaliṅga.[28] It occurs frequently in the Pāli Canon, but again not in the sense of a great king. Its earlier use often suggests chiefs and kings according to the context of use; its later use, when as *mahārāja* it claims greater royal authority, suggests a kingdom.[29]

Kingdoms, when they emerged, were hostile to the *gaṇa-saṅghas*, which they saw as an alternative system challenging the new polity. The major conflict in the fifth century BC in eastern India was between the Vṛjjis—a confederacy of *gaṇa-saṅgha* clans—and the newly emerged kingdom of Magadha, the victory of Magadha being a turning point in favour of kingship. This hostility is also highlighted in the *Arthaśāstra*.[30] The *aṭavikas*, regarded as inferior, meet greater hostility from both Kauṭilya and Aśoka.[31] The ostensible reason seems to be that they were resisting the encroachment of the king's armies into their forests. However, the two were not always at the extremities of political relations, and there were some convergences—although these generally meant the acceptance of kingship by the clan society.

Kingdoms are easier to define since they are frequently mentioned in the texts. The contrast with clan society is perhaps best captured in Kauṭilya's definition of a state, where he lists its seven limbs or constituents, the *saptāṅga*: *svāmi*, *amātya*, *janapada*,

[27] *Śatapatha Brāhmaṇa*, 1.6.4.21, 2.5.4.9, 4.3.3.17.

[28] A coin of Eucratides carries the title. Recently, the date has been taken to 180 BC with the legend on a coin of Apollodotus I Soter as *mahārājasa trātarasa apaladātasa*; Hathigumpha Inscription of Khāravela, *Ep. Ind.*, XX, 72ff.

[29] D.C. Sircar argues that *mahārāja*—as a title, as against being just a reference to a respected *rājā*—goes back to translations of Indo-Greek titles, and that there may also have been some influence of Achaemenian titles: *Indian Epigraphy*, 1965, 33ff.

[30] *Arthaśāstra*, 11.1.

[31] J. Bloch, *Les Inscriptions d'Asoka*, 129.

durga, *kośa*, *daṇḍa*, *mitra*. The *svāmi* (king) emerges as the head of a ruling family and the focus of power, and is generally expected to be of *kṣatriya* status—although Kauṭilya does not make this point. The king is assisted by *amātyas* (administrators and senior ministers), who are not his kinsmen and are selected from other competent persons. This is distinctly different from the chief relying on his kinsmen. The *janapada rāṣṭra* (territory of the kingdom) had to be defined and boundaries were generally frontier zones. The centre of governance is the *durga* (the capital), where the king resides and which is also the location of the *kośa* (the treasury), where the revenue is brought and stored. This again differs from clan society, where offerings brought to the chief were either consumed or distributed but not accumulated. The lack of accumulation accounts in part for the continuation of clan society, since it prevents resources being controlled by a single person.

What is meant by access to resources and the revenue thereof was significantly different in clan societies and kingdoms. The revenue in kingdoms came from regularly collected taxes by designated officers, and initially the terms used for taxes were the same as those used for offerings—*bali*, *bhāga*, *śulka*. The taxes came from land, some individually cultivated for the state, some for wealthy landowners. Common ownership by the clan was not the norm. Items produced for sale and exchange were also taxed. The system was sustained by a larger range of activities, demanding labour and greater specialization.

The collection and utilization of resources as revenue, differentiated in the two systems, are sometimes referred to as reciprocity and redistribution. Reciprocity is a one-to-one exchange on various occasions where resources are transferred formally from the recipient to others who are participants in the action. Rituals of sacrifice, such as the *rājasūya* and the *aśvamedha*, are such occasions. Offerings, constituting the wealth of the clan, are collected by the *yajamāna*, the patron of the sacrifice, and used in the ritual. What remains is given as a gift and a fee to the priests. The system of redistribution, on the other hand, is more appropriate to kingdoms where wealth, in the form of revenue, is collected by officers and brought to the treasury, from where the king disperses it to support functions of state.

The two remaining constituents are *daṇḍa* (force), and *mitra* (ally). Governance required maintaining an army of professional soldiers. This was a departure from the clan system, where all clansmen fought when the need arose. Now the king, the capital, and the treasury had to be constantly protected. Sometimes the word *daṇḍa* is used in place of *bala*. This includes punishment and, by extension, the rule of law. The right to coercion was a concession to the king, who was governing subjects with varied identities. And finally, there was the need for an ally, cultivated through diplomacy: allies were required for relations between kingdoms, and on occasion formalized through a matrimonial alliance.

Kingdoms and state systems are characterized by strong political and social hierarchies that are evident in various forms. From the Gupta period onwards, when there is a quantitative and qualitative change in the complexities of state authority and governance, the range of intermediaries (some would call them feudatories) increased, accompanied by an increase in the titles used and permitted. In some cases they became quite lengthy, but the length of a title was more a convention of status than a literal reflection of power. *Rājā* and *mahārāja* gave way to the superior *mahārājādhirāja,* one among many other titles.

These were a reflection of a further political and economic change, which took the form of gradually increasing numbers of grants of land in post-Gupta times. Such land grants were to *brāhmaṇas* who had performed rituals to legitimize power, or to ward off evil; and in similar numbers to administrators who had served the king well; and to Buddhist monasteries. These grants created a category of intermediaries, or feudatories, who occupied the space between the cultivator and the king, and who became recipients of what had earlier been revenue for the king. The merchant and the artisan was a partially parallel system in terms of providing revenue to the state. This was the broad basis of the relationship, although there were variants and adjustments at each level. The well-established and better-off intermediaries saw themselves as potential kings and competed with one another to acquire a throne. In the establishing of these relationships and claims, there was much recourse to earlier historical traditions for purposes of legitimizing rule.

The emergence of a caste-ordered society represented another form of control. Social divisions and distinctions were now sharper than they had been among clans. The hierarchy was more marked, with an emphasis on the subordination of those at the lower end of society. The relatively egalitarian tendency of clan society was eroded. This is sometimes referred to as the movement from *jana* to *jāti*, or from clan to caste. Competition for political authority being relatively open, its legitimation was sought from myths of origin and lineage links. Control over narratives about the past therefore became useful, if not necessary.

Caste society endorses *varṇāśrama-dharma*, the code defined by one's social status and age. These were duties and obligations in accordance with one's caste, and encapsulated social hierarchies. *Varṇa* has been defined as ritual status, which automatically accentuates hierarchy. This was underlined in the importance given to the *dvija* (the twice-born), a term initially used only for the *brāhmaṇa* but later sometimes extended to the next two, the *kṣatriya* and *vaiśya*. The term *kṣatriya* drew on *kṣatra* (power), and *vaiśya* on *viś* (the clan). The fourth, the *śūdra*, was invariably rated low.

In this hierarchy, those outside the system of the four castes were placed outside the pale of caste society and referred to as *mleccha*. This category included forest-dwellers, *caṇḍālas*, and others ranked below the *śūdra* and treated as untouchables, and those seen as alien to the prevailing culture. This was the normative framework of the *varṇāśrama-dharma* which a society was expected to observe. But in fact it was not universally observed. At the lower levels the important component was not *varṇa* but *jāti*, closely identified by birth and occupation. This was in many ways more central to the functioning of caste. What is of interest is that the rules of *jāti* functioning had some affinity with those of the clan. The permanency of segregation between caste groups and those outside the system was maintained by insisting that the *brāhmaṇas* were the purest, the *śūdras* much less so, and the untouchables maximally polluted. The latter two provided labour and this was ensured by insisting on their exclusion.

In the post-Gupta phase the focus shifted to the kingdom and the varied forms that this kind of state could take, the movement being towards control by the few, leading to greater complexity. Clan society was now subordinate. The expansion of kingdoms occurred through two main processes. One was the usual and familiar act of conquering and annexing new areas. The other was more subtle and perhaps particular to the Indian experience. Clan societies were converted to caste societies and incorporated into the kingdom, a historical process brought to the attention of historians by D.D. Kosambi.[32] This change could come about through assimilation, involving changes in occupation, or through confrontation. The range of societies thus incorporated into the caste structure included those that had earlier been hunter-gatherers, forest-dwellers, pastoralists, shifting cultivators, and peasant groups, where clan affiliation was not too distant. The record of confrontations between relatively egalitarian clans, or of conquest, is evident in the sources. However, the confrontation between kingdoms and the societies to be incorporated through the appropriation of resources and conversion to caste is less evident. Yet the historical tradition records this change as well.

Ideologies play a significant role in these processes, drawing on a range of ideas—from belief systems to rational enquiries. Frequently, the coercion is carried out through a hegemonic ideology, generally of a religious sect. This hegemonic form of control is evident in some constructions and representations of the past which provide legitimacy to an authority either already established, or just prior to being so.

Constructions of the past gradually took shape. The movement from lineage-based societies at various stages to kingdoms was a continuous process of historical change even in the centuries AD—although by now kingdoms had become the norm—with clan societies continuing to exist in the more remote areas.

5. Continuities in Historiographical Traditions after AD 1300

The long section above attempts to provide the background to why one may expect a change in historical perceptions over the period of two millennia which may be called early India. The forms that

[32] D.D. Kosambi, *The Culture and Civilisation of Ancient India in Historical Outline*, 140ff.

I have underlined change roughly halfway through. But it is not as if in AD 1300 the forms from the latter part of this period died out. They continued as parallel traditions or were transmuted. I would like to mention these, although they will not be discussed further.

The arrival of the Turks, Afghans, and Mughals did not terminate the importance of the *itihāsa-purāṇa* tradition, which, although no longer dominant at the capitals of these new kingdoms, was still fostered in those where legitimation continued to be drawn from an earlier historical tradition. Sometimes the new rulers were incorporated into the old tradition. Although the Buddhist tradition died down in the kingdoms of the plains, it continued in the Himalayan region and Tibet. That of the Jainas continued in western India, where there were large Jaina communities. The bardic tradition underwent reinvigoration, as evident in the many compositions on kings and local heroes.

Historiography linked to Islamic ideology in India is treated as a monolith. Yet, as I have suggested, there are at least three ideological variations that gave shape to different facets of this historiography: the Arabic, the Turkish, and the Persian, all of which had diverse antecedents. Such diverse legacies would have produced histories with nuances reflecting diversity. These nuances were important to the internalizations of Islamic historiography in India. Historical texts from the courts of the Sultans, and later of the Mughals, were an extension of the chronicle form but with more detail on events and persons. Together with these, inscriptions in the languages of those in authority continued as historical records.

An inscription of the thirteenth century provides an example of how some of the essential features of earlier official documents and chronicles were continued into later times.[33] The inscription was not a royal document, for it was issued during the reign of Ghiyāsuddīn Balban (1266–86), then Sultan of Delhi, by a merchant, Uḍḍhāra, who lived in Ḍhillī/Delhi and is described as a *ṭhakkura*, i.e. a man of status. His family came originally from

[33] Palam Baoli Inscription, in P. Prasad, *Sanskrit Inscriptions of Delhi Sultanate 1191–1526*, 3ff.

Ucca, located in the confluence zone of the rivers of the Punjab and the Indus. This suggests commercial links between that area and the Doab. The inscription records the building of a *dharmaśālā* or inn for travellers (used by travelling merchants) as well as a *baoli* or large step-well.

The inscription opens with a salutation to the deities Gaṇapati and Śiva. It states that the land of Hariyānaka (where Delhi is located) was earlier ruled by the Rajput Tomaras and Cauhānas and is now ruled by the Śakas. The latter term is used sometimes for Turkish and Afghan rulers and harks back to the Śakas of antiquity, who also came from Central Asia via Afghanistan. The previous sultans are correctly listed, even if the conquests of some among them are poetic fancy, and in this the listing recalls the hyperbole of some earlier Sanskrit inscriptions, where it was also required that the current ruler be mentioned. The highpoint is the remark that even Viṣṇu now sleeps peacefully because of the (righteous) reign of Sultan Balban. The donor's genealogy is given, both of his father and mother, as well as details about his siblings, stepbrothers, and sisters. Significantly, mention is made of a separate *vaṃśāvalī* (chronicle) which records the genealogies of the families in greater detail; the reference is doubtless to a precursor of the family genealogies of the dominant castes, maintained to this day at various pilgrimage centres. It further states that Pandit Yogeśvara composed the inscription and gives the precise date of 1333 in the Vikrama era, the equivalent of AD 1276.

Similar inscriptions are available from other sites in the vicinity of Delhi, and of the same century.[34] Hariyāna is described as the territory where Kṛṣṇa Vāsudeva and Arjuna roamed, thus recalling a connection from the *Mahābhārata* and the *Purāṇas*. The sultan, Muhammad Tughluq, is referred to as a Śaka and as "a crest jewel of all the rulers of the earth", a phrase familiar from earlier times. A detailed genealogy is given of the merchant who had had the well built. The inscription concludes with the name of the author and is dated with precision. Another inscription, also a eulogy on a merchant family responsible for constructing a well, carries

[34] Naraina Stone Inscription, in P. Prasad, *Sanskrit Inscriptions of Delhi Sultanate 1191–1526*, 22ff.

the statement that the city of Delhi had been built by the Tomara Rajputs, who were succeeded by the Cauhānas, who were in turn conquered by Shahabuddin Muhammad of Ghor.[35] The latter is referred to as a *mleccha*, indicating someone outside the pale of caste society and, by extension, generally of low status. But here it was probably being used merely as a term of social demarcation. It is unlikely that a term of contempt would be used for a sultan in such an inscription. The current ruler, Muhammad Tughluq, is described as a *turuṣka*, the term used for Turks and for those coming from Central Asia.[36]

On other occasions attempts were made to trace the ancestry of sultans to *kṣatriya* lineages, or to link the origins of local dynasties to Islamic historiography. For example, the Kotihar inscription of 1369 from Kashmir records the construction of a *dharma-maṭha* and refers to the ruling king Shahabadena/Shihab-ud-din. The eulogy evokes Gaṇeśa and Śiva and then refers to Shihab-ud-din as having been born in the house of the Pāṇḍavas, and goes on to list his conquests.[37] This new historiographical tradition was available in the chronicles often maintained in the courts of the Sultans. The earlier fashion in Sanskrit for writing biographies surfaced occasionally even in these courts. Chronicles in the regional languages were written along the traditional lines. This literature requires to be investigated in historiographical terms, as well as for its articulation of local perspectives, and is likely to yield interesting insights on historical perceptions.

Such inscriptions indicate that, even among those who were not members of the ruling families or part of the nobility, there was a continuation in the format of the record from pre-Islamic times. Some chronicles in the courts of the Sultans and the Mughals

[35] Sarban Stone Inscription, ibid., 27ff.

[36] Interestingly, Kalhaṇa refers to the Kuṣāṇas as *turuṣkas*, which probably related to their Central Asian origin since they were not Turks. The use of the term is a back projection for those who came from Central Asia: *Rājataraṅgiṇī*, 1.170, 8.3412.

[37] B.K. Kaul, *Corpus of Sharada Inscriptions from Kashmir*, 113–18; J. Tod, *Annals and Antiquities of Rajasthan*; Veraval Inscription at Junagadh of AD 1264, where the Hijri era is referred to as *rasūla-muhammada-samvat*: *Ep. Ind.*, 34, 141ff.

stemmed from a different historiography, but these did not oust the earlier forms. An understanding of the earlier forms therefore provides insights even into later writing. The inscriptions point to the continuation of a tradition in some formal documents which accompanied the making of grants, gifts, and charitable endowments, as well as those commemorating a notable act.

It is significant that not merely was the form continued, but that it was thought necessary to provide what we today would call a historical context to the statement, with the inclusion of a brief history and precise date. Into this historical context is set the immediate history of the individual donor through the genealogical details of his family and a reference to his caste. One has the impression that this "history" was essential in order to give authenticity to the statement. That such history was more on the model of the earlier tradition, than on that of the contemporary court chronicles of the sultans, would be partly conditioned by it being the statement of a merchant and not a member of the court, and by it being composed in Sanskrit and not in Turkish or Persian—which were yet to take root even in the court at Delhi. This lack of uniformity again seems to reflect the many parallel coexisting ways for the expression of historical consciousness.

An aspect of the continuing presence of history which is seldom recognized is the use made of objects from the past. The most dramatic example is the pillar erected by Aśoka Maurya, originally placed in Kauśāmbi but later shifted to the Allahabad fort. The date of shifting is uncertain. Firuz Tughluq shifted some Aśokan pillars but it is unlikely that he moved this one as the fort at Allahabad was built by Akbar in the late sixteenth century. The pillar just outside the gateway of the fort may have been shifted around this time. Jahangir's inscription dates to 1605. The pillar carries many inscriptions, the important ones being the Pillar Edicts of Aśoka, the long *praśasti* (eulogy) on the Gupta emperor Samudra Gupta, and one giving the genealogy of the Mughal emperor Jahangir. Whether or not Samudra Gupta knew the contents of the Pillar Edicts, no reference is made to them. His own accomplishments—of conquest through wars—were precisely what Aśoka had condemned. Jahangir certainly had no knowledge of the contents of the earlier inscriptions. Yet the pillar in each case was recognized as a statement of history to which a ruler added his own statement, and through this historical function claimed further legitimacy. So the pillar was an object of power and demanded secular respect. It was an act of inheriting and translating the past, as is also evident from the frequent re-use of Aśokan pillars during the Sultanate.[38] Some of these pillars, located at Fatehabad probably by Firuz Tughluq, carry inscriptions on the history of the Tughluq dynasty, which makes the point.

From the early second millennium AD there are narratives in the regional languages pertaining to historical events.[39] These incorporated genealogies, succession lists, and references to events. They were written in various languages of northern India, such as Old Gujarati, Marathi, Dingal, and Oriya. Such texts were, until recently, largely ignored by historians concerned with historiography because they were not written in Sanskrit, or for that matter in Persian or Turkish.

The poem *Kanhadade Prabandha* in Old Gujarati, with the imprint of a Jaina style and composed by a *brāhmaṇa* called Padmanābha, focuses on the resistance of the Cauhānas of Jalor to Ala-ud-din Khilji, an event of 1310. (A comparison has been made between this and the *chansons de geste* of medieval France.[40]) Material of a similar sort in Marathi took the shape of *kaiphiyatas* and *bhakhars*, from the fifteenth century collected in the western Deccan and inspired by ballads on Shivaji and the Maratha chieftains.[41] The most widely quoted composition in this genre from Rajasthan was the *khyāt*, composed in Dingal, by Nainsi, and dates to the seventeenth century. The *Mahārāṣtra Purāṇa*, in

[38] F.B. Flood, "Pillars, Palimpsests and Princely Practices", 95–116.

[39] J.P. de Souza and C.M. Kulkarni (eds), *Historiography in Indian Languages*; R. Aquil and P. Chatterjee (eds), *History in the Vernacular*.

[40] I.M.P. Raeside, "A Gujarati Bardic Poem: The *Kanhadade Prabandha*"; V.S. Bhatnagar (trans.), *Padmanābha's Kanhadade Prabandha: India's Greatest Patriotic Saga of Medieval Times*.

[41] N.K. Wagle, "Heroes in the Charitra-bhakhar, Povada and Akhyana of Seventeenth and Eighteenth Century Maharashtra", 219–36.

Bengali, refers to Maratha incursions into Bengal in the eighteenth century.[42] This harks back to the style of the *Purāṇas* but is more closely concerned with a narrative of contemporary events. Chronicles and temple records from Orissa, such as the *Mādalā Pañjī*, refer to historical events.[43] These texts were written parallel to the court chronicles of the various sultanates and a comparative study might prove instructive.

These were compositions that drew in part from earlier traditions with their multiple sources: the records of the bards and genealogists—the *bhaṭ* and *chāran*—as well as the court records of the scribes. Added to this were doubtless the narratives recorded at the courts of the Sultans and the Mughals in Persian and Turkish, whose authors were familiar with Arabic and Persian histories from further west. These texts of the later half of the second millennium drew together many strands of what they themselves probably saw as histories of families of status, dynasties, and significant events.

But in the nineteenth century, in some places, the style was beginning to change under the influence of Mughal historiography and colonial writing.[44] Mritunjaya Vidyalankar's *Rājabali,* written in 1808, is a narrative of the history of Delhi and Bengal. Time is measured in *tithis* and space is viewed as that of Jambudvīpa and Bhāratavarṣa. The somewhat summary narrative starts with the *Mahābhārata* and continues to the Mughals. Akbar is praised and Aurangzeb carries the contradiction of being both a destroyer and a patron of temples. An oblique reference is made to the *Rājataraṅgiṇī*, perhaps because it was being discussed in Orientalist circles. The stamp of Islamic historiography comes in the statement that all rulers are appointed by Divine Will. Later in time, the model of colonial writing becomes apparent in the *Bhāratabarṣer Itihāsa* of Taranicharan Chattopadhyaya, written in 1878, and in the writings of Bholanath Chakravarti. The latter explains that Hindu society was corrupt and decadent owing to long years of Muslim rule. The coming of Yavana rule

[42] E.C. Dimock and P.C. Gupta (eds), *The Mahārāṣṭra Purāṇa*.

[43] H. Kulke, *Kings and Cults: State Formation and Legitimation in India and South Asia*.

[44] P. Chatterjee, *The Nation and Its Fragments*, 75ff., 95ff.

terminated the decadence. This was precisely the line given by Eliot and Dowson in their *History of India as Told by Its Own Historians.*[45]

The break with the indigenous tradition is more evident with the introduction of European concepts of historiography. With the assumption that there was no historical tradition, let alone information on the past, a structure of historical narrative was seen as necessary. The narrative now begins to describe a different plane of being from what had existed before.

6. Summing Up

I should like to attempt defining historical consciousness as differing from historical traditions and these from historical writing, especially as these terms will recur often. All three make a distinction between a believed past and the present. In the first case it may not be sharply articulated, but it is indicated. My example would be what I have called embedded histories, or more evidently the inscriptions on the pillar of Aśoka at Allahabad. Historical traditions by contrast are not just aware of a believed past but have some understanding of the uses of a past, and these are then employed in texts that draw on the functions of the past. The three traditions that I referred to—the *itihāsa-purāṇa*, the Sramanic, and the bardic—do precisely that. The elision from a historical tradition to historical writing is an unflustered change, not always recognized right away. Historical writing of pre-modern times is sometimes articulated in new literary genres (as in early India), whose prime purpose is to present persons and events in a manner that pertains to the present but may be useful in the future, even if the data draw upon the past. Methodological tests may be applied to historical writing, but with the proviso that the demands we make on historical writing today were not known in those times. Some contextual judgement is a prerequisite.

I shall be arguing that there is a historical consciousness in societies which is expressed in the manner in which they perceive

[45] H.M. Elliot, *The History of India as Told by Its Own Historians*, vol. I, Preface.

and wish to present their pasts. Where this becomes an important part of identity and legitimacy, and is represented as such, with claims of recalling the past, it can take the form of historical traditions. These have to be assessed in terms of their agenda, their use of historical evidence as available to them, and whether the ensuing narrative follows a systematic argument. Where these requirements are met and the texts written as history, they constitute historical writing. Historical consciousness, therefore, is an underlying feature of all societies. Historical traditions may be constituted from this and may initially take embedded forms. Such is the case with poems about heroes, and with epics, and with patterns of the past stitched into ritual texts. By contrast, in Buddhist and Jaina historiographies, prominence is given to events connected with monastic Elders and the history of the Saṅgha, and, by correlating these with the history of rulers and persons of authority, history becomes a powerful statement of a different kind of tradition. The same would hold for the post-Gupta texts that pertain to historical writing, such as the inscriptions, the *carita* literature, and the *vaṃśāvalīs*.

This study is not an exercise in *mentalités*. Nor is it an attempt to reinstate an indigenous interpretation of early Indian history, or to argue that there is an "authentic" version of Indian history in such sources. That kind of enterprise would be neither possible nor worthwhile. It is not my intention to claim that my analysis reflects what the authors of the texts were stating. I am searching for and highlighting those facets in the texts that could represent the ways in which the authors were commenting on what they believed was the past, and on its interface with the period when the texts were composed. In the embedded tradition the narrative was updated more than once through interpolations. When genres of distinctive historical writing emerged, updating and changing was no longer necessary. Since the texts were not associated with the sacred, other texts could be written if so required to confirm or contradict the earlier ones.

Nevertheless, an awareness of the perceptions which earlier authors had of the past does seem to be necessary for understanding early society and culture, and possibly even for the comprehension of "the Indian reality" in early times. To the extent that a historical tradition is a search for and a record of identities, there can be more than one such tradition. The juxtaposition of such traditions and their priorities carries its own message. In the hierarchy of hegemonic discourses, their ranking would vary in time and place.

A historical tradition places events in a chronological framework, although the chronology may not carry dates; it is conscious of past events which are relevant to the society; and these events are recorded in a form which meets the requirements of that society. The form is based on its intellectual and social assumptions—these include the social purpose of the record and the ideological concerns of the society with reference to its understanding of the past. And it is not devoid of some excusable element of fantasy about the past.

My discussion of the texts in this book is from a single dimension: the role of such texts in creating a historical tradition. The central focus is on historical consciousness and changing forms within a society's perceptions of the past. In this sense, my study is limited. It is not an attempt to discuss every major text of a historical tradition, but only to consider a few representative examples. The attempt is to see the earlier traditions as coherent; as possessing some continuities despite changing forms; to analyse some of their constituent forms; to perceive their relation with the society from which they emerged; and to recognize the nature of historical consciousness articulated in multiple ways—which, in any society, is meaningful to the understanding of social culture. The search is for the past looking at its present. The points at which this is viewed become the lineages of their present, linked to nodules of the past, created and reformulated momentarily or over a span of time.

PART II

The Embedded Tradition

3

Fragmentary Narratives from the *Vedas*

1. The Vedic Corpus

The Vedic corpus is so far the earliest body of texts from the Indian past. Much of it was initially transmitted orally and later in a written form. It can be viewed as the point of commencement of the *itihāsa-purāṇa* traditions, initiating forms that eventually became germinal to these traditions. Among them, mention is made of the *dāna-stuti* hymns, included in the earliest of the *Vedas,* the *Ṛgveda*; and, subsequently, of *gāthās* and *nārāśaṃsīs*, all poems in praise of heroes; and *ākhyānas,* narratives that are associated with *itihāsa*. This in itself may not have been the commencement: the *Ṛgveda* may have incorporated some themes from the oral tradition going back to earlier times, and reflecting some integration with other prior cultures. Until the Harappan pictograms are deciphered we can, at best, assume only a marginal continuity of earlier traditions in the Vedic corpus.

The problem in using these texts as historical sources is that the area they cover is vast and their chronology uncertain. Spatially, the area of languages related to Indo-Aryan would include north-eastern Iran, northern Afghanistan, and north-western India.[1] Subsequently, there were migrations into the Ganges plain where, most

[1] Unless otherwise stated, India in this book refers to the Indian subcontinent.

likely, the existing languages were not Indo-Aryan. The Harappan cities date to about 2600–1700 BC. The Vedic corpus is subsequent to this. The *Ṛgveda* is frequently dated to *c.* 1500 BC, although it might even be later, given that its cognates in Old-Iranian and parallels from northern Syria date to about the fourteenth century BC. The substantial presence of Indo-Aryan speakers in north-western India is from this period, although some minimal contact may have existed from the borderlands just prior to this.

Some archaeological cultures have been associated with the period of the later Vedic compositions—such as the Painted Grey Ware culture—overlapping with the Late Harappan at a few sites in the Punjab;[2] and with some Black-and-Red Ware cultures contemporary with a late phase of the Harappan in Gujarat. If some elements of the earlier traditions had continued despite the decline of the Harappan cities, they could have been incorporated into the emergent cultures. The same would apply to whatever may have been brought by Indo-Aryan-speaking migrants from the borderlands. These fragments from the past could include aspects of mythology and rituals, as well as observances based on astronomy; as also some names of clans that might have survived, even if only in memory. This does not mean that the *Ṛgveda* was contemporary with the Harappan culture, but that logically, being post-Harappan, it may include partial survivals from the believed past.

The chronology of the *Vedas* is difficult to sift, for not only were the hymns composed over a long span of time, some fragments could be later interpolations.[3] Thus, even in the *Ṛgveda*, which is earlier than the other three *Vedas*, sections of the first and last of its ten *maṇḍalas* are dated later than the intervening ones. The verses, although composed in the latter part of the second millennium BC, were compiled and edited in various recensions in the early first

[2] J.P. Joshi, "Interlocking of Late Harappan Culture and PGW Culture in the Light of Recent Excavations", 100ff.; R. Thapar, "Puranic Lineages and Archaeological Cultures", in idem, *Ancient Indian Social History: Some Interpretations*, 249ff.

[3] M. Witzel, "Tracing the Vedic Dialects"; idem, "Substrate Languages in Old Indo-Aryan (Rigvedic, Middle and Late Vedic)"; G. Erdosy (ed.), *The Indo-Aryans of Ancient South Asia: Language, Material Culture, Ethnicity*; J.F. Staal, *Discovering the Vedas: Origins, Mantras, Rituals, Insights*.

millennium BC, as was the one of Śākalya, now commonly used.[4] These recensions of the *Ṛgveda* could perhaps have been contemporary with the earlier sections of the later *Vedas*—the *Sāma* and *Yajur Vedas,* constituting the *triveda,* to which the *Atharvaveda* was then added. The *Vedas* came to be accepted as divinely revealed.[5] They were probably codified when their oral reproduction needed to be systematized. Regardless of their chronological uncertainty, what is important is that the process of compiling and editing them suggests the existence of a perspective on the past.

The corpus was edited with reference to people of diverse origins. Since there were earlier settlements of non-Aryan-speaking peoples, whose presence is recorded through non-Aryan linguistic elements in Vedic Sanskrit, and from earlier archaeological sites, the societies reflected in the Vedic corpus were not culturally homogeneous, as is often assumed.[6] A multilingual situation, with the mixing of speakers of more than one language, resulted in linguistic mingling, also reflected in part by mention of many teachers and editors of the Vedic compositions in the *Nirukta* and the *Pratiśākhyas*—the early grammars and etymologies.

Each of the four *Vedas* was identified by a school determined by its editor, and by a set of texts:

- *Saṃhitās*, hymns associated with each *Veda*
- *Brāhmaṇas*, largely exegeses on rituals
- *Āraṇyakas* and *Upaniṣads*, philosophical texts on matters arising from the *Vedas,* and from more general concerns of philosophical thinking
- *Śrauta-sūtras*, concerned with the performing of public rituals, such as the important *yajñas* (sacrifices)

[4] M.M. Deshpande, "Genesis of Ṛgvedic Retroflexion: A Historical and Sociolinguistic Investigation"; *Nirukta* of Yāska, 9–23; *Aṣṭādhyāyī of Pāṇini*, 1.1.16, 4.3.106, 4.3.110.

[5] J. Gonda, *Vedic Literature*, 9.

[6] T. Burrow, *The Sanskrit Language*; F.B.J. Kuiper, *Aryans in the Ṛgveda*; R. Thapar, "Society in Ancient India: The Formative Period", in *Cultural Pasts*, 336ff; idem, "The Archaeological Background to the *Agnicāyana*", in F. Staal (ed.), *Agni*, vol. II, 1–40; R. Thapar, "The Ṛgveda: Encapsulating Social Change", in K.N. Panikkar, *et al.*, *The Making of History,* 11–40, included in R. Thapar, *The Aryan: Recasting Constructs*.

Table I

Texts of the Vedic Corpus Referred to in this Chapter (based on F. Staal, *Discovering the Vedas*, 80–1)

Veda	*Saṃhitā*	*Brāhmaṇa*	*Upaniṣad*	*Śrauta Sūtra*
Ṛgveda				
	Ṛk	Aitareya Kauśītaki		Āśvalāyana Śāṇkhāyana
Yajurveda				
(Kṛṣṇa)	Taittirīya	Taittirīya		Baudhāyana Āpastamba
	Kāṭhaka Maitrāyaṇi		Kaṭha	
(Śukla)	Vājasaneyī	Śatapatha	Bṛhadāraṇyaka	Kātyāyana
Sāmaveda				
		Pañcaviṃśa	Chāndogya	Lāṭyāyana
	Sāma	Jaiminīya	Jaiminīya-Upaniṣad-Brāhmaṇa	
Atharvaveda				
	Atharva	Gopatha		

The Vedic corpus was substantially manuals of ritual, and of exegeses on these. The *Brāhmaṇas* and the *Śrautasūtras*, for instance, composed later than the *saṃhitās*, were more appropriate for priestly recitation and chanting, referred to as *chandas*. Other associated texts were the *Grihyasūtras*, concerned with the domestic rituals of the individual's life-cycle; and the *Dharmasūtras*, which focused on the ordering of society through codes of duties and obligations. The *dāna-stuti* hymns, *gāthās*, *nārāśaṃsīs*, and *ākhyānas* are just a small part of this vast compendium of ritual texts, but the fact that they are included points to their significance.

In the process of stabilizing the corpus a prominent linguistic feature was the separation of the liturgical language/s from the popular language. This was, not overtly but in effect, literate elites acquiring and maintaining a certain kind of social control. That there were already problems in comprehending the language of the liturgical compositions in the early half of the first millennium BC is evident from the need for etymological and explanatory texts, such as the *Nighantus,* the *Nirukta* of Yāska, and the explanation of narratives—as in the *Bṛhad-devatā*. The increasing distance of the liturgical from popular usage was reiterated in Pāṇini's fourth-century BC grammar of classical Sanskrit, where he distinguishes between the more commonly used language, the grammar of which he systematized and which he calls *bhāṣā,* as distinct from the more liturgical language of *chandas*.

The transmission of these compositions, seen essentially as ritual requirements, became the special preserve of the *brāhmaṇas*. For long periods, the compositions were memorized orally. A complex set of mnemonic devices was (and are still) used to ensure the correct articulation of each syllable, since the power of sound was fundamental to the efficacy of the formulae. There is, however, a debate as to whether or not these devices presumed literacy.[7] The earliest evidence of an indigenous script dates to the third century BC with the use of both *kharoṣṭhī* and *brāhmī* in the edicts of Aśoka. The scripts are likely to have emerged just prior to this.[8]

Because of the power believed to lie in the recitation of these hymns, their availability was restricted. There was in theory a careful check maintained on who could legitimately be included among the priests, the criteria being birth and the use of Indo-Aryan speech. However, there were exceptions. References are made to *brāhmaṇas* born of women of low status or alien, as, for example, the *dāsyaḥ-putraḥ brāhmaṇas*. The revered *ṛṣi* Dīrghatamas Māmateya of the *Ṛgveda* is said in the later texts to have married a *dāsī* by whom he had a son, the well-known poet Kakṣīvant. A frequently narrated story refers to the two sons of the *ṛṣi* Kaṇva, one of whom is said to have been of a *śūdra* mother and who walks unhurt through a fire to prove the quality of his

[7] J.F. Staal, *Nambudri Vedic Recitation*; R.T. Oliver, *Communication and Culture in Ancient India and China*; L. Renou, *The Destiny of the Veda*; P. Kiparsky, "Oral Poetry: Some Linguistic and Typographical Considerations".

[8] *Brāhmī* graffiti on potsherds from recent excavations at Anuradhapura in Sri Lanka have been dated to the fifth century BC, but the date and the nature of the evidence are still being debated.

birth.[9] This would be expected in a situation of the commingling of people, and doubtless it acted as an entry point for cultural notions and practices from local sources. Thus, it seems feasible to suggest that the oral traditions of earlier times and of other peoples would have gradually found their way into the immense corpus of Vedic compositions.[10]

All oral sources do not constitute oral history. In order to qualify, the material must reveal an attempt to transmit an awareness of some common historical consciousness.[11] Because the *Vedas* were ritual texts, their preservation and transmission entailed what might be called a closed oral tradition, where, in theory at least, few interpolations could be admitted. This, it was thought, could be ensured by careful mnemonic devices for memorizing the hymns. This was a contrast to the open oral tradition of the epics, where additions and changes were made, although not readily admitted to.

2. The Authors and the Audience

Historical consciousness is articulated in two forms to be discussed here. One is that of the *dāna-stuti* hymns in praise of heroes, which are scattered in various parts of the *Ṛgveda*, although the largest number is in the Eighth *maṇḍala*, associated with the Kaṇva family of *brāhmaṇas*. The Kaṇvas in later texts were linked to the Aṅgirasas who, together with the Bhṛgus, are regarded as keepers of the narratives relating to past events. The late *maṇḍalas* of the *Ṛgveda*—the First and Tenth—also have *dāna-stutis,* in some cases looking back to the past. Such a looking back is more evident in the later Vedic corpus, where *rājās* are said to have performed sacrificial rituals in earlier times, and are upheld as exemplars, such as Sudās Paijavana,[12] also mentioned in the *Ṛgveda.*

[9] E.g. Dīrghatamas in *Ṛgveda,* 1.147, 1.158; A.A. Macdonell and A.B. Keith, *Vedic Index*, vol. I, 336; *Aitareya Brāhmaṇa*, 2.8.1; *Pañcaviṃśa Brāhmaṇa*, 14.6.6. See also *Jaiminīya Brāhmaṇa*, 3.233–5; W. Caland (ed.), *Das Jaiminīya Brāhmaṇa*.

[10] R. Thapar, *From Lineage to State*, 116ff.; D.D. Kosambi, *An Introduction to the Study of Indian History*, 96ff.

[11] D.P. Henige, *Oral Historiography*; B.A. Stolz and R.A. Shanon (eds), *Oral Literature and the Formulae*.

[12] *Aitareya Brāhmaṇa*, 8.21; *Ṛgveda*, 7.18.

The ritual content of the *Vedas* made it inevitable that the authors would be the priests who performed the rituals—the *brāhmaṇa śrotriya* priests. Mention is made of *kavis* (poets), a category that would probably have included *brāhmaṇas* and bards. The *brāhmaṇas* were at this point a caste of ritual specialists and therefore provided paradigms embodying rules, norms, status, and hierarchy which could either be observed, as by the orthodoxy, or rejected, as by the heterodoxy.[13] Ritual was, in turn, locked into *mantras* which, with their emphasis on correctness of sound, constituted a special kind of language.[14] That the Vedic tradition focused on ritual did not of course promise complete authenticity, since ritual itself undergoes change. These were compositions describing and explaining rituals, accompanied by commentaries, all authored by families of priests: therefore their worldview was limited. This was not literature reflecting a large range of social concerns.

Editing and compiling would have involved sorting out authorship, and ascribing authorship either to individuals, which is infrequent, or to families, which is more common. What led to the arrangement of the compositions—doubtless accompanied by diverse opinions on the matter—would have been another experience.[15] Presumably, with each increase in the number of hymns there would have developed a system of farming out the memorization to families of priests, and including new *paṭhas* as mnemonic devices.

Some distinction in authorship can be made between poets and ritual specialists. In one hymn there is a personification of *raibhī, nārāśaṃsī*, and *gāthā*.[16] Also associated with these were the songs of praise recited by *kavis*.[17] Whereas in the *Ṛgveda* there is some overlap between the functions of the priest and the poet,

[13] Cf. J.F. Staal, "The Independence of Rationality from Literacy", 301–10.

[14] Ibid.; K.G. Ghurye, *Preservation of Learned Tradition in India*; C.G. Kashikar, *A Survey of Śrauta-sūtras*.

[15] There have been diverse opinions even in recent times. Among the more representative views are those of L. Renou, *Etudes Vediques et Paninéennes,* Paris, 1956–; and M. Witzel, "Substrate Languages in Old Indo-Aryan (Rigvedic, Middle and Later Vedic)".

[16] *Atharvaveda*, 14.1.7; *Ṛgveda*, 10.85.6.

[17] *Ṛgveda,* 10.114.5.

this was gradually bifurcated in the later corpus and the *brāhmaṇa* grew distinct from the *sūta,* who was in some senses a successor to the *kavi*.

Nevetheless, many poets are named, such as Babhru,[18] Śyāvāśva,[19] Nābhānediṣṭha,[20] and Kakṣīvant. The last is also described as a *vipra, kavi*, and *stotṛ,* and claims Nāhuṣa and the Sindhu *rājā* Svanaya Bhāvya among his patrons.[21] Referred to often and reverentially, Kakṣīvant is both a presser of *soma* and a eulogist.[22] One hymn narrates the restoration of his youth—a common enough legend in many early literatures.[23] Kakṣīvant Auśija is a descendant of Uśij, a *dāsī* who is said to have been sent to his father Dīrghatamas,[24] this being another instance of a *brāhmaṇa* born of a *dāsī.*

The narratives refer to the exploits of the *rājās*, justifying their authority. At this early stage there may, on occasion, have been a tension between the *brāhmaṇa* and the *kṣatriya* in their respective claims to authority.[25] The *brāhmaṇa* was the recipient of gifts—tangible wealth—from the *kṣatriya,* and in return held out to the donor the possibility of rewards, such as going to heaven, attaining power, strength and territory, and controlling labour.[26]

Bards in the *Ṛgveda* were regarded as more than just professionals singing praises of the *rājās.*[27] They are respected *kavis*—*tvam viprastvam kavi*[28]—judged by the quality of their poems and recitals. A comparison is made between the juice of the *soma* plant being "decked" with milk in the same way as the *rājās* are graced with eulogies.[29] *Stutis* (praise) could therefore be fantasy, but references to person and event reduced the fantasy. Eulogies

[18] *Ṛgveda*, 5.30, 8.22.10; *Atharvaveda*, 4.29.21.

[19] *Ṛgveda*, 5.52–61, 8.35.38, 9.32, 8.2.40; *Pañcaviṃśa Brāhmaṇa*, 13.7.12.

[20] *Ṛgveda*, 10.62.

[21] *Ṛgveda,* 4.26.1, 10.143.1, 1.116.10, 117.13, 118.6, 112.11, 1.126, 4.26.1.

[22] *Ṛgveda*, 1.18.1, 1.112.11.

[23] *Ṛgveda*, 10.143.1.

[24] *Ṛgveda*, 1.18.1.; *Pañcaviṃśa Brāhmaṇa*, 14.11.16; *Bṛhad-devatā*, 4.21ff.

[25] *Śatapatha Brāhmaṇa*, 4.1.4.1–6.

[26] *Aitareya Brāhmaṇa,* 8.40.2.

[27] 9.18.2.

[28] *Ṛgveda*, 1.177.5, 1.178.3, 3.33.8, 3.39.7, 5.33.7; *Śatapatha Brāhmaṇa*, 12.1.5.1, 12.4.3.5.

[29] *Ṛgveda*, 9.10.3.

on Indra, victorious over the *dasyu*, represent the deity as hero.[30] Their compositions bring them wealth and the *rājās* are exhorted to give generously to the bards.[31] The *adhvaryu* priest is required to direct singers who sing in praise of the *yajamāna* and the *rājās* of earlier times.[32]

Among those who compose eulogies, mention is made of the Bhṛgus. The Bhṛgu and the Aṅgirasa are sometimes referred to jointly in the phrase Bhṛgvāṅgirasa. As a distinct category of priests they are associated with the *Atharvaveda* and the worship of Agni.[33] It is significant that, in one text, it is explicitly stated that the *hotṛ* for the *rājasūya* should be a Bhṛgu; the *hotṛ* is required to recite the *pāriplava* narratives referring to the past, and these include the *ākhyānas*.[34] Were the Bhṛgus the repository, as it were, of these narratives? They are connected with the *yatis*, whom Indra disliked, and yet they were priests of the Druhyus.[35] The Druhyus were opposed to the Tṛtsu and Bharata.[36] This suggests local political confrontations. Bhṛgus are also said to be the keepers of narratives relating to the *itihāsa-purāṇa* tradition despite being associated with the unorthodox—the *yātudhānas* and the *vrātya*. This situation seems likely to have encouraged many strands in the tradition. Is this a hint that part of the tradition came from non-Vedic sources?

It has been suggested that some priests of the *dāsas* were adopted by the Indo-Aryan speakers.[37] Among these were the Bhṛgus and the Aṅgirasas. They were exempted from the usual rules of marriage for they often married *kṣatriya* wives,[38] thus introducing a category that came to be called *brahma-kṣatra,* a combination of *brāhmaṇa* and *kṣatriya*. This notion may not have been altogether

[30] *Ṛgveda*, 3.34.5–6, 5.33.7.

[31] *Ṛgveda,* 5.10.3, 6.3.7.

[32] *Śāṅkhāyana Śrautasūtra*, 16.1.25; *Śatapatha Brāhmaṇa*, 13.4.3.3.

[33] *Śatapatha Brāhmaṇa*, 1.2.1.13.

[34] *Śāṅkhāyana Śrautasūtra*, 15.12.2, 16.1.22.

[35] *Ṛgveda*, 8.3.9, 6.18.

[36] *Ṛgveda,* 7.8.4, 7.18.

[37] D.D. Kosambi, "On the Origin of Brahmana Gotras", 98–166; R.K. Chaudhury, *Vratyas in Ancient India,* 24.

[38] D.D. Kosambi, "On the Origin of Brahmana Gotras"; J. Brough, *The Early Brahmanical System of Gotra and Pravara,* 4; R.P. Goldman, *Gods, Priests and Warriors.*

unconnected with rights over clan resources and associated authority. They are said to have been the priests of the enemies of the gods—the *daityas, dānavas* and *asuras*—to begin with, and later ministered to those on the side of the *devas* (the gods).

The Aṅgirasa and Atharvan priests are associated with the *Atharvaveda,* viewed as somewhat different from the other three *Vedas,*[39] and are in later texts referred to as Atharvāṅgirasaḥ. The endorsement in the *Atharvaveda* of *yātu* and *abhicāra* (sorcery), as well as *bheṣaja* (healing), hints at its origins as a manual for shamans. There is a telling statement on the relationship of the Atharvāṅgirasaḥ to *itihāsa-purāṇa* when it is said, "*atharvāṅgiras eva madhu kritah iti purāṇam puṣpam* . . ." (the *atharvāṅgirasaḥ* draw out the honey from the flower that is the *purāṇa*).[40] The reference here seems to be less to the text and more to the authors.

Even more striking is the implied association with sorcery of both the Bhṛgus and the Aṅgirasas in references to *yātudhāna.* The *Atharvaveda* is described as *yātuvid,*[41] and the *yātudhāna* are associated with the *rākṣasas.*[42] The two are propitiated through sacrifice.[43] The derivation of *rākṣasa* is from **rakṣa* (to guard). One of the things that was being guarded initially may have been a secret knowledge essential to sorcery, and those having this knowledge could have been the *rākṣasas.*

The closeness of the Bhṛgu and the Aṅgirasa is further illustrated in variations on a myth of origin. The great god Prajāpati performed a sacrificial ritual in the presence of Varuṇa. On beholding the goddess of speech, Vāc, the semen of the two gods fell on the fire. From the flames arose Bhṛgu, and from the embers Aṅgirasa.[44] This myth may have been a later invention, although both the fire and *soma* cults are common to the *Avesta* and the

[39] A.B. Keith, *Religion and Philosophy of the Vedas and Upanisads*, 223–6; A.A. Macdonell and A.B. Keith, *Vedic Index*, vol. I, 18.

[40] *Chāndogya Upaniṣad*, 3.4.1

[41] A.A. Macdonell and A.B. Keith, *Vedic Index,* vol. II, 190.

[42] *Ṛgveda*, 10.87, 10.182, 7.104.1; A.B. Keith, *Religion and Philosophy of the Vedas and Upanisads*, 237–8.

[43] *Taittirīya Brāhmaṇa*, 3.4.1.5.

[44] *Bṛhad-devatā*, 5.97–101; cf. *Aitareya Brāhmaṇa*, 3.34.1; *Nirukta* of Yāska, 3.17.

Ṛgveda.[45] Was one of the claims to ascendancy of the Bhṛgu-Aṅgirasa derived from a believed tradition of knowledge from earlier times? Whatever the case, the association with magic, whether beneficial or hostile, remains dominant.[46] Thus it is mentioned that the Aṅgirasa who was oppressed by the *kṣatriyas* ruined his oppressors.[47]

The migration of some clans eastwards to the middle Ganges plain seems to have led to the induction of local bards and poets, referred to as the *sūta* and the *māgadha*, and yet another group known as the *vrātyas* whose identity, despite speculation, remains enigmatic. But they seem to have some links, however tenuous, with the Bhṛgvāṅgirasas. The term is generally explained as deriving from the root **vrata*, to wander, as they roamed around in bands,[48] a tendency which has led to them also being described as renouncers. The *yati* is sometimes associated with the *vrātyas*.[49] If this association is valid, then the *yatis* may also be linked to the Bhṛgvāṅgirasa.[50] The *vrātyas* are said to speak the language of the consecrated, although they are unconsecrated themselves and require a *vrātyastoma* ritual in order to be made ritually acceptable. The ability to pick up the speech of the Indo-Aryan speakers was crucial.[51] Their having to adapt to Indo-Aryan may suggest they were people from the east, from Magadha and Aṅga, and therefore initially unfamiliar with the speech of those from the Ganga–Yamuna Doab.

[45] *Ṛgveda* 5.11.6.

[46] A.B. Keith, *History and Philosophy of the Vedas and Upanisads,* 224–5; A.A. Macdonell and A.B. Keith, *Vedic Index*, vol. I, 11.

[47] Of the Aṅgirasas mentioned in the Vedic corpus, perhaps the most intriguing is the reference to Kṛṣṇa. Ghora Aṅgirasa is said to have communicated the knowledge of the *Upaniṣads* to Kṛṣṇa, the son of Devakī, and he is said never to have thirsted after knowledge again. *Chāndogya Upaniṣad*, 3.17.6. A Kṛṣṇa, son of Devakī, was to play a major role as the incarnation of Viṣṇu in subsequent times.

[48] This is emphasized in the later meaning of the word, as in the *Aṣṭādhyāyī of Pāṇini*, 5.2.25. See also *Mahābhārata*, Sabhāparvan, 13.55.

[49] R.K. Chaudhury, *Vratyas in Ancient India*, 56.

[50] *Ṛgveda*, 10.72.7, 8.6.18.

[51] N.N. Ghose, *Indo-Aryan Literature and Culture*, 6ff.; *adikṣita-dikṣitavācam-vadanti-aduruktvākyam-duruktamahuḥ*, in *Pañcaviṃśa Brāhmaṇa*, 17.1.9.

It would thus seem that there were people who, although regarded as *mleccha* or outside the pale by the *brāhmaṇas,* were of some consequence. It is just possible that they were the shamans and priests of the earlier culture, and that their claims to power led to their continuation as practitioners of rituals within the Vedic system, thereby also introducing changes in Vedic belief and ritual. A major concession was the inclusion of the book of the Vrātyas in the *Atharvaveda* (Book XV).

Mention is made of the *itihāsa* and the *purāṇa*, the *gāthās* and the *nārāśaṁsīs*, in association with the *vrātyas*.[52] Did such groups then bring their own narratives, introducing their own past? And were these incorporated into the *ākhyānas* of the Vedic corpus so as to appeal to a larger audience at the time of the sacrificial ritual? Such narratives would act as a bridge between the earlier people and those migrating into the area. Yet the *Atharvaveda* was also associated with the Bhṛgvāṅgirasa. The *vrātya* tradition appears to have been an independent tradition which was gradually, although perhaps unwillingly at first, included in the Vedic corpus.

The *Dharmaśāstras*, composed later, came to use the word *vrātya* to refer to groups which had failed to perform their prescribed social and ritual duties. They were therefore thought degenerate, and *brāhmaṇas* were advised to dissociate from them.[53]

Even more directly linked as authors to the seminal historical traditions were the *sūta* and *māgadha*, mentioned only in the later Vedic corpus. The *māgadhas* belonged to Magadha (south Bihar), a land regarded as alien and impure.[54] There is a connection with the *vrātyas* since the *brahmabandhus,* inferior *brāhmaṇas* of Magadha, are recipients of a *dakṣinā* in the form of items belonging to *vrātyas*.[55] *Brahmabandhus* were those claiming to be *brāhmaṇas* but not trained as such, and the same definition was sometimes used for the *vrātya*.[56]

[52] *Atharvaveda*, 15.6.4.

[53] *Manu's Code of Law*, 10.20–3, 11.63; *Patañjali's Vyākaraṇa-Mahābhāṣya*, 5.2.21.

[54] *Śatapatha Brāhmaṇa*, 1.4.1.14ff. The land had to be purified by Agni before it could be settled.

[55] *Lāṭyāyana Śrauta Sūtra*, 8.6.28; *Kātyāyana Śrauta Sūtra*, 22.4.1ff. and 24.

[56] *Pañcaviṃṣa Brāhmaṇa*, 17.1.2; *Chāndogya Upaniṣad*, 6.1.1.

Of the two, the *sūta* had a somewhat better standing, and the word came to be used for a bard. He was not only a bard but one who had a connection with the *rājā* as his charioteer—the chariot was a symbol of status, apart from being military equipment. This proximity allowed him to narrate the exploits of the *rājā*. He is mentioned together with the *grāmaṇi*—the head of the village—and is listed among the eight *vīras* (heroes) and the eleven *ratnins* (jewels) who were important to the *rājā* in the ritual of the *rājasūya* (consecration).[57] The *sūta* is referred to as *rājakṛt*, literally a maker of the *rājā*, presumably through his eulogies on his patron.

The origin of the word *sūta* remains unclear. Linked to the root **su*, it can either mean to consecrate or to impel. The first meaning links it to the recitation by the *sūta* of the *gāyatrī mantra*, which was intended to give energy to the *rājā*.[58] The word has also been explained as denoting the one who preserved the *śruta* and *stuti*, aspects of the tradition.[59] It could also be argued that it had some connection with *sūtra*, or thread, where the other function of the *sūta*, which was to keep the genealogies of the *rājā*, may have been seen as maintaining the thread which ran through succession.[60] Presumably it was in this capacity, as the genealogist of the *rājā* and therefore his legitimizer, that he was also regarded as inviolable.[61]

It has been suggested that *sūtas* were drawn from the Bhṛgvāṅgirasa families, but this plausible suggestion lacks definitive evidence.[62] The *sūtas*, moreover, are not associated with brahmanical training. In subsequent centuries their status is lower, as also that of the *māgadha*, until in the *Dharmaśāstra* of Manu, written at the start of the first millennium AD, the *sūta* comes to refer only to the profession of the charioteer, or to those associated with the keepers of animals.[63] This thus has a bearing on who controlled the historical tradition once it came to be more clearly constructed.

57 A.A. Macdonell and A.B. Keith, *Vedic Index*, vol. II, 462–3.

58 *Kāṭhaka Saṃhitā*, 28.3.

59 F.E. Pargiter, *Ancient Indian Historical Tradition*, 15.

60 R. Thapar, *From Lineage to State*, 137.

61 *Taittirīya Saṃhitā*, 4.5.2.1: *namaḥ sūtāyāhantyāya*.

62 V.S. Pathak, *Ancient Historians of India*, 4, 15ff.

63 *Manu's Code of Law*, 10.11, 17, 26, 47.

There is certainly a contradiction between the status of this group as given in the later *Dharmaśāstras* and that recorded in earlier traditions. Yet the narratives in the *Purāṇas* are often attributed to *sūtas*, and they are central to the epics as well. The *sūtas* were to take up other professions as soldiers, physicians, keepers of horses, and elephants. The *māgadhas*, by comparison, decline.

As regards the audience, the poem in praise of the *rājā* would have been recited at two kinds of gatherings. One was the occasion when the *yajña* was performed, when the clan would have gathered, the poem being part of the larger recitation linked to the ritual. The other would have been a smaller gathering, perhaps intended only for the chief and his kinsmen. In either case the audience would have comprised other poets and the clan. Such hero-lauds were also intended to be heard by later generations, hence their location in ritual texts.

The authors of the fragmentary references to past and contemporary *rājās* seem to have been people who were keepers of a tradition that was distinct from the rituals, even if the tradition was incorporated into ritual texts. They came from groups such as the Kaṇvas, Bhṛgus, Aṅgirasas, and *sūtas*, that initially had a marginal status but who nevertheless worked their way into the mainstream. It is possible that the compositions they controlled, which were historical in nature, came to be seen as a potentially valuable component of power, but not with the same value as ritual. This may possibly explain why the *itihāsa-purāṇa* is referred to as the Fifth *Veda*.

3. The Social Universe of the Vedic Corpus

Events and relations of power are embedded in the Vedic corpus, but they have to be teased out. Such teasing out requires some familiarity with the kind of society and politics it encapsulates. The Vedic corpus illustrates a clan society (as defined in Chapter 2), although there is within it a mutation from the relatively more egalitarian system of the *Ṛgveda* to a more hierarchical system of the later *Vedas*. Eventually, as noted, this was to evolve into kingship and the creation of states from the mid-first millennium BC in post-Vedic times. Since the remembrance of past heroes and events is referred to, it might be useful to keep in mind the historical context of these societies. Some further familiarity with the historical background at this point will also be useful in drawing out elements of historical consciousness from the texts.

The *Ṛgveda* describes cattle-herding agro-pastoralists, whose geographical horizon was the north-west of the subcontinent. The wider horizon was narrowed down to the land between the Sindhu/Indus and the "two grassy banks of the river Sarasvatī".[64] The latter has been identified by some scholars with the Haraxvati to the west and by others with the Hakra to the east of the Indus, or in that vicinity. Some clans migrated eastwards to settle in the Ganga–Yamuna Doab, perhaps because of hydrological changes in the former region.[65] This transition also resulted in greater agricultural activity, which gradually superseded pastoralism.

This would have meant settling in areas which, judging from the archaeological evidence, were in some cases inhabited by an existing sedentary population familiar with agriculture. Seasonal sacrifices point to increasing agricultural activities. A settlement required clearing forested areas, which involve encroaching into the hunting grounds, if not the habitat of existing forest-dwellers. Relations between the various communities involved in such activities changed. The difference between the *grāma* (settlement) and *araṇya* (wilderness) is sharply demarcated. The dichotomies, therefore, were not just between earlier inhabitants and newcomers, but also between the diverse existing societies.

The clan society of the *Ṛgveda* is different from the urban cultures that came before and after—the Harappan cities prior to it and the subsequent kingdoms of the mid-first millennium BC. The unit of society, the *viś* (clan) was located in small localized settlements. A group of clans formed the *jana*, sometimes translated as "tribe", although it might be better understood as "a constituent of a segmentary society". Identity came from the clan one was born into. The mainstay of clan wealth was cattle, alongside horse livestock.[66] The horse's speed made it essential to fast transportation and therefore more valuable than other animals. Increases in wealth required proficiency in herding, involving proximity to pasturelands and water resources. Controlling access

[64] *Ṛgveda*, 7.96.1–2.

[65] M.R. Mughal, *Ancient Cholistan*; R. Thapar, *From Lineage to State*, 21.

[66] Horses of quality, however, have never been successfully bred in India and have generally been imported from Central Asia and Arabia.

to these led to skirmishes. When they proved difficult to come by, cattle-raiding became the simpler way out. Cattle raids and the ensuing violence were almost endemic to pastoral communities. Each clan saw itself as a potential node of power and was vying for authority until such time as it fell by the wayside. Since the focus of authority could shift and the pastoral system required a balance between the clans, raiding was a way of preventing the concentration of power and the accumulation of wealth in one clan. Nevertheless, this could not be avoided and some clans emerged as more powerful and wealthy, and their clansmen became the heroes of the epic poems. The person who protected the resources or led the raid was crucial to the clan, and this was in most cases the chief, the *rājā/rājan*.

A more peaceful access to resources comes about at times when the relationship between pastoralists and cultivators is symbiotic instead of combative. In this, pastoralists follow a defined circuit whereby they move their herds to fields recently harvested. The animals feed on the stubble and their droppings manure the fields. This is not a relationship described in the hymns, but it seems to have been frequently practised. It is a plausible hypothesis that if the cultivators spoke a language different from that of the pastoralists, then some degree of bilingualism may have emerged; and this may have been one factor accounting for non-Indo-Aryan elements in the language of the Vedic corpus.[67] Given the occurrence of non-Aryan agricultural words in the Vedic corpus, it could be suggested that the *dāsas* were the cultivators, with whom eventually a symbiotic relationship emerged.[68]

If this body of clans was to be referred to conjointly, it is just possible that the term used was *pañca-janāḥ* (the five peoples), although its meaning remains something of an enigma. Some have argued that these are the five tribes occasionally mentioned together—the Pūrus, Anus, Druhyus, Turvaśas, and Yadus[69]—as

[67] T. Burrow, *The Sanskrit Language*, 373ff.; F.B.J. Kuiper, *Aryans in the Ṛgveda*.

[68] R. Thapar, *From Lineage to State*, 34ff.; idem, "Society in Ancient India: The Formative Period", in *Cultural Pasts*, 310–35.

[69] B.R. Sharma, "The Pañca-janas in the Vedas", 244–64; M.V. Patvardhan, "Pañcajana", 169–82; *Ṛgveda*, 1.108.8, 7.18.14, 8.10.5.

opposed to the Bharatas.[70] In the *Purāṇas*, the five are described as the sons of Yayāti, a connection which is not made in the *Ṛgveda,* where Yayāti is referred to as a *yajamāna* (patron of the sacrifice) from ancient times.[71] Others have suggested that the five represent the four *varṇas* and those outside the *varṇa* ordering; or various categories of human and celestial beings; or the four fires of the sacrificial ritual and that of the *gṛhapati* (head of the household).[72] Since the number five is sometimes used to represent a spatial totality—four quarters and the centre—by extension *pañca-janāḥ* may be idiomatic for all the clans.

Given the primacy of kinship, recording generations changed from just mentioning individuals as fathers or sons to listing an ancestor or two and a couple of descendants. Generations therefore become time-markers. Depending on the context, such references can be helpful in suggesting the chronology of the hymns.

The *rājā/rājan* was the title of a single person, although clans with multiple *rājās* are mentioned in later sources that refer to them more as governing families.[73] The term is generally translated as "king", but in the context of the *Ṛgveda* "chief" seems more appropriate. Chiefships could last for a considerable time before mutating into kingships. Sacrificial ceremonies, such as the *abhiṣeka*, *rājasūya*, *aśvamedha*, and *vājapeya*, could well have been the initiation and articulation of chiefly power: they need not be seen only in terms of kingship. The context determines whether the reference is to a chief or to a king. The constituents of the state mentioned in the later texts—when states and kingdoms had come to be established[74]—are not evident in these earlier compositions. Elements of impending kingship probably date to a period closer to the mid-first millennium BC.

The *jana* was the larger unit incorporating both the *rājan/rājā* and his kinsmen, as well as the *viś,* and possibly more than one clan. The *rājā* received offerings and prestations (*bali*) from the

[70] *Śatapatha Brāhmaṇa,* 13.5.4.14; *Aitareya Brāhmaṇa,* 8.23.

[71] *Ṛgveda,* 10.63.

[72] 7.67ff.; *Bṛhad-devatā*, 7.51ff.; *Nirukta* of Yāska, 3.8.

[73] As, for example, the many Cedi *rājās* mentioned in the *Cetiya Jātaka,* no. 422, in *The Jātaka.*

[74] *Arthaśāstra,* 6.1.1ff.

viś at the sacrificial ritual,[75] and the produce of the *viś* was for the clan and the *rājā*. The latter in turn acquired additional wealth through cattle raids and predation, which was distributed at rituals where the clan assembled, such as that of the *vidatha*. Cattle raids were also a means of acquiring labour when herders were captured along with their animals. The emergence of the *rājā* as protector distinguishes between those under his protection, his *prajā* (literally: children), and those who were likely to be captured in a raid and were therefore alien. The ability to retain the *prajā* came to be crucial, because raids required a body of followers, as did claims to land newly cleared and settled. The charisma of the chief drew on rituals which, in part, acted as legitimizing devices. Eulogies of the chief, providing exaggerated accounts of his exploits, as in the hero-lauds, were always to his advantage.

A dual social division was that of the *ārya* and the *dāsa*. This has been much debated, particularly in the context of the theory of an Aryan race. From an overview of the evidence it can be suggested that the distinction had less to do with skin colour and racial type, despite occasional references to darkness in connection with the *dāsas*, and more to do with differences in language, belief systems, and cultural norms.[76] The term *ārya* is more frequently associated with status and used for a respected person, and implicitly connected with wealth and possessions.[77] Incorrect use of the Indo-Aryan language is one characteristic of the Other, although not the only one. The emphasis when making the distinction seems to be less on ethnicity and more on Otherness.

The *dasyu*, whom some take to be identical with the *dāsas* (others distinguish between the two terms), are said to be *amantur-anyavrato-amānuṣah* . . .; and elsewhere they are said to be *adevam* and *ayajyavan,* the words suggesting differences in belief, worship, deities, and human concerns.[78] Deities, especially Indra and Agni, help to destroy the *dāsas*. The cattle wealth of the *dāsas* is often the reason for skirmishes. There is hostility towards the *dāsas*,

[75] *Śatapatha Brāhmaṇa*, 1.3.2.15.

[76] R. Thapar, "The *Ṛgveda*: Encapsulating Social Change", 11–40; see also idem, *The Aryan: Recasting Constructs*, 121–60.

[77] H.W. Bailey, "Iranian *Arya* and *Daha*", 71ff.

[78] *Ṛgveda*, 10.22.8, 9.105.6.

but some powerful *dāsa* chiefs find respectable mention. Priests, as recipients of gifts from clan chiefs, refer to the magnanimity even of *dāsa* chiefs. The *śūdra* caste, the lowest and linked to the notion of servility, possibly originated largely from their ranks. *Dāsa* comes to connote a slave, and together with the *śūdra* later became a distinctive functional category, outside the lineage system, providing labour.

Another duality was between the *ārya* and the *mleccha* or *anārya*.[79] The latter was a broader group than the *dāsas* and included those that did not speak the Aryan language, or who spoke it incorrectly, or who did not observe custom as practised by Aryan speakers.[80] This duality was to have widespread geographical ramifications with the rippling outwards of the Aryan language. The term *mleccha* does not always connote contempt, because sometimes it merely means one who is outside the social pale of caste. *Dāsa* came to be used for those thought of as servile.

Vedic society was not egalitarian. The differentiation between the *rājā* and the *viś* becomes sharper in the later *Vedas*. The distinctive roles of the chief and the *ṛtvij* (the ritual specialist) were being accentuated. Kinship determined distance from labour and wealth. Prestations were made at sacrificial rituals and the distribution of these gifts involved larger shares for *brāhmaṇas* and *rājās*. The *rājā*, selected as the representative of the clan, was the repository of wealth, which was computed in cattle, horses, chariots, gold, and *dāsīs*. However, he was not encouraged to accumulate wealth as a means of enhancing his power. The *yajña* (sacrificial ritual) was the occasion for wealth to be periodically displayed, consumed, and destroyed. Rituals that were meant to facilitate the acquisition and consolidation of power actually ensured that the acquired resources were exhausted from time to time, preventing a concentration of authority among the ruling clans. But this gradually changed. The retaining of resources and power by the *rājā* encouraged the eventual emergence of kingship and of the state.[81]

79 *Ṛgveda*, 7.5.3, 7.5.6, 4.16.3, 1.101.1, 10.22.8.

80 *Ṛgveda*, 3.53.14; *Nirukta* of Yāska, 6.32.

81 R. Thapar, "Sacrifice, Surplus and the Soul", in idem, *Cultural Pasts*, 809–31.

Small settlements close to each other were replaced with a clustering of settlements around larger centres in the middle Ganges plain.[82] This appears to have been accompanied by a rise in the population. Rights over land—largely still rights of usage—are held by the clan. Territory as a political unit of subsistence is no longer unbounded but identified as that of the *jana*—the *janapada*: literally, where the *jana* places its foot—and generally named after the ruling clan, thus recognizing territory as a source of power. The differentiation between *kṣatriya* and *viś* is evident in similes, such as one which says the former eats the latter as the deer eats grain.[83] Indra is proclaimed as the prototypical *kṣatriya* and is said to be the sovereign of all creation, the one who attacks the settlements of the *dāsas* and the *asuras* and guards the law.[84]

The stratification of society is frequently referred to in terms of *varṇa*, literally "colour", but used symbolically to differentiate between groups; the word is translated as caste in modern times.[85] Of the four *varṇas*, the *brāhmaṇas* were most frequently identified through *gotras* which were patrilineal, exogamous sibships whose members traced their descent to a common eponymous ancestor.[86] The *kṣatriyas,* from the root **kṣatr*, pointed to power. They claimed status on the basis of genealogical bonds and descent, which comes to be represented in the notion of *vaṃśa* (succession; lineage) and confirmed by marriage alliances with families claiming the correct status. *Kṣatriya* was the term which, in the

[82] G. Erdosy, *Urbanisation in Early Historical India.*

[83] *Śatapatha Brāhmaṇa*, 3.3.2.8, 8.7.2.2, 9.4.3.5.

[84] *Aitareya Brāhmaṇa,* 8.12.17.

[85] The translation of *varṇa* as caste, although current today, raises the problem of the translation of *jāti*, used in some texts more frequently in the sense of caste. A distinction can be made between *varṇa* and *jāti*, where the former relates more to ritual status and the latter to actual socio-economic status and occupation. There is no reference to *jāti* in the *Ṛgveda*, and sparse references to it even in the later parts of the Vedic corpus. This is not altogether surprising since the *Vedas* are essentially ritual texts, and therefore *varṇa* as ritual status would be mentioned more frequently.

[86] P.V. Kane, "Gotra and Pravara in Vedic Literature", 1–17; D.D. Kosambi, "Early Brahmins and Brahminism", 87–97; idem, "On the Origin of the Brahmana Gotras", 98–166; J. Brough, *The Early Brahmanical System of Gotra and Pravara*. In the *Dharmaśāstra* texts *gotras* are said to be important for marriage and for the worship of *pitṛs* (ancestors), i.e. for asserting identity of descent.

later Vedic corpus, superseded the earlier *rājan* or *rājanya* used in the *Ṛgveda*. The function of the *kṣatriya* as the warrior protecting territory and people was gradually extended to governing both. The initial separation between *brāhmaṇa* and *kṣatriya*, and the subsequent interdependence of the two, is indicated in various statements.[87] The interdependence also leads to some tension in the relationship.[88] Eventually the two co-operate in subordinating both the *vaiśya* and the *śūdra*.

The *rājanya* and the *brāhmaṇa* live off the *vaiśya*, whose occupations were cattle-raising, agriculture, and trade. The *vaiśya*, from *viś*, could be oppressed by those in power by being pressed into service or by being made to provide prestations.[89]

The exclusion of the *śudra varṇa* from the first three higher *varṇas* is made clear in the later texts, the *Dharmasūtras,* even by the fact that the *śūdra* cannot trace an ancestry through a *gotra* or a *vaṃśa* (lineage). His ancestry is limited to his parents, who are usually said to be of different castes; therefore he is of mixed caste and this in itself lowers his status.

Such a system of stratification is in part a carry-over from a lineage-based society. Interestingly, the specific hostility of Indra to the *dāsa* and the frequent prayers to Indra in the *Ṛgveda* to destroy the *dāsa,* are mentioned less frequently in the later Vedic corpus. The social ordering of society had now acquired other mechanisms of claiming status and creating subordinated groups. The term *dāsa* continued to be used but the connotation seems to shift from meaning "the Other", to "one who has to be servile".

Caste stratification was also made effective through ensuring that regulations regarding marriage were observed. Rules of marriage were also a form of control over women. Women provided not only progeny but also labour, and patriarchal control was seen as necessary on both counts.[90] The functioning of caste was dependent on this control.

[87] The *adhvaryu* (priest) proclaims the *yajamāna* as *rājā* to the *ratnins*, followed by the statement, *somo'smākam brāhmaṇāh rājā*, that Soma is the *rājā* of us *brāhmaṇas*. *Vājasaneyī Saṃhitā*, 9.40.10.18; *Taittirīya Saṃhitā*, 1.8.10.2; *Baudhāyana Śrauta Sūtra*, 10.56, 58.16; *Āpastambha Śrauta Sūtra,* 18.12.7.

[88] *Atharvaveda,* 5.18, 12.5.

[89] *Aitareya Brāhmaṇa*, 7.29.

[90] There has been some romanticization of the freedom of women in Vedic

Women who are assertive in the narratives tend to be *apsarās/ apsarāses*. Their celestial origin may explain why they are not subservient to male control. The *apsarā*, born of the waters (and therefore often translated as "water nymph"), appeared from the churning of the Milk Ocean, which is symbolic of fertility and plenitude. *Apsarās* can insist on the hero fulfilling their conditions before they agree to live with him, as did Urvaśī.[91] Their repeated transgression of the social norms of human society is a comment on the norms. In terms of lineal descent, the intervention of the *apsarā* in the story often marks a break in the lineage, or the induction perhaps of a new clan, since she is by definition alien. Therefore if a woman of obscure background bore a son to the *rājā*, a possible way of conferring status on her could be that, in recapitulating the story at a later time, she was said to be an *apsarā*.

Genealogical connections and descent gradually come to be mentioned more often because they are a means of conceptualizing rights over areas of subsistence, resources, and even territory. Channelling power into a family or a cluster of families could be through kinship connections. The need for a clan to select its *rājā*, as in the *Ṛgveda*, could act as a counter to this power, but it was unlikely to topple families once so established. Claims to status increase in situations where status cannot be taken for granted and has to be wrested through confrontation. Contending groups often resort to remembering multiple pasts, some claiming to be more authentic.

The diversity of societies disallowed a uniform, unchanging cultural ideology. What was being sought was a system that could provide an identity to those in authority but which was, at the

---

sources. It is emphasized because of the insistence that "Vedic times" were a Golden Age. The occasional Gārgī who was a philosopher is the proverbial swallow who does not a summer make. That women were gifted as wealth, as chattel slaves, is of course not discussed as that would tarnish a Golden Age. The later and even more evident subordination of women in the *Dharmaśāstra* literature drew its legitimacy from the Vedic corpus. U. Chakravarti, "Whatever Happened to the Vedic Dāsī?"

[91] *Ṛgveda,* 10.95.

same time, flexible enough to permit, if required, other groups to be assimilated as part of the identity. This would mean having to readjust, from time to time, accounts of the activities, idioms, and social assertions of those who claimed a particular identity: for example, when those earlier depicted as non-*āryas* in speech and ritual come to be included in the lineages of the *āryas,* the respected ones. Such readjustments had recourse to a presumed history.

The *rājā*'s link to *kṣatra* becomes evident. The selection of the *rājā* is referred to in the context of a war between the gods and the demons when the former decide that Soma, or in other cases Indra, the deity with the greatest prowess, should lead them or appoint a *rājā* to do so.[92] Initially, in the *Ṛgveda,* the *rājā* is seen as a protector, claiming the obedience of those he protected. But beyond this his power was hemmed in by a range of assemblies—the *vidatha, samiti, sabhā*, and *pariṣad*—some select and some open, which acted in multiple ways as bodies of deliberation, as avenues for the redistribution of wealth and booty, as agencies for conferring status, or as the hub of festivity.

Subsequently, special status was conferred on the *rājā* via a series of elaborate *yajñas*—sacrificial rituals discussed at length in the *Brāhmaṇas* and the *Śrautasūtras*: the *abhiṣeka,* which was the initiation into the status of the *rājā* and was included in many sacrificial rituals; the *rājasūya*, which established a *rājā*,[93] and therefore involved the conquest of the four quarters or the *digvijaya* and the bringing of tribute, as well as the lavish consumption and distribution of wealth as part of the proceedings of the ritual; the *aśvamedha,* which combined claims to territorial control with fertility rites; the *vājapeya,* or rejuvenation rites of a *rājā*. These rituals, among others, were elaborate and continuous, in some cases lasting many months, and required an extensive outlay of resources.

The attempt to divinize the *rājā* through these rituals, or at least associate him with deity, became a counterweight to the political

[92] *Aitareya Brāhmaṇa*, 1.14.2ff., 8.12–17; *Śatapatha Brāhmaṇa*, 3.4.2.2–3; *Taittirīya Brāhmaṇa*, 3.1.5.9.

[93] *Śatapatha Brāhmaṇa*, 5.2.3.1ff.: *rājasūyenetva rājā bhavati.*

role of some of the assemblies of the *viś*, and to isolate him by this connection, bringing him even more under the influence of priests. The move towards kingship as divinely sanctioned was assisted by ideas—such as that the *rājā* was the representative of the god Prajāpati and could therefore rule over people.[94]

This introduces two levels of power: abstract power and functional power. The greater his dependence on divine intervention as abstract power, the less was his actual, functional power. The *rājā*, in his isolation through associating with a deity, was increasingly dependent on retainers, such as the *ratnins* (literally "jewels"), who also served to set him apart. Because of his supposed access to a deity, he was said to control events over which ordinary mortals had no control: for example, the ability to terminate a drought. But this special power required that he be physically unimpaired so as to be acceptable to the deities. Physical imperfections disqualified *rājās*, and many a narrative hung on this.

The ritual of sacrifice came to involve both those who offered the sacrifice, the patron or *yajamāna*, and a large range of ritual specialists constituting different categories of priests, in particular the *hotṛ, adhvaryu, udgātṛ*, and *brāhmaṇa*. The larger and longer-lasting sacrificial rituals became occasions for the clan to gather, the legitimizing of the status of the *yajamāna*, the channel for propitiation of and prestations to deities, and the occasion for redistributing wealth. The last was often limited to reciprocal exchanges between the *yajamāna* and the priests, where the former was the recipient of intangible "wealth", such as legitimacy and status, whereas the latter's wealth was only too tangible in the form of *dāna* (gifts) and *daksiṇā* (sacrificial fees).[95]

The performance of a *yajña* resulted in a generalized reciprocity among the *kṣatriyas* and a competition in the establishing of their status on par with a successful cattle-raid. He who bestows the largest gifts on the priest wins undying fame through eulogies and hymns of praise. The best of warriors was invariably the one who also gave most generously of his wealth.[96]

[94] *Śatapatha Brāhmaṇa,* 5.1.5.14.

[95] *Ṛgveda*, 1.48.3–4, 8.63.12, 8.67, 1.18.1ff.

[96] M. Patel, *Die Dānastutis des Rigveda.*

The rituals were also a means of collecting wealth before it was dispersed, and to that extent the *rājā* becomes the focus.[97] The sharing of wealth, implicit in the lavish consumption during the ritual and the subsequent gift-giving, converted the *yajña* into establishing dominance and subordination. This is complicated by the unequal exchange: tangible wealth is bestowed, intangible authority is procured. Legitimation ensuing from the gifting of wealth had a recorded historical continuity from the *dāna-stutis* to the royal *praśastis* (eulogies) of later times.

Despite references to the storing of wealth, such accumulation of wealth remained tenuous. *Brāhmaṇa* recipients, with their healthy expectations and praise of gift-giving, doubtless acted as a check on this accumulation by *kṣatriyas*, the rituals ensuring a depletion of their stores. The acquiescence of the *kṣatriya* in these rituals was in part a consequence of belief in their efficacy, and in part that it kept the wealth in their hands until it was dispersed. This prevented others from tapping the reserves and becoming a rival source of power. In fact, the destruction of wealth was a sign of status and prevented a wider distribution of wealth. This was in some ways a parallel to the potlatch.[98]

At this stage there was no systematic revenue collection backed by authority. Terms such as *bali, bhāga*, and *śulka*—later to be used for taxes on the area of land held, on its yield, and on the value of commodities—were at this time used largely for voluntary first fruits of the harvest, i.e. prestations which tended to become more regular with the establishment of an agricultural cycle or where the power of the *kṣatriya* drew on gift-giving. The association of deities with his legitimation began to change the concept of the *rājā* as chief, with a momentum leading eventually to kingship. However, the instituting of a state in the form of a kingdom was still distant in time.

The gradually changing relationship between the *rājā* and the *viś* becomes apparent. The *Ṛgveda* speaks of the *rājā* eating the *ibhyas* (wealthy ones) in the same way as Agni consumes the

[97] R. Thapar, "*Dāna* and *Dakṣiṇā* as Forms of Exchange", in idem, *Cultural Pasts*, 521–35.

[98] R. Thapar, *From Lineage to State*, 65ff.

forests.[99] This simile continues into later texts.[100] The *rājā* or the *kṣatriya* who, for the sake of victory, may once have eaten from the same vessel as the *viś*,[101] is now implicitly separated. The increasing importance of the *grāmaṇi* (head of the village) indicates a decline in the negotiating ability of the *viś*. *Kṣatra* now combines political power with charisma, hence the more frequent use of the term *kṣatriya* in preference to *rājā*.[102]

Conflicts between the *rājās* are often described as battles, such as the much-quoted battle of the ten kings—the *dāśarājña*—but battles on any large scale were rare; most conflicts were skirmishes involving small numbers. When the sacrificial horse of the *aśvamedha* was released to wander and thereby claim territory for the patron, it was guarded by a troop of only four hundred. The major heroic exploit was still the cattle raid. The pre-eminent Kuru-Pañcālas, said to be speakers of the best Sanskrit, set out on cattle-raids in the dewy season and returned after some weeks. Descriptions of really fearful battles had to wait for the epic literature. The notion of professional soldiers shows a gradual reordering of conflict, as do the declining instances of one-to-one contests between *rājanyas*.[103]

My intention in providing this brief survey of the societies reflected in the Vedic corpus is to suggest the relevance of embedded history in these texts (as also incidentally in the subsequent epics); it also suggests that such history is most often found in lineage-based societies. References to matters of historical import may remain fragmented, but when placed in the context of the society to which they refer their documentary usefulness can be made more apparent. That said, embedded history is not recognizable as history. Nevertheless, what it does reveal is a certain perception of the past which provides evidence for the existence of historical consciousness. Consequent to this, references specifically claiming to be historical—to persons and events in earlier times—can lead to the germination of a historical tradition. These projections of

[99] 1.65.4.

[100] *Śatapatha Brāhmaṇa,* 13.2.9.6–9; *Aitareya Brāhmaṇa,* 8.39.3.

[101] *Śatapatha Brāhmaṇa*, 4.3.3.15.

[102] *Śatapatha Brāhmaṇa*, 2.4.3.7, 6.6.1.7, 9.3.1.13.

[103] *Ṛgveda*, 4.24.4.

the past become increasingly relevant as legitimating strategies to societies and groups aspiring to power when they are in situations of conflict, or when situations demand the accommodation of contending groups through narratives of adjustment. Because these societies comprised multiple competing groups, such narratives of the past were functionally necessary as ideological and hegemonic counterparts of their competition for supremacy.

4. Embedded History in the *Dāna-stuti* Hymns

When the historical context of certain categories of compositions is analysed, their forms provide clues to the society from which they emanate. The *dāna-stutis*—literally, "in praise of gift-giving"—in the form of hymns or verses in the *Ṛgveda,* provide an example. Being essentially a collection of ritual hymns, it is to this function that studies generally draw attention. However, the *dāna-stutis*, although few in number, had an importance of their own. For this reason they were preserved by being embedded, as it were, in a compilation of essentially ritual hymns.

The *dāna-stutis* refer to earlier or current patrons and are the prototype of forms that became praise poems involving heroes, actual or fictive. They are included as fragmentary narratives but mention is also made of them as a specific category in subsequent texts that comment on some of the narratives of the *Ṛgveda*, such as the *Bṛhad-devatā, Nirukta*, and *Anukramaṇīs.* These texts mention the *gāthās, nārāśaṃsīs*, and *raibhīs* being of the same genre as the *dāna-stutis*. But the first three are found more frequently in the later Vedic corpus and the last in the *Ṛgveda*.

Unlike the hymns to Soma, the *dāna-stutis* were not collated into a single *maṇḍala*, but like all compositions showcasing patronage, came to be treated almost as property. They were claimed by particular families, the assumption being that even the recitation of ancestral generosity may result in a gift—at least a milch cow.[104] Clan societies generally recorded the activities of the *rājās*/*rājans*.[105] Their claim to high birth, enhanced through

[104] *Ṛgveda*, 2.2.9, 10.64.12.
[105] T. Earle (ed.), *Chiefdoms: Power, Economy and Ideology.*

a heroic act, was eulogized by the poet, for which he received a gift from the *rājā.*

When the performance of *yajñas* became essential to initiation as *rājā,* the maintenance of that status also became a reason for eulogizing the chief. The rituals created a bond between the chief and the ritual specialist, the fulcrum of which was the act of giving by both to each other, although the gifts so exchanged were not identical. Gradually, a *dakṣinā* or fee was given to the priest and Dakṣinā, the fee personified, in a late hymn indicates this change.[106] To drive home the point, it is said that *dakṣinā* does not come from misers, it comes from those who wish to avoid the dishonour of being called so.[107]

Wealth and prestige require widespread dissemination of the recognition; poems of praise composed by the priests and the panegyrists, as well as by poets—the *kavi, rebha*, and *kāru*—perform this function. If the eulogy pleased the chief, the poet was rewarded, thus creating the nexus of patronage, central to the *dāna-stuti* hymns.

Many *dāna-stutis* are in the form of specific verses. A *rājā*, generally a contemporary, is praised for his munificence in bestowing gifts on the composer.[108] A few are complete hymns, with praise being their sole intention.[109] Many are placed in the late *maṇḍalas*—the First and the Tenth—although the concentration is in the Eighth Book of the Kaṇvas. Some of those in the late *maṇḍalas* refer to patrons of earlier times. Hero-lauds are referred to interchangeably as *stuti, stoma*, or *stotra,*[110] terms that are also used in praising the gods, which may have given rise to the idea of praising the chief. The exploits of Indra—the attacker of *purs*, the winner of cattle, and the lord of wealth—are imitated by the *rājās.*[111]

The event eulogized is rather mundane and hardly occasions

[106] *Ṛgveda*, 10.107.

[107] *Ṛgveda*, 10.107.3.

[108] M. Patel, *Die Dānastutis des Rigveda*; P.V. Kane, *History of Dharmasastra*, vol. II, 837ff.

[109] *Ṛgveda,* 8.1.31–3, 2.41–2; *Bṛhad-devatā,* 3.142ff., 5.62ff.

[110] *Ṛgveda,* 7.32.18–19, 5.18.5.

[111] *Ṛgveda,* 8.5.10ff.

inclusion in a compilation of ritual hymns. However, an association with the deity may, in some instances, be the justification. It has been suggested that these hymns may have been added later.[112] But the sentiments they evoke are intrinsic to clan societies and their concerns. Equal, if not more significant, is the importance of their role as a record of what was assumed to have happened—what is said to be *itihāsa*, and this was likely to be better preserved if embedded in a ritual text.

The composer of the *dāna-stuti* would claim that the hymn made the *rājan* immortal—*rājano amṛtasya.*[113] If immortality is understood as undying fame, then this is a valid claim; today we know about these *rājas* largely through this category of hymns. Such *dāna-stutis* were said to ensure the glory of the *rāja* even in heaven.[114] In a late hymn a bard states that he was the eulogist to Mitrātithi, grandfather of the current *rājā,* Upamaśravas.[115] This suggests that some bards were attached to the family or clan of the *rājā*, a hoary tradition continuing even into the recent present. Authorship of such hymns could be that of a single poet or a group of poets.[116]

Sometimes there is an invocation of the deity with the appeal that the composer rapidly acquire a generous patron. Of the deities invoked, the two most popular are Indra and Agni, although the Maruts, Vāyu, Uṣas, the Aśvins, and Mitra-Varuṇa are also described as assisting the donor to victory, or as witnessing the gift given, or even as exemplars of gift-giving.[117] The poet claims that the intervention of the deity is the result of the poet's invocation.

The more munificent *rājās* were projected almost as gods in their generosity. Deities can be unimaginably generous— doubtless a hint to encourage extravagance among the *rājās*. Praise of

[112] H. Grassman, *Worterbuch zum Rigveda*, vol. II; A.B. Keith, *History of Sanskrit Literature*, 49ff.

[113] *Ṛgveda*, 1.122.7–15.

[114] *Ṛgveda*, 1.126.2.

[115] *Ṛgveda*, 10.33.6–7.

[116] *Ṛgveda*, 8.1.16, 1.126.4, 7.18.

[117] *Ṛgveda*, 6.47.22, 6.27.9, 6.37.4, 5.52.17, 1.122.14, 8.24.28–30, 6.63.9–10, 8.5.37, 5.18.3, 5.27.1, 5.34.9, 1.122.7–9.

the deity elides to praise of the donor. The status of the donor had to be high, even if he was a *dāsa*, and his name had to be mentioned. This gives the narrative a hint of authenticity. The notion of the bard as the moral conscience of the hero was as yet absent.

A recitation of the exploits, past or current, of the human hero follows, together with a listing of the gifts which the composer received. A particularly generous patron, Kuruśravana, is gratefully remembered after his death by the bard, and the patron's son and grandson are reminded of his generosity.[118] The Bharadvāja priests are said to have been handsomely rewarded.[119] The assumption is that if the gifts from past occasions are magnified, those in the present will enlarge.

Of the many patrons, some are singled out for special mention. Abhyāvartin Cāyamāna attacked the Vṛṣīvants at Hariyūpīyā.[120] Successive generations of a family—Sṛñjaya, Sahadeva, and Somaka—claim exploits.[121] Sudās, the son of Pijavana,[122] was of the Bharata clan. Sudās defeated the *rājās* Varcin and Śambara. The Sṛñjayas were his allies and helped him overcome the alliance of ten *rājās*, referred to as the *dāśarājña.*[123] The ten clans opposing Sudās are described as those who do not perform *yajñas*, which gives them an ambiguous cultural identity. The ten consist of those mentioned often—the Yadu, Turvaśa, Anu, Druhyu, and Pūru; as well as those mentioned infrequently—the Pakthas, Bhalānas, Alinas, Śivas, and Visānins. Of the first five, the Anu and the Druhyu seem less important. The Bhṛgus are the priests of the Druhyu but are linked also to the *yatis* whom Indra tried to feed to jackals.[124] The Yadu and the Turvaśa are often coupled, especially when being rescued from a flood by Indra.[125] The Yadu were generous patrons and fought against both Sudās and Śambara. Of the Pūrus, Trasadasyu—whose father was Purukutsa and

[118] *Ṛgveda*, 10.33.4; cf. 10.32.9, 1.33.4.
[119] *Ṛgveda*, 6.47.22–5, 8.46.21–3, 10.33.4–5.
[120] *Ṛgveda*, 6.27.4–8, 4.15.7–10.
[121] *Ṛgveda*, 6.47.
[122] *Nirukta* of Yāska 2.24.
[123] *Ṛgveda*, 7.18, 7.33, 7.83.
[124] *Ṛgveda*, 8.3.9, 6.18.
[125] *Ṛgveda*, 1.174.9, 4.30.17, 5.31.8.

son Kuruśravaṇa—were settled in the Suvastu/Swat region of the north-west. Another *rājā*, Bhāvya, dwelt on the banks of the Sindhu.[126] Pṛthuśravas, the son of Kanīta, gave handsomely.[127] Kaśu, son of the Cedi *rājā*, is said to be particularly generous.[128] A hundred buffaloes come as a gift from another Cedi.[129] Many of these clans are referred to in later texts and their activities treated as having happened in the past.

Among the *dāsa* chiefs, Śambara was feared since he was targeted among those attacked with the aid of Indra. He controlled a large number of *pur* (enclosed settlements).[130] His main foe was Divodāsa Atithigva. Śambara referred to himself as *devakā*, a more honourable title than given to most *dāsas*, and is remembered for his immense treasures.[131] Divodāsa gives the poet the booty taken from Śambara.[132] On another occasion, the *dāsas* Balbūtha and Tarukṣa are mentioned as givers of wealth.[133] It seems apparent from this that the battle lines were not drawn on the basis of ethnic identities, if these did in fact exist; the panegyrists were happy to receive gifts from whoever was willing to give them.

Where the patrons are niggardly, they are described in a satirical manner, such as Śāra, the son of Suradeva, who gave only a single calf to three poets.[134] Possibly, this was in fact the order of wealth that came the way of poets, and the extravagant descriptions need to be taken with a pinch of salt.

In the information provided on the *rājās*, the genealogical depth is shallow and rarely exceeds four or five generations; even these are not listed as a succession. Descent is usually not given within single hymns but has to be collated from scattered references. In an earlier hymn, Trasdasyu is described as the son of Purukutsa; and

[126] *Ṛgveda*, 1.126.1.
[127] *Ṛgveda*, 1.116.21, 8.46.21.
[128] *Ṛgveda*, 8.5.37.
[129] *Ṛgveda*, 8.5.37–9.
[130] W. Rau, "The Meaning of *Pur* in Vedic Literature", 1ff.
[131] *Ṛgveda*, 1.51.6.
[132] *Ṛgveda*, 6.47.22; A.A. Macdonell and A.B. Keith, *Vedic Index*, vol. II, 355.
[133] *Ṛgveda*, 8.46.32.
[134] *Ṛgveda*, 8.70.15.

in a later hymn mention is made of Upamaśravas as a descendant, suggesting an authentic lineage link. Repeated references to the same fathers and sons but in different contexts, as in the case of Sṛñjaya or Sudās, could suggest that some at least of these may have been known persons and not mythical figures.

The Bharatas and the Pūrus who were not allies in the *Ṛgveda* are prominent as lineages in later texts, such as the *Brāhmaṇas* and the *Mahābhārata,* and as part of the prominent Kuru–Pañcāla confederacy. Among the Bharatas, Divodāsa is mentioned a few times but the more authoritative *rājā* was Sudās.[135] The *Brāhmaṇas* have fragments of narrative associated with these *rājās*. The *Mahābhārata* stories, however, revolve around later descendants. The Pūru descent in the *Ṛgveda* is not repeated at any length in the epic.[136] There is a suggested identity between the Pūrus and Purukutsa.[137] Pūru is part of the alliance against Sudās. The epithet *mṛdhravāc* (of harsh or incorrect speech) is used for Pūru, whose ancestor is said to be an *asura rākṣasa,*[138] thus indicating a difference in speech and descent. The clans who allied against Sudās are nevertheless described as *ayajyavāḥ*, meaning "those that do not perform the sacrificial rites".[139] One of the composers is said to be Kavaṣa, possibly the Kavaṣa Ailūṣa mentioned in the *Aitareya Brāhmaṇa* as the son of a *dāsī.* The internal evidence points to the coexistence, whether harmonious or hostile, of clans not identical in culture. The *dāna-stuti* hymns provide one version of this coexistence.

The *Ṛgveda* tends to speak of single clans but the need for self-protection and exploiting resources probably encouraged the idea of confederation; but alliances changed, in part because the enemy was not constant and in part because migrations were essential to the search for pastures and water.

Of conflicts, two in particular stand out. One is the much discussed *dāśarājña*, when Sudās leading the Bharatas and Tṛtsus

[135] *Ṛgveda*, 3.53.9, 33.11.12, 7.18, 7.20, 7.33.

[136] *Ṛgveda*, 8.19, 10.33.6–7; *Bṛhad-devatā*, 7.35–6.

[137] *Ṛgveda*, 6.20.10 and 1.63.7.

[138] *Ṛgveda*, 7.18.13. Even if he was speaking Prākrit, as has been suggested, it was different from Vedic Sanskrit. *Śatapatha Brāhmaṇa*, 6.8.1.14.

[139] *Ṛgveda*, 7.83.7.

defeated a confederacy of ten clans.[140] Although it is translated as "battle", it was hardly of a formal order and was more a defence of the water sources on the river Paruṣṇī, with a skirmish on its banks. The description of this event comes from hymns in the *maṇḍala* attributed to the Vasiṣṭhas. The latter were closely associated with the Tṛtsus, and this may have contributed to the narration of the rout of the enemies. Another conflict involved Abhyāvartin Cāyamāna defeating the Vṛṣīvant at Hariyūpīyā.[141] These were victories over other clans and chiefs who were not invariably fantasized into demons, even though the conflict was sometimes between those described as *āryas* and at other times between *āryas* and *dāsas*.

The heroic exploit that compelled the composition of a eulogy is described in glowing terms, followed by an enumeration of the wealth bestowed by the *rājā* on the poet as reward for the eulogy. Wealth is listed as cattle, horses, camels, chariots, wagons, garments, treasure chests, pieces of gold and jars with gold, and *dāsīs*; dogs, sheep, calves, colts, and asses carry less value. Mention is also made of copper utensils, bamboo objects, and the skin from the *soma* plant after pressing.[142] By far the most valuable of these were horses and cattle, sometimes listed in clearly exaggerated figures. Horses range from a single steed to many thousands. Some poets claim to have received 1000 cows and others 60,000 head of cattle.[143] Such figures are formulaic, as are 100, 1000, and 10,000, since the same figure is at times repeated for an entire list. The wish for more and more cows is the dream of cattle-herders.

The reference to *vadhū*, fifty in number, among the gifts of Kuruśravaṇa,[144] was read as "women" by Sāyaṇa, the commentator on the *Ṛgveda* of medieval times, but others have read it as the female of any species. *Dāsas* are rarely listed as wealth in these hymns, but *dāsīs* are. Did the *dāsī* refer at this point to a captured woman from the *dāsa* community, as seems likely in the context, or was the term already being used for a woman slave in a household?

[140] *Ṛgveda*, 7.18.
[141] *Ṛgveda*, 6.27.4–8.
[142] M. Patel, *Die Dānastutis des Rigveda*, 64ff.
[143] *Ṛgveda*, 8.4.19–20, 6.63.10.
[144] *Ṛgveda*, 8.19.36.

The wealth as listed was largely associated with pastoralism and with chiefdoms and was utility wealth. The *dāna-stutis* reflect the wishful thinking of a society eager for wealth.[145]

The notion of an exchange of wealth here assumes reciprocity. Exchange creates a bond between donor and recipient, and this in turn creates a variety of greater or lesser obligations. Reciprocal gifts can be of equal value or, as in this case, of unequal material value but of equal significance, although different in form and kind. There is, however, a nucleus of the concept of redistribution in the processing of this wealth. The booty collected from skirmishes and raids seems to have been taken to a central place, possibly the assembly of the *vidatha*, where it was distributed. Hymns addressed to Bhāga, literally "the share", clarify the personified Bhāga as the distributor.[146]

The poet, however, was given his gift directly by the *rājā*. The figures mentioned by the poets are doubtful as it would have been unlikely for an agro-pastoral community to produce such wealth—even if only animal wealth. Later too, when the performance of a *yajña* demanded the expending of wealth, the actual gift-giving is likely to have been much less than stated. The elaborate rituals in the later corpus call for prestations and offerings—*bali*, *bhāga*, and *śulka*. These come from the *viś* and are directed to the *yajamāna*. The *rājā*'s control over the *viś* had increased by this time, facilitating the extraction of wealth.[147] Nevertheless, the *yajña* could curb the acquisition of wealth by a *rājā,* thereby enabling a balance between the authority of the *rājā* and the *brāhmaṇa.*

The gifting of land, which was to be introduced some centuries later, is conspicuously absent, as it also is in the listing of wealth in the *Mahābhārata*.[148] The clan had the right to use the land it claimed to control but none had the right of individual ownership. Even in the later corpus, where mention is made indirectly of land being given by the patron to the ritual specialist to establish a

[145] Archaeological sites ranging from 1700 to 600 BC have not revealed great wealth. Burials, unfortunately for historians, are absent, but were unlikely to have yielded dramatic wealth.

[146] *Ṛgveda*, 7.41.2, 9.97.55.

[147] *Śatapatha Brāhmaṇa,* 8.7.2.3, 5.1.3.3, 13.2.2.15.

[148] *Mahābhārata*, Sabhāparvan, 47–8.

settlement, it is not an outright gift, and furthermore requires the approval of the *viś*.[149] Grants of land even as *dakṣinā* are debated and at one point strongly contested.[150] Generally, the best in *dāna* and *dakṣinā* consisted of gold, cattle, garments, and horses.[151] Land is a permanent investment and changes the status of the donee as well as his relationship with the donor.

Wealth actually or even supposedly given on such occasions becomes a form of social gradation, as well as a part of the gift exchange implicit in the relationship between patron and poet.[152] There is an awareness of the distinction between those with wealth and the rest of the clan. Patrons are generally the *rājās* and rarely others. The access to wealth and its acquisition is an evident concern. It has been argued that the word *arya* refers to one who is wealthy.[153] This is also suggested in Pāṇini, who glosses *arya* as *aryaḥsvāmivaiśyayoḥ,* meaning "a lord or a *vaiśya*", i.e. a man of wealth.[154] Can the argument be taken further that the association with a magnanimous gift, even if fictive, could be used as a way of raising the status of those whose origins were obscure, both of the donor and the recipient?

Gift-giving was to remain a nexus between political authority and priestly function, and was intensified when the *yajña* became the pivot in this relationship. In a vertical division of society into lineages with an absence of overall central authority, gift obligations kept a check on those desirous of acquiring the greatest resources. Since gift-giving symbolized mutual dependence and reciprocity, the gift could, up to a point, take on the dimensions of a ritual item: its quantity or financial value need not be taken literally.[155] What was important were the social and economic consequences of the act.

[149] *Śatapatha Brāhmaṇa*, 7.1.1.4.

[150] *Śatapatha Brāhmaṇa*, 13.7.1.13–15.

[151] *Śatapatha Brāhmaṇa*, 4.3.4.7.

[152] R. Thapar, "*Dāna* and *Dakṣinā* as Forms of Exchange", in idem, *Cultural Pasts*, 521–35.

[153] H.W. Bailey, "Iranian *Arya* and *Daha*", 71ff.

[154] *Aṣṭādhyāyī of Pāṇini*, 3.1.103.

[155] M. Mauss, *The Gift*; C.A. Gregory, *Gifts and Commodities*; R. Thapar, "*Dāna* and *Dakṣinā* as Forms of Exchange", in idem, *Cultural Pasts*, 521–35.

It is axiomatic that the wealthy person must give of his generosity when requested: *dado maghāni maghavaniyanaḥ*.[156] If the figures given by the poets were in any way accurate, then they in turn would have been required to gift wealth to others. But we hear none of this, which indicates that the actual wealth gifted to them was probably small. The nuances change somewhat when the gift-giving is linked to the *yajña*. The axis of the sacrificial act could be the gift, where the reciprocation is implicit.[157] This is summarized in the statement *dehi me dadāmi te me dehi te dadhe.*[158]

5. The *Yajña* as the Occasion for Invoking the Past

Of the generous patrons described in the *dāna-stuti* hymns, some continue to be remembered in later sources where they are described as *pūrve mahārājāḥ śrotriyāḥ,* the great *rājās* who were patrons in ancient times. The *rājasūya* ritual required reciting the list of earlier consecrated *rājās*, some of whom performed *yajñas*. Mention is made in particular of Purukutsa the Ikṣvāku, Trasadasyu, Kakṣivant Auśija, Janamejaya the son of Parikṣit, Marutta Avikṣita the Ayogava, Kraivya the Pañcāla, Bharata Dauḥṣanta, Dvaitavana the Matsya, and Para Āṭṇāra of Kosala.[159] The identity of the *rājā* was linked to the clan. Where the ritual was a prayer for progeny, each ended up with a thousand sons. Therefore, the effectiveness of the sacrifice was also endorsed! These references cover a large geographical area of the western and middle Ganges plain, and therefore incorporate traditions from an extensive region.

That this material was embedded in ritual was, as earlier suggested, in part because the ritual gave it longevity and status and was a means of eliding change: old practices could give way to new ones, or new ones could enter relatively unobtrusively and give a

[156] *Ṛgveda*, 7.29.1.

[157] J. Gonda, "Gifts and Giving in the Rigveda", in idem, *Selected Studies*, vol. IV.

[158] *Taittirīya Samhitā,* 1.8.4.1; cf. *Śatapatha Brāhmaṇa*, 2.5.3.19.

[159] *Jaiminīya Upaniṣad Brāhmaṇa*, 2.6.11; *Pañcaviṃśa Brāhmaṇa*, 25.16.3; *Taittirīya Saṃhitā*, 5.6.5; *Aitareya Brāhmaṇa*, 8.21–3; *Śatapatha Brāhmaṇa*, 13.5.4.1ff.; *Atharvaveda*, 20.127.7; *Śāṇkhāyana Śrautasūtra*, 16.9.

new or additional meaning to the ritual. The names of *rājās* and their clans participating in the public rituals are correlated with the names of the priests performing the ritual for them. Such lists could well have been arbitrarily adjusted since accuracy was not their function. They sought sanction from the past for the present. The lists became a way of legitimizing *rājās*' claims to links with earlier ones. They could have resulted either from some *rājās* being challenged, or others maintaining that innovations were traditional. The perceived past had to be carefully memorized. A link with the past is also sought in the rituals dedicated to ancestors, such as the *piṇḍapitṛ yajña.*

A comparison of gift-giving in the *Ṛgveda* with that in the *Brāhmaṇas* suggests that, although the cultural emphases of language and rituals had undergone change, the *rājās* of earlier times continued to be evoked. The preservation of separate identities among clans from past times gave way to a considerable mingling of peoples in the creation of new identities. The trend was towards confederation, involving larger territorial units—one among other factors that encouraged the creation of kingdoms by the mid-first millennium BC. The emerging culture was an amalgam of *ārya* and *dāsa*, with their diverse languages and ritual practices but with different degrees of proximity or separation.

A continuation of the idea of the *dāna-stuti,* and perhaps recognition of the usefulness of the form in creating a perspective on the past, is referred to in the *Śatapatha Brāhmaṇa*.[160] In the context of the *aśvamedha* ritual, two *vīnāgāthins* are mentioned, *rājanya* and *brāhmaṇa*, who sing the praises of the patron, the sacrifices he offered, his victories, and the gifts he distributed. The bifurcation of the task of eulogizing the patron gave a new dimension to the relationship and in some ways made it more important, with both a *brāhmaṇa* and *rājanya* now reciting the *rājā's stuti,* accepting the legitimacy of its role.

Similar to the *dāna-stutis* were the compositions referred to as *raibhis*, *gāthās*, and *nārāśaṃsīs*, which are on occasion linked.[161]

[160] *Śatapatha Brāhmaṇa*, 13.1.5.1–6.

[161] *Śatapatha Brāhmaṇa*, 13.4.3.3–5, 13.4.2.8, 13.5.4.1–24; P. Horsch, *Die Vedische Gatha und Sloka Literatur*; *Atharvaveda*, 15.6.4; *Taittirīya Brāhmaṇa* 1.3.2.6, 7.5.11.2, 13.2.6; *Bṛhad-devatā*, 3.154; *Ṛgveda*, 1.126.1, 2.34.6, 6.24.2, 8.32.1, 9.99.4, 10.85.6; *Aitareya Brāhmaṇa,* 6.32; *Gopatha Brāhmaṇa,* 2.6.12.

The *gāthās* are thought to be epic fragments that may have been added later to the *Vedas* at appropriate places. The emphasis shifts from extolling the heroic exploit to extolling the *rājā* for holding a sacrificial ritual and giving a handsome *dakṣinā* to the priests, regardless of whatever heroic exploits he may have performed. The poetic function is subordinated to the priestly, but the need to remember precedents is emphasized. This emphasis is new when compared to the *dāna-stutis* of the *Ṛgveda*.

With the ritual running over many days, the recitation of narratives became a way of retaining the attention of the participants and the audience. The reward for the poet, where not explicitly stated, was implicit in the act of composing and reciting the narrative. The eulogistic content is so evident that the compositions are sometimes dismissed as untrue, although it is not clear whether the falsity refers to the size of the gift rather than the exploit.[162] It could suggest that there was an accepted version, or perhaps a memory of an event, with which these versions were being compared.

The *gāthins* who sang the *gāthās* were the precursors or associates of the professional bards of later times, the *vīnāgāthins* composing verses on "battles". The *gāthā* was also incorporated into the *gṛhya* or domestic rituals, especially in rites to ensure heroic offspring.[163] The prototypes were the Indra-*gāthā*, the song in praise of Indra as the deity who destroys the strongholds of the enemy and helps various *rājās* against their foes, a similar sentiment to that expressed in the *sūktas*, such as those of Nābhānediṣṭha.[164] A few of the *rājās* who feature in the *dāna-stutis* are also referred to in the *gāthās.* Others are new names of a later date.

The composition of the *gāthās* has been linked to the Kaṇva *brāhmaṇas.* This would not be surprising as the *dāna-stuti* hymns are found largely in the Kaṇva book of the *Ṛgveda.* Some *gāthās* recall *rājās* who performed the *aśvamedha* in the past,[165] such as

[162] *Taittirīya Saṃhitā*, 5.1.8.2; *Kāṭhaka Saṃhitā*, 14.5; *Maitrāyaṇi Saṃhitā*, 1.11.5; *Aitareya Āraṇyaka*, 2.3.6; *Taittirīya Brāhmaṇa*, 1.3.2.6–7.

[163] *Āśvalāyana Gṛhya Sūtra*, 1.14.6–7.

[164] *Śatapatha Brāhmaṇa,* 13.5.4.1ff.; *Aitareya Brāhmaṇa*, 6.32.1ff.; *Atharvaveda*, 20.128.12–16.

[165] *Aitareya Brāhmaṇa,* 8.21–3; *Śatapatha Brāhmaṇa*, 13.5.4.1ff.; *Śāṇkhāyana Śrautasūtra*, 16.9.

the Kuru-Pañcāla. The poems praised heroes as conquerors of the earth,[166] and as performers of the *aśvamedha.*[167] But they were not restricted to *rājās* and could refer to others; and they could be recited individually or as a cluster.[168]

The rituals in the later corpus expand in number, complexity, and time, becoming central statements of the political and assertive aspects of power—both sacred and profane. The heroes are sometimes ascribed the status of *pitṛs* (ancestors) because they belong to the past. They are listed in the commentaries on the ritual.[169] A specific set of ten *nārāśaṃsīs* (hero-lauds) has to be sung at a particular point in the ritual.[170] Of these, the better known are those of Śunaḥśepa's release from being sacrificed and his induction into the clan of the high-status Viśvāmitra; Kakṣivant attaining the status of a *brāhmaṇa* despite being of *dāsī* descent; Vasiṣṭha being the *purohita* of Sudās and replacing Viśvāmitra; Vatsa, although initially dismissed as the son of a *śūdra* woman, successfully claiming brahmanhood; and Nābhānediṣṭha obtaining gifts from Aṅgirasa. The shift in these narratives lies in the emphasis not being on heroic acts alone but on the acquisition of high status, sometimes projected as the obtaining of a special gift. Some were mentioned in the *Ṛgveda* but are now backed with narratives to provide precedents and refresh memories. Where the verse is addressed to a living recipient,[171] the *kavi* is said to have a tongue of honey![172]

The process of acculturation is evident whenever there is an interface among varying societies. The acquiring of status involves eulogizing those that both bestowed and received status. Its significance is reflected in later texts that relate the narratives, sometimes expanding on a passing reference in the *Ṛgveda.* That status had to be acquired, sometimes through elaborate means, tends to give a

[166] Yāska defines it as *yena narāḥ praśasyante sa nārāśamso mantrāḥ*: *Nirukta* of Yāska, 9.9.

[167] *Śatapatha Brāhmaṇa*, 11.5.6.8.

[168] *Śāṅkhāyana Śrautasūtra,* 16.2.

[169] *Aitareya Brāhmaṇa,* 7.27ff., 7.34, 8.14, 8.21–3; *Kauṣītaki Brāhmaṇa,* 26.5, 28.4ff.

[170] *Śāṅkhāyana Śrautasūtra*, 16.11.1ff.

[171] *Bṛhad-devatā,* 3.154 [T-3.125]; 7.139 [T-7.109]—'T-' here in square brackets, and hereafter, indicates the translation by M. Tokunaga.

[172] *Ṛgveda*, 10.62, 5.5.2, 1.13.3.

touch of credibility to the story, although of course these elaborate means could be part of an understood rhetorical practice.

To the extent that the *nārāśaṃsī* narratives focus on status and are linked to a *yajña*, they differ somewhat from the *dāna-stuti* and the *gāthā*. The narrative is not radically changed in these later texts, even where it is not too complimentary to those involved. Was this intended as a hint of authenticity?

The *nārāśaṃsīs* were incorporated into the large sacrificial rituals,[173] some referring to *rājās* and settlements,[174] mentioning the name of the *rājā*, the *jana* to which he belonged, his priest, and often the location of the sacrifice.[175] References are made to earlier performances of the ritual, as when Śatānika Śatrajita performed the *aśvamedha* after taking away the sacrificial horse from the *rājā* of Cedi; or that Māthava the Videgha went eastwards with Agni to the area of what later was called Videha, which had to be cleared and settled.[176]

The significance of these compositions was that they preserved a notion of past personalities and events which they wanted posterity to remember. This also meant recalling the believed history of those who had been inducted into the society of the *ārya*, as for example the *dāsyaḥ putraḥ brāhmaṇas*. Thus, prior to the *rājasūya*, mention is made of the important *brāhmaṇas* who had conducted sacrificial rituals for important *rājās*. Tura Kavaṣeya sacrificed for Janamejaya Parikṣit, a name echoing the Kavaṣa of the *Ṛgveda*; or Parvata and Naraka, who sacrificed for Somaka, Sahadeva, and Babhru; or Vasiṣṭha for Sudās Paijavana, familiar from the *Ṛgveda*.[177] Further in the same text there is a list of *rājās* who underwent the *mahābhiṣeka* and then performed the *aśvamedha*. Included among these were Janamejaya Parikṣit, Sudās Paijavana, Marutta Āvikṣita, Bharata Dauḥṣanti, and Durmukha Pañcāla. An attempt was being made, first, to endow such names and their narratives with some claim to historicity; second,

[173] *Śāṅkhāyana Śrautasūtra*, 16.10.1ff., 16.11.1ff.

[174] U.N. Ghoshal, *Beginnings of Indian Historiography and Other Essays,* 17ff.

[175] *Aitareya Brāhmaṇa*, 8.21–3.

[176] *Śatapatha Brāhmaṇa*, 13.5.4.19, 1.4.1.14–17.

[177] *Aitareya Brāhmaṇa*, 7.34.

ensure their preservation by ensconcing them within rituals; and third, through reciting the narrative as part of the ritual, deliberately connecting a believed past to the present.

At a more mundane level there was also the element of comparison. Thus if the munificence of earlier patrons were extolled, contemporary patrons might be provoked into following their example. There was an obsession with the correct performance of the ritual and the correct pronunciation of the *mantras*. The Sṛñjayas were defeated because of a mistake in the ritual.[178] The perfection of the ritual also gave added importance to the priest. Bolstering this, attempts were made to explain what were believed to be the historical origins of certain ritual sacrifices, thus providing a rationale for their performance should their efficacy be doubted. Evidently, there was a need to propagate the rituals to ensure livelihood, status, and authority for those performing them, and the fragmentary historical tradition as it was then perceived was brought into service.

6. The *Ākhyānas*

The *dāna-stuti* hymns, *gāthās*, and *nārāśaṃsīs* were fragments of heroic poetry and became part of the material which went into the making of larger poetic narratives, the *kathās* and the *kāvyas*. But heroic exploits, situations of political authority, and the acquisition of status by individuals were narrated as *ākhyānas*, included in the later Vedic corpus. This genre is especially characteristic of the rituals in the *aśvamedha*, where the *pāriplava* is a year-long cycle of *ākhyānas*,[179] and is also recited in the *rājasūya*.[180]

The distinction between *nārāśaṃsīs* and *ākhyānas* was not sharp and some themes were listed variously in these categories. But the function of the *ākhyāna* as part of a ritual focusing on sovereignty and supremacy, almost cosmological in intent, lends a different connotation to this category.[181] *Ākhyānas* were recited

[178] *Atharvaveda* 5.19.1; *Kāṭhaka Saṃhitā*, 12.3; *Taittirīya Saṃhitā*, 6.6.2.2.3.
[179] *Śatapatha Brāhmaṇa*, 13.4.3.2ff.
[180] *Śatapatha Brāhmaṇa*, 13.4.3.2ff.
[181] *Śāṅkhāyana Śrautasūtra*, 15.12.1ff.

at particular points of the ritual or were part of its commentaries. Or else an event from the past was linked to the efficacy of the ritual, as for instance in the statement that because a particular *rājā* did not perform a Soma sacrifice, the Kurus were forced out of Kurukṣetra.[182] Some *ākhyānas* are specifically referred to as *itihāsa.*

The context of gift-giving gradually changed from *dāna*, a gift, to including *dakṣinā*, a fee to the ritual specialist for performing a ritual of legitimation for the *rājā*. The *dāna-stuti* hymns were seminal to the *praśasti* (eulogy), most often linked to kings in later periods.

Because the *ākhyānas* are a regular part of certain rituals, the rituals may be summarized here.[183] The *rājasūya* was generally performed after a *digvijaya* (conquest of the four quarters), conducted by the *rājā* and his kinsmen. It could only be performed by a *kṣatriya* and was a consecration ritual. The earlier rituals included the *ratninām havīṃśi*, with the *rājā* briefly visiting the homes of the twelve jewels—professionally differentiated members of the community on whom the *rājā* was dependent for various functions. These included the *sūta*/charioteer or bard. The consecration ritual took five days and had to be performed by a *hotṛ* who was a Bhṛgu. The announcement was then made that the *yajamāna,* the patron of the sacrifice, was in effect the *rājā*. The story of Śunaḥśepa is recited, perhaps symbolizing an elevation in status by his induction into a superior clan; wealth is donated by the *rājā* to the priests; his son is recognized; and he conducts a mock cattle-raid. Equally significant is the game of dice as part of the ritual, umpired by all those connected with the distribution of wealth in the society—the *saṃgrahītṛ, bhāgadugha, kṣattṛ*—and clearly the game is symbolic of allotments of resources and the wealth that each carries. These are the essential actions in claims to chiefship. There is a further period of offerings to the gods and *dakṣinā* to the priests. After a full year, the rituals of consecration move towards completion.

[182] *Śāṅkhāyana Śrautasūtra*, 15.16.11.

[183] See P.V. Kane, *History of Dharmasastra*, II.2.1214ff.; II.1.1228ff.; J.C. Heesterman, *The Inner Conflict of Tradition.*

The *aśvamedha* is perhaps hinted at in a seminal form in a couple of late hymns of the *Ṛgveda.*[184] In the later sections of the corpus it is described as an elaborate ritual lasting many months and performed by those who qualified as consecrated *rājās.* The intention was to claim territory, sovereignty, and prosperity, and conclude with an evocation of fertility. After due rituals, a white horse was let loose to wander where it willed, protected by a troop of four hundred, and the *rājā* was entitled to claim the territory over which the horse wandered for a year. However, if the horse was captured, the sacrifice was void. Hence the advice, in passing, that the reins of the horse should be firmly held! Meanwhile, the *hotṛ* was to recite narratives for a year in cycles of ten days each—the *pāriplava* cycle. The audience was the *rājā* and his kinsmen, other priests, and the community of householders. Much of what was recited was linked to eulogies of the *rājā*, and the more generous the patron the more exalted the praise. After a year the horse was brought back, the *rājā* consecrated again, animals sacrificed, and the horse ritually killed. This was followed by fertility rituals involving the chief wife of the *rājā* and the dead horse. The many priests involved were recipients of much wealth from the *rājā*. Despite the centrality of the *aśvamedha*, kings in later periods claiming to perform the *aśvamedha* were more likely treating it as a symbolic ritual.

The origin of the *ākhyāna* has been sought in the dialogue hymns of the late sections of the *Ṛgveda* arguing that the prose portions are lost and only the verses survive.[185] Examples of dialogue hymns are the Yama-Yamī;[186] Saramā and the Paṇis;[187] and, pre-eminently, Purūravas and Urvaśī .[188] The *ākhyāna* of Śunaḥśepa first finds mention as a name in the *Ṛgveda*,[189] and is elsewhere listed as *nārāśaṃsī*,[190] with the *ākhyāna* being an elaboration of

[184] 1.162, 1.163.

[185] L. Alsdorf, "The Ākhyāna Theory Reconsidered", 197ff.

[186] *Ṛgveda,* 10.10.

[187] *Ṛgveda,* 10.108.

[188] *Ṛgveda*, 10.95.

[189] *Aitareya Brāhmaṇa,* 7.13ff.

[190] 5.2.7, 1.24.13; *Śāṅkhāyana Śrautasūtra*, 16.11.1. See 15.17–27 for the narrative.

a narrative thought to be significant. There is a qualitative difference between the *gāthās* and *nārāśaṃśīs* and the *ākhyānas*. In the *Nirukta,* Yāska refers to the *ākhyānas* and *itihāsas* of earlier times.[191] In still later sources, both *ākhyāna* and *ākhyāyika* seem to be used in the context of *itihāsa-purāṇa*.[192]

The *pāriplava* was a revolving, recurrent, cycle of narratives incorporating *ākhyānas*. These were narrated at specific points in the ritual, in part to fill in time between the rites.[193] They were recited by the *hotṛ*, or later by the *paurāṇika sauti,* the bard familiar with old narratives. Power and fertility are common themes.[194] Mention was made of the *rājās* of the past who, it was claimed, had performed the *aśvamedha* and the cycle became thereby a mechanism for remembering a past. These recitations were the likely forerunners of the reciting of *kathās*, some of which eventually evolved into epics. Remembering the narratives was probably thought necessary for new generations, or newly inducted people who formed part of the audience at the ritual. The *ākhyānavid* was proficient in narrating stories of the past. The *aitihāsika* commented on the stories and was familiar with the *ākhyānas*.[195]

A few of the *ākhyānas* concern deities and may have been intended as prototypes.[196] Others, categorized as *itihāsa*, are narratives about humans such as Devāpi and Śantanu, as related in the *Bṛhad-devatā*.[197] The story of Devāpi is preceded by the statement that Yāska regards the *ākhyāna* as a *samvādam* (dialogue), whereas Śaunaka regards it as an *itihāsa*.[198] Devāpi is mentioned earlier in a late hymn of the *Ṛgveda* which focuses on a prayer

[191] *Nirukta* of Yāska, 2.10, 2.24, 5.21, 7.7, 9.13, 10.26, 11.19, 11.25, 12.10. See also *Bṛhad-devatā*, 1.53 [T-1.49].

[192] *Aṣṭādhyāyī of Pāṇini*, 6.2.103, 4.2.60. The *Arthaśāstra* of Kauṭilya includes *itihāsa* as important to the education of a prince and adds that it consists of *purāṇa, itivṛtta, ākhyāyika, udāharaṇa, dharmaśāstra*, and *arthaśāstra*: 1.5.12.

[193] *Śatapatha Brāhmaṇa*, 13.4.3.2ff.; *Taittirīya Brāhmaṇa,* 3.9.14.4; R.D. Karmakar, "The Pāriplava at the Aśvamedha", 26–40.

[194] *Śāṅkhāyana Śrautasūtra*, 16.1.22, 16.2.36, 16.10.13; *Lāṭyāyana Śrauta Sūtra,* 9.9.10ff.

[195] *Nirukta* of Yāska, 2.10, 12.1, 5.21.

[196] *Bṛhad-devatā,* 3.156ff. [T-3.126; 4.66; 4.59; 6.99; 6.75–82].

[197] 7.155-9 [T-7.125ff.; see pp. 281–2].

[198] 7.153 [T-7.124].

for rain.[199] This story is enlarged in later sources to refer to two brothers, Devāpi and Śantanu, of the Kuru lineage. The elder is said to have had a *tvagdoṣa* (skin disease), which disqualified him from ruling. He anointed Śantanu and went to the forest. But this was such a severe infringement of primogeniture that it brought on a twelve-year drought. Śantanu therefore sought out Devāpi in the forest and requested him to be the *rājā*. Devāpi again declined but agreed to officiate as the priest in the sacrificial rituals invoking rain.[200]

The *ākhyāna* highlights the rules of succession and the possible combination of *rājā* and *ṛṣi* (king and seer). Devāpi as the "rainmaker" ended the drought, a concept very central to high office in lineage-based societies. This narrative occurs in a variety of later texts but is altered to suit a changing context.[201] That this story comes to be called *itihāsa* is probably because of its association with fundamental requirements of an earlier society.

The *ākhyāna* of Śunaḥśepa is also listed as *nārāśaṃsī* in some texts, and was to be recited to the king by the *hotṛ* after the ceremony of anointing in the *rājasūya* sacrifice whilst both he and the king were seated on golden seats—these were later given to the priest.[202] The purpose of the recitation was to ensure victory as well as the birth of sons.

The story is as follows.[203] Hariścandra, an Ikṣvāku *rājā,* was without an heir and appealed to the gods for a son. Varuṇa granted him a son but on condition that the son so born should be sacrificed to him. On the birth of his son, Rohita, Hariścandra delayed the sacrifice. Rohita meanwhile came upon a seer, Ajīgarta, an Aṅgirasa *brāhmaṇa*, who because of extreme hunger was willing to sell his middle son, Śunaḥśepa, to Rohita for a hundred head of cattle. Rohita thus redeemed himself by handing over Śunaḥśepa to Varuṇa and the sacrifice was prepared. Ajīgarta was asked to bind his son to the stake, which he agreed to do for a further

199 10.98.

200 V.G. Rahurkar, "Devāpi and Śantanu in the *Ṛg Veda*", 175ff.

201 *Mahābhārata,* 1.89.53, 1.90.46; *Viṣṇu Purāṇa*, 4.20.7ff.; *Bhāgvata Purāṇa*, 9.22.14–17.

202 *Aitareya Brāhmaṇa*, 7.13–18.

203 See also *Śāṅkhāyana Śrautasūtra,* 15.17–27.

hundred head of cattle, and to slaughter him for yet another equal amount.

At this point, on the advice of the priest Viśvāmitra, Śunaḥśepa prayed to the gods, and the prayer is largely of verses from the *Ṛgveda* (suggesting them as a source).[204] His prayers heard, the bonds were released. Viśvāmitra refused to return him to Ajīgarta and adopted him as his own son, appointing him to the status of *sreṣṭha* (the best), and *jyeṣṭha* (the eldest). Śunaḥśepa agreed on condition that the hundred sons of Viśvāmitra accept him as such. The elder fifty being unwilling were promptly exiled to become the ancestors of various peoples outside the social pale, such as the Andhras, Pulindas, Śabaras, Puṇḍras, Mutibas, and many Dasyu tribes. The younger fifty, who were addressed by Viśvāmitra as *gāthins*, accepted Śunaḥśepa, who was given the name of Devarāta and initiated into the sacred lore of the *gāthins* as well as overlordship of the Jahnus—Viśvāmitra's family.

The narrative of Śunaḥśepa relates the origin of clans. Viśvāmitra emerges as the powerful figure reordering the relationship of Śunaḥśepa to the various persons in the story, demonstrating the dependence of royal power on priestly power.[205] In later texts Viśvāmitra is described as a *kṣatriya* attempting to acquire the status of a *brāhmaṇa*. Śunaḥśepa claims to be an Aṅgirasa *brāhmaṇa*. Viśvāmitra performs the sacrifice as the *hotṛ* but is complimented as being a bull of the Bharatas, a metaphor used for *kṣatriya* heroes.

The narrative points to clans taking in outsiders as kinsmen if they are found acceptable. The reactions of Viśvāmitra's sons reflect the conflict between those who are conscious of kinship in relation to whatever is regarded as property, in this case access to sacred lore, and those who are not. Those who do not accept Śunaḥśepa are removed from kinship by being given the low status of *dasyus*. The adoption of Śunaḥśepa requires that the entrant be given a new name, indicating a change of identity, rights of lineage in his overlordship of the Jahnus, and access to the secret lore of the *gāthins*. All these features recur often in later times,

[204] *Ṛgveda*, 1.24.
[205] A.B. Keith, *Ṛgvedic Brahmanas*, 62ff.

although reformulated somewhat. The historicity of the story is in some ways irrelevant. Its significance lies in its encapsulating a historical process—that of assimilation into a clan—central to early society. In later times the story provided a precedent for the induction of new groups into existing castes, and in that sense too is part of *itihāsa*.

The reference to Śunaḥśepa as an Aṅgirasa would make him a member of the priestly group associated with the *Atharvaveda*. The name Śunaḥśepa (dog's tail or penis), and those of his brothers meaning the same, Śunaḥpucha and Śunaḥlāṅgala, and their patronymic, Ājīgarti, suggest a very different identity from the one he acquired as the son of the exalted Viśvāmitra. The intention of the narrative might have been to explain the closeness of the Aṅgirasa to *kṣatriya* interests, assuming that the Bhṛgvāṇgirasa *brāhmaṇas* were the keepers of the *kṣatriya* tradition. The outcast sons in other sources are referred to as the *mleccha* or impure people, with a location outside the Ganges plain in western and central India and the peninsula. Does the narrative record a split in the clans, with some migrating and others accommodating themselves to change? Or is it recording the presence of clans other than those accorded status in Vedic sources? Was this a legend that was tagged on later with its curious play on phallic names?[206]

Another narrative regarded as *itihāsa* was that of Purūravas and Urvaśī,[207] first referred to as a dialogue between the two in the *Ṛgveda*.[208] Purūravas is described as the son of the ancestress Ilā, a deviation from the patriarchal norm of giving the father's name rather than that of the mother, the name being a personification of the sacrificial oblation. Her son, a *rājā*, loved to distraction the *apsarā* Urvaśī. She was banished to earth by the *gandharvas*, and when Purūravas pleaded his love for her she agreed to live with him provided that he would tend her two rams and ensure that she never saw him naked. One night, the *gandharvas* stole one of the rams and Purūravas ran after the thief, at which point there was a flash of lightning and Urvaśī, seeing him naked, vanished.

[206] J.C. Heesterman, *The Ancient Indian Royal Consecration,* 158ff.
[207] *Bṛhad-devatā,* 7.147ff.
[208] 10.95.

Purūravas spent many years searching for her and eventually found her. The hymn in the *Ṛgveda* encapsulates their dialogue: he implores her to return, to which she agrees, but only to meet him once in the year. This she does over the next five years and consequently bears him five sons.

Interpretations of the legend are many.[209] Max Müller saw it as a nature myth with the dawn vanishing at the approach of the sun.[210] Another view is that Urvaśī is symbolic of matriarchal cults dying under the patriarchy of the Aryans.[211] This has led to a further interpretation that the story records the marriage of an Aryan male to a non-Aryan woman.[212] The entry of the *apsarā* could mark a break in succession, or a marriage alliance which deviates from the norm. The association of an *apsarā* with trees and water may be read as her being from the community of low-status forest-dwellers; she was elevated when necessary and described as an *apsarā*.

The legend is retold repeatedly in subsequent centuries in various texts.[213] It is a theme well known to mythology and parallels the Greek myth of Cupid and Psyche, although the roles are reversed.[214] Yet it has an importance in the historical tradition since Ilā and her son Purūravas are, as we shall see, said to have founded one of the major lineages in the reconstructed version of the past as given in the *Purāṇas*.

Parallel to the *ākhyānas* and the descent list of lineages was

[209] J.C. Wright, "Purūravas and Urvaśī", 526–47; R.P. Goldman, "Mortal Man and Immortal Woman", 273–303.

[210] *Chips from a German Workshop,* vol. I, 98ff.

[211] D.D. Kosambi, "Urvaśī and Purūravas", in idem, *Myth and Reality*, 42–81.

[212] R.C. Gaur, "The Legend of Purūravas and Urvaśī: An Interpretation", 142ff.

[213] M. Winternitz, *History of Indian Literature*, 91ff.

[214] In the Greek myth, Psyche was a mortal, and Cupid, the son of Venus, falls in love with her. He visits her after dark and leaves before dawn, which has her puzzled. Urged by the curiosity of her sisters, she attempts to see him by lamplight, whereupon a drop of oil falls on Cupid, who awakes and disappears. The distraught Psyche performs many tasks for Venus, including a visit to Hades, in the hope of winning back Cupid. Eventually this is achieved by Psyche joining him as an immortal.

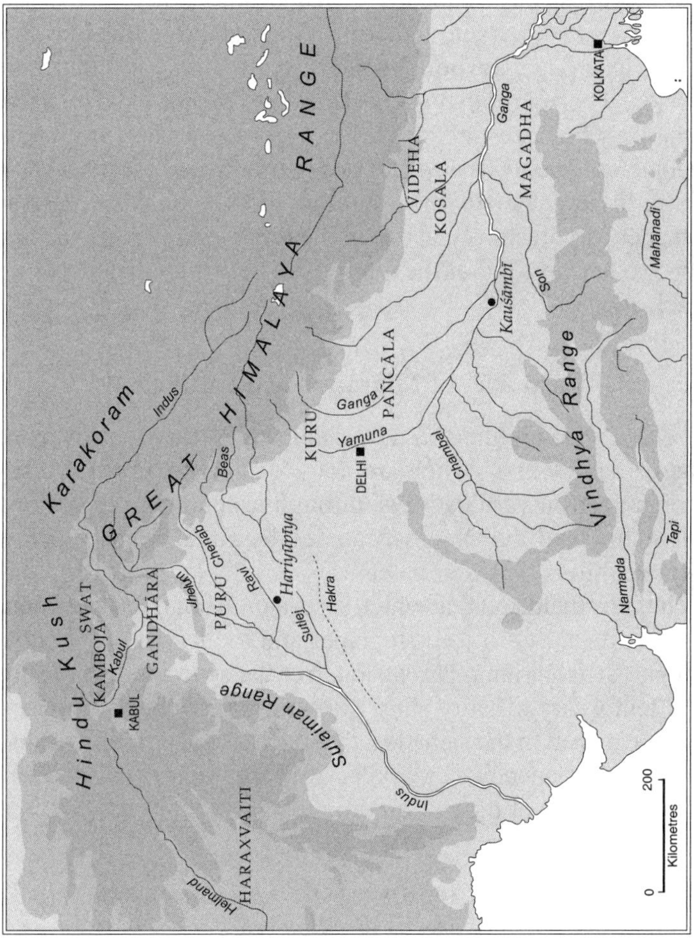

Map 1: Locations of the More Important Places, Clans, and Dynasties

the succession of teachers recorded in the *Upaniṣads*. These texts incorporate, for the first time, the *vaṃśas* (succession lists) of those regarded as important *brāhmaṇa* teachers.[215] Such lists in the *Upaniṣads* may well have been required, apart from other reasons, because of the questioning of the *Vedas* by heterodox sects.[216] Ancestry is frequently traced back to a deity which sets the *brāhmaṇas* apart and underlines their status, as well as that of their teachings, as more ancient than the rest and therefore superior. There are also succession lists of *ṛṣis*.[217] The same mechanism for asserting status was to be used later in *kṣatriya* genealogies. The *Upaniṣads* do not list familial descent, as was done in the *kṣatriya* tradition, but they list the lineal succession of teachers. Interestingly, in one of the *brāhmaṇa vaṃśas,* the first forty-two teachers out of the total of fifty-eight are listed as sons of their mother.[218]

7. Narratives of Migration and Settlement

Space and time are the two dimensions of history that focus on "where" and "when". They are not absent in these texts. They are organized in various ways, through accounts of migrations, settlements, and the spaces occupied by ritual activity. These define relations between categories of people, indicating that which binds them and that which separates. Rituals are occasions for the collectivity to come together and to identify itself either through participation or exclusion. Yet the space so demarcated had a temporary sanctity since public rituals were not required to be performed in the same location each time—settlements had a greater permanency as markers of space—but rituals also incorporated ways of measuring time.

[215] *Śatapatha Brāhmaṇa,* 10.6.5.9; Max Müller, *A History of Ancient Sanskrit Literature*, 229ff.; U.N. Ghoshal, *Studies in Indian History and Culture,* 2; idem, *The Beginnings of Historiography and Other Essays*; *Jaiminīya Upaniṣad Brāhmaṇa*, 3.40–2, 4.16–17.

[216] *Bṛhadāraṇyaka Upaniṣad*, 2.6.1–3.

[217] *Āśvalāyana Gṛhya Sūtra*, 3.4.1–5; P.V. Kane, *History of Dharmasastra*, vol. II, 690ff.

[218] *Bṛhadāraṇyaka Upaniṣad*, 4.6.1.

Settlements were given to fission or breaking away if demographic imbalances or confrontations required diffusion. In this process new settlements, in imitation of earlier ones, would be established in adjoining territory. Confederation and fission were mechanisms of reducing aggression. Major conflicts are often located on rivers, understandably so, given the need to control water resources. In some cases it is possible to trace the migration of clans by comparing their locations in the *Ṛgveda* with references to locations in the later sections of the Vedic corpus.[219]

The Pūrus, originally located in the Suvastu/Swat valley in the north-west, became part of the large Kuru tribe linked to the Pañcāla in the western Ganges plain. The Bharatas on the Paruṣṇī (Ravi) river move to the Vipāś and Śutudrī (Beas and Sutlej) rivers, and finally to the western Ganges plain, again as part of the Kuru tribe. Some clans opposed to each other in the *dāśarājña* were unified a few centuries later. Despite Pūru's language being harsh and incorrect, the language of the Kuru-Pañcāla is now said to be the best and they observe the required Vedic rituals—although earlier they were said to be *ayajyavāḥ* (not performing the required rituals).[220] The Kurus are often mentioned as the most eminent among the clans, the pace-setters of the culture that had now emerged.

There is by now the much-quoted story of Māthava the Videgha going from the region of the Sarasvatī in the Indo-Gangetic watershed all the way across to the Sadānīrā river (generally identified with the modern Gandaka). He carried Agni in his mouth and was accompanied by his *purohita*, Gautama Rāhugaṇa, who was an Aṅgirasa. The land was uncultivated and marshy. He crossed the river when the land on the other bank had been purified by Agni and established himself to the east of it, whence the name Videha, derived from Videgha.[221] The presence of Agni could refer to both the purification of the land through sacrificial rituals as well as the clearing of the land by fire, in this case the forests of the foothills. There is a reference to *brāhmaṇas* who had now settled around the Sadānīrā. It is said that, at the time when the sacrifice

[219] *Ṛgveda*, 3.23.4; *Śatapatha Brāhmaṇa*, 13.5.4.11ff.
[220] *Śatapatha Brāhmaṇa*, 3.2.3.15, 1.7.2.8, 5.2.3.5.
[221] *Śatapatha Brāhmaṇa*, 1.4.1.14ff.

was begun, Agni issued forth from the mouth of Videgha Māthava. This could be a way of saying that this migration brought both the ritual of sacrifice as well as the Indo-Aryan language to a region earlier unfamiliar with both.

This is the region which in later centuries came to be associated with the Ikṣvāku lineage. There is a single reference in the *Ṛgveda* to Ikṣvāku as a *rājā*,[222] and the *Atharvaveda* refers to him as an ancient hero. Rāma is part of the name of some teachers listed in the *Brāhmaṇas*. Janaka as the *rājā* of Videha is known to the same texts.[223] This migration and subsequent settlement is a prototype story in the narratives of later times.

Tentative efforts at narrating origins and giving an initial form to the past comes from the intriguing story of the Flood first told in the *Śatapatha Brāhmaṇa.*[224] This was elaborated upon in later texts, with some changes to become the starting point of the *itihāsa-purāṇa* tradition in the *Purāṇas*.

The earliest version relates briefly that Manu, generally described as the first man, the patriarch—the word itself being linked to *mānava*, meaning mankind—performing his morning ablutions, found a fish in his cupped hands and reared it until it reached an enormous size. Growing larger, it had to be changed from a jar to a tank to the sea. It divulged the intention of the gods to drown the earth in a deluge for no apparent reason. Wishing to save Manu from this disaster it ordered him to build a boat which, when the flood came, was tied to its horn. It then swam through the waters and lodged the boat on a northern mountain. From here Manu returned when the waters subsided. Being alone and desirous of sons he performed a sacrifice from which a daughter was born, whom he significantly named, Idā /Ilā, literally a libation or a sacrificial food offering. Through her in turn were born his descendants.

Of all the multiplicity of Flood stories from various parts of the world, this version most closely parallels the story in earlier Mesopotamian texts, and is elaborated in the *Purāṇas*.

[222] *Ṛgveda*, 10.60.4.

[223] *Śatapatha Brāhmaṇa*, 11.3.1.2ff.; *Bṛhadāraṇyaka Upaniṣad*, 3.1.1; 4.1.1; 4.4.7; 5.14.8.

[224] 1.8.1.1–10.

8. Early Concepts of Time

Descriptions of creation included references to concepts of time.[225] Time is the progenitor of creation, beginning with the day and the night, counting to the year, and requiring the existence of the sun and the moon.[226] The calendar measures time. In some later texts *kāla* (time) is said to control the universe. The span was the *yuga*, initially calculated as a five-year period, although this did not preclude a longer span. Five is a significant number linked to the five seasons, five directions, five deities, five peoples.[227] The computation of time was not as yet a central concern to the pattern of the past. This was to come later.

The theory of the four *yugas*, as demarcated periods of time and visualized as cycles of time, is not mentioned. What were to become the labels of the four *yugas* in post-Vedic texts—Kṛta, Tretā, Dvāpara, Kali—are mentioned, but as throws of dice (*akṣa*). The alternative name for Kali referred to the single dot on the dice.[228] There is a hint here of chance being associated with time. Spans longer than the *yuga* were said to be periods of a hundred years and multiples of this. In the absence of cycles of time, the idea of the repetition of events was unknown.

Creation is attributed to Indra, to the separation of earth and sky, to primeval Man—*puruṣasūkta*, to the golden embryo, *hiraṇyagarbha*.[229] It is also said that Time begets heaven and earth.[230] The reiteration of the centrality of time comes about through the performance of seasonal rituals. This emerges from a luni-solar calendar, the notion of a cyclic return each year. Mention is made of the figure 360 in a riddle, as well as what has been interpreted as a twelve-month year with an intercalary month. However, it was essentially also observing a linear reckoning. This coincided with the more frequent domestic rituals involving the listing of *tithis*/days, the new and full moon which was to become the basis

[225] *Ṛgveda*, 10.129, 10.130, 10.190.

[226] *Ṛgveda*, 10.190.

[227] *Taittirīya Saṃhitā,* 4.3.3.

[228] *Śatapatha Brāhmaṇa,* 5.4.4.6; *Atharvaveda*, 7.114.1, 7.52.

[229] L.Gonzales-Reiman, "Cosmic Cycles, Cosmology and Cosmography", 411–28.

[230] *Atharvaveda*, 19.53.5–6.

of the *pakṣa* or fortnight—of which two constituted a *māsa*/month; *cāturmāsa* were the three four-monthly seasons; and larger periods were changes in the position of the sun such as the *uttarāyana* and the *dakṣiṇāyana.* This interplay was of lunar and solar measurements as well as linear and cyclic notions of time. These were to remain a continuing feature.

9. In Sum

The *dāna-stutis, gāthās,* and *nārāśaṃsīs* can be viewed as fragments of a tradition, similar to the epic, claiming some semblance to persons and events. The *ākhyāna* provided the possibility that the legend could be used, as indeed it was, as a precedent for other times and other contexts. Its close association with the *itihāsa* and the *purāṇa* is reiterated in the *pāriplava* cycle where, in the ten-day cycle of *ākhyānas*, the eighth day is reserved for *itihāsa* and the ninth for *purāṇa.*[231]

Over time the conjoint *itihāsa-purāṇa* referred to an all-enveloping category, delineating specific texts. It was important enough to be part of the ritual compendium but was also associated with the Kaṇvas and Bhṛgvāṅgiras, and later the *sūta* and *māgadha,* who may have been distanced from the orthodox. Initially, the heroic act is at a premium, but this is gradually modified by the focus shifting to *yajñas*. However, the expected gift always has primacy.

The fragments narrated here are but a few examples. As messages relating to the past they require to be interpreted both by their authors and by their audience.[232] The significance of the past was recognized by clan societies, but the ordering of the past as history was not a requirement. Nevertheless, elements of what eventually went into the making of a historical tradition were woven into what was projected as the past in the literature of these early societies.

Ritual becomes an avenue of indicating the presence of the past and for ordering the present. What is sought to be recorded and remembered from the past is the power of those who conducted

[231] *Śatapatha Brāhmaṇa*, 13.4.3.2ff.; *Taittirīya Āraṇyaka*, 2.10.
[232] D.P. Henige, *Oral Tradition and History*, 194.

raids to enhance wealth and were later patrons of the sacrifice, and those who performed rituals for the patrons. The attempt was to suggest a continuing identity of power among some clans from earlier to later times, irrespective of whether this was actually so. Those that endorsed these claims could not be part of the same identity, and the separation of the *kṣatriya* from the *brāhmaṇa* facilitated the *brāhmaṇa*'s endorsement of the *kṣatriya*, even if it increased the latter's dependence on the former. The rituals focused on the *kṣatriya,* the access of the *vaiśya* was limited, the *śūdra* was excluded. Kavaṣa Ailūṣa was the son of a *dāsī*, therefore he was expelled from the ritual and was only invited back to conduct the ritual when it was discovered that he was favoured by the gods.[233]

It has been argued by some scholars that the stories of *kṣatriya* heroes and their patronage were originally gathered as a kind of *kṣatriya* tradition distinct from the brahmanical, with texts possibly composed in Prākrit.[234] This version was then rendered into Sanskrit and portions of it entered the *Vedas*, the epics, and the genealogical section of the *Purāṇas*. Others hold that Prākrit and Apabhraṃśa were always second-order languages.[235] Since the popular use of Sanskrit in inscriptions, for example, is late, it is likely that the earlier common languages consisted of various regional Prākrits (as in the Aśokan inscriptions). Sanskrit may well have been the ritual language. In that case it is likely that the *kṣatriya* tradition would have been kept by the Bhṛgus, who could be described as *brahma-kṣatra* and the *sūtas,* who were not *brāhmaṇas,* but the former had access to the compiling of the *Vedas*. This may explain the initial authorship of the *itihāsa* tradition.

The Vedic corpus includes various forms of narratives, a few of which can be regarded as seminal to the idea of historical tradition. Whatever the genesis of these narratives, their eventual attribution, when they were included in the *Vedas*, was to *brāhmaṇa* authors. What is curious is that these authors were not always impeccable

[233] *Aitareya Brāhmaṇa*, 2.19.

[234] F.E. Pargiter, *The Purana Text of the Dynasties of the Kali Age*, x.

[235] S. Pollock, *The Languge of the Gods in the World of Men*, 104.

brāhmaṇas with unquestionable credentials. It is almost as if the *itihāsa-purāṇa* tradition was regarded as a trifle alien. That it could not be ignored or superseded is evident from its incorporation. Was the *itihāsa-purāṇa* tradition initially a non-brahmanical tradition that was gradually appropriated by the *brāhmaṇas*, or did the authors of the tradition use their access to this knowledge about the past and its political potential in contemporary affairs to work their way into the main tradition? This might explain why the authors of the *itihāsa-purāṇa* tradition sought links with rituals until such time as ritual moorings became unnecessary to asserting control over the tradition.

Such questions have been asked in earlier times. Yāska, for instance, refers to *aitihāsikas* and *nairuktas* (etymologists and commentators).[236] The former were those who maintained that many of the *itihāsas* that are narrated in the Vedic corpus had a historicity, but they were opposed by the *nairuktas*, such as Skandāsvamin, who insisted that the *itihāsas* had to be interpreted figuratively. For the orthodox the *Vedas* are revealed, and therefore need have no elements of historicity. That this was debated in those times points to seminal concerns about historical consciousness. That these compositions can be regarded as embedded history is suggested by a few features that, though by no means conclusive, are nevertheless indicative. The continuity from the past to the present lay in eulogizing the heroes, initially for their success in acquiring booty and in later times for their generous patronage of sacrificial rituals, both activities becoming agencies not only for gift-giving, which was the ostensible reason for the compositions, but also for remembering the heroes and their actions. The later composers were familiar with the earlier references but were also aware of the changed contemporary context. Elaborate sacrificial rituals were added to cattle-raids as occasions for eulogies and gift-giving. The earlier context, in a sense, legitimized the later, since the later drew upon the earlier. The legitimacy was based on events that were believed to have been historical.

Narratives in elementary forms which encouraged a familiarity with the past are embedded in the Vedic corpus and claim to refer

[236] *Nirukta* of Yāska, 2.16, 12.1, 4.6, 6.11, 12.10.

to what happened in contemporary and in past times. These forms and their narratives, however fragmentary, did contribute towards a perception of the past, particularly later when they were incorporated into more recognizably historical texts, even if by then they had undergone a change. Some themes, occasionally altered, are repeated in later texts. Seminal ideas of what constitutes a narrative about the past, and which is not thought of as fictitious, and the need to maintain such a tradition—all of which suggest a historical consciousness—are contained in some of these fragments. The *dāna-stuti* hymns were in many ways seminal to the *praśasti* sections of the later inscriptions. The historicity of the narrative continues to be uncertain, but the fragmentary components of a historically oriented perception of the past becomes evident.

4

The *Mahābhārata*

1. Creating the Epic

Epics, when not composed as a formal literary genre, carry by their very nature an element of embedded history. These are not histories *per se*, but they incorporate fragments of narratives pertaining to what was believed to have happened. Initially, and thereafter for some time, they are often oral compositions, until they are collated and connected through a narrative. They therefore tend to be compositions later in time from the events described, among their functions being the recalling and reconstruction of earlier events. There is in their evocation of the heroic glories of earlier times an almost nostalgic view of the past. Neither the events nor the personalities are necessarily historical; nevertheless, the assumptions of an earlier society are evident in them. In part this is due to the gradual evolution of the different forms within what we call the epic genre: the epos, the narrative prior to the epic form; the panegyric, the eulogy of a person who may not be present; and the epic, with the layered meanings of its narrative.[1]

The *Mahābhārata* and the *Rāmāyaṇa* are described as epics; insofar as the term suggests the work of a single author, this is a

[1] N. Frye, *Anatomy of Criticism*, 113. See also B.K. Lewalski, *Milton's Paradise Lost and the Rhetoric of Literary Forms*, 9–11; idem, *Renaissance Genres: Essays in Theory, History and Interpretation*; R.L. Colie, *The Resources of Kind: Genre-theory in the Renaissance*.

misnomer for both carry later interpolations, some small and some quite substantial.[2] These interpolations emerge from a changing present that seeks sanction from the past, and therefore presents it differently from the way it may have been presented earlier. To that extent they offer evidence of the existence of a historical sense.

Historical consciousness in these epics is expressed in the representation of two socio-political forms: a society of past times and the society of the present—although the earlier in some places survives as parallel to the later. The two are not starkly distinct, there is considerable fluidity between them. Nevertheless, the difference is recognizable. The historicity of event and person may therefore be less important than the portrayal of the bigger change. The juxtaposition is of lineage-based societies and chiefships of earlier times with the incipient kingdoms of later times. Mutation from one to the other provides a historical flavour. The perception of this juxtaposition—which is from a later age looking back on the earlier—is part of the representation of the past.

In the *Mahābhārata* this dichotomy is graduated. But it is apparent from what have been called the narrative sections, which assume a background of clan societies, and which differ somewhat from the later didactic interpolations holding forth on the merits of kingship.[3] The *Rāmāyaṇa* treats this dichotomy differently and there is, as will be seen later, a confrontation between the two woven into the story itself. This recognition of difference may be seen as a perception of historical change, as well as awareness that the juxtaposition of the two is an attempt at constructing the past in a particular way. The transition, in a sense, becomes the historical perception.

The origins of epic poetry have been traced to the *dāna-stuti* hymns, *gāthās, nārāśaṃsīs*, and *ākhyānas* of the Vedic corpus. Events centre on the lives of *rājās*. Fragments were probably brought together, juxtaposed, and interleaved. This is suggested by the retelling of familiar narratives from earlier times, or by the men-

[2] Some scholars argue for the texts having been composed at a particular point in time without later additions. Discrepancies and contradictions weaken this argument. It is difficult to believe that a text as lengthy, diverse, and complicated as the *Mahābhārata* was composed at one point in time.

[3] R. Thapar, "The Historian and the Epic", in idem, *Cultural Pasts*, 613–29.

tion elsewhere of narratives included in the epic, such as those of Yayāti, or the birth of Bharata,[4] and by a comparison of these with Buddhist and Jaina versions. The retellings carry changes. Sixteen *rājās* of earlier times are listed in the later sections of the epic, but of these only six are referred to in the Vedic corpus.[5] The rest, including Rāma and the Pāṇḍavas, must have come from other traditions. Described as powerful *samrāṭs* and *cakravartins*, they reflect the later images of kings. There is passing mention of the Kauravas in the *sūtra* literature,[6] but there is no mention of the Pāṇḍavas, although a cattle-wealthy *rājā*, Janamejaya Pārikṣita, was famous for performing an *aśvamedha*.[7] It has been suggested that the Pāṇḍava narrative could originally have been independent but was later knitted into the epic.[8] Pāṇini, in the fourth century BC, mentions the Kuru territory, Kuntī, Yudhiṣṭhira, and the *Mahābhārata*.[9]

Such narratives emanate from two kinds of situations: they were recited at the *yajñas*, where the ritual is central; or when bards recited hero-lauds in the *sabhās* (the assembly halls) of clan chiefs, and where the focus was on the hero. The *Mahābhārata* was recited initially at ritual occasions; nevertheless the focus is on the heroes.

The early groping towards what eventually went into the making of a historical tradition is embedded in the *Mahābhārata* and the *Rāmāyaṇa*. The former is referred to more often as *itihāsa*, although also described as *ākhyāna,* as well as the fifth *Veda* or *Kṛṣṇa Veda*—that of Kṛṣṇa Dvaipāyana Vyāsa, the compiler. *Itihāsa* is *smṛti* or remembered tradition—and not *śruti* or revelation, as are the *Veda*s—therefore calling the *Mahābhārata* the fifth *Veda* is somewhat problematic. The *Rāmāyaṇa* is referred to more often as *kāvya* (poem), or even *ādi-kāvya* (the first poem). Both texts grew out of narrating stories, the *kathā*, and in their

4 H. Winternitz, *History of Indian Literature*, 279ff., 378ff.

5 The story of Rāma is told as representing courage in distress: *Mahābhārata*, 3.258–75.

6 *Śāṇkhāyana Śrautasūtra*, 15.17–27.

7 *Aitareya Brāhmaṇa*, 4.27, 7.34, 8.21; *Śatapatha Brāhmaṇa,* 13.5.4.1–3.

8 J.L. Fitzgerald, "No Contest between Memory and Invention".

9 *Aṣṭādhyāyī of Pāṇini*, 4.1.172, 6.2.42, 6.2.38, 8.3.95, 4.1.176.

earliest and shorter forms were referred to as the *Bhārata* and the *Rāma-kathā*.[10]

The early forms of both texts could have been part of the oral tradition, recited and preserved by bards. The *Mahābhārata* may subsequently have been compiled and composed in literary form by Vyāsa/Kṛṣṇa Dvaipāyana, and other compilers (if Vyāsa was their generic name). It has been argued that this text was redacted by Bhṛgu *brāhmaṇas,* but this view is not universally accepted, there being many views on its composition and authorship.[11] My argument draws on the epic having undergone three phases of change—the original oral composition was given a literary rendering by Vyāsa, subsequent to which were added the interpolations by later redactors, probably the Bhṛgus. This last phase propagated kingship and the worship of Viṣṇu.

The epics are revered by some but regarded with contempt by others. Buddhist commentaries refer to them as *nirarthakathā* (meaningless narrative) and state that places where they are recited are not to be visited.[12] Floating bardic fragments appear as stories in the *Jātaka* literature and in Jaina narratives. The Buddhist *Jātaka* stories, probably compiled in about the second century BC and incorporating earlier verse sections, show some familiarity with the protagonists of the epic,[13] but with less empathy—and the stories differ.

The Jaina versions brought some fragments together in the

[10] J. Brockington, *The Sanskrit Epics*; idem, "Issues Involved in the Shift from Oral to Written Transmission of the Epics: A Workshop Report", 131–8; Y. Vassilkov, "The Mahabharata's Typological Definition Reconsidered", 249–56.

[11] V.S. Sukthankar, "Prolegomena", in the Ādiparvan, *Mahābhārata*, vol. 1, i–cx; idem, "The Bhṛgus and the Bhārata: A Text-Historical Study", 1–76; idem, *On the Meaning of the Mahābhārata*: these have argued for the Bhṛgu redaction, but others disagree, e.g. A. Hiltebeitel, *Rethinking the Mahābhārata*; M. Biardeau, "The Salvation of the King in the Mahābhārata", 75–97. See also R.P. Goldman, *Gods, Priests and Warriors: The Bhṛgus of the Mahābhārata*; J.L. Fitzgerald, Introduction to The Book of Peace in *The Mahābhārata*, vol. 7, 79–164.

[12] *Sammoha-Vinodini*, 490, as quoted in G.P. Malalasekera, *Dictionary of Pali Proper Names*, vol. 1, 372.

[13] *Jātakas: Dhūmakāri Jātaka* 413; *Dasa-brāhmaṇa Jātaka* 495; *Kunāla Jātaka* 536.

Pāṇḍava Purāṇa, and in an eighth-century AD work, the *Harivaṃśa Purāṇa* of Jinasena.[14] But even these are variants and differ in characterization, events, and intentions. They introduce the Mathura legends of Kṛṣṇa. The war is attributed to Jarāsandha seeking revenge on Kṛṣṇa, who had killed his son-in-law. It has been said that the Jaina *Purāṇas* are an intentional rewriting of the brahmanical *Purānas*.[15] Jarāsandha is in them the valorous adversary of Kṛṣṇa, and the heroes eventually seek liberation through renunciation, demonstrating the centrality of Jaina ethics. Creating an acceptable version was the task of the compiler, even if it meant discarding the variants. Vyāsa's attempt was presumably to cull and refashion the events into a retrievable whole, and to underline brahmanical ethics.

Some of the important persons in the epic, barring the Pāṇḍavas, find mention in the *Vedas*, but often in passing and linked with other locations and events. The Bharatas moved from the Ravi to the Sutlej–Beas rivers, and may then have moved into the Doab, where there could have been a conflict with existing settlements. A possible genesis of the epic in the *dāśrājña,* the conflict of the ten *rājās* described in the *Ṛgveda*, has been suggested.[16] Stories about the earlier conflict may have survived, been exaggerated and a local conflict could have been enlarged into a war. Alliances and identities would have taken other shapes in the course of stories going from the *Ṛgveda* via the *Brāhmaṇas* to the epic. The locations of the battle would change with migrations.

An oral tradition meant that the story could be added to or subtracted from through various renderings. The text was not frozen until it was written, and even then it could be added to.[17] The oldest core, according to one opinion, may have been that composed in the *triṣṭubh* metre.[18] Subsequent emendations and interpolations

[14] B.N. Sumitra Bai and R.J. Zydenbos, "The Jaina Mahabharata", 251ff.

[15] P. Jaini, "Jaina Puranas: A Puranic Counter Tradition", 207–46.

[16] *Ṛgveda*, 7.18; M. Witzel, "The Vedas and the Epics: Some Comparative Notes on Persons, Lineages, Geography and Grammar", 21–80; S.S.N. Murthy, "The Questionable Historicity of the Mahābhārata", 1–15.

[17] V.S. Sukthankar, *On the Meaning of the Mahābhārata*; I. Morris, "The Use and Abuse of Homer", 81–138.

[18] M.C. Smith, "The Mahābhārata's Core", 479–82.

would have continued for a few centuries, as is characteristic of open oral traditions. The preservation of these texts was therefore very different from the more meticulous memorization of the ritual compositions of the Vedic hymns, virtually a closed oral tradition. Memorization is not the key factor in an oral composition since there can be improvisation in the course of a recital.[19]

It has been argued that societies with a lively oral tradition live in the present and slough off those bits of the past which are irrelevant. Oral literature is therefore heavily dependent on its immediate social context.[20] Updating the context of the story would explain the presence of peoples contemporary with the updaters, such as the Yavanas, Śakas, and Hūṇas of the post-Mauryan period, the retaining of what they viewed as pertinent, introducing an element of historical consciousness. Irrespective of whether what is described is factual or not, there is a sense of the past, and of carrying a tradition of information on the past which is of significance to later reconstructions of the past. Most oral epics, as noted earlier, take a written form much after the events they are narrating, and this turning to the past has to do with marshalling the past for the purposes of the present—a feature even of some modern historical writing.

The epic tradition can be consciously archaic, given that heroic poetry reminds its audience of deeds that are assumed to have happened in an earlier "heroic age". It is a narrative focussing on individuals, generally members of the elite patriline, with an emphasis on martial values,[21] and where heroism becomes a social necessity.[22] The conflict is frequently between such societies and those less well configured and seen as alien, as in the *Rāmāyaṇa*; or between fairly equally matched families for political supremacy,

[19] R. Finnegan, *Oral Poetry*, 52; A. Parry (ed.), *The Making of Homeric Verse: The Collected Papers of Milman Parry*; A.B. Lord, *The Singer of Tales*. There is a discussion on the validity of the views of Parry and Lord in relation to the oral forms in the Indian epics in W. de Jong, "Recent Russian Publications on the Indian Epic", 1–42.

[20] R. Finnegan, *Oral Poetry*; W.J. Ong, *Orality and Literacy*.

[21] G. Thomson, *Studies in Ancient Greek Society*, 527ff.; S.P. Brodbeck, *The Mahābhārata Patriline*.

[22] J. Redfield, *Nature and Culture in the Iliad: The Tragedy of Hector*, 99ff.

as in the *Mahābhārata*; and alongside there is a grappling with the problems of historical change. Are the chiefdoms of the *Mahābhārata*, which possibly date to the early first millennium BC, fearful of the socio-political change inherent in the transition to kingdoms, which they begin to glimpse in the Magadhan kingship of the mid-first millennium BC?

Epic literature traces origins and provides data for the recognition of beginnings. To that extent, lineages and the origins of social groups are of substantial interest. This is expressed in the use of the symbols of a warrior aristocracy and the delineation of a world imbued with its values; a universe where status and birth are seemingly synonymous yet also negotiable through legends; where the purity of lineage is important enough for some heroes to be fathered by the gods, but where this purity can also be fabricated through a genealogy; where legitimacy is crucial to the claim to political power, but the latter precedes the former; where the resolution of problems is often through conflict; and where ordinary people, with some exceptions, are not involved in the events other than at subservient levels.

Myth is sometimes differentiated from epic: myth evokes the remote past and deals with the origin, nature, and destiny of the cosmos and in it the deities have functions; an epic on the other hand evokes the more recent past with a specific time and place, and deals with the origins, nature, and destiny of man, and heroes are role models.[23] Immortalizing the current hero would also be of benefit to the bard, who anticipates lavish gifts from the hero, as earlier in the *dāna-stuti* hymns. Questions of origins and identity are pertinent to the roots of the community and can become the reason for the sanction which lies behind the necessity of the transmission. The difference between the remote and recent past is also significant to notions of time.

2. The Narrative

The *Mahābhārata* as we have it now is of enormous length and consists of eighteen *parvans* (books).[24] Some constituted the core

[23] A. Hiltebeitel, *The Ritual of Battle*, 31–2.

[24] V.S. Sukthankar, S.K. Belvalkar, and P.L.Vaidya, *et al., The Mahābhārata*,

story as narrated in the Ādi *parvan* (1), and Sabhā *parvan* (2), and the descriptions of the battle in later *parvans*; some were the encasing of this story in a variety of discourses on polity, social codes, rebirth, and such like, as given in the Śānti *parvan* (12) and Anuśāsana *parvan* (13). It is thought the latter two and the early part of the Ādi *parvan* are additions of a later period. Such interpolations occur elsewhere in the *parvans* as well, but not always at such great length. The epic refers to itself as the fifth *Veda* and is referred to as such in other texts.[25]

The core of the epic is a family feud over control of territory and resources. The epic narrative is in part a continuation of actions pertaining to societies as described in the *Vedas*, and in part the induction of other clans and customs alien and subsequent to the *Vedas*. It is, overall, an attempt at the reconstruction of some of the believed history of the clans. It focuses on the descendants of Ilā/Iḍā, the hermaphrodite child of Manu, constituting one of the two major lineages of *kṣatriyas*, the ruling clans in clan societies. (In later times this was to be called the Candravaṃśa or Lunar lineage; the other being the Sūryavaṃśa or Solar lineage. The *Mahābhārata* narrative revolves around the first and the *Rāmāyaṇa* story figures as the second.)

The central narrative involves the Kauravas and Pāṇḍavas, cousins who are descendants of Pūru. Their identification as Bharatas may have been intended to link them with the Bharatas of the *Ṛgveda*. The cousins confront each other in a war which, it is said, exterminated the *kṣatriya* clans. Associated with the Pāṇḍavas is Kṛṣṇa of the Vṛṣṇi clan, descended from Yadu; Kṛṣṇa is eventually projected as an incarnation of Viṣṇu. The lineages are not mentioned as such in the Vedic corpus, but the names of clans and persons exist in scattered references. The descent groups could be inventions, as doubtless some were. However, the more important ones feature in narratives in Buddhist and Jaina texts as well,

---

For the First Time Critically Edited, 19 vols; translation of *parvans* 1–5, of the Critical Edition, J.A.B. van Buitenen (ed. and trans.), *The Mahābhārata*, Chicago, 1973, 11, 12 (i), J.L. Fitzgerald, 2004.

[25] J.L. Fitzgerald, "India's Fifth Veda. The *Mahābhārata's* Presentation of Itself", 251–73. See also D.D. Kosambi, "The Autochthonous Element in the *Mahābhārata*", 31–44.

although the stories differ, as do the worldviews. This suggests a common source of stories—but not necessarily historicity.

The narrative of the family feud in the *Mahābhārata* begins with Śantanu marrying Gaṅgā, who unfortunately for him does away with each of her children at birth. Only one son, Bhīṣma, is rescued, after which the mother disappears. Later, Śantanu marries Satyavatī, who demands that Bhīṣma remain celibate so that her sons succeed Śantanu. Bhīṣma agrees, but nevertheless he is referred to as *pitāmaha*—paternal grandfather, the respected patriarch.

The sons of Satyavatī die childless, two widows surviving them. The crisis of succession requires that the two submit to bearing a son each from Vyāsa, himself the illegitimate son of Satyavatī born through a liaison with the *ṛṣi* Parāśara, prior to her marrying Śantanu. The two step-brothers, Dhṛtrāṣṭra and Pāṇḍu—the sons of Vyāsa by the two widows—are therefore born out of wedlock, although the fathering of the two boys has been explained as a form of *niyoga* or levirate.[26]

Vyāsa is an affinal kinsman and has no blood connection with the lineages, nor have the widows. Neither of the two sons can succeed since the first is born blind and the second has an abnormally pale skin and is possibly an albino. Physical defects are a disqualification for the status of *rājā,* an echo of the story of Devāpi. Ironically, the only child with no physical defects is the one fathered by Vyāsa on a *dāsī*, and therefore ineligible on grounds of status. Vyāsa's mother, Satyavatī, is the paternal great-grandmother to the heroes of the epic, but neither she nor the father of Vyāsa is part of the lineage of the Pūrus. Dhṛtrāṣṭra is father to the Kauravas, and Pāṇḍu gives his name to his five sons, although they are not born of him: he is unable to father children because of a curse. The two sets of cousins are not related by blood to the Pūru lineage. Nevertheless, Bhīṣma ensures a succession against

[26] 1.97.7ff. (In this chapter, numbers without reference to a text pertain to the *Mahābhārata*.) There is a difference of opinion in the *Dharmaśāstras* regarding the rules of levirate. *Manu's Code of Law*, 9.57, states that an older brother cannot cohabit with a younger brother's widow but *Gautama Dharmasūtra*, 18.4–8, and *Viṣṇu Dharmasūtra*, 15.3, allow it. In this case Vyāsa was the elder stepbrother.

heavy odds and insists on it. One wonders why there should have been such insistence. Was the story of paternity through Vyāsa an attempt to veil the real *pitāmaha*? If the latter was Bhīṣma, there would have been a continuation of the blood-line.

The birth of the Kauravas and the Pāṇḍavas is also abnormal. The Kauravas, numbering a hundred brothers, emerged as a ball of flesh from their mother Gāndhārī's womb, which ball was then divided into a hundred pieces, and each placed in a jar; the Pāṇḍavas were fathered by various deities, called up by a formula given to Kuntī, the wife of Pāṇḍu. Kuntī's first son, Karṇa, was the child of Sūrya the sun-god, but being born out of wedlock was never given the status of a *kṣatriya* or of a Pāṇḍava, although in fact he was in no way inferior to the rest. He grew up in the family of a *sūta*—a bard or a charioteer—and became an ally of the Kauravas. Kuntī bore three sons from three different gods and passed the formula onto her co-wife Mādrī, who called up the twin-gods, the Aśvins, and bore twin sons. Some have explained Kuntī's actions also as a resort to *niyoga* (levirate), but none of the gods so called upon were kinsmen and Kuntī herself does not acknowledge it as *niyoga*.[27] The twin sons have no blood relationship with the three older brothers but are regarded as related.

From the perspective of a society underlining kinship connections, as was this society, the lapses in the connections are quite striking. They are ignored in favour of political claims. The annulling of kinship as actual identity hints at a proto-caste identity, since they all claim to be *kṣatriyas*.

On the death of Pāṇḍu, his five young sons go to the residence of their uncle at Hastināpura and are brought up with his hundred sons. The eldest among the latter, Duryodhana, is determined that he should inherit the entire patrimony. He lays various plans to kill the Pāṇḍavas: these plans and their consequences fill out the early part of the epic narrative. The five Pāṇḍava brothers, together with the matriarch Kuntī, have to go into hiding for a year. During this period they attend, in disguise, the *svayamvara* of Draupadī, the daughter of the *rājā* of Pañcāla, and win her. She becomes the joint wife of the five brothers—an act of fraternal polyandry.

[27] 1.112.2ff.; 113.30.

They return to Hastināpura, and it is decided that, because of the continuing conflict among the cousins over succession, the territory should be divided into two; and so the Pāṇḍavas establish themselves at neighbouring Indraprastha. This requires burning down the surrounding forest in an extensive, graphically described conflagration.[28] Having established themselves, their friend Kṛṣṇa encourages the eldest, Yudhiṣṭhira, to hold a grand sacrificial ritual, the *rājasūya*, to mark their authority. This involves a preliminary *digvijaya*, with his brothers going out to conquer in different directions. This is ostensibly to conquer territory, but actually to coerce other *rājās* into bringing tribute for the *yajña*.

The treasury of the Pāṇḍavas, having become so full that it would be impossible to empty it in a hundred years, Yudhiṣṭhira expends his wealth on a *rājasūya*.[29] *Brāhmaṇas* coming from all over repeat their continuously heard refrain, *diyatam* (give).[30] The *rājasūya* requires the consent of the *kṣatriyas*. Kṛṣṇa recites their history, starting with their slaughter by Paraśurāma, down to the contemporary Jarāsandha who was attacking *kṣatriyas* as if he was a clone of Paraśurāma. Yet the *rājasūya* is required if there is a claim to being the one above all others—the *samrāṭ*. This is a claim to sovereignty. The question of status comes to the fore when deciding who should be the honoured guest. The Pāṇḍava choice, Kṛṣṇa, is opposed presumably because the Vṛṣṇis have a low status among the lineages. Significantly, Kṛṣṇa is called *arājā* (not a *rājā*).[31]

There are problems with the powerful Jarāsandha ruling in Magadha, in the middle Ganges plain.[32] He and Kṛṣṇa have been enemies despite a matrimonial alliance with the Vṛṣṇis. Finally, he is put to death in a rather unheroic manner by the Pāṇḍavas at the instigation of Kṛṣṇa. Śiśupāla of the Cedis objects to the Pāṇḍava choice of Kṛṣṇa as honoured guest since he is not of a sufficiently high status, but he is silenced by Kṛṣṇa beheading

[28] 1.215ff.
[29] 2.30.7.
[30] 2.30.50, 13.61.11ff., 64.3, 68.2.
[31] 2.34.1–10.
[32] 2.13–22.

him.[33] The somewhat laboured passages describing Kṛṣṇa as even greater than the great gods are surely later interpolations.[34] The conflict between and among some descendants of Yadu and Pūru is significant, not entirely unrelated to an earlier conflict over descent where Yadu, the eldest son of Yayāti, was superseded by Pūru, the youngest.

The *rājasūya* is successfully completed, to the irritation of the Kauravas, who later challenge the eldest of the five brothers to a game of dice. This is normally part of the ritual of the *rājasūya*,[35] replete with symbolic meaning, but is here narrated as a separate and significant event subsequent to the ritual.

The highpoint of the game of dice is when Draupadī is placed as a stake. She questions the legality of this action, given that the Pāṇḍavas have already been staked and have lost. They not only lose their territory and their wealth but have to go into exile for thirteen years, which period they spend substantially in the forest. They finally return to reclaim their territory and rights, but the Kauravas refuse to concede these. This leads to the war in which all the *kṣatriya* clans are ranged on either side. Insistence on battle is also because Draupadī had been insulted by the Kauravas and she wants revenge.

Much of the epic is then taken up with the details of the eighteen-day battle. Kṛṣṇa is advisor to the Pāṇḍavas and they emerge victorious. But the war has taken its toll on the *kṣatriya* world, the world of the heroes, which virtually comes to a close. Kṛṣṇa makes the appropriate historical comment to Dhṛtrāṣṭra: *tav'aparādhān nṛpate sarvam kṣatram kṣayam gatam* (because of your wrong actions as ruler, all the *kṣatriyas* have been destroyed).[36] Events subsequent to the war gradually lead to a pallid ending, with the protagonists going to their respective afterlives: the anti-climax to many stirring epics.

The narrative of a family feud over succession becomes an involved text incorporating the participation of virtually every clan,

[33] 2.37ff.

[34] 3.186.13–16, 187.1–55, 256.29ff.

[35] J.A.B. van Buitenen, *The Mahābhārata*, vol. 2, 5ff.

[36] Śalyaparvan, 62.43.

interwoven with mythology, with discourses on how best to govern with passages on ethical behaviour, and with the glorification of Kṛṣṇa as the incarnation of Viṣṇu. Why Kṛṣṇa is chosen remains a puzzle, given his ambiguity in relation to ethical norms, a matter which has been much commented upon.[37] The story moves sometimes easily and sometimes in a jagged fashion between the essentials of a clan chiefship, with the anticipated authority of emerging kingship waiting in the wings—as represented in the Śānti and Anuśāsana *parvans*.

According to some, the epic is the glorification of a grand potlatch;[38] according to others it is, in its later form, the popular text of devotional religion. But, above all, the narrative is a version of the past focusing on the perspective of the *kṣatriya* component of clan societies, perhaps of the early first millennium BC. The extensive sacrificial rituals of the heroic cult are not merely a propitiation of deity but are also a form of legitimation for the *rājā*. Of the accumulated wealth, some was consumed in the ritual, the rest given as gifts to the priests. Pāṇini mentions the veneration of *kṣatriyas*,[39] which may have been associated with the *pañca-vīra* cult of the Vṛṣṇis. The hero cult was sought to be strengthened by equating battle with the ritual of sacrifice.[40] The narrative borrows occasionally from earlier sources, and reformulates what is borrowed, both of which hint at the attempt to create a seminal historical tradition.

3. Occasions for the Initial Recitation of the *Mahābhārata*

The recitation of the *Mahābhārata* is associated with two special occasions which suggest the phases of composition. The first occasion was when the *brāhmaṇa* Vaiśampāyana, one of the disciples of Kṛṣṇa Dvaipāyana Vyāsa, the compiler of the epic,

[37] B.K. Matilal, *Moral Dilemmas in the Mahābhārata*.

[38] G. Held, *The Mahābhārata: An Ethnological Study*; M. Mauss, *The Gift*.

[39] *Aṣṭādhyāyī of Pāṇini*, 4.3.99.

[40] *Mahābhārata*, 12.97.10 to 98.53, 12.99.12ff.; *Ṛgveda*, 10.154.3; *Manu's Code of Law*, 5.98; P. Filliozat, "The Afterdeath Destiny of the Hero According to the Mahābhārata", 3–8.

recited it at the famous *sarpa-sattra* (snake sacrifice) performed by Janamejaya. *Sattras* were distinctive because, frequently in their performance, only *brāhmaṇas* were the patrons and no gift was given to the ritual specialist. But on this occasion the patron was a gift-giving *kṣatriya.*[41] The narrative was being recited to Janamejaya, the great-grandson of Arjuna, and was the story of his immediate ancestors.[42]

Possibly the snake sacrifice is symbolic of obliteration: on this occasion of the heroes.[43] This, in effect, had taken place both recently, in the battle at Kurukṣetra, as well as earlier, when Paraśurāma exterminated the *kṣatriyas*. The recitation of *itihāsa* and *purāṇa* was prescribed as expiation when an elder of the family passed away, presumably to pass on the tradition to the next generation.[44] Was this Janamejaya's gesture at the passing away of his elders, where the *Mahābhārata* would be recited as an *itihāsa*?

On the second occasion it was recited by a *sūta*, Ugraśravas, at a sacrificial ritual performed some time later in the Naimiśa forest by a group of *brāhmaṇas*, pre-eminently Śaunaka.[45] The bard began the recitation by providing a narrative of the Bhṛgu ancestors of Śaunaka. This is virtually stating that the Bhṛgus made a later rendering of the text, a statement they could not formally admit to. There is therefore the curious anomaly of two recitations at two different occasions,[46] each said to be the initial one, although the second recitation is claimed as exactly the same as the first. The composition was originally proclaimed (*proktah*) by Vyāsa, and narrated (*kathitah*) by Vaiśampāyana. The first recitation was a literal repetition of the composition of Vyāsa by Vaiśampāyana. In a sense, Vyāsa was narrating the story of his grandsons. Ugraśravas had learnt it from his father Romaharṣana (also a *sūta*), who had learnt it as a pupil of Vyāsa. It is once

[41] C.Z. Minkowski, "Snakes, Sattras and the Mahābhārata", 384ff.

[42] 1.54.18–20.

[43] C.Z. Minkowski, "Janamejaya's Sattra and Ritual Structure", 401–20.

[44] *Āśvalāyana Gṛhyasūtra*, 4.6.6.

[45] 1.1.15–19.

[46] *Mahābhārata*, 1.1.50ff.; see also G. Held, *The Mahābhārata: An Ethnological Study*, 59ff.

removed, although Ugraśravas claims he is reciting it exactly as his father learnt it. It is described as an ancient narrative and its diverse forms. This gives the story a flavour of the historical. There are some differences,[47] and the time gap between the two makes one later than the other.

It is curious that the two occasions were not coalesced in the editing of the epic, unless this was deliberate, the intention being to indicate that there was a second and later version for a different purpose. Was the second a recitation of the Bhṛgu version—therefore the recitation of Bhṛgu ancestors—claiming to be the original composition of Vyāsa? The *brāhmaṇa* recites the narrative to the *kṣatriyas* and the *sūta* recites it to the *brāhmaṇas*. The interplay of the role of *brāhmaṇas* and *sūtas* was to be a continuing feature of compositions associated with *itihāsa*.

For such a text to be put together, the burden fell on the compiler rather than the author. Vyāsa may have been doing just that: compiling rather than authoring. Vyāsa listens to fragments being recited off and on,[48] for it is said that this *itihāsa* has been recited before by *kavis* and will be recited by them again in the future.[49] Although it is described as the *Veda*,[50] unlike the *Vedas* expansion is allowed and encouraged. Those who recite it should support their narrative from the earlier *itihāsa* and *purāṇa*.[51]

Vyasa was traditionally thought of as the learned *ṛṣi* (sage) who is said to have edited a variety of compositions, such as the *Vedas*, the *Mahābhārata*, and the early *Purāṇas.* In fact this statement may mean that a recognized oral composition was taken out of the hands of its original authors, the *sūtas*, and ascribed to a *ṛṣi*, putting it into a brahmanical framework. Vyāsa, despite his mixed parentage,[52] was evidently acceptable as a *brāhmaṇa*. Once again there are echoes of *dāsī-putrāḥ brāhmaṇas*. There were

[47] A. Hiltebeitel, *Rethinking the Mahābhārata*, 96ff.

[48] B.M. Sullivan, *Seer of the Fifth Veda*.

[49] 1.1.24.

[50] 1.1.2, 1.1.16–19, 1.1.205, 1.56.17.

[51] 1.1.204.

[52] As noted above (in section 2 of this chapter), he was born to Satyavatī, a woman of the fisherfolk said to be the daughter of an *apsarā*, and the *ṛṣi* Parāśara, the son of a *brāhmaṇa* father but of a low-caste mother. Attempts were made later to suggest that Satyavatī was actually the daughter of a *kṣatriya*.

attempts later to improve his caste status through other legends of his parentage. The recitation by the bard Ugraśravas sounds more authentic, except that his name, meaning "loud-throated", seems a trifle sarcastic.

Its recitation at a sacrificial ritual linked the epic to the *ākhyānas* of earlier times, also recited at ritual occasions. Was the *Mahābhārata* in origin a collation of *ākhyānas*?[53] The shift would have been from unconnected scattered stories to a continuous one linked by a narrative framework. The *sūta* says that whereas the *brāhmaṇas* recited stories from the *Vedas* during pauses in the ritual, Vyāsa recited the *Mahābhārata*.[54] A summary of the core narrative given by Vaiśampāyana was presumably based on the *kathā*.[55]

The *brāhmaṇa* Śaunaka, presiding over the *sattra* in the Naimiśa forest, asked Ugraśravas to begin by reciting the genealogy of the Bhṛgu *brāhmaṇas* who were his ancestors.[56] Once again, the invocation is of a believed past. This was in accordance with the practice, as it had evolved, of authors initially reciting the genealogy of patrons. Subsequent to the Bhārgava genealogy, with its claims to status, there followed claims for the hero's ancestry, that of the Pūru lineage as given in the Ādi *parvan* of the *Mahābhārata*. The replay of earlier narratives takes new forms. Thus, mention is made of Devāpi and Śantanu in the *Ṛgveda*, which is elaborated in the *Nirukta* and *Bṛhad-devatā*, where they are said to be Kurus.[57] Devāpi's skin disease is omitted in the *Mahābhārata* but is reflected in the physical infirmity of Pāṇḍu. The role of the "rain-maker", symbolic of magical power, is now absent, not being required in later polities.

The function of the *sūta* was being gradually differentiated, making it professionally important to the *rājās* of the time, even if it was lower than that of the *brāhmaṇas*. Ugraśravas is deferential towards the *brāhmaṇas* and addresses them as *dvija* and *vipra*,

[53] R.C. Hazra, "The Aśvamedha, the Common Source of Origin of the Purāṇa Pañca-lakṣaṇa and the Mahābhārata", 190–203.

[54] 1.53.32.

[55] 1.53.27 to 1.56.30.

[56] 1.5.

[57] *Ṛgveda*, 10.98; *Nirukta* of Yāska, 2.10; *Bṛhad-devatā*, 7.154, 8.7; *Mahābhārata*, 1.97.1.ff., 1.50.42–3, 5.149.15.

and the bard is referred to as *sūtanandana*.[58] Mention is made of the *sūta, māgadha,* and *kuśīlava*, all categories of bards, and all of whom tend to have a low status. Possibly this change also reflected the incorporation of local bards attached to lesser *rājās*, and the status of these would perforce have to be kept distanced from a rising brahmanical strata.

4. Dating the Epic

Analyses of the epic go back to the earliest discussions on its date. In these, incidents and descriptions are shown to be of varying dates, which makes the chronology of the narrative uncertain.[59] There are diverse views on dating the epic. Some tend to assign it to a short period, whereas others argue that the different fragments have each to be dated separately. In the latter view, the collation as we have it today spreads across a few centuries, from the mid-first millennium BC—at which time the early bardic version would have been familiar—to the early first millennium AD, by when the accretions relating to the worship of Viṣṇu and of the pre-eminence of kingship had been written in.[60] The later sections can be seen as justifying the change to incipient kingship, which differed from the social infrastructure of the earlier clan society.

Much has been written on the possible origins and versions of the *Mahābhārata* before the present one, and the radical changes introduced in each, and where this process implies historical change.[61] The dichotomy suggested between the epic and the pseudo-epic was explored at length and has been revived by some, pre-eminently in the separation between the narrative and didactic sections.[62]

[58] 1.2.1ff.

[59] E.W. Hopkins, *The Great Epic of India*, 386–9.

[60] V.S. Sukthankar, *On the Meaning of the Mahābhārata.*

[61] See the summary of views in V.S. Sukthankar, *On the Meaning of the Mahābhārata*; A. Hiltebeitel, *Ritual of Battle*; J.F. Fitzgerald, Introduction to Śāntiparvan, *Mahābhārata* (Book xii, trans.).

[62] E.W. Hopkins, *The Social and Military Position of the Ruling Caste in Ancient India as Represented in the Sanskrit Epic,* 57ff.; also idem, *The Great Epic of India.*

Whether the text was composed in a unitary form by a single author, or put together by a group of authors over a short period of a century, between *c.* 150 and 0 BC, has been much discussed.[63] Some of this discussion questions Sukthankar's view of a long period of composition and compilation. That there was an attempt at some unity would be the purpose of editing the text, but as a historical source it is difficult to concede that it was a one-time composition since an epic by its very nature incorporates variant views and contradictions. Obviously, therefore, to speak of an "epic age" as historians did, not so long ago, makes little historical sense.[64]

There is no agreement on the date of the central event, the war at Kurukṣetra. One view holds that it marks the end of the Dvāparayuga (the third age) and the beginning of the Kaliyuga (the fourth and final age of the great cycle). This has been calculated as the equivalent of 3102 BC.[65] The theory of the four *yugas* or time cycles described in the epic is, however, late and is dated to around the Christian era.

The Puranic genealogies would contradict the date of 3102 BC,[66] stating that there were either 1015 or 1050 years between Parikṣit ruling soon after the war, and Mahāpadma Nanda, known to be ruling in the fourth century BC. Kalhaṇa dates the Kurus and Pāṇḍavas to 653 years after the start of the Kaliyuga.[67]

Another somewhat uncertain method used in recent times is that of counting the generations in the genealogies and calculating a certain average number of years per generation, which results

[63] M. Biardeau, "Some More Considerations about Textual Criticism", 115–23; A. Hiltebeitel, *Rethinking the Mahābhārata*.

[64] By way of comparison it should be pointed out that the attribution of single authorship of the Greek epics to Homer is now doubted, with other poets prior and subsequent to Homer thought to be contributing to the composition. This also brings historicity into doubt even in an event as central to the Greek epic as the Trojan war. K.A. Raaflaub, "Epic and History", 55–70.

[65] See D.C. Sircar, "Myth of the Great Bhārata War", 18ff. For earlier views on the date of the Kaliyuga, see Āryabhaṭṭa in D.C. Sircar, *Indian Epigraphy*, 222; Aihole Inscription, *Ep. Ind.*, 6.1ff.; *Varāhamihira's Bṛhat-saṃhitā*, 13.3.

[66] F.E. Pargiter, *Dynasties of the Kali Age*, 74.

[67] *Rājataraṅgiṇī*, 1.51.

in a date close to the second millennium BC.[68] Astronomical data has been used to calculate the date to 2449 BC.[69] Yet none of these early dates fit the contextual evidence. Given the structure of the epic, the Bhārata *ākhyāna/kathā* was doubtless known by the mid-first millennium BC, and the inclusion of the Bhāgavata cult would date to the rise of Bhagavatism at the end of the first millennium BC.

There appear to have been two strands in the epic. The bardic material referred to events which were believed to have happened, and these are therefore associated with *itihāsa* and familiar. The other was the brahmanical input, largely expressed in the didactic sections. The Bhṛgu *brāhmaṇas* are thought to have introduced aspects of the *dharmaśāstra* tradition—discussions on *dharma* and *nīti* (polity)—and on the worship of Viṣṇu as part of the Bhāgavata ideology.[70] The *Mahābhārata* sometimes used *atīta, ākhyāna,* and *kathā*, all referring to narratives—both cosmological and others—synonymously.[71] The early sections are referred to as *itihāsa*.[72] In the later sections it is said that the past is an exemplar to the present, *atrāpy udāharantīmam itihāsam purātanam* . . .[73] This becomes a formula for referring to the past and looking back into a more remote past, and is quite consciously introduced in the interpolated sections.

Examples quoted from the past, to illustrate a point being made in the present, consist of narratives which begin with the statement that they are *itihāsam purātanam,* i.e. narratives of what happened in the past, a phrase also used in the *Upaniṣads*. A reference to the Pāṇḍavas, as having through their own valour regained the realm that they had lost to the sons of Dhṛtrāṣṭra, is treated as something from the distant past, unrelated to current events.[74] This would

[68] S.N. Pradhan, *Chronology of Ancient India*, 258–60; P.L. Bhargava, *India in the Vedic Age*; R. Morton-Smith, *Dates and Dynasties in Early India*.

[69] D.C. Sircar (ed.), *The Bhārata War and Puranic Genealogies*, 19.

[70] V.S. Sukthankar, "The Bhṛgus and the Bhārata: A Text-Historical Study", 1–76.

[71] E.W. Hopkins, *The Great Epic of India*, 48.

[72] 1.1.17, 1.54.23.

[73] E.g. 12.259.2, 13.137.2.

[74] 13.6.40.

reinforce the argument that much of the Anuśāsana *parvan* was an addition of the early Christian era. The Śānti and Anuśāsana *parvans* carry statements that are sometimes similar to those in the Manu *Dharmaśāstra* and the Kauṭilya *Arthaśāstra*, which further suggest a date of post-Mauryan times.

The function of *itihāsa* is not necessarily to provide what we would today call "authentic history", but to project an earlier age and its ideals, as well as to introduce the different context of the later time when the composition was re-edited. (Bhīṣma, lying on a bed of arrows, in the throes of dying, but holding forth for days on matters of *dharma, varṇa*, and *mokṣa*, would be one such mechanism.) Thus, the archaeological search for material culture as the counterpart of the epic becomes something of a chimera. The manipulation of time in the epic is too complex for there to be a correlation with archaeological periodization. At most, artefacts may provide tangible forms to some descriptions in the epic.

An attempt was made to date epic events by referring to the silt deposit at the site of Hastināpura, and correlating it with mention of a flood of this town soon after the war, which led to a migration south to Kauśāmbi. The silt deposit dates to about the eighth century BC,[75] a date at variance with other suggested dates. The story of the shifting of the capital may have been invented by those who founded Kauśāmbi, to claim a link with Hastināpura. Comparisons with archaeological material require more than the juxtaposition of artefact with text.[76]

Heroic society prior to the rise of states is doubtless the context to the earlier narrative. The intermingling of various cultures is such that texts looking back on the past would inevitably have to be multi-layered.[77] The epic was probably in origin localized and known initially in the western Ganges plain, from where it spread to other parts. Various local narrative fragments are likely to have been added on, becoming part of the text, ensuring them both status and continuity.

[75] B.B. Lal, "Excavation at Hastinapur and other Explorations in the Upper Ganga and Sutlej Basins", 4ff.

[76] G. Lad, *Mahābhārata and Archaeological Evidence,* 65ff.

[77] M. Witzel, "The Vedas and the Epics . . .", 21–80.

There is a popular opinion that the Vālmīki *Rāmāyaṇa* is earlier than the *Mahābhārata* since the latter gives a version of the story of Rāma in the Rāmopākhyāna section of the text. However, this could be a later interpolation. Events in the *Mahābhārata* are set in an earlier socio-political system.

5. The Authors

The *Mahābhārata* in its present form suggests the possibility of phases in its authorship: the oral compositions of the *sūtas,* their rendering into a literary form by Vyāsa, and the introduction of new political, social, and religious ideas perhaps by Bhṛgu *brāhmaṇas.* That the latter did not expunge the former would point to the propagation of Bhāgvatism being facilitated by converting an established and popular narrative. The bardic material was probably viewed as a kind of history and therefore could not be discarded, especially if the *kṣatriya* tradition thought it important. This pattern of authorship implies that there may originally have been compositions in Prākrit which were then rendered into Sanskrit, the redactors being aware of the political potential in appropriating this material.

Within this possible dual authorship there is also the tension between the non-*brāhmaṇa* element where, for example, *varṇa* rules and the *dharmaśāstra* norms seem absent and the counterpart views of the *brāhmaṇa* redactors, who, if they were Bhṛgus and earlier associated with magic, sorcery, and marginal groups such as the *vrātyas*, were now moving into the foreground of brahmanical social functioning.

There is no agreement on the length of the text. The earliest version may have been the *Jaya* of 8800 verses; then the *Bhārata,* attributed to Vyāsa, consisting of 24,000 verses; this was later inflated to 100,000 verses and came to be called the *Mahābhārata*.[78] The theory of three different versions of the *Jaya, Bhārata*, and *Mahābhārata*, composed variously, has been questioned.[79] While

[78] van Buitenen, *The Mahābhārata*, 1, xxiii, 1.1.61.

[79] A. Mehendale, "A Review of Yardi, M.R., *The Mahabharata: Its Genesis and Growth*". Yardi attempts a statistical analysis based on metre and argues

some sources refer to two texts,[80] the *Bhārata* and the *Mahābhārata*, the epic itself makes no such distinction. It states that the prefix of *mahat* is applied to the *Bhārata*.[81]

The epic has many stock items of the bardic repertoire, such as descriptions of halls and residences, the grandeur of guests invited on special occasions, and the recital of conflicts.[82] Another feature is the constant boxing in of stories, which provides the opening for infinite tales, not to mention the repetition of the same stories in different contexts, such as that of Paraśurāma.[83]

Other segments show the bardic presence through the inclusion of genealogies. A *gāthā* called the *anuvaṃśya* carrying genealogies is associated with a *ṛṣi*.[84] Later sources refer to the *sūta* maintaining genealogies.[85] The *sūta* and the *māgadha*, numbering some eight hundred, are said to be employed by Yudhiṣṭhira, reminiscent of the musicians accompanied by the *vīnāgāthins*.[86] Theirs were songs of victory, recitations of genealogies and eulogies on the gifts received and their donor.[87] The function of charioteer associated with the *sūta* may have contributed to lowering his status by the time of Manu.[88]

The sanction of the bard also derived from the belief that the epic was a record of what had happened. This belief is significant, even though we know today that the factual element in the epic was limited. Events can be confused or genealogies telescoped or extended since the compiler has the licence to rearrange his material. What we now have is a generalized view of the past, but worked over by redactors.

The *sūtas*, as bards, had a distinct and separate status. That they

---

for four recensions of the original text. See also N.J. Shende, "The Authorship of the Mahabharata", 67–82.

[80] *Āśvalāyana Gṛhyasūtra*, 3.4.4.

[81] 1.1.209.

[82] E.g., 2.7.1ff., 2.8.1ff., 2.31.1–9, 3.175–6.

[83] E.g., 1.98.1ff., 12.50.

[84] 3.86.5.

[85] *Vāyu Purāṇa*, 1.26–31; *Padma Purāṇa*, 5.1.27–8.

[86] Cf. *Śatapatha Brāhmaṇa*, 13.4.3.3–5.

[87] 1.206.2, 3.43.15ff.

[88] *Manu's Code of Law*, 10.11, 17, 26, 47.

were initially respected and associated with various immunities such as personal inviolability—they could not come to harm—is one indication.[89] This may have been a concession to the representation of the actions of the *rājā* crucial to his reputation. Perhaps they were inviolable in the *kṣatriya* domain because, as charioteers of the *rājā*, when visiting other *rājās* on special missions they were representing their patron. Their status tended to rise with the status of their patrons, but when the compositions were taken over by other groups in society the status of the bard was deliberately lowered, as evident in the *Dharmaśāstra* of Manu.

In the vision of the bard the agents of history are in part historical, in part allegorical, and in part mythical.[90] Thus he comes to be seen at times as the inheritor of the shaman, and as a mantic, both merging into the seer. For such a person the knowledge of the past lies in events and genealogies, and of the future in prophetic utterance and inspired speech.[91] The finest recitations were thus performances by him on special occasions before a select audience.

If the epic was at some stage added to by the Bhṛgus, their interest in doing so needs to be known. Their status in the Vedic corpus is unclear. Bhṛgus are priests to the *asuras*—the force of evil, they married *kṣatriya* women, were associated with violence, sorcery, and the violation of norms;[92] yet they are also *brāhmaṇas*.

The pre-eminent Bhṛgu, Śukra, was superior to the priest of the *devas* because he knew how to revive those who had died, so those that fell in battle rose up again to battle further.[93] His magical power is reminiscent of the power of shamans. The *kavis* bestowed immortality through their compositions, and this carefully guarded knowledge was passed on to their sons. However, because it was realized that immortality can also be acquired through history, memory, and records, the control of these becomes crucial.

[89] *Taittirīya Saṃhitā*, 4.5.2 *ahantya*; *Vājasaneyī Saṃhitā*, 16.18 *ahanti*. Both forms suggest *ahanya*: not to be slain. A.A. Macdonell and A.B. Keith, *Vedic Index*, vol. II, 463.

[90] M. Abrams, *Natural Supernaturalism,* 332.

[91] N.K. Chadwick, *Poetry and Prophecy*, 14ff.

[92] R.P. Goldman, *Gods, Priests and Warriors*, 144ff.

[93] G. Dumezil, *The Plight of a Sorcerer*.

As *brāhmaṇas* who had married into *kṣatriya* families, and as occasional warriors, they could have been motivated to maintain and reconstruct the *kṣatriya* tradition. They placed themselves above the *kṣatriyas*, and as among those *brāhmaṇas* who could challenge even gods such as Agni and Indra. They were particularly concerned with discourses on *dharma* and *nīti,* theories of the functioning of society and polity. This could in part explain the induction of these into the Śānti and Anuśāsana *parvans*, and occasionally elsewhere. Yet they themselves were not averse to acting contrary to these codes, perhaps to demonstrate that they were above the norms.

The *Mahābhārata* has many myths about the Bhṛgus in which they are generally in conflict, and successfully so, with the *kṣatriyas* or even the gods.[94] They are said to be proficient in the functions of the *kṣatriyas,* but were also their priests. However, since they married into *kṣatriya* families they could have become *brāhmaṇas* of a lesser, *brahma-kṣatra*, status. Paraśurāma (also known as Rāma Jamadāgni) was of Bhṛgu descent, and in his fury destroyed all the *kṣatriyas* twenty-one times.[95] The destruction began with matricide.[96] It took place in Kurukṣetra, as did the second destruction of the *kṣatriyas* in the battle. If Paraśurāma destroyed the *kṣatriyas,* then *kṣatriya* women would have had to procreate through *brāhmaṇas*, resulting in the mixing of the two *varṇas*.[97] This strengthens the notion of the coming into being of *brahma-kṣatra.* These *kṣatriyas* were predictably superior, as would have been their descendants.[98]

It has been plausibly argued that the story of the destruction of the *kṣatriyas* reflects the Bhṛgus taking over the *kṣatriya* history and tradition.[99] To argue for a Bhṛgu redaction is not to suggest that the Bhṛgus went through the text with a fine comb, systematically eliminating what they disapproved of and substituting, in every case, their own views. More likely, they inflated the

[94] 3.115–17.
[95] E.g., 12.49.30ff.
[96] 3.116.5ff.
[97] 1.58.1–29, 1.98.1–6.
[98] 1.58.4ff., 12.49.55ff.
[99] R.P. Goldman, *Gods, Priests and Warriors*, 112ff.

text by inserting what they thought was appropriate at particular points and including extensive additions. Some sentiments of the previous authorship would therefore have continued into the later text.[100] The induction of the didactic sections and their worldview signalled the need to justify kingship eventually replacing clan society.

The adding on of material was not limited to heroic narrative but included, among other things, large swathes of instructions pertaining to kingship, and the introduction of Vaiṣṇava Bhāgavatism. The Śānti and Ānuśāsana *parvans* are didactic in character, purporting to matters relating to kingship, governance, and social obligations These passages have some parallels in existing *Dharmaśāstras* and the *Arthaśāstra*.

The worship of Vedic deities gave way to deities which had earlier remained relatively backstage, such as Śiva and Viṣṇu.[101] Vaiṣṇava Bhāgavatism is different from the religion of the *Vedas*, even if it sometimes evokes their authority. Kṛṣṇa becomes an *avatāra* of Viṣṇu. The obvious addition of the *Bhagavadgītā* was said to be the teaching of Kṛṣṇa as this incarnation.[102]

It was possible to appropriate the literature of the earlier stage and adapt it to contemporary needs through interpolations. The continuity of the text required the retention of some sections so that an ancient authenticity could be claimed. The attempt is not to homogenize but to provide diverse situations with which incorporated groups can identify and find their own reflection in this compendium. It becomes a text with multiple voices.

This process was in part the reverse of the *dāna-stuti* hymns. The narratives of heroes, culled as a category outside ritual compositions, were now made to absorb a sacred ambience. Bhāgavatism was being embedded in the epic. Why this was done was in part

[100] N. Hein, "Epic *Sarvabhūtahite Rataḥ*: A By-word of Non-Bhārgava Editors", 17-35, makes much of this phrase and argues that delighting in the welfare of all beings was not a Bhārgava sentiment. But it is, at the same time, not offensive to the Bhṛgu view.

[101] V.S. Sukthankar, *On the Meaning of the Mahābhārata*, 63, 71; M. Winternitz, *History of Indian Literature*, vol. I, 422ff.

[102] This smaller text was also not composed at a single point in time but was added to on more than one occasion. See A.L. Basham, *The Origins and Development of Classical Hinduism,* 82–97.

to control the believed history of the heroes and in part to ride on the popularity of the heroes to preach a new sectarian religion by converting them into representing and endorsing it. This idea may have been borrowed from the heterodox sects, where biographies of the Buddha and Mahāvīra were helpful in propagating their teachings and asserting their historicity.

The new religion required devotion to the deity. Legitimation was therefore through the intervention of the deity, as in the case of Kṛṣṇa assisting the Pāṇḍavas. Being sired by gods did not make the heroes either gods, or their incarnations, but it gave them a special status. What continued to hold from earlier belief was that after a heroic death the hero lived eternally and blissfully in the heaven of Indra. The end of the *kṣatriyas* by whatever means was in effect symbolic of the end of the clan system and a way of introducing historical change.

This was not just an incidental change. The period from the Mauryas to the Guptas, when the present form of the epic was finalized, witnessed many confrontations between *gaṇa-saṅghas* and kingdoms. Inscriptions refer to kings destroying *kṣatriyas.* These are likely to have been references to the *kṣatriyas* of the *gaṇa-saṅghas*. The Nanda and Maurya states absorbed those of the middle Ganges plain, such as the Vṛjjis, Śākyas, and Licchavis, who are subsequently not associated with this region. Others in Rajasthan, Gujarat, Punjab, the Upper Doab and Central India survived until Gupta times. The political economy of kingship had to subordinate if not uproot the *gaṇa-saṅghas*.

The other challenge came from heterodox sects that received extensive patronage from dynasties described in brahmanical sources as *śūdra* and *mleccha.* That the redactors did not support Jarāsandha, despite his representing the transition to kingship in Magadha, was possibly because the rulers of Magadha supported heterodox sects, and where such sects had a following. In the delineation of Yudhiṣṭhira there appears to be an attempt to appropriate righteous rulers.[103] There was competition between the heterodox and brahmanical sects, and the latter's view of the

[103] In AD 449 an inscription from eastern India quotes Yudhiṣṭhira's protection of land given to *brāhmaṇas* as a precedent for current donation. Damodarpur Inscription no. 2, *Ep. Ind.*, 15, 134.

governance of society, different from the heterodox view, had to be propagated. The denial of the *Vedas* and of Vedic deities by the heterodox led to the latter being called *nāstika* by the *brāhmaṇas.*

Clan societies resisted the change to kingship and were seen as an ideological threat by established kingdoms. Kauṭilya advises the decimation of clan society. Not only was their political form a threat, so too was their not conforming to the *varṇāśrama-dharma*. Buddhism and Jainism were initially rooted in the *gaṇa-saṅghas* of the middle Ganges plain, but from the Mauryan period their *saṅghas* attracted the patronage not only of royalty but also of wealthy artisans, merchants, and land-owners. Their substantial monastic establishments must have raised the ire of those without such patronage.

And there were also the people of the forests resisting the encroachment of settlers. The *Arthaśāstra* and Aśokan inscriptions both record the hostility of the state towards such people.[104] Exile in the forest has many meanings, but one among them was to enable the *grāma* (the village settlement) to justify its encroachment into the *araṇya* (the forest). The people of the forest are therefore often demonized so as to deepen dichotomous categories.

The definition of *dharma* as expounded in the *rāja-dharma* and the *varṇāśrama-dharma* had to be differentiated from the Buddhist definition rooted in the universal application of social ethics irrespective of caste status. The definition of *dharma* becomes pivotal to a debate in which the orthodox demanded that kings destroy *dasyus.* In Buddhist and Jaina thought, *dharma* is the ethic born of relatively egalitarian social norms; and because it is authorized by humans it is not subjected to any other authority. Brahmanical thought was governed by social inequality and required both divine authority and Vedic sanction.[105] The debate touches on the acceptance or non-acceptance of the *Vedas*, a matter that was repeatedly raised in philosophical discussion. *Dharma* also raises issues of fate and *karma* which affect the human condition. The basic difference is over whether humans can

[104] *Arthaśāstra,* 2.1.36, 7.2.19, 8.1.54, 1.16.29, 8.4.41–2; Major Rock Edict 13; J. Bloch, *Les Inscriptions d'Asoka,* 129.

[105] *Manu's Code of Law,* 2.6.

control their fate. Kṛṣṇa accuses Dhṛtarāṣṭra of being the cause of the killing.[106] Dhṛtarāṣṭra invokes the power of both *dhatṛ* (fate) and *karma* (causally connected actions). In a sense, both are impersonal and beyond control, since even *karma* is an inheritance from a previous birth.

The Bhṛgu intervention touches on many changes of the time. The importance of *āpad-dharma* could refer to *brāhmaṇas* losing out on royal patronage given at this point more frequently to heterodox sects. Vedic Brahmanism was appropriate to its brahmanical practitioners and the society that it endorsed, but with change and the need for popular support—which had become characteristic of the heterodoxies—a reformulation may have been thought necessary. This was reflected in the emergence of Puranic religions. The propagation of the *Mahābhārata* seems to have been at two levels. The narrative of the heroes became a familiar story, referred to in many later sources and in popular repertoires of story-telling.[107] The *sūta* was peripatetic and recited portions of the epic to assembled groups or at places of pilgrimage.[108] The propagation of the ideology of the *Mahābhārata*, as redacted later, was encapsulated in the *Gītā* but more expansively explained in the Śānti and Anuśāsana *parvans*. This required more labour and an intensive effort.

The Bhṛgus emerge as efficient propagandists and their intention was to intervene in the reading of the past so as to make it support their own ideology. The Pāṇḍava victory is largely dependent on advice from Kṛṣṇa, the incarnation of Viṣṇu. His intervention is also beneficial to them at many crucial situations in the story. Although the Bhṛgus break the rules of *varṇāśrama-dharma*, they make it a focus in their interventions in the *itihāsa-purāṇa* tradition. Such intervention, therefore, is concerned less with demonstrating the historicity of persons and events, and more with presenting a view of the past, as well as a reading of it in a manner recognizable to contemporaries—as encapsulating a changing society.

[106] *Mahābhārata*, 9.62.38ff.

[107] Nasik Cave Inscriptions, *Ep. Ind.*, 8, 2, 60ff.

[108] Y. Vassilkov, "Indian Practice of Pilgrimage and the Growth of the Mahābhārata".

6. Genealogies as Frames of the Past

The *Mahābhārata* is a story within a frame, recited as part of a ritual. It is an extension therefore of the notion and function of the *ākhyāna*, where the narrative momentarily supersedes the ritual. It is presented as the past of the pre-eminent lineage of the Bharatas, and, by extension, as an exposition of *dharma* for kings and men as appropriate to the fifth *Veda*. The story of the Bharatas is the

Table II

Abbreviated Descent List

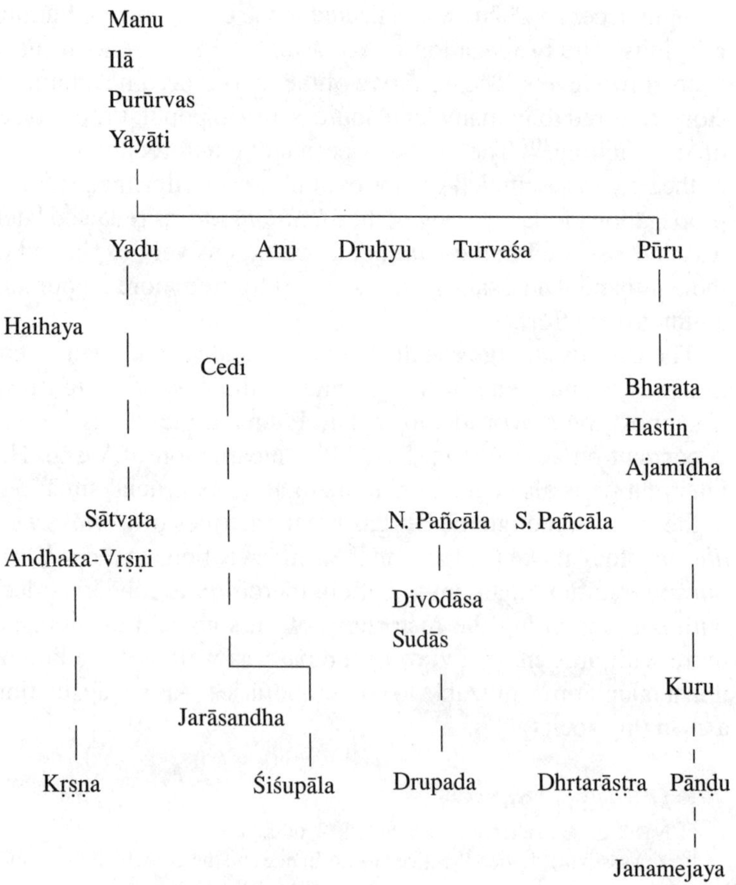

spine of the narrative which holds together the stories of other *kṣatriya* descent groups. An elaborately constructed narrative of the Bharatas is central to the perception of the past, gathered from the Vedic corpus and other oral traditions.

The Ādi *parvan*, as the first book of the *Mahābhārata*, sets out the descent lists of the clans. The Sabhā *parvan* is a logical sequence as it is concerned with establishing the legitimacy of the Pāṇḍavas to rule, the Kurus having contested this. But, more importantly, it represents the functioning of a chiefship. The building of a *sabhā* (assembly hall) encapsulates a dynamic aspect of this function, the hub of decision-making, as exemplified in the *sabhā* of another clan, that of the Vṛṣṇis. The *sabhā*, a structure too sophisticated for a simple assembly hall, is built by the enigmatic Asura Maya. Nārada arrives at this point and speaks on the principles of kingship and kingdoms, hinting at an imminent change. Such interventions are preliminary to the more extensive discourses in the Śānti and Anuśāsana *parvans*.

The descent comes in segments and is interspersed with legends. The bardic form has clearly been worked over by later authors acknowledging the importance of *itihāsa* and *purāṇa*.[109] Creation starts with the cosmic egg, out of which come the orders of deities and men, of the universe, and of time. The descent of the Kurus is suggestively associated with the deities. A brief history of the Bhṛgus is included at this point, hinting at a special connection. Genealogies of various celestial and supernatural beings, such as *devas, dānavas, gāndharvas, apsarās*, and *yakṣas* follow, as does a list of *asuras* born as kings. Subsequent to this comes the lineage of Bharata. There is some logic to this sequence, covering creation, the gods and the presumed early history of the heroes. These concerns mark the epic as a departure from the Vedic corpus. In the latter, such references and narratives are scattered, whereas in the epic there is at least an attempt at order and sequence, suggesting a homogenizing of the theme and a move towards seeing a pattern in the past.

The *sūta* Ugraśravas recites the lineage of the Bhṛgus to their descendant Śaunaka. It has only eight generations going from

[109] 1.1.15.

father to son. In almost every case there is the story of some exploit associated with the person. Such a brief succession list hardly calls for the expertise of a bard; nevertheless, the Bhṛgu *brāhmaṇa* asks the *sūta* to provide the information, hinting at the need for a professional record.

There is a fuller account of the lineage of the heroes and associated legends. Manu, who had ten sons, is mentioned briefly as a founding ancestor.[110] One son, Ila/Ilā, was a hermaphrodite and as a woman gave birth to Purūravas. Of his sons and grandsons, the eldest was Yayāti.

With the descent of the Bharatas, the information becomes more detailed. The *sūta* claims to be repeating what had been recited by Vaiśampāyana. The genealogy earlier given in a shortened version is then repeated in more detail.[111] The two versions agree in part, but not entirely—which contradicts the claim. Both telescoping and extending are recognized bardic techniques in the making of genealogies.

The longer genealogy begins with the claim that the god Dakṣa was the ancestor, and then proceeds with the descent list. Yayāti is important, as are the eldest and youngest of his five sons: Yadu, Turvaśa, Druhyu, Anu, Pūru (familiar names from the *Ṛgveda*). Yayāti banishes the eldest, Yadu, and appoints the youngest, Pūru, to succeed him. So the line continues through Pūru. Of the five the first two are the sons of Devayānī, the daughter of a Bhṛgu sage, and the last three the sons of Śarmiṣṭha, the daughter of a powerful *dānava*. This meant that these sons had *asura* links on the maternal side. In one Vedic text Pūru is referred to as descended from an *asura rākṣasa*.[112] The Bhṛgu connection is introduced with this lineage, and there is a fair amount of intermixing.

Further down the line, Duḥṣanta marries Śakuntalā, the daughter of an *apsarā*. Bharata is his son, after whom the line is named. Bhumanyu is recognized as a son by Bharata in the shorter list, where it is made clear that he was actually not the son of Bharata but of Bharadvāja. This was a significant difference and perhaps

[110] 1.70.13ff.
[111] Cf. 1.89.1ff. with 1.90.1ff.
[112] *Śatapatha Brāhmaṇa*, 6.8.1.14.

signalled a disjuncture in the descent. Hastin is said to have founded Hastināpura, the main settlement of the Kurus. The son of Ajamīḍha founded the Pañcāla line. We finally come to Devāpi and Śantanu, which brings us to the epic events.

Succession goes through the sons, fathered by Vyāsa on the two widows of Vicitravīrya.[113] Technically, these sons do not belong to the bloodline and this should mark a break, but the succession is seamless. The Pāṇḍavas, in addition to their joint wife, marry other women. The line continues through Arjuna's marriage to Subhadrā, the sister of Kṛṣṇa, and the birth of their son Abhimanyu, which unites the Yadu and Pūru lineages. He is the father of Parikṣit, whose son in turn is Janamejaya, to whom the epic events are being narrated.

The shorter version lists all the sons in each generation, although the succession generally, but not invariably, goes through the eldest—Arjuna's descendants being one such exception. Frequently, the wives are mentioned with an inclusion of the clan or the region of their provenance. Women as the link between clans were more characteristic of these societies. In the earlier part of the longer genealogy there are names which are familiar from the Vedic corpus. The more famous names from the *Ṛgveda*—such as Sudāsa or Trasadasyu or Purukutsa—are not included in the lists, although they are mentioned individually elsewhere in the epic. There seem to have been some attempts, however, to draw a few names from the *Vedas* and fit them into the genealogical framework of the epic, as for example the five sons of Yayāti.

The two versions of the descent lists attempt a continuous succession, with no break from the time of Manu to events after the war. In fact, however, there are breaks which are barely papered over. If the list were entirely fictive, breaks would not be necessary: their existence suggests other clans being stitched onto the main lineage. At such seeming points, there are stories. The first major break appears to be that of Pūru, the youngest son, succeeding Yayāti. This decision was questioned by the *brāhmaṇas*

[113] The names of the wives of Vicitravīrya recall the *tryaṃbaka mantra*—*ambā ambikā ambālikā*—in the *Śatapatha Brāhmaṇa*, 13.2.8.1–3, associated with a fertility rite.

because, according to the law, the eldest son by an official wife could not be superseded.[114] The compromise agreement was that the son who showed concern for the welfare of his father should succeed, and Pūru had agreed to confer his youth onto his ageing father.

The next break seems to come with Bharata, who adopted Bhumanyu, a son of Bharadvāja. Adoption, when referred to in genealogies, is frequently an indication of a new line.

The establishment of Hastināpura by Hastin would suggest a concentration in the Doab and an assertion of power in this area, or again the incorporation of local people into the settlement. Ajamīḍha is said to have had six sons, one of whom was ancestor to the Pañcālas, literally meaning "the five peoples" or "the five houses", presumably a confederacy of five clans. One curious parallel to earlier narratives is the story of the Pañcālas attacking the Bharatas, who then fled to the Sindhu region, where they lived for a long while until Vasiṣtha helped them win back their territory.[115] This echoes the story of the *dāśarājña* in the *Ṛgveda*.[116] Eventually, the descendants of the Bharatas returned to the western Ganges plain, where Kuru is said to have bestowed his name on the region, which was called Kurujāṅgala—the Kuru forest—and where the great war was fought on the "field of the Kurus", Kurukṣetra. Kurujāṅgala giving way to Kurukṣetra suggests a significant change in the history of land use. The final segment, subsequent to Śantanu, is quite obviously a break, for the lineage actually terminates with Bhīṣma. The descendents of Dhṛtarāṣṭra and Pāṇḍu are clearly added on.

The lists of succession indicate other interesting features as well. The descent list of the Yadus is not given in the chapter on origins, even though they are related to the Pūrus, and Kṛṣṇa is important to the epic. Despite Yayāti's centrality in the lineage, he does not marry into *kṣatriya* clans. Devayānī was the daughter of a Bhṛgu *brāhmaṇa* and Śarmiṣṭha was of *dānava* origin. The Pūrus are described as *kṣatriyas* despite their ancestry from *asura*

[114] 1.80.12–15.
[115] 1.89.34–42.
[116] *Ṛgveda*, 7.18, 7.33.6.

rākṣasas. The descendants of Yadu, however, are not given the same status. Their descendants include the Vṛṣṇis, the somewhat inferior clan of Kṛṣṇa, and the Bhojas, the clan of Kuntī, the mother of the Pāṇḍavas.[117] The people of Saurashtra in western India where Dvārakā, the main centre of the Vṛṣṇis was located, are elsewhere referred to as *sankīrṇa yonayāḥ,* namely, of mixed and therefore low caste.[118]

There is also a seeming difference in political status. Śiśupāla, the *rājā* of the Cedis, taunts Kṛṣṇa for not being a *rājā* or a priest.[119] He is merely a clan member of the Vṛṣṇis. In Buddhist sources the Cedis are also chiefs but their status is high.[120] Status seems to have been generally on an uneven keel and could vary from text to text, depending on the author's patron.

The genealogical data is an attempt to provide origins and an identity to the protagonists of the story over a period of time through pinning together the variant fragments and connecting them through legends. The genealogies were doubtless worked over repeatedly and updated. They reflect a variety of concerns about the past.

Some of these descent lines may have been collaterals which were also shuffled into a single line of descent. Some segments relate to other peoples who were amalgamated, confederated, or in some way associated and therefore brought into the genealogy. There was also the likelihood of the invention of names to fill out and lengthen the period of the genealogy, and thus also create a greater distance in time between the events and the editing of the epic.[121] One of the techniques used for such lengthening—the addition of spurinyms—is evident in the longer genealogy, where there is a succession of unlikely names ending in *-ayus* after Ayus, or in *-yāti* after Yayāti. The insistence on a genealogy and latching heroes onto genealogies is a clinging to a lineage-based society, since genealogies are central to lineage. Reckoning by

[117] 7.118.14–15.

[118] *Baudhāyana Dharmasūtra*, 1.2.13.

[119] 2.34.1–10.

[120] *Cetīya Jātaka*, no. 422, in *The Jātaka*.

[121] D.P. Henige, *The Chronology of Oral Tradition*; J. Vansina, *Oral Tradition as History*.

genealogies also introduces a linear concept of time, and this becomes almost contrapuntal to another innovation in the epic, which is the description of time as cyclic.

The lineage-based system drew on kinship, but the descent is marred by breaks and therefore it is necessary to knit genealogies together and present a seamless succession. Adoptions and marriage alliances help in this. Repeated patterns in the genealogies are giveaways of such attempts. Thus the figure five occurs repeatedly in the descent list. The action begins effectively with the five sons of Yayāti and closes with the five Pāṇḍavas. The succession, although it goes to the grandson of Arjuna, is shrouded in a myth of his being revived as a dead foetus. Is this a cover-up for a disjuncture in the lineage and power being appropriated by another clan or another kinsman?

Where new settlements are involved, there again Uparicara has five sons who settle in Central India and Bali has five sons who establish themselves in the east. This is reminiscent of terms such as the *pañcajanāḥ,* or the *pañcavīras* associated with the Vṛṣṇis, or names such as Pañcāla. Within the five there is the additional pattern of two wives, one bearing three sons and the other two, as in the case of the wives of Yayāti and Pāṇḍu. Genealogies are also useful in rights to territory, as in the claims of the Kauravas and the Pāṇḍavas to descent from identical genealogically attested clans. The irony is that if blood ties were crucial to inheritance, then neither the Kauravas nor the Pāṇḍavas had rights of inheritance to the territory of the Pūru lineage.

The authenticity of the descent lists is not of primary importance: only a modicum of authenticity would have sufficed. What are being represented are the social and political systems of clan societies. The attempt is to capture a past that was different from the present as reflected in legends linked to genealogies. They are, significantly, often those narratives and *ākhyānas* which might have had a bearing on the eventual working out of a perception of the past. For example, the story of the Flood, first briefly mentioned in the *Śatapatha Brāhmaṇa*, is repeated in the *Mahābhārata* but with some change.[122]

[122] 3.185ff.

The fish orders Manu to place the seven seers (*saptarṣi*, Ursa Major) and the seeds of all creatures in the ship and embark on the sea. The fish announces that it will tie the ship's rope to its horn.[123] It will navigate the ship through the deluge, mooring it safely to the highest peak of the Himalaya. This it does and, when the flood subsides, Manu disembarks. The fish, having declared itself as being the god Brahmā, then disappears. Manu proceeds with his asceticism and creation is reborn. This is somewhat different from the earlier Vedic version and is even closer to the Mesopotamian story.[124] It comes to be seen as seminal to the beginnings of history.

The story of Purūravas and Urvaśī, unlike the version in the Vedic corpus, is not sympathetic to Purūravas.[125] That of Devāpi and Śantanu also changes from the Vedic version.[126] The parallel between the story and the succession in the Kuru line is evident. It also reinforces the statement that there is rainfall in the kingdom if the king rules justly,[127] or that in the absence of a *rājā* there is no rain. By extension, the "rain-maker" signalled a person of immense power and legitimacy where kingship is not established. The story of Śunaḥśepa receives a bare mention, although the latching on of clans remains a feature of the epic.[128]

References to Vena in the *Ṛgveda* praise him as an early *rājā*.[129] There is no reference to Vena being evil and therefore deposed. But the *Mahābhārata* has an elaborate story about the two sons born from his body. This becomes a prototype story to explain the rejection of forest-dwellers and the acceptance of settled communities. Vena was made *rājā* by the *ṛṣis*, but he gradually took to evil ways and did not perform the required rituals.[130] The *ṛṣis*

[123] The eventual size of the fish and the horn is suggestive of the narwhal, of the whale family, and the male grows a spiral horn. But these are generally limited to the Arctic waters. M. Allaby (ed.), *The Oxford Dictionary of Natural History*, entry under "Monodontidae".

[124] W.G. Lambert and A.R. Millard, *Atra-hasis*.

[125] 1.70.16ff.

[126] 5.147.16ff.

[127] 1.99.40ff., 1.163.14–22.

[128] 13.3.6–8.

[129] *Ṛgveda*, 10.93.14, 8.9.10, 10.148.5, 10.171.3.

[130] 12.59.94ff.

decided to do away with him by piercing him with the sacred *kuśa* grass. His death resulted in a condition where there was no ruler, a condition of chaos (*arājya*), which was unacceptable. So they churned his left thigh and there emerged a short, dark, ugly man the colour of antimony, with bloodshot eyes and thick lips whom they named Niṣāda and banished to the forest. Niṣāda, together with Śabara and Pulinda, became generic names for people of the forest treated as outside the social pale.

They then churned the right arm of the dead Vena (in contrast to the left thigh earlier) and there sprang up a tall and handsome man, Pṛthu, fit to be a *rājā*. The *ṛṣis* came to an agreement with him: he would be allowed to rule provided he observed the appropriate rituals and laws of *varṇāśrama-dharma* preventing the mixing of castes, and that he would punish the unrighteous. Pṛthu agreed and made a successful *rājā*, introducing cattle rearing and cultivation. The earth was so pleased with him that she took his name, Pṛthvī.

The agreement was between the *brāhmaṇas* and the *kṣatriya*, and no others were consulted. The initiative was with the former, both in the killing of Vena—using a sacred object—as well as in the banishing of Niṣāda and the appointing of Pṛthu. But what is also emphasized is the separation between those that are banished to the forest and those that are part of the settled community. The idiom of the settlement (*grāma*) and the forest (*araṇya*) is reiterated.

Such stories suggest that *ākhyānas* were known to the oral tradition or were picked up and refashioned as required. The differences in the Vedic and epic versions also reflect the interests of authors who were not identical, nor was the historical context. There may have been a mutual borrowing, or else a common source.

Mentioning shifts in location and referring back to earlier locations can introduce a historical perspective. Migrations, initially notional, can be given a geographical base after a passage of time. Migration is also linked to exile. The geographical focus of the epic is the area around Hastināpura and Indraprastha and the forests in the vicinity, although exile and skirmishes inevitably move the location to more distant parts. The main line, that

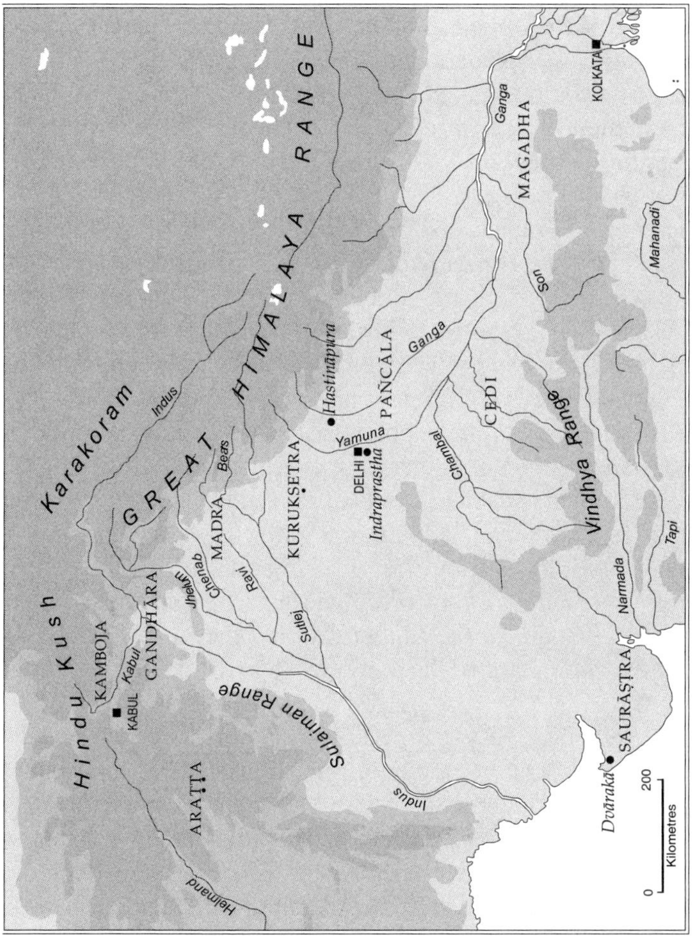

Map 2: Locations of the More Important Places, Clans, and Dynasties

of the Kurus, occupied the watershed and the Upper Doab, and their neighbours to the east and south-east were the Pañcālas. Kuntī was of the clan of Bhoja settled in Rajasthan, and close to the Vṛṣṇi and Andhaka.

The listing of places conquered by the brothers of Yudhiṣṭhira at the time of the *digvijaya* is partly accurate and partly fantasy, incorporating the place names known to those times, and the dispersal of the clans even if not precisely. The ranking of the clans and their *rājās* in terms of the tribute which they bring subsequent to the *digvijaya* indicates the nature of their economies and status.[131]

Mentioning Jambudvīpa (the land of the rose-apple tree) has no geographical exactitude but envisions an ideal space inhabited by a variety of people. Recognizable place names give it a semblance of geography and link the actual space with imaginary space. Interestingly, in referring to peoples, tribes, communities, the *digvijaya* makes no differentiation between *ārya* and *anārya*. It gives the names of the peoples conquered, and only some are listed as *dasyus*.[132] Nor is there a specification in identifying the *mlecchas*, which is used as a collective word.[133]

There is a scatter of references to other clans, such as that of Gāndhārī, wife of Dhṛtarāṣṭra, who lived in the north-west, in the region which was known to history as Gandhāra; or Mādrī, the wife of Pāṇḍu, of the Madra clan located in the Punjab; or the Āraṭṭa who inhabited the borderlands and did not observe the *dharma*.

In the region of the Vindhyas and the Narmada were the Cedis, and to the east was the powerful ruler of Magadha, Jarāsandha. Ambiguity regarding relations with Magadha is a marked feature of the politics of the epic. Magadha being part of the eastern region was different from the western Ganges plain; and state systems in the form of kingdoms were beginning to emerge in the eastern region, and Magadha was pre-eminent among these.

The kingdom of Magadha was a threat to the *gaṇa-saṅghas*. Was

[131] R. Thapar, "Some Aspects of the Economic Data in the Mahābhārata", in idem, *Cultural Pasts*, 630–46.

[132] 2.24.14–16.

[133] 2.28.44–50, 2.29.15–16.

Jarāsandha seen as seeking to expand and consolidate Magadha at the expense of the chiefdoms? The segment on Jarāsandha is thought to be late.[134] The enmity between Magadha and the Vṛṣṇis in the epic may reflect the rise of Magadha from the time of Bimbisāra and his son Ajātaśatru.

There are echoes of the history of Magadha in this episode which recall narratives involving its early rulers, Bimbisāra and Ajātaśatru, from other sources. Yudhiṣṭhira is referred to as Ajātaśatru,[135] possibly intended literally as an epithet. Initially disliked by the Buddhists and the Jainas, Ajātaśatru was later claimed as a patron of the Buddha. Rajgir was the capital of these kings prior to the establishment of Pāṭaliputra under the Nandas. Jarāsandha and his allies sow dissension among the *kṣatriya* lineages,[136] echoing the story in the Buddhist sources of Vassakara, the minister of Ajātaśatru, sowing dissension among the Vṛjji clans.[137] The episode involving Jarāsandha possibly reflects aspects of contemporary events.[138] Were contemporary events being imposed on data of earlier times? Kṛṣṇa, as adviser to the Pāṇḍavas, suggests a way of getting rid of the ruler by assassination rather than conquest.

The genealogy attempts not only to knit the other *kṣatriyas* and almost-*kṣatriyas* into a series of relationships, it also sets out the geography of the time before the war. In a comparison of the status of clans and groups mentioned in both the Vedic corpus and the *Mahābhārata*, there are discrepancies or changes in status. Migration is also linked to the notion of exile.

Exile, apart from being a useful bardic device for prolonging the story, introduced descriptions of new areas as they came onto the geographical horizon of the narrative. New peoples, when incorporated into the epic and located geographically, could acquire a myth of origin and links to established clans. Exile was

[134] J. Brockington, "Jārasandha of Magadha, Mbh. 2.15–22", 73ff.; A. Hiltebeitel, *Rethinking the Mahābhārata*, 5ff., 73ff.

[135] 2.12.8.

[136] *Mahābhārata*, 2.13.6ff.; G.P. Malalasekera, *Dictionary of Pali Proper Names*, 31ff.

[137] *Dīgha Nikāya Aṭṭakathā*, 2.72ff.; *Sumaṅgalavilāsinī*, 2.522ff.

[138] 2.15–22; J. Brockington, "Jarāsandha of Magadha", 73ff.; A. Hiltebeitel, *Rethinking the Mahābhārata*, 5ff.

generally to living in the forest, which was in itself a counterpoint to the settlement and therefore an indicator of distance. It was also the habitat of "the other" society, regarded as alien and inferior, but nevertheless feared: peoples who were seen, or else deliberately projected because of animosity, as still distant from civilization in the perception of the society of the heroes.

The dichotomy of settlement and forest, first referred to in the Vedic corpus,[139] is reiterated in the epic. Unlike the specificity of the settlements, the forest in the epics becomes the central space, geographically vague, but the backdrop to important happenings. This is where the authors could locate the semi-imagined "Other" and where the fantasies about the wider world could be played out. The forest in the Sanskrit epics parallels the "wine-dark sea" in Homer.

There is here a merging and mixing of peoples and cultures of separate origins. The *Mahābhārata* becomes the perceived history of various clans at different levels of the social hierarchy, evident in the observances and political forms of these clans. A move towards a clearer historical perception would require reordering this material—as happened later in the *Viṣṇu Purāṇa*.

7. Chiefdoms and Incipient Kingship

The broadly differentiated earlier narrative section, and later didactic sections of the text hint at historical intention. The world of *kṣatriyas* is concerned with the ethics and values of the heroic society, whereas the latter tries to imprint the normative models of the brahmanical social codes wherein kingship is pivotal. The juxtaposition is of two kinds of societies, differentiated through discourses and some tampering with the narrative, but not by a radical restructuring of the text. The perception and use of the past is important to the construction of a historical consciousness.

In clan society, identity is through lineage, actual or fictive; kinship; claiming to be *kṣatriyas*; instant wealth comes from raids, and more slowly through agro-pastoralism; and the *yajña* is pivotal

[139] *Śatapatha Brāhmaṇa*, 13.2.4.1; C. Malamoud, *Cooking the World*, 74–91; R. Thapar, "Perceiving the Forest: Early India", 1–16.

to belief and community. Clans tend to break away and migrate when the pressures of population and competition for resources become too great. The power of the *rājā* also comes from implicit control over drought, famine, and disease—all disastrous for agro-pastoralism.[140]

Lineage links had a direct connection with two aspects of political power—legitimacy and territory—claims to both being largely based on kin connections: hence the importance of genealogies and the need to continually reiterate them, even if it sometimes meant inventing fictive connections.

Equality of status is not absolute among the Vṛṣṇis, the Kurus, and those who are members of the *gaṇa-saṅghas.* The least equal among them were the *dāsas* and *dāsīs*, domestic and household slaves who were employed to a lesser degree in either pastoral or agricultural production. Reciprocity gradually becomes characteristic of the economy, symbolized in gift-giving.

Political forms are not sharply differentiated. The epic seems to veer from pre-state chiefship to incipient kingship, indicating that perhaps the earlier epic was initially put together in times of chiefships and then moved to the twilight period of transition between the two; and that the later interpolations draw from the more complex societies of established kingdoms. Advice on the benefits of kingship is sporadic and scattered. The Śānti and Anuśāsana *parvans* are meant to imprint and enlarge these advantages and negate other political systems. The discussion on kingship is projected more at the conceptual level than with reference to historical examples. This may not have been the case with clans.

Elements of chiefship can be recognized in the functioning of various clans: for instance, in the *saṅgha* (assembly) of the Andhaka-Vṛṣṇis who are said to be constituted of eighteen *rājakulas* (ruling families); the *kula* of Kṛṣṇa-Vāsudeva had a subdivision of eighteen lesser groups and of eighteen *vratas*.[141] The *saṅgha* was governed by the *rājanya vṛddha* (elders of the

[140] R. Thapar, *From Lineage to State*.

[141] 2.13.35; *vrata* has been translated as "bands" and as "soldiers". The numbers should not be taken too literally, since eighteen in particular was a frequently used number, almost notional, with little attempt at accuracy.

ruling clans) and were divided into other groups, such as the *varga, pakṣa, gṛhya, gaṇa*, and *dvanda,* generally headed by a *śreṣṭha* (the one acknowledged as the best). The continued existence of such groups is referred to even in the later sections, where the working of the *gaṇa* is described.[142] It is said that only dissension could destroy its corporate and collective working. This is precisely what happens in the narrative when the Vṛṣṇis attack each other. Sowing dissension is recommended by Kauṭilya as a method of bringing down a *gaṇa-saṅgha.*[143] The *gaṇa* assembly consisted of members of the *rājakula*, and the consensus of kinsmen was crucial to decisions. Succession could still be disputed among kinsmen, as in the case of the collateral lines of the Kauravas and the Pāṇḍavas.

The duality of *kṣatriya* and non-*kṣatriya* was maintained by the access of the former to resources, and to status through birth and by marriage alliances. Legends of birth and marriage covered up the transgressions. The *kṣatriya* identity focused on the clan and the household, over and above which were mores, customs, and social obligations.

The link with power also lies in descent from father to son, ensuring the continuation of lineage, this being basic to heroic society. At a symbolic level, the weakness of the link between Pāṇḍu and his sons makes them almost subliminal personalities, continually on the edge of definition. Tied into the notion of succession was primogeniture, the violation of which is one of the essentials on which the narrative hinges. The "disqualified eldest" becomes a recurring theme.[144] The household, which holds together lineage and property, is disrupted in exile.

The activities of the heroes lie at the intersection of two economies, the pastoral and the agricultural. These are areas of political confrontation. Birth into a clan gave rights to participation in clan ownership of animals and land. Encroaching into existing settlements, or clearing forests for agriculture, or claiming pasture-

[142] 12.108.6–31.

[143] *Arthaśāstra*, 11.1.

[144] J.A.B. van Buitenen, *The Mahābhārata*, I, xviiff. The practice has antecedents in the replacement of Yadu by Pūru.

lands, could be conflicting and could require the need to defend territories and rights. The frontier is often the forest, a no-man's land with which the relationship is never neutral and in which the first claim is established when the land is settled. It is also the fantasy world inhabited by demons. Frontier ecologies have their own code of ethics derived from local practices.

Cattle raids are fair play, but if the raider is caught he is liable to be enslaved or killed—as would any predator. Single combat takes on the quality of a hunt, without recourse to allies and armies. This increases the urgency of the action, which is often more exaggerated than required. Pasturing and swidden agriculture need large territories because returns come from extending the area rather than intensifying the investment and labour. Larger territories are more difficult to conquer and protect than the compact arable land of plough cultivation. Thus, territory was claimed preferably through kinship ties and alliances.

A distinction is maintained between gathering and producing economies. The former remains important, judging by the tribute brought by a range of people prior to the *rājasūya* sacrifice. Property can be tangible—herds of cattle and horse, gold, grain, and other material objects; it can also be intangible—authority over a household and those both dependent on it and labouring for it, such as kinsmen, women, servants, and slaves. The heroes lived off the labour of those regarded as lesser men and women, namely,the *śūdras* and the *dāsas* and *dāsīs,* male and female slaves, all shadowy figures in the wings. Aliens were sometimes also reduced to this status. When Yudhiṣṭhira stakes the wealth of the Pāṇḍavas in the game of dice, all these categories are included.

In such a society, gift-giving becomes, as earlier noted, a form of circulating wealth. The more one gives the more one receives: this was axiomatic. The *rājasūya* was an occasion for extensive gift-giving. The lists of items echo the earlier exaggeration of the *dāna-stuti* hymns. The new items are elephants and textiles and increased numbers of slaves.[145] When Yudhiṣṭhira stakes his wealth, he stakes his *janapada* (territory), but agricultural lands are not

[145] R. Thapar, "Some Aspects of the Economic Data in the Mahābhārata", in idem, *Cultural Pasts*, 630–46.

mentioned.[146] The ritual context makes the gift significant as an item of exchange, of establishing status and alliances between clans, and a mechanism of integration. The gift also provides political legitimacy, even if tenuous. The *rājasūya* is counterposed to the major event which succeeds it, namely, the game of dice. By losing this game, the Pāṇḍavas are deprived of their wealth and status. Draupadī's questioning of Yudhiṣṭhira's right to place her as a stake actually has a wider implicit significance related to the legitimacy of the Pāṇḍavas to rule after they have lost.

The *kṣatriya* receives prestations in the form of voluntary tribute from the others and is expected to give this wealth as gifts or *dāna*. The *kṣatriya*'s prime function, apart from protecting his people, is to make gifts, especially to *brāhmaṇas*. This continues to be underlined even in the later sections of the epic.[147] Gift-giving in this form carried the germ of what was to become a redistributive economy, characteristic of kingdoms, where the redistribution was more formally organized: the revenue was systematically collected and then spent on the structures that supported the state system. This required the accumulation of wealth. However, the major sacrificial rituals were inimical to such accumulation. This impasse could only be broken either through a far greater access to wealth where the surplus remained with the *yajamāna*, accompanied by a new concept of wealth, namely, immovable and permanent property in land; or through a decrease in the performance of rituals. In either case, the nature of the *kṣatriya*'s dependence on the *brāhmaṇa* had to be formulated differently.

These changes began to take place from about the fifth century BC in the middle Ganges plain. Rice cultivation in this region, despite its requirement of co-operative labour and irrigation, produced a big yield, which increased the availability of wealth to the *rājā* as *yajamāna.* So too did the introduction of new technologies.[148] The efficacy of the *yajña* was questioned in some *Upaniṣads* and in the teachings of heterodox sects. There was now

[146] R. Thapar, "The Historian and the Epic", in idem, *Cultural Pasts*, 613–29.

[147] 13.7.14, 13.8.9; cf. *Manu's Code of Law*, 7.85.

[148] R. Thapar, *From Lineage to State*, 70ff.

an interest in the possibility of belief and activity that required neither patron, nor priest, nor ritual, nor gift-giving.[149] The change from cattle wealth, and a sharing of rights in clan land to private ownership of land in the context of kingdoms,[150] led gradually to a changed situation—as reflected in the later books of the epic. The propagation of a social ethic that did not require *yajñas* but emphasized the individual's social actions, tended to marginalize sacrificial rituals and questioned codes based on emerging caste identities.

Kingship seems to have been an adjunct to the core society of the *Mahābhārata.* But the brahmanical concept of the divine sanction of power was being challenged by Buddhist and Jaina ideas. This was a major ideological concern in the post-Mauryan period, probably parallel with the later additions to the *Mahābhārata.* As such, it was essential to visualizing a past without kingship and then justifying the brahmanical definition of the change.

The transition from chiefship to incipient kingship can be seen by comparing the contexts of the Sabhā and Śānti *parvans.* That some parts of the epic refer to an earlier society is indicated by social norms that differ substantially from those prescribed in the Śānti and Anuśasana *parvans*, generally following the codes of the *Dharmaśāstras*. This becomes particularly evident in the varied forms of marriage and in the way women are depicted. Some social practices as narrated would have been unacceptable to *kṣatriyas* conforming to the normative prescriptions.

The Pāṇḍavas seem to digress quite frequently from the normative prescriptions. Pāṇḍu's marriage with Mādrī did not require a dowry, being of the *asura* category in which bride-wealth is given.[151] The Madras are said to be part of a group in the northwest, including the Āraṭṭas and the Bāhlikas and sometimes the Gāndhāras and Sindhu-Sauvīras as well, who do not observe the *dharma* and whose women are relatively free.[152] Women

[149] R. Thapar, "Sacrifice, Surplus and the Soul", in idem, *Cultural Pasts*, 809–31.

[150] R. Thapar, *From Lineage to State*, 116ff.

[151] 1.105.5ff.

[152] *Mahābhārata*, 8.30.52–9.

such as Kuntī, Gāndhārī, and Draupadī are fiercely independent. Marriage forms such as the *svayamvara,* where the woman chooses a husband from a limited few,[153] and the *gandharva*, by mutual consent, are regarded as appropriate only to *kṣatriyas*. Pāṇḍu's sons are all fathered by deities, a contingency not included in the marriage codes. This does not make them into incarnations of gods, a different status used in later times.

The fraternal polyandry of the Pāṇḍavas was unusual. It is questioned in the epic.[154] Elaborate and curious explanations follow, involving deities. The brothers married other individual wives and the sons from these marriages are more visible in the narrative. Arjuna has a *rākṣasa* form of marriage by abducting his bride, the sister of Kṛṣṇa, from which marriage the lineage continues. The objection of the Vṛṣṇi clans was to Arjuna abducting Subhadrā and not that it was a cross-cousin marriage, practised fairly widely.[155] This was despite the disapproval of the normative texts.[156] Was Bhīṣma's abduction of the brides for Vicitravīrya a *rākṣasa* form of marriage for them?[157] Draupadī questioning the right of Yudhiṣṭhira to stake her in the game of dice—when he had already lost his independence and that of the Pāṇḍavas to Duryodhana—was a turning point in the story. This contradicts the subservient position of women in the normative texts.

[153] 1.211.21. It is not always listed among the eight recognized forms of marriage. It becomes a feature of courtly literature in later times, often more symbolic than actual, and a stage prop to romantic exploits.

[154] 2.61.35, 1.146.34.

[155] A detailed study, *The People of India*, carried out by the Anthropological Survey of India, provides evidence of the frequency of cross-cousin marriage in North India among the lower levels of the social hierarchy. This would suggest that cross-cousin marriage has not been limited to South India. The *Dharmaśāstra* opposition to it may have been *brāhmaṇa* hostility to a custom practised by those of lesser status: quite apart from the inherent objection to marrying a close kin, which was seen as incestuous.

[156] One text describes cross-cousin marriage as causing a loss of caste or a sin: *Baudhāyana Dharmasūtra*, 1.2.4.6; that it was a custom peculiar to the South: *Baudhāyana Dharmasūtra*, 1.2.2–3ff.; and that it is forbidden in *Manu's Code of Law*, 11.172–3. Kumarila, writing much later, tries to argue that Arjuna's marriage to Subhadrā was not a cross-cousin marriage: P.V. Kane, *History of Dharmasastras*, vol. II.1, 459–60.

[157] C.R. Deshpande, *Transmission of the Mahābhārata Tradition*, 22.

Among the Vṛṣṇis, there is a frequency of cross-cousin marriage with the daughters of maternal uncles and paternal aunts.[158] The role of Śakuni is significant in advising Duryodhana in the game of dice and actually throwing for him, for Śakuni is Duryodhana's mother's brother, and but for him the Kauravas were unlikely to have won the game.[159] The range in forms of marriage and resulting kin relations was probably an attempt to acknowledge variants and make them acceptable. Such variations, current in earlier societies or in other societies, were validated by their introduction into the family of the heroes.

The necessity for kinsmen to stand together, particularly on the battlefield, is repeatedly emphasized.[160] It is kinsmen who take decisions in the *sabhā*, perform the functions of administration, and are crucial decision-makers, as for example in the decision of the Kauravas to exile the Pāṇḍavas.

Beyond the kinsmen was the *jana*, where behaviour is conditioned by an audience wider than just the close kin. Thus, the decision on the part of Yudhiṣṭhira and the Pāṇḍavas to hold a *rājasūya* sacrifice, or the description which Kṛṣṇa gives of the defeat of the Vṛṣṇis at the hands of Jarāsandha of Magadha and their migration to Dvārakā, involved the *jana*. Clan assemblies were also involved in choosing their *rājās*, as in the cases of Kuru and Janamejaya.[161]

The meaning of the word *rājā* gradually undergoes change. In the Śānti *parvan*, the root of the word *rājā* is said to be **rañj*, to please, to be accepted as the one who established *dharma*, a meaning that carried little connotation of political authority.[162] This is an incorrect etymology, the word deriving from **raj*, to shine. Except where the constituents of the state as a kingdom are mentioned as part of the narrative, it might be more appropriate to assume that *rājā* should be taken as chief and not king.

The references to cattle raids in the narrative would point to

158 These practices have been explained as due to the South Indian recensions of the text: T. Trautmann, *Dravidian Kinship*, 316ff.

159 2.45.36, 2.53ff.

160 3.232.1–5.

161 1.89.42ff., 1.40.6.

162 12.59.125ff., 12.56.36ff., 12.137.103ff.

societies still associated with herding. These were well-organized raids lasting many weeks. The term *gāviṣṭhi* (desire for cattle) is used for skirmishes in the Vedic corpus.[163] The *ghoṣa-yātra,* in the *Māhabhārata,* an expedition to brand cattle, is another source of potential conflict between the Kauravas and the Pāṇḍavas since they personally attend to this activity—an unlikely act for established royalty.[164]

The insistence on Yudhiṣṭhira being the *dharmarāja*, both because he is the son of the deity Dharma and because the title implies that he follows the *dharma*, would point to the gradual significance of kingship and its association with *dharma*, an association which becomes very clear in the sections added later, by which time kingship was becoming the norm. However, the disestablishing of the wicked *rājā* is a theme more familiar from the narrative sections.

8. Defining Kingship

The Śānti and Anuśāsana *parvans* are discourses on various aspects of governance such as *rāja-dharma*, or the origin and principles of kingship; *daṇḍa-dharma,* or coercion, punishment, and armed strength; *āpad-dharma,* or governing in times of distress; *varṇāśrama-dharma,* or the duties and obligations of various castes, particularly those of the *kṣatriyas*, and their relations with *brāhmaṇas*; *vyavahāra-dharma,* or the rules of correct behaviour; *dāna-dharma,* or how to give gifts, to whom, when and what to give; and *mokṣa-dharma,* or the liberation of the soul from the cycle of rebirth. The discussions on these subjects also mark a change from earlier times, when these would not have been so relevant to earlier societies, governance, and belief.

Āpad-dharma recognizes that laws are flexible in time and space and have to be modified according to whether the times are normal or not.[165] Abnormal times would be when the other

[163] *Taittirīya Brāhmaṇa*, 1.8.4.

[164] 3.224–36. If the later tradition of the epic genre in India provides a clue, the narratives of pastoral heroes such as Ālha, Pābujī, and Ghāzi Miyān are the epic forms of medieval centuries. Associated with these are the large numbers of hero-stones, many of which memorialize a hero who died defending the cattle of the village.

[165] 12.128.11–13.

aspects of *dharma* are not being observed as defined. This could be a reflection of the visibility of heterodox sects of Buddhism and Jainism, not to mention the memory of Aśoka's *dhamma* with his definition of social ethics being so different to that of the *varṇāśrama-dharma*.[166] There is a reiteration of the message of the *Gītā* that the *kṣatriya* as the ruler has on occasion to kill, else he cannot carry out his *dharma* as a ruler.[167] In the same sense, the accumulation of wealth essential to kingship is necessary to the king,[168] a subject not referred to earlier.

In order to reiterate the necessity of kingship, Bhīṣma narrates the rise of the system. There was chaos in human society as a result of error, desire, and passion. This frightened the deities who were, in addition, bereft now of offerings that came to them from the performance of sacrifices. The gods appealed to Viṣṇu to appoint a ruler, and he did so. A few generations later came Veṇa, and the story of Niṣāda and Pṛthu is repeated, but with some additions that link it to the *itihāsa* tradition. Pṛthu appointed Śukra, a Bhṛgu, to be his priest. From his sacrificial fire there sprang the *māgadha* and the *sūta*, the first bards who immediately began reciting the eulogies of Pṛthu,[169] which had prime importance. The story points to a link between the Bhṛgu and both the *rājā* and the *sūta*, such that it would validate the Bhṛgu reformulating the composition of the *sūta* pertaining to the activities of the *rājā*.

It is said that a *brāhmaṇa* can only be considered learned if, apart from the *Vedas* and *Upaniṣads,* he also knows the *ākhyāna*.[170] The more the interpolations, the more significant the text for mobilizing the past to the needs of the present. The interpolations were tied to the ideology of power, which made the text polemical. It was still a portrait of the ideal *kṣatriya*, but he was no longer essentially the *kṣatriya* of the *gaṇa-saṅghas*, he was now gradually becoming the *kṣatriya* of the *rājya* (kingship).

With the coming of kingship, institutions begin to differ from

166 J.L. Fitzgerald, Introduction to Book 12, *Śāntiparvan*, Part I, *The Mahābhārata*, vol. 7, 109–28.

167 12.128.25–35. The debate on war and peace in the Udyoga *parvan* is discussed in A. Malinar, *Bhagavad-Gītā*, 38ff.

168 12.120.30–5.

169 12.59.118.

170 1.2.235.

their earlier forms. The existence of the state and kingship is assumed in the advice that Bhīṣma gives to Yudhiṣṭhira. The theory of the state is crystallized in other texts in the concept of the seven limbs or elements (*saptāṅga/saptaprakṛti*) constituting the state.[171] Yudhiṣṭhira in asking "what is a king" requires Bhīṣma to give a version of the theory of the state: a king is the single man who is powerful and exceptional.[172] His right to coerce and punish is conceded. He is assisted by ministers who need not be kinsmen but constitute the royal court located in a fortified urban centre. Revenue comes to the treasury as taxes and is redistributed through the maintenance of an army and administration, and extensive gift-giving. Punishment is essential to good administration.[173]

It is said that in the earliest times there were no *varṇas.* With the falling off in *tapas* (ascetic austerities), the four *varṇas* came into being and subsequently there was a mixing of the four which resulted in the many low mixed castes—the *sankīrṇa jātis*.[174] There is a more detailed formulation of *varṇa* society in which the role and function of the four *varṇas* are stated in terms similar to those of the *Dharmaśāstras*. *Varṇāśrama-dharma* is defined as the obligations of each *varṇa,* and, together with the *Vedas,* as the foundation of society.[175] The interface between the *varṇas* is thought to be necessary and is clearly defined, with the *brāhmaṇa* advising on rules of conduct for all. The welfare of the *brāhmaṇa* is now a major concern for the king.

The transition is apparent from the comparison between the kingless state and the need for a king.[176] The king takes exalted titles, such as *samrāṭ, cakravartin, adhirāja,* but the reality behind these titles is seldom so exalted. Primogeniture is the preferred succession; where this is not possible a legend covers the break.[177] There is still a concession, however, to subjects being allowed to kill a *rājā*, although the actual killing is done by the *brāhmaṇas*,

[171] *Arthaśāstra*, 6.1; *Manu's Code of Law*, 8—*rājadharma*.
[172] 12.59.5ff.
[173] 12.70.
[174] 12.285.1ff.
[175] 12.60.6ff.
[176] 12.59.120ff., 12.67.2–17.
[177] 1.80.12–15, 1.107.24–7, 5.147.16–26.

as in the story of Vena.[178] The treasury is the root of the state—*kośamūla hi rājanaḥ.*[179]

The explanations for the establishing of the office of *rājā* as incipient kingship are varied and narrate the history of the concept. It is said that people in a state of anarchy agreed among themselves to observe certain rules, but failed to do so. Therefore anarchy increased. They then requested a god to give them a clone who would rule and protect them and whom they could worship.[180] Manu was requested, but he initially refused. He was persuaded when it was agreed that a percentage of the produce and a quarter of the merit of the people would accrue to him. (In another version, the king was required to take upon himself a quarter of their sins.[181]) In return, he was to protect the people and maintain the rules of caste. There is therefore a contract in which Manu is answerable only to the gods, since the intervention of deity establishes kingship. Those who claim to represent deities claim to know how the king should function.

The story of the origins of kingship in the epic parallels the contractual element in the Buddhist narrative, the contract having been made sometime in the remote past. There are also similarities in the process leading to kingship. But the *Mahābhārata* initiates it with an appeal to Brahmā for someone to govern who would draw upon the *varṇāśrama-dharma*. He appoints Manu, taking a cue from the *Vedas.*[182] The king is viewed as a deity in human form when he is described as *mahtī devatā hyeṣā nararūpeṇa tiṣṭhati.*[183] In the case of Yudhiṣṭhira, divinity is reinforced by a divine paternity, the deity Dharma.

Protection becomes a central element. Loss of property and confusion in the social order are the reasons for the creation of a state. The *Dharmaśāstras* emphasize *daṇḍa* as essential to political power. This was not merely a reference to external aggression but also to controlling those who resisted assertions of power.

178 12.59.98–100.

179 12.119.16, 12.128.35.

180 12.59.94, 67.20–9, 69.24–5, 88.10–16.

181 12.76.6–8.

182 12.56.22–4.

183 12.68.40.

That the origin of kingship was being debated is evident from there being more than one explanation. These explanations point to its emerging historically. Another story maintains that, to begin with, *dharma* prevailed in society, but this situation changed when the *asuras* destroyed it. The resulting loss of utopia made *daṇḍa* necesary.[184] Who were these *asuras*? Were they literally believed to be demons, or was it a synonym for prevailing heterodoxies, which in the post-Mauryan period received extensive patronage? The right of the government to exercise coercion is reiterated in another statement: when human society began, neither *rājyam* nor *daṇḍa* were required because people protected each other.[185] *Daṇḍa* is now necessary for maintaining law and protecting property. The abolition of *daṇḍa* would lead to total chaos and destruction, as would the absence of a king.[186] The legitimacy of kingship is now extended from lineage to the wielding of *daṇḍa*.

The theory of *mātsyanyāya* is quoted, that in a condition of drought the big fish in a pond eat the little fish. Therefore, in a condition of anarchy, where there are no *rājās*, the big consume the small, a condition in which neither wives nor wealth can be enjoyed. To avoid this injustice, kingship was necessary and the king protected the weak from the overbearing as well as the aggressors.[187] Kingship is the solution to anarchy.

These conditions are distanced from the narrative sections which contain the occasional reference to *prajā, prakṛti*, and *puravāsino janāḥ* (people), participating in the choice of a *rājā*, or the friendliness between the Kauravas and the cowherds when the cattle are being branded, or the mourning at the funeral of Pāṇḍu.[188] The closeness of the clansmen gives way to the distance between king and subject. The king exercises control over activities, regulates labour, demands taxes, and can rule through coercion. These were not the norms of a lineage-based society.

The notion of wages introduced into the contract becomes a justification for taxes and is a new feature. Taxation necessitates

[184] 12.283.7–8ff.
[185] 12.59.13–14.
[186] 12.15.2–3 and 12.67.3–19.
[187] 12.67ff., 87.9.
[188] 3.229.6ff., 1.118.25.

officers and ministers who are functionaries rather than kinsmen, and who are required to keep the more complex system going. There is an elaborate declaration on the obligations of kingship and the rights it bestows.[189] The *rājā*, as a functionary,[190] introduces the idea that his rule has to maintain the structures of the state. The final arbiters are no longer clansmen but ideologues of the state.

Wealth remains a precondition to the sacrificial ritual. But whereas earlier the ritual was eulogized, now wealth becomes the source of well-being and only a part is used in ritual. The renouncing of wealth is unacceptable as it negates social obligations.[191] Wealth has to be given in *dāna*, as a gift in charity, but only to discerning persons. This is not the same as the *dāna* encouraged by the Sramanic sects, which is not intended for particular recipients but for the institution, the Saṅgha. Generating more wealth requires employing more labour and the supervision of its work. The ritual status of *varṇa* has to be extended to redefining the status of the *sūdra*, perhaps better viewed as *jātis* covering a range of labour-providing occupations.

Mention of gifts of land and digging tanks begin gradually to be added to earlier gifts of cattle and gold. The capital city, although still the residence of the ruler, became the hub of the state as well as a centre for the exchange of goods. Coercive authority need not refer only to the army but could include all forms of state coercion, including the enforced observing of laws. Centralization of power also involved alliances outside the kingdom with neighbours. Insisting on a *digvijaya* would not have been conducive to alliances unless it became symbolic, as it gradually did. Underlying the discussion on kingship is the right of the king to rule as a single source of power.

Given the extensive discussion on these matters, its historical context becomes significant. This was neither the single nor even the dominant view of kingship. The notion of kingship was also the subject of discussion in Buddhist circles, as well as among others whom the *brāhmaṇas* referred to as *nāstikas*—essentially

[189] 12.56.10ff.
[190] 12.8.8–25.
[191] 12.9.4-11.1ff.

those who denied the *Vedas,* or the role of deities, or opposed brahmanical views of caste and its practice.

By the time the epic was put into its present form, there had been both discussion and experience of various kinds of power in the half-millennium before. Doubtless some awareness persisted of the attempts of the Mauryan emperor Aśoka to govern with a difference. In the Buddhist view the king is appointed by the people and there is no intervention by either *brāhmaṇas* or deities. *Dharma*, the law of social ethics, gives direction to governance. The universal observance of an egalitarian social ethic applicable equally to all, which was the Buddhist *dharma*, was an implicit recognition of the priority of this ethic over caste. Where social ethics were determined by caste, there the controllers of caste had authority in the state. They probably recognized that the Buddhist Saṅgha had access to power wherever it received patronage. But the social ethic of the Sramana sects relied on an ethic of virtue, with caste not being a determining factor.

There was probably also the realization in the post-Mauryan period that an ideology of governance focused on a single teaching was more effective in consolidating power than diffused ideologies. This might in part explain why the *brāhmaṇas* referred to all other belief systems as *nāstika*, even when the supporters of other systems, such as Aśoka, called for equal respect towards *brāhmaṇas* and *śramaṇas*. The power of the state was certainly more dazzling than that of a clan chief.

An obsession with *āpad-dharma* runs like a thread through the discourse on the requirements of a good king. To live with societies that do not abide by the *varṇāśrama-dharma,* and do not respect the *Vedas,* would have been a reason for distress.[192] This could be a reflection of kingdoms ruled by what the *brāhmaṇas* regarded as *śūdras*, *vrātya-kṣatriyas*, and *mlecchas*—such as the Nandas, Mauryas, Indo-Greeks, Śakas, and Kuṣānas. Another aspect of distress was where, at one place in the text, a Caṇḍāla quotes the rules from the *śāstras* to a *brāhmaṇa* in order to persuade the *brāhmaṇa* not to act contrary to his *svadharma*.[193]

[192] 12.110–11.
[193] 12.139.12ff.

Yudhiṣṭhira, filled with remorse at the killing of his kinsmen in the war, wishes to renounce kingship but is dissuaded and is consecrated king. As has been pointed out, this echoes the story of Aśoka and his remorse at the killings in the Kaliṅga war.[194] Yudhiṣṭhira argues that the law of the *kṣatra* is evil as it endorses the killing of people—*kṣatradharmānna pāpīyāndharmosti bharatarṣabha abhiyāne ca yuddhe ca rājā hanti mahājanam*.[195] Parallels to Aśokan thoughts seem not too distant.[196] He is told that kings are cleansed by upholding the righteous and holding back evil, by conducting *yajñas* and giving *dāna*. A Cārvāka curses Yudhiṣṭhira for causing the killing and is put to death by the *brāhmaṇas*.[197]

There must have been some comment on the story of the Pāṇḍavas killing their kinsmen, as this episode suggests. The historical background would involve not only the policies of Aśoka but other contradictory political theories; as also the change from clan to caste, from chiefships to kingships in various places, where the more localized laws of the former competed with the attempted uniform regimen of the *Dharmaśāstras*. The killing of the *kṣatriyas* may also have been a metaphor of the success of Vedism over the *nāstikas*, given that many *kṣatriyas* in the *gaṇa-saṅghas* followed what the *brāhmaṇas* regarded as heterodoxies.

The Śānti *parvan* reflects a debate on what constitutes *dharma* with an endorsement of the need to oppose and kill the non-believers.[198] This debate had implications for the legitimacy of

[194] If the point of reference was Aśoka's *dhamma*, then this would be a reference back to the past, assuming that the Śānti *parvan* is post-Mauryan—as is likely. In this connection mention is made of a *svayamvara* in Kaliṅga where, among the kings listed, are Aśoka followed by Śatadhanvan. This hints at some knowledge of the later Mauryas as given in the *Purāṇas*, not to mention the link with Kaliṅga: 12.4.7.

[195] 12.98.1.

[196] J.L. Fitzgerald, *The Mahābhārata,* Book 12, Śāntiparvan, Part I, 98ff.; I. Selvanayagam, "Aśoka and Arjuna as Counterfigures Standing on the Field of Dharma: A Historical-Hermeneutical Perspective", 59–75; N. Sutton, "Aśoka and Yudhiṣṭhira. A Historical Setting for the Tensions in the *Mahābhārata*", 331–41; A. Hiltebeitel, *Rethinking the Mahābhārata,* 262–3; idem, "Buddhism and the *Mahābhārata*", 107ff.

[197] 12.39.22–35.

[198] 12.34.13–20.

kingship. The discussion introduces the diverse meanings of *dharma*. Violence is evil, but evil is so defined as to apply to those who do not follow the *Dharmaśāstras*. The *kṣatriya*'s duty is to kill in battle and kill the *dasyus—nityodyukto dasyuvadhe raṇe kuryātparākramam.*[199] What appears to have been an audible debate on violence is made inaudible, but nevertheless can be heard through contradictory statements. War as a form of sacrifice, where the hero fights and kills for *dharma*, is often mentioned without any questioning, as is the analogy of battle with *yajña*.[200] The morality of war is a central subject of discussion, with Arjuna raising it before the war and Yudhiṣṭhira after. The debate evidently had a history.

Confrontations by subject people were not frequent, although advice to the ruler against oppressive taxation is frequent. The barb is sought to be removed by the changed relationship between the *rājā* and the rest, where the latter are referred to as *prajā* (children), in this case of the *rājā*, in the midst of a receding echo of kinship. Aśoka extends the boundaries of those he includes to all human beings when he says, *save munisse pajā mamā*.[201]

Such changes were neither sudden nor uniform. There were overlapping situations and some converging functions. But the general trends were apparent. As the power of the state condensed, the obvious area of confrontation was from those who opposed or broke away from the norms and structures introduced by the coming of the state. This was done in many alternative ways of thinking and acting in relation to *dharma* and to *rājya*. Among these were renouncers and ascetics who foreswore social obligations and either went away to live in isolation or else established alternative societies, as was the case with Buddhist and Jaina monks. Renouncers claimed a parallel moral authority by moving out of the system. This was different from the autonomy claimed by *brāhmaṇas* as the most superior within the system. Yudhiṣṭhira posing renunciation as his alternative to kingship was a crisis for orthodoxy and dangerously close to the teaching of the heterodox.

[199] 12.60.14.
[200] 12.99.12–21.
[201] Separate Edict I, in J. Bloch, *Les Inscriptions d'Asoka*, 137.

It would seem, therefore, that somewhere along the line the *Mahābhārata* changes course. From legitimizing a lineage-based society and the clan systems of earlier times, some of which were still in existence, it turns to endorsing the new rules of the nascent kingdoms that were superseding the former. The lineage-based society is part of a presumed history; the kingdom is concerned with contemporary matters. The change is being legalized in the new orientations to *dharma*. The contrast between the two systems had to be retained in order to demonstrate the change between what was and what could be with the change to kingship.

If the intention had been only to legitimize the latter, then the text would have been entirely rewritten to present the Pāṇḍavas and the Kauravas as full-fledged monarchs. But this would also have involved changing the entire context of the events, possibly a degree of reordering which was too extensive, since the oral tradition had by then already accreted to itself a vast number of fragments relating to a variety of *rājās* and *janas*. And there were other versions of this tradition familiar to Buddhist and Jaina sources. Had this been done then the change implicit in the narrative and didactic sections would have been negated. Such a rewriting was more feasible with a shorter narration of events, as in the case of the *Rāmāyaṇa*. If there is a perception of historical change, and this is sought to be conveyed in the manner in which the epic is edited, then this also raises related questions of concepts of time in the redacted *Mahābhārata*.

9. The Reckoning of Time

The *Mahābhārata* has a more detailed reckoning of time than the Vedic corpus. Time now becomes important to narration. This change would seem to date to around the Christian era, characterized by explorations in Indian astronomy and some familiarity with ideas emanating from the eastern Mediterranean.[202] At one level, the reckoning is simple and goes by the seasonal calendar, as it did earlier, with the movement of the sun and the moon determining periods of time. The year is divided into the Uttarāyaṇa—the northern or rising cycle—also referred to as the *devayāna* (the way of the gods); and the Dakṣināyaṇa—or

[202] D. Pingree, "Astronomy and Astrology in India and Iran", 229–40.

downward cycle—this being the *pitṛyāna* (the way of the ancestors).[203] Within each year there were three seasons—the rains, winter, and summer—each of four months (*cāturmāsya*), which had earlier marked domestic sacrifices in the *Veda*s. The agricultural calendar determined many activities. At another level there was some attempt to count by generations; occasionally, references are made to stages in a descent list, although this is not developed consciously as a form of time reckoning.

Apart from routine calendrical time, the concept of what may be called cosmological time, perhaps first discussed in the Manu *Dharmaśāstra*, also occurs in a late section of the *Mahābhārata*.[204] It envisages time as a *mahāyuga* (great age), or cycle.[205] Each cycle begins afresh after the destruction of the universe at the end of the previous great cycle. Each *mahāyuga* consists of four lesser *yugas* of decreasing length which run sequentially and the figures follow a mathematical pattern. The first is the Kṛta/Satya, lasting 4800 years, followed by the Tretā of 3600 years, then the Dvāpara of 2400 years, and ultimately the Kaliyuga, which is the present cycle or age and will last 1200 years. To the basic figures of 4000, 3000, 2000, and 1000 were added the two twilight figures of an equal number of hundreds. The decline is in geometrical progression. The total of 12,000 years was regarded as an eon. A thousand eons were equivalent to one day of Brahmā or a *kalpa*, a term familiar from Buddhist texts as well. The numbers have to be multiplied by 360 to convert them into human years. In human years this would work out to:

Kṛta	4800 =	1,728,000
Tretā	3600 =	1,296,000
Dvāpara	2400 =	864,000
Kali	1200 =	432,000
The four constituting the *mahāyuga*	12,000 =	4,320,000

[203] G. Held, *The Mahābhārata: An Ethnological Study*, 189ff.

[204] L. Gonzales-Reiman, *The Mahābhārata and the Yugas*; *Mahābhārata,* 12.216–20. It is also added to the narrative when the Bhārgava *ṛṣi* Mārkaṇḍeya recites it to Yudhiṣṭhira: 3.188.10–189.1ff.

[205] 3.148.10ff., 186.16ff., 187.31, 188.10,64, 188.89ff., 189.1–15.

The numbers are drawn from various sources. Sometimes they are the same as those quoted for the number of bricks to build a fire-altar or the number of syllables used in a Vedic text, but they also coincide with Mesopotamian figures used in cosmology. There seems to have been a dialogue between cosmographers and astronomers of the time in discussing these numbers.

Characteristic of the four *yugas* was also an increasing moral decline and a falling off of the rules of social behaviour from the first to the fourth. Towards the end of the Kaliyuga, the world of *dharma* is turned upside down. The notion of the decline of *dharma* was central and causally connected to the coming of Kalki, ushering in a return of *dharma* at the end of the Kaliyuga which leads eventually to the return of the Kṛta of the next *mahāyuga*. Time is therefore linked to the utopia of the past, from which there is a downward slide to the present and an eventual return of utopian conditions at the start of the next great cycle. The end of the eon is heralded by unseasonal climate and cataclysms. The decrease in the length of the *yuga* and of *dharma* is partly inherent and partly attributed to the infiltration of *mlecchas* into society. Kalki, the tenth and final reincarnation of Viṣṇu, brings about the end of lawlessness and the usurpation of power by the low castes. There is an implicit eschatology in the scheme of the *mahāyuga*, moving from utopian beginnings to an ultimate end. Just prior to the termination of the great cycle comes the saviour figure of Kalki, who makes possible the return of utopia and a new great cycle. Orientalist scholarship denied this as eschatology since there is a return to a *mahāyuga* and not the termination of time. However, the length of each great cycle is so enormous that it annuls the measurement of time. It is a fantasy that remains symbolic, as indeed does that of the Judaeo-Christian tradition, invoking the teleology of the Garden of Eden ending with Judgement Day. Nevertheless it has to be seen as eschatology, even if dissimilar from the Judaeo-Christian. There is a distinct relation to the past and present.

The significance of this concept also lies in areas other than the measurement of time. The names of the *yugas*—Kṛta, Tretā, Dvāpara, and Kali—are the same as those used for successive numbers in the throw of dice.[206] They indicate descending numbers that suit the declining length of each cycle. Implicit in this scheme is the suggestion of fate unfolding in time. The word for time—*kāla*—although etymologically linked to the root **kal* (to calculate), is also used in the sense of destiny. Thus, references to the *yugas* and to time are frequent in the text.

Even more important is the description of the *yugas*. The Kṛta, which is the winning throw in dice, is an age when law reigns supreme, there are no gods and anti-gods, no *Vedas*, no transactions, no need for labour, an absence of disease and conflict, and the four *varṇas* are respected. The Tretā registers a small decline in moral values with a reduced observance of laws and sacred duty by a quarter, and with motivation becoming the purpose of action. In the Dvāpara the law is further reduced, and lust, disease, and untruth are observed. In the Kali age only a quarter of the law survives and there is a moral degeneration among people. Detailed descriptions of the problems of this age emphasize an overturning of the rules of sacred duty, with lower castes taking on the function of the higher. Misbehaviour is attributed to this time-cycle. Whereas *dharma* declines in each age, the need for labour increases. It is a world turned upside down. Even the complexion of the gods changes colour in each *yuga*! This construction of time cycles is of the later period, when kingship and caste had become characteristic features of society, and this description was probably added to the epic.

The use of time concepts as a key to viewing social change is common to many cultures, where there is an image of the remote past as utopian, and utopia can take the form of negating present conditions. Hesiod, for example, uses the myth of the metallic ages: gold, silver, bronze, and iron, to reflect on Greek society. The golden age was when men lived like gods, with land providing grain without labour, with an absence of sickness and old age, and with a gentle death. The age of silver brought a reduction in longevity, and a turning away from the gods and from offering sacrifices. The age of bronze was violent and fierce. The present age, of iron, is depicted in negative terms and it is said that

[206] *Aitareya Brāhmaṇa*, 7.15.

nothing will be as it was in the past, customary social behaviour having been overthrown. The contrast is between the gold and the iron, with the silver and the bronze providing a passage between them.[207]

Some scholars maintain that cyclic notions of time are characteristic of India and the recurring cycle is a refusal of history. All events are liable to be repeated in the next cycle, so no event can be particular or unique.[208] But a different reading can be given of cyclic time. Cyclic or cosmological time becomes the circumference of social activity, seen sequentially as units within which a society is created, lives out its history, and is extinguished. Change therefore is evident. It also necessitates an increase in the span of time from a five-year *yuga* as it was in the *Ṛgveda* to one of 12,000 divine years. This reflects a constant expansion in the scope of the past, where the past can then be variously compared with the shorter and more limited present.

Cyclic cosmology therefore marks a growing concern with the relationship between past and present. It fits with the narrative of the Bharatas since the story deals with the passing of an earlier age, the annihilation of many clans, and the preservation of the few who are responsible for creating the present Kali age. Because the events narrated took place in the earlier Dvāpara age, the narrative is firmly a narrative of the past. Placing the epics in the Tretā and Dvāpara is also meant to evoke a distant past for the events. The timespan of the *mahāyuga* is so immense that the repetition of events becomes irrelevant. The notion of these *yugas* allows the projection of a cosmic struggle where the intervention of the deity, Viṣṇu, becomes imperative.

There is also in the epic the initial notion of linear time. This is evident in the recording of descent through genealogies. These are not elaborate, but they record a sense of the chronology of person and event. The word for lineage is *vaṃśa*, a bamboo or cane, capturing the idea of a linear form with nodes, each node giving

[207] *Hesiod's Theogony: Works and Days*, 106–201.

[208] M. Eliade, "Time and Eternity in Indian Thought"; M. Eliade, *Cosmos and History: The Myth of the Eternal Return*. For an alternative view, see R. Thapar, *Time as a Metaphor of History*.

rise to a stem: a precise parallel to a generation and its descent to the next generation. It is also possible to argue that linear time is a segment of the cyclic arc but has a different trajectory.

Seen differently, three elements of time have been suggested for the epic genre: heroic time, which is the background to heroic society; narrative time, which is when the epic is believed to have been first composed and is therefore a witness to the events described; and documentary time, which relates to the various recensions of the epic.[209] There is therefore a continuum between the three elements. This questions the notion of there being only two points of time in a text, that of the events and that of the composition describing them. These three events seem more logical in that they refer to the time of the events, that of the composition, and that of the reformulations of the composition. Seeing the past in this way evokes perspectives which, subsequent to the first, hint at history.

The movement back and forth in time is evident in the epics. Events and social patterns sometimes have to be explained with reference to a previous cycle of time. In this there is, at one level, a continuum of time in that events move back and forth; but at another level there is a disjuncture in time in that events belong to different time cycles. More manageable is the continuum within the single *yuga,* with the same characters moving from one birth to another, a device used on occasion to explain an otherwise inexplicable situation.

That the period towards the end of the Kurukṣetra war ushered in the fourth and last time cycle is yet another way of separating the time of the heroes from the aftermath of the war, of distancing the past from the present. The passing away of the elders of the family of the heroes is held in transit, as it were, whilst the Śānti and Anuśāsana *parvans* are recited. Bhīṣma lying on a bed of arrows, wounded and about to die, holds forth for days on various *dharmas*. This can only be a disjuncture in the narrative, of both intention and authorship. Was this the major brahmanical intervention, which is also reflected in lesser forms elsewhere? The

[209] Victor Turner, "Comparative Epic and Saga", quoted in A. Hiltebeitel, *The Ritual of Battle*, 50.

dominance of the notion of time beyond the cyclic and the linear lies in statements such as that the death of a person who is killed is determined by Time; or that Time itself is the great killer.[210] The authorship of the *Mahābhārata* suggests that later redactors as authors were looking back at the earlier composition, and were adding to it in accordance with their intention of changing its function, but not so as to obliterate the purpose of the original composition. The attempt was to use the earlier composition as history in order to legitimize its later purpose. Cosmological time cycles are so deployed as to introduce the notion of time as a feature of social change through the various ages—a process that is characteristic of historical writing today. But the intention is also to accommodate the linear time of genealogies in the age that precedes the emergence of dynasties—the Dvāpara prior to the Kali. As reviewed by the redactors, the termination of the *kṣatriyas* is a time marker separating these two ages. The battle at Kurukṣetra marks the end of clan societies just prior to the coming of dynasties.

There is, at many levels, an interplay of what came before and what came later. The narrative section is in any case subsequent to the events described and is looking back at what was believed to have happened earlier. The didactic sections incorporate a more recent perspective of the narrative. The two changing perspectives are not merely those of a change in time but also project two views of society, one subsequent to the other; and in highlighting the difference they incorporate a consciousness of historical change.

[210] *Mahābhārata*, 12.34.4ff.

5

The *Rāmāyaṇa*

1. Epic

The epic form, as I have suggested, can be viewed as the articulation of a consciousness relating to the historical past, even if the events which it narrates may not all be historically authenticated. As part of an oral tradition, its form is relatively freer than written forms. Variants in narrative or characterization—which can become apparent through a comparison of the epic's recensions—suggest changes in historical context. The new looks back on the old, and often does so nostalgically. The epic has a potential role in the making of a historical tradition since there is, as we have seen, a relation between history and the epic, however ambiguous. Is the epic meant to narrate what happened, or is the mythical and heroic gloss on the narrative so extensive that what may have been historical becomes opaque? Does the epic represent actual events—the "hard facts" as some historians would call them—which permit of the historicity of an epic age? Or are the epics essentially born of imagination and so heavily interpolated in later periods that even the episodes can hardly be dated or set in a historical context?

Whereas in the previous chapter my attempt was to show how the text depicts two different kinds of polities—the clan system and the kingdom—the first earlier than the second and the two as ideologically opposed, my intention in this chapter is to show the two in actual confrontation, encouraged by their ideological opposition. I shall also argue that where a variant version questions the authenticity of the hegemonic, the explanation it provides to support its views may shed light on the historical purpose of the hegemonic version and the contradiction thereof.

The narrative of the *rāma-kathā*—what might have been the original story of Rāma—has many more variants than the *Mahābhārata*. Although the Vālmīki *Rāmāyaṇa* has become the hegemonic text, the variants point to a choice of narratives that existed at various times. The chronology of the variants suggests some consciousness of a historical process. I have selected three variants, all important in their own traditions and closer in time to each other. I shall examine the degree to which they can be seen as charters of validation referring to discrete moments of time and reflecting the perspectives of alternative historical traditions.

The three are the Buddhist *Dasaratha Jātaka*,[1] contemporary with and perhaps even prior to the second version to be discussed here—namely the Vālmīki *Rāmāyaṇa*—and which may have been one among the many tellings known to Vālmīki;[2] and the third is the Jaina version of the story, the *Paumacariyam* of Vimalasūri.[3] This last contests the Vālmīki version and is the only one of the three that claims to be historically authentic. Irrespective of when the earliest oral tradition was current, these three versions were established by the early Christian era.

The variants do not build on a single uniform story. In the *Dasaratha Jātaka*, one part of the *Rāmāyaṇa* story is narrated. The Jaina version questions the veracity of the existing versions. The *Jātakas,* composed in Pāli, date to about the second century BC; the different phases of the *Rāmāyaṇa,* composed in Sanskrit, are dated to *c.* 400 BC to AD 400; and the *Paumacariyam*, in Prākrit, dates to the early centuries AD. The authorship differs too—as will be discussed for each version. And then there are differences of context. Apart from all else, the first of these reflects a clan-based society; the second is essentially the conflict between

[1] *Dasaratha Jātaka*, no. 461, *The Jātaka*, IV.78.

[2] *The Vālmīki Rāmāyaṇa*, General Editors G.H. Bhatt and U.P. Shah, 7 vols; *The Ramāyaṇa of Vālmīki*, Critical Edition, trans. R.P. Goldman, *et al.,* vols I–VI and VII forthcoming. All future citations of the *Rāmāyaṇa*, unless otherwise specified, are to the G.H. Bhatt and U.P. Shah version.

[3] *Paumacariyam*, ed. H. Jacobi.

a kingdom and a chiefship; and the third assumes a universality of kingdoms.

Both in terms of chronology and content, there is a perception of historical change and the later text becomes a commentary on what has preceded it. This perception is not sufficient in itself to demonstrate a sense of history. Each represents a different perspective on historical change. The Jaina text specifically denies historicity to the other two but claims it for itself. Whereas historical consciousness has to be extracted when it is embedded in a text, a statement such as this suggests more clearly the recognition of a historical tradition.

What seems significant therefore is to ask why there was a need for diverse versions. What were the reasons for the dissimilarities? And what was the nature of the historical statements (if they can be called that) which each version was making? Variant versions of the *rāma-kathā* are prolific through the centuries. The three selected are expressions of a consciousness of the historical moment rather than historicity: by this I mean that they show an awareness of the time during which they were composed, not that they contain facts which can be verified. Since the *Rāmāyaṇa* was of a more manageable size than the *Mahābhārata*, it was possible to maintain parallel versions of the story, or parts of it.

Nineteenth-century interpretations of the *Rāmāyaṇa* saw it as the narrative of a confrontation between Aryans and Dravidians, of North Indian Aryan invaders pushing aside the Dravidians and forcing their way into South India and Sri Lanka.[4] The Aryan, it was maintained, is represented as the orderly and advanced society of Ayodhyā and the Dravidian by the uncouth wildness of the *rākṣasas*. This dichotomy was influenced by that of the civilized and the primitive, central to the nineteenth-century concept of civilization, and was a transplant from European ideological obsessions with "the Aryan". Since "Aryan" and "Dravidian" do not refer to a race or ethnic group but to a language identity, the historical process of establishing a language becomes a far more complicated matter of why languages are spoken and by whom.

[4] C. Lassen, *Indisches Alterthumskunde*, vol. I, 596ff.; M. Monier Williams, *Indian Epic Poetry*, 9–10.

The perspective from the epic itself poses the distinction as being between two political forms, social codes, belief systems, and ecologies.

Some modern ideologies of nationalism in their more extreme forms insist on the historicity of epic events and persons and seek to construct history from these. The epic can be treated as among the genres reflecting a past, but this does not permit it being read literally as history. The debate on the historical versus the legendary can become a central concern of politics in a nation-state.[5] Associated with this is the attempt to authenticate the contents of the epic by searching for archaeological counterparts. This has yielded no viable results—as was to be expected, since fantasy plays an immense role in epic compositions and is not reflected in excavated artefacts, although it may influence their interpretation. The sites excavated yield too many discrepancies and the interpretations of such excavations remain controversial.[6] A further problem is that the present-day place names need not be those of earlier locations.[7]

The *Rāmāyaṇa* of Vālmīki was converted from a narrative epic to the sacred literature of the Vaiṣṇavas when Rāma was transformed into an incarnation of Viṣṇu, which in turn distanced it from the variants.

[5] Witness the controversy over the birthplace of Rāma in the conflict at Ayodhyā: Sarvepalli Gopal (ed.), *Anatomy of a Confrontation*.

[6] *Indian Archaeology—A Review*, 1976–7, 1979–80; B.B. Lal, "Historicity of the Mahabharata and the Ramayana: What has Archaeology to Say in the Matter"; idem, "The Two Indian Epics *vis-à-vis* Archaeology", 27–34. Recent excavations at Ayodhyā (2002–3) to determine whether there was a temple beneath the Babri Masjid have not revealed the remnants of such a temple—judging by what has been reported. Excavations at Ayodhyā date the earliest levels to *c.* the seventh century BC, with an early form of the Northern Black Polished Ware at the lowest levels. The material culture of this level does not conform to the descriptions in the text of Ayodhyā as an urban centre, and such centres date to c. the fifth century BC from excavations. This would of course be in conflict with the later tradition, which takes the events of the *Rāmāyaṇa* back to an impossibly distanced past located in cosmology, the Tretā *yuga*, the second of the four time-cycles of many millennia ago.

[7] B.B. Lal, "Was Ayodhya a Mythical City?", 45–9; M.C. Joshi, "Ayodhya: Mythical and Real", 107–9; G. Roth, "Ayodhyā and Ganga", 121–34.

The theme of the *rāma-kathā* was treated in a variety of ways.[8] The changes introduced in the retelling are of other times and draw on other ideologies. These versions incorporate a change of perception, both of personalities and the events known to the early epic. Each variant version is making a statement; often, these are implicitly historical statements since they reflect the social assumptions of a particular segment of society at a point in time. It becomes difficult to argue that there is a single authentic version, for every version claims authenticity. Comparing versions also makes it possible to see the raw material of epic episodes and the way in which these episodes or incidents are introduced into what becomes the hegemonic text in a given tradition.

The composition of an epic changes with repeated recitation, the changes being either innocuous or substantial depending upon the person reciting it, the audience, and the occasion. When fragments are collated into an epic, which then takes a written form, the recording is relatively uniform. There were therefore changes in the oral composition. What we have now in manuscript versions of the Vālmīki *Rāmāyaṇa* are the outcome of reformulations from the oral, together with interpolations into the written.

The intensity with which the many variant versions were propagated through the centuries makes it apparent that the *rāma-kathā*, though not necessarily the Vālmīki *Rāmāyaṇa*, was one of the thematic dialogues of Indian civilization. It occurs wherever the more elite Indian culture touched local cultures, resulting in narrative variations that reflect the vast span of cultural intersections.[9] The dialogue registers historical change both in terms of space and time, the location and date of the variants being significant. Differences in narrative are not accidental, for they are either affirming or contesting each variation, whether marginally or centrally.

The literary currency of the poem is evident from allusions in other literature and epigraphs. Comparisons have also been made between the conflict of Rāma and Rāvaṇa with that between Indra and Vṛtra in the *Ṛgveda*. Aśvaghoṣa's *Buddhacarita,* a biography

[8] R. Thapar, "A Historical Perspective on the Story of Rama", 141–63; J.L. Brockington, *Righteous Rāma*.

[9] Its continuing centrality to South East Asian societies, and the Indonesian in particular, is a case in point.

of the Buddha, seems in a few instances to have borrowed from the Vālmīki version. These link the past with the present.

With the geographical spread of the epics, local landmarks were associated with the story. Episodes familiar to a local audience could find their way into the main narrative, so that the events of the epics are in a sense localized. The nuances and emphases change in accordance with the requirements of the local culture, and sometimes even the narrative is altered. The story could be appropriated by a different authorship and be given a different rendering. By including the genealogical portions and maintaining that the epics recorded a slice of the *itihāsa-purāṇa* tradition, an element of believed history was introduced. However, there could at most be a sliver of historicity, enveloped to the point of near invisibility in the many embellishments within the narrative. Nevertheless, the embellishments provide the narrative with a different historical perspective.

2. The *Jātaka* Variants

In the Buddhist commentaries and texts of the early centuries AD, references to the epic stories—the *bharata yuddha*, *sītāharana*, and other such stories—are uncomplimentary and described as "purposeless talk".[10] But the stories which make up the *Jātaka* anthology include scattered fragments which either echo episodes from a *rāma-kathā* or are narratives of clans that were eventually coalesced into an epic story. If these fragments, or *ākhyānas*, were put together in the larger epic, the implication would be that both categories of texts derive from a common oral tradition.

The *Jātaka* stories were, with a few exceptions, brief narratives looking back at the past and relating incidents of a past life of the Buddha. Some are fantasy, some mention clans and persons. The dialogue of the protagonist, generally the Buddha in a previous birth, approximates some aspect of his teaching: hence their inclusion even as folk literature in the Buddhist Pāli Canon. Composed in Pāli prose, some include verses from earlier times. Their locations are largely the initial area of the spread of Buddhism—the

[10] *Buddhaghosācārya Papañcasudāni (Majjhimanikāya-aṭṭakathā)*, 1.163; *Culavaṃsa*, 75.59, 83.46.

Ganges plain and Central India. As recast in their present form, their authors were monks. The audience was the lay community of Buddhists and others who heard the teachings in an accessible form. The *Jātakas* were familiar stories recited in the context of Buddhist ethics, and the claim that they pertain to previous lives of the Buddha provided an opportunity to proselytize. This is also evident from their visual depiction at *stūpa* sites during the same period.[11]

That the *Jātaka* versions were not an attempt at an alternative version of the *Rāmāyaṇa* is evident from the absence of narrating the same events from a Buddhist perspective. The historical contexts of the Buddhist compositions were often the *gaṇa-saṅghas* (chiefdoms) and incipient kingdoms, and urbanism of the mid-first millennium BC, the written forms being subsequent. Heroic societies were part of an ancient past for Buddhist authors. Whether some of the *Jātaka* stories were based on a currency of the Vālmīki *Rāmāyaṇa*, or drew from an earlier oral tradition of episodic tales that went into the making of the latter, has been debated. The details of the stories, where they differ, become significant statements.

Mention of persons associated with the *rāma-kathā* in these stories often come from the earlier verse sections. There are, for example, verses describing the sorrow of Rāma's mother when he is exiled;[12] Sītā's devotion to Rāma when accompanying him into exile;[13] and the description of Rāma as Daśaratha's royal son.[14] There are also episodes similar to those in the *Rāmāyaṇa*, such as Daśaratha accidentally killing the young ascetic whilst on a hunt,[15] has its parallel in the *Sāma Jātaka*.[16] It has been viewed as the hidden power of fate in the epic narrative,[17] but in the *Jātaka* the

[11] V. Dehejia, *Discourse in Early Buddhist Art*.

[12] *Jayaddisa Jātaka*, no. 513, in *The Jātaka*.

[13] *Vessantara Jātaka*, no. 547, in ibid.

[14] *Dasaratha-rājaputta*, in V. Fausboll, *The Jātaka*, vol. VI, 558.

[15] *Rāmāyaṇa*, 2.57.8ff.

[16] *Sāma Jātaka*, no. 540, in *The Jātaka*.

[17] *The Rāmāyaṇa of Vālmīki, Vol. II: Ayodhyākāṇḍa*, ed. and trans. S. Pollock, gen. ed. R.P. Goldman. It could also be viewed as the unexpected in the adventure narrative as analysed by M.M. Bakhtin, "Epic and Novel", in idem, *The Dialogic Imagination*.

Buddhist ethical perspective is underlined through the remorse of the king at his action, his decision to look after the blind parents, and the eventual return to life of the dead son.

An important episode concerns Ayodhyā which in the Buddhist texts is located on the Ganges and is distinct from Sāketa. On one occasion it is said to have been attacked by the Andhavenhuputta, who besieged and subjugated the city, after which they returned to Dvāravatī in western India.[18] The Andhavenhu/Andhakavṛṣṇi are said to be *dāsaputtas*, therefore of low birth or alien culture,[19] and are also mentioned in some *Purāṇas* as *kṣatriyas*, but of a lesser status. The Haihayas, another segment of this lineage, also attacked Ayodhyā.[20]

Videha and its capital, Mithilā, are mentioned,[21] Mithilā as a prosperous city reminiscent of Ayodhyā in the *Rāmāyaṇa*.[22] Videha is a rich land of 16,000 villages with full granaries and 16,000 dancing girls. Names such as Nimi and Janaka occur in the later Puranic genealogies of the Videha branch of the Ikṣvāku or Sūryavaṃśa/Solar line.[23]

The *Jātaka* story which comes closest to the main frame of the *Rāmāyaṇa*, but nevertheless differs in significant ways, is the *Dasaratha Jātaka*, and this has been commented upon at length.[24] Dasaratha rules from Varanasi and not from Ayodhyā. He has two sons, Rāma-paṇḍita and Lakkhana, and a daughter, Sītā-devī, from his eldest queen. After her death he raises another wife to the status of queen consort, and she demands that her son Bharata be made the heir-apparent. The king, frightened that the new consort will harm the older sons, suggests to them that they flee to the neighbouring kingdom and claim their rights after Dasaratha has died,

[18] G. Malalasekera, *Dictionary of Pali Proper Names*, vol. I, 165.

[19] *Ghaṭa Jātaka*, no. 454, in *The Jātaka*.

[20] F.E. Pargiter, *Ancient Indian Historical Tradition*, 153.

[21] *Sādhīna Jātaka*, no. 494; *Suruci Jātaka*, no. 489; *Mahā-ummagga Jātaka*, no. 546; *Vinīlaka Jātaka*, no. 160; *Mahāpanāda Jātaka*, no. 264; *Makhādeva Jātaka*, no. 9; *Nimi Jātaka*, no. 541; *Kumbhakāra Jātaka*, no. 408: all in *The Jātaka*.

[22] *Rāmāyaṇa*, 1.5.6ff., 1.6; *Mahājanaka Jātaka*, no. 539, in *The Jātaka*.

[23] F.E. Pargiter, *Ancient Indian Historical Tradition*, 145ff.

[24] *Dasaratha Jātaka*, no. 461, in *The Jātaka*; V. Fausboll, *The Dasaratha-Jātaka, being the Buddhist Story of King Rāma*.

it having been prophesied that he would die after twelve years. Sītā accompanies her brothers and the three go to the Himalaya. Dasaratha dies after nine years. Bharata, refusing to become king, goes in search of Rāma and tries to persuade him to return. Lakkhana and Sītā, on hearing of their father's death, faint, but Rāma preaches to them on the impermanence of life. This is the core teaching of this *Jātaka*, where Rāma-paṇḍita was the Buddha in a previous incarnation. Rāma insists that he will return only after twelve years have been completed and therefore gives his sandals to Bharata, to symbolically guide him in taking decisions. Finally, they all return to the kingdom. Rāma makes Sītā his queen consort and they rule righteously for 16,000 years. The kidnapping of Sītā is not part of this narrative.

This *Jātaka* is in part a parallel to the second book of the *Rāmāyaṇa*, the Ayodhyākāṇḍa. Superimposed on the story are themes from the origin myths of the *kṣatriya* clans, particularly those of the Śākyas and the Koliyas from Buddhist sources.[25] These constitute the charter of validation from the Buddhist perspective. Some of their features are anathema to brahmanical views—as for example that Rāma and Sītā are siblings, yet rule as consorts.

An ancestral figure in some stories is king Okkāka, who is said to have sent for the daughter of the *rājā* of the Madras for his son Kuśa. She arrives together with a hunchback nurse, reminiscent of the story in the *Rāmāyaṇa*.[26] The Madras were neighbours of the Kekeyas in northern India. The name Okkāka is said to derive from *okkamukha*, light seemed to come from his mouth.[27] In one Buddhist tradition Okkāka is equated with Ikṣvāku and the etymology of this name is derived from *ikṣu* (sugarcane), the usual etymology as given in Puranic sources.[28] The association with the Ikṣvākus may have been a later attempt to link *kṣatriya*

[25] See Chapter Nine.

[26] *Kusa Jātaka*, no. 531, in *The Jātaka*.

[27] *Sumaṅgalavilāsinī*, 1.R258; "... *kathanakāle ukkā viya mukhato pabhā niccharati tasmātam okākkoti sanjanisu ti* ..." The *Śatapatha Brāhmaṇa*, 1.4.1.14–17, describing Videgha Māthava travelling east to the middle Ganges region, states that he carried Agni in his mouth. This could be a reference to bringing the fire sacrifice to the region or it could be, as I have suggested elsewhere, a reference to bringing Aryan speech to the region.

[28] S. Beal, *Romantic History of Buddha*, 18ff.

clans which supported Buddhism with one of the two major royal lineages of the Puranic *kṣatriya* tradition.

The theme of exile and kidnapping occurs more than once in the *Jātakas,* with the *Sambula Jātaka* being close to the *Rāmāyaṇa* story.[29] It focuses on the hesitant reconciliation of a husband to his wife who had been kidnapped by a *rākṣasa* and eventually rescued by Sakra/Indra. The *Vessantara Jātaka* is most frequently quoted in connection with the theme of exile.[30] Vessantara is the epitome of the gift-giving *rājā* since he bestows his wealth on all who ask for it. Finally, he even gifts his famous rain-inducing elephant to the *rājā* of Kaliṅga, who is in need of it to terminate a prolonged drought in his kingdom. The subjects of Vessantara, incensed by this act—which symbolizes the loss of prosperity—banish him. His wife, in emulation of Sītā, accompanies him into exile. They travel to the distant territory of the Cedis and live in the forest. But even here he is beset by greedy *brāhmaṇas*. They take away his children and his wife to work for them. A passing comparison is made to Sītā. Eventually Sakra appears, and it turns out that the tribulations of Vessantara were to test his ability to gift even those whom he loved. The emphasis in this story is on *dāna,* the gift-giving much propagated in Buddhist ethics. The ethical underlining is different from that of the *Rāmāyaṇa*, which is more focussed on familiar heroic values encapsulated in the destruction of the evil *rākṣasas*.

Underlying the many stories, some themes seem parallel to ideas that shaped the *Rāmāyaṇa*. Events take place in a known geographical area. The geographical dimension is emphasized in the theme of exile where the banished *rājās* either go north to the Himalaya or south towards the Vindhyan region. The Cedi *janapada* was clearly important and the *Cetīya Jātaka* gives the lineage of the Cedi *rājās*.[31] They were descended from the primeval ruler in Buddhist origin myths, the Mahāsammata, and one of their more famous ancestors had been gifted an aerial chariot. After him the lineage was segmented, and his five sons are said to have ruled in

[29] *Sambula Jātaka*, no. 519, in *The Jātaka.*

[30] No. 547, in *The Jātaka*; R. Gombrich, "The *Vessantara Jātaka*, the *Rāmāyaṇa* and the *Dasaratha Jātaka*", 427–37.

[31] *Cetīya Jātaka*, no. 422, in *The Jātaka.*

five different regions of Central India, a statement also made in the *Purāṇas*,[32] and in the *Mahābhārata* in connection with the ancestry of Jarāsandha. The *Vessantara Jātaka* mentions that the land of the Cedis was replete with meat, wine, and rice, and inhabited by 60,000 *khattiyas/kṣatriyas* who lived there as *rājās*, suggesting that it was a chiefship.[33] The *Jātaka* stories reflect transitional stages between the polities of chiefships and kingdoms.

Exile in these stories could symbolize migration and settlement in new areas. Even if the exiles return to their original home, there continue to be connections with the area of exile. Colonization was probably expressed in the form of exile, perhaps to dramatize the explanation for migration. The actual process of colonization would be similar in each case, irrespective of the narrative which provided the justification. The process is described in the *Jayaddisa Jātaka*, where land is settled by the king through clearing, digging a lake, preparing the fields, bringing in a thousand families, and founding a village such that it could support ascetics through alms.[34] New settlements also led gradually to the growth of new cities, and this introduced a different culture.

The etymology of *khattiya/kṣatriya* in the Buddhist texts derives not from being a warrior but from being the lord of fields. Thus, those who go into exile are described as belonging to the *rājakula* (ruling clans). In some cases, as in that of the *Cetīya Jātaka*, fragments of their genealogy are given to indicate their status; in other cases it is enough to say that they belong to the Ikṣvāku lineage.

The occurrence of sibling incest in origin myths may symbolize many things: marriage between two exogamous phratries or tribal subdivisions from the period of the original settlement; a hint of cross-cousin marriage; or a method of stressing purity of descent where ancestry is traced back to a single set of parents

[32] F.E. Pargiter, *Ancient Indian Historical Tradition*, 118ff.

[33] The link between the Cedis and Kaliṅga is interestingly attested to in the Hathigumpha inscription: see D.C. Sircar, *Select Inscriptions*, 214ff. Khāravela, the king of Kaliṅga, describes himself as a descendant of the Cedi king and takes the title of Mahāmeghavāhana, as did other kings of Kaliṅga.

[34] *Jayaddisa Jātaka*, no. 513, in *The Jātaka*. This is similar to the statement in the *Arthaśāstra*, 2.1, referring to the settling of land by *śūdra* cultivators under the control of the state in order to start cultivation and collect revenue.

and is therefore a symbolic demarcation of distinctive status. The theme of sibling marriage may also suggest some traces of a system of succession where a brother and sister merely rule jointly. Sibling marriage was not intended to be taken literally but was a way of underlining high status, as in the *Dasaratha Jātaka*. That the theme is common to many Buddhist origin myths places the story in a recognizably Buddhist context.

In terms of political sanction, these stories reflect a mixture of the *gaṇa-saṅgha* chiefships or oligarchies and incipient kingship. Members of the ruling clan can be removed by angry subjects, as was Vessantara. Other *Jātakas* refer to *rājās* being either banished, or to situations of crisis where they are called upon to abdicate. Some were elected by popular opinion. The Cedis boast of many thousand *rājās*, suggesting a large *gaṇa-saṅgha*. Where individual *rājās* are mentioned, kingship is still not so familiar.

The social ethic in the Buddhist ethos is implicitly emphasized in the qualities that make the ideal hero. *Dāna* becomes a major criterion of morality, often associated with *karuṇā* (compassion). Central to this ethos is the ideal of the *bodhisattva* who postpones his *nirvāṇa* in order to help others attain theirs. Any identification of Rāma with a deity is noticeably absent. The link between the past and the present is maintained in the *Jātaka* stories through the belief that these referred to the Buddha's previous births. This eliminated a sudden disjuncture or abrupt termination of the past and allowed for a sense in which the past seemed to glide into the present.

Many *Jātakas* narrate stories of the kings of Kosala: Pasenadi and Viḍūḍbha; and the kings of the powerful state of Magadha: Bimbisāra and Ajātasattu.[35] These kings ruled prior to the Nandas of the fourth century BC. But there is no association of Rāma with the kingdom of Kosala as an earlier ruler. He is merely one of many in the *Jātakas*, and of no particular significance. This would suggest that the epic names, if not fictional, claim to be earlier than the chronology assigned to the Buddhist oral tradition. Alternatively, if the *rāma-kathā* was "purposeless talk", it would not have been given prominence.

[35] G.P. Malalasekera, *Dictionary of Pali Proper Names*, vol. II, 285ff.

3. The Vālmīki *Rāmāyaṇa*

The Text

The story of Rāma is narrated by Nārada to Vālmīki in the opening *sarga* of the Vālmīki *Rāmāyaṇa*. It would seem to have had links with the earlier *rāma-kathā*,[36] perhaps a floating bardic tradition of fragmentary stories from which Vālmīki composed a single text. This is infrequently referred to as *itihāsa* in the earlier section of the text, but much more frequently as *kāvya* (poetry) in the later sections and sometimes as the *ādi-kāvya* (the first poem), where it is also on occasion referred to as *ākhyāna* or even *purāṇa*.[37] This might suggest a change from a past that was thought of as having actually happened, to recognizing the layers of creative imagination that went into the making of an early literary masterpiece—prior to its being converted into a sacred text. It was initially part of an open oral tradition, as were most *ākhyānas*, until they were recorded later in a written form.[38] Since the text has been interpolated at various times it cannot be dated to a particular period and only the occasional episode can find a possibly verifiable historical counterpart. This again has led historians to discard the notion of an "epic age" firmly rooted in chronology.

It may be suggested that the *Rāmāyaṇa*, as we have it today, went through various forms, as did the *Mahābhārata*. Fragmentary narratives from the oral tradition were probably selected and recomposed and compiled as an epic poem by Vālmīki; this poem then absorbed interpolations defining the accoutrements of kingship and introducing the worship of Viṣṇu—here presented as the Rāma-avatāra as part of the newly emerging Bhāgavata religion. Both were developments of the late first millennium BC

[36] *The Rāmāyaṇa of Vālmīki, Vol. I: Bālakāṇḍa*, ed. and trans. R.P. Goldman, 31ff.

[37] 1.4.6–7, 1.4.21–6.

[38] C. Bulcke, *Rāmakathā*; H.D. Sankalia, *Ramayana: Myth or Reality*; G. Bailey and M. Brockington, *Epic Threads*; J. Brockington, *The Sanskrit Epics*; J. Brockington, *Righteous Rāma*, examines carefully the many layers in the text and suggests five stages which went into the making of the present text. N. Sen, "Comparative Studies in Oral Epic Poetry and the Vālmīki *Rāmāyaṇa*: A Report on the Bālakāṇḍa", 397–409.

and the early centuries AD. The attempt therefore was to condense the fragments into one text.

The two foci of the *Rāmāyaṇa* are the events which centre on the kingdom of Ayodhyā, and those which narrate the period of exile culminating in the battle at Laṅkā.[39] Within each a number of sub-fragments can be detected.[40] Apart from specific interpolations, which are many, there are two substantial additions, the first and last books. The attribution of these to Bhṛgu redactors remains a matter of controversy.[41] These are extraneous to the story and appear to have been added mainly for didactic purposes. Both additional books carry some of the stock-in-trade narratives also found in the Vedic corpus, the *Mahābhārata*, and later in the *Purāṇas.*

It has been argued that the Vālmīki *Rāmāyaṇa* evolved in five stages. The initial version of the story was the narrative in Books 2–6. This was put together in the fifth-fourth centuries BC and revised with periodic interpolations from the third century BC to the first century AD. The text was by then in written form. In the subsequent two centuries, Books 1 and 7 were added. From the fourth to the twelfth centuries AD small passages were incorporated.[42] The Rāmopākhyāna from the *Mahābhārata* seems to be based on the second stage.[43] The Bālakāṇḍa (Book 1) narrates the antecedents to the main story. The Ayodhyākāṇḍa (Book 2), as the name implies, focuses on the kingdom of Kosala. The Araṇyakāṇḍa (Book 3) appropriately sees the *rākṣasas* in action and the kidnapping of Sītā. The Kiṣkindhākāṇḍa (Book 4) is essentially the book of the *vānaras*. The Sundarakāṇḍa (Book 5) sees Hanumān in Laṅkā. The Yuddhakāṇḍa (Book 6) narrates

[39] A.K. Warder, *Indian Kavya Literature*, vol. II; R. Thapar, *Exile and the Kingdom*; Introduction in *The Rāmāyaṇa of Vālmīki, Vol. II: Ayodhyākāṇḍa*, ed. S. Pollock (gen. ed. R.P. Goldman).

[40] C. Bulcke, *Rāmakathā*; J. Brockington, *Righteous Rāma*.

[41] 12.57.40; N.J. Shende, "Authorship of the Ramayana", 19–24.

[42] J. Brockington, *Righteous Rāma*, 348ff.; N. Sen, "Comparative Studies in Oral Epic Poetry and the Vālmīki *Rāmāyaṇa*", 397–409; R. Antoine, *Rama and the Bards: Epic Memory in the Ramayana*; *The Rāmāyaṇa of Vālmīki, Vol. I: Bālakāṇḍa*, ed. and trans. R.P. Goldman, 14ff.

[43] J. Brockington, *Righteous Rāma,* 301.

the battle between Rāma and Rāvaṇa, the fire ordeal of Sītā and Rāma's triumphant return to Ayodhyā. The Uttarakāṇḍa (Book 7) carries a kind of postscript on Rāvaṇa.

The last book also has the add-on of Sītā's second fire ordeal and the recitation of the epic by the sons of Rāma. Highlighting heroic qualities, and the initial characteristics of a kingly hero so evident in the Ayodhyākāṇḍa, the epic gradually absorbs the idea of Rāma as an *avatāra* of Viṣṇu. Some have argued that this is emphasized more in the later books than the earlier. The references may be occasional in the earlier books but the insistence is more emphatic in the later. Association with a deity becomes an additional way of glorifying kingship. This kind of kingship came to be more recognized by the Gupta period, but its projection earlier was also a counter to other political systems.

The first and last books also present the major evidence for the brahmanization of the text in the form of frequent references to the four *varṇas*, the importance of *dharma* and *daṇḍa* to the functioning of the king, Rāma as an *avatāra* of Viṣṇu, and Rāma-bhakti being as important if not more so than the performance of *yajñas*.[44] Being put together over a period of time meant that the context of the narrative changed with historical change—from heroes in conflict to the complexities of kingdoms.

The basic story contains the raw material of all epic tales. But I would like to suggest that, unlike the *Mahābhārata,* the *Rāmāyaṇa* is not essentially the story of a family feud but rather of a confrontation between two types of society: the kingdom of Kosala and the more diffused society of the *rākṣasa*.[45] It is possible to place the many other societies in the epic along a spectrum between these two. The hero, Rāma, is the eldest son of king Daśaratha, who rules from the city of Ayodhyā over the kingdom of Kosala situated in the middle Ganges plain. Daśaratha's sons are born after the performance of a special ritual and grow up as accomplished princes. The forests in the vicinity are the haunts of the *rākṣasas*, who interfere with the sacrificial rituals of ascetics living in forest

[44] "*Rāmo dharmabhṛtām varaḥ*", in G. Bailey and M. Brockington, *Epic Threads*, 250–64; J. Brockington, *Righteous Rāma*, 425ff.

[45] This has been commented upon by earlier scholars. See A.A. MacDonell, *History of Sanskrit Literature*, 312–13.

hermitages. Rāma and his younger brother Lakṣmaṇa are called upon to rid the forest of these demons. This they do and then proceed to the court of the neighbouring king, Janaka of Mithilā.

Here a *svayamvara* is being held for Janaka's daughter Sītā. The choice of husband is dependent on which of the princes gathered there can lift and bend a massive bow. Rāma alone does so and Sītā becomes his bride. On their return to Ayodhyā, Daśaratha announces the installation of Rāma as the future king. But Rāma's stepmother Kaikeyī, prodded by her hunchback maid, reminds her husband of a promise which he had made to her earlier. Kaikeyī therefore demands that her own son, Bharata, should succeed Daśaratha, and that Rāma be exiled for fourteen years. Daśaratha, true to his word, sadly gives in. Rāma, Sītā, and Lakṣmaṇa, the latter two voluntarily, go into exile, wandering in the forests of the Vindhya hills. Bharata tries to persuade Rāma to return but he refuses as it would be contrary to his father's order.

Descriptions of the idyllic life in the forest are interrupted by the kidnapping of Sītā by the powerful *rākṣasa* Rāvaṇa, who takes her away in his aerial chariot to his home in Laṅkā. Rāma and Lakṣmaṇa discover her whereabouts with the help of their monkey ally Hanumān. In order to recover Sītā, Rāma goes into battle against Rāvaṇa and, after a fierce confrontation, Rāvaṇa is killed. Sītā is rescued but has to go through a fire ordeal to prove her chastity. The three then return to Ayodhyā where, the period of exile being completed, and Daśaratha having died meanwhile, Rāma is crowned. His reign, projected as utopian, has been encapsulated in the phrase *rāma-rājya.*

The role of Rāma as the incarnation of Viṣṇu is highlighted, particularly in the first and seventh books, converting the epic into a Bhāgavata text. The first book includes the appeal by the gods to Viṣṇu to incarnate himself as Rāma in order to destroy the evil Rāvaṇa. The seventh book narrates Sītā's exile to the hermitage of Vālmīki, where her twin sons, Kuśa and Lava, are born and raised, and the poem is composed. This addition would also have highlighted the status of Vālmīki.

The names of Sītā's sons are curious since *kuśīlavah* was the term used for bards, hardly an appropriate status for scions of royalty. Vālmīki teaches the boys his epic poem of the deeds of

Rāma, and they recite it at Rāma's *aśvamedha* sacrifice. The latter is much moved and sends for Sītā but insists that she undergo yet another fire ordeal, whereupon she protests her innocence and appeals to her mother, the earth, and is immediately taken back into the earth from where she was born.

In the earlier text, therefore, the lineage ended with Rāma, who was still childless. By adding the story of his two sons, and his bequeathing the northern and southern kingdoms of Kosala to them, there was the possibility now of other descent groups latching themselves onto one of the sons, and attempting thereby to establish their status—as indeed happened later. The seventh book also elaborates upon the high status of Rāvaṇa, making him a suitable enemy for Viṣṇu incarnated as Rāma. The fading out of the ruling lineage in both epics is crucial, suggesting the end of an age. In the *Mahābhārata* succession goes through Parikṣit, the still-born foetus revived by Kṛṣṇa, and in the *Rāmāyaṇa* it goes through Kuśa and Lava, effectively low-status bards.

The question of whether the *Rāmāyaṇa* was a collation of *ākhyānas* currently familiar and therefore remaining a trifle disjointed in the epic, or whether it was conceived as a single narrative, remains controversial.[46] Where the *Dasaratha Jātaka* initially parallels the story of the Ayodhyākāṇḍa, there is also the much-discussed Rāmopākhyāna in the *Mahābhārata* which concentrates on later events, the central feature being the kidnapping of Sītā, and follows more closely the Vālmīki narrative.[47] Rāma refuses to take Sītā back, irrespective of her relations with Rāvaṇa.[48] But the gods, joined by the spirit of the dead Daśaratha, proclaim her innocence. This is reminiscent of the celestial voices which proclaim the innocence of Śakuntalā in the *Mahābhārata*.[49] It appears to have been an early epic device which was later changed to fire ordeals, and rings associated with memory.

[46] Discussed in *The Rāmāyaṇa of Vālmīki, I: Bālākaṇḍa*, trans. R.P. Goldman, 29ff.; *The Rāmāyaṇa of Vālmīki, Vol. II: Ayodhyākāṇḍa*, trans. S. Pollock, 9ff.; see also R. Gombrich, "The *Vessantara Jātaka*, the *Rāmāyaṇa* and the *Dasaratha Jātaka*", 427–37.

[47] 3.258–75.

[48] 3.275.14.

[49] I.62ff.

If the story is seen analytically in terms of the constituents of a folktale, then it is strikingly consistent. The *Rāmāyaṇa* seems to combine an original adventure narrative with a romance genre, and the interweaving is so effective that it passes for a single story based on the structure of a folktale. Embedded in the story is the epic narrative, which follows the stereotype common to such narratives, focusing on the trials and tribulations of the hero in many cultures. He has to be of an aristocratic or warrior family and his birth comes about as a result of a specially performed ritual: this marks him out as unique. He shows his prowess in attacking enemies, demons, and supernatural beings, and also in performing a feat by which he wins the hand of the heroine.[50] He is denied his legitimate inheritance through the machinations of a close kinsman or kinswoman and goes into exile. The heroine frequently accompanies him. She is kidnapped, and this forms the second part of the story. She is located and allies are found to help the hero recover her. The battle with the villain is described at length and is followed by the victory of the hero. The action moves out of cosmological time and, momentarily at least, enters linear time.

Exile is a frequent device in epics as it provides a condition outside the normal. This allows a play of fantasy on person and event, the breaking of convention and an occasion for the bard to extend the story by weaving in other narratives. Given that every forest was said to be infested with predators, demons, and supernatural beings, and could be a place of extreme pain, exile in a forest allowed for the display of heroic qualities.[51] The heroes are less the boastful warriors given to sumptuous consumption and more the ideal *kṣatriyas*. Nevertheless, the forest poses something of a challenge not only from the *rākṣasas* but also from the *ṛṣis* whom the heroes are protecting, and who symbolize a different kind of authority—a moral authority feared even by the gods. If the forest is the background to the romantic narrative it is also the haunt of renouncers, opters out, ascetics, those who have forsaken social

[50] V. Propp, *The Morphology of the Folktale*; idem, *Theory and History of Folklore*; S. Thompson, *Motif-Index of Folk Literature*.

[51] *Rāmāyaṇa,* 2.25.4, 13.

obligations.[52] The culture of the *rākṣasas* is depicted as alien, and this is enhanced by their being demonized and thereby treated with contempt. Rāma has to protect the *ṛṣis* but also come to terms with their power—to accept their authority. The forest is an area of ambivalence where the future of chiefdoms and kingdoms is being contested prior to the main contest on the battlefield. But neither can claim a clear articulation of its aspirations.

The Authors

The first and seventh books carry some information of a biographical nature on Vālmīki, which is in keeping with the general practice that some information be given about the author. But the information is sparse to the point of being almost negligible and largely fanciful. He is said to be a *ṛṣi* living with other such in an *āśrama* on the banks of the Tamasa. He observes a pair of *krauñca* birds courting, and one of them is shot by a Niṣāda hunter. The grief of the other inspires him to compose a verse which becomes the prototype *śloka* and is immediately memorized by his Bharadvāja disciple.[53] The grief of the surviving mate evokes in Vālmīki the empathy to tell the story of another grief, the story of Sītā.[54] It is ironic that the composition eventually undermined the grief of Sītā by glorifying the actions of Rāma, whose rejection of Sītā was the cause of her grief.

As in the *Mahābhārata*, the frame of the story is a ritual occasion and there is an echo of earlier times when the recitation of *ākhyānas* punctuated the rituals of the *aśvamedha*. Here too the epic recitation overwhelms the ritual. The *Mahābhārata* refers to Vālmīki as a distinguished *ṛṣi*, as the author of a particular form of *śloka*, and as the son of Garuḍa.[55] The antecedents of Vālmīki are unclear, although he is mentioned as a Bhārgava in the Uttarakāṇḍa, as also by Aśvaghoṣa, and in the *Viṣṇu Purāṇa*.[56]

[52] R. Thapar, "Renunciation: The Making of a Counter-culture", in idem, *Cultural Pasts*, 876–913.

[53] 1.2.4ff.

[54] 1.4.6–7.

[55] 2.7.14, 3.83.103–4, 6.59.29, 5.99.11; G.H. Bhatt, "On Vālmīki", 1–4.

[56] *Rāmāyaṇa*, 7.84.16; *Buddhacarita* 1.43; *Viṣṇu Purāṇa*, 3.3.18; J. Brockington, *The Sanskrit Epics*, 394; C. Bulcke, "About Materials for the Biography of

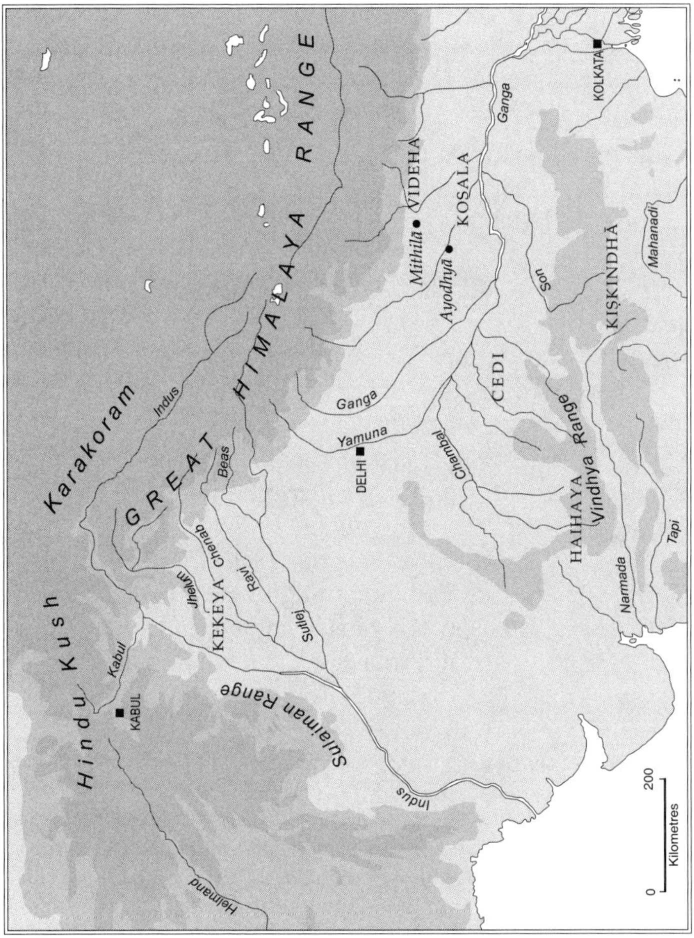

Map 3: Locations of the More Important Places, Clans, and Dynasties

If the story was taken over from the bards, a concession seems to have been made to them by *brāhmaṇa* authorship in naming Rāma's twin sons Kuśa and Lava. As such, their caste ranking should create a problem.[57] In a lineage-based society the bards had a high status, but later, when caste society is well established, their ranking is low.

Both terms have another meaning and are used for the sacred grass in the ritual of sacrifice: the upper grass being *kuśa* and the lower, *lava*. The *kuśa* is also a small wooden pin used as a marker in recitation.[58] In one text they are treated with suspicion. Their low status made them suitable recruits as spies for the state. It also recommends that a courtesan's son from the age of 8 should work as a *kuśīlava.*[59]

The *kuśīlava* are included among professional actors, as are *cāraṇas*, and they are paid wages so that they do not take to robbing people.[60] Such occupations are not normally associated with *kṣatriyas,* but the *kṣatriya* ambience might have given them status. However, this was not generally conceded. One text says that they have to be treated as *śūdras*, another that they are a *sankīrṇa-jāti* (mixed caste), and in yet another that they should be banished from towns.[61]

The *Rāmāyaṇa* mentions that the *sūtas* and *māgadhas,* as bards, should awaken the king in the morning by their compositions.[62] Daśaratha's *sūta,* Sumantra, is his friend as well as his eulogist but also has the status of a minister.[63] Mention is made of the

---

Vālmīki, Author of the First Rāmāyaṇa", 346–8; see also R.P. Goldman,"Vālmīki and the Bhṛgu Connection", 69ff.

[57] J. Gonda, *History of Indian Literature*, vol. III, 333; H. Jacobi, *Das Rāmāyaṇa: Geschichte und Inhalt nebst Concordanz der gedruckten Recensionen,* 62ff.; G.H. Bhatt, "On Vālmīki", 1–4; *Manu's Code of Law*, 3.155, 158; *Gautama Dharmasūtra*, 15.18; *Āpastamba Dharmasūtra*, ed. G. Buhler, 1.1.3.11–12, 2.25.4; *Rāmāyaṇa*, 1.4.4–9ff.

[58] 7.58.4–9; cf. 1.4.3–11, 7.84.6–15.

[59] *Arthaśāstra*, 2.27.6–7.

[60] *Arthaśāstra*, 4.1.58–65.

[61] *Arthaśāstra*, 3.7.32; *Mahābhārata*, 12.69.49.

[62] 2.82.8.

[63] 1.7.1–2, 1.8.2–5.

purāṇavid, the *vedavid*, and the *sārathi*.[64] The story of Sītā's sons would tend to confirm the uneven relationship between the *brāhmaṇas* and the bards. Is the recitation by the twins a hint that the composition was originally by the bards and was then reformulated by Vālmīki, a *brāhmaṇa*, as an epic poem? There is once again the curious play on authorship and kinship. If Vyāsa was both the author of the *Mahābhārata* and the grandfather of the heroes, here Vālmīki was both the author of the *Rāmāyaṇa* and the foster-father of the sons of Rāma.

Table III

Abbreviated Descent List

Manu	
Ikṣvāku	
Vikukṣi	Nimi
	Mithi Janaka
	Devarata
Sagara	
Dilīpa	
Raghu	
Aja	
Daśaratha	Sīradhvaja
Rāma	

64 2.13.17, 2.14.1, 2.29.4, 6.116.19.

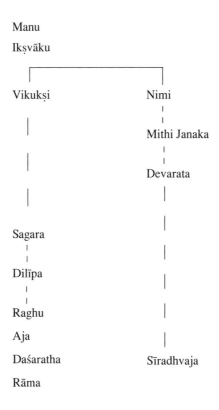

Genealogy and Caste

The epic is a validation of *kṣatriya* society, so its social concerns are limited to an elite and not to ordinary people. The focus is on the kin groups of the *rājās*. In the transition to kingship the group expands to include non-kin. Rituals of legitimation continue to be a necessity. Daśaratha has to perform the *putreṣṭi-medha* and the *aśvamedha* to obtain sons.[65] This is not the world of ordinary people. *Kṣatriya* status derives from birth, so genealogies are appended for both Daśaratha and Janaka.[66] They are recited at the wedding, an appropriate occasion to claim status.

Rāma's ancestry begins with Brahmā and comes down via various *ṛṣis* to Manu and his son Ikṣvāku, and continues with this lineage. The next segment is a descent list of heroes covering many generations. Some are just names, and a few other—such as Mandhātṛ, Sagara, and Dilīpa—performed heroic acts. The genealogy is repeated with marginal changes in the Ayodhyākāṇḍa, suggesting this might have been the earlier one.[67] This also parallels the repetition of the genealogy in the *Mahābhārata*. The lineage is described as that of the Ikṣvākus. A break is suggested by Asita attacking the Haihayas, Tālajaṅghas, and others of the Yadu lineage, which would have included the Vṛṣṇis and Cedis. His relationship to the successor Sagara is not clear. Both epics suggest hostility between the lineage of the heroes and that of the Yadus, which might reflect an age-old enmity, a difference in polity, or competition to control valuable territory, as for example the route going to the peninsula—the *dakṣināpatha*—traversing the Vindhyas and crossing the Narmada. The binary is underlined in their belonging to two different major lineages—the Sūryavaṃśa and the Candravaṃśa.

Janaka's genealogy is shorter and, significantly, does not go back to a deity. It begins with the Nimi, also descended from Ikṣvāku, thus making them collateral lineages. Only the eldest sons are named in both descent lists. Association with the gods underlines status and divine connections, but genealogies seek to establish legitimacy, and it is important that legitimacy be maintained

[65] *Rāmāyaṇa*, 2.40.19–20.
[66] 1.69.15ff., 1.70.1–14.
[67] 2.102.2ff.

throughout. The central event focuses on rightful succession, with the right of the eldest son being subverted when Rāma is sent into exile. Problems over succession occur between paired brothers, Rāma and Bharata, Rāvaṇa and Vibhīṣaṇa, and Vālin and Sugrīva.[68] Genealogies are intended to underline kinship connections and clearly the emphasis here is on the two collateral lines of Daśaratha and Janaka.[69] By including the genealogical portions and maintaining therefore that the epics recorded a slice of the *itihāsa-purāṇa* tradition, an element of believed history was introduced.

With the establishing of a kingdom, caste becomes an important source of identity. Interpolations, even when mentioning caste, are not altogether arbitrary or without a historical context. A heightened consciousness of caste in the late books parallels the Śānti and Anuśāsana *parvans* in the *Mahābhārata*. This is noticeable in the elevated status of the *brāhmaṇa* in contrast to the *śūdra*, and the prohibition on the mixing of castes.[70] The reign of Rāma will ensure the system of *varṇas*;[71] and references to *varṇas* and *śūdras* increase in the later sections. The abject condition of the *sūdra* is clear from the story of Rāma killing Śambūka, the *śūdra* who had dared to become an ascetic (Book 7). Rāma's action is justified as conforming to the rules of *varṇa*.[72] This contrasts with Rāma's earlier acceptance of food from Śabarī of the forest-dwellers,[73] who is described as a *śramaṇī* and is therefore of the heterodox group. Interestingly, his first ally in exile is Guha, the chief of the *niṣādajātyaḥ*, the Niṣāda clan.[74]

Chiefdoms

The function of the Vālmīki version in the propagation of Vaiṣṇava belief and practice has received great attention. This has tended to divert interest from other aspects which are significant. I would

68 2.16.33, 2.97–8, 6.10.1–11, 6.51.1–26.

69 N.R. Wagle, "A Study of Kinship Groups in the Ramayana of Valmiki", 17–142.

70 1.6.16–17, 7.65.6–7.

71 1.1.75, 5.33.11, 6.113.29.

72 7.67.

73 3.70.6–9; J. Brockington, *Righteous Rāma*, 158.

74 2.44.9ff., 2.78.1ff.

like to argue that Vālmīki's original version of the story symbolizes the triumph of kingship, and the epic therefore becomes a charter of validation for kingdoms, which would be one reason among many for its currency in later times. This introduces the perception of what is believed to be the past, as expressed in the epic, and as an element of the historical tradition. This element is further expressed in different versions in different periods over recompositions of the story, and the variations reflect historical change.

I have tried to show in the previous chapter that the consciousness of historical change in an epic form is articulated in the *Mahābhārata* by the two types of societies which emerge from the narrative and didactic sections, indicating the change from lineage-based chiefships to kingdoms. In the *Rāmāyaṇa*, the consciousness of historical change uses the same categories but expresses it by a sharper contrast. Here, kingship is not an abstract notion but a functioning reality. The *rākṣasa* and the *vānara* communities, to which respectively Rāvaṇa and Hanumān belong, are closer in form and spirit to chiefships, whereas the kingdom of Rāma is the exemplar of early kingship. The hostility or the alliances in some instances are symbolic of the fading away of the earlier society and the increasing success of kingdoms.

The dichotomy, however, is neither deliberate nor always consistent. Within each there is more of some and less of some. Thus, the kingdom of Ayodhyā, recently evolved, is one where the institutions of monarchy are present but perhaps not as yet fully entrenched. This can sometimes result in anachronisms or contradictory situations. Similarly, the depiction of *rākṣasa* activities in the forest is different from their activities in the city of Lankā, where the context appears to approximate kingship although it is not actually so. The society of the *rākṣasas* tends to conform to the organization of chiefships. There is also a variety of forest-dwellers, such as *vānaras*, who would be included in this range.

The later editors, familiar with kingdoms and courtly norms, were nevertheless attempting to retain a sense of the earlier narrative and its depiction of a different social context. This would suggest the awareness that the text being redacted related to a different and earlier kind of society, else once again it would have been recomposed in an idiom of contemporary times—as happened in later adaptations of the narrative.

Vālmīki's *rākṣasas* may well have been entirely fanciful. But since they are described as having the appurtenances of a human society, the assumptions implicit in these descriptions need to be analysed. Their polity and society follows a distinctive pattern. In the earlier books, the societies of both Kosala and the *rākṣasas* are relatively simple and the *rākṣasas* approximate closely to human society. The *rākṣasas* are seen more as enemies than as demons, although they magically transform themselves into animals and creatures of fantasy. Rāvaṇa's wife refers to him as *āryaputra*, indicating status and nobility.[75] The differences were of form and patterns of living in two contesting societies.

Unlike kingdoms, there are no boundaries to their territories and they wander at will, claiming the forests as their territory. The city of Laṅkā, being an island, is perforce bounded but the territorial control of Rāvaṇa is never clearly defined. The location of Laṅkā, however well-fortified, remains vague and somewhat fictitious in its exaggerated wealth. The *rākṣasas* are widely distributed and tied by kinship links rather than territorial proximity. In place of kingship they seem to function as a chiefship, and when in groups they are referred to as *gaṇas*.[76]

The *rākṣasas* have virtually no genealogies, although reference is made to some ancestors. In a late book, some of the *rākṣasas* are said to belong to the Paulastya line which also originated in the middle Ganges plain at Vaiśāli, but little is said of their descent.[77] Nevertheless, kinsmen are of considerable importance, as for instance in the deliberations of Rāvaṇa when Laṅkā is under attack.[78]

The term *senā* is used for the army in the early sections and military formations such as the *akṣauhīni* are more frequently mentioned in the later sections.[79] The four wings of the army are

[75] J.L. Brockington, "Religious Attitudes in Vālmīki's *Rāmāyaṇa*", 108–30.

[76] 5.41.12, 5.46.14.

[77] *Rāmāyaṇa* 7.2.3ff.; F.E. Pargiter, *Ancient Indian Historical Tradition*, 241ff.

[78] 6.6.1.ff., 6.7.1ff.

[79] J. Brockington, *Righteous Rāma,* 134–5.

listed,[80] but these appear to be formal descriptions. Among weapons, the largest number of references is to bows and arrows, which would rather contradict the conventional four wings.[81] Whereas the armies had regular weapons, the monkey forces fought with trees and stones, as did some of the *rākṣasas*.[82]

The association with magic allows the *rākṣasas* to assume various forms and to materialize weaponry of an exalted kind, suggestive of poetic fantasy. Thus, the aerial chariot is a characteristic feature of Rāvaṇa's equipment. The demonizing of the *rākṣasa* and an association with magic could be born of fear of the enemy. The *rākṣasas* have the characteristics of supernatural beings, but can more often perhaps be viewed as fantasized aliens. The physical descriptions of the *rākṣasas*, including Rāvaṇa, deploy phrases that are conventionally used in other texts for forest-dwellers such as Śabaras and Niṣādas. Thus, it is repeatedly said that Rāvaṇa or the *rākṣasas* look like a mass of black antimony—*nīlāñjana*; they are short-statured and with bloodshot eyes; they resemble mountains and roar like the thunder—a formulaic description of forest-dwellers.[83] Hence also the frequent epithet of *megha* in their names, as for instance Meghanāda. The elements highlighted are their violence, their magical power to metamorphose like the gods, and their intemperate sexuality.[84]

To these may be added the even more significant characteristic, which is that they do not observe the *varṇāśrama-dharma,* and therefore rules of social hierarchy, commensality, consanguinity, and pollution. In fact they reverse the rules. They do have some social differentiations, but not deeply marked and not derived from caste. Śūrpaṇakhā's actions suggest that their women are forthcoming, and she is a contrast to the submissive Sītā. Rāma and his brothers are monogamous but Rāvaṇa is polygamous and picks up wives wherever he chooses. Rāma was expected to protect the four *varṇas*.[85] By implication, he would be opposed

[80] 2.73.9, 2.107.11, 3.28.2.

[81] J. Brockington, *Righteous Rāma,* 140.

[82] 6.95.17–18.

[83] 5.47.7, 6.48.36, 5.1.29.

[84] *The Rāmāyaṇa of Vālmīki, Vol. III: Araṇyakāṇḍa*, trans. S. Pollock, 68ff., 2.108.8ff.

[85] 5.33.11.

to those that did not organize their society accordingly, such as the *rākṣasas*.

There is a small distinction, however, in the depiction of the *rākṣasas* of the forest and those of Laṅkā. The latter observe some of the familiar forms, such as Rāvaṇa living in a palace, although they can relapse into ways regarded as uncivilized. The contrast is made apparent in the Sundarakāṇḍa, where the recitations and the *yajñas* of the *rākṣasas* in Lankā resemble those of *brāhmaṇa* ascetics. But these are called *yātudhāna,* referring to sorcery rather than to ritual.[86] A difference in religion is indicated by the association of the *rākṣasas* with *caityas*. These were the locations of non-*brāhmaṇa* cults and centres of *yakṣa* worship, among others. As sacred spaces and funerary mounds they were segregated from Vedic ritual. Laṅkā has a large *caitya* covered with jewels.[87]

As a general category the *rākṣasas* are referred to as *anārya,*[88] where *ārya* is one who is to be respected. Their being alien is heightened by a different set of norms, but their magical powers and violence are feared, a fear which is exaggerated by their habitat being the unknown forest. All that is thought to be contrary is imputed to them. This makes them different from other *anāryas* or *mlecchas*, who are outside the pale of the *varṇāśrama-dharma* but are still familiar—such as some clans of the north-west.

There is mention neither of plough agriculture nor of merchants, yet Laṅkā is said to be fabulously wealthy, its buildings adorned with trimmings of gold and gems.[89] The source of this wealth is not mentioned nor any association with wealth-producing activities. It may therefore have been poetic exaggeration. The *rākṣasas* who lived off the forest require large tracts for hunting, for grazing, and for swidden agriculture; they would therefore see encroachers wishing to clear and settle in the forest as natural enemies. Even when there is a distinct shift in their representation, as for instance Rāvaṇa in Laṅkā, and they are not restricted to the forest, they represent a different political and social system, one which was required to be terminated in the interests of the extension of kingship and the sources from which kingdoms derived

[86] 5.3.26–8, 5.4.12.

[87] 5.13.15–17.

[88] 3.17.19.

[89] D.R. Chanana, *The Spread of Agriculture in Northern India*.

their sustenance. The *rākṣasas* seem to derive their wealth only from forests and mineral resources. Vālmīki's demonizing of the *rākṣasas* is both the demeaning of clan society as well as of the earlier polities prior to kingship. This becomes more obvious in the later alternative versions.

However, a sharp dichotomy between the two societies is not invariably present and there is a gradation from the *vānaras* to the forest *rākṣasas*, to the *rākṣasas* of Laṅkā, to the people of Ayodhyā. In the positioning of various societies, conquest would more likely have brought about a disruptive cultural change. The *rākṣasas* were undergoing a slow mutation in adapting to the culture of kingdoms, cities, and castes. This was accelerated by the enclaves of settlements in the form of the *āśramas* of *ṛṣis*. Such settlements seemingly allowed various cultures to coexist. But, with increasing patronage to the hermitages by royalty, their presence would have aggravated the pressure of change on the forest-dwellers. This is reflected in a comparison with the *Paumacariyam*, as we shall see, where the descriptions in the later text refer to a changed landscape from the forests of the *Rāmāyaṇa*.

The Enhancement of Kingship

The geographical horizon of the text extended from the kingdom of Kosala in the middle Ganges plain into Central India. The northern links are implicit in the Kosala–Kekeya alliance and are referred to marginally, as when Bharata visits his maternal uncle. The forest to which Rāma goes is a few days' journey from Ayodhyā and across the Ganges. The boundary of Kosala is known to Rāma, who refers to their first night outside the territory of Kosala.[90] The major part of the narrative, the theme of exile, seems to be geographically located in the Ganges plain impinging on Central India.[91] The condition of exile also serves to emphasize

[90] 2.47.2.

[91] This question relates to the complex discussion on the location of Laṅkā. Most scholars have located it in the Vindhyas or in the Amarakantaka region, and some locate it more to the east of this region. I have suggested a location in the region of Kaliṅga rather than the popularly believed Sri Laṅkā. See R. Thapar, "The *Rāmāyaṇa*: Theme and Variation", in idem, *Cultural Pasts*,

the contrast between the kingdom and the forest. The kingdom is the *rājya* and the territory is the *deśa/rāṣṭra/janapada/viṣaya* with its town (*pura* or *nagara*), the term *paurajānapada* denoting the people of the territory. The *paura* (townspeople) are different from those of the territory of Kosala, the *paurajānapada*.[92]

Economic differences are apparent. Kosala is associated with agriculture and its wealth is measured in terms of storehouses stocked with grain together with the activities of traders and merchants.[93] Although agriculture, cattle-rearing, and trade are mentioned as the three occupations of the *vaiśya*, the plough is referred to in the later books.[94] Merchants active in the city and the span of occupations associated with urban life occur more naturally in descriptions of Ayodhyā, and in the first and last books, although passing mention is made of shops and markets in other parts of the text.[95] Descriptions of Ayodhyā mention the royal highway—the spine of urban centres—as also open spaces, gardens, orchards, many-storeyed buildings and palaces, horses, elephants, and chariots. Courtesans are another characteristic feature and accompany the retinue that bids farewell to Rāma when he leaves for the forest.[96] Incidental references, however, indicate that palaces were perhaps still rather simple buildings. The distraught Kauśalyā who grieves on Rāma's departure is said to fall on the dust-covered floor.[97]

Wealth is demonstrated by quantities of grain—*dhanadhānya*—while grain and jewels fill the *kośa* and the princes gave magnificent gifts.[98] Coins are not referred to, although they existed at the

---

647–79. A recent and plausible attempt has been made to plot the geography of this exile using topo-sheets, Google Earth, and field surveys, and this confirms the area of the Vindhyas. S. Agashe, *The Geography of the Ramayana*, forthcoming.

[92] 1.12.10–12.

[93] 1.5.17.

[94] 1.38.19, 7.17.30.

[95] 1.5, 1.6, 2.6.12, 2.13.2, 2.106.13, 1.31.4–7, 4.32.5, 2.61.7ff., 2.77.12–15, 7.62.11–12.

[96] 2.32.3, 45.19–21.

[97] 2.17.8, 37.10, 40.25.

[98] 2.30.17–18, 2.15.2–3, 2.29.5–17, 1.6.6.

time of the text. Even the word *niṣka*, sometimes taken to be a coin, occurs sparingly.[99] The description of Ayodhyā as an urban centre is familiar from descriptions of other cities elsewhere. Wealth is also measured by the giving of gifts, either to *brāhmaṇas* on the conclusion of a ritual (such as the funeral rites for Daśaratha), or to bards when patrons are pleased with their eulogies, or even when elder kinsmen wish to show their affection for the younger ones (such as the gifts to Bharata from his maternal kinsmen, the Kekeyas). Cattle, horses, elephants, and gold are the preferred objects of gift-giving, and although land is referred to, as are houses and grain, these are limited to the kingdom of Kosala.[100]

The emergent state was dependent on economic activities bringing in revenue and ensuring a full treasury. Administration was necessary for regular collection of revenue and its redistribution to the agencies of governance. Agricultural taxes are not mentioned but were probably known as reference is made to *viṣṭi* (labour tax).[101] Coercion was a fallback should peasants, artisans, and merchants resist providing revenue. Such resistance is referred to in the *Jātakas*, where peasants migrate from a kingdom that imposes oppressive taxes.[102] The city was now the centre of administration and exchange, reflecting a socio-economic change. Its prosperity and multiple activities could have been exaggerated, as obviously were the measurements of its size. These were more a metaphor of expansion than meant to be taken literally. There is no mention of the known cities of the time, such as Rājagṛha in Magadha, or Takṣaśila in Gandhāra, or Śrāvasti and Vaiśāli nearer home.

The concern with primogeniture reflects a kingship in which hereditary authority has passed into the hands of a particular family whose legitimacy is based on descent—hence Daśaratha's anxiety at not having a son to succeed him.[103] Status is further emphasized by the introduction of legends narrating the lives of royal ancestors, even though the actual order of descent in the

[99] J. Brockington, *Righteous Rāma*, 62ff.
[100] 2.64.17ff., 2.28.7, 29.11–16, 71.2–3, 6.113.41.
[101] 6.115.4.
[102] *Gaṇḍatindu Jātaka,* no. 520, in *The Jātaka.*
[103] *Rāmāyaṇa*, 1.8.1ff.

Rāmāyaṇa does not tally with those in other texts.[104] Whereas in the *Jātaka* story Vessantara is exiled by the angry subjects of his father, in the *Rāmāyaṇa* the citizens of Ayodhyā, unhappy with Daśaratha's decision to exile Rāma, can do nothing to change it.

The Ayodhyākāṇḍa is the validation of kingship.[105] Genealogy as one agency of this record becomes more important than before and has to be underlined and repeated. The king is the protector of *dharma* and of the *prajā*.[106] This involves enforcing the *varṇāśrama-dharma*, a use of authority that is different from the system of the chiefships, or from that of Buddhist thinking that prevailed in many *gaṇa-saṅghas* of the middle Ganges plain. The concentration of power is expressed in the will of the king—which should not be opposed.[107]

The characteristics of an acceptable kingdom lie in fulfilling its norms: economic prosperity where revenues exceed expenditure, the observance of *varṇāśrama-dharma,* the prevalence of justice so that crimes are punished, and the welfare of the subjects.[108] The *sabhā,* or assembly of the heads of clans central to the functioning of chiefships, was replaced by the *mantrīs, amātyas*, and *pariṣad* of the royal court.[109] The absence of kingship and the evils of a kingless state—*arājya*—are conditions of chaos. Kingship poses new problems for the epic genre, the focus being now on hereditary royal power as an established norm,[110] in the hands of a single family. Rāma, the hero, becomes the ideal king because of his concern for the *dharma* necessary to dynastic stability and power. However, listening to public opinion has less to do with politics and focuses on the chastity of Sītā, which Rāma is unwilling to defend.

Rāma is required to seek legitimacy through performing Vedic rituals. The narrative is generally not interrupted by homilies,

[104] *Viṣṇu Purāṇa*, 4.5, 4.2.

[105] *The Rāmāyaṇa of Vālmīki*, *Vol. II: Ayodhyākāṇḍa*, trans. S. Pollock.

[106] There is a dire description of a land without a king, 2.61.7–25.

[107] *Rāmāyaṇa*, 2.46.18.

[108] Cf. 2.94.37–58.

[109] 2.30.15–20.

[110] 2.61; Introduction in *The Rāmāyaṇa of Vālmīki*, *Vol. II: Ayodhyākāṇḍa*, trans. S. Pollock, 10ff.

but there is an interesting list of errors that a king should avoid.[111] It starts with patronage to people who are *nāstika* and *anṛtaka*—those who do not believe and who lie—indicating a clear sectarian turn with opposition to heterodoxy. In a state without a king there would be no one to protect the subjects and maintain the laws.[112] Qualities of kingly concern and administration are significantly different from the ethic and practices that ensure the success of oligarchies.[113]

A distinction between the two societies of Kosala and Lankā, therefore, lies in the centrality of kingship in the first and the absence or at best the marginality of this in the second. This absence means no rain and therefore no cultivation, no authority, wealth, gardens, sacrificial rituals, festivals, sages, and no security for the rich. Justice would be denied, the tellers of tales would lack an audience, and the army would be ineffective. Destructive atheists would thrive. The law of the fishes—*mātsyanyāya*—would prevail. The reign of the righteous king, *rāma-rājya*, is in sharp contrast with all this.[114]

The power of the king of Kosala is somewhat circumscribed by the assembly, because Daśaratha has to consult the *sabhā* when he decides that Rāma should succeed him and be crowned.[115] At the same time, he speaks of primogeniture being the norm among the Ikṣvākus. Bharata refuses to take up the kingship during the lifetime of his elder brother.[116] Exiling Rāma, on the other hand, is fulfilling a personal promise: Daśaratha takes a unilateral decision and does not consult those whom he did on the earlier occasion. The question of primogeniture also triggers off Lakṣmaṇa's suggestion that Rāma should not acquiesce so easily to his exile and that the two brothers could consider reversing the decision.[117] This suggests a palace coup, the likes of which would not have been easy in a chiefship.

[111] 2.56–58.
[112] 2.61.7–22.
[113] Cf. *Rāmāyaṇa*, 2.94.9.ff., 2.56–8, with *Dīgha Nikāya*, II.76.
[114] 6.116.80–90.
[115] 2.1.35–6.
[116] 2.107.1ff.
[117] 2.18.8–12.

The importance of councillors and functionaries, i.e. *mantrīs* and *dharmapālakas*, is more marked in the late sections of the text. It was the king's duty to protect the people, and in return for this he received the *ṣaḍbhāga* or one-sixth share of the produce as tax.[118] The *sabhā* is also addressed as the *pariṣad.* The *paura-jānapada-janāḥ* suggests a continuity with the earlier assemblies and with *janapadas.*[119] The latter also occur as units of territory, together with *rāṣṭra, deśa*, and later *viśaya*. Towns are mentioned as *pura, paṭṭana*, and *nagara*, and are more frequently associated with activities in Kosala than with those of the *rākṣasas*—even those inhabiting the town of Laṅkā. *Grāmas* and *mahāgrāmas* are different categories of villages in Kosala.[120] Scattered in the countryside of Kosala are a variety of forts and the boundaries are well defined.[121]

The forest is also home to the hermitages of the *ṛṣis* and this serves to highlight two features. One is the dichotomy between the settlement and the wasteland. The *grāma* was the known, the orderly, the predictable, and the *araṇya* was unknown, with no recognizable order; it was where the unexpected could happen. Those who habitually live in the one were unfamiliar to the other, hence the contrast between the people of Kosala and the *rākṣasa*. Hermitages became the vanguard of the settlement encroaching into the forest and not unexpectedly are attacked by those who live in the forest. The hermitage is a threshold condition between settlement and forest, for it is peopled by ascetics who do not fully conform to the mores of either the settled habitations or the forest-dwellers. The *rākṣasa* attacks on the hermitages are consistent. The resentment seems also to have arisen against the *ṛṣis* bringing in a new culture, changing the habitat of forest-dwellers through agriculture, exchange, and the clearing of forests. Rāvaṇa performing sacrifices seems to have been an afterthought.

The *Rāmāyaṇa* eulogizes the kingdom as nurturing the sources of wealth and its administration, maintaining the distinction of caste and hierarchy, and supporting those who were the

[118] 2.69.18, 3.5.10–13.
[119] 2.103.24, 2.2.18.
[120] 2.1.35, 2.51.3.
[121] 2.94.44, 6.3.19, 2.43.7.

legitimizers of the system.[122] This is not characteristic of *rākṣasa* society. In juxtaposing two systems and endorsing one as historically superior to the other, the *Rāmāyaṇa* can be seen as a charter of validation for kingdoms established in areas of erstwhile chiefships. Alternative polities had to be discredited.

Yet another theme introduced into the text through interpolations, which became a powerful support to the political and historical role of kingship, was Vaiṣṇava *bhakti*. It heightens the transformation of the hero. Whether the idea of the divinity of Rāma can be traced to the earliest composition, or whether it was introduced in the later revision, has been debated.[123] The emphasis on divinity is much heavier in the later sections.

The depiction of Rāvaṇa in the late books contradicts the early ones. He is said to be of *brāhmaṇa* descent who undertook the severest asceticism for a thousand years.[124] Subsequent to this he obtained a boon that he would not be killed by either god or *asura*, but did not include man in the request as he thought no man would have the power to kill him. Perhaps it was the confidence which the boon gave him that led to his misdemeanours.[125] Thus, it was a god in the form of a man who was responsible for his death. This image of Rāvaṇa was an oblique projection of the greatness of Rāma in bringing low such a powerful figure.

The text changes its function when Rāma becomes primarily an *avatāra* of Viṣṇu, and as such a necessary part of the literature of Vaiṣṇavism through the new cult of Bhāgavatism. The preferred popular mode of worship was *bhakti* (devotion). Indra, earlier associated with Vedic hymns and sacrificial rituals, is now cut to size in the redacted versions. In one place, Rāma is said to have divine virtues that equate him with Indra; elsewhere, when Indra and Brahmā speak of Rāma as the creator of the universe, the

[122] *Rāmāyaṇa*, 2.61.7ff., 2.94.10–59ff.

[123] *The Rāmāyaṇa of Vālmīki, Vol. III: Araṇyakāṇḍa*, trans. S. Pollock; L. Gonzales-Reiman, "The Divinity of Rāma in the *Rāmāyaṇa* of Vālmīki", 203–20.

[124] *Rāmāyaṇa*, 3.30.17–18, 6.80.22.24, 1.14.5ff., 7.10.10ff.; *Mahābhārata*, 3.259.22ff., 3.265.23.

[125] 3.30.6–20.

reference is to Viṣṇu.[126] It has been argued that the Rāma–Rāvaṇa conflict was an updating, as it were, of the Indra–Vṛtra conflict of the *Ṛgveda*,[127] where Indra destroys the *rākṣasas*.[128]

The *avatāra* grew out of the historical process of acculturation, both in channelling Vaiṣṇava beliefs and values into new areas as well as by incorporating cults from these areas into Vaiṣṇavism. This was useful to the functioning of a state, providing a new identity, binding diverse groups into focusing on a single deity, and giving direction to ritual and belief. Its technique was less to proselytize directly, as did the Buddhists and the Jainas, but to incorporate and absorb. Organizational techniques were probably borrowed from the Sramanic sects, especially the reference to a text and the association of visual representation with the text. But these developments evolved slowly.

Making Rāma an *avatāra* of Viṣṇu reflected on the nature of kingship. Incarnation introduced the idea of the divinity of the king—although Rāma is treated as a mortal in the earlier sections.[129] The epic hero in the early composition had a relationship with the gods that was close but distinct. In a further stage the hero can, on occasion, act like a god. In the final revised version he is the incarnation of a god.[130] The king's analogy with a god stems from his function to protect, which goes back to the early *rājā,* and to ensure the welfare of his subjects.[131] Prior to the full divinization of Rāma, reference is made to kings with elements of the divine, such as the king having a quarter of Indra in him, or that kings are gods who walk the earth in the guise of men.[132] Yet if divinity is required for Rāma to protect his *prajā,* and if the fight against evil is personified in Rāvaṇa, then the heroic ideal is diminished.

[126] 2.2.19, 6.105.5–28.

[127] F. Whaling, *The Rise of the Religious Significance of Rama,* 76ff.

[128] *Ṛgveda*, 7.94.12.

[129] S. Pollock, "The Divine King in the Indian Epic", 505–28; also *The Rāmāyaṇa of Vālmīki, Vol. III: Araṇyakāṇḍa*, trans. S. Pollock; see also *Mahābhārata*, 3.265.28.

[130] J.L. Brockington, *Righteous Rāma*, 218–25.

[131] 1.61.7ff.

[132] 2.95.4, 4.18.38.

Rāvaṇa's recourse to magic and the supernatural distinguishes him from Rāma, who functions as a mortal. The counter-hero often does have these powers which in a sense enhance the glory of the hero, since he has to combat what is more than human. In the opening sections of the first book, Rāma is a man of every virtue. It is only later that the notion of an incarnation of deity is emphasized.[133] Rāma was moving from being an epic hero to becoming the exemplar of a post-epic society. In the circumstances, his decision to accept exile does not arise out of an event, as for example a game of dice, but from a situation which poses a moral dilemma where primogeniture is pitted against his father's agreement that Kaikeyī's son would succeed as king. Rāma has to behave as the exemplar, and this prepares him for the essential function of the king as protector of *dharma.*

A historical change is also being underlined in the association of kingship with divinity. *Rājās* were earlier permitted to share activities with gods but were not gods. The *rājā* as protector was initially the heroic figure governed by heroic values. The *rājā* as king is also a protector but gradually he becomes the protector of *dharma* and can have associations other than mortal. The protector is now also the nourisher. The last stage in the metamorphosis is the king who is the incarnation of divinity, an idea which becomes increasingly frequent in later centuries. It isolates the king from the normal sources of power, and the king's divinity becomes dependent on those who represent the deity on earth.

The change to kingship involved a different manipulation of power from that of chiefships. The obtaining, maintaining, and functioning of power was more focused on the king and the institutions that emerged as the infrastructure of a kingdom and state. Literature associated with the court as the hub of power takes on a different character from that associated with the *sabhā* or assembly-hall of the chief. But some remnants of the clan society do surface. Bharata's legitimacy in succeeding Daśaratha was based on the *rājyaśulka*, an agreement made to Kaikeyī's kinsmen at the time of her marriage by which her son would

133 1.14.; see also C. Bulcke, "The Genesis of the Bālakāṇḍa", 327–31. This has also been taken to suggest that some parts of the Bālakāṇḍa may be old: *The Rāmāyaṇa of Vālmīki, Vol. I: Bālakāṇḍa*, trans. R.P. Goldman, 67ff.

succeed Daśaratha.[134] Such an agreement, hinting at bride-price and an earlier form of polity, may have been unlikely had the Kekeyas also had a hereditary kingship. The "disqualified eldest" is a theme in both epics.

Kingship also raises the question of who legitimizes the king. The idea of his acceptability to the people over whom he rules gradually gave way to *brāhmaṇas* being his legitimizers. The king had to be given the status of a *kṣatriya,* or else be content with the label of *vrātya kṣatriya* (degenerate *kṣatriyas*), as were the Yavanas and Śakas said to have been created by Vasiṣṭha's magical cow.[135] Legitimation was needed where, as in later times, the *kṣatriya* status became relatively open, and where those with some power could consolidate it by resort to fanciful origins and connections. But it would also have been required in earlier times, in the transition to kingship, where the aspirant would wish to claim more than the normal share of power. Thus, when the *kṣatra* is eating the *viś* (as the *Vedas* put it), this act has to be legitimized.[136]

Kingship obviously has its own basis of authority, but it can be buttressed by brahmanical support. In the *Mahābhārata*, legitimacy was acquired through links with the established descent group—the line of Pūru—even though the heroes are unconnected by blood, and through the performance of the required sacrificial rituals, such as the *rājasūya*. The *Rāmāyaṇa* points to a significant shift. The genealogies are brief, the *aśvamedha* is performed by Daśaratha and later by Rāma, but essentially Rāma's qualification is his conforming to *dharma*. The notion of *rāja-dharma*, which enters both epics through the didactic interventions, readjusts the meaning of legitimacy. Rāma asserts his authority more often through his reactions to crises, and his *aśvamedha* is mentioned towards the end of the appended narrative.

The *aśvamedha* he performs is truncated without the presence of the chief queen, since Sītā is no longer present. There is a vast audience of a cross-section of people, as well as *pauraṇikas*, grammarians, dancers, and singers. It is the occasion for Kuśa and Lava to sing the first version of the *Rāmāyaṇa* composed by Vālmīki.

134 2.99.3.

135 1.53.18ff., 1.54.3. Such references are clearly late.

136 *Śatapatha Brāhmaṇa*, 8.7.1.2, 8.7.2.2, 9.4.3.5.

Notions of *dharma* seem to be edging out the centrality of *yajñas*. *Dharma* comes to be defined by the *brāhmaṇas* and the many texts on the subject, some with specific *rāja-dharma* sections, become the manuals of kingship. Was the *Rāmāyaṇa* attempting to be an independent assertion of the king's *dharma* before the interpolations brought it into line with the *Dharmaśāstras*? The significance of *dharma* has also been seen by drawing attention to the concern with *dhamma* by the Mauryan king, Aśoka.[137] But Aśoka's *dhamma* is not that of the *Dharmaśāstras*: it is an ethic that applies universally and assumes social equality. It touches on the same issues as the *rāja-dharma* but differs in its understanding of the functions of the king and the conduct of his subjects.[138]

Dharma as a legitimizing factor—the king's actions being in accordance with a required pattern of governance—introduces a new feature in the political authority of the king and demarcates him from the epic hero. It could have released the king from the dictum of brahmanism, but as it turned out the control over defining the king's *dharma* remained in the hands of the *brāhmaṇas* in most kingdoms. Aśoka endorsing diverse views was not problematic to many kings, but the people of Kosala, described as *dharmaśīla* (righteous), are praised for not tolerating *nāstikas* and *anṛtakas* (unbelievers and those opposed to the truth). Who defines the truth is an implicit question.

The insistence on defining *dharma* and twinning it with *daṇḍa*—the right of the king to punish and coerce—hints at opposition to the brahmanical definition of *dharma*, possibly deriving from *nāstika* views. The rule of the Mauryas and their patronage of the *śramaṇa* sects would have been known to the redactors. The more effective incorporation of the perception of the past, in historical terms, is not merely the *rājya* confronting the *gaṇa-saṅgha* or its manifestations but the assumption that the *gaṇa-saṅghas* or their like were of the past, and that they would have to give way to the more recent and more powerful form of state power—the kingdoms.

The question of what is legitimate becomes an issue, as for instance in the killing of Vālin. Sugrīva agreed to help Rāma in

[137] *The Rāmāyaṇa of Vālmīki, Vol. II: Ayodhyākāṇḍa*, trans. S. Pollock, 69.
[138] R. Thapar, *Aśoka and the Decline of the Mauryas*, 137–81.

retrieving Sītā. So Rāma bestows legitimacy on Sugrīva, and in doing so has to kill the elder brother, Vālin, thus transgressing primogeniture. Vālin had abducted Sugrīva's wife. A convoluted argument is used to justify the killing. It involves the difference between *āryas* and *anāryas*, the fact that monkeys being *anāryas* do not observe *niyoga* (levirate), but that nevertheless Vālin had sinned—*pāpamkarmakṛt*—but then he was after all only an animal (*mṛgo hyasi*).[139] There is much slippage here between different categories. The essential feature is that both *anāryas* and *mṛgas* have to be subservient. Hanumān's subservience is later converted into *bhakti.*

The new redactions consider the *ṛṣis* who can, on occasion, show greater power than the gods. *Apsarās* are sent by the gods to seduce them and weaken the power accumulated by asceticism. The curse of the *ṛṣi* can be neutralized, but never erased. This effectively underlines the claim to moral authority by the ascetic. In the epic the ascetic is not he who renounces the world and moves off the pages of history, but rather he who uses the power of asceticism to direct the unravelling of action. This presents another facet of the notion of power in human action different from the obviously political.

Episodes from the *Rāmāyaṇa*, and more so than even from the *Mahābhārata,* became the focus of later compositions in various literary forms. From the thirteenth century onwards there were commentaries on the Vālmīki *Rāmāyaṇa*, such as those of Varadarāja, Maheśvara, Govindarāja, Nageśa Bhaṭṭa. There is an awareness in them of contradictions within the text. Some of the statements are investigated in terms of real time and space. Occasionally, these reflect a concern with the underlying question of whether the events in the text actually took place. Some attempts seem to have been made to differentiate between an original text and additions. Comments are also made on the chronology of the text. By now it was being said that it was written in the Tretā *yuga*, which was of course fantasy, but emphasized an enormous distance in time. The commentaries are an indication that it had acquired the status of a hegemonic text.

[139] *The Rāmāyaṇa of Vālmīki, Vol. IV: Kiṣkindhākāṇḍa*, trans. R. Lefeber, gen. ed. R.P. Goldman, 37ff.; *Rāmāyaṇa* 4.18.19–36.

The remoulding of the *Rāmāyaṇa* into a text for the sacred made it less an epic. Used metaphorically as the personification of good and evil, it was occasionally applied to historical situations. In the late first millennium AD, enemy rulers of any category, local and Turks, were on occasion referred to as Rāvaṇa. The Turks were not singled out, as has been argued by some scholars.[140]

5. The Jaina *Paumacariyam*

The Vālmīki version of the story, significantly different from the *Jātaka*, seems to have stimulated yet another version, namely the Jaina text of Vimalasūri, the *Paumacariyam* in Prākrit, or the *Padmacarita* if referred to by a Sanskrit title. This takes the form of a counter-epic. Its date, as given by Vimalasūri, is 530 years after the death of Mahāvīra, which would make it around the Christian era, but most scholars prefer a slightly later date of the early centuries AD.[141] The *Paumacariyam* was the earliest among a long line of Jaina versions, which suggests that the rewriting of this story was of considerable importance to the Jaina tradition. If the Vālmīki text was redacted by Vaiṣṇava propagandists, the Jaina version is equally didactic in using the story to propagate Jaina views. At the same time, its variants on the story are strikingly significant statements from a historical perspective.

Vimalasūri informs us that he is narrating the traditional story of Padma/Rāma as told by Mahāvīra to Indrabhūti, who narrated it to his disciples.[142] The initial narrator is either a deity or a person of status, and this underlines the importance of the text. The story is also called *Rāghavacarita*; based on the *nāmāvalis* and *caritas* of Nārāyaṇas and Baladevas available in the Jaina *āgamas*, it is sometimes referred to as a *purāṇam ākhyānam*.[143] The genre remains the same as in the brahmanical tradition but the narratives and their intentions differ.

[140] S. Pollock, "Rāmāyaṇa and Political Imagination in India", 261–97.

[141] *Paumacariyam*, ed. H. Jacobi, vols I and II; V.M. Kulkarni, *The Story of Rama in Jaina Literature*; idem, "Origin and Development of the Rama Story in Jaina Literature", 189–204; *Pariśiṣṭaparvan*, Introduction, xix; K.R. Chandra, *A Critical Study of Paumacariyam*.

[142] *Paumacariyam*, 118.102–3.

[143] 118.118, 118.111, 1.32, 118.117.

Vimalasūri's purpose in writing his version of the story is, he says, to give the true facts of what happened instead of the lies and silly stories, contrary to reason and belief, with which the existing narrative is replete.[144] He does not specifically mention the Vālmīki *Rāmāyaṇa*, but perhaps it is implied. He proceeds by going back to the earlier writings which he uses as source, and whose versions he then questions and conradicts.

His personal background is that he was himself of the Nailakula-vaṃśa, with no clear affinity to either of the two Jaina sects, the Digambara or Śvetāmbara. Possibly he was a resident of Mathura, which features in the story and which was a flourishing Jaina centre.[145] The text in Prākrit was clearly intended for a much wider audience than if it had been written in Sanskrit.

The *Paumacariyam* is said to be part of the *ācārya-paramparā* (the tradition of teachers), and it would be expected therefore to incorporate much of what might be called the prehistory of the Jaina tradition in the form of cosmology, creation legends, and early mythological material. The book opens with a salutation to Mahāvīra and the *tīrthaṅkaras* who are associated with the teaching of Jainism. In Puranic fashion, it begins with the history of the universe, the cycles of time, and the biographies of the *tīrthaṅkaras*. It is therefore at the intersection of the epic and Puranic genres. It then proceeds to describe the origin of the major ruling families involved in the story and gives their genealogies, some of which are closer to the lists in the *Purāṇa*s than the genealogies in the Vālmīki *Rāmāyaṇa*.

The story of Rāma is introduced in a provocative manner. The initial scene is that of Magadha, a prosperous kingdom located in Jambudvīpa, with its capital at Rājagṛha and ruled by king Śrenika (Bimbisāra).[146] Śrenika doubts the authenticity of the story as told in the existing versions and asks for the correct version from a disciple of Mahāvīra. This is a claim to historicity, Bimbisāra being a near-contemporary of Mahāvīra. Buddhist sources refer to Bimbisāra as a contemporary of the Buddha, and he is included in the Puranic dynastic lists, all of which suggest his historicity.

144 2.116ff.

145 V.M. Kulkarni, *The Story of Rama in Jaina Literature*, 60.

146 *Paumacariyam*, 2.1–20.

Many of Śrenika's doubts centre around the characterization of the *rākṣasas*, and of Rāvaṇa in particular, but he also questions various other statements.[147] The implication of such a beginning would be that there was some historical basis to the story, but that the existing versions were deliberate falsifications. The notion of historicity here is open and central, not embedded. This is not unconnected with the general attitude towards the past among Sramanic sects.

What is at issue in the *Paumacariyam* is not only a Jaina rendering of the story but also an attempt to present a sympathetic narrative of "the Other"—the *rākṣasas* of Vālmīki—if not a narrative from the perspective of the other side. It is clearly stated that the *rākṣasas* are not demons and that the word comes from the root **raks*, meaning "to protect".[148] Rāvaṇa was neither ten-headed—the Daśagrīva of the Vālmīki version—nor a meat-eating fiend. All that has been said about him by foolish poets is untrue.[149] The *Paumacariyam* is a conscious attempt at rewriting the existing versions of the story and depicting the *rākṣasas* as they actually were before being demonized. And it claims historical authenticity for its version of the story.

The narrative begins with a description of the land of the Vidyādharas— literally, the bearers of knowledge—of whom the *rākṣasas* and the *vānaras* form a part. The early chapters provide a detailed account of the genealogies of these two groups, and it is not until well into the story that we are introduced to the episodes involving Daśaratha and Ayodhyā. The geographical focus is essentially that of the Vindhyan region, with extensions southwards towards the Godavari river. All the main characters are pious Jainas, and therefore people who try to avoid violence; nevertheless, aggressive heroic values cannot be entirely eliminated and the kings and princes in this version do show their valour in combat.

In the genealogical section, which is technically more efficient than in the *Rāmāyaṇa*, it is stated that the four important descent groups are those of the Ikkhāga/Ikṣvāku, Somavaṃśa, Vijjāharāṇa/

147 3.7ff.
148 5.257.
149 3.14–15.

Vidyādhara, and Harivaṃśa.[150] The Ikṣvāku is also called the Ādityayaśa, an alternative name for Sūryavaṃśa, the Solar lineage, of the *Purāṇas*. This was one of the two major lineages as visualized in the *Purāṇas*, the other being the Candravaṃśa/Somavaṃśa or Lunar lineage. The genealogies from the *Mahābhārata* and the *Rāmāyaṇa*, and possibly the early *Purāṇas*, were doubtless familiar from the oral tradition. It was, however, not so necessary at this point for the genealogies to tally.

The inclusion of the genealogy was an underlining of claims to status by birth and connections between clans. Whether it was accurate beyond a few generations was not of central concern. The Vidyādhara appears to have been the most important, since their genealogy is given in greater detail than the others. Even the etymologies of the names are sometimes included.[151] The Vidyādharavaṃśa traces its ancestry back to the great Ṛṣabha who, in his later life, became a monk and divided his kingdom between his two sons, Nami and Vinami. Being the recipients of many *vidyās* (sciences and knowledge), they are called Vidyādhara (bearers of knowledge).

The most important among them is Meghavāhana who, because of certain complications, has to flee to Laṅkā where he establishes the Rākṣasavaṃśa.[152] Many of the names in the long list seem to have been arrived at through free association with a multiplicity of prefixes and suffixes, but all of a similar kind, such as *vajra* (thunderbolt), *vidyuta* (lightning), and *megha* (cloud), although the immediate forefathers of the main personalities remain consistent. Another segment of the Vidyādharavaṃśa important to the story was the Vānaravaṃśa, which is again founded by a Vidyādhara prince who is exiled to Vānaradvīpa and where, at Kiṣkindhā, outside the Vindhyan region, he establishes a kingdom. The *rākṣasas* and the *vānaras* are therefore related. It is called the Vānaravaṃśa not because they are monkeys but because the prince takes a monkey emblem for his standard.[153] There are confrontations as

[150] 5.1–2.

[151] 5.250ff.

[152] 5.14ff.; R. Thapar, "The Rāmāyaṇa: Theme and Variation", in idem, *Cultural Pasts,* 647–79. The *rākṣasas* as well as Khāravela, the king of Kaliṅga, both have a Meghavāhana lineage, and the latter is associated with the Cedis.

[153] 6.60–92.

well as marital and political alliances between these segments of the Vidyādhara line.

The Ādityavaṃśa is also called Ikṣvāku because Ṛṣabha taught his subjects to process sugarcane. Of its genealogy, only a few names are common to the *Rāmāyaṇa*. The Somavaṃśa, the equivalent of the Candravaṃśa, is not described in detail and draws less interest. The Harivaṃśa, to which Janaka, the father of Sītā, belongs, is relatively minor and is not related to the Ikṣvākuvaṃśa of Daśaratha. Of the earlier Ikṣvāku kings, the *Paumacariyam* gives prominence to Sagara, who is said to have married a Vidyādhara princess.[154] This would have been unlikely in the Vālmīki version.

Rāvaṇa is described as an *ardhacakravartin*—i.e. an almost universal monarch, having conquered vast areas of Bhāratavarṣa. He is also an ardent Jaina and a protector of Jaina shrines. The conflict between him and Rāma is virtually predetermined since Rāma is the eighth Vāsudeva and Rāvaṇa is the eighth Prativāsudeva, the two groups being inherently antagonistic according to Jaina belief. He is handsome and brave and attractive to the *apsarās*. He does not have ten heads but his single head is reflected in each of the nine large gem-stones which he wears as a necklace, hence the sobriquet of *daśagrīva* or Ten-headed.[155] He has the ability to fly and is therefore called *akāśamārgi*—he who travels through the sky. Rāvaṇa owns a *puṣpakavimāna*, an aerial chariot which he uses on occasion and which endorses his Cedi connection.[156] Rāvaṇa is no less a hero than Rāma. His relationship with Sītā is of a more sensitive kind as compared to the rather terrifying overtures and threats which he makes in the Vālmīki version.[157]

The first major exploit of Rāma is the expulsion of the *mleccha* threatening the kingdom of Janaka,[158] an exploit similar to that of Sagara of earlier times expelling the Haihayas. Daśaratha, impressed by the teachings of a Jaina *muni*, decides to renounce the world. This leads Kaikeyī to demand that her son succeed to

[154] 5.62ff.

[155] 7.96.

[156] *Paumacariyam*, 8.1–28.

[157] *Rāmāyaṇa*, 5.20–4.

[158] *Paumacariyam*, 27.4ff.

the throne.[159] Daśaratha had granted a boon to Kaikeyī because of her skill in driving his chariot when he was contesting for her hand. Kaikeyī tries to dissuade Rāma from going into exile, since she merely wants the succession for her son, and even follows Rāma into the forest together with Bharata to persuade him to return, but to no effect.[160]

The exiles arrive in the Vindhyan region and the conditions of exile are dissimilar from those described in the Vālmīki version. Whereas in the latter it was the *āśramas* of the *ṛṣis* which had to be protected, now it is Jaina shrines which replace the *āśramas*. The period of exile includes attention to innumerable smaller problems relating to the royal families of the kingdoms of the Vindhyan region, which are now scattered in the area earlier described as wilderness. The *araṇya* has in parts given way to the *grāma*, which in itself would give a later date to this text. Exile here is hardly a condition of long periods of austerity in the forest. Much time is spent at local courts and the interweaving by the author of what purports to be local history.[161]

In many ways the *Paumacariyam* is a mirror image of the late *Rāmāyaṇa*. This is so not only in its Jaina didactic content, which has been commented upon by scholars, and which is a counter to the Vaiṣṇava didacticism of the Vālmīki version, but also in the thematic structure of the text. The theme of exile occurs at two levels. One is the familiar narrative of the exile of Rāma, where the hero lives in the forest for a stipulated period and then returns home. The other is exile as migration and the settling of new areas, which is referred to not in connection with the Ikṣvāku line but with the Vidyādharas.

Meghavāhana establishes himself at Laṅkā and gives rise to the Rākṣasavaṃśa, and another hero founds the kingdom of Vānaradvīpa. The new settlement is demarcated by the term *dvīpa*, literally an island, but perhaps used metaphorically in these cases, as it often was in the geographical sections of the *Purāṇas* to denote a distinctive territory. Each had its capital city and some

[159] 31.59ff.

[160] 32.38ff.

[161] 33.25ff., 34.38ff., 36.8ff., 38.22ff., 40.1ff.

distinguishing topographical feature. Exile is caused by some conflict with people established in the area, and the rulers of the new settlement derive their status from kinship connections with the older lineage.

Unlike the vast wilderness through which the *rākṣasas* roam in the Vālmīki text, the territories of the Vidyādharas are more clearly defined in the *Paumacariyam*. The kingdoms of the north tend to be hazy, but there is a greater familiarity with the more prosperous towns of the northern plains and with the valleys and plains of Central India. The area of exile in the Vindhyas is no longer the forest haunt of demons, for it now boasts of some cities and kingdoms. Inevitably, kingship is as much the norm among the *rākṣasas* now as among the Ikṣvākus. Even the institution of *sāmantas* (neighbouring rulers and intermediaries) is mentioned.[162] Marriages are an agency of political alliances, so Rāma, Lakṣmaṇa, Hanumān, and Rāvaṇa make marriage alliances, or in some cases consider possibilities.[163]

Forest peoples such as Pulindas and Bhillas are sometimes referred to as *anārya*.[164] Other *anāryas* include the *mleccha/milakkha*; these are listed as Śabaras, Kirātas, Kambojas, Śukas, Kapotas, and suchlike,[165] where the main difference was language. The *rākṣasas* are depicted as hostile to Vedic sacrifices. This would have endeared them to the Jainas, who disapproved of the sacrificing of animals. Another striking difference in the *Paumacariyam* is the absence of the need to uphold the *varṇāśrama-dharma* and the status of the *brāhmaṇa*. The *brāhmaṇas* here are the killers of animal life in their sacrifices, eaters of meat, indisciplined, sunk in sensual delights instead of living according to moral laws, heretics and preachers of false doctrines who have acquired their status by cheating people.[166] The term used for the *brāhmaṇas* as heretics—*pāṣaṇḍa*—is the same that the *brāhmaṇas* use for the Sramanic sects.[167] Interestingly, the Bhṛgus and the Aṅgirasas and

[162] 38.51ff.

[163] 51.12ff., 33.139, 11.100, 19.32, 77.55.

[164] 98.63, 104.20, 12.13.

[165] 27.5–8, 27.29–33.

[166] 4.85ff., 105.46, 11.23–8, 105.43ff.

[167] 89.48, 4.64–90.

their disciples come in for a pointed attack as teachers of silly doctrines that make fools of people.[168] This would suggest that Vimalasūri's criticism is particularly aimed at the redacted version of the *Rāmāyaṇa*.

The *kṣatriyas* are also called *rayaputta/rājaputra*, and their function is to govern and protect. The protection is extensive and covers the fending-off of the *mlecchas*, attacks from the chief of a tribe, freeing people from an oppressive king, and fighting rebels.[169] The most respected social groups other than royalty are the merchants, and princes are said on occasion to have been merchants in their previous births.[170] This is not surprising, given that the Jaina *saṅgha* had many Jaina merchant families as its patrons.

The greatest reverence is naturally given to the Jaina *munis* who weave their way through the narrative. Although there is no well-defined theory of incarnation, as in Vaiṣṇava Bhāgavatism, the tripartite complex of Vāsudeva–Prativāsudeva–Baladeva serves a similar function. The inevitability therefore of the predetermined relationship between Rāma and Rāvaṇa erodes some of the brutality of the conflict and reduces thereby the occasions for heroic stances. The Jaina *muni* is frequently found to be preaching renunciation. Finally, both Daśaratha and Rāma renounce the world and Sītā becomes a nun, the Jaina ethic triumphing over the *kṣatriya* ethic.

The vehemence with which the *Paumacariyam* denounces the known versions of the *Rāmāyaṇa* and sets out to give a different version does suggest that, apart from the existence of alternative versions, there may have been a historical need for such a treatment. The *Paumacariyam* may well have been attempting to legitimize the Vidyādhara lineage. It could be acting as a charter of validation for the kingdoms which arose in the Vindhyan region and its fringes in the early Christian era. These were the Traikūṭaka in western India, rising on the decline of the Sātavāhana and the Ābhira; the Bodhi in Bundelkhand and Tripuri, which area later saw the rise of the Kalacūri; the Bhoja and the

168 4.86.

169 3.115, 27.28ff., 34.44, 33.115ff., 26.29.

170 5.81–92.

Vākāṭaka in Vidarbha; Dakṣina Kosala under various rulers; and the Cedi in Kaliṅga. Linking many of these was what appears to be a Cedi connection, with some among them using the Cedi era of AD 248–9 in their records.[171]

Jainism was becoming more popular in this region during the early centuries AD and was doubtless seeking royal patronage. Many dynasties were beginning to seek genealogical links with the more established *kṣatriya* lineages. Those claiming Haihaya origins may have encouraged the questioning of the Bhārgava versions of the tradition.[172] The Jaina version may well have been more acceptable if the dynasties which claimed Cedi and Meghavāhana connections were claiming a radically different identity for the *rākṣasas*.

The Jaina background to the *Paumacariyam* would not be averse to Cedi connections. In suggesting that Śrenika was conversing with Jaina teachers, Vimalasūri was projecting a Jaina association with Magadha to an earlier period. The *Mahābhārata* endorses a link between the Cedis and Magadha. Among early royal patrons, the Jainas claim Candragupta Maurya, during whose reign their focus was on Magadha. That the Kaliṅga Cedis were patrons of the Jainas is stated in their inscriptions. At about the same time, Mathura emerged as a centre of Jaina worship.[173] By the early centuries AD, Vidiśā had Jaina centres and gradually such centres were established in Bundelkhand and Rewa as well.[174] The Jaina context of the *Paumacariyam* therefore was familiar in North India.

Surprisingly, little attention is given to the real time of these historical events that are associated with Jaina activity. The concept of time remains close to that of the cyclic *yugas*. It points to a familiarity with the concepts of the epics and the *Purāṇas,* but there are differences. Time is divided into *kalpas*—the longest

[171] V.V. Mirashi (ed.), *Corpus Inscriptionum Indicarum*, IV.1.1ff.

[172] F.E. Pargiter, *Ancient Indian Historical Tradition*, 197ff.

[173] G. Buhler, "New Jaina Inscriptions from Mathura", 371ff., 393ff.; idem, "Further Jaina Inscriptions from Mathura", 195ff.; V.S. Agrawala, "Catalogue of the Mathura Museum . . .", 36ff.

[174] K.D. Bajpai, "Development of Jaina Art in Madhya Pradesh"; U.P. Shah, *Jaina Art and Architecture*, vol. I, 128; V.V. Mirashi, *Corpus Inscriptionum Indicarum*, IV, clxi–ii.

unit—and each of these is conceived as a cycle with an upswing (*utsarpini*), which leads to prosperity, and a downswing (*avasarpini*), which moves towards a decline. The analogy is to the waxing and waning of the moon.[175] The length of the *kalpa* is 20 *koṭakoṭisagara* years, where 1 *sagara* equals 10 *koṭakoṭi palyopama* years and 1 *palyopama* is the time taken to empty an area 1 *yojana* wide and deep-filled with the hair of new-born children, and where 1 hair is removed annually.[176] Each half-cycle is divided into 6 periods of time, the duration of which changes in the ratio of 4, 3, 2, 1 *koṭakoṭisagara* years, and each of the last two are 21,000 years. Once again, the immensity of measurements tends to annul time.

Utopian conditions existed in the remote past when wish-fulfilling trees provided for all wants.[177] The decline in the downswing brought about the need to labour, and also the introduction of caste as *varṇa* and *jāti*.[178] These are listed as *kṣatriyas*, *vaiśyas*, and *śūdras*. Mention is also made of *purohitas* and *bhaṭṭas*. Time therefore is virtually infinite, and the decline from utopian beginnings makes it necessary to have law-givers.[179] The scheme recognizes change over time and tries to rationalize the need for law and the functionaries of law-giving, such as, presumably, the king.

6. The *Rāma-kathā* as Part of a Historical Tradition

It would seem possible to argue that the epic literature is describing the bifurcation of chiefdoms and kingdoms and the gradual fading away of the first with the establishing of the second. Pāṇini is aware of the two systems when he says that ruling *kṣatriyas* were either *ekarāja* or *ekādhīna*, or else they were *gaṇādhīna* or ruled by a *saṅgha*. The *saṅgha* was a corporate body without distinctions of high and low. The intention in the epics, apart from other concerns, is to evoke the earlier societies whose form in some places was

[175] 3.49ff.
[176] 20.63ff. One *yojana* can be anywhere between 2.5 and 9 miles.
[177] 3.37ff., 102.126–32.
[178] 3.111ff.
[179] K.R. Chandra, *A Critical Study of Paumacariyam*, 316.

still current, and to record the historical change to more recent forms; as also to claim legitimacy for the change.

The further proliferation of the story in variant forms and languages was linked with both the spread of Vaiṣṇavism and processes of cultural assimilation. But it served other purposes as well. The Gupta and post-Gupta period saw the subjugation of forest tribes by various kingdoms, where the latter either extended their territory or tried to intensify their control over all areas of the existing kingdom, including those inhabited by forest-dwellers.[180] The conflict between Kosala and the *rākṣasas* doubtless was seen, even subconsciously, as a metaphor and justification of encroachment into forests. The texts would therefore be topical, and provide a validation from the past for such encroachments.

Another feature is connected to the genealogical links claimed by many new dynasties at this time. Rituals such as the *rājasūya, aśvamedha*, or *vājapeya*, which were once the only legitimation ceremonies, began to be superseded by genealogical connections. This led to *brāhmaṇas* gradually taking over custodianship of the genealogical data from which they could provide the necessary links for their patrons among the ruling families. The *vaṃśānucarita* section of some early *Purāṇas,* listing descent and succession of clans and then dynasties, were constructed to go back to the earliest origins.[181] Two lineages, as noted earlier, dominate the pattern: the Sūryavaṃśa/Solar lineage, and the Candravaṃśa/Lunar lineage. Rāma, his ancestors and descendants, belonged to the Sūryavaṃśa, whereas the clans of the *Mahābhārata* were in the main members of the Candravaṃśa. Thus, all those dynasties which claimed descent from the Solar line would also claim Rāma as their ancestor, and the genealogical link was made through one of his two sons, Kuśa or Lava. The story of Rāma would therefore become the ancestral epic. That Rāma was an incarnation of Viṣṇu strengthened the notion of kings being associated with the divine.

Courtly culture involved heroic actions similar to those in the

[180] As for example in the Allahabad pillar inscription associated with Samudragupta, and the later Khoh plates of Hastin: J.F. Fleet (ed.), *Corpus Inscriptionum Indicarum*, vol. III, 1ff., 93ff.

[181] See Chapter Six.

epic and also encouraged loyalty and devotion to the king. He was not only a terrestrial ruler, he also had elements of the divine and an impeccable ancestry and occasionally was an incarnation of deity. Loyalty and devotion to the king constituted a useful norm, to be inculcated among the many intermediaries—the *sāmantas*. These formed the nobility, where the term *sāmanta* was ceasing to mean a neighbour and was used more frequently for a subordinate ruler.

The epic is a saga of heroes and focuses on chiefships in competition over territory, status, and rights, although the ostensible reason in the narrative may be the kidnapping of the heroine or the losing of a game of dice. The reformulation of the story may happen on occasions of major historical change, such as with the emergence of the state in the form of a kingdom, or of new states with fresh incentives, or when states require ideologies that mark out the king as having divine elements. Such changes required validation from the past, and the story was recast to provide this. New territory may be incorporated into the geographical circumference of epic events, where such territory has to be described as having been rightfully settled or conquered. The legitimacy of the new rulers has to be ensured through origin myths, genealogical links, and events held to be significant to the tradition. Mythology is used to draw the territory and the personalities into a circle of known and familiar forms. Kingship is used to establish links between the new rulers and the territory which is to be incorporated. The ideological-religious background is provided by those religions—Buddhism, Bhāgavatism, and Jainism—whose spread coincides with the power of kingdoms, each with its court, capital, and ability to bestow royal patronage.

If a kernel of historicity is sought in the *Rāmāyaṇa*, it may lie in the references commonly made in the *Jātakas*, the *Mahābhārata*, and later the *Purāṇas*, to conflict among the clans. Clans descended from Yadu are associated with attacks on Ayodhyā. These are the Andhavenhu/Andhakavṛṣṇis and the Haihayas, who are not associated with kingdoms but with *gaṇas* (chiefships), and are said to be *dāsaputtas*—a low status.[182] In the *Mahābhārata* there

[182] *Ghaṭa Jātaka*, no. 454; *Kumbha Jātaka*, no. 511, in *The Jātaka*.

is a confrontation between the Vṛṣṇis and the Cedis, expressed through the animosity of Kṛṣṇa towards Jarāsandha and Śiśupāla, located in the middle Ganges plain. But the Vṛṣṇis are absent in the *Rāmāyaṇa*. Rāvaṇa, being of Meghavāhana descent according to the *Paumacariyam*, may have been a Cedi. The Cedis, also of Yadu descent, have a high status in Buddhist sources and claim the primeval ruler, Mahāsammata, as their ancestor. Rāvaṇa being airborne is reminiscent of the Cedi chief Vasu having been given an aerial chariot by Indra. According to Puranic accounts the Haihayas, associated with the Cedis, who were in turn linked to Meghavāhana, attacked Ayodhyā and were eventually defeated by Sagara.[183] The *Rāmāyaṇa* refers to the Haihayas and other clans attacking Ayodhyā.[184] The Bhṛgus are said to have been priests to the Haihayas but to have left them after an altercation.

Interestingly, in the transition from lineage-based societies to states, it is Magadha and Kosala which emerge among the earlier states that move towards kingdoms.[185] In the first century BC, Khāravela, the Jaina king of Kaliṅga, claims a Cedi origin and a Meghavāhana lineage.[186] Kaliṅga is the territory earlier conquered by the Nandas and the Mauryas. Did the establishment of monarchy in the middle Ganges plain treat the alternative existing chiefdoms initially with animosity, until such time as they too mutated into kingdoms, or were absorbed into larger states?

The identifications suggested here hinge on the *Paumacariyam* describing Rāvaṇa as a Vidyādhara of the Meghavāhana lineage. The historical link is provided by the inscription of Khāravela, where he claims Cedi links and descent from Vasu, and a Meghavāhana lineage. Given the historical evidence, the Cedis by the early centuries AD were distributed along the southern Vindhyas and Central India from the west coast to the east. Most scholars argue for the location of Laṅkā in the Vindhyan or Amarakantaka or the Mahanadi region, which would not be a problem. The epic therefore would not be concerned with the

[183] F.E. Pargiter, *Ancient Indian Historical Tradition*, 153; *Rāmāyaṇa*, 1.37–40, 2.102.14.

[184] 2.102.14.

[185] R. Thapar, *From Lineage to State*, 110ff.

[186] Hathigumpha Inscription, *Ep. Ind.*, 20, 71–89.

historicity of Rāma but with representing the more important event, namely, the confrontation between the clans where the descendants of Ikṣvāku were trying to get their own back on the raid of the Yadu clans. The demonizing of the Cedis into *rakṣasas* was partly poetic imagery, and partly the politics of the conflict with the Cedis, with the delineation of the *rakṣasas* drawing in part on the alien culture of the forest-dwellers. The descriptions of the two are similar.

From this perspective, the *Paumacariyam* depicts the establishment of kingship in those very areas where previously there had been chiefships, or at most early forms of kingship. The three versions of the narrative refer to three different historical moments; and the latter two are well aware of a distance in time and the reconstruction of the past. They register a historical statement of change in the area. There is a much sharper and stronger assertion of identity and a different identity among the *rākṣasas* in the *Paumacariyam* than in the earlier two. In the *Jātakas* they are demons, goblins, and magical beings, and their role tends to be minimal. The Vālmīki text depicts them as similar to human society in some ways but as lurid creatures of the imagination. The *Paumacariyam* has no doubt about their being a recognizable human group with rights over a specific geographical area, governed by the institutions of kingship. The conflict in this version is one between equals. The revelation of this identity in all its facets would have required a rewriting of the story to incorporate the changes. The rewriting coincides with the period when such changes were taking place either in areas of erstwhile *gaṇa-saṅghas,* or some previously forested areas.

The literary construction of a given reality may not be historical fact, but it offers insights into that reality. The importance of cultural survivals in some societies are not pristine and unchanged in form because survivals accumulate and internalize contemporary events. They also point to historical implications in the nature of the changes they undergo. Variants illumine each other and the modern historian has to be cautious in accepting any single one as central for all time. The dialogue may not refer to the totality of the text. Fragments may be more pointed in terms of making new statements. Variants are essentially in dialogue with each other, and since the dialogue extends over time it includes elements of perspectives on the past and constructions of the past. The new has greater acceptability if it is seen as a transformation of the old, although in fact it may be making a statement which is a departure from the old. Each change reflects the politics of culture, for these versions were meant for popular audiences and also had a political function which included the legitimation of monarchy, religious sectarianism, and dissenting heterodoxy.

In the variants discussed above a major innovation is the notion of historicity. The Vālmīki text and the Buddhist stories make no mention of this, although they may intend it. The first text to claim historicity is the Jaina version. It insists on this not only by associating the text with the historical king Śrenika/ Bimbisāra, but by denouncing the other versions as fabrications. The Jaina variant alone is attempting to present what it claims is an authentic historical account; therefore the endorsements which it suggests are significant from the point of view of a perspective on the past. The claim of historicity for this story connotes a new concern with the past.

PART III

Interlude: The Emerging Historical Tradition

6

Genealogies in the Making of a Historical Tradition

The *Vaṃśānucarita* of the *Viṣṇu Purāṇa*

1 The Context of the *Purāṇas*

The *Purāṇas,* partially incorporating historical traditions, are texts on the threshold, as it were, of the recognizable genesis of one kind of historical writing in early India—the *itihāsa-purāṇa* tradition. In their lists of succession, the *vaṃśānucaritas*—which form one section of these texts—cull their data from the embedded narratives in the *Vedas* and the epics, which they use as sources. These succession lists, although again embedded in religious sectarian texts, can nevertheless also be seen—which they often were later—as statements independent of the texts in which they had been placed.[1] The data in them is reformulated in accordance with what was more appropriate to contemporary social forms, a change due in part to recognizing the political and social potential of creating a historical tradition.

[1] R. Thapar, "The Purāṇas: Heresy and the Vaṃśānucarita", 28–48; idem, "Genealogical Patterns as Perceptions of the Past", in idem, *Cultural Pasts*, 710–53; idem, "Clan, Caste and Origin Myths in Early India", in ibid., 782–96.

It probably also arose from observing the actual usefulness of reconstructions of history, as had become evident from the Buddhist perspective.

The *Purāṇas* mark a new phase in the making of a historical tradition. *Purāṇa* being literally "that which is ancient", these texts claim links to the past. Their historical concern, in the shape of their succession lists—seek to provide a continuous genealogical construct of lineages, followed by dynasties of rulers from earliest times to approximately the mid-first millennium AD. The historical past emerges through these lists.

The *Purāṇas* took shape as a distinctive genre in the first millennium AD, some composed in the early part of the millennium and some later. The material incorporated may, once again, have existed originally as part of an oral tradition. Each section of the text has a distinct theme with a discernible pattern. Some segments occur in other texts as well, such as discussions on kingship and on concepts of time. Intertextuality between the *Purāṇas* becomes important.[2] They claim to evolve from the *Vedas,* a connection claimed largely to ensure status. They reflect much that is marginal to the *Vedas*, and some that comes from the non-Vedic, although the latter is not conceded. Incorporation was one mechanism of overcoming the influence of the other. The teaching of the *śramaṇas* is regarded as evil. Nevertheless, the antagonism suggests that the reformulation of historical data was in part motivated by the historical traditions propagated by Sramanic ideas. There can therefore be contradictions in the Puranic discourse. That the old can become the new encapsulates the notion of change.[3] The early narratives were intended to construct an image of the past.[4]

Each *Purāṇa* focused on a deity and became a compendium of its worship, subject to interpolations.[5] The *Viṣṇu, Vāyu, Brahmāṇḍa, Matsya*, and *Bhāgvata Purāṇas* included genealogies

[2] G. Bailey, "Intertextuality in the Purāṇas: A Neglected Element in the Study of Sanskrit Literature", 179–98.

[3] *Nirukta* of Yāska, 3.19: *pura navam bhavati iti purāṇam.*

[4] *Śatapatha Brāhmaṇa*, 11.5.6.8: *puravṛtta pratipādikam purāṇam.*

[5] R.C. Hazra, *Studies in the Puranic Records of Hindu Rites and Customs*; L. Rocher, *The Puranas*.

of ancient heroes and king-lists of early dynasties. Concepts of time, which have a bearing on the notion of history and in constructing chronologies, were also described.

Initial studies of the *Purāṇas* in the late eighteenth and nineteenth centuries took them to be second-order knowledge, as compared to the *Vedas*, in accordance with brahmanical views. William Jones compared their chronologies with Biblical ones and the dynastic lists with data from non-Indian sources, but he made few connections. For purposes of history the focus was on the *vaṃśānucarita*, set of course in the wider context of the other contents of the genre.

Attempts at establishing an order in the genealogies were made by H.H. Wilson in the nineteenth century and by F.E. Pargiter almost a century ago.[6] Wilson was frustrated by the questionable authenticity of the *Purāṇas,* yet had to concede that they were a basic source of early history. Pargiter was less interested in the genealogical patterns and what these may be stating, and more in trying to identify the different descent groups. This was easier for the third part, dealing with dynasties, since quite a few could be correlated with other categories of sources. Pargiter's plea that the data be treated seriously was well taken; unfortunately his identifications of the descent groups were misleading.

Defending the *Purāṇas* as historical records, Pargiter argued that even as part of the oral tradition some memory of early kings would have remained and that, however garbled the genealogies, they would still have been based initially on some authentic versions. This provided the *Purāṇas* with a degree of respectability in the eyes of modern historians; nevertheless, the debate remained heated.[7] Pargiter's readings became unacceptable as he argued, on the basis of current theories, that Indian history began with the Aryans, and that the genealogies recorded the story of Aryan expansion.[8] By this argument some lineages were of the

[6] *Śrīviṣṇupurāṇa*; *The Vishnu Purana*, ed. and trans. H.H. Wilson; idem, "Analysis of the Puranas", 61ff.; F.E. Pargiter, *Ancient Indian Historical Tradition*; idem, *The Purana Text of the Dynasties of the Kali Age* (hereafter *DKA*).

[7] U.N. Ghoshal, *Studies in Indian History and Culture*, 37–52.

[8] F.E. Pargiter, *Ancient Indian Historical Tradition*, 295–6, 306, 311–12.

Aryan race, some Dravidian, and some of the Austro-Asiatic groups. This was at a time when the notion of such "races" was acceptable to historians.

Whether or not Puranic genealogies should be taken seriously as historical material remains controversial. Some have stated that "to extract either chronology or history from such data, must be an operation attended with equal success as the extraction of sunbeams from cucumbers by the sages of Laputa."[9] Vincent Smith, on the other hand, spoke of their dynastic lists as a "near approach to accuracy", particularly in relation to the Andhra kings, although other historians have been more sceptical.[10]

Historians of the later twentieth century have attempted to put together a narrative of history from these genealogies. Pusalker in the 1950s also treated the data as mapping the spread of the Aryans, despite the fact that none of the groups listed is specifically described as "ārya".[11] Pradhan, Bhargava, and Morton-Smith attempted to work out definitive chronologies, calculating time periods on the basis of what is said about chronology and on the generational length.[12] But this was arbitrary because of variations in the lists and there being few close correlations with other sources.

These readings have hinged on a literal understanding of history as a chronicle of rulers and the genealogies get treated as factual, whereas it might be more useful to understand why genealogies, factual or not, came to play such a central role in the perception of the past. The unsuccessful attempts to cull what may be regarded

[9] V. Kennedy, *Researches into the Nature and Affinity of Ancient and Hindu Mythology*, 130.

[10] V. Smith, "Andhra History and Coinage", 649–75; idem, *The Early History of India*, 11–12; H.C. Raychaudhuri, *Political History of Ancient India*, uses the Puranic lists for reconstructing early history, particularly dynastic history. For a sceptical view of history in these sources, see D.D. Kosambi, *Ancient India: A History of its Culture and Civilisation*, 174.

[11] A.D. Pusalker (ed.), *History and Culture of the Indian People, Vol. I: The Vedic Age*, 271–322.

[12] S.N. Pradhan, *Chronology of Ancient India*; P.L. Bhargava, *India in the Vedic Age*; A.D. Pusalker, *Studies in the Epics and Puranas*; idem, *History and Culture of the Indian People, Vol. I: The Vedic Age*; R. Morton-Smith, *Dates and Dynasties in Earliest India*; M.N. Yajnik, *Genealogical Tables of the Solar and Lunar Dynasties*.

as reliable history from the *Purāṇas* has underlined the need to look at the Puranic sources from a different perspective. Evidently, the genealogies were not invariably meant to be taken literally.

Chronologies of Indian history, and the more linear concepts of time, begin with genealogies, as also with records in the form of inscriptions. But the veracity of the *vaṃśānucarita* cannot be assumed, except perhaps in patches. The argument has been that since dynasties of the third section are largely historically attested, the earlier genealogies should also be taken literally.

Generational length in India has been computed as averaging fourteen or even twenty-seven years.[13] Reign lengths vary according to the stability of the polity, and stable dates tend to support longer reigns—as has been suggested in studies of genealogical data from elsewhere.[14] Uninterrupted direct descent from father to son among dynasties rarely exceeds five or six reigns.[15] The Puranic lists were not meant to be treated as chronologically precise, although time is important to genealogical reconstructions, however approximate. The *kṣatriya* descent lists are dated to the Dvāpara *yuga* and the dynastic lists to the succeeding Kaliyuga, the point of change being approximately the battle at Kurukṣetra in or just after most *Purāṇas*.

2. The *Purāṇas*

The format of the *Purāṇa*, ideally, was that it should consist of the *pañca-lakṣana* or "the five facets" which set it apart from other literature. These were the descriptions of the *sarga* (primary creation), *prati-sarga* (secondary creation), *manvantara* (the time cycles), *vaṃśa* (succession, in this instance, largely of deities and sages), and the *vaṃśānucarita*. The last is regarded as an important component of the ideal *Purāṇa*, although it is not common to all.[16]

[13] T. Trautmann, "Length of Generation and Reign in Ancient India", 564–77; A.L. Basham, *Studies in Indian History and Culture*.

[14] D.H. Jones, "Problems of African Chronology", 161–76.

[15] D.P. Henige, *The Chronology of Oral Tradition*, 120.

[16] R.C. Hazra, *Studies in the Puranic Records of Hindu Rites and Customs*, 4–5; idem, *Studies in the Upa-Puranas*; L. Rocher, *The Puranas*, 115–32; S.H. Levitt, "A Note on the Compound *Pañcalakṣaṇa* in Amarasiṅha's *Nāmalingānuśasana*", 5–38.

In fact, only one, the *Viṣṇu Purāṇa,* conforms to the format of the five. Sometimes there is even mention of ten facets, but these are less evident in the texts.[17]

Each *Purāṇa* focuses on a deity and its worship. Apart from myths, this includes rules relating to gift-giving, fasts, pilgrimages, rituals, and sectarian religious data. The older *Purāṇas* are the *Matsya, Vāyu, Viṣṇu*, and *Brahmāṇḍa,*[18] and these have much in common. The *Bhaviṣya* claims to narrate the dynasties of the future,[19] but the title "Bhaviṣya Purāṇa" is something of an oxymoron.

There is a difference between the eighteen *mahāpurāṇas* and the lesser ones which, in a later period, came to include a wide variety of subsidiary texts, such as the *Upa-Purāṇas,* often focusing on lesser deities. Associated with these were texts on sacred topography and places of pilgrimage, such as the *Sthala-Purāṇas* and the *Mahātmyas,* incorporating the believed history of the sites. Still later, the caste *Purāṇas*—as for example those of the Mallas, the Śrimālas, and the Dharmāranyas—provided glimpses of the past arising out of social concerns. Of the non-brahmanical sects, the Jainas produced their *Purāṇas*, presenting a different perspective from the brahmanical.

Hinduism, as reflected in the *Purāṇas*, has come to be called Puranic Hinduism to differentiate it from Vedic Brahmanism. The prominence of deities such as Viṣṇu and Śiva, earlier marginal, is new, as is the depiction of deities as icons housed in temples, and the act of worship being an offering to the icon accompanied by hymns and prayers in the commonly spoken languages. The later *Purāṇas* gave more space to religious sects: for example, the *Samba Purāṇa* to the cult of the Magas, or those of erstwhile tribal areas, such as that of Vindhyavāsinī (Central India). However, my

[17] *Bhāgavata Purāṇa,* 2.10.1ff. All citations, unless otherwise specified, are to the edition by V.L. Pansikar.

[18] R.C. Hazra, *Studies in the Puranic Records of Hindu Rites and Customs*, 8 ff.; *Matsya Purāṇa*, ed. H.N. Apte; V.S. Agrawala, *Matsya Purana: A Study*; S.G. Kantawala, *Cultural History from the Matsya Purana*; *Vāyu Purāṇa*, ed. R. Mitra; V.R.R. Dikshitar, *Some Aspects of the Vāyu Purāṇa*; *Brahmāṇḍa Purāṇa*, ed. K. Srikrishnadas.

[19] F.E. Pargiter, *DKA*, viiff.

concern is only with the *vaṃśānucarita* section, and specifically the one in the *Viṣṇu Purāṇa*.

3. The Authors

The *Purāṇas* claim an ancient ancestry.[20] Brahmā is said to have compiled them even before the *Vedas* were revealed.[21] Revelation emphasizes a different origin, and compilation facilitated each *Purāṇa* becoming a sectarian text. A Vedic link is suggested in the earlier statement that the *itihāsa-purāṇa* was the fifth *Veda*. The beginnings of the *Purāṇas* seem to have been diverse, with various groups elbowing in. The transmission of the *Purāṇa* went from Brahmā via the sages to Parāśara, the grandson of Vasiṣṭha.[22] Initially, the *sūta* (bard) narrates that Maitreya asked Parāśara to explain to him the origin of the universe and all that followed. Other *Purāṇas* maintain that they were recited by the *sūta* to the *ṛṣis* in the Naimiśa forest—thus imitating the *Mahābhārata*.

Elsewhere, we are told that Veda Vyāsa, having edited the earlier Vedic material and authored the *Mahābhārata*, subsequently gathered together the *itihāsa-purāṇa* and compiled the original *Purāṇa*.[23] The possibility of an *ur*-text has not been accepted by most scholars, who hold that there has always been a diversity of *Purāṇas*. Associating them with Vyāsa gave them a higher status.

There is a parallel between some forms in the *Purāṇas* and the *Mahābhārata*. A *sūta* arrives in the forest. Here, a sacrifice is being performed, and he is asked to recite the story of former times—*purāṇam*. The *Purāṇas* drew on the narratives of earlier *rājās* from the Vedic texts, although often with some change.[24] Whether they were intended as commentaries remains controversial.[25] There are references in the *Viṣṇu Purāṇa* to the use of

[20] *Vāyu Purāṇa*, 1.183; *Matsya Purāṇa*, 53.63.

[21] *Vāyu Purāṇa*, 1.54.

[22] *Viṣṇu Purāṇa*, 1.2.8–9. This and all future citations are to the Gorakhpur edition.

[23] *Viṣṇu Purāṇa*, 3.6.15ff.

[24] P. Horsch, *Die Vedische Gāthā und Śloka Literateur*, 12–13.

[25] L. Rocher, *The Puranas*, 14ff.

earlier forms, such as the *ākhyāna, upākhyāna, gāthā*, and others, as sources.[26]

The earlier *Purāṇas* are the more important ones in terms of genealogical data, although the details vary. Genealogies were enlarged from the shallow lists of the Vedic corpus to the longer ones of the epics, and thence to further generations, interspersed with familiar legends.[27] Contradictory statements suggest that these texts do not conform to a particular orthodoxy. Some claim that the *Purāṇas* are the *sāra* (essence) of the *Vedas*, others that they precede the *Vedas—purāṇam sarva śāstrānām pratham.*[28] Additions are claimed as that which came from the past (*yathāśruta*).[29]

The *Viṣṇu Purāṇa* has more on the Mauryan dynasty (fourth to second centuries BC), the *Matsya* on the Andhras (second to third centuries AD), and the *Vāyu* attempts to bring the dynastic lists up to the Guptas (fourth to sixth centuries AD).[30] Because they were not regarded as revealed, they could be changed and brought up-to-date with contemporary social needs, which makes it difficult to date them. Their claim to authenticity is that their contents come from ancient times.[31]

The *Viṣṇu Purāṇa* states that for compiling the four *Vedas* Kṛṣṇa Dvaipāyana consulted one *brāhmaṇa* for each. But for the *itihāsa-purāṇa* he asked the *sūta* Romaharṣaṇa. This was despite the *itihāsa-purāṇa* being referred to as the fifth *Veda.*[32] This suggests that the source of the *Purāṇas* lay in the compositions of the *sūtas*, even if the recital is attributed to a *brāhmaṇa.*

In attributing the composition of the *Purāṇas* to Vyāsa and various *brāhmaṇas*, there is interplay between the *sūtas* and the *brāhmaṇas*, both linked with the authorship. If the genealogical sections were originally composed in Prākrit, as has been suggested, they are more likely to have been composed by the *sūtas.*[33]

[26] A.S. Gupta, "Purāṇa, Itihāsa and Ākhyāna", 451ff.; *Viṣṇu Purāṇa*, 3.6.15ff.

[27] *Mahābhārata*, 4.20.8ff., 1.69.29ff.; *Viṣṇu Purāṇa*, 4.1.11ff.

[28] *Devī-Bhāgavata Purāṇa*, 12.13.26; *Matsya Purāṇa*, 53.3.

[29] *Padma Purāṇa*, 5.2.53.

[30] V. Smith, *The Early History of India*, 11ff.

[31] *Vāyu Purāṇa*, 1.183; *Matsya Purāṇa*, 53.63.

[32] *Viṣṇu Purāṇa*, 3.4.7–10; 3.6.15ff.

[33] F.E. Pargiter, *DKA*, x–xi.

On *brāhmaṇas* recognizing the importance of appropriating the records of the past, they may have taken these over, rendered them into Sanskrit, and incorporated them in the early *Purāṇas.* Such a process would point to the recognition of the importance of creating a historical tradition. The information is generally given in the form of a dialogue, with one person asking a question and the other replying, as with Maitreya and Parāśara in the *Viṣṇu Purāṇa.*

Echoing the *Mahābhārata*, it is also said that an original *Purāṇa* was taught by Vyāsa to his fifth disciple, the bard Lomaharṣaṇa/ Romaharṣaṇa—literally "causing the hair to stand erect in excitement"—who was not a *brāhmaṇa.*[34] He is praised and respected and requested to narrate past events.[35] The connection of the *purāṇa* with the *sūta* would seem to be so necessary that, even when it is attributed to *brāhmaṇa* authors, the *sūta* remains central. Lomaharṣaṇa divided the original *Purāṇa* into six parts, each of which he taught to all his six disciples. These six, curiously, were all *brāhmaṇas*, curious because the high-caste *brāhmaṇa* would not have taken instruction from the lower-caste bard. In addition, Lomaharṣaṇa also taught the entire *Purāṇa* to his son, Ugraśravas, who recited it for a living, his disciples being *brāhmaṇas* and bards. Clearly, there is ambivalence over whether the authorship be ascribed to *brāhmaṇas* or to bards, and this is also an echo from the *Mahābhārata*. Doubtless, this was aggravated by the genealogical material coming from the oral tradition of the bards. Most existing *Purāṇas* claim the stereotyped origin that they were revealed by a deity to a *ṛṣi*, who then recited the text at a sacrifice.[36] Many of the early *Purāṇas* suggest that they were first recited in some part of northern India, sometimes the Naimiśa forest, but this was probably just convention.[37]

The *sūta* is said to have been honoured by the sages, even

[34] *Viṣṇu Purāṇa*, 3.4.10, 3.6.15ff.; *Vāyu Purāṇa*, 1.1.13–33; *Brahmāṇḍa Purāṇa*, 2.35.63ff.; V.S. Agrawala, "Original Purāṇa Saṃhita", *Purāṇa*, 232–45. The caste status of Vyāsa remains somewhat ambiguous. See B.M. Sullivan, *Krishna Dvaipayana Vyasa and the Mahabharata: A New Interpretation.*

[35] *Vāyu Purāṇa*, 1.13–33.

[36] G. Bonazzoli, "Puranic Parampara", 33–60.

[37] G. Bonazzoli, "Places of Puranic Recitation According to the Purāṇas", 48–60.

though he is not entitled to knowledge of the *Vedas* or to recite them.[38] Status in this case seems to have been different from caste, since it is said on one occasion that the killing of a *sūta* was as heinous as killing a *brāhmaṇa*: and yet the same text refers to the bard as being of low caste.[39]

The other term for a bard used occasionally is *māgadha,* even more obscure etymologically, perhaps linked to Magadha in south Bihar. The *māgadha* is sometimes called *brahmabandhu*, suggesting a dubious brahmanical link. Could this be a hint of these being low-level priests whose importance depended on their knowledge of the oral tradition?

The Manu *Dharmaśāstra* ascribes a low status to the *sūta* and the *māgadha* owing to their being of mixed caste (*varṇasaṃkara*), with a *kṣatriya* father and a *brāhmaṇa* mother, and therefore born of a hypogamous union (*pratiloma)*, regarded as particularly low.[40] Did the lowering of status reflect the bardic tradition having been taken over by the *brāhmaṇas*? The *Arthaśāstra*, however, distinguishes between the ordinary *sūta* and the one who recites the *Purāṇas*, but the *māgadha* remains low. In a largely oral tradition, it would seem normal for there to have been large numbers of persons associated with the profession of reciting narratives and compositions of various kinds, such as the *gāthaka* and the *gāyanah*, both of whom were singers;[41] the *kuśīlavah* and the *vāgajīvana*.[42]

The origin of the *sūta* and the *māgadha*, as described in the *Purāṇas*, is linked to the consecration ritual of the primeval ruler Pṛthu Vainya.[43] The two bards, when emerging from the sacrificial fire, were addressed very respectfully, appointed hereditary

[38] L. Rocher, *The Puranas*, 49ff. He is said to have been addressed as *medhāvin, vaṃśakuśala, kalpajña*, and *mahābhāga*: *Vāyu Purāṇa,* 1.13–29.

[39] *Bhāgavata Purāṇa*, 1.18.18.

[40] *Baudhāyana Dharmasūtra*, 1.9.17.8; *Manu's Code of Law*, 10.11, 17, 47; *Arthaśāstra*, 2.30.42, 3.7.27–9.

[41] *Aṣṭādhyāyī of Pāṇini*, 3.1.146–7.

[42] *Arthaśāstra,* 3.13.30, 2.27.6. The rather uncomplimentary associations with these professions were probably because the author of the text treated all professions which were itinerant as suspicious.

[43] *Viṣṇu Purāṇa*, 1.13.41ff.

chroniclers, and asked to recite the lineage of Pṛthu. Their names would associate them with the territories of Aṅga and Magadha, located on the fringes of the *ārya-varta*, said to be inhabited by the *mleccha* and the *vrātya*, the impure people of low culture. The story provided an exalted status to the original keepers of the tradition, even if associated with a culture regarded as somewhat alien. Despite their low status they were gradually acculturated.[44] Possibly, at this stage, the genealogical tradition was separate, to be later amalgamated with other traditions, when taken over by *brāhmaṇa* authors as part of the Puranic texts.

A distinction has to be maintained between the high-status, learned *brāhmaṇa,* and the one who reworks data collected from the *sūta.* A generalized link is made to Vedic authority,[45] but the essentials of these texts are different. It is claimed that they are transmitting that which in some cases has not so far been revealed. This is a way of validating new information.

4. The Contents of the *Viṣṇu Purāṇa*

From the perspective of the *itihāsa-purāṇa* tradition, the *Viṣṇu Purāṇa* is probably the best example, for it appears to have fewer interpolations. Its composition is consistently that of a single text.[46] The structure of the *Viṣṇu Purāṇa* conforms more closely to the five *aṃśas* (parts) required of a *Purāṇa.*[47] A description of the creation of the world, as well as the geography of the universe, precedes the genealogical section thus providing both a temporal and spatial context to the past. It also provides a context to the eschatology of the *Purāṇas*.

The opening section, on primary creation, considers the origin of the universe and of human society within an all-encompassing cosmology.[48] The world was created by Viṣṇu, with *kāla* (time)

[44] The *Mahābhārata* uses the epithet *vrātyam sūtam*: Anuśāsana *parvan*, 48.10.

[45] G. Bonazzoli, "Remarks on the Nature of the Purāṇas", 77–113.

[46] R.C. Hazra, *Studies in the Puranic Records of Hindu Rites*, 18.

[47] *The Vishnu Purana*, ed. and trans. H.H. Wilson, rpnt with an Introduction by R.C. Hazra; V.R.R. Dikshitar, "The Age of Visnu Purana", 46–50.

[48] *Viṣṇu Purāṇa,* 1.

as a causal factor. The symbolic measurement of time, both human and divine, described in some detail provides the framework for cosmological time. The earliest events take place in the first time cycle of the Kṛta *yuga*, and are essential to the beginnings of Puranic eschatology.

Legends are narrated with purposeful intent. The birth of Manu Svayambhu, the self-born, is described, as is the descent of the celestials.[49] Interspersing genealogies with legends and myths created a transition between myth and that past which was perceived to have happened. It also extended the story—always useful to bardic recitations—covered up breaks in succession, explained alliances and enmities, and validated unusual social customs. The *Vedas* are revealed, followed by the creation of the four *varṇas*, to enable the performance of sacrifices— which gives them a ritual context. In the third time cycle, the Tretā *yuga*, sin enters human life through the agency of those opposed to the *Vedas*.[50] Implicit in this is the equation of time with change. The perfection of the Golden Age of the Kṛta *yuga* is now tarnished.

The story of Pṛthu Vainya, frequently related in many texts, is recounted in a Puranic version.[51] This was important because Pṛthu was a descendant of the earliest rulers, the Manus, and an ancestor of Manu Vaivasvat, seventh in the line. In the *Purāṇa* the story is extraneous to the *vaṃśānucarita* as the relationship with Manu is ambiguous. It seems to illustrate the contention between ritual specialist and ruler, as well as explain the expulsion of forest-dwellers from mainstream society and their ensuing low status,[52] as with those who dwell in the Vindhya mountains.[53] The forest-dweller preceded the cultivator and may on that account too have been seen as the earlier inferior person.

Pṛthu became the legitimate ruler, was given the title of *rājā* because he pleased—*anurañjita*—his subjects, the same etymology as given in the *Mahābhārata*. Characteristic of utopian

[49] *Viṣṇu Purāṇa,* 1.7.1ff.

[50] *Viṣṇu Purāṇa,* 1.6.29ff.

[51] *Viṣṇu Purāṇa,* 1.13.8ff.

[52] *Manu's Code of Law*, 10.39, 4.79.

[53] *Viṣṇu Purāṇa*, 1.13.36ff.; *Bhāgavata Purāṇa*, 4.14.45–6; *Brahmāṇḍa Purāṇa* 2.36.11–46.

conditions was that grain and milk were produced without labour.[54] Pṛthu carried the mark of Viṣṇu's *cakra* (disc) on his hand and is therefore described as a *cakravartin*, as powerful as the gods and associated with conquest. The Buddhists used it for a universal monarch whose rule was associated with the wheel of law.

Brahmā performed a *yajña* at the birth of Pṛthu. Out of the sacrificial fire there sprang the *sūta* and the *māgadha*, who were instructed to praise the lord of men.[55] The *sūta* was recording the past, making predictions, and to that extent commenting on the present. This version of the myth captures many features of the historical perceptions of the time, such as states incorporating forest lands into their domains, and forest-dwellers being dismissed as inferior.

The disjuncture between *grāma* and *araṇya*—the settled village and the forest—is a running thread in social history.[56] The myth provides a justification for treating forest-dwellers with contempt. Niṣāda, together with Bhilla, Śabara, and Pulinda, becomes a generic term, connoting those for whom the forest is their habitat. Also included here is a caution against states without rulers bringing about lawlessness.[57] Such a condition is set right with establishing a *rājā* and the emergence of *varṇas*, which bring order into society. The *rājā* is invested with the power of *daṇḍa* (coercion). This picture is contrasted with that of a pristine age, when there was an absence of both *varṇas* and coercion,[58] there being no need for either.

Multiple myths follow, tracing the descent of deities and suggestive of the merging of traditions. Reference is made to the mind-born progeny of Brahmā, among whom are the Bhṛgu and Aṅgirasa *brāhmaṇas*,[59] who play an important role in the historical tradition.

The duties of the four castes as given may in times of distress be modified. The four *āśramas* or stages of life—student,

[54] *Viṣṇu Purāṇa*, 1.13.50.
[55] *Viṣṇu Purāṇa,* 1.13.51–7.
[56] R. Thapar, "Perceiving the Forest: Early India", 1–16.
[57] *Viṣṇu Purāṇa*, 1.13.30–2.
[58] *Vāyu Purāṇa*, 1.8.60, 1.8.155, 1.8.55–8.
[59] *Vāyu Purāṇa*, 1.59.88.

householder, anchorite, ascetic—are listed, as well as the rites of passage for each, as are other matters pertaining to social obligations. This section reads like an encapsulation of the *Dharmaśāstras*, setting forth the normative position but with the addition of some features from contemporary belief and custom.

The section on *prati-sarga* (secondary creation) is essentially concerned with the cosmos and the geography of the earth. The universe is shaped like an egg, its size measuring infinite space. The earth lies at the centre, with seven nether regions (*pātāla*) below it, where evil-doers are sent after death and which is peopled by demons. Above it are another six directions, the *lokas*. At the centre of the earth is Jambudvīpa, circular and surrounded by seven concentric oceans and continents, at the core of which is Mount Meru, the centre of the universe. Jambudvīpa is divided by mountain ranges into seven parts, among which one is Bhārata-varṣa. Whereas the wider geography is fanciful, that of Bhārata-varṣa is less so, even if not always precise,[60] a mix of imagination and some geographical names. Places referred to as *janapadas* (settlements of clans and peoples) are a trifle more accurate. Geographical information, whether accurate or not, is set in a larger canvas of cosmology referring to other continents, nether regions, space, planets, and constellations, the movement of the sun and the moon, and the seasons.

The third *aṃśa* (section) of the *Purāṇa* treats of the time dimension of cosmology in some detail.[61] An attempt is made to reconcile various forms of time-reckoning, such as the *kalpa*, *manvantara*, and the *yugas*. The *kalpa* covers the creation and the destruction of the universe. We are told that Brahmā created Manu Svayambhu, the self-born, who was followed by a sequence of Manus, each of whose time-period, the *manvantara*, is described and is almost a reckoning of infinite time. Each is associated with

[60] D.C. Sircar, *Studies in the Geography of Ancient and Medieval India*; M.R. Singh, *Geographical Data in the Early Puranas*; S.B. Chaudhuri, *Ethnic Settlements in Ancient India: A Study of the Puranic Lists of the Peoples of Bhārata-varṣa*.

[61] *Viṣṇu Purāṇa*, 3.1.7ff.

a group of deities, of *ṛṣis* and of sons, culminating in the seventh Manu, Vaivasvat, in the present cycle of time. There are still more *manvantaras* to follow after the destruction of the present. Each *manvantara* is a repetition of an earlier one and the *Vedas*, when they disappear at the end of this period, have to be revealed afresh. The *ṛṣis* teach the *dharma* and the *Vedas* in each *manvantara*; continuity is maintained by each group repeating what it has heard from the one in the preceding *manvantara*.[62] But the *manvantara* is not intended as a specific unit of time. The universe is tied to time and since Viṣṇu incorporates time, time is also a creator, preserver, and destroyer of the universe.[63]

The *manvantara* was one form of time-reckoning, more closely tied to the Manus, but different from the *mahāyuga*—the cycle of four *yugas*. It has been suggested that time was structured in two ways, perhaps indicating a different authorship and narrative. Eventually, the concept of the four *yugas* prevailed. The *manvantara* reckoning may have been intended initially for the period of the Manus, whereas the *mahāyuga* was more closely tied to *kṣatriya* descent groups and dynasties.

This is followed by a fierce denunciation of sects that do not follow the *Vedas* and the *Dharmaśāstras*. These are the *nagna* or naked mendicants—presumably Digambara Jainas and those clothed in *raktāmbara* (red cloth), the Buddhists. Viṣṇu creates "Māhāmoha", a false teacher of delusory ideas who preaches anti-Vedic beliefs to the sinful and ensures their damnation. The teaching is evil because it gives equal validity to theories that contradict Vedic belief, that oppose animal sacrifice, and that question the efficacy of caste rules. Many *pāṣaṇḍas* (false sects) are created by Māhāmoha. There was thus a currency of opposing ideologies. Eventually, these are among the reasons that bring about the dystopia that leads to the calamitous decline of the universe, coinciding with the end of the time-cycle.

The fourth *aṃśa* of the *Purāṇa* contains the descent lists of the

[62] J.E. Mitchiner, "The Evolution of the Manvantara Theory as Illustrated by the *Saptarṣi* Manvantara Traditions", 7–37; L. Gonzales-Reiman, *The Mahābhārata and the Yugas*, 3–4.

[63] *Viṣṇu Purāṇa*, 1.2.15ff.

ruling families, the *vaṃśānucarita*. It begins with the Manus, then moves to the genealogies of the *kṣatriyas*, and the final section lists the dynasties and kings of each.

The fifth describes the Kṛṣṇa incarnation of Viṣṇu and is replete with legends on his life. A brief sixth section considers the theories on the four ages and the ultimate destruction of the world. Possibly, this section was added when the theory of the four *yugas* overtook that of the *manvantaras*. Thus the text itself completes the cycle and the reader can return to the beginning with the description of primary creation.

5. The *Vaṃśānucarita*

A significant question would be why genealogies, whether actual or invented, came to be important to the perception of the past. Why were they embedded in texts with a religious sectarian identity? The timeframe is continuous, but the patterns within the succession lists indicate historical change. The pattern is not arbitrary, nor the time when it was formulated. (Incidentally, such patterns suggest a perspective different from that of the colonial construction of the early Indian past, which was based on racial identities.)

That this perspective was expressed through genealogies has to do with the centrality of clan and caste in Indian society: a system in which genealogical connections (actual or fictional) are social imperatives. It comes to form what might be called a genealogical mode of recording the past. That it was embedded, but not firmly, in religious sectarian texts was probably for the same reasons that the hero-lauds of earlier times were part of the Ṛgvedic hymns—they received attention and were preserved. The genealogies are more frequently found in Vaiṣṇava *Purāṇas*, and this in a sense links them to the Bhāgavata redactions of the epics.

Until recently, genealogies had little respectability as historical data among historians. It was only with the work of anthropologists and some social historians that what was earlier regarded as fanciful concoction began to be subjected to serious study.[64] Genealogy

[64] J. Vansina, *Oral Tradition as History*; D.P. Henige, *The Chronology of Oral Tradition*.

is not just a matter of real or fanciful history. Genealogies claim to be past records, although their preservation or even invention can derive from the social institutions of the present, including kingship, for which they are legitimizing mechanisms. Thus the *kṣatriya* descent lists recall clan society, yet some later dynasties claimed *kṣatriya* status by linking their ancestry to one of the lineages. Genealogies need not be taken as faithful records of the past, but they can claim to be memories of social relations and therefore have an important social function since succession can relate not only to transfer of property but also status. Genealogies can be rearranged if need be in accordance with the requirements of later times, as in the sorting out of *kṣatriyas* into the Solar and Lunar lines—the Sūryavaṃśa and the Candravaṃśa. Where they record migration, fission or assimilation, they do so by separating or incorporating lineages in relation to the established ones. Myth and history in such perceptions of the past run parallel, occasionally intersecting.[65]

Genealogies are also a commemoration of those who have passed away and hint at a cult of the dead. Supposed ancestors do not necessarily have to be biological. Frequently, the earlier portions of lengthy genealogies are fabricated. They are required in order that status be bestowed on those making the claims. Therefore, the nature of connections sought by those constructing the genealogy is significant.

Genealogies become important at points of historical change, either with the entry of new social groups or factions, or in periods of competition when existing authority feels threatened. Treating them as legal charters and rearranging the fragments or compiling them into a coherent whole is closely tied to the changing political status of the person or family which is the subject of the genealogy. The historical reasons for the compiling of genealogies are therefore as significant as the actual pattern of the compilation.[66] Genealogical lists claim to be arranged chronologically. This involves time reckoning, where even a confused genealogy may

[65] J. Goody and I. Watt, "The Consequences of Literacy", 304–45.

[66] M. Fortes, "The Structure of Unilineal Descent Groups", *American Anthropologist*, 17–41.

nevertheless suggest a period of time. They need not be seen as a record of what happened—although in the later phases they often are seen as such—but they do implicitly in representing the past become a perspective on it. Other sources mention a tradition of maintaining genealogies in India in early times. Megasthenes, a friend of Seleucus Nicator, wrote an account of India in the fourth century BC, where he states that up to the time of Sandracottos (later identified as Candragupta Maurya) the Indians counted 153 kings over 6042 years.[67] Pliny has the figure at 154 kings over a period of 6451 years.[68] Despite the heavy inflation in numbers, the focus on genealogies is striking.

From the Puranic perspective the *vaṃśānucarita* is a book of genesis. It begins with myths of creation and cosmology but concentrates on the succession of those who are presumed to have wielded power. It assumes for the earlier periods the centrality of high status through birth and therefore access to power, and claims to provide the genealogies of all the *kṣatriyas* of Bhāratavarṣa, although in effect it is largely limited to parts of northern India.

The reciting of the *vaṃśānucarita* is attributed to Parāśara, in response to a request by Maitreya. There is no mention of a *sūta* at this point, although in some *Purāṇas* the *sūta* recites a portion.[69] An indirect reason for maintaining these lists is perhaps the fear that the past will be forgotten. A comment is made on the impermanence even of great heroes, of *yajamānas* (patrons of the sacrifice), and the *tapasvi* ascetics. It is said that even Pṛthu has vanished like a cotton pod thrown into the fire.[70] Was this a fear also born from the fact that alternative historical traditions were becoming prevalent?

An attempt will be made here to analyse the *vaṃśānucarita* of the *Viṣṇu Purāṇa*. Its construction appears to have been based on three sequential periods with distinctly different patterns. The first narrates the period of the Manus narrating myths of creation and cosmology. This period is set aside because of the great Flood, subsequent to which comes the second period. This constructs a

[67] Arrian, *Indica*, 9.9; Solinus 52.5.
[68] Pliny: *Natural History*, 6.21.4–5.
[69] *Viṣṇu Purāṇa* 4.1.1–4.
[70] *Viṣṇu Purāṇa*, 4.24.144–5.

record of what was perceived as the lineages of ruling clans. It traces the descent of the *kṣatriya* lineages from their progenitor Manu, via the two main descent groups, the Sūryavaṃśa and the Candravaṃśa. These include, among others, the families and clans of the *Mahābhārata* and the *Rāmāyaṇa*. The third section is a listing of kings and dynasties, reflecting the establishment of kingship and the state. It focuses initially on Magadha and continues up to the Gupta rulers of the mid-first millennium AD, and possibly a little later.[71] These three distinctive patterns reflect a perception of historical change in northern India.

6. Manu and the Flood

There is much in the first part—the time of the Manus—that conforms to reconstruction through myth. Time is seen as infinity and the narrative is almost chronos-free, a time when gods and men mingled. The narrative, in the form of a dialogue between the bard and the sage, begins with the god Brahmā. Descent is traced from the gods via Dakṣa, Aditi, and the seven Manus who ruled at the beginning of time, associated with enormous timespans. During the reign of the seventh Manu there occurs the great Flood which destroys everything. But Manu survives to become the ancestor to the two main *kṣatriya* lineages, the Sūryavaṃśa and the Candravaṃśa.[72] The Flood is a time-marker.

The story of the Flood, first mentioned in the *Śatapatha Brāhmaṇa* and repeated in the *Mahābhārata,* is elaborated upon in the *Matsya Purāṇa*, although the versions differ in details.[73] The story was clearly important, repeatedly narrated with some modification. The Puranic version centres on the perspective of the past.

In the *Matsya Purāṇa* the fish becomes an incarnation of Viṣṇu. In this form Viṣṇu predicts first a drought and then a flood. The ship, tied to the horn of the fish, carries Manu, various deities,

[71] A.B.L. Awasthi, *History from the Puranas*, maintains that there are references to post-Gupta history in some *Purāṇas*, but these suggestions are not convincing.

[72] Table IV (p. 318) summarizes the Puranic pattern.

[73] *Śatapatha Brāhmaṇa*, 1.8.1.1–10; *Mahābhārata*, 3.185; *Matsya Purāṇa*, 1.16ff.

the seed of all creatures, some embodied rivers, *ṛṣis*, the *Vedas* and *Purāṇas*, and various branches of knowledge. The inclusion of the Puranic texts is crucial to the status of the *Matsya Purāṇa* itself. The change of deity from Brahmā in the *Mahābhārata* to the *matsya*, the fish incarnation of Viṣṇu, marks a departure.[74]

Manu, returning after the waters subsided, was desirous of sons, so he performed a sacrifice. The first child (although in some texts this was the last child) was Ilā, literally the name for sacrificial food or libation,[75] who was born a woman because of a fault in the ritual! Other versions state that the male Ila was transformed into the female Ilā to eventually become a hermaphrodite, *kiṃpuruṣa*, or that Ila was alternately male and female for specific periods.[76] The female Ilā was the eponymous ancestor of the Candravaṃśa, and Manu's eldest son Ikṣvāku of the Sūryavaṃśa. The restoration of life after the Flood has to be brought about through ritual, and there is an interweaving of sacrifice and procreation.[77]

Of all the multiplicity of Flood stories from various cultures, these versions parallel most closely the story in the earlier Mesopotamian texts.[78] The latter speak of the seven pre-diluvian kings with inordinately long reigns, and the survivor who is associated with the descent of kingship onto various cities of Mesopotamia. The seven sages are also mentioned. Regnal years use figures similar to those given in the later Puranic time cycles, such as 1200, 32,400, and 64,800. The figure of 1200 is mentioned as the last segment of time, in which the population increased and became a source of irritation to the gods. Each successive cycle is said to be of 4800 years. These figures are repeated by the Babylonian Berossus with reference to Chaldean chronology, where mention

[74] A fish with a horn is known in the whale family—the narwhal—and now only in the Arctic. Greek authors refer to huge sea animals like whales near the Makran coast. Arrian, *Anabasis Alexandri, Books V to VII, Indica*, 30.

[75] *Ṛgveda*, 5.41.19.

[76] *Matsya Purāṇa*, XI.40 to XII.50.

[77] J.C. Heesterman, "The Flood Story in Vedic Ritual", in idem, *The Inner Conflict of Tradition*, 59ff.

[78] W.G. Lambert and A.R. Millard, *Atra-hasis*. This story was also the source for the Biblical version of Noah and the Flood (Genesis 6.5–8.22); E.A. Speiser, *Genesis*, 9, 55.

is made of 36,000 and 64,800 years. Berossus writes of ten patriarchs from Adam to Noah and of ten kings from the creation to the Flood, ascribing to them a period of 432,000 years, a figure that features in the *mahāyuga* theory of time.[79] He also mentions eight sages, and the first of these is fish-like in appearance. The Sumerian god Enki, who saves mankind, is often represented as a fish in later Mesopotamian mythology. As a contrast to the enormous length of the pre-diluvian regnal years, the post-diluvian drop to credible figures. The Flood seems to mark a past which is more mythical, as distinct from the later one, which is more real.

Given the close connections between the Harappans and the Mesopotamians, the story may have been current in Harappan times and come down as part of an earlier tradition. Alternatively, it may have become familiar from Assyrian sources closer in time to the *Śatapatha Brāhmaṇa*, which is later than the Sumerian source. Flood legends seem to have been common in the eastern Mediterranean and are mentioned by Plato and Strabo.[80] What is significant is that the beginning of history in Puranic terms is traced to a myth which has links not with Indo-European sources but with those in West Asia. The Iranian variant of the Flood story—which might have been included in Vedic mythology given the closeness between Old Iranian and Indo-Aryan—is absent. This is not the narrative of a flood but of a freeze resulting from endless winters which brings life to a standstill. The earth also suffers from overcrowding, thus echoing the Mesopotamian version. The ark is not a ship but a cubical enclosure which eventually is placed inside a mountain.

The Flood in the *Purāṇa* assumes the primary precondition of water, out of which the known creation arises. The reason for including it in the myth of genesis is perhaps because it represents the *pralaya*, the calamitous termination of the previous creation, from the ruins of which the new creation arose. No reason is given for the Flood, unlike the Mesopotamian version where it is a punishment. The Puranic version suggests a cleaning away of the past, but Manu, and those that survived in his boat, represent continuity.

[79] S.M. Burstein (ed. and trans.), *The Babylonica of Berossus*, 19–21.

[80] *Geography of Strabo*, 13.1; Plato: *Timaeus*, III, 677–80.

The Flood can also be a stage in the cycle of time, perhaps what Eliade would call the abolition of profane time,[81] where the Flood is a marker separating the ending of one creation and the starting of another, or even the time of origins, seen from the perspective of later events. The remote past of the Manus is narrated through myths, not through genealogical connections. The beginnings of history emerge from a condition which has no antecedents. Manu/*mānava* would inevitably have survived, but he acquires prestige through being chosen to survive. This, in turn, gives added prestige to those who claim descent from him, and who are listed in the second part of the genealogical record.

7. The Lineages

The second part of the *vaṃśānucarita* introduces the children of Manu. They are eponymous ancestors of the various lineages listed in detail, the *vaṃśam rājñyam,* and this "succession of *rājās*" is not grouped into dynasties but into lineages. Many of these are kin-related, literally claiming a line of descent from a common ancestor. They are also referred to as *kṣatriyas,* those with *kṣatra* (power). The descent groups are worked out in a neat structure of genealogical patterns. Interspersed within the lists are legends and myths, suggesting perhaps points of change or break. The inclusion of genealogies in a ritual text is again an attempt at using sanctification to ensure preservation.

These legends are not arbitrary. Some are variants on what were referred to as *itihāsa* in earlier sources, their choice thus being deliberate. They provide clues to social custom and define the ethos of the *kṣatriya*, among which are the *digvijayas* of Mandhātṛ and Sagara; and the *svayamvaras.* Both are expressive of heroic societies, but change their meaning in later periods. The *digvijaya* begins to reflect a fantasy of conquest with a rhetoric of names.

Listing conquered areas is also a mechanism for defining one's own territory, but the lists should preferably be read as statements on what was known of the wider world and current relationships between clans. When reference is made to the parentage of Bharata, there is a quotation from the *Mahābhārata* version of the

[81] M. Eliade, *Cosmos and History*, 115ff.

story, the epic being treated as a historical source.[82] The descent list of the Pūrus is substantially from the *Mahābhārata*, although there are deviations. A few names echo the Vedic corpus.[83] Was this an attempt to include these names to give them continuity and a hint of historicity?

Manu's eldest son, Ikṣvāku, the progenitor of the Sūryavaṃśa, had three sons, two of whom were important and established themselves at Kosala and Videha, contiguous territories in the middle Ganges plain and important to the narrative of the *Rāmāyaṇa*. The rulers of Kosala and Videha are therefore of collateral lines. The *Rāmāyaṇa* is an epic of the Sūryavaṃśa. The form of this genealogy is the presumed record of descent from father to eldest son. Younger sons are not mentioned barring exceptional cases. Collaterals can be set aside when the purpose is to record the transmission of property and office going from father to eldest son. Patrilineal descent is heavily underlined, as also the unchallenged right to succession of the eldest son. Thus the narrative of the *Rāmāyaṇa* becomes all the more meaningful in this context. The initial genealogy would have terminated with Rāma, but the addition to the epic takes it to his sons.

The *Rāmāyaṇa* preserves a list which differs from the *Purāṇas* both in numbers of generations and the ordering of succession.[84] Lengthening and shortening of the lists is not uniform. In this process, a few relationships may be altered while others are omitted, and some new names added. Synchronizing generations in different lineages is not thought necessary. Lengthening through added numbers of generation is generally associated with more centralized polities. Whereas such succession need not be accurate over an extended period, it does point to an attempt to project a relatively stable political society.

The descent lists in the *Purāṇas* and the epics are not identical. The *Purāṇas* appear to have telescoped the earlier generations, a technique often used by genealogists and which has been described as structural amnesia. The *Rāmāyaṇa* reflects a more durable

[82] *Viṣṇu Purāṇa*, 4.19.12–14; *Mahābhārata*, 1.69.29ff.

[83] *Viṣṇu Purāṇa*, 4.19ff.

[84] *Rāmāyaṇa*, 1.70–1.

polity in the kingdom of Kosala through its lineage, as compared to the area of exile such as Kiṣkindhā and Daṇḍakāraṇya where lineages are absent. The society associated with the Sūryavaṃśa lineage was being shown as politically more stable.

The lineage of Janaka suggests fabricated genealogies. Janaka, descended from Ikṣvāku, emerged from a *manthana* or churning, since his father was Videha, literally "without a body". The myth echoes the story of the churning of Vena. Sītā was found in a *sītā* (furrow) and adopted. The genealogy terminates with this.

The genealogical pattern of the Candravamśa (the Lunar line) is a contrast to that of the Solar. From Manu's female child Ilā is descended a vast spread of clans classified as Candravaṃśa. Women standing at the apex of a clan, or myths of celestial women as the mothers of heroes, may suggest a different kind of clan organization.[85] The genealogical pattern of the Candravaṃśa records the descent of all the sons in the early part of the genealogy, and each forms a segment of the main lineage. The lists of descent do not come down in neat parallels but fan out laterally and inevitably cover a larger geographical space. This is similar to what has been described as segmentary lineage systems.[86] The obvious suggestion is that segments of these clans were given to migrating or fissioning off. But this pattern can equally be seen as attempts to assimilate other groups by inducting them into the lineage. This would have enlarged the geographical extent of the lineage identity. The Candravaṃśa has a larger number of clan names than personal names.

The descendants of Yadu, as segments of the Candravaṃśa, seem particularly prone to fanning out or incorporating new groups. The fanning out involved situations of conflict. These are referred to—even the attack on Ayodhyā by the Haihayas, a branch of the Yadus who are said to have had their stronghold at Mahiśmati on the Narmada river.[87] This is a contrast to the comparatively static nature of the Ikṣvāku descendants, who seem not to move away from the middle Ganges plain, suggesting a more

[85] This is said to be common in patrilineal polygynous societies. Personal communication from S.C. Humphreys.

[86] M.D. Sahlins, "The Segmentary Lineage: An Organisation of Predatory Expansion", 332–45.

[87] This episode has been discussed in Chapter 5.

stable kingdom. Presumably, this was how Kosala was viewed in retrospect at the time when the early *Purāṇas* were written.

Sometimes the founding ancestress of a segment is an *apsarā*, such as Urvaśī or Menakā, whose identity remains obscure. This becomes a ploy to paper over breaks. Some descent groups are named from ancestors, and some among these become clan names. Repeated patterns include that of five sons, three from one wife and two from another. The five sons of the famous Yayāti, the eldest Yadu and the youngest Pūru, are ancestors to the two most significant segments of this lineage and form a substantial part of the Candravaṃśa.[88]

Pūru, despite being the youngest son, inherits the core of the territory and Yadu has to migrate to the south-west. A myth is introduced to explain this reversal of primogeniture in which Pūru, unlike Yadu, agrees to exchange his youth for his father's old age. Yadu, Turvasa, and Pūru are mentioned as *rājās* in the *dāna-stutis.* Some others are also mentioned with Kuru as a prefix in their names, and Kasu the Cedi is especially wealthy. The main line of the Pūrus controls the Ganga-Yamuna Doab. Their descendents at a much later generational date are contestants in claims to this territory as narrated in the *Mahābhārata*. The descendents of both Pūru and Yadu have ambiguous caste identities since few are recognized as *kṣatriyas* in other sources, although they are listed as such in the *vaṃśānucarita.*

However, despite the projection of a seemingly smooth descent, there are also some barely disguised breaks in succession. An obvious break is the story of Bharata adopting a son, Bharadvāja, on the grounds that none of his sons were suitable. Further along in the line of Pūru descent, Hastin is followed by three sons, each of whom has the suffix *-mīḍha* in their names, suggesting "spurinyms".[89] Another break is the story of Devāpi and Śantanu, which takes us back to the *itihāsas* of the Vedic corpus.

Artificial lengthening of the descent list is evident from the

[88] Yayāti's five sons—Yadu, Anu, Turvasa, Druhyu, and Pūru—appear almost at the start of the descent list. Towards the end of the list come the five Pāṇḍavas—Yudhiṣṭhira, Bhīma, Arjuna, Nakula, and Sahadeva.

[89] D.P. Henige, *Chronology of Oral Tradition*, 40ff. A spurinym is a clearly spurious name.

use of toponyms and geographical names, such as the five sons of Bali—Aṅga, Vaṅga, Kaliṅga, Suhma, and Puṇḍra.[90] The genealogical construction in the *Purāṇas* ties together the scattered stories of persons, placing them in a framework that draws on the past. This can also be seen as an attempt at unifying the segments. In this process of restructuring, strangers get grafted in and others get detached.[91] The new entrants either come in laterally via a marriage alliance, or vertically as inheritors and successors. Recognizing these processes remains problematic.

Such recognition could come from customs, such as bride-price, marriage by abduction, cross-cousin marriage, and fraternal polyandry—not prominently propagated in the normative *Dharmaśāstra* texts. These occur in the stories punctuating the descent lists of the Candravaṃśa, reflecting a variety of kinship systems, some dissimilar from those of the Sūryavaṃśa.[92] Could some of these have come from societies different from the familiar agricultural communities?[93] The dichotomy between the normative texts and actual social forms becomes a pointer to recording social change through specific peoples, even if not historically accurate over their particulars.

The story of the Syamanta jewel, bestowing prosperity upon its owner, encapsulates the Yadu clan system.[94] There appears to have been competition and suspicion among the clans, therefore the jewel is closely guarded by one among them. At the point when it is lost, it is recovered by Kṛṣṇa, who is then welcomed by all the Yadu clans—*sakalayādavaḥ*—and the women of the clans. In order to make clear that he had not stolen it, Kṛṣṇa explains the events to the *yādavasamāja* (the gathering of the Yadu clans). This starts a series of intrigues involving clan hierarchies and rivalries as well as alliances. There are continuous references to Yadusamāja, Yadukula, Yaduvaṃśa, Yaduloka. The legends that punctuate the genealogies are taken from earlier Vedic and epic sources but are not identical. Linking earlier tradition with the

[90] *Viṣṇu Purāṇa*, 4.18.13ff.

[91] L. Bohanan, "A Genealogical Charter", 301–15; E. Peters, "The Proliferation of Segments in the Lineage of the Bedouin of Cyrenaica", 29–53.

[92] E.g., 4.7.21; T. Trautmann, *Dravidian Kinship,* 238ff.

[93] K. Gough, *Matrilineal Kinship*.

[94] *Viṣṇu Purāṇa*, 4.13.111ff.

current reconstruction gave authority to both. The Yadu clans are mentioned as a collective and in the plural, whereas the Pūrus are mentioned more frequently by name.

Candravaṃśa descent does not invariably claim to list a father to son succession. The relationship between generations is frequently left ambiguous, with statements such as "B" followed "A", or "B" was the heir of "A", or "B" was of "A" or "B" was after "A".[95] This is in contrast to the more specific mention of "B" being the son—*putra* or *ātmaja*—of "A".[96] There is a frequency in the use of forms connoting "being of", such as *tatasca, tasya, tasmād, tena, tata, tattanya.*[97]

The geography and migration of the Candravaṃśa lineages, and of the Yadus in particular, would include West and Central India, the Narmada and the Vindhyas, and large parts of the edge of the Ganges plain—a far wider spread than the more concise circuit of the Sūryavaṃśa in approximately the middle Ganges plain. The inclusion of some geographical locations could be the attempt of genealogists grouping varieties of peoples into neat genealogical packages, not entirely arbitrary. A consciousness of geographical space is apparent in the apportioning of space through the locations of the clans.

Barring the names and generational descent that occur in other sources as well, the rest of the names could be arbitrary and listed as fillers. These genealogies indicate the distribution of clans, their claims and alliances, prior to the rise of the kingdom of Magadha in the mid-first millennium BC. Such kinship links may have some veracity, but essentially the representation is of what was believed to have been the political and social co-ordinates of earlier times. The seamless genealogies suggest pre-state societies, or those in the process of mutating into kingdoms. The *kṣatriya* clans are of relatively equal status; the connections are through birth, even if they are fictional. Legends woven in from the *Mahābhārata* are attempts to draw on the authority of *itihāsa.* These are necessary to cover up breaks, to explain alliances to validate unusual customs, or even caricature some activities. The grand finale of this section is the war at Kurukṣetra, where all the clans face each

[95] F.E. Pargiter, *Ancient Indian Historical Tradition*, 89.
[96] *Viṣṇu Purāṇa*, 4.16.1ff.; 4.19.1ff.
[97] E.g., 4.8.18–21, 11.10, 12.2, 14.2–5, 21.12–16.

other and the war becomes the time-marker terminating *kṣatriya* clan societies.

A little digression at this point is perhaps in order, touching on aspects significant to the patterns of these two descent groups and attempting to explain why a genealogical mode of recording the past was appropriate. Apart from the question of the veracity of genealogies as a form of remembering the past, such forms were central to the society of the Ganges plain and its fringes in the period prior to the rise of states. The oral tradition had, in its repertoire, recitations in praise of heroes past and present. Occasions for displaying prowess such as cattle raids gave way to disputes over clearing and settling land, where settlements would be subject to attack especially if they encroached on existing habitations.

Settlement called for an organized migration, often led by *kṣatriya* families who lent their name to the territory and amalgamated clan, territory, and claims to sovereignty. This was seminal to the eventual instituting of the state. The clan chief or *rājā* could gradually evolve into a king but retaining the title "*rājā*".

The lineage claimed by the dominant clan determined the identity of those most respected. The Kuru, Pañcāla, Vatsa, Kāśī, Kosala, and Videha occupied the area from the watershed to the middle Ganges plain, bestowing their names on the territorial *janapadas*. Those of lesser status were on their fringes. The Yadus, based in West India, had some branches in Central India or even further east in Orissa. Geographical knowledge had expanded at the time when these texts were written, so there was a larger expanse to choose from in locating clans.[98] With the growth of urbanization in the mid-first millennium BC, the network of the Ganges plain draws closer together, and Magadha gradually emerges as the dominant region.[99]

There was now a distance between those who had access to or claimed private ownership over economic resources, and those

[98] Incidentally, there are hints of this from the distribution of archaeological cultures that appear to parallel this picture in the first millennium BC, although no definitive correlations can be made. R. Thapar, "Puranic Lineages and Archaeological Cultures", in idem, *Ancient Indian Social History: Some Interpretations,* 240–67.

[99] For a general discussion of the background to these historical conditions, see R. Thapar, *From Lineage to State*.

who worked on obtaining produce from these resources. The genealogies relate to the former. Even when claims to an extensive territorial identity declined, genealogies still functioned as important indicators of social links, especially those that were underwriting political power.

Current ideas on the origin of government supported the notion of a single person holding office as king, whether as a nominee of the gods or as elected by the community. The right to collect taxes ensured further power, as did the right to coerce, which was given to the ruler on the assumption that it was necessary for the preservation of law and order. Such an accumulation of rights points to the establishment of states defined as kingdoms similar to that at Magadha—on which there is much evidence. The epics, through their later interpolations, become charters of validation. They support the legitimacy of such states as a new form of political organization. The *Purāṇas* were of course written at a time when kingdoms were well established.

The reconstruction of the past in the form of genealogies provides pointers to how its social and political concerns were viewed. The *vaṃśānucarita* is both a construction of the past and a potential source for links with the future. Despite some names being common to all these texts, there is little evidence of a systematic borrowing in the later sources from the earlier.

The notion of kinship in a genealogy was extended through links over time. Genealogies, in any case, shift attention back to an archaic period where eponymous ancestors and legendary heroes are the protagonists. Nevertheless, there is a sense of time which links this past to later generations and to contemporary personalities. The significance of literacy can be deduced from the length and complexity of the genealogical pattern. The Puranic genealogies appear to have been deliberately constructed from smaller fragments and the overall form points to presenting a distinct perspective on the past.

What is important, therefore, is not that the genealogies do not always tally in various sources, but that the function of this data suggests an awareness of a changed historical situation represented in this attempt to construct the past. Genealogies, creating a continuous and seemingly unbroken past, relate to societies where descent groups are more important than institutions. This pattern, however, changes in the third and last part of the *vaṃśānucarita*, when a new form comes to be recorded.

8. The Dynasties

The war at Kurukṣetra is a catastrophe, and catastrophes are time-markers. As the *Purāṇas* put it, the war ends the splendour of the *kṣatriyas*. The world and its polities are not the same thereafter. This is reflected in distinctly new features of the record of succession. The *kṣatriya* clans now give way to the pedigrees of kings.

Subsequent to the war, statements about what follows are made in the future tense, even though the text was compiled after the events. The *Viṣṇu Purāṇa* maintains that it is being composed in the reign of Parikṣit, three generations after the war. The prophetic form includes occasional lapses into the past tense, suggesting that it was originally written in the past tense, as was the rest of the *vaṃśānucarita*, but that at some point the dynastic section was changed to the future tense.[100] The narrator of the *Viṣṇu Purāṇa* says, "I will now enumerate the *bhupālas*, who will reign in the future periods. . ."[101] A distinction is perhaps being made between referring to the clans as *kṣatriyas* and the terms now used for kings, such as *bhupāla* and *nṛpa* (protector of the earth and of men).[102] The past lay in events which took place before the war. The Pūru line surviving the war terminates with Kṣemaka in the Kali age.

In using the future tense the narrator claims the power of prophecy and the author's ability to foresee events. It might also suggest the uncertainty of the shift to dynasties, made inevitable by the power of prophecy. The implication seems to be that those who control the past have access to the future. Happily, the switch to the future tense provides us today with a clue as to approximately when the text was compiled, since the prophecy stops with contemporary dynasties.[103]

100 F. E. Pargiter, *DKA*, ixff.

101 *Viṣṇu Purāṇa*, 4.21.1: *atah paraṃ bhaviṣyānaham bhūpālān kīrtyiṣyāmi*; *Vāyu Purāṇa*, 2.37.256ff.

102 F.E. Pargiter, *DKA*, 2–3, 57.

103 The *Bhaviṣya Purāṇa*, composed some centuries later, carries further information of some post-Gupta dynasties.

The prophetic form did not, however, prevent variations among the *Purāṇas* on what was to follow. A few further descendants of the Sūryavaṃśa and the Candravaṃśa are listed, but more as a rounding off of the descent groups. Among the former, mention is made of the Buddha's family, of Siddhartha as the son of Śuddhodana and grandson of Śākya, and of his own son Rāhula. Nothing further is said in this section about the Buddha.The focus shifts from the upper Doab to the Ganga–Yamuna confluence, a migration necessitated by a flood of the Ganges and the destruction of the earlier capital at Hastināpura, leading to a new settlement at Kauśāmbī.

Dynastic history is traced through the line of Magadha, and the first dynasty mentioned, together with individual regnal years, was that of the Bṛhadrathas. The reckoning by regnal years was a concession to a plausible, measured concept of time. Magadha is no longer the *mleccha-deśa* of earlier sources but is seen as the region where ruling dynasties were first established. We are told that the kings listed in this section of the *vaṃśānucarita* shall include those who are of mixed caste, those regarded as of low status (*vrātya*), those who are of lower caste (*a-dvija*), the *śūdras*, foreigners and others of impure origin (*mleccha*), and those who are of *udit-odit vaṃśa* (upstarts). There would thus be a mixing of *ārya* and *mleccha*. This was a concession to political power being negotiable and open to those who did not even have to claim to be *kṣatriyas* in origin. Regnal years accompanying the list of *bhupālas* and *nṛpas* do not necessarily agree in the various *Purāṇas*, but are characteristic of kingship and indicate the increasing centrality of linear time in the historical tradition. Whereas previously the succession was that of the *vaṃśam rājñyam*, the later lists are of dynasties and enumerate names and regnal years of individual kings.[104]

Subsequent to the Bṛhadrathas, the Pradyotavaṃśa ruled for 138 years and are described as *pṛthivīm bhokṣyanti* (enjoying the earth), a phrase not associated with the *kṣatriya vaṃśas* but now occurring in association with dynasties.[105] The early Śiśunāga

[104] *Viṣṇu Purāṇa*, 5.1.1: *nṛpāṇām kathitassarvo bhavatā vaṃśavistaraḥ/ vaṁśānucaritam caiva yathāvadanuvarṇitam.*

[105] *Viṣṇu Purāṇa*, 4.24.2, 7.

dynasty is permitted a minor concession in that the kings are described as having *kṣatriya* kinsfolk—*rājanah kṣatra bāndhavah*—or being *kṣatrabandhu* (so-called *kṣatriyas*). Of the Nandas it is specifically said that the founder, Mahāpadma, will exterminate all *kṣatriyas*—*kṣatra vināśa kṛt*—as did Paraśurāma of old, and subsequent kings will be *śūdras* and *adharmakah*. This could be a reference to his destroying the clan societies. The *gaṇa-saṅghas* of the middle Ganges plain play no political role after the Nandas. Mahāpadma is described as *eka-cchātram* (sole ruler). The *brāhmaṇa* Kauṭilya, we are told, will uproot the Nandas and anoint Candragupta as king, who will found the Maurya dynasty that will enjoy the earth (*pṛthvīm bhokṣyanti*) for 137 years. The enjoyment of the earth is more frequently associated with kings. No comment is made on the Mauryan kings, especially Aśoka, being patrons of the heterodox. References to the low origin of the Mauryas increase in the later commentaries on the *Purāṇas*.[106]

Puṣyamitra Śuṅga will assassinate his king Bṛhadratha, the last of the Mauryas. Vasudeva, the minister of the Śuṅgas, will overthrow the last of the Śuṅgas and establish the Kāṇva dynasty. This is referred to as the Śuṅgabhṛtya, literally the servant of the Śuṅga, but perhaps better rendered as "in the service of . . .",[107] these being people in administrative office who, relying on the use of force as well as the authority of office, rose to kingship. The last Kāṇva will be assassinated by his *bhṛtya*, who has the unusual name of Balipuccha, and will inaugurate the Andhra dynasty. The Andhras, *bhṛtyas* of the Kāṇvas, are succeeded in turn by their *bhṛtyas*. The political ambitions of the upper bureaucracy would seem to have often met with success in this account.

A long list of successors follows, among which feature the Śakas, Yavanas, and Turuṣkas. The last was doubtless a reference to Central Asians such as the Kuṣāṇas. The Guptas, mentioned towards the end of the list, will rule over the *janapadas,* of Gaṅga, Prayāga, Sāketa, and Magadha. This is followed by a list of territories across northern India. Those ruling in these territories are described as kings of Vidiśā, Bāhlikas, Mekala, Kosala,

[106] S.N. Roy, "Textual and Historical Analysis of the Puranic Chronology Relating to the Maurya Dynasty", 94–106.

[107] *Bhṛtya*, from the root *bhṛ*, to bear or to carry, means being dependent on, or a servant of, and refers to one who is to be maintained or nourished.

Niṣāda, and suchlike. It is likely that these territories were recording their histories in local inscriptions and court chronicles, and were not part of the Puranic scheme—which was anyway petering out at this point.

At the time when the *Purāṇas* were being written, the *kṣatriya* status could be claimed by anyone who could be legitimized by acquiring genealogical links. This involved fewer Vedic sacrificial rituals and more *mahādānas* (large-scale gifts), *praśastis* (eulogies on the ruler), and genealogies—a few of which could have been fabricated. The dynastic lists are followed by a list of miscellaneous castes, territories, and communities, a contrast to the ordered form of the dynasties. Either the dynastic data was now too voluminous, or else there were too many states to be accounted for in a regular manner. Recent rulers tend to be treated with contempt. This was perhaps the logic of the Puranic eschatology—in the Kaliyuga, *dharma* was on the way out.

Yet curiously this was the time when *brāhmaṇas* were beginning to acquire more royal patrons than before, and although the competition with heterodoxy continued, the latter was in decline. Even if the *Viṣṇu Purāṇa* is dated to the early Christian era, when heterodoxy was in the ascendant, the text would have been revised for later times. In some *Purāṇas* the Yavanas are described as following evil ways, bereft of *dharma*, *karma*, and *artha*, and mingling *ārya* with *mleccha*, killing women and children, their rule coinciding with that of upstarts.[108] The misrule of these kings contributes to the dystopia of the Kali age. The prelude to the dystopia, prior to the arrival of Kalkin, the last incarnation of Viṣṇu, is strikingly similar to conditions described in Buddhist texts prior to the coming of the Buddha Maitreya, with people fleeing to the hills for refuge.

Such statements are new to the account and underline the capturing of political power by families with claims to pedigrees different from the *kṣatriya* clans. Dynasties described here as evidently foreign, such as the Śakas and Yavanas, do however sometimes add *kṣatriya* suffixes to their names in inscriptions.[109]

[108] *N'aiva mūrdh ābhiṣiktās te bhaviṣyanti narādhipāḥ yuga dośa durācārā* . . ., F.E. Pargiter, *DKA*, 56; *Matsya Purāṇa*, 273.25–34.

[109] E.J. Rapson (ed.), *The Cambridge History of India, I: Ancient India*, 577.

Foreign rulers are sometimes treated with contempt in the *Purāṇas*, gentle contempt in some texts, but harsh and hostile aggression in others.[110] The *Yuga Purāṇa* comes down heavily on the Yavanas, the Hellenized Greeks, and others from West Asia.[111] The three middle sons of Yadu, generally of little consequence, are sometimes made progenitors of these alien rulers.

The reckoning of kings by regnal years was a recognition of measured, linear time. The exaggerated lengthening of regnal years in the early part of the dynastic section was probably to give the sanctity of antiquity to kingship. The concept of generations was the listing of the name of the successor. In the dynastic section, a generation was counted when a king assumed office, since only regnal periods are recorded. Dynastic lists are also open to manipulation but this is different from the manipulation of lineages and generations in a genealogy. Succession can be changed by collapsing collaterals or erasing interregnums. The function of the genealogy remains twofold: setting out the presumed chronology, and presenting a charter of legitimation. The dynasties are named and sometimes bunched together in a large time bracket; and although names and regnal years are not consistent in every *Purāṇa,* the discrepancies are generally small.

This third part of the *vaṃśānucarita* is essentially one of non-*kṣatriya* kings where dynasties changed either with the arrival of new families or through conquest, or where administrators usurp power, or a combination of these. The power of a minister in a kingdom is clear from the occurrences of ministers assassinating kings and founding dynasties, such as the Pradyotas, Śuṅgas, Kāṇvas, and Āndhras. Both the Śuṅgas and Kāṇvas were *brāhmaṇa* families, but presumably because they were administrators and servitors and not priests they were overlooked in the generalization about low-caste dynasties. *Brāhmaṇa* ministers and officers were obviously not ritual specialists. The justification for *brāhmaṇas* removing an ineffective king goes back to the story of Vena. There is a gradual increase in dynasties which do not

110 *Matsya Purāṇa*, 273.25–33; *Viṣṇu Purāṇa*, 4.24.70–80; F.E. Pargiter, *DKA*, 56.

111 J. Mitchiner, *The Yuga Purāṇa*; D.C. Sircar, "Problems of the Yuga Purāṇa", in *Studies in Yugapurāṇa and Other Texts*, 1–17.

even claim to have been *dvijas* (twice-born), pointing to a new understanding of political power. Some *Purāṇas* have a small subsection on *rāja-dharma* to instruct the king.[112]

Legitimation was now recognized less through sacrificial rituals and more through the assertion of power. The latter was either through conquest or through exercising administrative control, as in the case of those described as *bhṛtyas*. This social condition would conform to the statement that in the Kaliyuga caste hierarchies and functions are overturned; inevitably, therefore, those in power would be of lower castes or outsiders who had no caste identity to begin with. However, in subsequent times, latching onto the *kṣatriya* genealogies was to become one of the methods of legitimizing a dynasty. Kings are no longer said to have a portion of deity as it might have been embarrassing to make this concession to *śūdras* and *mlecchas*.

The succession lists were not continued soon after the Gupta period because each dynasty probably sought its own record, and this was frequently in the form of royal inscriptions and chronicles. The *vaṃśānucarita* section, therefore, provided easy access to claims of status through families linking themselves to ancient heroes. The claim required legitimation by *brāhmaṇas*. The *brāhmaṇa* therefore had to control the information in the lists of heroes and kings.

The *vaṃśānucarita* ends with Pṛthvī reflecting on the future.[113] Kings acquire exaggerated notions of power when they conquer territory, but they frequently lose power when they fight over what they have won. Their desire to enjoy the earth overwhelms all else.

9. Concepts of Time

The dimension of time, inevitably present in all attempts to structure the past, is central to patterns of succession as well. Succession lists placed within the outer framework, as it were, of cosmology, are differentiated from those perceived as historical. Included in the *Purāṇas*, therefore, are theories of time where the

[112] *Matsya Purāṇa*, 215–20.
[113] *Viṣṇu Purāṇa*, 4.24.128–36.

sequence of time is viewed in different ways, cosmological and cyclic, genealogical and linear. The grand theory of time, the theory of the *yugas*, is a play on the concept of time, a metaphor at many levels, suggesting chronology.[114] It is used in varying contexts: from the vastness of the aeons running into thousands of years, to the minutiae of the blinking of an eye; from time originating as part of the cosmos to time determining the ethics of an age or to time seen in a spatial form.[115] This is not time which is subject to calibration. Nevertheless, it cannot be ignored as it impinges on historical consciousness.

The cyclic concept was obviously derived from observing the regular recurrence of seasons in the rhythm of nature and the movement of stars in the night sky. There appears to have been an attempt to draw on figures used in contemporary studies in mathematics and astronomy, perhaps to suggest exactitude, given that the mid-first millennium AD was an active period in Indian astronomy. Time as part of the cosmic view is also a tangential reflection of the then current exploration of mathematics and astronomy developing on the ideas of the *Jyotiśa-vedāṅga*, as also on the dialogue with Alexandrine and Hellenist astronomers.

The concept of cyclic time is of course common to many early cultures. Greek notions of the repeated destruction of the world occur in Plato.[116] More elaborate views are discussed by those in favour of Mithraism, popular in pre-Christian Europe. Time is depicted as a *quadriga* which travels in a circle, and the four horses are the elements—fire, air, water, earth. The fastest of these is the first and the cycle ends with destruction.[117]

Cosmological time in the *Purāṇas* reiterates the three cycles of time: the almost immeasurable span of the *manvantara*, the immense length of the *kalpa*, and the lesser four ages or *yugas*.[118]

[114] C.D. Church, "The Myth of the Four Yugas in the Sanskrit Puranas", 5–25; R. Thapar, *Time as a Metaphor of History*.

[115] *Matsya Purāṇa*, 124.13–91; *Viṣṇu Purāṇa*, 1.3.6ff.

[116] Plato: *Timaeus*, III.22.

[117] F. Cumont, *The Mysteries of Mithra*, 116ff.

[118] Apart from references in the *Mahābhārata* and Manu mentioned in the previous chapter, there are also descriptions in the *Gārgiya Jyotiṣa*, all dating to between the third century BC and second century AD. L. Gonzales-Reiman, "Cosmic Cycles, Cosmology, and Cosmography", 411–28.

The *kalpa* is first referred to in the inscriptions of Aśoka. The other two come with brahmanical redactions of the epics and *Purāṇas*.

Puranic chronology refers to the *manvantara*, as also to the calculation based on the Kaliyuga of *c.* 3102 BC and the Saptarṣi of *c.* 3176 BC as calculated in later sources.[119] The two eras seem to act as a bridge between the infinity of the *manvantara* cycles and the shorter spans of descent groups and dynasties. The unit is the *yuga*, the measurement of which changed from possibly meaning one generation or even a short span of five years—according to some, in the *Ṛgveda*—to 12,000 divine years or 4,320,000 human years in Manu.[120] The calculation of the start of the Kali age as equivalent to 3102 BC made by Āryabhaṭa is further confirmed by its use in the Aihole inscription of Pulakeśin II.[121]

The *mahāyuga* encompassing the theory of the four *yugas* is the same as given in the *Mahābhārata* (Chapter 4). The decline of *dharma* remains central to the theory, a decline that proceeds systematically to the end. A thousand *mahāyugas* make a *kalpa* (an aeon), each of which is followed by the destruction of the world, often through a great deluge. This further underlined the myth of the Flood.

The reckoning based on the *kalpa* is also tied to the *manvantara* calculation where each *manvantara* is equal to a little more than 71 *mahāyugas*. This is truly infinite time, or almost a sense of time which is without beginning or end,[122] what might be called "deep time", or timeless time. Human history in the current *mahāyuga* is in the period of its ultimate decline. A long view of the past inevitably has to project it as a decline from a golden age, an initial utopia of the Kṛta age to the present Kaliyuga. Decline reinforces this sense of the end of an age.

Figures such as those of 4,320,000 for the *mahāyuga*, the calculation of the precession in the ecliptic of 360 degrees, would have been widely discussed among astronomers. Some figures

[119] J. Mitchiner, "The Evolution of the Manvantara Theory . . .", 7–37.

[120] *Ṛgveda*, 1.139.8; *Arthaśāstra*, 2.20.29ff.; *Manu's Code of Law*, 1.69ff.

[121] L. Gonzales-Reiman, "Cosmic Cycles, Cosmology, and Cosmography"; Aihole Inscription, *Ep. Ind.*, 6.1ff.

[122] M. Biardeau, "Etude de Mythologique Hindoue", 19–45.

also occur in Babylonian astronomy, and it has been argued that Indian astronomers were familiar with Babylonian ideas by about *c.* 400 BC.[123] The basic parameter of the *yuga* system was the Kaliyuga of 432,000 years, which is the figure for the pre-Diluvian kings in Babylonian sources and further quoted in Greek sources, and which in turn is based on the sexagesimal system (2 x 60/3), a system also in use in India. The figure 432 has as its fractions 2x2x2x2x3x3x3. To this was added the decimal system commonly known to Indian mathematics, and a *kalpa* was calculated as 1000 *mahāyugas* or *caturyugas*. The four *yugas* were placed in a descending order of 4:3:2:1.

The cyclic notion was closely related to the idea of the revolution of heavenly bodies and a number of cycles of time were in use. Among the more popular were the five-year luni-solar cycle of the *Jyotiśa-Vedāṅga* texts on astrology reconciling the lunar and solar calendars, and the Saptaṛṣi era, an imaginary cycle of about 2700 or 2800 years based on the theory that the constellation of the Saptaṛṣi (the Great Bear) stays for 100 years in each of the 27 or 28 *nakṣatras* (asterisms). From the sixth century AD, the cycle of Bṛhaspati or Jupiter became popular and was often computed as a complete cycle of sixty years.

There was, however, a difference of opinion among astronomers regarding the length of the *yuga*, and Āryabhaṭa for instance argued for an equal length of all four in the *mahāyuga*. There were also differences between Puranic cosmology and the cosmology of the astronomers, as is evident from texts by the latter questioning the former.[124]

The notion of this infinite scale of time as built into cosmology was different from measured time. Did this reflect a tension between those who sought the sanction of cosmological time for a record of the past and those who wanted a more precise time reckoning? Or was the association of cosmic time with the past yet another device to maintain, at one level, the otherness of the past? Cosmological time can circumscribe other systems, such as generational and linear time, but does not exclude them. The fantasy of numbers in this scheme of cosmological time has been

[123] D. Pingree, "The Purāṇas and Jyotiḥśāstra: Astronomy", 274–80.
[124] Ibid.

read as a "refusal of history".[125] It would seem more appropriate to suggest that it was an attempt at distancing a mythical past by framing it in a time concept which was palpably unreal. Not all the Puranic versions agree on the details of the four *yugas*,[126] thus underlining the symbolic character of the idea. In the *Viṣṇu Purāṇa*, cosmological time is described in an early section of the text which deals with creation. Genealogical chronology is in a separate section, the *vaṃśānucarita*.

Varying concepts of time can also be used to demarcate historical change. Time cycles of immense scale can be ways of pushing back the past so that primary creation, as in this case, belongs to a time which is virtually beyond human intervention. The Golden Age, located in this early time period, is also easier to handle and describe since it has no limits on fantasy. Resolving conflict between *smṛti* texts was by maintaining that some—recording customs in contradiction of those currently practised—were legislating for a bygone age. Such an age would have to be extremely distant in time to relegate the practice to the past. The form of narration can also suggest time concepts, such as the question and answer format of the *Purāṇas*, which can create the impression of linear time.[127]

The cyclic concept is not discussed in the *vaṃśānucarita* where time would be inherently linear. Was this a method of keeping cyclic time distinct from linear? Genealogies become a form of sequential reckoning. To record the past in a genealogical form could suggest that there was a core tradition which might have been relatively fixed, but that other material could have been changed. This was a system based on a sense of time not as clearly historical as the precise dating of the documents of contemporary courts or of later periods. It could also be a way of suggesting that linear time is a segment of the arc of the larger span of cyclic time, and that the two can intersect.

Linear time is also used in reckoning regnal years and in calculating dynastic time brackets.[128] In locating these as part of the *yuga*

[125] M. Eliade, *Cosmos and History*, 117.

[126] *Viṣṇu Purāṇa*, 1.3.2ff.; *Vāyu Purāṇa*, 8.18–63; *Matsya Purāṇa*, 142–4.

[127] G. Bailey, "Intertextuality in the Purāṇas: A Neglected Element in the Study of Sanskrit Literature", 197.

[128] *Viṣṇu Purāṇa*, 4.24.104ff.; *Vāyu Purāṇa*, 98.409–12.

system, there is simultaneous use of cyclic and linear time. Was this to accommodate a tension between mythical and measured time, where cosmic time was used to indicate the otherness of the past? But the past was not rejected since it was now appropriated by recourse to linear time. Cosmological time circumscribes time systems but does not exclude them. Was cyclic time in this form an attempt at distancing a mythical past?

Regnal years and dynastic time periods in the third part of the *vaṃśānucarita*, computed in linear time, were of a different order from cosmic time and even from the genealogical time of lineages. This may have had to do with the currency of eras and dates used in other contemporary sources. The commonly used ones among these were the Vikrama Samvat of *c.* 58 BC, the Śaka era of AD 78, and the Gupta era of AD 319–20. Equally popular were the Kaliyuga era later traced back in some reckonings to the equivalent of 3102 BC and the Laukika era of 3076–5 BC,[129] both of which are mentioned in official records in the post-Gupta period.

The use of eras would also have had to do with the impact of a culture given increasingly to literacy. The event that inaugurates the Kaliyuga shifts from the date of Manu after the Flood, to the last stage of the war, to the death of Kṛṣṇa.[130] The parallel with the date of the death of Mahāvīra and the Buddha as the basic era in the Jaina and Buddhist historiography cannot go unnoticed. But the date of the Kaliyuga is not the stable date from which eras are calculated. These derive their identity from diverse events, the most frequent being the most secular, namely the establishing of a dynasty or a reign.

Time as a *mahāyuga* does not eliminate the past and the future, since the cycle terminates in destruction and a new cycle follows. The inordinate length of the cosmological time-cycle underlines timelessness. The universe had a beginning in cosmological time which is described as a generative factor. But the immensity of the cycle virtually eliminates time. Within this are the four lesser cycles, each of which does not return to its beginning but moves into the next. The form is a spiral or a helix and this form, if

[129] The Laukika era was particularly common in Kashmir and Punjab and was also used in Rajasthan in the period towards the end of the first millennium AD.

[130] *Viṣṇu Purāṇa*, 5.38.8.

stretched, becomes a wave and even a not-too-straight line. But simultaneously time measured by generations and therefore different, and under human control, comes into historical reckoning. A distinction is implicit between the history of the universe viewed in infinity and human history subject to more exact measurement. The latter was also linked in the meticulous measurement of time as used in astrology, which centres on the past and future of the individual.

In terms of eschatology, the Golden Age was in the remote past, in the beginnings of time, after which there has been a steady decline, from *dharma* to *adharma*. The link between time and the moral condition is described in the social decline which will prevail towards the latter part of the Kaliyuga. The rulers will be of impure origin, and their subjects will be oppressed; the *varṇa* ordering will be discarded and castes will move away from their allotted functions. Vedic rites will not be observed and even the *brāhmaṇas* will lose their code of ethics. Money will be the criterion of status. Women will be liberated and will no longer obey their husbands. *Śūdras* will take over upper-caste functions. The need to labour will increase. People will live for fewer years. In this almost Spenglerian vision it will indeed be a world turned upside down. The change in the social condition becomes an allegory of a sense of historical change. This would require that those who ruled in earlier periods were of the appropriate social status and are all clubbed together as *kṣatriyas*. The *kṣatriya* identity of these is a striking contrast to the non-*kṣatriya* identity of most of the dynasties.

Degeneration over time is again an idea familiar from other cultures. Hesiod speaks of the four ages as being of gold, silver, bronze, and iron.[131] The *Avesta* has a similar concept.[132] In Buddhist and Jaina texts people will be forced to labour for the king and this oppression lasts until the coming of the saviour figure.[133] Written into cyclic time is of course the inevitable decline with the downswing of the cycle.

The insistence on a dire condition in the Kaliyuga is difficult

[131] *Hesiod's Theogony: Works and Days*, 109–201.

[132] R. Zaehner, *The Dawn and Twilight of Zoroastrianism*, 26.

[133] *Mahāsupina Jātaka*, no. 77, in *The Jataka*; Jinaprabhāsūri, *Vividhatīrthakalpa,* 14.

to explain since the time when the *Purāṇas* were being written was when the Vaiṣṇava and Śaiva sects were beginning to attract patronage and were becoming popular. However, Vedic Brahmanism was threatened by the success of the Sramanic sects, the Cārvāka/Lokāyata and such like, who were called heretics. Cults such as those of the Śāktas were rivals for patronage. Although hidden, the anxiety becomes apparent in some parts of the texts.

The notion of social decline is very useful and can be used whenever necessary. Curiously, the reason often given for the decline in the Puranic texts begins with a crisis in agriculture—over-taxation, drought or torrential rain, famine, among other things—and it is accompanied by the migration of the population.[134] There is no reference to peasant revolts in these texts but only to migrations, perhaps because it was the more effective method of registering protest.

The slow restoration to the Kṛta age will come about with the arrival of Kalkin as the final *avatāra* of Viṣṇu. He will destroy the *mlecchas* and the *dasyus* and proclaim the *dharma* once again. This is a close parallel to the coming of the Buddha Maitreya. The *kṣatriya* lineages will be restored through two *kṣatriyas* who survive time and live through the *yuga*.

The creation of Kalkin may not have been only a counterpart to the Buddha Maitreya. The early centuries AD was when many figures emerged in the current religions as saviours whose predicted coming was to bring back utopian conditions. The idea had currency in the areas that had close contact through trade—West and Central Asia.[135]

10. An Interpretation

What are we to make of all this information? The theories of racial identification do not hold because of contradictions within the texts, apart from race now being a discredited concept. Pūru, for example, whose "aryan" identity is doubtful since his speech is *mṛdhra vāc* (impure language) and he is said to be descended

[134] *Viṣṇu Purāṇa*, 6.1.38.

[135] R. Thapar, "Millenarianism and Religion in Early India", in idem, *Cultural Pasts*, 946–62.

from the *asura rākṣasa*,[136] is nevertheless given an eminent status in the genealogies. Equally important were those descended from Yadu, yet their status is also low in other texts: the Vṛṣṇis and the Andhakas are referred to as *vrātyas* and the people of Saurāṣṭra, associated with the Yadus, as belonging to mixed castes.[137]

The contradiction between the *Purāṇas* listing them as *kṣatriyas* and *rājās* and other sources referring to their lower status, can perhaps be resolved if the Puranic lists are only of those who constituted the chiefs of clans. Irrespective of the caste ranking given them by *brāhmaṇa* theoreticians, from the historical perspective of the dynastic lists they were seen as societies with *rājās* and were located within particular descent groups. The epics and the *Purāṇas* appear to have been far more flexible in their social formulations than the *Dharmaśāstras*. This may have been more than just the contrast between accepted practice and normative texts, and may have had to do with their initial authorship. The authors of the former were bards and *brāhmaṇas* of rather ambiguous origin, whereas the authors of the *Dharmaśāstras* were orthodox *brāhmaṇas*.

The differentiation between lineage-based society and kingdoms is clear in the differing patterns of succession and in the chronological separation through the Flood and the war. The construction of the descent group set out the location, alliances, and politics of clans as perceived from a later perspective. Inclusion in a particular descent group was also a pointer to the kind of political society associated with the clan. It is worth noting that a number of motley clans is included under the Candravaṃśa but not so in the Sūryavaṃśa.

The *Viṣṇu Purāṇa* states that the *vaṃśānucarita* section is a brief account of all those who have ruled on earth, and the account shows the futility of aspiring for extensive power or assuming that one can be immortal. All is transient and passes, and this includes the rulers of earlier times. The individual urge for possession is meaningless since it cannot last. The text goes on to ask rhetorically: What has happened to the heroes of old, Rāma and

[136] *Śatapatha Brāhmaṇa*, 6.8.1.14.

[137] *Baudhāyana Dharmasūtra*, 1.1.2.13.

Yudhiṣṭhira among others. We do not know where they are now, did they actually live?[138] All present and future rulers are subject to the same fate of being forgotten; unless, as is the assumption here, only inclusion in the *vaṃśānucarita* can prevent that fate. This would be an appropriate conclusion to a text purporting to relate the list of the rulers of the past.

The *Purāṇas* have to keep pace with changes in every *yuga*,[139] therefore a fixed tradition was not required (which incidentally makes it difficult to date them). Their data makes them sources for later writing. Their contents were not sacrosanct, as were those of the *Vedas*, which perhaps encouraged a sense of historical change.

The gods and the sages are associated with the beginnings of history. The founder of a descent group has a special relationship with a deity that establishes his unique position and status. Built into the function of kingship, with its exercise of power over diverse communities, was the notion of the king's patronage to more than one sect. This may have been resented by *brāhmaṇas* or by the Sramanic Saṅgha; nevertheless it was a political reality commonly practised.

Descent from the founder has a noticeable pattern, differentiated in the Candravaṃśa and the Sūryavaṃśa, and this presumes a historical difference. The difference possibly points to variant forms of political power and becomes both the source and the expression of the legitimation of such power. Attempts to chart the major *kṣatriya* clans after the Flood are also attempts to fill in geographical space.

To name the lineages after the sun and the moon seems predictable, denoting permanence in the iconography of this period and associated with calendrical time. Both the Solar and the Lunar calendars were in use, but for different social functions: the agricultural year or the ritual calendar. Their associations are often contrasted: the sun is seen as the male symbol and the moon as the female, endorsed by the ancestress Ilā at the head of the Lunar line. Seniority may have been given to the Sūryavaṃśa, since Ikṣvāku

[138] *Viṣṇu Purāṇa*, 4.24.149.
[139] *Matsya Purāṇa*, 53.8–9.

is frequently mentioned as the eldest son of Manu and there is some confusion over the gender of Ila. Taken more literally, the sun outshines the moon. In Tantric and Yogic texts, the sun and the moon symbolize the two main nerve centres to the right and the left in the human body, and their unity is sought in certain Yogic practices.[140] There is mention of *iḍā* as the left vein and *piṅgala* as the right vein. The taking over of such symbols reinforces the interaction with Śākta and Tantric sects.

The sun and the moon, when referred to jointly in inscriptions, often stand for eternity. A grant of land where it is irrevocable, the hope is expressed that it will last as long as the moon and the sun endure. As such they continue to be depicted for centuries on hero-stones, commemorating dead heroes. As planets they host the brilliance of sovereignty.

The recording of dynasties after the Kurukṣetra war indicates a perception of difference in the nature of power in kingdoms. The war is a watershed in the Puranic periodization of the past. Whereas earlier all were included under the umbrella terms of *rājā* or *kṣatriya*, now the social status of individual dynasties is given separately, with ksatriyahood not being a prerequisite for kingship. The acquisition of power in itself confers rank. Therefore a dynasty of Hellenistic origin, the Yavana, quite clearly *mleccha*, is nevertheless described as *vrātya kṣatriya* (degenerate *kṣatriya*). Dynastic succession is a pointer to the existence of states that take precedence over non-state, clan-held territories. The eventual establishment of the monarchical state involved a different set of institutions from those of preceding political forms, and therefore a different basis of royal power.

If the relationship between descent groups was somewhat opaque, that between dynasties is clear. Where a ruling family was subordinate to the previous dynasty, it is described as the *bhṛtya*. Overlordship is explicit. There are no lineage links connecting dynasties, thus negating the importance of such links. However, the links were within each dynasty with its shorter span than the lineage. Political power seems to be a sufficient base for claiming legitimacy. Claim to descent, if it was accepted, was sufficient: it

[140] S.B. Das Gupta, *Obscure Religious Cults*, 235ff.

did not have to be represented as a biological fact. The claim was important because a genealogy was the king's legal title to rule.

An important and not unconnected statement towards the end of the account of dynasties reads that a king of Magadha, having overthrown the *kṣatram*, will create another *kṣatram.*[141] This concedes that although the traditionally accepted *kṣatriyas* had declined, it was still possible for there to be a new category of *kṣatriyas*: a statement which has interesting consequences for the future form of the *itihāsa-purāṇa* tradition. Implicit in this statement is the fact that since *nṛpah* rather than *kṣatriya* frequently qualifies dynasties, claims to being *kṣatriya* would seek links with the Sūryavaṃśa or Candravaṃśa. The genealogical chapter provided a peg on which to hang the status of the families who in later times claimed to be *kṣatriyas*.

Interestingly, the list of other *varṇas* converted to *kṣatriya* status through this new caste are the Kaivarta, Pañcaka, and Pulinda, fisherfolk and barbarous peoples otherwise ranked as low castes outside the pale of caste society. As a projection of the decline of what was viewed as an earlier aristocracy, even if *śūdra* in caste, and its replacement by newcomers and upstarts, the statement could not be more explicit.

The statement seems to reflect the change in the polity of the post-Gupta period, from about the seventh century onward, which led to an increase in kingdoms. New claims were made to *kṣatriya* status by families even of obscure origin. Where a *brāhmaṇa* recipient of a land grant lurked in the ancestry, as was often the case, there the likelihood could be of a *brahma-kṣatra* caste. This makes an interesting counterpoint to the more than occasional statement in the descent lists, where *kṣatriyas* are said to have been the founders of *brāhmaṇa varṇas*, especially *kṣatriyas* of the Pūru lineage, prior to Bharata. The interchange of *kṣatriya* and *brāhmaṇa* is striking, suggesting grounds for accepting *brāhmaṇa* kings or what the inscriptions refer to as *brahma-kṣatra.* The *kṣatriyas* are also sometimes given *brahma-kṣatra* status.[142]

[141] F.E. Pargiter, *DKA*, 53.

[142] *Viṣṇu Purāṇa*, 4.21.18: *brahma kṣatrasya yo yonir vaṃśo rājarṣisatkṛtaḥ*...

This also raises the question of the changing connotation of *kṣatriya*. The earlier function had been that of the heroic ideal and eventually the king. Were dynasties listed as *śūdra* and non-*kṣatriya* because they were patrons of non-brahmanical sects, such as the Mauryan kings? Or should this be read as a statement that those kings who could not or did not wish to trace their ancestry to the clans were disapproved of by the *brāhmaṇa* authors? In the claim to being *kṣatriya*, as reinvoked in the post-Gupta period through assumed genealogical links, was royalty seeking support from *brāhmaṇas* for validation? Alternatively, the term as applied to earlier *rājās* may have been used more in the sense of a designation rather than as a caste, since not all that were so called met the eligibility qualifications. The caste of some was distinctly ambiguous. In later periods *kṣatriya* appears to have become more closely a *varṇa* usage.

There is an element of uncertainty if not disjuncture towards dynastic kingdoms in the *vaṃśānucarita*. This strikes a different note from the endorsement of kingship, albeit as an ideal system of government, in the later sections of the epics, as well as what might be regarded as the exploitation of kingship in the texts to be discussed in subsequent chapters. The *vaṃśānucarita* can perhaps be seen as a watershed where, in the long perspective on the past, the earlier *kṣatriya rājās* were viewed, from the brahmanical perspective, as the more prestigious and the later dynasties projected largely as families of low origin or servitors.

There could even have been an initial distancing between Vedic Brahmanism and the way kingship was evolving, because in effect, during the course of this change, the political takes precedence over the ritual as a significant articulation. The righting of this condition in the literature was to come about when dynasties began to bestow largesse on the *brāhmaṇas*, often for validation as *kṣatriyas*.

The full-throated endorsement of kingship in the Śānti *parvan* of the epic may well have coincided with the initial attempts at envisioning the *vaṃśānucarita*. Legitimacy now lay not just in rituals but also in conquest, marriage alliances, and the establishing of a caste-based society. The earlier prestation economy of the *kṣatriya rājās* was at an end. It had been replaced by peasant economies incorporating hereditary rights over land and by more complex systems of exchange and trade. Nevertheless, the generosity of kings was expressed in gift-giving to *brāhmaṇas*.

11. Historical Functions of Genealogies

The *vaṃśānucarita* as a chapter on succession is an attempt at giving an overview of the past, the Puranic view of pre-Gupta history. The historical perspectives are expressed in the genealogical patterns. The data is taken from the Vedic corpus and the epics but is reformulated as a continuous narrative in a genealogical form. This became a substantial source in the post-Gupta period for constructing links between dynasties and the earlier lineages, as is evident particularly in inscriptions.

The possibility of there having been a distinctive *kṣatriya* tradition has been debated.[143] This would not be altogether surprising, given the emergence of caste *Purāṇas* in many sections of Indian society seeking to provide a history and a status for their caste. Without going over the old debate again,[144] it does seem possible that, similar to the succession lists of teachers maintained by *brāhmaṇas*, some *kṣatriya* succession lists, such as those in the epics, were maintained by bards. These may well have been taken over by *brāhmaṇa* authors and reconstituted, together with later material, into the *vaṃśānucarita* in the *Purāṇas*.

The potential of a believed past as recognized by *brāhmaṇa* authors goes back to mention of *itihāsa* and *purāṇa* in Vedic texts. But giving distinctive form to the tradition was a later development. The Bhṛgu and Aṅgirasa *brāhmaṇas* hovering over the tradition could have bridged the difference. The *Purāṇas* can perhaps be seen as an attempt to appropriate some of the legitimacy of Vedic Brahmanism, while at the same time drawing on a tradition from non-brahmanical sources. Thus, the history of those claiming political power was being embedded in the form of a *vaṃśa*.

There was the added parallel that dynasties patronizing brahmanical sects such as the Guptas could be projected in a favourable light, whereas those who were not patrons were described in

[143] F.E. Pargiter, "Ancient Indian Genealogies and Chronology", 1–56.
[144] L. Rocher, *The Puranas*, 125–9.

unflattering terms, if at all. The inclusion of historical succession in sectarian texts was a common practice wherever the sect had some links with rulers, as is evident from Buddhist histories pertaining to monasteries and the Saṅgha. Initially, the record of the *vaṃśa* or succession would have been orally maintained, hence the possibility of restructuring it at some point. When compiled as texts, the brahmanical worldview would have been influential, especially in countering heterodox teaching.

The Vaiṣṇava sects, in endorsing the assimilation of selected cultures, assisted in the emergence of states and the change from clan to caste. This was helpful to the ideological justification of social inequalities, as also the vesting of power in kings, who were increasingly compared with deities but from whom they were predictably differentiated. The sectarian teaching became more universalized when it was in textual form. The recitations by *paurāṇikas* in temples and at gatherings on special occasions were opportunities to address a wide audience. The inclusion of a genealogical section (if it was also recited) meant that it was open to more people than through bardic recitals alone. The genealogical mode was more than just a list of succession when seen as a historical statement.

Why did the *brāhmaṇas* eventually take over this tradition? And why does this come to be associated particularly, but not invariably, with the Bhṛgus? At an obvious level, this may not have been unconnected with literacy. The transmission of the *Purāṇas*, in a literate form, made them texts for reference. Although they could be recited on ritual occasions, or even as an act of acquiring merit, a more developed historical sensibility required written records. Writing introduces changes in the transmission of that which is believed to be significant to a culture. However, the form which writing takes and the degree to which it is diffused in society influences historical sensibility. Further, although an account can be changed, such change can be less radical in a written than an oral form.

However, the more significant reason has to do with the function of a historical perspective. The historical tradition becomes an instrument of social control and is maintained by a specific category of people whose power derives from their ability to provide those in authority with an identity. A historical tradition therefore establishes group consciousness. As a person recording the past, or transmitting the past in an oral or literate form, the historian is an informant. Gradually, however, as his control over the past increases, he acquires a perspective and takes on the role of a participant as well, although not literally.

The need for a historical perspective probably had much to do with the challenge from the histories being written by Sramanic sects. Buddhism had its version of clan societies, and kingdoms dominated by a historical figure. The *brāhmaṇa* version of this was a deity, Viṣṇu, in the guise of a hero attempting to do the same. But this was less effective as history. The challenge was intensified by having to acquire an identity in a new historical situation, and when history came to be recorded in inscriptions. The contradictions between *brāhmaṇa* and Buddhist authors become apparent if the *Yuga Purāṇa* is compared with the *Milinda-pañho*, both virtually contemporary works.[145] The first condemns the Yavanas as alien whereas the second is an attempt at persuading a Yavana king to become a Buddhist.

It may also be argued that the way in which the notion of deity as an element of kingship—although rooted in Vedic notions of deity and power—was developed may have been part of the competition with Buddhism. The close identity of king and deity is evident in Manu.[146] The form it takes differs from the way Aśoka, for instance, marginalized deities as part of social functioning. The question has been asked whether the *aitihāsika paurāṇikas* were the ones to develop the idea of the divine king in the form it was to take in the mid-first millennium AD.[147] The major *aitihāsika paurāṇikas* could have been linked to Bhṛgu *brāhmaṇas*.

Association with political power was recognized as a method of enhancing the authority of other groups. This association was assisted by providing a history for the rulers which could gradually replace rituals as a source of legitimation. The opening up of new

[145] J. Mitchiner, *Yuga Purāṇa*; *Milinda-pañho*.

[146] *Manu's Code of Law*, 7.1–35.

[147] M. Tokunaga, "Structure of the *Rājadharma* Section in the *Yājñavalkya-smṛti*".

areas with consequent settlements became a feature of the political economy from the Gupta period. This would have required some historical back-up in providing identity to the new rulers.

If we decode the *vaṃśānucarita* as a perception of the past, a number of patterns emerge. The past is set out in distinct periods, with the consciousness of a change in the historical context as the causative factor of difference. Implicit in the pattern is the shift, in many instances, from clan to caste. *Varṇa* or *jāti* are not noticeable identities of the *kṣatriya* heroes, for even *kṣatriya* seems to have a different connotation initially from that of only *varṇa* ranking. But *varṇa* is specifically mentioned in association with the dynasties. This is parallel to some degree with the mutation of non-state systems to states taking the form of kingdoms. The perception of who could legitimately acquire power and how is distinctly different in the third period from the second. This is now a more impersonal act. It not only does not require kinship links between one dynasty and another, but successors sometimes emerge from situations of disjunction. The association of this perception with the *Viṣṇu* and *Matsya Purāṇas* raises the question of the extent to which Vaiṣṇavism was an assimilative ideology and Bhāgavatism played a role in the mutation.

The *vaṃśānucarita* becomes a ready reference for later use. Legitimation through genealogical connections is reflected in inscriptions and chronicles. Claims are made to Sūryavaṃśa and Candravaṃśa origins, or to other invented "*vaṃśas*". Such claims become necessary to those of obscure origin for establishing status, providing a presumed history and arranging marriage alliances with established families already having claimed *kṣatriya* status. It points to the implementation of the *varṇāśrama-dharma* as a somewhat different stratification from what had existed before.

The focus shifts to courts and to the new feature of the worship of Puranic deities in temples. The king had to maintain those who were the source of his legitimacy—generally the *brāhmaṇas* propagating Puranic Hinduism and forging worship in the temples. A closeness to kingly authority required the appropriation of the authorship of the tradition, with the texts of the tradition becoming essential to the new form of royal legitimation, and the claims of the latter to particular pasts. They could dictate the content and form of the records pertaining to the past. Texts could also be copied and multiplied and gifted to *brāhmaṇas*.[148] Special readings were held, and since these were open to *śūdras* and women, the audience was large. The *paurāṇika* who read them is also called *itihāsa-vid*. This doubtless would have increased the tension between *brāhmaṇa* and bard.

The tension would have stretched to that between the oral tradition and texts. Where the historical process uses both, it emerges from an accommodation and negotiation between the two. The narratives of the *Purāṇas* are often reported narratives—composed by Brahmā, taught by Vyāsa, recited by the *sūta*; but each has a written text to back it up, as it were.[149] Narratives from the past, therefore, are not random. The narrators are aware of their role in transmitting a process that has the implications of being historical and linking the past to the present. The mode of discourse is not altogether arbitrary: it has some coherence in terms of continuity and a larger than local outlook.[150]

Why did the *vaṃśānucarita* stop with the Guptas? This was probably the point at which it was composed and, the third segment being in the future tense, it could not be continued. Dynastic succession was now beginning to be recorded in inscriptions issued by rulers, who most likely used the *vaṃśānucarita* as a source. New genres of texts were to emerge from the royal courts, such as the *caritas* (biographies of kings and ministers), and the *vaṃśāvalīs* (chronicles). The *Purāṇas* became more central as religious sectarian texts. As such they parallel the Buddhist *avadāna* literature, where each text focused on one person or on an *arahant*, and it was the literature of propagation.

The emergence of *itihāsa* from out of an embedded tradition, at a particular period of time, requires us to look more closely at that point in time. Constructing the past is a normal activity in most societies, as are changes in these constructions from earlier to later periods. This process is necessitated by new political forms, such

[148] *Agni Purāṇa*, 63.13–20.

[149] V. Narayana Rao, "Purāṇa as Brahminic Ideology", 90ff.

[150] F. Hardy, "Information and Transformation—Two Faces of the Purāṇas", 159–85.

as, in this case, the uprooting of chiefdoms in favour of kingdoms (the proud boast of Samudra Gupta); changes in the structure of the economy that sustained kingdoms, resulting in a decentralization in the control of economic resources despite the revenue that accrued to the king; the mutation of clans into castes where this happened; the political requirement of assimilating outsiders into what was normatively projected as a closed social structure; and the confrontation between Vedic and non-Vedic ideologies that eventually resulted in Puranic Hinduism superseding Vedic Brahmanism as the religion of a larger number.

The genealogical material could be used to identify groups and provide them with historical antecedents. But the genealogies were more crucial to political functions and to the status and acceptability of office-holders.[151] The perception of the past is expressed in the association of places of origin, links with lineages, and the counting of generations. Newcomers are grafted on or segments detached. The genealogy therefore becomes a useful historical and political tool. This necessitates that those who keep the genealogical tradition are aware of their closeness to political power.[152] Genealogy was among the king's legal titles to rule.

In the composition of the *vaṃśānucarita* an attempt was made to reconstruct a past, constituted for a purpose. Was this perhaps to establish a brahmanical version of the past, distinct from that put together in other traditions such as the Buddhist or Jaina, traditions that were seen as rivals to the brahmanical *Purāṇas*? The oral tradition of the bards was incorporated in this version. Yet the bards were not banished at this point, for the bard often foretells the narrative of dynasties. Nevertheless, the perspective endorses neither the bardic view nor the Sramanic.

Constructing a view of the past doubtless arose from the recognition that religious authority is assisted by association with political power—as demonstrated in the establishing of Buddhism. One of the strengths of such an association lay in controlling the construction of the past. The taking over of the tradition by the *brāhmaṇas* was to ensure that this construction was perceived as important to contemporary politics. The genealogical section drew

[151] M.D. Johnson, *The Purpose of Biblical Genealogies*, 77–82.
[152] D. Dumville, "Kingship, Genealogies and Regnal Lists", 72–104.

attention to data, and to the structure facilitating the legitimacy of ruling families. The ideological location of this construction was in the texts of the new Puranic religions which were the recipients of royal patronage. This was not only a counterpoint to Buddhism in a period when Puranic sects were making a bid to compete with Buddhism in seeking support, but it also encouraged the notion of the interface of political power with religious authority.

If situations of competition or confrontation increase sensitivity to historical perceptions, then this would be expected in the mid-first millennium AD. In the competition between Buddhism, the Śaiva sects, and the Bhāgavata religion, the Gupta dynasty, being supporters of the latter, would have been regarded as appropriate patrons. A past would then be constructed in which there would be a claim to historicity. Even if not factually historical, this claim took the form of genealogies as a summary of the historical past. Genealogies therefore become important at particular points in time, demonstrating their importance by increasing in frequency.

As a construction of the past, this section of the *Purāṇas* encapsulated a consciousness of history and was used as such, being elaborated upon in the subsequent period. The forms, however, changed from the bare bones of a genealogical skeleton to the far fuller forms of inscriptions, biographies, and chronicles.

Table IV
Historical Change Suggested in the *Vaṃśānucarita*

I. The Seven Manus—from Svayambhu to Vaivasvat, ruling for extraordinarily long periods, suggesting mythical time

The Flood as a time-marker

II. *Kṣatriya* lineages:
Sūryavaṃśa: from Ikṣvāku to Rāma
Candravaṃśa: from Ilā to the Pāṇḍavas

The Kurukṣetra war as the time-marker

III. Sequential order of dynasties with lists of rulers and regnal years: initially of Magadha but soon after of northern India

7

Early Inscriptions as Historical Statements

(Up to *c.* the Sixth Century AD)

1. The Data

Among the documents that record events and refer to the past, the more reliable are thought to be inscriptions. They generally reflect the views of those in authority, are located in public places, and are addressed to subjects of the state. This probably requires them to be more accurate in what they are saying, although this requirement is not always met. They can also be the statements of less-well-established groups. Early inscriptions tend to be fragments of historical information, and this is the manner in which they have been used. But inscriptions also assume some sensitivity to historical consciousness expressed in a variety of ways, which is what is assumed here. Inscriptions as annals date to a later period.

As textual records, inscriptions have varying functions, requiring diverse languages, and spoken by different people. In nineteenth-century India they were listed under archaeology because they were engraved on an object and came to be treated as artifacts. The texts were sieved for data on dynastic succession and chronology. A century later they were recognized as important documents providing information on society and economy. Their extensive information on grants of land has been discussed at length in the last few decades, leading to an incisive debate on whether or not the post-Gupta period saw the establishing of a feudal society. Here, I would like to give them additional recognition in relation to the study of historical writing.

The early inscriptions reflect an awareness of a past linked to the present in a historical manner. This is a departure from the ambiguities of the epics and *Purāṇas*. On occasion, inscriptions confirm what may be stated in a text, but they also provide a parallel text. In a marginal way they are artifacts and can be examined as material culture, but in effect they are texts and should be regarded as such. Considering that a major part of the history of India prior to *c.* AD 1000 comes from inscriptions, it is surprising that they have so seldom been studied as documents providing a sense of history.[1]

Inscriptions in early India are of many kinds: royal edicts, votive inscriptions recording gifts, brief biographical statements, eulogies of rulers, records of particular events, legal documents pertaining to rights and obligations over land, and suchlike. As with all categories of historical data, they reflect historical change. The context of a text involves asking many questions, such as: Who is the author? What is the intention of the text? Who is the intended audience? How does the language reflect history? Where there is a change of language, what determines the choice? The same questions can be asked of inscriptions.

The earliest forms of writing were the Harappan signs, engraved in the main on small seals found in abundance mostly at the city sites.[2] These were discontinued with the decline of cities. This disjuncture suggests a language change in north-western India. Whatever the Harappan language may have been, the successor languages as recorded were predominantly Indo-Aryan in that area.

Language change is not an isolated phenomenon but is tied to other historical events. Who uses which language and for what purposes is basic to understanding societies of the past, since

[1] D.C. Sircar, *Early Indian Epigraphical and Numismatic Studies*, 91; R. Salomon, *Indian Epigraphy*, 226–32.

[2] A. Parpola, *Deciphering the Indus Script*.

there was no uniform use of a single language. This is interestingly reflected in early Indian inscriptions. Those up to the early Christian era are exclusively in Prākrit (a widely used and varied vernacular form of Old Indo-Aryan), although Sanskrit was simultaneously being used for other purposes, such as in Vedic rituals. Later, at the turn to the first millennium AD, Sanskrit came into use in inscriptions, coinciding with it becoming the court language, although Prākrit remained a commonly used language.[3]

Scripts also evolved and changed over time. Initially, two were used for writing Prākrit: *brāhmī*, which was widespread and had some similarities with the southern Semitic script; and *kharoṣṭhī,* derived from Aramaic, current in Achaemenid Iran, which was limited to north-western India and Central Asia; the use of this gradually declined. *Brāhmī* remained the primary script and gave rise to others. Modifications of the script became marked after the mid-first millennium AD. This was in part due to adaptations to emerging regional languages. The *brāhmī* script evolved to the point where it gradually became impossible to read the earliest inscriptions.

In the late nineteenth century many inscriptions began to be read and variations in the script were recognized. Since many were dated, the focus was on obtaining a reliable chronology. Mention of the ruling king made it possible to reconstruct dynastic history. This was especially so of the period subsequent to the Guptas, when the *Purāṇas* ceased to carry dynastic information, but a substantial increase in inscriptions compensated for this. The growing awareness of there being sources of power other than ritual is evident from the deliberate drawing on the past and using it to legitimize the present. This was to become an important aspect of the data in inscriptions, quite apart from their information on the present.

Early authors of inscriptions varied, but generally conformed to either of two categories: the monks, nuns, and householders who wished to record the bare essentials of their gift to the monastery or *stūpa*; or scribes to whom the king dictated the text of his statement and who would in turn pass the text on to the engraver.

[3] R. Salomon, *Indian Epigraphy*; A.H. Dani, *Indian Palaeography*.

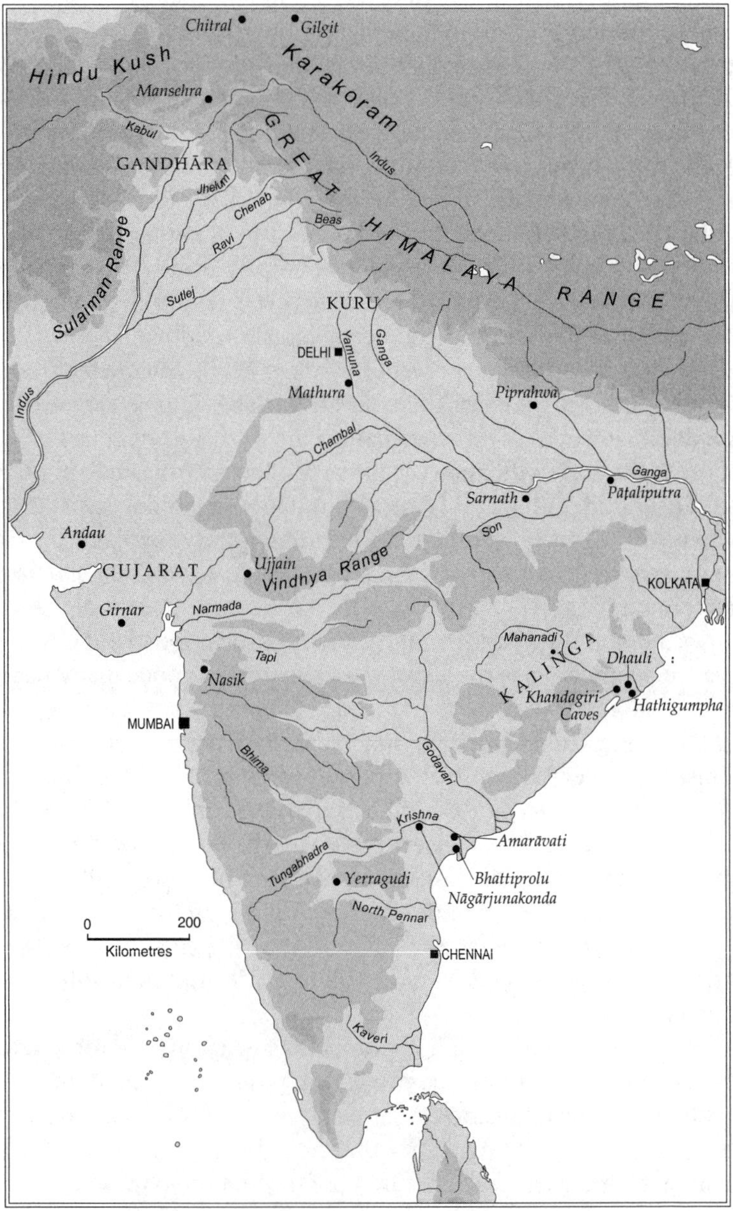

Map 4: Locations of the More Important Places, Clans, and Dynasties

Inscriptions tend to be explicit about the source of their authority. The audience for the first category was substantially the common people who either visited the Buddhist site or who read or heard what the king and others had to say. The audience for the royal inscriptions would have included the royal court. Compared to texts, the inscriptions have a wider reach. Royal inscriptions, therefore, are mostly statements on governance or, more often, grants, but other aspects of life also get recorded.

Inscriptions were recorded on varied surfaces according to their function. The earliest were royal edicts, engraved on rock faces in locations where people gathered. Subsequently, these edicts were engraved on monolithic pillars with finely sculpted capitals. Inscribing royal edicts came to be seen as significant to governance.

Almost parallel to this were votive inscriptions, initially found at *stūpa* sites. Small caskets or vases containing post-cremation relics were frequently placed at the base of the central shaft of the *stūpa*. The lid of these would be inscribed, explaining the contents. Votive inscriptions were engraved on the exterior surface of the *stūpa* or the railings, the donation being a contribution to its construction. The assumption of literacy and the need to record the action is impressive.

A third category was the copper-plate inscriptions generally recording grants of land. The grant was inscribed on two or more hand-sized plates of copper, held together by a ring which passed through a hole on one side. The idea may have been an imitation of birch-bark and palm-leaf manuscripts held together by stringing the leaves. These are late inscriptions dating to the centuries AD.

2. The Inscriptions of Aśoka

The earliest deciphered inscriptions are the edicts of the Mauryan emperor Aśoka dating to the third century BC.[4] These edicts, as royal proclamations, are in three languages—Prākrit, Greek, and

[4] E. Hultzsch, *Corpus Inscriptionum Indicarum,* vol. I; J. Bloch, *Les Inscriptions d'Asoka*; R. Thapar, *Aśoka and the Decline of the Mauryas*, 271–5; H. Falk, *Aśokan Sites and Artifacts.*

Aramaic; and four scripts—*brāhmī, kharoṣṭhī*, Greek, and Aramaic. The largest number is in Prākrit, with locations all over the subcontinent. The Greek and Aramaic inscriptions are located in Afghanistan, in the area ceded to the Mauryas by Seleucus Nicator.

The conversational tone of the edicts would have been inappropriate in Sanskrit since the audience would have been largely Prākrit-speaking. This is made apparent by the king mentioning that his officers were to read the edicts wherever people gathered and wished to hear what he had said. There were areas where literacy was not sufficient among people to read the edicts, although literacy in Prākrit among state officials, Buddhist monks, traders, and some others is attested to. Regional differences of dialect point to the language being widely spoken. Probably the edicts were sent out in Māgadhi Prākrit, current in the capital at Pāṭaliputra, and local scribes and engravers introduced local dialect usage.

One of the interesting variations is that in Māgadhi, the "r" is replaced by "l". Thus *rājā* is written as *lājā*. This replacement has a long history. It is mentioned in the Vedic corpus five centuries earlier as characteristic of the speech of the *asuras*, the *mlecchas*, barbarians who cannot speak Sanskrit correctly.[5] From the orthodox Sanskritic perspective the language used by the emperor Aśoka was that of people outside the social pale.

The Aśokan edicts written in Aramaic had incorporated some elements of Prākrit, reflecting the presence of Prākrit speakers in that area. An Aśokan bilingual Aramaic-Greek inscription indicates the presence of a Greek-speaking population, which is further endorsed by translations of the Major Rock Edicts from Prākrit into Greek. These become epigraphic cross-references to events in Hellenistic West Asia, made more firm by the mention in one edict of five Hellenistic kings who were contemporaries of Aśoka.[6] The type of Greek used was generally the *koine*, which was the lingua franca of the Hellenistic world, registering regional variation, and it therefore parallels the use of Prākrit in India. The variants used in the languages become historical statements.

[5] *Śatapatha Brāhmaṇa*, 3.2.1.23.

[6] MRE XIII, in R. Thapar, *Aśoka and the Decline of the Mauryas*, 40ff.

The five Hellenistic kings are mentioned as:

atta aṃtiyoge nāma yonalā [ja] palaṃ cā tenā aṃtiyogenā cattalī 4 lājane tulamaye nāma aṇtekine nāma makā nāma alikyaṣudale nāma . . .[7]

[. . . where reigns the Yona king named Antiochus and beyond that Antiochus four kings named Ptolemy, Antigonus, Magas, and Alexander . . .]

This reference to the *yonarājās* has come to be the bedrock of ancient Indian chronology because the dates of these kings as contemporaries of Aśoka are well established. The certainty of this evidence supersedes the equating of Sandrocottos with Candragupta Maurya—which was suggested by William Jones. The keystone of chronology comes from inscriptional evidence, which gave a firm base to historical reconstruction.

What is remarkable about these edicts is that the king touches on many facets of Indian life and history that had been and were being acted upon in later centuries. Without saying so directly, there was much that later had its genesis in these ideas. In more senses than one, the edicts can be regarded as an introduction to the historical traditions of early India. There are references to ideas and actions as they prevailed in the past and the manner in which they were now being changed, and why.

A historical document of great significance is the inscription identifying the birthplace of the Buddha at Lumbini.[8] The most expansive of the inscriptions are the Major Rock Edicts and the Pillar Edicts which are in effect the statements of a *cakkavatti*, a universal monarch discoursing on the code of social ethics or *dhamma* that he wishes his subjects to follow. He does not call himself a *cakkavatti* but he acts as one. The edicts are partly autobiographical, articulating his thoughts and activities, reflecting on awareness of royal functions in past times in the light of contemporary concerns, and the relevance to posterity of what he says. This gives the edicts a flavour of historical consciousness.

[7] J. Bloch, *Les Inscriptions d'Asoka*, 130; R. Thapar, *Aśoka and the Decline of the Mauryas*, 40–1.

[8] J. Bloch, *Les Inscriptions d'Asoka*, 157.

Aśoka's edicts fall into two categories. The smaller in number is addressed to the Buddhist Saṅgha and focuses on matters pertaining to the activities of the Saṅgha. For instance, in one of these he specifies the teachings of the Buddha that the monks should know. He does not refer to these as parts of the Canon, thus suggesting that it may have been unfamiliar in the form we know it. The larger category of edicts is mainly that of the Rock and Pillar Edicts, apart from various small edicts. The Major Rock Edicts were issued after his twelfth regnal year (*dbādasa vāssābhisittena*).[9] Another set of edicts was issued, after his twenty-sixth regnal year, this time on pillars, some *in situ* and some specially erected at important locations in the Ganges plains. These latter are a retrospective, reviewing what he has achieved and commenting on his earlier actions. They emphasize social ethics as defined by Aśoka in his explanation of *dhamma*, and, although not identical with Buddhist teaching, were nevertheless in dialogue with it. They do not limit themselves to endorsing Buddhist teaching but incorporate the ethics of tolerance relating to diverse views, as well as the nurturing of wide social relationships.

The distinction between the two is also evident from the smaller number of the first category being located at specifically Buddhist sites, since they were addressed to the Saṅgha, and the larger number of the second category being located more often at places where people congregated, but which were generally not places of pilgrimage for Buddhists in the Mauryan period. In the Buddhist historiographical tradition, however, as we shall see, Aśoka came to be projected as the royal patron par excellence of the Buddhist Saṅgha and the doctrine. The authors of the tradition either did not read the edicts, or could not do so with the *brāhmī* script having changed, or chose to ignore them.

The Aśokan inscriptions usher in a pattern of correlating events to regnal years, thereby underlining a sharper chronological focus. Regnal years are also indicative of linear time. Frequent mention is made of past times (*purā*) or, more specifically, in times past many years ago (*atikkātam aṃtaram bahūni vāssastāni*), when kings indulged in pleasures that have now declined (MRE I, IV, VIII). The penchant for hunting among previous kings has been replaced

[9] MRE III, ibid., 95.

by his missions teaching ethics and speaking of *dhamma*. Where once there was no presence of the gods, they now mingle with the people. Some activities however are to continue until the end of the *kalpa*, the existence of the universe (*samvaṭṭa kappā*).

Aśoka refers to his domain as *vijaye*—that over which he rules (MRE XIV). Friendly references are made to his western neighbours, the five Hellenistic kings (MRE XIII), and to various peoples within the imperial territories: the Yonas, Kāmbojas, Nābhakas, Nābhapaṅktis, Bhojas, Pitinikas, Andhras, and Pārindas; and in the South the Cholas, Pāṇḍyas, Keralaputras, and Satyaputras. These latter references, in contrast to those pertaining to the Hellenistic rulers, contain no names of kings, and the suffix *putra* is often used for a clan. This may explain why the region was not treated on par with the Hellenistic kingdoms.

Mention is also made of the forest peoples—the *aṭavikas.* It is said that the king is like their father and feels for them and that they will be forgiven by the king in so far as they can be forgiven. But what they are to be forgiven for is not stated and the threats seem uncalled for (SE II). Presumably, forest-dwellers were resisting the encroachment into forests by kingdoms desirous of cutting down forests and converting them into cultivable land in order to establish new settlements and enhance revenue. This is implied in some of the remarks on forest tribes in the *Arthaśāstra,* the text on political economy, a part of which is thought to be of this period.[10] Forest produce included flora, fauna, and mineral wealth, and had to be strictly guarded against private exploitation. The confrontation between the state and forest-dwellers was constant, resolved either by the latter ceasing to be clan entities and becoming law-abiding peasants with caste identities, which meant changing their way of life or, alternatively, by some of them moving deeper into the recesses of the forest.

3. Inscriptions Recording Royal Statements

Post-Mauryan inscriptions provided information on rulers and on events associated with them, either through a direct reference or indirectly. Others referred back to earlier kings and their activities.

[10] *Arthaśāstra,* 2.17.

Some of this information came to be included in the *praśasti* section— the eulogy or panegyric on the king and dynasty—which became a normal preliminary in the format of certain inscriptions, and in the royal seals of some dynasties. Yet others on occasion used the site of a previous inscription for adding further inscriptions, the whole being regarded as historically important.

Prākrit was widely used for almost four centuries from the Mauryan period. Dynasties of the immediately post-Mauryan period issued inscriptions in Prākrit. Coin legends of the Sātavāhanas, Indo-Greeks, and Indo-Scythians used other languages as well, such as Greek in the north-west. This is not surprising at a time when trade was in the ascendant, encouraging bilingualism. Royal inscriptions recorded donations to Buddhist monasteries and *brāhmaṇas*. The inscription was a statement of status as well as the record of a pious gift. For example, grants recorded at Nasik include a substantial investment by a member of the Kṣatrapa royal family in two weavers' guilds, the interest of which was to be used in diverse ways: for purchasing robes for monks;[11] for planting 32,000 coconut trees for a congregation of monks; and for making lavish donations to *brāhmaṇas,* including providing some with wives.[12]

An innovation in royal inscriptions was the inclusion of a brief biography of a ruler in an inscription from western India, and in another a somewhat longer autobiographical statement from a king of Kaliṅga in the east, both issued at about the same time. Gotami Balasiri, a Sātavāhana queen, refers to the achievements of her son Siri Sātakaṇi Gotamiputa.[13] The reigning king took the title of Vāsiṭhiputa Siri Pulumāyi.[14] Whereas he is referred to as *raño,* Gotamiputa is given the title of *rājaraño*—king of kings—later

[11] *Ep. Ind.*, 8, no. 12, 82ff.

[12] Ibid., no. 10, 78ff.

[13] Ibid., no. 2, 60ff.

[14] Vāsiṭhiputa is the Prākrit for the Sanskrit Vāsiṣṭhīputra. The other name, Pulumāyi, does not appear to be of Indo-Aryan origin. The use of bilingual coins in Tamil and Prākrit by the Sātavāhanas would suggest some component of Dravidian speakers. A possible Dravidian etymology could be *puliñan* or *puliyan* (forest-dwellers or mountaineers; *DED* 3547, 3548) and may also have provided the root for the Sanskrit name Pulinda, referring to such people.

to take the form of *mahārājādhirāja*. Gotamiputa is said to have revived the glory of the Sātavāhana dynasty—*sātavāhana-kula-yasapatithāpana*—by defeating the Yavanas and rooting out the Khakharāta clans. He also stopped the contamination of the four *varṇas*, as required by the orthodox brahmanical social code, a phrase that had become more politically formulaic than reflective of actual social observance. This inscription anticipates the *praśastis* of later inscriptions and also carries the seminal notions of what were to develop as biographies of kings.

Conquests and the protection of caste society were to be requirements of kingship. Nevertheless, it is also on record—and was often to be so—that the royal patron supported the Saṅgha, a link which was to be emphasized in the Buddhist historical tradition. Gifts and grants, given separately to *śramaṇa* (Buddhist and Jaina) and to *brāhmaṇa* grantees, were a common practice and remained so until grants to Buddhist and Jaina recipients declined.

Another prototype of the *praśasti* is the unusual Hathigumpha inscription from Orissa, a brief autobiography of Khāravela, the Cedi ruler of Kaliṅga, dating to the first century BC.[15] It is virtually a year-by-year account of his achievements in early life. The location of the inscription near a Jaina centre was perhaps because the king was a Jaina. Khāravela refers to conflict with the Sātavāhanas over territory in the Deccan. He also refers to the *Yavana-rājā Dimita*—probably the Indo-Greek king Demetrios, whose presence in Central India is mentioned in other sources, and who refers to himself in his coins as Dime[tra] in Prākrit. Other conflicts included campaigns against the kingdoms of South India, and closer home against those of the middle Ganges plain.[16] He takes an interest in the compiling of Jaina texts, doubtless on the model of what was being done in the Buddhist monasteries at the time, and which was to give rise to a distinctive historical tradition. Khāravela's reference to holding an assembly of ascetics and monks coming from every direction, to describing himself among other things

[15] *Ep. Ind.*, 20, 71ff.

[16] D.C. Sircar, "Problems of the Yuga Purāṇa", in idem, *Studies in Yugapurāṇa and Other Texts*, 1–19.

as *bhikkhu-rājā, dhama-rājā* (the *rājā* of monks and of *dharma*), and to his revering all sects—*sava-pāsaṃḍa-pūjako*—suggests an attempt to emulate the actions of Aśoka Maurya, of which he would have known from his edicts and from Buddhist texts. Most of the place names that he mentions have been identified.

The Hathigumpha inscription introduces features that were to become characteristic of inscriptions in the later period. In speaking of his origins he refers to himself as *airena* which, as *ailena*, could mean the descendant of Ila/Ilā, a lineage ancestor/ancestress of the Candravaṃśa from the Puranic tradition. He identifies his own lineage as that of the Mahāmeghavāhana, which in the Jaina tradition is particularly illustrious.[17] He claims links to the Cedi descent group, as do a number of dynasties of this region, such as the Kalacuri and the Haihaya. The title *kaliṅgādhipati* makes him the lord of Kaliṅga, of substantial importance in eastern India.

A group of brief inscriptions in the Manchapuri cave (Khandagiri in Orissa) contain references to the cave of (presumably donated by) the *mahārāja* Kaliṅgādhipati Mahāmeghavāhana.[18] The Mahāmeghavāhana seems to have been the lineage ruling in Kaliṇga at this time. The literal meaning of *mahāmegha*, the great cloud and vehicle, hints at the story of the Cedis to whom this lineage was linked and who used a flying chariot (a great cloud?) to traverse the skies! His claim to a Cedi connection marks a significant historiographical point. The Cedis were one of the sixteen major states of northern India in Buddhist sources. In the genealogical lists of the *Purāṇas*, as we have seen, they are said to belong to the wider Yadu lineage. But Khāravela's claim doubtless comes from Jaina sources, and may be prior to the construction of descent groups in the *Purāṇas*. The comparison of Khāravela to Vena is also of interest since Vena was opposed to brahmanical orthodoxy. Mention of the Raṭhika and the Bhoja evokes Aśokan inscriptions. The reference to the Nandas of Magadha is to the pre-Mauryan dynasty, here said to have constructed a watercourse in Kaliṅga, dated to *ti-vasa-sata*—read as either the year

[17] This is evident from the *Paumacariyam*, the Jaina version of the *Rāmakathā*. See Chapter 5 above.

[18] *Ep. Ind.*, 13, 160.

103 of a Nanda era (?), or 300 years from the Nandas. Khāravela is anxious to make connections with earlier rulers and events, in an assertion of authority.

Autobiographical statements such as that of Khāravela are rare, as also are pen-portraits of rulers until later times. Even portraiture does not seem to have been particularly fashionable. Occasionally, when earlier rulers are depicted in sculpture, the intention is not to make a portrait or represent the person through a recognizable likeness. The identity is established through a label giving the name. Thus *rāyā asoko* is represented on two panels at the *stūpa* in Kanaganahalli, and the two portrayals are not identical. The figures are the conventional depiction of royalty from that period.[19] Representations of more than one ruler do occur at a couple of places. At Mat, near Mathura, there are statues of Kuṣāṇa kings—perhaps of Vima Khadphises and Huviṣka, with a headless statue of Kaniṣka identified from the label inscription. The place is referred to as a *devakula*, family/house of the gods/kings. This shrine is similar to the Kuṣāṇa shrine at Surkh Kotal in Iran, described as the house of the gods.[20] At Junnar, near Nasik, there are representations of some Sātavāhana rulers.[21] Portraiture on coins is absent although there was a familiarity with the many Greek and Roman coins with their fine portraits found in various parts of the subcontinent.

4. Votive Inscriptions

The most widespread use of Prākrit was in votive inscriptions at Buddhist and Jaina sacred places. The donations are recorded at *stūpa* sites, on icons, and on pottery. Rulers are not donors in significant numbers, nor are they given grandiloquent titles. The donors are mainly ordinary people of varied professions whose donations are either individual, or often as a family or community group.

[19] R. Thapar, "Rāyā Asoko from Kanaganhalli: Some Thoughts", 249–62.

[20] G. Fussman, "The Māṭ *Devakula*: A New Approach to its Understanding", 193–9.

[21] J. Burgess and B. Indraji, *Inscriptions from the Cave Temples of Western India*.

From the second century BC to the third century AD, there is a flood of votive inscriptions recording donations made by many people to the building and adornment of Buddhist *stūpas.* Other inscriptions on the pedestals of Jaina icons also record donations and acts of piety. Such inscriptions are important as sources recording the splits in the Saṅgha, in ownership of property that accompanied the importance of the site, and in reconstructions of the history of Buddhism and Jainism. Apart from mentioning the name, family, and occupation of the donor, as well as the place of origin, the nature of the donation, and sometimes the sect to which the donor belonged, the ruling king is occasionally mentioned. The title of the ruler continues to be a form of *rājā* and nothing grander, perhaps because the context is a pious act or because kings were spoken of simply as *rājās.* These inscriptions record an act taking place in the present, but are not oblivious of the future that will look back on them as a record from the past.

Such inscriptions provide data on the honorand, what was being honoured, by whom, and often also the kinship networks of those doing the honouring. Extended families can be joint donors, as can a monk or a nun together with their kinfolk. Occupations are mentioned prominently and include small land-owners, artisans, merchants. In the construction of a pavilion by the son of a merchant, the list of donors includes the father, mother, wife, brothers, daughters, daughters-in-law, grandson, kinsmen, and friends.[22]

Here, genealogy is not a source of status but rather an expression of a companionable donation covering family members past and present, and even extending to the community or the guild. This is particularly so of the category referred to as *gahapati*, i.e. a householder owning land, livestock, and labour.[23] The *gahapati* in turn gave rise to the *seṭṭhi-gahapati*, the entrepreneur who used his property as capital for establishing trade networks.[24] The importance of women donors, both nuns and lay women,[25] and the

[22] *Ep. Ind.*, 10, Appendix: H. Lüders, "A List of Brahmi Inscriptions from the Earliest Times to About AD 400" (henceforth Lüder's List), no. 1024.

[23] U. Chakravarti, *The Social Dimensions of Early Buddhism,* 69ff.

[24] *Ep. Ind.*, 10: Lüder's List, nos 1056, 1073, 1075.

[25] K.K. Shah, *The Problem of Identity: Women in Early Indian Inscriptions*; K. Roy, "Women and Men Donors at Sanchi: A Study in Inscriptional Evidence", 209–33.

frequency of metronymics in some dynastic inscriptions, such as those of the Sātavāhanas, is noticeable. Discussions on these range from their being pointers to matrilineal forms, to their indicating cross-cousin marriage.

The most striking of the votive inscriptions is the much discussed Piprahwa Buddhist Vase Inscription of about the late third century BC found in Basti District.[26] A vase was donated by a family to a Buddhist *stūpa*. The claim made in the inscription is that it contained the relics of the Buddha—*iyam salīla nidhane budhasa bhagvate sākiyanam*. It echoes the story in the Buddhist texts that the relics of the Buddha were divided between the clans that revered him and a *stūpa* was built over each collection. Was this intended (apart from being an act of piety) to record the distribution of the relics to give it historicity?

This claim is repeated on a casket inscription within a set of caskets found in the *stūpa* at Bhattiprolu in Guntur District.[27] It would seem that relic worship had become so important that claims of the relics being those of the Buddha were not questioned. Relics are also regarded as proof of the historicity of the person. Reference is made to a *gothi* (a community of Buddhists), and to a *negama* (guild), whose members are named. They were obviously local personages, some officials but also many others, who gave various objects to be included in the donation and were handling the caskets. Community donations meant that contributions were made to construct the monument or acquire the caskets, and these were acknowledged individually. Such donations would give a sense of identity and history to the community.

The Buddhist veneration of a bodily relic contrasts with brahmanical practice. The worship of a post-cremation relic would be anathema to *brāhmaṇas*, for whom death was a source of impurity. Yet it was widely practised in the megalithic and other local cultures contemporary with the Vedic corpus. Attitudes to death differed. Maintaining continuity through an artifact with a person who had died also suggested historical continuity. This would be part of the reason for the maintenance and veneration of

[26] *Ep. Ind.*, 10: Lüder's List, no. 931; F. Barth, "The Inscription of the Piprahwa Vase", *Ind. Ant.*, 1907, 36, 117ff.

[27] *Ep. Ind.*, 2, 323.

stūpas. The lack of burials of the dead from the first millennium AD also eliminated the possibility of funerary orations recorded as inscriptions—as were common in, for example, Greco-Roman cultures.

As a parallel to the votive inscription at Buddhist sites, an unusual inscription at Mandasor records the building of a temple to Surya by a silk-weavers' guild that had immigrated from further west. The author of the inscription had pretensions to being a poet, but that apart a change in epigraphic style becomes apparent. The eulogy is of the city of Daśapura, where the temple was located. Praise is lavished on the local kings, although the Gupta overlord is mentioned. The date is 493 in the Mālava era, i.e. AD 436. The temple, having fallen into disrepair, had to be renovated thirty-seven years later, in AD 473, the date of the inscription. Members of the original guild, now in other occupations, nevertheless came together to restore the temple and recalled their earlier association in the inscription. The guild here is the equivalent of the extended family of the Buddhist votive inscriptions.

Some inscriptions refer to Buddhist texts and teaching such as the *Nikāyas*, stating that they go back to an earlier period. This is reminiscent of Aśoka, in an inscription addressed to the Buddhist Saṅgha, listing the teachings of the Buddha with which monks should be familiar,[28] the teachings being of an earlier period. References to the rulers in inscriptions are in part to give an indication of the date, and in part to provide an association with the male donor of the royal family. Thus an inscription by a *gahapati* mentions the year of the *raño vāsiṭhīputa sāmi siri pulumāvi*—the king Vāsiṣṭhiputra Pulumāvi.[29]

Many considerations led to the choice of sites of *stūpas* and *vihāras*, these being located in every part of the subcontinent. There could be an existing sacred place that went back to prehistoric times. The more obvious of these were the sites of

[28] Bhabra Edict, in J. Bloch, *Les Inscriptions d'Asoka*, 154–5.
[29] *Ep. Ind.*, 10, Lüder's List, no. 1248,

megalithic burials, such as Amaravati, which was appropriated by a large Buddhist structure engulfing the earlier one but the sacredness of which became a historical continuity. This was a process that continued throughout Indian history, with Hindu temples built at the site of Buddhist *caityas* (halls of worship), as at Ter and Chezarla; or Muslim mosques built at sites of Hindu temples, as at Delhi and Ajmer. The inscriptions may not refer to the taking over of such sacred spaces, but the archaeological and architectural evidence for this is a historical statement.

Prākrit votive inscriptions were not limited to Buddhist sites. Among others is a pillar inscription dedicated to Viṣṇu at the turn of the Christian era.[30] The pillar was established by Heliodorus, the son of Diya/Dion, a native of the city of Takṣaśilā (Taxila) in the north-west; he describes himself as a Yona/Yavana, the term used for Greeks and West Asians. He is the *dūta* (ambassador) of the *mahārāja* Amtalikita/Antalkidas to the *rājan* Kāsiputa. The pillar is his declaration of being a follower of the Vāsudeva cult, one of the many forms of the worship of Viṣṇu. It is worth noticing that he refers to his king as *mahārāja*, whereas the local Indian king is simply *rājan*, in keeping with the current Indian usage.

Another important set of inscriptions in Prākrit was the group found at Andau in Saurashtra which date to the early second century AD.[31] Issued during the reign of Rudradāman, three generations of his ancestors are named, information that was becoming common in inscriptions. The date is given as the year 52 but the era is not mentioned. If it was issued in the currently popular Śaka era, this would work out to AD 130, which would be in agreement with the palaeography. The inscriptions have a Jaina association and are funeral monuments of a family. As reminders of the past these would become the historical records of the family.

There are many reasons for the extensive use of Prākrit as the language of inscriptions. State administration wishing to communicate with a range of people, and not just the elite, made Prākrit the language of polity; as the language of merchants and artisans it was tied into trade crucial to the economy of the time;

[30] Lüder's List, no. 669, Besnagar Garuda Inscription, in D.C. Sircar, *Select Inscriptions*, vol. I, 90–1.

[31] *Ep. Ind.*, 16, 23.

both Buddhism and Jainism, which had a considerable following, used Prākrits, including texts that dealt with the past; the extensive donations to *stūpas* and *vihāras* were from the *upāsakas*—lay followers, who were Prākrit speaking, and among them women were conspicuous. From the third century BC to the second century AD, Prākrit was the language of the cosmopolitan discourse of the South Asian region and its neighbourhood in virtually every direction.

5. Sanskrit Inscriptions: A Different History

In the early centuries AD, Prākrit was gradually replaced by Sanskrit as the language of the court and of some public discourse. With all the activity involving Prākrit and its pre-eminence in epigraphs, one wonders at the absence of inscriptions in Sanskrit. The use of Sanskrit in inscriptions begins tentatively in the early centuries AD, and increases when Sanskrit comes to be associated with the royal courts. The language of the ritual texts was distinct. The more commonly used Sanskrit of Pāṇini included a wider range of texts that could be sources on the past, since even some heterodox sects, such as those of Northern Buddhism, were writing in Sanskrit.

Inscriptions in the Mathura region using Prākrit, but veering close to Sanskrit linguistic forms, have been labelled Epigraphical Hybrid Sanskrit.[32] One among these inscriptions commemorates the setting up of an image of a *bodhisattva* (a Buddha to be) by the daughter of a local *mahārāja* and is dated to the twenty-third year of the Kuṣāṇa king Kaniṣka. Another slightly later *kharoṣṭhī* inscription gives the day, month, and year, again in an unknown era, possibly the Śaka era of AD 78. The king is given elaborate royal titles—*mahārājasa rājātirājasa devaputrasa kaisarasa* (the great king, the king of kings, the son of the deity, the *kaisara*)—indeed a far cry from the simple *rājā* of earlier inscriptions.[33] The use of these titles has been debated. Their frequent occurrence in the north-west was perhaps the influence of Roman imperial titles,

[32] Mathura Inscription, *Ep. Ind.*, 28, 42ff.

[33] Ara Inscription of Kanishka II, *Ep. Ind.*, 14, 130ff.

where *kaisara* may be a version of Ceasar, and *devaputra* suggests the Chinese "son of heaven". The Kuṣāṇa kingdom had transactions both with the Roman and the Chinese empire. Other than adopting a fashion, it was an indicator of a change in the perception of kingship: the king was now a far greater focus of authority and power than had been the earlier *rājā*.

An inscription of the Śuṅga period from Ayodhyā records the performance of *aśvamedhas,* followed by an ambiguous statement that may refer to a person sixth in descent from the *senāpati* (commander of the army), Puṣyamitra.[34] In literary sources the *senāpati* Puṣyamitra is said to have usurped the Mauryan throne and founded the Śuṅga dynasty. The inscription corroborates the designation and seems to refer back to a period prior to his being king, possibly based in the Puranic dynastic list. As a *brāhmaṇa* family, the Śuṅgas would have given preference to the use of Sanskrit, however bowdlerized. The publicity and significance given to the performance of Vedic rituals in association with emerging kingship at this time would have been qualitatively different from the same rituals being performed by the *rājās* of earlier centuries. The wealth expended on the ritual was most likely greater, even if the ritual was performed in a different manner. The concept of wealth was slowly beginning to include land, which had not been the case earlier.

The use of a Sanskrit, not quite conforming to rules, is evident from some early Sanskrit inscriptions.[35] These refer to heroes of the Vṛṣṇi clan and mention Saṃkarṣaṇa and Vāsudeva, and are linked to the Puranic religion.[36] However, a notable exception is the well-known Bala inscription, which commemorates the establishing of a statue and monastery at Sarnath at the instance of a Buddhist member of the Saṅgha claiming that it was on the spot where the Buddha himself used to stroll.[37] Such claims, more common among sects asserting historicity, was clearly the inventing

[34] *Ep. Ind.*, 20, 57ff.

[35] Gosundi Inscription, *Ep. Ind.,* 16, 25ff.; Hathibada Inscription, *Ep. Ind.*, 22, 198ff.

[36] R. Salomon, *Indian Epigraphy*, 86–7.

[37] *Ep. Ind.*, 8, 176–7.

of a tradition. We may dismiss it as such, but its significance lies in being an attempt to appeal to history, however garbled.

The initial spurt in Sanskrit inscriptions comes from an unlikely quarter—the dynasties that ruled in the north-west, linked to Central Asian origins. These would most likely have been included under the label "*vrātya kṣatriyas*" (degenerate *kṣatriyas*). The first inscription in standard Sanskrit, which marks the gradual turning of public discourse from Prākrit to Sanskrit, was that of Rudradāman, the *mahākṣatrapa* (the great *satrap*) of western India. It was issued in 72 of the Śaka era, the equivalent of AD 150, and engraved on the same rock as the set of Aśokan edicts at Girnar in Saurashtra.[38] The valley had been dammed by the Mauryan administration to create the Sudarśana Lake, presumably as a source of irrigation. The inscription describes the restoration of the embankment after it had been destroyed during a fierce storm, and is located where the edict of Aśoka was engraved.

The inscription mentions the builder of the dam as *mauryasya rājnaḥ candraguptasya rāṣṭriyena vaiśyena Puṣyaguptena kāritam* (the act of Candragupta Maurya's governor, the *vaiśya* Puṣyagupta). Subsequently, after another storm, it was restored by *aśokasya mauryasya te yavanarājena tuṣāsphena adhiṣṭhaya* (Aśoka's administrator the *yavanarāja* Tuṣāśpa); and the current breach was restored by his own governor Suviśākha. This awareness of the history of the dam makes it evident that the location of his own inscription juxtaposed to that of Aśoka Maurya was deliberate, and intended as a continuation of the history. It is impressive that an event of the fourth century BC was being recalled in the second century AD and was to be remembered still later. The inscription makes a particular point of stating that the restoration of the dam did not require forced labour or extra taxes, for the finances from the treasury were sufficient and the administrator Suviśākha was an upright man and not susceptible to corruption.

Rudradāman's inscription mentions his father, Jayadāman, and his better-known grandfather, Caṣṭana. He acquired the title of *mahākṣatrapa* through his conquests in the area and makes a point of referring to defeating the Yaudheyas, who claimed to

[38] Ibid., 42ff.; R. Salomon, *Indian Epigraphy*, 89.

be *kṣatriyas.* Presumably, this referred to the Puranic use of the term *kṣatriya* to mean the clans of old, since the Yaudheyas were known to be a chiefdom. He defeated Sātakarṇi the Sātavāhana, but let him off because of a close relationship. He donated cows to *brāhmaṇas*, which would have brought him the support of the brahmanical orthodoxy. In listing the characteristics of a king he mentions some of the requirements of a state system as given in texts on political economy, such as the army and the treasury. It is also noticeable that, although the dynasties of this period were beginning to take grandiose titles, Rudradāman refers to Candragupta Maurya as *rājā.* The latter part of the inscription is more conventional in describing his good looks and the number of *svayamvaras* where he won the hand of many a princess!

An obvious question is why a *mahākṣatrapa* whose title indicates that he was not a local ruler, or for that matter other *kṣatrapas*, should use Sanskrit for inscriptions. Prākrit was still used and the earlier inscription of Aśoka at Girnar was in Prākrit. Was the new ruler making a claim that although of alien stock he was not a *mleccha* and that his status was as good as that of any other ruler? Or was it becoming fashionable to use Sanskrit at court to demarcate its membership, and he therefore chose it for his inscriptions as well? What is surprising is that it took so long for the language to attain status in administration.

Sanskrit became the established language of court and administration from the mid-first millennium AD. Texts exploring mathematics, medicine, and astronomy, as well as forms of creative literature, had already begun to use Sanskrit. The inferior status of Prākrit is strikingly set out in the dramas of these times, where upper-caste men spoke Sanskrit—all except the *viduṣaka,* the uncharacteristic *brāhmaṇa*—whereas the women and lower-caste men spoke Prākrit.

A few of the early Hybrid Sanskrit epigraphs are linked to the emerging worship of Puranic deities, in particular Śiva and Viṣṇu. Was the use of Sanskrit a method of identifying with the orthodox against the earlier patronage to the heterodox sects, particularly if one was not of the upper caste oneself? But the latter were also using a Hybrid Sanskrit; why they were doing so is in itself a question that needs an answer. Was the legitimizing of kingship more accessible through brahmanical rituals? According to the rules of the the *Dharmaśāstras*, Rudradāman would have been a *mleccha*. In the previous period such rules were less adhered to, but perhaps now they had become a part of the play of political power. The possibility of a *mleccha* seeking or being given lineage links with the Puranic descent groups was yet to come.

An entirely different category of inscriptions that begin as brief records in the mid-first millennium AD but become more frequent and elaborate in later centuries were those commemorating the death of the hero and of the woman who became a *satī*.[39] The setting up of an upright stone slab as a memorial may go back to the menhir of megalithic cultures, followed later by Buddhist memorials to the dead. A generalized depiction of a hero in action, often on horseback, is a new addition and gradually a brief inscription is added. The *satī* is memorialized by stylized symbols. The minimum information mentions a place and the date. Gradually, the hero-stone began to carry sculptured panels representing the battle, or frequently the cattle raid, and the hero being taken to heaven by *apsarās*. The sun and the moon at the top invariably represent eternity. This elaboration was accompanied by longer inscriptions recording the identity of the hero, the date and the event. These changed from brief mention in Sanskrit to long accounts of the event and the person in the regional languages. Local ballads and short epics were the counterpart to the memorial stones and sustained the memory of the person in greater detail. Such hero-stones are found all over the subcontinent, particularly in frontier zones subject to changes in political control.

6. The Centrality of the *Praśasti*

The efflorescence of Sanskrit as the language of the court and of inscriptions in Sanskrit was established by the Gupta period. The best known among the early ones was the retrospective inscription on Samudra Gupta of the Gupta dynasty at Allahabad.[40] It

[39] R. Thapar, "Death and the Hero", in idem, *Cultural Pasts*, 680–95; S. Settar and G.D. Sontheimer (eds), *Memorial Stones*.

[40] J.F. Fleet (ed.), *Corpus Inscriptionum Indicarum*, vol. III, 195ff.; S.R. Goyal, *A History of the Imperial Guptas*, 122ff.

is regarded as an exemplar of the *praśasti*—the eulogy or panegyric—and according to some scholars was issued by his son Candra Gupta II in the fourth century AD. Samudra Gupta is given the full imperial title of *mahārājādhirāja*, although even lesser rulers were to take extraordinarily grand titles, much of which was hyperbole. *Praśastis* refer back to dynastic origins, involving deities and ancient *ṛṣis*, as well as short genealogies, drawn possibly from the records now maintained in royal courts. The exaggeration of the formulaic can be separated from that which is more historical. Conquests over kingdoms and over chiefdoms are listed. The latter seem to have been politically more important than is conceded by modern historians. The author of this *praśasti* was the court poet Hariṣena.

The location of the inscription raises many questions. It is engraved on the pillar erected by Aśoka, which carries his pillar edicts in Prākrit—it is the one moved to the fort at Allahabad built many centuries later. Apart from the edicts, and a couple of other Aśokan inscriptions, and this *praśasti,* it also carries a brief Persian inscription giving the lineage of the Mughal emperor Jahangir. The inscriptions date to three different millennia and are in three different languages. There are a few brief miscellaneous inscriptions by sundry others, some in the nature of grafitti.

Why was Samudra Gupta's *praśasti* engraved on this pillar? If Aśokan *brāhmī* could still be read in the Gupta period, which is possible, the message of the Gupta inscription, extolling military conquest, contradicted Aśoka's opposition to violence. Was it an attempt to denigrate Aśoka and show Samudra Gupta as the great conqueror? But that might have been more effective on a separate and equally imposing pillar. Was the Aśokan message seen as a Buddhist discourse which needed to be overwritten? Or was it, on the contrary, an attempt at historical continuity evoking the legitimacy of the Mauryan emperor?

Attempts were made in Gupta art to emulate some Mauryan forms, especially in the capitals of the pillars.[41] Such attempts at

[41] Joanna Williams, "A Recent Aśokan Capital and the Gupta Attitude Towards the Past", 225–40; idem, *The Art of Gupta India: Empire and Province*, 96ff.

historical continuity also led to inscribing *praśastis* in juxtaposition with other earlier inscriptions. Another Aśokan pillar, now located on the citadel of the Sultan Firuz Shah at Kotla (Delhi), carries a *praśasti* of Viśāla Deva, the Chauhan ruler of the Delhi region, dating to the twelfth century, prior to the pillar being shifted to Delhi in the fourteenth century. He mentions defeating the *mleccha*, yet it was the *mleccha* that gave prominence to his *praśasti*. These pillars highlight the importance of inscriptions as historical memory, even if subconscious.

Various sultans brought pillars of earlier times to places of importance in their territory, as for example the iron pillar of Candra of the fifth century was brought to the Quwwat al-Islam mosque at the Qutb in Mehrauli (Delhi) by Iltutmish. This is further underlined when, in the fourteenth century, Firuz Shah Tughluq shifted other Aśokan pillars to prime locations in the proximity of mosques in an attempt to link the Sultanate with the Indian past.[42] The pillar at Fatehabad (Hissar) was engraved with a lengthy Persian inscription giving an account of the history of Firuz Shah, emulating in some ways the kind of history recorded earlier on the pillars. It was said to have been crowned with a golden *kalaśa* (cupola), as is done in Hindu temples. Pillars are referred to in earlier times as *jayastambhas* and *kīrtistambhas*, symbolic of victory and fame, even if, as in the case of Aśoka, he disapproved of fame through conquest. Samudra Gupta's inscription is a claim to conquest but that of Jahangir is a claim to a respected ancestry.

There is a curious political ambiguity in the placement of the Samudra Gupta *praśasti* on the pillar of Aśoka. The puzzle is that in the brahmanical *itihāsa-purāṇa* tradition Aśoka is barely mentioned, except as a name in the dynastic list of the Mauryas. Presumably, this was because he was a patron of the Buddhist Saṅgha. The title which Aśoka took, *devānaṁpiya* (beloved of the gods), was treated with contempt in much of brahmanical

[42] M. Shokoohy, "Haryana I: The Column of Firuz Shah and Other Islamic Inscriptions from the District of Hissar"; F.B. Flood, *Objects of Translation*, 247–55; E. Hultzsch (ed.), *Corpus Inscriptionum Indicarum*, I, xv–xvii; J. Irwin, "Aśokan Pillars", 706–7; C.B. Asher, "Appropriating the Past: Jahangir's Pillars", 8.

literature. Only in Buddhist historiography is he a figure of exceptional historical importance. His historical importance was known but not reflected in brahmanical texts. The representation of Aśoka as a respected ruler is not confined to Buddhist texts, as is evident from the proximity of later inscriptions to those inscribed by him. This was not merely a question of finding a convenient surface on which to engrave a statement, but of deliberately choosing to be associated with the earlier ruler or event. The choice of the site of an inscription was made after much thought. It also underlines the importance of a historical tradition that differs from the Puranic.

Imitating the Mauryan style in pillars is not the only example of the Guptas making connections with the Mauryas. At Girnar there is a third inscription of the later Gupta, Skanda Gupta, who records that the embankment of the Sudarśana Lake burst, once again due to heavy rain, in AD 457, and the local governor Cakrapālita had it repaired.[43] These are three sets of inscriptions spanning 800 years, but they are clearly linked to the building and breaching of the same dam. What is impressive is that the previous breaches were known and recorded. There is a suggested continuity in the engraving of the inscriptions, and it would seem that the earlier ones could still be read. References to the previous repairing of the dam were not based on hearsay but on a precise record of what had happened in the past.

The record-keepers of the state are referred to in a set of grants from Damodarpur in eastern India. Issued during the late Gupta period, the grants range from AD 443 to AD 533. The dates are recorded in detail, mentioning the name of the Gupta ruler and the date in the Gupta era. This was a requirement for legal documents, which is what the copper-plate inscription was meant to be. The chronology was based on linear time.[44] The grants pertain to the purchase of various qualities of land which will enable the purchasers to make benefactions.[45] These copper-plate inscriptions mark a departure: sale deeds and grants of land transactions are

[43] Junagadh Inscription of Skandagupta, in J.F. Fleet (ed.), *Corpus Inscriptionum Indicarum,* III, 56ff.

[44] R. Thapar, *Time as a Metaphor of History.*

[45] *Ep. Ind.*, 15, 113ff.

a new and significant feature from this period. Land is purchased by private persons to be gifted to religious beneficiaries in order to acquire merit for the donor and his parents. The beneficiaries here are *brāhmaṇas* and land is the item being purchased and donated. Most of the requests are for tax-free fallow land which has not been previously gifted. This required the checking of the records relating to the land, and the price was doubtless fixed in accordance with the state's demand.

The dates given for the Gupta rulers provide a chronology and a genealogy. Royal titles are most elaborate—*parama-daivata parama-bhaṭṭāraka mahārājādhirāja*. This is not merely the influence of earlier Kuṣāṇa titles but also marks a demarcation between the self-perception of the earlier *rājās* and the exaggerated sense of persona of the current ones. These inscriptions are symptomatic of a different kind of state. Even if the territory involved is on the periphery of the kingdom, the legalities of its ownership are controlled by a hierarchy of officials involved in both recording and permitting the grant. The matter had also to be passed by the civic administration of the governors and advisors who were officials, such as the *mahattaras*, *aṣṭa-kula-adhikaranas, grāmikas*, and *puṣṭapālas* responsible for maintaining the records. Civic patrons such as the chief merchant, artisans, and various scribes were also consulted. Grants of land began to be given frequently in the post-Gupta period, often for the performance of rituals or because of the magnanimity of the ruler. Since some were quite substantial grants, one has to examine possible political reasons as well.

Originally, the grant was of the revenue from the land in lieu of salaries, so it was the provision of an income. Gradually, however, these being grants in perpetuity, the land itself came to be claimed by the grantee. Grants of land were made to religious and ritual specialists and to selected officers. *Brāhmaṇa* grantees were being recompensed for performing rituals to enhance power, or to ward off evil, or to provide a genealogy legitimizing the ruler with acceptable genealogical links. The last of these meant a familiarity with the *vaṃśānucarita* of the *Purāṇas* and whatever else was thought relevant in providing a *kṣatriya* genealogy. If the grant was of wasteland or forest, it encouraged the grantee to convert it to agricultural use. *Brāhmaṇas,* although forbidden from being agriculturalists, did at least supervise the cultivation of these lands, even if they did not cultivate them, as is clear from the *Kṛṣiparāśara,* a manual in Sanskrit for wet rice cultivation, the most lucrative crop in areas where water was available.

Kings conquering neighbouring kingdoms converted the defeated king and made him a *sāmanta*. Derived from *sīmā* (boundary), it originally referred to a neighbour. It is now often translated as "feudatory", but should perhaps more correctly refer to an intermediary. A hierarchy of intermediaries of differing rank and function came into being, intervening between peasant and king. The latter had the power to revoke the grant, even if categorically stated to the contrary by the original grantor. Cancellations of grants were infrequent since they created a nucleus of political opposition.

In setting out the statement of a grant, together with the rights and obligations of both grantor and grantee, and the occasion of the grant, the statement encapsulated a historical event. An example of such a grant at a relatively earlier period is one issued by Prabhāvatī Gupta, the daughter of Candra Gupta II, married into the Vākāṭaka royal family and ruled as the queen regent until her son came of age.[46] The grant is written on two copper-plates that measure approximately 9 x 6 inches, originally held together by a ring on which the royal seal was attached, authenticating the inscription as being her command.

The grant provides the essential information. It invokes the deity Viṣṇu. It provides the credentials of the donor, the queen-mother, by giving her family connections as also a résumé of the Gupta kings where, interestingly, she makes specific mention of the queen Kumāradevī and her own mother, Kuberanāgā. The Licchavi princess Kumāradevī was socially a cut above the obscure Gupta family, as is indirectly conceded by the early rulers. She

[46] The Poona Plates of Prabhāvatī Gupta, in V.V. Mirashi (ed.), "Inscriptions of the Vākāṭakas", in *Corpus Inscriptionum Indicarum*, vol. V, 5ff.; H.T. Bakker (ed.), *The Vākāṭaka Heritage: Indian Culture at the Crossroads*; N. Sinha Kapoor, "State Formation in Vidarbha: The Case of the Eastern Vākāṭakas"; K.M. Srimali, *Agrarian Structure in Central India and the Northern Deccan (c. AD 300–500): A Study of Vākāṭaka Inscriptions.*

also explains why she has the authority to make the grant, being the queen regent for her son. As is normal in such inscriptions she mentions the village granted and indicates its exact location. The purpose of the donation is the acquisition of religious merit, and the donation is sanctified by the pouring of water into the hands of the donee. The latter is a *brāhmaṇa* well versed in the four *Vedas.* The duties, obligations, and exemptions of the donee are listed, and it is specifically stated that they are in accord with the grants of former kings. Earlier records would therefore have been consulted. The perpetuity of the grant is wished for, with punishments for those who obstruct it. The name of the engraver is mentioned.

Such grants of land on a bigger scale were often the nucleus of what were later to become principalities and small kingdoms. One such group is recorded in the well-known Khoh copper-plate inscriptions of the *mahārājā* Hastin issued in the Gupta era of 156 equivalent of AD 475, and the later inscription of Samkṣobha of AD 529.[47] He claims to have come from a *nṛpati-parivrāja-kula* (a family of royal ascetics) and was generous with his gifts. Samkṣobha mentions Hastin having inherited an ancestral gift of a *brahmadeya* grant (land given to a *brāhmaṇa*), which in this case consisted of eighteen forest kingdoms. He was thus well able to establish himself as a semi-autonomous ruler with his own feudatories, to whom he refers, and gifts a village to a *brāhmaṇa* in turn. This is one example of how states and kingdoms encroached into forests and cleared them for cultivation, by coercing the forest dwellers to become their peasants, or settling cultivators from elsewhere to labour on the land, with the grantee acquiring a source of revenue. Many grants were of land already under cultivation, or even a village, which was an immediate source of income for the grantee. These inscriptions have been used by modern scholars to suggest a new periodization of Indian history, differentiating the late first millennium AD from the earlier period.

The inclusion of genealogies in the inscriptions begins in a

[47] Khoh Copper-Plate Inscription of the Maharaja Hastin, in J.F. Fleet (ed.), *Corpus Inscriptionum Indicarum*, vol. III, 93ff. Khoh Copper-plate inscription of the Maharaja Samkshobha, ibid., 112ff.

small way with references to a few generations; it becomes more prominent in the *praśastis*, and more so in the royal seals. Members of ruling families such as the Guptas had their own seals.[48] A number of clay sealings of the later Gupta rulers help reconstruct the declining years of the dynasty. In the course of creating genealogies, there was an increasing tendency to claim descent in the Sūryavaṃśa or Candravaṃśa lineage, a reflection of using the *vaṃśānucarita* of the *Purāṇa* as a source. Some families go further and latch themselves to a particular descent group, and among these many claim to be of the Yadu lineage.

The *vaṃśānucarita* of the *Purāṇas*, contemporary with some of these inscriptions, projects the past in the form of genealogies and dynastic lists. The epigraphic data is different, since genealogies, although important, are not sole representations of the past. Historical thinking was now beginning to shift towards recording persons in the context of events as well as part of a dynasty. Nevertheless, there is space for genealogies and they have a function in the multiple claims to status, territory, and associations with the past. There is a gradual move towards what may be called externalized history, where the narrative is not embedded in a religious text but is recognized independently as a distinct genre and a historical record.

7. Historical Time in Inscriptions

A central feature of the inscription as a record was the fact that it was generally precisely dated and followed one of many eras current at the time.[49] Initially, calendrical time was based on the lunar year, each with twelve months in accordance with the *nakṣatras* (constellations). Later there is a shift to the solar year, although some reckonings continue to be made in the lunar year.

[48] Nalanda Clay Seals of Budhagupta, Narasiṃhagupta, and Kumāragupta, in J.F. Fleet (ed.), *Corpus Inscriptionum Indicarum*, III; B.C. Chhabra and G.S. Gai, *Corpus Inscriptionum Indicarum*, III, 350–5; Bhitari Seal of Kumāragupta, ibid., 358ff., 364ff., 319ff.; H. Sastri, "Nalanda and its Epigraphic Material", 49–53; J. Marshall, *ASI (Annual Reports)*, 1911–12, 44–60.

[49] D.C. Sircar, *Indian Epigraphy*, 119ff.; R. Salomon, *Indian Epigraphy*, 180ff.

The division of time that covers the existence of the universe is, as earlier discussed, into four *yugas*: the Kṛta, Tretā, Dvāpara, and Kali. The calculation of the start of the present Kaliyuga as equivalent to 3102 BC was finding acceptance.[50] The *yugas* are referred to but rarely used in defining a precise chronology in inscriptions. They were tied to the time calculations used in astronomy. But historical eras commemorate persons or events.

Time in the inscriptions is measured in a more linear form. Many of the early inscriptions, such as those of Aśoka, Khāravela, and some Sātavāhana rulers, mention regnal years. Others provide a date but do not mention the era. Precision in dating through using an era becomes more common from the fifth century AD. The most commonly used era is the *samvat* (era), first referred to as Kṛta, then Mālava, and finally and most frequently as Vikrama. This is the equivalent of 58–57 BC. Who instituted it is still debated. It may commemorate the accession of Azes I, as is the explanation of modern scholars, even if Azes was not a particularly important king. Or it may be a calculation used by astronomers at Ujjain, the location of the meridian, and which was also the capital of Mālava. In the inscription of the silk weavers at Mandasor it is described as having been founded by the clan of the Mālavas. It was subsequently renamed Vikrama, but the reason for this remains unexplained. The other commonly used era was the Śaka era of AD 78, as also the Kalacuri-Cedi era of 248–9 and the Gupta era of 319–20. Eras used after the sixth century, which were plentiful and of which some became obsolete, often commemorated events of regional significance.[51]

8. Inscriptions as Historical Records

It has been argued that Sanskrit became a public political language in the post-Gupta period and came to form a cosmopolis—a cultural formation that transcended political boundaries and religious affiliations.[52] The use of Sanskrit linked politics to a political

[50] J.F. Fleet, "The Kaliyuga Era of BC 3102", 479–96, 675–98; *Varāhamihira's Bṛhatsaṃhitā*, 13.3; *Rājataraṅgiṇī*, 1.49.

[51] D.C. Sircar, *Indian Epigraphy*, 251ff.

[52] S. Pollock, "The Cosmopolitan Vernacular", 6–37.

culture beyond the region, whereas the later inclusions, of regional languages in inscriptions, were records of specific local powers. Could the same not be said of Prākrit in the Mauryan and post-Mauryan period? Why then did Sanskrit become the hegemonic language during this period?

Epigraphic Sanskrit was not of a uniform standard. A major stylistic departure from earlier inscriptions was the *praśasti*. Techniques of *kāvya* were used in *praśastis*, whose authors sometimes were court poets. The *praśasti* gradually became formulaic. But it had a purpose. Obscure families claiming to be royal used it to latch themselves to *kṣatriya vaṃśas* (lineages) given in the *Purāṇas* or an equivalent status. The *praśasti* accommodated upward mobility among ruling families. The inscription terminated with a statement in Sanskrit mentioning the author, the scribe, and the engraver—who were virtually the witnesses—and added to the legitimacy. The use of Sanskrit in these inscriptions was to become something of a formality in later periods, but also a source of validating claims drawing from the past. The *praśasti* had some affinities with, and was in some ways germane to, the *carita* literature of royal biographies from the seventh century.

The functional portion of such inscriptions, such as the details of the grant, was less literary, although crucial as a legal document. In later centuries, it was optionally written in the regional language to ensure accessibility to local administration. This was reminiscent of the variants of Prākrit used in early inscriptions. The Sanskrit passages were more formal. The wider use of Sanskrit also evolved from the growing importance of literacy and appreciation of literary composition even when providing historical material. A change in language could mean a change in authorship and audience, and a consequent change in function. Buddhist and Jaina monks and the laity gave way ultimately to court poets and officers of the administration. Particular languages used for particular statements reflect social hierarchy.

The multiplicity of kingdoms, each with a court cloning the more powerful ones, evolved through expansive grants of land. Inscriptions attempt to encapsulate the political order of the time, where sovereignty had to be acquired and protected. Dependent on a hierarchy of political relationships, frequently founded on a control of economic resources, those who could extend these resources were central to the polity. Some *brāhmaṇa* grantees therefore became agricultural entrepreneurs. Since land was permanent wealth, it became hereditary, enabling the *brāhmaṇa* to participate in the political culture and stamp it with the accoutrements of his own culture—such as Sanskrit as the language of authority. Sanskrit-knowing scribes, officials, and ritual specialists were at a premium.

Added to this was the claim to controlling the supernatural and the unforeseen through ritual. This brought the *brāhmaṇa* into competition with the shaman and the priests of local cults, and the former was not averse to incorporating some of the techniques of the latter. The resulting religious practices were unpredictably different from earlier ones.

Parallel to this was knowledge of various kinds, preserved or rendered into Sanskrit, and going back many centuries, now reinforced by the functional use of Sanskrit. The polity became a play between those appropriating the expanded agricultural economy, the underlining of caste status (which included a large range of occupational and status identities becoming castes), and the emergence of the many sects of Puranic Hinduism as a result of religious incorporation from various sources.

Patronage gradually began to centre on the royal court, with kings and the royal family and those associated with them as ministers and administrators as the main players. The keeping of records shifted from monasteries and local centres to courts and prestigious families. As a semi-biographer the court poet writing on the ruler altered the relationship between political authority and its legitimizer. The poets were often *brāhmaṇas*, requiring ample maintenance from a prosperous court. The less wealthy courts probably had to make do with a bard. Brahmanical learning, even of the non-ritualistic kind, flourished in *āśramas* and *agrahāras,* the latter being based on substantial royal grants. A surfeit of educated *brāhmaṇas* by the late first millennium AD led to their migrating out from Gauḍa, Kanauj, and Kashmir to Gujarat, the Deccan and elsewhere. This helped spread Sanskritic culture at elite levels. It might also account in part for the multiple commentaries on Sanskrit texts from the early second millennium AD.

The royal court also maintained record keepers who were part of the administration. The *akṣa-paṭala-adhikaraṇa-adhikṛta*, for example, maintained the legal documents. These included the royal seals and inscriptions, both of which had to be verified before being issued. Forged inscriptions (*kūṭaśāsana*) were known and there was enough literacy to manipulate records from the past. Copper-plate grants would be the obvious target for forgeries. But sometimes even inscriptions on stone were tampered with to change ownership.[53] The composers of the inscriptions were from the upper castes, but the engravers were less literate and of the lower castes, such as goldsmiths. The importance of literacy and of the court poet was enhanced by the occasional ruler who claimed competency or more in the writing of plays and poetry, such as Harṣa of Kanauj and Mahendravarman the Pallava king. Harṣa wrote a fine calligraphic hand if the signature on one of his inscriptions stating *svahasto mama mahārājādhirāja śri harṣa* (by my own hand, *mahārājādhirāja* Harṣa) is his.[54]

Parallel to the *āśramas* and the *agrahāras* were the Buddhist and Jaina *vihāras*, where there had been a premium on literacy and learning since early times. Much of the monastic activity was given over to copying texts. This is attested to by the large number of manuscripts collected by Chinese Buddhists who travelled to India in search of Buddhist teaching in the first millennium AD. Jaina teaching similarly retained an interest in its early Prākrit texts, but also shifted to writing in Sanskrit. Literacy and the wider resort to inscriptions were interrelated.

Early inscriptions in themselves do not constitute a historical tradition, but they reflect an obvious sense of historical consciousness. I have touched on the articulation of four aspects of this. Inscriptions are records and can therefore be consulted in the future for information on the past. Thus, the record of the repairs to the embankment at the Sudarśana Lake are available for 800 years.

[53] As, for example, in the inscriptions at the Barabar and Nagarjuni caves, where the original donation of the caves was by Aśoka and his grandson Daśaratha, to the Ājīvika sect, but a later sect tried to obliterate this name: H. Falk, *Aśokan Sites and Artifacts*, 258ff. and 270ff.

[54] Banskhera Copper-Plate Inscription, in *Ep. Ind.*, 4, 208.

There is an evoking of the past in order to make statements about changes in the present. The Mauryan emperor Aśoka reminds us that what he is doing now is new and different from the same activity's connotation in the past. Kings of past times went on hunts and campaigns but he travels and spcaks about the *dhamma*, the social ethic that he is propagating. The past can also be remembered by venerating the relics stated to be of those who lived earlier.

And then there is the clear evocation of the past for calling upon the legitimacy of history and the value of continuity. What is remarkable is the consistency with which the pillars of Aśoka are used for this purpose—by Candra Gupta II inscribing the *praśasti* of Samudra Gupta, by Viśāladeva the Rajput, and even more forcefully by Firuz Shah Tughluq and Jahangir. Evidently, such pillars were the embodiment of a sense of history.

The inscriptions of the Gupta and immediate post-Gupta period mark a departure from earlier statements on the past and anticipate the form that state records were to take in later centuries. Relevant information is given at some length. Care is taken over a reasonably accurate chronology. Mention is made of author and subject. There is awareness of providing a relatively complete record, perhaps because inscriptions were becoming legal documents and the purpose had to be clearly stated. There is a conscious introduction of the past as part of the formula for legitimizing persons and actions of the present. The reuse of inscriptional locations and inscribed objects with references to what happened in earlier times points to the consultation of records. Inscriptions are also aware of communicating information to posterity. By the late first millennium, these developments were to be formalized into a recognizable pattern which allows us to refer to inscriptions as annals.

8

History as Literature

The Plays of Viśākhadatta

1. Drama

A preliminary turn towards treating *itihāsa* as a possible literary form and not just the record of lineages and dynasties was the writing of plays based on historical themes. The past was now to be remembered and recalled by reading the texts that referred to it, and in the process being made relevant to current historical concerns as well. A few of the plays, different from the dramas of Sanskrit literature, are to that extent a distinct turn to the historical, although not history.

The texts of the Gupta period which can be included in the broad category of *itihāsa* constitute in some ways a watershed between what I have called embedded history and externalized or embodied history. The latter takes the form of distinctive genres associated with historical writing. Historical consciousness slowly gives way to the recognition of a historical tradition, initially in the *vaṃśānucarita* section of some *Purāṇas* and in the early inscriptions. These had a distinctly different function from ritual texts inasmuch as they recorded events connected with political and other activities of rulers and/or their patronage, even where the royal gift contributed to the performance of a ritual. The political context superseded the ritual.

Another contribution to historical consciousness came from the Sramanic literature, within which Buddhist and Jaina authors distanced themselves from brahmanical views. They forged an alternative narrative on the events of the past. This sharpened the need to examine the past from a different perspective, or else represent it in a different way. Such representation of the past was not arbitrary and incorporated an ideological function. In terms of the past as part of the Puranic worldview, the challenge from the Sramanic perspective would have further loosened the ties to ritual texts.

At this point the historical tradition was tentatively introduced into literature. Of the many literary forms emerging in the first millennium AD, the dramatic genre deployed themes from the historical tradition, even if infrequently. This is not altogether unexpected, since this form lent itself more easily to projecting actions and persons from the past. A variety of plays categorized as *nāṭakas* came to be written, some of which hinted at historical themes. Among the authors of these, Bhāsa of the early centuries AD stood out. Apart from stories taken from the epics, two of his best-known plays, *Pratijñāyaugandharāyana* and *Svapnavāsavadatta*, hinted at historical themes wrapped in the romantic exploits of Udayana of Vatsa.

A couple of centuries after Bhāsa, the *Mālavikāgnimitra* of Kālidāsa draws on the past. The play touches on the hostility between the Mauryas and the Śuṅgas, although the plot is centrally about the romance of the Śuṅga prince Agnimitra, and Mālavikā. Kālidāsa also drew on believed history in his epic poem *Raghuvaṃśa* (the lineage of Raghu, ancestor of Rāma). This refers to seven generations of the lineage, ending with the descendants of Rāma. The historical content of the poem is not to the fore, but it carries a strong endorsement of brahmanical values, especially in relation to the duties of kingship.

Plays were generally court romances involving kings and princesses, gardens and palaces, gently entangled plots and happy endings. There are exceptions, but not many. The story-line was largely fiction, and the plays occasionally touched on what were perhaps incidents with historical connections. Beyond that, there is little evidence of history. Strands of history become opaque when enveloped by romance.

The audience for these plays would have been the court circles.

Plays were performed at court, and some may also have been performed in homes of the wealthy, where the audience would extend to respected townspeople, the *nāgarakas*, merchants, administrators, and fashionable young men, some of whom met regularly in parks and at the homes of *gaṇikās* (courtesans). The ambience of the audience was essentially urban, and the plays assumed a degree of sophisticated taste in literature and culture.

2. The Plays of Viśākhadatta

In the rich tradition of the writing of plays in Sanskrit at this time, it is strange that there should have been only one dramatist of note who wrote plays that were specifically on historical themes with a strong political orientation. With Viśākhadatta we have two plays that are focused on what, in other accounts, were historical situations. The first, *Devīcandragupta,* has survived only in fragments, passages from it being quoted in a later work, the *Nāṭya-darpana*, which discusses drama. These passages provide a flavour of the original. There are other passing references to an incident in various texts, which dramatizes a court intrigue and an act of bravado that eventually assisted Candra Gupta II of the Gupta dynasty becoming king.[1] The other play, *Mudrārākṣasa*, has survived as a complete text.[2] It has an entirely political focus and is thus exceptional. The two plays differ in that the first emphasizes conflict within the royal family, while the second explores the actions of two ministers, each with his candidate for royal succession. A lost third play, *Abhisārika-vañcitaka/Abhisārika-bandhitaka,* is also mentioned in some commentaries, such as those of Bhoja and Abhinavagupta of the ninth-tenth centuries, but it appears to have been quite unlike the other two in that it was a romance similar to those of the earlier kind.

We know little about Viśākhadatta barring the couple of lines

[1] S. Levi, "Deux nouveaux traits de dramaturgie Indienne", 193–218; R.C. Majumdar and A.S. Altekar (eds), *New History of the Indian People*, vol. VI.

[2] M.R. Kale (ed.), *Mudrārākṣasa of Viśākhadatta*; K.H. Dhruva, *Mudrārākṣasa or The Signet-ring*; G.V. Devasthali, *Introduction to the Study of the Mudrārākṣasa*; C.R. Devadhar and V.M. Bedekar, *Mudrārākṣasa of Viśākhadatta*; V. Raghavan, *The Mudrārākṣasa of Mahādeva*; R.S. Pandit (ed.), *Viśākhadatta's Mudrārākṣasa or The Signet-ring*; M. Coulson (trans.), *Rākṣasa's Ring*.

traditionally mentioned in the opening of a play. His grandfather was a *sāmanta*. The family acquired status in the next generation: his father took the title of *mahārāja*. Their name suggests that their ancestor could have been a *brāhmaṇa* who had been given a grant of land, this being common among *sāmantas.* With this background it is likely that Viśākhadatta had links to the court and the politics of his time. These may have given him a taste for history.

His date remains uncertain, but there is a mention in the colophon of the play to a *pārthivaścandraguptaḥ*: this is likely to have been Candra Gupta II of the Gupta dynasty, although some would identify it with Candragupta Maurya. The Gupta identification is strengthened by his associating a verse on Viṣṇu with Varāha, the boar incarnation, which has Gupta connections, but none with the Mauryas. This would date the author to the fifth century AD. It has even been suggested that there may have been a kin relationship between him and the royal family through marriage.[3] If Viśākhadatta and Kālidāsa were close contemporaries, then the former was overshadowed by the poetry of the latter. Viśākhadatta has also been dated to a later century on the basis of alternative readings of *candragupta.* Some of his plays carry different names—*avantivarman / rantivarman / dantivarman.* These are names that range from possible kings of Kashmir to South India over a long period, and therefore are of little help in dating the author. Since the verse in question is a *praśasti* of the king, it is likely that the name was changed each time that the play was performed before a new patron. If his patron was Avantivarman—the Maukhari king and father of Grahavarman who married Harṣa's sister Rājyaśrī—it would date Viśākhadatta to the seventh century and make him a near-contemporary of Bāṇa, another formidable literary figure.

3. *Devīcandragupta*

The story of the first play, *Devīcandragupta*, seems to be a defence of the actions of Candra Gupta II, who, together with Samudra

[3] R.S. Pandit, *Viśākhadatta's Mudrārākṣasa or The Signet-ring*, Appendix C, 171.

Gupta, was one of the two most prominent kings of the dynasty. So in writing this play Viśākhadatta was either justifying the action of his patron Candra Gupta II, or if he lived later he was praising the actions of Candra Gupta II as an earlier and much renowned king of the Gupta dynasty. More likely, it was the latter. In either case it would seem that the actions had been criticized by some members of the court, and it is more likely that the criticism was in retrospect. Viśākhadatta was dramatizing the action of a past king.

Candra Gupta claims in an inscription that he was "accepted by his father"—*tat-pari-grihīta*—an unusual phrase where it would normally have been *tat-pāda-anudhyāta* (meditating on the feet of his father). It has been argued that this may have been a covert way of stating that the accession was contested, making it a euphemism for usurpation. The discovery of the play identified Rāma Gupta as the elder brother of Candra Gupta II, and the latter may have eventually usurped the throne, omitting Rāma Gupta from his inscriptions. The plot of the play is as follows: Rāma Gupta, the son of Samudra Gupta, is associated with a rather scandalous story. At the termination of a conflict with the Śaka ruler of western India, he surrendered his wife Dhruvadevī to the Śaka. This act enraged his younger brother, the *kumāra* Candra Gupta, who went in disguise to the Śaka king's palace and rescued Dhruvadevī by killing the Śaka ruler.

As regards a possible historical context to the play, it is known that the Śakas ruled in western India and that there was conflict between the Śakas and the Guptas over the control of the region. The hostilities were probably over acquiring ports that gave access to the lucrative trade of the Arabian Sea. Rṇma Gupta could well have been the Gupta heir-apparent appointed to govern the troublesome territory of Mālava, which brought him into conflict with the Śakas. Copper coins were discovered in Mālava, in western India, issued by a certain Rṇma Gupta.[4] The name was not known to the dynastic lists. It is unclear whether the coins were issued by Rāma Gupta as king or as governor of Mālava. It is just possible that Rāma Gupta had not yet been crowned, in which case

[4] S.R. Goyal, *A History of the Imperial Guptas*, 226–7, 252–3.

the events would have taken place prior to the accession of either. That he did become king is suggested by some inscriptions. These are from three Jaina statues mentioning Rāma Gupta as *mahārājādhiraja.*[5]

Primogeniture was upheld in the epics, but in the literature of this period it was either glossed over or else explained away in situations where it had not been observed: in theory, it was the accepted law, but may have been different in practice. Authors of the *carita* literature could suppress what they felt was inconvenient. In the play it is said that he surrendered his wife for the sake of *prakṛtīnām āśvāsa-naya* (pleasing the people).

Other versions of the story occur in later texts, such as the *Harṣacarita* of Bāṇabhaṭṭa, the *Kāvyamīmāṃsā* of Rājaśekhara, the *Śṛṅgāraprakāśa* of Bhoja, Abhinavagupta's commentary on the *Nāṭyaśāstra*, and in some copper-plate inscriptions of the Rāṣṭrakūṭa kings.[6] In the latter, there is a comment on the morality of Candra Gupta, suggesting that this was discussed even into later times. There appears to have been a competition between the brothers for the love of Dhruvadevī; although she preferred Candra Gupta, she was married to Rāma Gupta. A similar story is told about a Bikramaris (thought to be Vikramāditya, a possible title for Candra Gupta II) in a Persian source of later times. Here, Rāma Gupta is said to have abducted Dhruvadevī at her *svayamvara* despite knowing that she loved his brother. Some passing references of a later time state that Candra Gupta killed Rāma Gupta and married Dhruvadevī. It seems to have became a cause célèbre.

Surrendering the queen to the enemy is something of a stereotype. It occurs later, for example as a variant in the medieval story of Padminī, the queen at Chittor, where she and other women are said to have immolated themselves to preclude being dishonoured by the enemy. In the earlier version, there was no question of the

[5] B. Chhabra and G.S. Gai (eds), *Corpus Inscriptionum Indicarum,* vol. III, 231–4; G.S. Gai, "Three Inscriptions of Rāma-Gupta", 247–51.

[6] *Harṣa-carita of Bāṇa,* ed. and trans. E.B. Cowell and F.W. Thomas, 194; Sanjan Plates, *Ep. Ind.*, vol. XVIII, 235, where Candra Gupta is condemned for his actions; H.M. Eliot and J. Dowson, *History of India as Told by her Own Historians*, vol. 1, 110.

queen immolating herself, and it would seem that customs were different. There is little said about what Dhruvadevī thought about all this. Some commentators have hinted that the younger brother marrying the widow of the elder was a form of *niyoga* (levirate), despite his having killed his elder brother. Others condemn it and describe it as an illicit act. In later years Dhruvadevī's royal seal identified her as the wife of *mahārāja-adhirāja-śrī-candragupta* and the mother of Govinda Gupta.[7] Such seals were stamps of status and carried formal administrative rights. To some extent the play portends the *carita* literature (yet to be written) which, as biography, focused on a contemporary king and explained why a younger brother usurped his older brother's throne. It could be said that Candra Gupta was saving the honour of the dynasty; but his action was rather drastic. It is more likely that the play was written during the reign of one of Candra Gupta's successors, when critical comment on him may have required his actions to be justified.

4. *Mudrārākṣasa*

The second play, *Mudrārākṣasa,* has little to do with politics in the Gupta court. It goes back 800 or more years to Mauryan times. Viśākhadatta's recreation of events is more imaginative than historical. The interest of the play lies not in its being used as a source for Mauryan history but as an attempt in the Gupta period to represent an event from earlier times. The intention is perhaps to provide a historical perception of this crucial period of change. The title literally translates as "the seal"—in this case the signet-ring—of Rākṣasa, the name of a minister of the Nanda king, being the dynasty prior to the Mauryas, ruling in the fifth–fourth centuries BC. The action of the play centres on the change of dynasty. In choosing this event, there was a distinct perspective on a past dating back to eight centuries or so. The choice of the name Rākṣasa is ironic since the person so called is far from demonic: in fact quite the reverse. It is Cāṇakya, the other minister and one of the historical characters who features in the play,

[7] *ASI, Annual Report*, 1903–4, 107.

whose machinations are demonic. Possibly the name refers to the root **rakṣ*, "to protect". But what was he protecting? The Nanda dynasty, or his own loyalty to the dynasty? Rākṣasa is not a name familiar from the Nanda administration.

The play attempts to reconstruct the events of a crucial few days when the Nanda dynasty was overthrown and the Maurya established in its place. This occurred in about 324 BC, just after the campaign of Alexander in north-western India. The Mauryan aspirant was Candragupta, who is presented in the play as the protégé of the *brāhmaṇa* Cāṇakya—also known as Kauṭilya and later as Viṣṇugupta—the author of the well-known text on political economy, the *Arthaśāstra.* Modern scholarship argues that the large kingdom of the Nandas gave way to what emerged as the first empire, that of the Mauryas. That Viśākhadatta chose this point in the past seems to show an insight into the mutation of kingdom to empire. The play enlarges the historical moment. There is no reference to this change, but given the interest in Mauryan history, especially in the Sramanic tradition, an awareness of it can be assumed. Viśākhadatta imagines and reconstructs the event, introducing some elements of its possible historical background. That in such dramatization a few anachronisms were also introduced was not a problem since the author was not a modern historian.

Writing a play on a historical event was different from other forms of representing the past. Historical biographies were still to come. In some ways, this play is at a point where believed memory has to incorporate the archive. A text claiming to be historical would have to be accepted as such by readers and audiences, and although there was scope for imagination, the imprint of the past would need to be reasonably authentic. A play generally focuses on a single major event, whereas the other forms we have discussed move through a series of events. The use of textual sources would have widened the range of what was being made visible from the past.

There is some evidence of interest during the Gupta period in forms created during Mauryan times. This may have arisen from a curiosity about antecedent dynasties and their artifacts, originating in approximately the same area in which the beginnings of Gupta power were located. For both the Mauryas and the Guptas, Pāṭaliputra was an important city. The use of the name Candra

Gupta for the first king echoes the Mauryan. Samudra Gupta's *praśasti* on an Aśokan pillar was not accidental; nor was the acknowledgement of Mauryan enterprise in constructing the dam in Saurashtra. The forms of the Aśokan pillars and their capitals were imitated by various Gupta kings. The lion capital from Udayagiri has been viewed as a possible Mauryan original re-cut a little to suit Gupta aesthetics.[8]

Nevertheless, the deliberate choice of a significant event from the past and the elaborate manner in which it is depicted suggests that it was seen as relevant to the present. The relevance doubtless lay in the politics of changing dynasties. A respected and responsible minister from the previous dynasty could be an asset to the newly established one, provided such a person could be inducted voluntarily to serve the new one. His re-employment would contribute to the dynasty's acceptance, its status, and to continuity of sovereign action.

5. Sources

Viśākhadatta used a variety of sources when constructing his play.[9] These included narratives that occur in the Buddhist and Jaina traditions, either of this period or just later. In the case of the latter, it would seem that there may have been a general borrowing from floating oral renderings of the stories. The *Purāṇas* state that the Śiśunāgas ruled over Magadha and founded the city of Kusumpura, which later came to be known as the imperial capital of Pāṭaliputra. They were succeeded by the Nanda dynasty—Mahāpadma and his eight sons. The family was of low caste, regarded as *śūdra,* as were their successors as well—*tataḥ prabhṛti rajāno bhaviṣyāḥ śūdra yonayaḥ* (subsequent kings will be born *śūdras*). The Nandas were uprooted by Kauṭilya, who then made Candragupta the first Mauryan king.[10] The immediate

[8] J. Williams, "A Recent Aśokan Capital and the Gupta Attitude towards the Past", 225–40.

[9] G.V. Devasthali, *Introduction to the Study of the Mudrārākṣasa*. For a discussion on sources that narrate stories about Kauṭilya and Candragupta, see T.R. Trautmann, *Kauṭilya and the Arthaśāstra*, 10–66.

[10] F.E. Pargiter, *The Purana Text of the Dynasties of the Kali Age*, 25ff.

events leading up to this are what Viśākhadatta imagines and dramatizes in the play.

In the succession lists of the *Purāṇas*, dynasties are generally not kin-related. Each is an independent family, often of a different caste: the *brāhmaṇa* Śuṅgas succeed the low-caste Mauryas. In the case of the Mauryas, however, there is an attempt to give Candragupta a kin connection with the last Nanda king, although not of a kind that would enable him to be a legitimate successor, with a hint of his being born of a *dāsī*.[11] Was this to emphasize the *śūdra* caste of these kings and thus contradict the Buddhist sources, which give them *kṣatriya* status?

The play describes Candragupta as *mauryaputra* (a scion of the Mauryas). The controversy over whether or not he was related to the Nanda family, legitimately or illegitimately, continued to later times—judging by commentators on the play, who accept the story of Candra Gupta being born of a Nanda king and Rākṣasa being a prominent minister. Had Viśākhadatta accepted this story, there would have been little conflict over succession.

Viśākhadatta evidently knew the *Arthaśāstra* well. There are a few parallel discussions in the play and the text, such as the one on the six expedients of policy, which are unlikely to be coincidental.[12] The role of a variety of secret agents in working out the actions of the plot is as advised by the *Arthaśāstra*. This text was revised as late as the third century AD and was then attributed to Viṣṇugupta, an alternative name for Cāṇakya referred to in the play. In drawing upon the *Arthaśāstra*, Viśākhadatta was also in a sense endorsing what the text taught. In condoning the immoral politics of Cāṇakya, the author was perhaps defending the text against other views of politics which may have been rooted in a more humanistic social ethic.

Cāṇakya is known to Buddhist authors but less so in the early texts. A reference is made in the *Mahāvaṃsa* to Cāṇakya assisting Candragupta, and this version or an oral one may have been known to Viśākhadatta.[13] The *Mahāvaṃsa* was composed about the fifth century AD. More detailed stories come from the later

[11] *Viṣṇu Purāṇa*, 4.24.17–28.

[12] *Arthaśāstra*, 1.11–12; *Mudrārākṣasa*, 7.1.1.

[13] *Mahāvaṃsa*, 5.16.

commentary on this text, the *Vaṃsatthappakāsinī*. The references to Cāṇakya are not the most complimentary, but it would seem that there was an oral tradition in which these stories were probably repeated and therefore survived. Viśākhadatta's projection of Cāṇakya as the mastermind behind the rise of the first Maurya could be seen as an attempt to diminish the Mauryas. The policies of Aśoka, for instance, much applauded in Buddhist texts, were ignored in the *Purāṇas*.

The *Mahāvaṃsa* narrates its version of the history of the first three Mauryas. The termination of Nanda rule is attributed to a conflict with Candragupta Maurya, where the latter was tutored by Kauṭilya, who had his own reasons for bringing down the Nanda dynasty. The Mauryan is described as a *kṣatriya* belonging to a clan related to the Śākyas. Cāṇakya is represented as a brilliant if shrewd strategist who was insulted by the Nanda king and therefore swore vengeance.[14] He is said to have faked a vast sum of counterfeit money and looted the hidden wealth of the Nandas. With this he acquired an army to overthrow them. He put the young Candragupta of the Moriya clan to various tests, recognized his potential, and made him his protégé for kingship. There is an element of grand adventure in a young man from a fairly unknown clan being trained for kingship by a politically astute *brāhmaṇa*. This doubtless became more common in Viśākhadatta's own time with the frequency of *sāmantas* aspiring to kingship.

Another Buddhist text of the early centuries AD, the *Milindapañha*, refers to a major conflict between the Nandas and the usurper Candragupta Maurya advised by Cāṇakya.[15]

Jaina sources also elaborate on these events but most of them were written subsequent to the play. The Nandas are *śūdras*, Cāṇakya is a Jaina. He has an altercation with the Nanda king, whom he then vows to overthrow, and which he does by adopting Candragupta, finally establishing him as king. In between there are many colourful episodes of their activities.[16]

[14] *Vaṃsatthappakāsinī*, 181.12, 186.26.

[15] T.W. Rhys Davids, *The Questions of King Milinda*, vol. II, 147; *Milindapañho*, IV.8.26 (292).

[16] *Sthaviravali/Pariśiṣṭaparvan of Hemachandra*, 6.231–2, 8.2, 8.194, 8.415ff.

It is unlikely that Viśākhadatta read the Greek and Latin sources, although their contents may have been known to him. These are generally biographies of Alexander written after his time, and therefore references to the Nandas and Mauryas are taken from other accounts. They mention Sandracottos/Candragupta and the Nanda king Xandrames or Agrammes, and give exaggeratedly huge figures for his army.[17] Sandracottos, in some accounts, is said to have met Alexander as a young man and he later overthrew the governors left behind by Alexander. The role of Cāṇakya in establishing Candragupta as king is conspicuously absent in these accounts.

The play filled out the sparse references and created a version of the history of these events. But it was a version that viewed them from the perspective of the Gupta period. The continuing association of the minister, Rākṣasa, with the last deposed Nanda king would have been an idea furthered by the play, as also the depiction of the character of Cāṇakya. The character of Rākṣasa and his dilemma are a creation of Viśākhadatta.

This poses some questions for the historian. We have to ask what was picked up from the sources—in terms of the selection of events and persons in constructing a statement concerning a particular event of the past—and why this was done. Having reconstructed the event in whatever form and associated it with history, how did this reconstruction in turn help formulate later views about the event? In other words, what is the agenda of the *Mudrārākṣasa*? The play attracted commentaries among later litterateurs.

In order to consider these questions, I would like to begin with a brief synopsis of the plot. It is immensely complicated, with moves and counter-moves, and disguised double agents and spies weaving in and out. Plays about conspiracies such as this one thrive on uncertainties keeping the audience in suspense. History requires explaining an event. The play attempts this, albeit indirectly.

[17] J.W. McCrindle, *The Invasion of India by Alexander the Great*, 221ff.; Quintus Curtius Rufus, *History of Alexander the Great*, 9.2; Justin, 15.4.10–21; Plutarch, *Life of Alexander*, vol. LXII, 403; R. Thapar, "The Role of the Army in the Exercise of Power in Early India".

6. The Text

The Prologue, as is usual in Sanskrit plays, has a *sūtradhāra* (stage manager) who announces a new play, *Mudrārākṣasa*, by the poet Viśākhadatta and provides the barest information about him. The intention of the Prologue is to introduce the persons around whom the play revolves. The time period of the play covers just a few action-packed days, although a longer preamble to these activities is assumed.

The opening Act informs us that the last Nanda king has fled and Cāṇakya is preparing the coronation of Candragupta. There remains however the problem that the most prestigious and highly respected minister of the Nanda ruler Rākṣasa continues to be loyal to the Nanda king and is working towards restoring the dynasty. It is imperative therefore that his loyalty be transferred to the young Maurya, to lend legitimacy to the change. This has to be done not by defeating him in battle but through diplomacy: defeat in battle would not permit him to become chief advisor to the young Maurya. It is to this end that Cāṇakya has to work out strategies of intrigue and counter-intrigue; he must trap Rākṣasa into having to support the new king. Yet he is aware of and envies the strength of Rākṣasa's loyalty to the previous dynasty.

We are told that Rākṣasa is supporting another claimant to the succession, a prince associated with the Nandas, Malayaketu, and is therefore opposed to Candragupta. One of Cāṇakya's spies picks up the signet-ring of Rākṣasa almost by accident and takes it to Cāṇakya. Cāṇakya can now send sealed letters in the name of Rākṣasa making all kinds of statements, adding to the confusion already created by the double agents.

A close friend of Rākṣasa, the jeweller Candanadāsa, is arrested on Cāṇakya's orders because he has sheltered Rākṣasa's family and refuses to divulge where they are. Cāṇakya knows that Rākṣasa was also loyal to his friends, and therefore any harm to a friend would lead to Rākṣasa intervening in his defence.

A snake-charmer, in fact a spy, visiting Rākṣasa speaks eloquently about the properties required to handle both snakes and kings. There is a need for administrative skills, knowledge of spheres of influence, the ability to draw on antidotes where errors occur, discrimination in the use of sorcery, and maintaining secrecy. The introduction of a snake-charmer into the plot becomes almost a subtle commentary on the persons and their activities. Cāṇakya is busy getting rid of Rākṣasa's supporters, one by one. The signet-ring is brought back to Rākṣasa and he gives it for safe keeping to a friend, who is actually Cāṇakya's spy. Cāṇakya and Candragupta pretend to have a dispute so as to confuse Rākṣasa, knowing that this will be reported back to him. This fans the rumour of a split between them, but is part of Cāṇakya's plot. Arguing over the qualities of Rākṣasa leads to another spat. Candragupta threatens to take over the government but soon realizes that he cannot do without his preceptor. This part of the play comes close to depicting the raw quality of politics and diplomacy beneath a veneer of politeness.

Rākṣasa consults a Jaina monk to ascertain an appropriate time for a counter-offensive, not knowing that the monk is a spy, and finds the monk's response curiously evasive. Cāṇakya through various moves succeeds in alienating Rākṣasa from Malayaketu, who was Rākṣasa's candidate and a rival to Candragupta. A man is caught with a letter, sealed with Rākṣasa's ring, purporting to be written to Candragupta by Rākṣasa and stating that the allies of Malayaketu are increasingly becoming disloyal to him and their loyalty can be bought. The letter deflects the plans of Rākṣasa.

Rākṣasa hears that his great friend Candanadāsa is going to be executed by Cāṇakya for not disclosing the whereabouts of Rākṣasa's family. So he decides to enter the capital city unseen, and try and save Candanadāsa, which is of course precisely what Cāṇakya wants. The execution of Candanadāsa is being prepared by the executioners, who are two Caṇḍālas—outcastes. Rākṣasa speaks of this with anguish to another person and states that he will save his friend, whose life is valuable to him. He seems to anticipate what the cost will be, because he adds that there remains little he can do to help the Nandas.

In the final Act there is a discourse on politics by the two Caṇḍālas, who are as cynical about politics as was the snake-charmer. It is interesting that the articulation of cynicism comes from those who are regarded as social inferiors. Rākṣasa enters and stays the execution by sending the two executioners to report to Cāṇakya that he is surrendering himself in order to save the life of his friend. Cāṇakya appears and praises Rākṣasa and states he wants him to be minister to Candragupta. He also adds that the two Caṇḍālas are really not Caṇḍālas but his spies. He reveals the intricacies of his espionage to trap Rākṣasa. Candragupta enters and is told to greet Rākṣasa with respect. Rākṣasa is informed that unless he agrees to support the Maurya, his friend Candanadāsa's life will not be spared. Rākṣasa reluctantly agrees, out of friendship and loyalty to his friend. The play ends with a verse in praise of a king, Candragupta.

7. Playing with History

The play takes on something of the imagery of a game of chess between Cāṇakya and Rākṣasa. Chess (*śatrañja*) was by now fairly widely known. Cāṇakya is the smarter player, takes nothing for granted, and anticipates moves well in advance. Rākṣasa is the gentler of the two, more humane and less clever. He is not averse to plotting moves but is a little surprised when he is double-crossed. His main strength is his unflinching loyalty to the Nanda dynasty now being overthrown, and this now becomes a dilemma for him. The pawns are easily knocked off. They are the spies in various guises and roles, switching identities and virtually creating many small plays within the play. The final Act moves towards the kill—the trapping of Rākṣasa—and culminates in Cāṇakya's success not only in trapping Rākṣasa but forcing him into becoming a minister to the Maurya king. Plotting on this scale makes even the army redundant. It would seem that Viśākhadatta understood the mind behind the *Arthaśāstra*. It is this that he transposes into his characterization of Cāṇakya.

Although Rākṣasa prepares for a campaign against Candragupta, Cāṇakya works successfully towards getting Rākṣasa to support the Mauryan prince without a campaign. Cāṇakya's determination to do this indicates that the authority of this minister was crucial to the establishing of the Mauryan polity and its acceptance by the people, at least in the eyes of Viśākhadatta. The emphasis on this continuity despite a change in the ruling family is significant. Yet Rākṣasa is merely one among other ministers and is rarely singled out until late versions of the story.

Winning Rākṣasa over would have been a political achievement since, apart from upholding the legitimacy of Nanda rule, he also had the support of the *prakṛti*—here, the people. This carried stability and legitimacy. The use of the word *prakṛti* for people, rather than the more common *prajā* (children or subjects), indicated something more than just subjects. The word also means nature, or that which is regarded as natural. Rākṣasa being the natural and better choice as minister is being hinted at, and he has the support of the people. There is a political significance, therefore, to Rākṣasa being inducted, by whatever means, to serve the new king, rather than merely being killed. This establishes the historical continuity between the two dynasties as stated in the *Purāṇas*. Perhaps Viśākhadatta was exploring the statement in the *Purāṇas* that Cāṇakya made Candragupta Maurya king and was trying to envisage how this could have been done.

The plot of the play raises many questions: Why did Viśākhadatta choose this particular historical moment? Did this reflect his understanding of the importance of the Mauryan system in the past? Or did it resonate with the politics of Gupta and immediately post-Gupta times, such as the possible tension between kings and ministers? Was he presenting a contrast via his representation of the two ministers? Cāṇakya was being projected as a counter to the former. Was the author's intention somewhat limited when it came to explaining how Rākṣasa came to be minister to Candragupta? Was his larger intention to project the dilemma of Rākṣasa, a dilemma that would have faced ministers whenever there was a change of dynasty? Was he suggesting that there were other ways than war to attain success—a perspective apposite within a world where conquest was the pre-eminent value, as set out in the *praśasti* of Samudra Gupta? Events of consequence had to be explained.

The transition to imperial governance by the Mauryas would have been another theme. Given the conspiracy and counter-conspiracy in the play, it was not thought of as an ordinary situation and required an intricacy of plots. Nevertheless, there is no anticipation of a forthcoming grand design in the political economy under the Mauryas, nor of a new civilizational culture. Candragupta is a pliant young man, a trifle childishly ambitious but anxious to please his preceptor. In the scene where there is pretence at altercation, there is a hint of the making of an independent king. It would be hard to believe from this characterization that—according to the Greek sources—Candragupta had already met, and in some versions opposed, Alexander; nor that he was to overthrow the Greek governors appointed by Alexander to rule the provinces in the borderlands, and to spend his reign in extensive conquests and the consolidation of these.

The focus is on the rather different character and activities of the two ministers. Loyalty, intelligence, and courage are the prime requirements of ministers. Rākṣasa is uncomplimentary about Cāṇakya since he refers to him as *baṭu/baṭuka,* terms sometimes used contemptuously for dubious *brāhmaṇas.* This is an apt description, in many ways, but it does lower his esteem as the minister counselling and guiding a young prince. The author seems to subscribe to the view that the name Kauṭilya came from the epithet *kuṭila,* meaning "crooked". Cāṇakya is single-minded in his objective of overthrowing the last Nanda. He is fulfilling his vow to dethrone the Nandas. He expresses both envy and appreciation for Rākṣasa's ability to be loyal. Rākṣasa, he says, is the lone wild elephant roaming the forest who has to be trapped and made to serve the new king.[18]

In some ways the play is about the centrality of loyalty even within political diplomacy. Was loyalty so strongly underlined because it was being devalued in contemporary courts with the increase in competition for power? Was the writing of the other play, *Devīcandragupta*, an act of loyalty on the part of Viśākhadatta towards Candra Gupta II? Yet it has been argued that loyalty was in fact at a premium at the time.[19] Rākṣasa had to sacrifice his loyalty to the Nandas in order to save the life of his friend. Possibly this requirement of loyalty was because of the turnover of *sāmantas* and the evaluating of patronage in terms of who was providing the greatest benefit. In using the term *bhakti*, a distinction has to be made between the devotion to a deity, which might be absolute, and that to an overlord, which might be more considered. Loyalty was not to be equated with servitude.

[18] Act 1, v. 27 ('v.' indicates verse).

[19] Daud Ali, *Courtly Culture and Political Life in Early Medieval India*, 104–7.

The importance of Rākṣasa is further indicated by the title of the play. The signet-ring was popularized in India by the Indo-Greeks at the turn of the Christian era and is referred to as a central object in more than one narrative, the more obvious ones being the Vālmīki *Rāmāyaṇa* and Kālidāsa's version of the Śakuntalā story. The symbolism of such a ring was that in capturing the identity of the person, the person himself was captured. Cāṇakya's sealing of the letter with Rākṣasa's signet-ring, once it is in his hands, is a turning point in the play. It signals Rākṣasa's loss of identity and presages the eventual capturing of this identity by Cāṇakya.

Cāṇakya has no illusions about being in effect a king-maker. This role, and that of preceptor to the king, often overlap. There is a play on the relations between kings and ministers. Historical drama also highlights the parallel representation of person and office in the same character. That there was a tension is apparent when Cāṇakya does not allow Candragupta to make a lavish donation to the bards, and the young prince says he feels a prisoner rather than a king—*bandhaniv rājyam na rājyamiva.*[20] Rākṣasa guesses rightly that the rift is more pretence than real, for ordinarily Cāṇakya would have stormed out if thwarted. But the play does suggest that such tensions were not unusual between kings and ministers.

The legitimacy given to the king through the support of a minister respected by kings and their subjects seems to have outweighed the legitimacy from rituals and genealogies, or the conquests of the king. Interestingly, none of these are mentioned in the play as the normal techniques of establishing legitimacy. Cāṇakya in the play consistently refers to Candragupta as *vṛṣala*, which is used both for *śūdra* or low-caste status and for heretics. Rākṣasa is equally scathing in referring to Candragupta as *kulahīna* (baseborn).[21] This contempt was the privilege of an upper-caste man when dealing with one of low caste. Ironically, the caste of the Nandas was no higher, yet Rākṣasa speaks of them as a family deserving respect.[22]

[20] Act 3, after v. 23.
[21] Act 2, v.7; Act 6, v. 6.
[22] Act 6, v. 6; Act 4, v. 11.

Kṣatriya status was obviously not required in these earlier times, even for a low-caste adventurer rising to power. In a sense, this is all the more impressive since his preceptor was a *brāhmaṇa*. It would seem that once a king was installed his caste was virtually irrelevant—judging by the complimentary epithets received by kings from their supporters. This could have been intended to point up a contrast to the current fashion, from Gupta times onwards, for dynasties to acquire upper-caste status when establishing a kingdom, whereas the historical reality was that few dynasties claimed *kṣatriya* status until post-Gupta times. Or else it was intended as an emphatic contradiction of the Buddhist sources, where the Mauryas were said to be *kṣatriyas*.

The observance of caste rules is uncertain, and perhaps they changed from the Mauryan to Gupta period. Both Rākṣasa and Cāṇakya were, as *brāhmaṇas*, technically serving *śūdra* kings, contravening the normative code. So too is the commitment and close friendship of Rākṣasa for Candanadāsa, a *vaiśya*. Candragupta, despite being called *kulahīna* (low born), speaks Sanskrit because he is slotted to be the king. Other low-born people in the play speak Prākrit, as the literary rules require. The language used carries implicit statements beyond just the use of a particular language, often formulaic.

Religious sectarianism of the Gupta period views Jaina monks as ill omens, and there are no Buddhists on the scene. This is a condition close to the Gupta period, not to the Mauryan. Both these heterodoxies were flourishing in the early period, but less so in post-Gupta times. The play has little recourse to religion, as at every move politics is the end game.

The two executioners remain Caṇḍālas, as from earlier times. Rākṣasa, in the last Act, despite all his tribulations, warns Cāṇakya not to touch him as he has been in contact with the Caṇḍālas, at which point Cāṇakya explains that they are not really Caṇḍālas. The concern of one *brāhmaṇa* for the ritual purity of the other is striking, given that they were, in a sense, enemies. Yet, interestingly, neither of the protagonists conforms to the conventional image of the *brāhmaṇa* as defined in the *Dharmaśāstras.* Their distance from the other castes is negligible, barring the Caṇḍālas.

The allies of Malayaketu, described as the *mleccha rājās*, are a bit puzzling. They are from the borders of the realm—Kulu, the hill country; Kāśmīra; the Indus land; and the north-west. In the period with which the play is concerned, these could have been borderlands prior to their conquest by the Mauryas. Some of these *rājās* want territory in return for their support to Malayaketu, others want horses and elephants.

Was the play a putting down of the Mauryas, the only dynasty of consequence from the Ganges heartland prior to the Guptas? The Mauryas did not conform to brahmanical norms and were patrons of the Jainas, Buddhists, and Ājīvikas. Aśoka had made a sustained attempt to introduce a social ethic divorced from divine sanction and dependent on human behaviour, which he expounded as *dhamma* in his edicts. He was eulogized in Buddhist sources. Given the high visibility of Buddhism in the post-Mauryan period, this would have been viewed as a threat to *brāhmaṇa* orthodoxy, with its ethic based on the primacy of *varṇāśrama-dharma* and caste obligations. Rākṣasa describes the Nandas as a family of status; the Mauryas are the reverse, although Cāṇakya does not agree.[23]

Or, alternatively, was this particular historical event being viewed as something that was in earlier times rare—a *brāhmaṇa* bringing a family of obscure origin to power—but was familiar now. Although the play does not present Candragupta as a Jaina, there is nothing to suggest that he was committed to orthodoxy of the brahmanical mould. Viśākhadatta's explanation of the event did not follow conventional lines. The intention was not to recite facts but to try and understand a situation by re-enacting the event—with the caveat that the re-enactment need not be "as it really was". This does not represent history, but it introduces the ethics which the event provokes. So it can be seen as part of historical explanation.

From the brahmanical perspective it was important to emphasize the power of Cāṇakya as king-maker. This would decrease the status of the Mauryan kings, all of whom were patrons of heterodoxy. It could also be suggested that Viśākhadatta represents Cāṇakya as using underhand means for installing Candragupta,

[23] Act 6.6, 4.11, 2.7, 3.18.

and therefore suggesting that the Mauryas should not be treated as role-models for the Guptas. Or is he justifying the means for a purposive end? Or does the play intend to highlight the role of *brāhmaṇa* ministers in a polity such as that of the post-Gupta period, when there was a competition for power between kings and ministers or intermediaries—the latter often being *brāhmaṇas*—and when the advantage was with the kings? Cāṇakya's methods were well known from the implicit intentions of statecraft, as set out in the *Arthaśāstra,* apart from the stories about him. Rākṣasa was the counterfoil.

Malayaketu is scathing about the duplicity of ministers.[24] Rākṣasa concedes that Cāṇakya is the great tactician when he says *ekamapi nītibījam bahu phalatāmeti yasya tava* (the single seed of polity producing multiple fruit).[25] The play is a contest between two ministers:the respective princes whom they support are marginal. Candragupta was informed by Cāṇakya that Rākṣasa was to be his *amātya-mukhyam* (chief minister). Candragupta was in conformity with this decision inasmuch as he respected Rākṣasa, but even such a major decision was in Cāṇakya's domain. The political function of the protagonists has its own criteria of evaluation and is extraneous to the normative texts. Did the author see the transition from Nandas to Mauryas as a continuity of the rule of lower-caste dynasties? Or was there a notion that, despite the kings, effective control continued to be in the hands of *brāhmaṇa* ministers? In effect, politics is being presented as outside ritual and normative requirements.

Cāṇakya, in conversation with Candragupta, refers to the three forms of government discussed by specialists in political economy: a dependence on the king, or a dependence on the minister, or the interdependence of both.[26] Here the dependence seems to be on the minister, although there is a suggestion of the prince moving towards greater independence. Rākṣasa rather dismisses him as being too dependent on Cāṇakya. Apart from *vṛṣala*, which carries more than a hint of contempt, Cāṇakya also refers to Candragupta

[24] Act 4, v. 8.
[25] Act 2, v. 19.
[26] Act 3, after v. 19.

as his *śiṣya* (pupil). On one occasion, when the young man touches his feet, he raises him up and calls him *vatsa,* an affectionate term for a child. Others address the young prince respectfully as *ārya-deva* (noble lord), or *deva* (lord). When all is in order at the end of the play, Cāṇakya calls Candragupta, *rājan* (king). Admittedly, the depiction of Candragupta in the play is prior to Candragupta becoming king, when he is still under the tutelage of Cāṇakya; but it is a far cry from the familiar projection of Indian kings as absolute monarchs and despots.

As a commentary on politics, the play borrowed much from the *Arthaśāstra*, and this is reflected in the snake-charmer's discourse: those who understand the function of administration and diplomacy can handle both snakes and kings. If, as a royal servant, one is given authority, it is like holding a snake but without knowing the right spells with which to control it; therefore holding it presages death. But in the play the royals are the innocents and the ministers are the snakes. Sovereignty—Śrī—is fickle and goes from one to another like a harlot.[27] A commentary on court hierarchy, moving from the king via the ministers to fawning favourites competing for small handouts, is said to be a dog's life. The court chamberlain speaks of some who flatter the king until they tire out, and others who are free of this and treat the king like straw.[28] He then himself proceeds to flatter the king as only chamberlains can. Given the ways of Cāṇakya, there is some irony in the statement made by a spectator to the effect that in the realm of Candragupta there is no tyranny, indicating also an awareness of the possibility of political tyranny.

The *Mudrārākṣasa* reflects historical consciousness and is aware of the historical tradition. Viśākhadatta is basically projecting history in a form different from the forms used earlier to project the past; and the form he chooses is not what we today would call historical writing. His is an attempt to capture an *itihāsa* reconstructed from various traditions. The effort is not free of historical anachronisms. There are references to items, objects, and concepts that betray a period well after the Mauryas. The

[27] Act 2, v. 6–7.
[28] Act 3, vv. 14–16.

signet-ring and the term for an underground tunnel—*suraṅga*—generally thought to have been derived from the Greek, *syrinx*, are probably from Indo-Greek times just prior to the Christian era. The references to the *kāyasthas* as a caste of scribes, as also to the Kali age, would again be post-Mauryan. This would also apply to the list of kings outside the realm of the Nandas, a list more likely in later times, when such persons are mentioned. In suggesting likely allies, the author seems to be confusing the past with the present. Nevertheless, Viśākhadatta is aware that he is writing on an event that has happened in the distant past and is providing an explanation for it.

8. Commenting on the Play

An assessment of the play as providing historical consciousness can also consider how the play and the event it tries to capture are treated in texts later than the play, even if such texts are often concerned mainly with literary theory. References to the play, commentaries on the characters of the play, and versions of the stories increase from the tenth century AD. They often incorporate a retelling of the story, but with variants that make it more fictional than the play. There is a sense in which this later period is looking back on the earlier one, even if the more important discussions relate to its observance of the rules of dramaturgy (and some make a passing reference to the historical event that it dramatizes).

The Jaina interest in the story was in part because of the claim that Candragupta became a Jaina in later years, although this idea is discussed in a late Jaina text—Hemacandra's *Pariśiṣṭaparvan*.[29] The focus is on the threat of the frontier kings to the Nanda kingdom, perhaps reflecting current politics. A twelfth-century Jaina version conflates narratives from Buddhist sources but retells the story more in keeping with contemporary views of what might have happened. Inevitably, in one version Cāṇakya becomes a Jaina monk, which is an ironical twist to the story.

The retellings in the eleventh century Somadeva's *Kathāsaritsāgara* and Kṣemendra's *Bṛhatkathāmañjari* are so changed as to be

[29] VIII.415ff.

barely recognizable. From the fourteenth century, commentators again retold the story, but in variant form. A major commentary is included in the writings of Dhundirāja at the court of Serfoji in Tanjore in the eighteenth century. He reversed the story in some ways, although the protagonists remained the same. Candragupta is insulted by the Nanda king so the young man swears revenge and teams up with Cāṇakya to overthrow the Nandas. Here the initiative is with Candragupta.[30] Dhundirāja's evaluation was that the play belonged to the category known as *prakhyāta*—which meant that it was derived from *itihāsa*. But unfortunately he does not elaborate on this. The events were by now familiar, hence the interest both in the stories and the play. Drama makes history more visible and the question of historicity surfaces, although perhaps not so frontally in those pre-modern times.

In later times, then, the play was recognized for its literary merit, but because reference was also made to various versions of the narrative, it came to be seen as a representation of the past. Was there an attempt to consciously look at the past given that, by now, literary genres and inscriptions were incorporating references to the past?

How historical then is the *Mudrārākṣasa*? Does it embody a kind of collective memory, or is it a narrative reconstructed from various traditions with an underlying sense of history? It can perhaps be said that within the framework of the tradition, the *Mudrārākṣasa* kept alive an interest in the Nanda-Maurya transition, a significant historical event. Both plays by Viśākhadatta evoke a perspective of the past which draws attention to the historical, rather than being entirely fictional, even though the form is a part of creative literature. To that extent, Viśākhadatta seems to represent the Gupta interest in what went before. What is equally significant is that the literati of the time were reading

[30] G.V. Devasthali, *Introduction to the Study of the Mudrārākṣasa*, 161; V. Raghavan, *The Mudrārākṣasa of Mahādeva*, 2. These issues are raised in the *Daśarūpāvaloka* of Dhanika, the *Śṛṅgāraprakāśa* of Bhoja, and in Abhinavagupta's commentary on the *Nāṭya-śāstra*. Other texts, such as the *Nītisāra*, mention that Kauṭilya terminated the rule of the Nandas, as does the *Bṛhatkathāmañjari* of Kṣemendra.

texts of the Buddhist and Jaina historical tradition, whose narratives were different from the brahmanical. Whether or not these were incorporated in the literature that emerged, their presence was recognized: and they might even have been viewed as an alternative tradition.

PART IV

Alternative Histories

9

The Buddhist Tradition

Monks as Historians

1. Buddhist Historical Traditions: The Background

The Buddhist and Jaina constructions of the past are strikingly different from the Puranic, and they are different in many ways—in their genres, in the initial languages used, and, more importantly, in the intentions of the authors. There is a concern for a reasonably acceptable chronology and a well-defined ideological purpose in the historical account. These historical traditions are an alternative to the Puranic. Jaina narratives too of the first millennium AD reflect a different presentation of events and persons from that of the Puranic, even when the genre is similar. An example of this difference, within an earlier text, is, as we have seen, the Jaina version of the *rāma-kathā*.[1] To demonstrate the contrast with the Puranic, the focus now will be on Buddhist attempts to write histories.

A multiplicity of reasons account for the difference: the Buddha was a historical person whose life was seen by Buddhists not only as ethically exemplary but also as a turning point in history. His teachings were at first scattered and derived from what his disciples remembered, but with the impressive growth of a following

[1] As discussed in Chapter 5.

the teachings had to be organized into canonical texts. Those maximally committed to the teaching became monks and were instituted into an order—the Saṅgha. This innovation, the coming into being of such orders among various renunciatory sects, had not existed earlier to the same degree. Events that led to the structuring of the Saṅgha had to be recorded. This was done through periodic meetings of monks who debated the teaching and its interpretation. This led to sectarian splits with each dissenting group recording its own version of this history. The histories therefore were similar up to a point, but registered divergence.

Dating to the mid first millennium BC, Buddhism and Jainism differed from Vedic Brahmanism. They emerged at a time when polities in northern India consisted of *gaṇa-saṅghas* (oligarchies/chiefships), and *rājyas* (kingdoms), their essential differences occasionally leading to confrontations. The oral tradition underlying these groups coexisted. Fragmentary narratives about characters from the epics occur in Buddhist and Jaina texts, but their activities are dissimilar.

Buddhist texts from the late first millennium BC to the early centuries AD frequently refer to kings ruling in Magadha and Kosala in the middle Ganges plain, and to the *gaṇa-saṅghas* of the region, associating them with the Buddha. Two kings, Bimbisāra and his son Ajātaśatru/Ajātasattu ruling in Magadha, and Prasenajit/Pasenadi in Kosala, are said to be contemporaries of the Buddha, with their capitals at Rājagṛha/Rājagaha and Śrāvasti. The contemporary Vṛjji/Vajji confederacy of eight clans had its centre at Vaiśāli and among them was the Jñātrika clan, to which Mahāvīra belonged. Ajātaśatru campaigned at length against the Vṛjjis and finally won by sowing dissension among the clans. This confrontation was clearly important and was described in the Canon.[2]

The chiefships gradually succumbed to the kingdoms that were emerging as the new and effective form of government. The Śiśunāgas were succeeded by the Nandas, who ruled over a major part of the plain. The last Nanda king gave way to the Mauryas, *c.* 321 to 180 BC, who consolidated most of the subcontinent

[2] Mahāparinibbāna-sutta, *Dīgha-nikāya*, II.72.

into their empire. Starting with Candragupta, the next king was Bindusāra, and then came Aśoka, after whom the succession is not listed uniformly. From the Buddhist perspective the great patron and monarch was Aśoka.

The Buddha came from a clan-based chiefdom and approved of this form of polity, and his teaching was primarily but not exclusively in an urban context. Broad discussions of a philosophical nature are said to have been held in parks on the edge of towns—the *kutūhala-sālās*, literally, "places for raising curiosity".[3] Many of the new ideas that challenged Vedic orthodoxy were part of the urban experience, discussed at the courts of *rājās*, as the *Upaniṣads* inform us. The recitation of Vedic texts in towns was discouraged, perhaps because there was the danger of their being reviled.[4] Given the large number of heterodox sects, the competition was intense and ideologies had to be distinctive. Rival sects even among *śramaṇas* are mentioned in the Buddhist Canon and in the inscriptions of Aśoka.[5] This doubtless required that the teaching, especially of peripatetic teachers, be recorded.

Śramaṇas, distanced from orthodoxy, are referred to as existing even in earlier times as individual thinkers. They denied the sanctity of Vedic rituals and of deities in general. Their preference was for the teachings of human authors. What they did have in common was the belief in *karma* (actions) associated with *samsāra* (rebirth), although even in this the Buddhists questioned the existence of an eternal soul (*ātman*). For some the only reality was the material world. The term *śramaṇa* derived from **śram*, "to labour", points to the requirement for attaining liberation from rebirth—*mokṣa* or *nirvāṇa*.

Groups of *śramaṇas* as monks could organize themselves under a teacher and constitute an assembly, a Saṅgha. They regarded themselves as outside the social code, maintaining their own laws and regulations, with prescribed punishments for indiscipline. It was a community within the larger society but somewhat

[3] *Dīgha-nikāya,* 1.78–9, 3.36.

[4] *Āpastamba Dharmasūtra*, 1.11.32.21, 1.3.9.4; *Gautama Dharmasūtra*, 2.7.45, 16.45.

[5] *Dīgha-nikāya*, 2.151; *Sutta-nipāta*, 5.381; Schism Edict of Aśoka, in Bloch, *Les Inscriptions d'Aśoka*, 152ff.

apart. Converting sectarian identities into an institution could lead to dissidence, which in turn encouraged hostility. That the individual renunciate remained conspicuous is evident even from the *Indica* of Megasthenes, a work purporting to describe Mauryan India.[6]

Monkhood grew out of the acceptance of asceticism and renunciation, as a solution to the ills of life, which required opting out of the mundane way of life and becoming a renunciate. Asceticism and renunciation are not identical. The former required isolation in order to contemplate the world and the self. The latter permitted the creating of a community of the like-minded who lived together in monasteries and convents, pursuing their reflections on life without totally discounting all else. Living at the edge of settlements, such groups became a part of society but remained distinctive.

Monks were dependent on alms for food and donations for the monastery, hence the location of monasteries on the peripheries of towns, on trade routes, and in fertile agricultural areas. Monks, not being ascetics, made some minimal demands on society and in return assisted the lay follower to acquire the merit so necessary to enlightenment.

When monasteries became institutions, their records had to be kept. This meant statements on the veracity and validity of the original teacher, together with some biographical information as proof. How and why the Saṅgha was formed and its relationship with society provided a history to the foundation of the sect. The relation with society was significant in the light of two innovations. One was the permission given to women to join the Saṅgha through the establishment of convents, whereas previously, although not unknown, it had been rare for women to leave home and become renunciants.[7] The second was the accepting of gifts from lay followers—especially when the gifts helped in building places of worship. The donation, whether in kind or coin, had to

[6] Megasthenes, Frag. XLI, and Strabo, XV.1.58–60, in J.W. McCrindle (trans.), *Arrian's Indica: Ancient India as Described by Megasthenes and Arrian.*

[7] E.g., the *paribbājakas*, mentioned in *Majjhima-nikāya*, 1.305; *Saṃyutta-nikāya*, 3.238ff.; Megasthenes, Frag. XLI.60.

be recorded as an act of merit. Buddhist and Jaina votive inscriptions are among the earliest. Gradually, the merit could even be transferred to those whom the donor wished to benefit.

This therefore is a different story from the lists of lineages, heroes, and royal pedigrees of the *Purāṇas*. The Buddhist record, although not invariably reliable, did have the semblance of a more historical form than, for example, the narratives of the epics. Records of donations from royal families and the heads of clans added to the authority of the Saṅgha.

The Buddhist construction of the past has elements of the *itihāsa-purāṇa* tradition in its earliest narratives, but subsequently there is a marked change in the record of the history of Buddhism and of its institutions. The nature of royal power, the kind of social ethic propagated, and the perceived relationship between Buddhist ideology and political and social authority meant that the persons and events highlighted were not the same as those in the *Purāṇas*. Buddhist versions of segments of the Indian past have been recorded in various categories of texts, such as in the Buddhist Canon in Pāli, in the later Chronicles of Sri Lanka together with their later commentaries, and in biographies of the Buddha which were more frequent in the Mahāyāna tradition of north-western India. Chronicles from Tibet and Ladakh dating to the second millennium AD, though including some narratives on the Indian past, focus on the history of Buddhism in the specific area. An attempt will be made here to discuss some representative texts that constituted a Buddhist historical tradition.

Although perceptions of the past derive from Buddhist religious concerns, the relation with political authority and reflections on society become the more imminent connections. There is therefore an interface with history, both as a record to be cited as well as a source of legitimation. The claim to factual material is introduced to strengthen sectarian authority, characteristic of many monastic chronicles. A historical perspective is suggested in various ways—in narrating the activities of the Buddha, believed to be factual; in explaining how the Saṅgha came about; in listing the various sects that emerged from the original organization; and narrating the relationship of the Saṅgha with the ruler. The question of whether they can be called histories has been debated and a number of questions have been asked pertaining to the early compositions and how the contradictions between sects encouraged writing history from a sectarian perspective.[8]

2. The Texts of the Canon

The systematizing of knowledge in a literary form was a preliminary step to organizing an assembly of followers. The better-endowed monasteries became centres of learning, apart from propagating sectarian religion. Written texts facilitated a discipline of learning. With this, both hermeneutics and exegesis became a major part of scholarship and of the Canonical record. The texts also provided some institutional continuity. The record of endowments, concessions, and privileges would have required an interaction with patrons, who were functionaries of the state, private householders together with their kinsfolk, and monks and nuns. As a property holder the Saṅgha had to train monks in administrative functions, and doubtless this required a sympathetic relationship with the local bureaucracy.

A number and variety of texts go into the making of the Buddhist Canon, which becomes the base for the emergence of a historical tradition, aspects of which are discussed here with reference to the texts listed below.

The teachings of the Buddha, originally probably recalled as an oral tradition, were gradually organized into a format composed in Pāli and referred to as the Pāli Buddhist Canon. The Buddha used the commonly understood Ardha-Māgadhi, closely related to Pāli and the Prākrits, in preference to Sanskrit. Texts composed in Prākrit and later in Sanskrit relate to other sects. Subsequent to the death of the Buddha there was a fear of losing his teaching and of indiscipline in the Saṅgha. The teaching had to be recorded, as also the regulations that governed the functioning of the monasteries. This activity was controlled by the Elders—the Theras. The sect that initially claimed eminence was the Theravāda, which maintained that the Pāli Canon encapsulated the original teaching of the Buddha, a statement inevitably contested by dissident sects.

[8] C.W. Huntington, Jr., "History, Traditions and Truth," 187–227; J.W. de Jong, *A Brief History of Buddhist Studies in Europe and America*.

The Pāli Canon was assembled from about the mid-first millennium BC and took a written form somewhat later. It consists primarily of the three *Piṭakas* (baskets), but includes other related texts. The three are:

1. The *Vinaya Piṭaka*, the text setting out the discipline and rules to be observed in the monasteries. The Mahāvagga section mentions rules which the Buddha expected monks to follow, often backed by reference to the occasion when the rule was formulated. This provided something of a historical context. The Cullavagga section has scattered references to events.
2. The *Sutta Piṭaka* is in some ways the more important, with five *nikāyas* (collections) which develop on the essential teaching of the Buddha and are crucial to the Canon. These are the *Dīgha-nikāya, Majjhima-nikāya, Saṃyutta-nikāya, Aṅguttara-nikāya,* and *Khuddaka-nikāya.* The last of these includes the *Dhammapada* and the *Sutta-nipāta*.

   Touching on the supposed previous lives of the Buddha are the *Jātakas*, which are refurbished popular stories, and the *Buddhavaṃsa*. The *Jātakas* indirectly reflect aspects of the teaching and also on occasion concede a degree of dissidence in the Saṅgha.

   The *Buddhavaṃsa* is an attempt to create a legend of the Buddha and of Buddhahood, as it were, apart from the lineage of Gautama. He is not an isolated teacher but is twenty-fifth in a succession of Buddhas, reminiscent of the succession of teachers listed in the *Vedas*. His coming is a historical event. The time of the earlier Buddhas goes back to many *kappas/kalpas* (eons), but their descent is linear and sequential. The focus being on succession, it has links with later texts that carry the label of *vaṃsas*.
3. The *Abhidhamma Piṭaka* elaborates on and organizes the teaching. It includes the *Kathāvatthu*, which has references to some historical persons.

The format follows a system of a ready reference for the questions that arose about the teaching. Determining the original Canon remains problematic, as also ascertaining the changes introduced and their chronology. Segments within a larger text could belong to an earlier period and therefore a single date for the whole becomes uncertain. Information on polities, territories, and societies, scattered in these texts, has been used to comment on the history of these times.

In terms of a historical tradition, some distinction can be made between the Canon and the later commentaries, notably the *Samanta-pāsādikā* by Buddhaghosa on the *Vinaya*, or the *Sumaṅgalavilāsinī,* attributed to the same author, on the *Dīgha Nikāya*. Commentaries are largely in the nature of clarifications, rectifications, and some editing of the text, all looking back at past events. Commentaries become necessary when the accepted interpretation of the original is questioned by dissidents within the Sramanic tradition, or when the historical context has changed over a few centureis, or when new explanations more in keeping with current times are sought. The contestations could have been between Buddhist and brahmanical views, as is evident in the *Purāṇa*s. Some of the commentaries are authored by *brāhmaṇas* converted to Buddhism. The link between the text and the commentary is of a historical nature, even if it is not actually history. Commentaries on the Pāli Canon and related texts follow sooner than those on texts of the Puranic tradition. The commentaries were frequently in Siṅhala/Sihala, the language of an early preservation of parts of the Canon. These were systematically collected and translated into Pāli by about the mid-first millennium AD. These commentaries were not merely glosses. Their explanations and elaborations in looking back at past events went into the making of the historical tradition. The Canonical writing will be discussed in this chapter, the post-Canonical in subsequent chapters.

The post-Canonical texts of the Theravāda sect are, for our purposes, primarily the Chronicles of the Mahāvihāra monastery in Sri Lanka. These are the *Dīpavaṃsa* and the *Mahāvaṃsa*, both dating to the mid-first millennium AD, and therefore later than the Canonical texts. The commentary on the latter, the *Vaṃsatthappakāsinī*, was written later. The *Cūlavaṃsa* continues the narrative of the *Mahāvaṃsa* and covers a broad span of the subsequent history of Sri Lanka, also focussing on monastic history. These texts are sometimes jointly referred to as the Ceylon Chronicles.

The post-Canonical texts of the Northern Buddhist tradition, and as such distinct from the Theravāda, include biographies of the Buddha, initially written in the early first millennium AD. They were therefore parallel in time to the narratives that went into the making of the Ceylon Chronicles, but they were rooted in regions distant from each other and used Gāndhārī Prākrit and Sanskrit rather than Pāli. The subject of the biographies was the Buddha; nevertheless, some biographical vignettes included the patrons of the Saṅgha. The *Buddhacarita* of Aśvaghoṣa virtually initiated the biographical form as an aspect of the past; also taken up in the *Mahāvastu* and the *Lalitavistara*; and the *Divyāvadāna*, where a few chapters, such as the *Aśokāvadāna,* narrate the glorious deeds (as the term *avadāna* implies) of Aśoka.

The biography became a convenient form to use for teaching from the early centuries AD, when Buddhist missions travelled to distant places. However, the biographies are not conspicuous in the Sri Lankan Buddhist literature, and chronicles are relatively absent in the early literature of the north-west.

The Buddhist Canon was an attempt at systematizing the teaching. In the course of doing so, much is stated about the history of the Saṅgha, the Elders, prominent lay followers, discourses of the Buddha with kings and monks, some chronology of events, and snippets of the Buddha biography.

3. The Dates of the Texts

Assessing these texts as reflecting a sense of history is problematic since many are chronologically layered works, composed over a span of time. Some sections are thought to be earlier compositions, such as the *gāthās* and parts of the *Nikāyas*. Anthologies are by definition the compositions of varied times, sometimes added to, or even edited, over a longer period, although they may claim to be chronologically specific. They are consequently later texts looking back at earlier times. Themes claimed as historical are of interest. The assessment is inevitably based not on the claims as much as on what the texts convey of the histories of the earlier and later societies, and whether there is a consciousness of change, and if so whether there is an explanation for the change.

The chronological range therefore extends from the oral tradition of the Buddha's time, or just later, to the mid-first millennium AD when commentaries begin to be written. The Buddhist tradition seems to switch more consciously to a literate form, as compared to the Puranic, which continues to show traces of the oral. Nevertheless, initially, on the death of the Buddha, his teachings were remembered, and only subsequently, from perhaps the second century BC, did they start to be written.

The current controversy about the date of the Buddha affects the dating of the texts.[9] The Buddhist texts tend to use three dates for the *mahāparinirvāṇa*: 544, 486/483 BC. The first of these has limited use and is generally seen as an error of the eleventh century AD in the Pāli texts, when an attempt was made to introduce a sixty-year cycle to adjust the calendar. Apart from this, either of the remaining two dates was regarded as established. 486 BC is based on the Dotted Record of Canton, where a dot was marked on a manuscript kept at Canton on each anniversary of the Buddha's death. A long chronology and a short chronology have been suggested, dating to 486 and 368 BC, thus introducing another date.[10] Recently, scholars have argued for various other dates, some as late as the fourth century BC.[11] Earlier, East Asian scholars had also suggested alternative dates, either earlier or later than the standard one.[12] The date of Aśoka is firmly established by his reference to the five *yona rājās* (Greek kings) in his Major Rock Edict XIII. These were his contemporaries and their dates are well established.[13] The date of Aśoka's edict is the mid-third century BC, *c.* 256. This suggests the possibility of the Buddha's death dating to 486 BC.[14]

The firm association of the Buddha with the pre-Nanda kings, and the absence of mention of the Nandas in the Pāli Canon,

[9] P.H.L. Eggermont, *The Chronology of the Reign of Aśoka Moriya*, 132–43.

[10] E. Lamotte, *History of Indian Buddhism*, 13–14.

[11] H. Bechert (ed.), *The Dating of the Historical Buddha*, vols I–II; L.S. Cousins, "The Dating of the Historical Buddha: A Review Article", 57–63.

[12] H. Nakamura, *Indian Buddhism*, 12–15.

[13] J. Bloch, *Les Inscriptions d'Asoka*, 130ff.; R. Thapar, *Aśoka and the Decline of the Mauryas*, 40–1.

[14] The contemporary Hellenistic and Greek kings mentioned in the edict date to *c.* 256–55 BC. It was issued twelve years into his reign. This would date his accession to *c.* 268 BC. The Chronicle mentions his accession as 218 years after the *parinirvāṇa*, which would give 483 BC.

would support the earlier date. Given the propensity of the monks to link the Saṅgha with royal patronage, it is hard to believe that, had the Buddha been a contemporary of the powerful Nanda king, the Canon and the subsequent biographies would not have emphasized this association. The significant point is not so much the variation in the dates suggested by modern scholars, but that in the Buddhist texts chronology tends to conform to a plausible date for the *parinirvāṇa,* generally 486/483 BC, and most events are calculated from that date. The chronological ordering and arrangement of the Canon remains problematic.[15] The Canon probably took its present form by the turn of the Christian era, and provides the elements of what was later to go into the making of the Buddhist historical tradition.

4. The Authors

The recalling and recitation of various texts continued into the early centuries AD. The *bhānakas,* among others, were the monks who preserved the oral recitation. Schismatic teachings could not be excluded and were mentioned. Where texts were translated into other languages, the inheritance of concepts from that language would have left some imprint.[16]

The varied languages made the texts more appropriate to regional dissemination but also encouraged alternative explanations of passages that were difficult to comprehend. The Theravāda maintained their record in Pāli, arguing that it was close to the language in which the Buddha had taught, although the early texts of Sri Lanka drew on a Siṅhala oral tradition.[17] Sanskrit texts were translated into the languages of the areas to which the Buddhist missions travelled, such as Sogdian, Khotanese, Chinese, and Tibetan. Occasionally these, in their survived form, are more complete than the original.

[15] G.C. Pande, *Studies in the Origin of Buddhism*, has attempted a stratification of the *nikāyas* which demonstrates the chronological uncertainty of sections of the texts.

[16] J.W. de Jong, *Buddha's Word in China*; E. Zurcher, *The Buddhist Conquest of China*.

[17] Other later sects kept their records in Sanskrit, Prākrit, and Apabhraṃśa as well.

Unlike the *itihāsa-purāṇa*, the authorship in most cases is neither that of bard nor *brāhmaṇa,* but usually of monks in monastic establishments or learned lay followers. The perspective is therefore not primarily of the court or the monarchy, but of the monastery and the Saṅgha. Often placed on the edge of an urban centre, these would also reflect the interaction with townspeople, householders, and merchants. This did not exclude the politics of the capital, except that the politics came filtered through monastic concerns. Political authority is seen as central, but it is also viewed from the perspective of the monastery, the sect, and the Saṅgha. The premium on literacy among monks made it imperative that the Canon, commentaries, and chronicles be copied at regular intervals to ensure their preservation. The narrative was updated either by interpolations, or by rewriting the text, or by writing a fresh text, in each case using the existing ones as among the sources. Later commentaries, not surprisingly, could give variant readings, so changes can be noticed.

The Pāli Buddhist Canon reflects the concerns of the Saṅgha subsequent to the death of the Buddha, when records were required. The oral tradition continued for a while, as is suggested by references to teachings in the Aśokan edicts, which are not always found in the Canon or which come under different names. Orality would have been conducive to interpolations.[18] The Buddha explained what he was teaching in a face-to-face situation, and this went back to his first forays into propagating his ideas. The spoken word was respected but debated. The focus therefore was on questioning and discussion, and, in these early stages, on arguments deriving from logical thinking, and not from a believed divine revelation.

5. Origin Myths

The seeds of the historical tradition are probably to be found in the *itihāsa-samvāda*, the dialogue stories which were counterparts to the dialogue hymns and narratives—the *ākhyānas*—of the *Vedas*, but formulated here in a recognizably Buddhist idiom. These are

[18] S. Collins, "Notes on Some Oral Aspects of Pāli Literature", 121–36.

to be found largely in the *Nikāyas* of the *Sutta Piṭaka*,[19] narrated in the course of explaining the beginnings of social institutions or to illustrate aspects of the Buddhist doctrine. They tend to centre on an event in the life of the Buddha, or a prominent disciple or person, all couched in a frame of purposeful persuasion about Buddhist teaching. In the early texts the Buddha biography is so entwined in the history of the religion that separating them is difficult.

The beginnings often go back to origin myths, not to be taken as history, but rather as persistent myths that incorporate the social assumptions of that society. In the Buddhist tradition there are origin myths about utopian beginnings and there are fabricated genealogies of the descent of clans. They provide a glimpse of what was significant to the authors of the texts and became seminal to later historical perspectives.

The primary myth narrates the origin of family, private ownership of land, status, and political authority—a myth narrated in what has been called the Buddhist book of genesis.[20] The myth is based on the recognition of social differentiation. When the Buddha was asked about the origin of government, he explained that initially there was a utopian condition where none laboured and time was passed in leisure. There were no planets or stars, no day or night, no gender, only self-luminous beings. Gradually, this golden age began to tarnish, with the creeping in of evil. The earth acquired colour and odour and tasted of honey and *ghī*. People began to eat it and their luminosity diminished. The planets appeared, so days were differentiated from nights and time was measured. Physical differences made some people beautiful and some ugly and this fostered vanity and conceit. Together with this came sexual differences, which induced passion and immorality and, above all, shame. Rice that had grown naturally and replenished itself began to be hoarded, so a constant supply needed cultivation, which in turn required labour. Stealing from

[19] M. Winternitz, *History of Indian Literature*, vol. II, 34ff.; R. Thapar, "Origin Myths and the Early Indian Historical Tradition", in *Cultural Pasts*, 754–80.

[20] Aggañña Sutta, in the *Dīgha-nikāya*, 3.80ff. and 3.93.21; T.W. Rhys Davids and J.E. Carpenter (eds), *Dialogues of the Buddha*.

each other's fields led to claims of ownership, so rice fields had to be demarcated and allotted to different groups. Evil took the form of desire and covetousness.

In an effort to control these negative features and curb desire, families were established and segregated, but contentions continued. Individuals claiming ownership of fields treated property as personal possessions. Ultimately, the situation became so chaotic that everyone gathered and then elected one from among them, the *mahāsammata*—the great elected one—in whom they invested authority to make and enforce laws and protect property. As recompense for performing this unenviable task, they agreed to give a percentage of their produce to him. He was called *khattiya/kṣatriya* because he was the lord of the fields (*khetta*), and *rājā* because he charmed everyone.

The mythic evocation of this past takes the form of an evolutionary process. The story separates the time between common ownership of land and the subsequent private ownership, the latter situation accelerating disputes and disequilibrium. The crux of the story relates to two areas of *kṣatriya* interest—landownership and the exercise of political authority. It emphasizes the election of the ruler and subsumes a contractual relationship. The person so elected had to be pure in descent for seven generations, which circumscribed the choice.[21] The origin of the *kṣatriya* was thus merged with rulership. It seemed necessary to narrate the evolution of clans into more complex societies in a seemingly historical fashion. The myths are not tangential to the narratives, nor are the narratives lost sight of in the myths. This significant historical change, from an egalitarian society to a hierarchical society which introduced government and the dominant status of the *kṣatriya*, was not divinely ordained but contracted by the people. Deities are absent and the explanation is based on causality and logic, conducive to viewing the past historically.

The origin myths of *kṣatriya* clans occur frequently. Included in these is the founding of the city, associated with a particular

[21] Kuṭṭadanta-sutta, *Dīgha-nikāya*, 1.137.13.; *Aṅguttara-nikāya*, 1.163; *Aṅguttara Nikāya*, ed. R. Morris and E. Hardy, 5 vols; F.W. Woodward and E.M. Hare (trans.), *The Book of Gradual Sayings*.

janapada or territory of the clan, as for example that of the Śākyas, Koliyas, and Licchavis. The Śākyas were especially important, being the clan of the Buddha, and in some versions of the myth intermarried with the Koliyas. The Licchavis were a part of the powerful Vṛjji confederacy and an obstacle to the increasing strength of the kingdom of Magadha. The Vṛjjis resisted the transition to monarchy, a transition which was taking place all around them.

The long excursus on the origin of the Śākyas takes in a substantial part of the Buddhist construction of origins. The context is that of a *brāhmaṇa* disputing the social status of the Buddha, a contention not uncommon in brahmanical circles. The intention may also have been to dismiss the view that Buddhist teaching was attractive only to those of low status. There are marginal variations in the accounts of origins, but the main lines of the story are broadly similar. The genealogical mode of historical thinking, also used in the epics and *Purāṇas*, is evident, although the lists of descent may differ.

The Śākyas are traced back to the lineage of Okkāka.[22] He had five sons and four daughters, but on the death of his queen his new wife also bore him a son. He was afraid she might harm the children of the first wife as she wanted her son to succeed, so he was persuaded to exile his older children.[23] The nine of them travelled to the Himalayan foothills. Here they met the sage Kapila, who advised them to build a city and settle there. The city so founded was called Kapilavastu in honour of the sage. The eldest brother remained unmarried while the other four married their four sisters; and from them was descended the clan of the Śākyas.

Okkāka is the Pāli for Ikṣvāku, but the story differs from that of Ikṣvāku in the *Purāṇas*. An Ikṣvāku ancestry was possibly an

[22] Ambaṭṭha-sutta, *Dīgha-nikāya*, 1.92.16; D. Andersen and H. Smith, *The Sutta-nipāta*, 420ff.; K.R. Norman (trans.), *The Rhinoceros Horn and other Early Buddhist Poems (Sutta-nipāta)*; *Sumaṅgalavilāsinī*, vol. I, 258–60; T.W. Rhys Davids and J.E. Carpenter, *The Sumaṅgalavilāsinī*, vols I and II. There is a variation on this in the *Mahāvastu*, vol. I, 348–52.

[23] This is a stereotype narrative and occurs at the start of the *rāma-kathā* in the *Dasaratha Jātaka*.

attempt to appropriate a known ancestral figure. The gloss on Okkāka in a later commentary is that when he spoke a light like fire came out of his mouth.[24] This is reminiscent of the Vedic description of the *rājā* Videgha Māthava who carried Agni in his mouth and, when invoked, Agni flashed out of the *rājā's* mouth and burnt a path purifying the land eastwards to the river Sadānīra where Videgha Māthava settled.[25] The Śākyas are said to have settled in the same area.

A later version of the myth reverses the story somewhat and states that the Śākyas had a close relationship with the Koliyas.[26] The Śākyas consisted of five sisters and four brothers. The eldest sister was appointed to the role of mother, the remaining eight paired off. The eldest sister developed leprosy and was left in another part of the forest, where she was rescued by a *rājā* who was also exiled because of leprosy but who had cured himself. He cured her too and they were married. They built a city at the site of a *kol* tree, hence the name Koliya. They sent their sixteen pairs of twin sons to Kapilavastu to marry the daughters of their maternal uncles. The young men kidnapped the Śākya women and were not prevented from doing so since they were kinsmen (cross-cousins). The settlements of the Koliyas and the Śākyas were separated by a river.[27]

The myth in each case attempts to explain the origin of a clan, and the city associated with its *janapada* (territory). From the fifth century BC, such cities were hubs of political and economic activity.[28] The city as the residence of the ruling families of the clan was virtually coterminous with the identity of the *janapada*. The attempt to explain the name of the clan is striking, if only because the etymologies are false. The original was either forgotten or lost, or disguised if it indicated a socially less respectable group, and new ones had to approximate the sound of the word in Indo-Aryan. This would also account for varied explanations,

[24] *Sumaṅgalavilāsinī*, I.258.
[25] *Śatapatha Brāhmaṇa*, 1.4.1.10–17.
[26] *Sumaṅgalavilāsinī*, I.260ff.
[27] *Kunāla Jātaka*, ed. and trans. W.B. Bollee.
[28] R. Thapar, *From Lineage to State*, 79ff.

as for example the name Śākya being derived from **śak* (to be able), or from the *śaka/śakota* tree.

The *kṣatriya* families had origin myths and the right to be represented in the *santhāgāra* (assembly hall). The *kṣatriya* members of these *janapadas* were sometimes related and their territories lay in geographical proximity. The genesis of the dynasties ruling in the neighbouring kingdoms of Magadha and Kosala is not the subject of myths, even though the Buddha is said to have preached in these areas and was received with honour by their kings.

The insistence on siblings, or, even better, sibling twins, as the procreators of the clan is necessary to arguing for the purity of lineage, tracing it back to those of identical blood. It is unlikely to have been meant literally. Marriages of sibling twins would be the closest simulation of a utopia where humans were born as couples, a condition equally familiar to *brāhmaṇa* utopias. Sixteen pairs make a special number, namely, 2 x 2 x 2 x 2, where the base of 2 would again convey the sense of a twin. Sibling incest was also a symbolic form of social demarcation, where those of high social status had a marriage pattern which was denied to those of lesser status. It suggests a diffusion of power within a small social group, as distinct from the larger clan. The concept is known to other cultures.[29]

In other situations the preference is for cross-cousin marriage.[30] In the non-Buddhist tradition, by contrast, even this is on occasion doubted or treated with contempt.[31] Brahmanical texts quote it as a customary practice in the South.[32] In northern India it may reflect an earlier substratum culture later overlaid by *dharmaśāstra*

[29] H.A. Hoffner, "History and Historians of the Ancient Near East: The Hittites", 290. The queen of Kanesh/Kultepe bore thirty sons in one year, whom she placed in baskets and floated down the river. They were reared by the gods. She then bore thirty daughters in one year but kept them. The sons eventually came to Kanesh and married their sisters. In this version, however, the sons were not recognized as brothers.

[30] J. Silk, "Incestuous Ancestors: The Family Origins of Gautama Siddhartha, Abraham and Sarah in Genesis 20.12", 253–81.

[31] *Bhāgavata Purāṇa,* 10.54.18. Rāma and Sītā as siblings, ruling as consorts in the *Dasaratha Jātaka*, was unacceptable to the brahmanical tradition.

[32] P.V. Kane, *History of the Dharmasastras*, vol. II, pt 1, 460ff.

norms. Or else it may have been routinely adopted in many texts that were composed in societies where cross-cousin marriage was the current pattern, as in Sri Lanka.[33]

The *kṣatriya* status of the clan is explicit by the origin always being from an established royal family, often of the Sūryavaṃśa. Kinship helped establish rights in landownership and, ultimately, political authority. The repeated theme of exile would either point to there being dissident groups or else segments breaking away from the clan and migrating elsewhere to establish new settlements. These myths could also reflect local families, not necessarily immigrants, who, having come to power, sought links with the more established families of the middle Ganges plain, as was to be frequent in later centuries. Myths claimed to establish social links, legitimacy of succession, the possible migration of important groups, and the social status to those who had acquired political power. Migration, sometimes disguised as exile, can be used to assert the rights and priority of a particular group over a specific region. This assumed significance in periods when new groups were moving in as entrepreneurs in either previously occupied areas or newly opened lands.

That there was some discord between the brahmanical and Buddhist traditions is evident from the Buddhist insistence on the *kṣatriya* status of these clans. Most are not listed in the Puranic descent lists. If it was merely a question of discounting those who were the fountainhead of heterodox movements, then surely the Puranic genealogies would have deliberately included them and described them as either *vrātya-kṣatriyas* (degenerate *kṣatriyas*) or as *śūdras*—as they did some early dynasties.[34] The Śākyas are listed among the Sūryavaṃśa, although elsewhere in the *Viṣṇu Purāṇa* the Buddha is reviled for opposing Vedic belief and ritual.[35] The use of a similar origin myth in more than one instance may have been deliberate—to emphasize their distinctive culture and exclusivity, which separated them from the *janapadas* observing brahmanical norms. The myth in this case becomes an alternative view of the past.

[33] T. Trautmann, *Dravidian Kinship*, 316ff.

[34] *Manu's Code of Law*, 10.22, refers to the Licchavis as *vrātya-kṣatriyas*.

[35] R. Thapar, "The *Purāṇas*: Heresy and the *Vaṃśānucarita*", 28–48.

The origins of castes were explained in a manner similar to the evolution of rulership and the pre-eminence of the *kṣatriyas*. The *brāhmaṇas* lived a simple life on the edge of forests and settlements, reciting the *Vedas*. The *vessa/vaiśyas*, as householders, took to various professions. Those that pursued the lowest occupations, such as hunting, were the *sudda/śūdras*. Caste was a human invention, as was governance, and required no divine intervention. The *bhikṣu/bhikkhu* (monk) could be from any group since caste identity was discarded in the homeless state. The *bhikkhu* was closer to freedom from rebirth than the *upāsaka* (lay follower).

The *Buddhavaṃsa* in a sense runs parallel to this material but focusing on Gautama Buddha in a succession of earlier Buddhas. History in the *Buddhavaṃsa* logically terminates with Gautama. The next step requires a history of his teaching and the institution through which the teaching was established, the Saṅgha. This moves us to other texts.

6. Early History of the Saṅgha

The *Piṭakas* were claimed as an authentic record of the teachings of the Buddha, collated after his passing away and approved of in the course of discussions held at three Councils at different places and times. The Councils were not descriptions of contemporary events but a record of what was remembered as the earlier history of the doctrine and the instituting of the Saṅgha. The Buddhist perception of the past moves from origin myths to events claimed as historical and essential to the history of the Saṅgha. The *Vinaya Piṭaka*, in discussing monastic rules and moral discipline, describes the formation of the Buddhist community. Events are given a chronology.[36] Dissident sects, as they grew in importance, tended to reformulate the *Vinaya* to their own ideas, the alterations being largely disagreements with the Pāli Theravāda Canon.

The history of the various Councils is narrated in the *Vinaya Piṭaka*. The recording of the doctrine begins with the First Council of the Saṅgha, held at Rājagṛha soon after the Buddha's demise.

[36] H. Oldenberg (ed.), *Vinaya Piṭakam*, vol. 5, 284; I.B. Horner, trans., *The Book of the Discipline*, 6 vols; T.W. Rhys Davids and H. Oldenberg, *Vinaya Texts*; Cullavagga XI, XII, in *Vinaya Piṭaka*, vol. III, 370ff.

Two disciples, Ānanda and Upāli, recited the *Piṭakas*, which were then recorded.[37] The authority of Kassapa, who claims to have been present at the Buddha's death, is invoked. It is thought that this Council had a nucleus of authentic tradition,[38] and was held to collect and organize the teaching and guide the Saṅgha. The elaboration of this doctrine was to change with the emergence of new sects, but the *Vinaya* was relatively constant. The *Abhidhamma Piṭaka*, more centrally concerned with doctrinal matters, may have been recorded later. The rules of monastic functioning, necessary to the discipline of the monastery, had to conform to what was stated by the Buddha, where and why, and to whom. Inevitably, there were some differences in what was reported.

The Canon has references to the Buddha's admiration for the oligarchies.[39] When Magadha attacks the Vajji confederacy, the Buddha states that the unity of the Vajjis depends on their assembling regularly, honouring the Elders and established laws, respecting existing shrines, avoiding misconduct against women, and welcoming new teachers. These are also necessary for the welfare and future existence of the Saṅgha, the organization of which he modelled on the *gaṇa-saṅgha* system of chiefships to ensure the Saṅgha would have been relatively democratic in its functioning. However, its existence required it to be authoritarian. The later commentaries on the *Vinaya Piṭaka* provide material on the schismatic trends within the Saṅgha and the resulting sects, which, by the early centuries AD, were said to number at least eighteen, frequently a symbolic number in Indian lists.

A Second Council was held a century later at Vaiśāli.[40] Kings are associated as patrons with the Councils, Ajātaśatru with Rājagaha, and a Nanda king with Vaiśāli.[41] This links the Saṅgha to political authority, and incidentally dates the Buddha to pre-Nanda

[37] L. de la Vallee Poussin, *The Buddhist Councils* (trans.); A.K. Warder, *Indian Buddhism*, 201ff.

[38] L. de la Vallee Poussin, *The Buddhist Councils*, 25ff.

[39] *Dīgha-nikāya*, vol. II, 73ff; T.W. Rhys Davids and J.E. Carpenter (eds), *The Dīgha Nikāya*; T.W. and C.A.F. Rhys Davids (trans.), *The Dialogues of the Buddha*, 3 vols.

[40] L. de la Vallee Poussin, *The Buddhist Councils*, 30ff.

[41] E. Lamotte, *History of Indian Buddhism* (trans.), 139ff.

times. Dissension surfaced among the monks at the Vaiśāli Council, especially on the crucial question of whether monks could accept donations of money. The monks of Vaiśāli, who favoured monetary donations, differed sharply from those who came from the more western monasteries, such as Kauśāmbī and Mathura, and who were opposed to such donations. The issue was referred to a committee which decided that monetary donations were unacceptable. Regulations about food and drink, seating protocol, rituals, and monastic procedures were also contentious. Problems in the routine organization of monastic life needed sorting out. Eventually there was a split in the Saṅgha.

According to the Theravāda tradition, 136 years later a Third Council was held at Pāṭaliputra, the capital of the Mauryan empire and was associated with the Mauryan king Aśoka, in *c.* 250 BC. The link between the Saṅgha and political authority now stands out. The famous Schism Edict of Aśoka calls for the expulsion of dissident monks and nuns and thus confirms dissidence.[42] The Theravāda unsurprisingly claimed that it represented the orthodox core of the doctrine, but this was unacceptable to other sects.

A schism in the doctrine was recognized. The majority of the monks came to be called the Mahāsaṅghika, and the minority, apparently largely the Elders, were called the Sthaviravāda/ Theravāda. Since the record of this Council comes only from the Theravāda tradition, it has been seen as a possible attempt to legitimize the priority and authority given to Theravāda teaching in its texts. Other sects of what came to be called the Northern Buddhist tradition speak in some cases of another Council being held in Kashmir as late as the first century AD, during the reign of the Kuṣāṇa king Kaniṣka. Once again, the association was with the most powerful king of the time. The locations of the Councils were cities linked to politically powerful patrons. There is logic in the need for calling Councils and recording decisions in accordance with the perspectives of particular Saṅghas. The attempt is to give historicity to the Councils and their decisions. This was quite unlike the Puranic sects, which had little in the way of an institutional base at this point and were not concerned with historicity.

[42] J. Bloch, *Les Inscriptions d'Asoka*, 152ff.

The division of the Saṅgha into sects was not the final identity of the splinter groups, for each in time was further segmented. The organizational form of Buddhism was not that of a centrally controlled uniform religion, but of sects breaking away and recording their interpretation of the Canon.

The schismatic movement, explained as due to doctrinal differences, was also related to the rapid spread of Buddhism, which made it difficult to consolidate the dispersed groups. Further, the preaching of the religion in new areas inevitably led to problematic assimilation of local belief and practice. The dispersal of sects takes a regional and geographical focus. The earlier Theravāda claims strength in Magadha, from where it is said to have sent missions not only to other parts of the subcontinent but also to Sri Lanka and Hellenistic West Asia. The Sarvāstivāda was more visible in the region of Mathura and Kashmir. Multiple sectarian fissions were sought to be kept under some control when the overarching religion of Buddhism was bifurcated into the Hīnayāna or Lesser Vehicle (of which the Theravādins were a part), and the Mahāyāna or Greater Vehicle which associated the Sarvāstivādins among other sects.[43] Schisms required a record of a historical kind to justify the existence of those claiming to be the inheritors.

7. Kingship, the *Dhamma*, and the Saṅgha

In the *itihāsa-purāṇa* tradition, the right by which the king rules lies in the concept of *rājadharma*—how the king is meant to practice the *dharma*. The Buddhist tradition introduces another aspect in this relationship, that of the king's relation to the Saṅgha. The Saṅgha is largely only a way of assisting in the practice of *dhamma* and therefore is subordinate to the *dhamma*. Nevertheless, it was a clearly defined institutional aspect of *dhamma*.

[43] Mahāyāna, literally, "the greater vehicle", and Hīnayāna, "the lesser vehicle", together with the Vajrayāna, or "vehicle of the thunderbolt", were the three major schools of Buddhism. Eventually the Hīnayāna was associated with Sri Lanka and South East Asia and parts of India. Mahāyāna spread in central and eastern Asia and in some parts of India. The Vajrayāna, which emerged later, remained popular in eastern India and Tibet.

The Pāli Canon mentions the conversations of the Buddha with people in many cities where he preached, such as Rājagṛha, Vaiśāli, Śrāvasti, Campā, Kauśāmbī, Kuśināra, Kapilavastu, and Vārānasi. The mention of Pāṭaligāma is of historical interest as this site was later to develop into Pāṭaliputra—the capital of the Nandas and the Mauryas. At Pāṭaligāma a town is being built as a defence against the Vajjis. Here the Buddha addresses lay followers who have gathered. Elsewhere, and later it would seem, a monastery is located at Pāṭaliputra, the town presumably having been settled by now.[44]

The conversations were with a range of people—monks, householders representing the lay followers or the community at large, heads of clans and kings. Of the latter, those more frequently mentioned are Bimbisāra of Magadha and his son and successor Ajātaśatru, and Pasenadi of Kosala. Mention is also made of the minister significantly named Vassakara—literally, "the rainmaker"—who was sent by the Magadhan king to live among the Vajjis and sow dissension between the clans. This he succeeded in doing, and the kingdom of Magadha was able to finally conquer the *gaṇa-saṅgha* of the Vajjis. Sowing dissension among confederacies in order to weaken them is also advised by Kauṭilya.[45]

Kings were the most prestigious category to whom the Buddha preached. Although kingship was a relatively new polity, its potential was being recognized and there are descriptions of the ideal king, the *cakkavatti*. These descriptions point to a difference from the brahmanical view of kingship. The king's prime possessions were seven precious objects of sovereignty: the wheel, elephant, horse, gemstone, woman, householder, and councillor, symbolic of law, royalty, force, wealth, fertility, work, and advice. Of all these, the wheel was crucial and enabled the king, if he governed wisely, to become a *cakkavatti*—a universal monarch.[46] The *cakkavatti's* power was so extensive that only one could rule at a time, and because he is a *dhamma-rājā* (righteous king), he is supreme among competitors.

[44] *Vinaya Piṭaka*, Mahāvagga, 6.28.6, 8.24.6.
[45] *Arthaśāstra,* 11.1.160–1.
[46] Mahāsudassana-sutta, *Dīgha-nikāya*, 2.172.

The king is not divine but is expected to be the epitome of righteousness, accountable to the people who elect him initially, and therefore the absence of a king (*arājya*) is a state of chaos.[47] The exemplar of kingship is the *cakkavatti/cakravartin*.[48] The idea evolved slowly and was given a distinctively Buddhist connotation different from the ideal brahmanical *kṣatriya*. The *cakkavatti,* the lord of the four quarters, rules in accordance with *dhamma*—the just law—and in righteousness rather than by might. Righteous rule involves justly assessed taxation, appropriate social actions at appropriate moments, and the well-being of society. Such a ruler is the protector of his people and of the seven precious objects associated with sovereignty. He is imbued with *iddhi*, a magical superhuman power which makes him handsome, long-lived, healthy, and popular, and is marked by the thirty-two auspicious signs of the great man.[49] This allows him the choice of either becoming a great monarch and a *cakkavatti* or else a monk, and eventually a Buddha. The counterposing of kingship with renunciation is axiomatic.

Brahmanical texts define the *cakravartin* as one aware of *dharma*, but emphasize the idea of *digvijaya*—literally the conquest of the four quarters—marking the quality of a ruler. For the Buddhist *cakkavatti* the wheel of law was primary. The moral authority of *dharma* in the brahmanical model required affirmation by the gods via the priests through the medium of ritual. For the Buddhist, moral authority overrides the ritual. The *cakkavatti*, therefore, because he propagates the *dhamma*, is less the coercive king and more the compassionate and concerned paternal figure. Hence Aśoka's emphasis on *savve munissā me pajā*—all men are my children.[50] *Daṇḍa* is subordinate to *dharma*. The king is not an opponent of the Saṅgha, nor is the Saṅgha an independent authority. What is sometimes referred to as the two wheels—the

[47] Aggañña-sutta, *Dīgha-nikāya*, 3.92.20–93.

[48] Mahasudassana-sutta, *Dīgha-nikāya*, 2.169ff., 2.198ff.; Cakkavatti-sīhanāḍa-sutta, 3.59ff., ibid.; Lakkhaṇa-sutta, 3.142ff., ibid., etc.

[49] *Majjhima Nikāya,* 2.134; V. Trenckner and R. Chalmers (eds), *The Majjhima Nikāya*, 3 vols; I.B. Horner (trans.), *The Collection of the Middle Length Sayings*, 3 vols; *Dīgha-nikāya,* 2.177.

[50] J. Bloch, *Les Inscriptions d'Asoka*, 137.

dharmacakra or the wheel of righteousness, and the *ājñacakra* or the wheel of authority—seemingly suggests a dichotomy between the Saṅgha and the king. In effect, the dichotomy is muted.

The symbol of the *cakkavatti* was the wheel, which was visible outside the hall of audience, where it had come to rest after having rolled through many territories in every direction. The wheel was not inherited but had to be earned through ruling in accordance with the *dhamma*, and eliminating evil activities and poverty, otherwise the wheel would disappear. If the king ruled justly the wheel would rest near the hall of justice. If the king was unjust, the wheel would sink into the earth and the king would lose it.[51]

It was then predicted that centuries later there would be an evil king who would not follow the norms of the *dhamma*, and people would be given to stealing, lying, violence, and lack of piety, with a drastic reduction in lifespans. Many would be murdered and the rest would flee to the forest. This echoes the dystopia prior to the *mahāsammata* and the myth of the declining cycles of time ending in the Kaliyuga. Eventually, there would be a rejuvenation, a return to the beginning, and a new *cakkavatti,* a wheel-turning king would bring order back. This is also tied to the statement on the decline of the doctrine and its revival through the coming of the Buddha Maitreya, a parallel to the saviour figure in other religions.[52]

The notion of the *cakkavatti* represents the kingdom and the state as paramount. But the Buddhist and brahmanical perspectives on the state differ. *Varṇāśramadharma* from the brahmanical perspective has to be instilled and protected by the state and society, despite it introducing a divisive ethic conditioned by *varṇa*. The Buddhist association of *dhamma* with the *cakkavatti* transformed the state from being solely an agency of authority to being an ethical category.[53] As a universal category the state allows the possibility of universal ethics. The king's good actions, such as largesse to the Saṅgha, bring him merit. Personal merit was not associated with elements of the divine.[54] The king's legitimacy

[51] Mahāsudassana-sutta, *Dīgha-nikāya*, 2.172-4; *Majjhima Nikāya*, 3.172–3.

[52] Cakkavatti-sīhanāḍa-sutta, *Dīgha-nikāya*, 3.74.

[53] T. Ling, *The Buddha*, 140–7.

[54] R. Heine-Geldern, "Conceptions of State and Kingship in South East Asia", 15–30.

was reiterated through closeness to the Saṅgha. Righteousness as a prerequisite of the king is endorsed in a late section of the *Mahābhārata*, when Yudhiṣṭhira is being persuaded to accept kingship.[55] This could be a concession to Buddhist thinking, being different from the *Arthaśāstra* upholding power. Buddhist theory disapproved of the *khattavijja/kṣatriya vidyā*.[56] The ideal was the *rājā-cakkavatti dhammiko-dhammarājā*. As a universal ethic it assumed the equality of all and this contradicted the *varṇāśramadharma*.

The establishing of the state as well as the authority of the Saṅgha was part of the historical narrative. Governance involved the interface between the two much more visibly than in other traditions. The state embodying *sasana/śāsana* was parallel to the Saṅgha upholding Buddha-*śāsana*. The state had to be a system that produced more than just the essential so that it could maintain the community, which in turn maintained the Saṅgha, and the king could be its patron. It was gradually conceded that a royal patron could assist in making laws for the *śāsana*. Patronage from individuals in the form of *dāna* (gift-giving) enhanced the patron's acquisition of merit. *Dāna* was a replacement of *yajña* and sacrificial rituals, and was the tie between the householder and the monk, where contrasting ways of living did not obstruct interdependence. The recording of donations was important to the history of the Saṅgha, apart from *dāna* furthering merit.

8. The Concept of Time

In Buddhist thinking there is both a separation and an intersection of cyclic and linear time, depending on its function. Yet this is not identical with the concept of time in Puranic thinking. Measurement in historical terms, i.e. the centrality of the *mahāparinirvāṇa* as the focal point to calculate chronology as well as the recording of genealogies and the succession of the Elders, conforms to linear time. Cosmological time viewed as a cycle tends to be similar to notions of the Puranic tradition. Cosmological time, generational

55 *Mahābhārata*, Śānti *parvan*, 90.3–5; 13–15; 91.3ff.
56 Brahmajāla-sutta, *Dīgha-nikāya*, I.9.18.n3; 80.1ff.

time, and linear time all exist but function in contexts different from the Puranic.

Cosmological time is cyclic and linked to the notion of *kalpas/kappas* (aeons). A *kappa* is a cycle of existence and plays on immense measures of time, such as *mahākappas*, *asamkheyya kappas*, and *antara kappas* (countless eons). This is the time that is recalled in the history of the Buddhas who preceded Gautama and the numbers are symbolic. Thus, Dipaṅkara lived for 84,000 lakhs of years in a period of 100,000s of unaccountable *kappas* ago. The figure of 84 is treated as magical in many cultures of the subcontinent. The last few *kappas* decline in length.

The *asamkheyya kappas* were divided into four—gold, silver, copper, and iron, with a gradual decline in the downward movement of the cycle and a gradual progress in the upward movement. The time scale involved is so vast that it cannot be comprehended in human terms. Only the last part of the *kappa* can constitute what might be called historical time. Cosmological time is the beginning of an evolution up to where we are now. The inevitability of the decline is also underlined in the decrease of the human life span from 80,000 years to 10. These ideas resonate with similar patterns in other traditions.[57]

The timelessness of time has sometimes to be described spatially as its span is incalculable. In one passage there are three sets of questions: how far back is the beginning of time; how long is a *kappa*; how many have already passed away? In answer to the first, it is said that if a man prunes all the grass, twigs, and boughs from the whole of Jambudvīpa and stacks them in piles to mark the generations counting back from his mother's mother, the material will not suffice. Similarly, if a man were to make clay balls out of the whole of this earth, they will not suffice to count the generations from his father's father back in time.

As for the number of *kalpas* that have passed, it is said that if the grains of sand which lie along the river Ganges from its source to the sea were to be counted, it would give the number of past *kalpas*. If there is a cube-shaped hill measuring one *yojana* each

[57] The Greek cyclic concept of time also refers to four ages or cycles differentiated as gold, silver, copper, and iron, with an inherent assumption of decline.

way and if the top were to be brushed with a scarf every hundred years, then the time it would take for the hill to disappear would still be less than a *kalpa*. If a city, cubic in form and with iron walls, was to be filled with mustard seeds, and if one seed were taken out every hundred years, the final seed would be taken out in a period which is still short of a *kalpa*. Clearly, this is not time that allows any calculation. It is a metaphor for time too distant to be real. It is deep time or timeless time and can only be explained spatially.

At the philosophical level, the Buddhist theory of time differed from brahmanical views. Arguing that reality was a flux and time was of the instant, it was held that real time was that of the *kṣaṇa*/ moment or instant. Time therefore is perishable and the duration of time is a fiction.[58] There was opposition to the Upaniṣadic view of the *ātmavāda*, the permanence of the *ātman*, and the notion of the unchanging eternal soul.[59]

The new cycle in Buddhist cosmology continued from the old with the completion of its upswing. If it bypasses the point of its beginning even marginally, it mutates into a spiral, and a spiral if extended takes the form of a wave. Such a form, although not strictly linear, has some of the characteristics of linear time. One of these is the notion of the utopia to come, the golden age that lies in the future. This is different from the utopia that initiated the cycle. The utopia to come is expressed in the concept of the Buddha Maitreya, the future Buddha who will re-establish the doctrine. Only then can the moral regression of the world from utopian beginnings be set right. To that extent this is the eschatology of the Buddhist view of time, presented in a chiliastic form.

Generational time as a form of linear time is invoked in the genealogies succeeding Mahāsammata, but this list is generally vague and lacks even the imagined precision of Puranic lists. The genealogical sections subsequent to the *mahāsammata* follow the same form as those of the Sūryavaṃśa in the *Purāṇas*. The genealogy sets out the ancestry of the Śākyas and provides a sequence. The succession lists of the Elders are constructed more carefully since

[58] N.A. Balslev, *A Study of Time in Indian Philosophy*, 80ff.
[59] T.V.R. Murti, *The Central Philosophy of Buddhism*, 74–5, 121.

they bear on succession to high office, are often correlated with ruling kings, and refer to rules of discipline and to dissidence. These also commanded rights to property when monasteries became landlords, all of which is better managed through records conforming to linear time.

In linear time no ambiguity is allowed in what pertains to history. There is a single, central date, the *mahāparinirvāṇa*, from which later events are calculated. This both reinforced and was reinforced by the appeal to history. The basis of the calculation remains unchanged, though the date could be shifted a little. In theory it was the chronological bedrock. What is important about this emphasis on the linear is that it is finite time. A single event occurs once in a limited timespan and has no cyclical recurrence. There was however no sharp dichotomy between different concepts of time.

9. Traces of Historical Thinking

The texts that suggest a Buddhist historiography are different in structure and content, and in the formulation of a historical tradition, from those discussed in the previous chapters. They are up to a point ecclesiastical, but, in relating this to a political presence, the secular becomes a part of their history. Their concern is with the history of the Buddha as a historical figure and with the Buddhist Saṅgha and its multiple sects with their particular historical associations. Neither of these can be isolated from the wider society, since both are recognized as rooted in a historical context.[60] This relationship is expressed in a continual interaction of intention and event where factual material is brought in to strengthen dogma. The resistance to persecution and being treated as heresy becomes important and may have furthered the link to political authority and the need for history. The political role of the sect was upheld not just by its closeness to royalty but also by its involvement in the community of lay followers. The Saṅgha's dependence on a lay following, articulate in votive inscriptions at *stūpa* sites in

[60] Cf. A. Momigliano, "The Origins of Ecclesiastical Historiography", 132ff.

particular, is a comment on the nature of the dependence[61] In later times, this was furthered through the participation of monasteries in commerce and activity related to grants of land.

Interaction with political order was more effective if backed by the *vihāra* (monastery) in its *sīmā* (boundary), in effect the territory that held the community with which it interacted. The Saṅgha often had fiscal and juridical rights over large properties that involved local communities, giving it a socio-economic identity pivotal to the community.[62] This is apparent by the mid-first millennium AD although its beginnings were earlier.[63] If kings and ministers were given to political intrigue, so were the monastic Elders. It was sometimes difficult to distinguish between heresy and political rebellion. The cry of heresy was often a means of unifying those that formed the original core, or those that had been excluded. Persecution often had its origins in competition, and the successful used it to enhance their power and attempt to include a larger number of the community.

That the history of the Saṅgha was also a wider history can be recognized in these texts. Dynastic succession is sometimes paralleled by the succession of the Elders, with cross-references to rulers. History comes to include biography, since the lives of both kings and Theras affect the Saṅgha. Texts were important to the institution, so they were read by monks and recited to the *upāsakas* (lay followers). Attracting an audience may have required including fragments of the oral tradition, such as origin myths and the existence of pre-Buddhist societies, although doubtless most monks would also have enjoyed these narratives. Rhetoric, literary style, and hyperbole were not seen as deviations from measured factual evidence but as marks of emphasis, demarcating the significant from the ordinary. For example, narratives about the emperor Aśoka included the miraculous where it could highlight a point.

[61] G. Schopen, *Bones, Stones and Buddhist Monks*, 72ff.; R.A.L.H. Gunawardana, *Robe and Plough: Monasticism and Economic Interest in Early Medieval Sri Lanka*.

[62] R. Thapar, "Patronage and the Community", in *Cultural Pasts*, 589–609.

[63] R.A.L.H. Gunawardana, *Robe and Plough: Monasticism and Economic Interest in Early Medieval Sri Lanka*.

The history of the Saṅgha was local in pertaining to its community and patron, but also had a vision of itself as universal in its reference. The closeness of the Saṅgha to what had been the community shows in its prototype—the *gaṇa-saṅgha*—and to which there is occasionally an imperceptible harking back.

Although the Buddhist texts give space to genealogies, they are nevertheless not as obsessive about them as were the *vaṃśānucarita* sections of the *Viṣṇu Purāṇa*. Genealogies were more pertinent to the description of earlier societies; for later periods they took the form of the succession of Elders. Such diminishing importance of kin connections reflects a society more familiar with established kingship and statehood rather than with clan chiefs and the kings of emerging kingdoms. The Buddha, in recommending the functioning of the clan societies as the ideal for the Saṅgha, had perhaps not anticipated how quickly Buddhist teaching would be located in kingdoms and their respect for the Saṅgha. This in itself would have made the Saṅgha a distinctive institution in the context of polities conforming to kingship.

In institutions where monetary wealth and property are gifted rather than acquired through inheritance, the emphasis on genealogies declines or has other meanings—since the origin of wealth did not have to be proved by genealogical links. The patronage of urban families, particularly of the *seṭṭhis* (financiers and traders), tended to release the hold of inherited property in land, and the rise of rich merchants disrupted the older lineage demands. Newly evolving urban cultures tend to be less circumscribed by antecedents. At the same time, lists of succession were important in identifying relations with political authority, for chronology, and for stabilizing the monastery in terms of claiming a past.

Something of the contractual element of the urban environment seeped through and there was less emphasis on status alone. There was a freer attitude to caste, frequently expressed in terms of *jāti* rather than *varṇa*. Sramanic religions such as Buddhism and Jainism emphasize the importance of the individual, particularly in attaining *nirvāṇa* or freedom from rebirth. There is, in this, much less dependence on the limitations imposed by the functions of caste.

The Buddhists were not invariably part of the heterodoxy. In some areas they were the prevalent religious group. It is said that in the Indian context the opposition of orthodoxy and heterodoxy is less relevant and the more appropriate term would be orthopraxy, since it is in the nature of rituals and social observances that these differences were central. This did not preclude arguments on some fundamental issues of belief. The Canon includes some antitheses to brahmanical doctrine that make it oppositional to the *Vedas*.[64] Among those mentioned more frequently were the impermanence of time, the negation of the *ātman* as soul, the absence of deities, and the centrality of causality to understanding the world.

It has been suggested that Buddhism was not given to treating history as important since the Buddha disapproved of popular chatter about historical subjects pertaining to kings, ministers, wars, and suchlike, and furthermore the impermanence of time—which was basic to Buddhist thinking—is not exactly conducive to creating a historical tradition.[65] Yet the Pāli Canon has something of an underlying historical logic. It goes back to the origins of being a Buddha in a mix of mythology, and a degree of logical reconstruction, moving to the history of the Buddha's activities. After this comes the establishing of the Saṅgha and its history through the Councils and the schisms. Narrated in a chronological order with some degree of causality in explaining events, there is recognition of the flow, and a concern with some rational explanations, even if interspersed with mythology.

The Buddha's fundamental teaching of *pratītya-samutpāda* (dependent origination) underlined *hetu* (cause) as essential to understanding the past. Events do not happen in isolation, there is an order to their sequence.[66] The pattern has to be recognized, given that the universe is impermanent and changing, a theory that doubtless encouraged the idea of historical change.

The creation of what might be called a Buddhist historical tradition is present in its views of the past as given in the *vaṃsa* (succession). Enlightenment was not a divine moment but an

[64] R. Gombrich, "Recovering the Buddha's Message"; K.R. Norman, *Pali Literature*, 8.

[65] B.G. Gokhale, "On Buddhist Historiography", 99–108.

[66] G.C. Pande, *Studies in the Origins of Buddhism*, 423–4.

enquiry basing itself on analytical reasoning and the importance of causation.[67] There are diverse views on the teaching of the Buddha but in its evolution the constituents of a historical tradition are evident.

The history recorded in Buddhist texts is initially the history of a person, but with the death of the person evolves into the history of an institution—the Saṅgha. Kings play a role in supporting it or undermining it, as is amply demonstrated in the narratives of texts such as those that refer to Aśoka, and others later that mention Puṣyamitra Śuṅga. But the Saṅgha remains the historical protagonist—as will become clear from the Chronicles of the Māhāvihāra monastery.

[67] T. Ling, *The Buddha*, 130ff.; *Majjhima Nikāya*, I, 160ff.

10

The Monastic Chronicles of Sri Lanka

1. The Chronicles

Putting together the story of the Saṅgha, and the claim that its Canon was the authentic teaching of the Buddha, was a necessary exercise for any Buddhist mission. When doing so, the advantages of having a presumed history of the Saṅgha became evident. In order to validate the narrative, evidence had to be quoted, particularly in an ambience where there were rival histories, and the more so if that version was linked to authority—as was the claim of the Theravāda.

Narratives underlined the authority of the Saṅgha within the Buddhist community, but for status in society as a whole a surer way was association with political authority—the king and the court. This was done in the Canon by linking ruling kings with the Buddhist Councils. It was furthered by drawing on a range of lay followers as patrons, all personable householders who owned land or were prominent merchants—the *gahapatis* and *seṭṭhis*. This association gave the Saṅgha status, but again validating it meant recording events pertaining to its connection with secular authority. Since the connection was through monastic establishments, writing the chronicle of the leading monastery, recording events important to its links with other authorities, and its competition with other monasteries, became a way of establishing recognition.

Representative examples of this are the Pāli Chronicles from Sri Lanka. The earlier ones include substantial references to the history of northern India to make the connection to the Buddha and the Saṅgha, and are a contrast to the record of the same history in the Puranic tradition. Monasteries, emphasizing literacy, encouraged the keeping and preserving of records. This was far less pronounced in the Puranic tradition of pre-Gupta times. It is also somewhat puzzling that similar chronicles were not maintained in Indian monasteries, particularly where Buddhism had effective patrons, especially in the period between the third century BC and the third AD. Possibly the Saṅgha was not that close to political authority, despite the patronage of rulers such as Aśoka, since its major donors were not limited to royalty. More importantly, political authority distributed its patronage to other sects as well: bonding with a single sect was not the pattern.

When the Chronicles were first studied in the early nineteenth century, there was a debate on whether or not they could be taken as history.[1] It was initially maintained by G. Turnour that these chronicles were a reliable historical narrative of events pertaining to Sri Lanka, their reliability meeting the test of modern historical writing.[2] This approach was debated but endorsed by scholars such as H. Oldenberg and more so by W. Geiger and G.P. Malalasekera. Recently, it has been argued that the context and purpose for which they were written should be discussed by scholars prior to accepting their statements.[3] One can, however, draw out the reflections of the Chronicles on the past in the context of constituting a distinctive historical tradition, with interests different from those in other parallel and contemporary historical traditions of the region.

The early history of the Saṅgha in Sri Lanka, and of the kingdom of Anurādhapura as available in the monastic Chronicles,

[1] J.S. Walters, "Buddhist History", 99–164.

[2] G. Turnour, *An Epitome of the History of Ceylon Compiled from Native Annals; and the First Twenty Chapters of the Mahawanso.*

[3] H. Bechert, *William Geiger: His Life and Works*; G. Obeyesekere, "Myth, History and Numerology in the Buddhist Chronicles", 152–82; P. Jeganathan, "Authorizing History: Ordering Land: The Conquest of Anuradhapura", 106–38; J.S. Walters, "Buddhist History", 99–164.

draws on the Canon in Pāli as well as non-Canonical sources.[4] The Chronicles are the *Dīpavaṃsa*,[5] the *Mahāvaṃsa*,[6] and the later *Cūlavaṃsa*.[7] The first two Chronicles narrate the history of the Mahāvihāra, the monastery central to Theravāda in Sri Lanka, located at Anurādhapura, and the early history of the kingdom. Events in India are treated as background, leading to events in Sri Lanka wherever there were connections. All three Chronicles present the history of the middle Ganges plain from a Theravāda perspective. Later commentaries on the Pāli Canon and on these Chronicles, such as the *Samantapāsādikā* and the *Vaṃsatthappakāsini*, provide further details.[8] These chronicles and commentaries reflect the history of the Saṅgha, its relations with the state, variants of the narrative, and glosses on the meaning of passages where these are thought necessary.[9] Collectively, they reveal the fact that established religions sprout sectarian confrontations, and sects need to write commentaries to explain their contestations. Such explanations are also needed to convince new converts.

The *vaṃsa* virtually became a generic form as a record of objects, events, persons, and activities. This was handy material, even if not always reliable for writing chronicles. The *Buddhavaṃsa* goes back to the Pāli Canon but as a *vaṃsa* it takes forward the idea of succession. It draw the Buddha into the narrative of the past almost as a proxy for deity. The *Buddhavaṃsa* becomes a source for other kinds of succession. Contemporary with the contents of

[4] G.C. Mendis, *The Pali Chronicles of Ceylon*; see also C.E. Godakumbara, "Historical Writing in Sinhalese", in C.H. Philips (ed.), *Historians of India, Pakistan and Ceylon*, 72–86; A.K. Warder, "The Pali Canon and its Commentaries as Historical Records", ibid., 44–56; S. Seneviratne, "Peripheral Regions and Marginal Communities . . .", in R. Champakalakshmi and S. Gopal (eds), *Tradition, Dissent, and Ideology*, 266–70.

[5] *The Dīpavaṃsa*, ed. and trans. H. Oldenberg.

[6] *The Mahāvaṃsa*, ed. and trans. W. Geiger.

[7] *Cūlavaṃsa*, ed. and trans. W. Geiger.

[8] *Samantapāsādikā: Buddhaghosa's Commentary on the Vinaya Piṭaka*, ed. J. Takakusu and M. Nagai; *Vaṃsatthappakāsini* (Mahāvaṃsa Ṭīkā), ed. G.P. Malalasekera; G.C. Mendis, *The Pali Chronicles of Ceylon*, 23.

[9] R.A.L.H. Gunawardana, "The Kinsmen of the Buddha: Myth and Political Charter in the Ancient and Medieval Kingdoms in Sri Lanka", 62; B.L. Smith (ed.), *Religion and the Legitimation of Power in Sri Lanka*.

the commentaries and chronicles are inscriptions, which constitute both comparative and corroborative data.[10] Inscriptions provide evidence of the social and economic support given to the Saṅgha by lay society. They also provide evidence on the organization and functioning of monasteries, the succession of Theras and the links with kings.

The *Dīpavaṃsa*, though composed over a period of time, was compiled by anonymous authors in about the fourth-fifth century AD.[11] It has been suggested that its authors may have been nuns. Given the early date at which women were ordained as nuns in Sri Lanka—attested to by inscriptions—their writing of portions of texts would not be surprising, and this chronicle gives much attention to the activities of nuns.[12] As the name implies, it purports to be a history of the island. The Pāli is of uneven quality, suggesting an authorship not completely at home with the language.[13] Possibly, the original was composed in Sihala and then translated into Pāli. *Vaṃsa* is used in a general sense of a chronicle narrating a succession of persons and events. It provides a prototype for the *Mahāvaṃsa*.

The *Mahāvaṃsa*, dating to the next century, is more detailed, with a better crafted text and finer literary style. The focus remains on the Mahāvihāra monastery and the Theravāda sect, but is intertwined with the history of the island. Authorship is attributed to a monk, Mahānāma of the Mahāvihāra monastery. Among its sources the *Sihala-aṭṭhakathā-mahāvaṃsa* is mentioned, but which has not survived. The *aṭṭhakathās* were commentaries on Buddhist matters in Sri Lanka, composed in various monasteries. They tended to be didactic and were meant for the edification of monks.[14] The *Porāṇas* and *Porāṇāṭṭhakathās* were also regarded as ancient and authoritative. There are some similarities in names and regnal years with the dynastic section of the *vaṃśānucarita*

[10] A pioneering work on these inscriptions is L.S. Perera, *The Institutions of Ancient Ceylon from Inscriptions: Vol. I, Third Century BC to 830 AD*. The work was put together half a century before it was published.

[11] *Dīpavaṃsa*, 8–9.

[12] *Dīpavaṃsa*, 18.1ff.; R.A.L.H. Gunawardana, "Subtile Silks of Ferrous Firmness", 1–59; G.P. Malalasekera, *The Pāli Literature of Ceylon,* 36–7.

[13] M. Winternitz, *A History of Indian Literature*, vol. II, 210ff.

[14] E.W. Adikaram, *Early History of Buddhism in Ceylon.*

in the *Purāṇas*.[15] The record of the monastery was apparently maintained until its desertion. These were not the only historical works, although they are earlier and more representative and establish a genre.[16]

The chronicle is distinguished from the popular narrative and epic poetry by its specific purpose, namely that the Buddha chose Sri Lanka to be a centre of Buddhism and that Theravāda as represented in the Mahāvihāra monastery contributed the essential teaching. Events moved to make this possible.[17]

2. The *Dīpavaṃsa*

The first event in the Chronicle had to be the coming of the Buddha to Sri Lanka in order to prepare the island, predestined to receive the doctrine. It is said that he flew thrice to the island to select locations for future monasteries and *stūpas*, thereby giving a special sanctity to such places. Prior to the establishing of a kingdom on the island, it was inhabited by *yakkhas*, *bhūtas, rākṣasas, nāgas*, and suchlike—supernatural creatures who dwelt in the forests and had to be subordinated to become worshippers of the Buddha.[18] The coming of the Buddha made it relevant to introduce the history of northern India. The genealogy of the Buddha is taken back to Mahāsammata, and mention is made of lineages similar to those of the *Purāṇas*, but occurring in different combinations. The Cedis and Okkākas/Ikṣvākus are part of the same lineage, which contradicts the *Purāṇas*, where the two are distinct.[19] The *Purāṇas* are used as a partial source but the narratives differ.

The story of Vijaya and his entourage coming as migrants from India and establishing a succession of rulers follows as a form of epic beginnings.[20] The name of the island, Siṅhala/Sihala, is

[15] *Mahāvaṃsa*, xli.

[16] L.S. Perera, "The Pali Chronicles of Ceylon", 29ff.

[17] S. Kiribamune, "The *Dīpavaṃsa* in Ancient Sri Lankan Historiography", 89–100.

[18] R.A.L.H. Gunawardana, "The Kingdom of the Buddha: Myth as Political Charter in the Ancient and Early Medieval Kingdom of Sri Lanka", 54ff.

[19] *Dīpavaṃsa*, 3.5; 3.41; F.E. Pargiter, *Ancient Indian Historical Tradition*, 144–9.

[20] *Dīpavaṃsa*, 9.20ff.

explained through Vijaya's ancestry being linked to a lion. In other sources the island is called Taṃbapaṇi/Taprobane—a name also used for southern India, with Sihala becoming common at the start of the Christian era. Subsequently, the name changed to Laṅkā.

Vijaya's formal marriage was to a South Indian princess. This would support the idea of the initial settlements and culture being associated with the mainland.[21] Vijaya has no heir, so a successor from a co-lateral line is sent for from India. The names of these rulers seem to be taken from the *Jātakas* and the *Mahābhārata*.[22] This segment is a prologue to the subsequent narrative about early history.

The scene then shifts to the middle Ganges plain. The ancestry of the Buddha is traced from Okkāka down to Daśaratha and Rāma to Śuddhodhana, followed by some of the kings of Magadha.[23] The chronology is Puranic, although precise sources are not mentioned.[24] The association with kings introduces further links between the Saṅgha and political authority.

Soon after the Buddha's death, the First Council is said to have been called at Rājagṛha to record his teaching. A century later, a Second Council meets at Vaiśāli, as also mentioned in the Canon.[25] Disagreement at this later Council splits the Saṅgha. Another correlation is made between the succession of Theras and kings of the Ganges plain in an attempt to establish a chronology. The conversion of Aśoka and associated miracles are described.[26] Given the presence of dissenters in the Saṅgha, Aśoka is made the patron of the Third Council at Pāṭaliputra.[27] The dissenters are expelled and the Theravāda is established as the true doctrine. Buddhist missions are sent to various places and Aśoka's son, Mahinda, brings Buddhism to Sri Lanka. This explains why the

[21] S. Kiribamune, "Buddhist Historiography: Sri Lankan Perception", 9–15.

[22] G.C. Mendis, *The Pali Chronicles of Ceylon*, 59ff.

[23] *Dīgha-nikāya*, 3.39, 3.52.

[24] S. Kiribamune, "The *Dīpavaṃsa* in Ancient Sri Lankan History", 89–100.

[25] *Dīpavaṃsa*, 4.1–25, 4.1.47, 5.16.

[26] *Dīpavaṃsa*, 5.76, 6.1ff.

[27] *Dīpavaṃsa*, 7.39ff.

earlier narratives were necessary as antecedents. Mention of the Third Council is omitted in the Canon, which is surprising as it would have further legitimized the Theravāda.

The one king of consequence in Sri Lanka at this point is Devānaṃpiya Tissa, a contemporary of Aśoka, who took the same title, *devānaṃpiya*. The two narratives of India and Sri Lanka are tied together with the coming of Mahinda, and his successful conversion of the king and court,[28] an event also recorded in inscriptions. This is followed by the arrival of Mahinda's sister to ordain the women, together with a number of relics, including a branch of the sacred Bodhi tree. Apart from the relics, the objects signifying kingship, such as the royal umbrella, turban, and sword, are all said to have come from Aśoka. The conversion is widespread—as also attested to, incidentally, by the votive inscriptions of the local gentry, the *pārumakas*. Up to this point the Chronicle is concerned with the establishing of Buddhism and the rise of the Theravāda. Much space is devoted to how Aśoka as a Buddhist ruler and exemplar of a *cakkavatti* upheld the *dhamma* and was a remarkable patron of the Saṅgha. Events are a mixture of hard politics and the miraculous.

On the death of Aśoka, the interest in northern India flags and the narrative focuses on the history of Sri Lanka. However, relations with South India are referred to. These would have been more relevant, the kingdoms of the South being neighbours, as becomes evident in the political disturbance of the subsequent period. The Damila/Tamil chief Elāra ousts the Sihala ruler. The hero Duṭṭhagāmaṇi defeats Elāra and the Chronicle becomes something of a heroic epic in praise of Duṭṭhagāmaṇi. He unifies the island, defends it against the Damilas, whose threats did not completely cease, and re-establishes the Theravāda. Having overcome its first crisis, a eulogy on the Mahāvihāra monastery is thought to be appropriate. This is followed by references to various monasteries and *stūpas* built by various rulers, as also irrigation works that aimed at the production of larger revenues to the monasteries, apart from the general expansion of agriculture. Soon after, in the reign of Vaṭṭagāmaṇi, close to the Christian era,

[28] *Dīpavaṃsa*, 12.16.

the text of the three *Piṭakas* and the *Aṭṭhakathā* were compiled and put into written form, doubtless to secure the teaching and to enable its being quoted. This may also have encouraged the idea of writing a history of the island.[29]

The *Dīpavaṃsa* is thought to conclude on a note that is aware of the conflict between the Theravāda and other Buddhist sects, competing for royal patronage and asserting their authority.[30]

3. The *Mahāvaṃsa*

The *Mahāvaṃsa* emerges as the narrative of the success of the Theravāda sect, after another crisis in its history. It is much more self-consciously historical than the *Dīpavaṃsa.* The first thirty-seven chapters, written by the monk Mahānāma, are generally dated to the fifth–sixth century AD.[31] The narrative ends in the fourth century AD with the reign of Mahāsena, who initially undermined the Mahāvihāra monastery. The history of the monastery is projected as so central that it becomes in effect the history of a kingdom. Mahānāma was directly linked to the royal family, being kinsman of the contemporary ruler, Dhātusena. The text is written in a different mood from the *Dīpavaṃsa.* It is a fine-tuning, as it were, of the history of the Mahāvihāra. Inevitably, the events selected and emphasized are not identical with those in the earlier Chronicle. The voice of the *Mahāvaṃsa* is more aggressively purposeful. The sequence in the *Cūlavaṃsa* was written still later. The *Mahāvaṃsa* starts with the statement that the earlier texts were either too brief or too long and repetitive, and have therefore been rewritten by Mahānāma.[32] Updating texts was part of the *paramparā* (tradition). The *Mahāvaṃsa* also states that the Canon was initially orally memorized and the written version came much later.[33]

[29] *Dīpavaṃsa*, 20.20–1.

[30] S. Kiribamune, "The *Dīpavaṃsa* in Ancient Sri Lankan Historiography", 89–100.

[31] S. Kiribamune, "The *Mahāvaṃsa*: A Study of the Ancient Historiography of Sri Lanka", 125–36.

[32] *Mahāvaṃsa*, 1.2ff.

[33] *Mahāvaṃsa*, 33.100–1.

The core events of the *Mahāvaṃsa* remain much the same as in the *Dīpavaṃsa*, but the emphases change. The genealogy of the Buddha and the synchronization with the early kings of Magadha is given in greater detail.[34] There is a preference for the Mahāsammata rather than Okkāka as the founding ancestor, possibly because Okkāka founded a lineage whereas the Mahāsammata inaugurated governance—which brought kingship and the state. The centrality of kingship had to be highlighted. *Kṣatriya* ancestry bestowed status, especially with the Buddha having declared the *khattiyas* as socially superior to all others. The notion of royalty was absent in the Buddha's explanation of *mahāsammata*, but by now what was initially a concept had become a royal person.

Mauryan history was a necessary frame for the coming of Buddhism to Sri Lanka. Coincidentally, it is the history of the metropolitan area—of the middle Ganges plain[35]—which is linked to the history of Sri Lanka. This was not only the area where Buddhism flourished but also had had the greatest political significance in the early history of northern India. There is little interest in Mathura, Gandhara, and Kashmir, the areas linked to the Northern Buddhist tradition. The link peters out after Aśoka is said to have virtually legitimized the Theravāda. The narrative then focuses on relations with South Indian neighbours who inevitably intervened in the politics of Sri Lanka, being physically present so close by.

Vijaya's retinue accompanies him from Magadha to Sri Lanka, involving some readjusting of the Buddhist origin myths—to the start of the history of Sri Lanka.[36] In some ways the Vijaya story is the prototype story of immigrants settling in a new land. The existing inhabitants are brought low, denounced as demonic, and sent to live in the forest, where they remain obscure. Marriages with their women are not formalized, although there is progeny and the migrants await women from their homeland. The children thus born were the progenitors of the forest-dwelling Pulindas. Was Vijaya more likely to have been from across the straits and not from northern India because his formal marriage was to the

[34] *Mahāvaṃsa*, 2.1–33, 4.1–8, 5.14–23.

[35] R. Thapar, *The Mauryas Revisited,* in *Cultural Pasts,* 462–518.

[36] *Mahāvaṃsa*, 6.47.

Paṇḍu princess from Madurai (a Pāṇḍya from Madurai?) in South India?[37] His North Indian origins were intended to link him to the land of the Buddha.[38] His arrival becomes auspicious as it is said to have coincided with the Buddha's *parinirvāṇa*.

Since Vijaya has no son, his brother's son, Pāṇḍuvāsudeva, is sent for. The name is archetypal and suggests a familiarity with the *Ghaṭa Jātaka*, the *Mahābhārata,* and the *Harivaṃśa.* The link is further endorsed by the curious story of his successor Paṇḍukābhaya, which echoes the legend of the birth of Kṛṣṇa Vāsudeva. The child is hidden at birth, reared by relatives, and comes into conflict with his maternal uncle, whom he finally kills. It may be argued that though this story carries the stereotype of the myth of the birth of the hero,[39] the details are too similar for it to have been a coincidence. It could have been an attempt to link the royal family of Sri Lanka with the Vṛṣṇi-Yādava clan of western India, reiterating what is said in passing in the Chronicle—that Vijaya sailed from western India. A possible Cedi connection also lurks in the background, becoming more visible some centuries later. At the same time, connection with the clan of the Buddha is maintained through the curious coincidence of Paṇḍuvāsudeva having married a Śākya lady![40] Thus, the ancestry of the royal house of Sri Lanka is traced to socially high antecedents. The consecration of Paṇḍukābhaya is described and his descendants listed up to the time of Devānampiya Tissa. If at all there is a resort to the formulaic, it occurs in the earlier portions of this narrative.[41] Since

[37] *Mahāvaṃsa*, 7.50.

[38] That there was close contact between south-west India and northern Sri Lanka is evident from the striking similarities in the Megalithic Black and Red Ware cultures in both areas. S. Seneviratne, "The Archaeology of the Megalithic Black and Red Ware Complex in Sri Lanka", *Ancient Ceylon,* 237–99.

[39] Otto Rank, *The Myth of the Birth of the Hero*. The myth of Kṛṣṇa's life has the same elements. His mother had been imprisoned by her brother since it had been prophesied that her son would cause his death. When Kṛṣṇa is born, he is exchanged for a girl-child, is brought up in a cowherd's village, and eventually he challenges his wicked maternal uncle to combat and kills him, to the great relief of the people of the city of Mathura who had been oppressed by the uncle.

[40] *Mahāvaṃsa*, 8.18ff.

[41] L.S. Cousins, "Pali Oral Literature", 1–11.

the Buddha was a *kṣatriya* from North India, royalty in Sri Lanka had perforce to be linked to the appropriate status irrespective of whether or not such connections existed.

The list of associated kings of Magadha probably came from Puranic data, although the dynastic order sometimes differs. Bimbisāra and Ajātaśatru were contemporaries of the Buddha, as is stated in the Canon, and they precede the Nanda dynasty. These details of political history attempt to set the chronological framework, and authenticate events, not to mention drawing on the status of those in power.

In the reign of Tissa the various narratives of the Indian and Sihala background are brought together with the mission of Mahinda to Sri Lanka. Tissa, as his title Devānaṃpiya suggests, knew about and admired the Mauryan king and the coming of a Buddhist mission led by Mahinda, the son of Aśoka, may have been a request.[42] Mahinda is said to be the son of the pious Devī, who did not go to Pāṭaliputra when Aśoka became king and brought up her son and daughter as devout Buddhists. That Mahinda was the first missionary is reiterated in the inscriptions, presumably to underline what was believed to be his eminent parentage. Mahinda converts Tissa, and the Mahāvihāra monastery is founded,[43] its location having been sanctified presumably by the Buddha's flying visits. Subsequent to this the relics of the Buddha arrive—his alms bowl and part of his collar bone—and these are duly enshrined. A branch of the Bodhi tree is reverentially planted, giving additional sanctity to the site of the monastery, now known as the Mahāmeghavanārāma. This is also symbolic of tradition and succession—the *paramparā* and *vaṃsa*—not being broken or diverted in coming to Sri Lanka. The relics recreate the sanctity of Buddhism in the newly converted region. The Sihala community had been selected to receive and maintain the teaching, and this necessitated a continuous history.

The representation of Aśoka is extensive. From an evil person—Caṇḍāsoka—he becomes a pious king—Dhammāsoka—and a patron of the Saṅgha. Curiously, no mention is made of the Kaliṅga campaign, referred to by the king in an edict as the event that

[42] *Mahāvaṃsa*, 11.7ff.

[43] *Mahāvaṃsa*, 14.6ff., 15.16ff.

encouraged him along the path of the *dhamma*. This is curious because it had the makings of high drama in the hands of a poet-monk. Aśoka's father and grandfather are referred to briefly, and mention is made of the minister Cāṇakya/Kauṭilya. A later commentary has many narratives of how Cāṇakya selected Candragupta Maurya, and through a series of intrigues and confrontations defeated the Nanda king and made the Maurya the founder of the new dynasty.[44] The expansion of the narrative may have used oral traditions.

Stories of the coronation of Aśoka are followed by his conversion to Buddhism, the actions of the Thera Tissa Moggaliputta, and the birth of Aśoka's first son and daughter, Mahinda and Saṅghamittā. These various threads are gradually knotted together in the story of Aśoka calling the monks for the Third Council at Pāṭaliputra, the expelling of the dissident monks, and the refutation of dissident doctrines.[45] Its significance to Sri Lanka lay in the Theravāda being declared the true doctrine and in Mahinda's mission to Sri Lanka. Because Aśoka is projected as a great patron of Buddhism, there is some discussion of Mauryan history.

The Śākyan ancestry of Aśoka and the Mauryan family is mentioned,[46] and its being *kṣatriya* contradicts the *Purāṇas*, where the Mauryas are said to be *śūdras*. This was necessary to the status of Aśoka's son, Mahinda, as coming from the clan of the Buddha himself, which magnified the value of Mahinda bringing Buddhism to Sri Lanka.[47]

[44] *Vaṃsatthappakāsini*, 1.5.181ff.

[45] An event of this kind may have been the context of the Schism Edict of Aśoka, as has been suggested. J. Bloch, *Les Inscriptions d'Asoka*, 152.

[46] This is elaborated upon in a later commentary, the *Vaṃsatthappakāsini*, ed. G.P. Malalasekera, 180ff. The Mauryas are described as those Śākyas who fled from Kapilavastu when the king of Kosala attacked the Śākyas for having deceived him into marrying a slave-girl, instead of the daughter of the ruling clan who had been promised to him. The group of fleeing Śākyas settled in a *pīpal* forest with an abundance of peacocks *(mora/mayura)*, from which their name derived. This was a later attempt to link the Aśoka of the Mauryan dynasty, and his son Mahinda, with the family of the Buddha.

[47] In a much later Tibetan tradition, the conversion of Sri Lanka is attributed to the *ārya* Kṛṣṇa, and no mention is made of any son of Aśoka. However, Kṛṣṇa sounds an unlikely name for a Buddhist monk. Tāranātha, *History of Buddhism in India*, ed. D. Chattopadhyaya, folio 24 A, 72–3.

The importance of Aśoka to Buddhist historiography lies in his being projected as a *cakkavatti*, ruling in accordance with *dhamma*. His virtuous deeds also make him something of a *bodhisattva*, thus symbolizing a combination of temporal and sacral power. The king is both the patron of the Saṅgha as well as a lay follower. Details of the later years of Aśoka are narrated, suggesting attacks on the Buddhist order, parried by Aśoka. Monasteries and constructions of religious buildings by royal patrons are mentioned to emphasize the importance of the Theravāda.[48] By this time the property of the Saṅgha was quite substantial, and a record of this becomes part of its history.

Another thread in the narrative that gradually assumes greater visibility is that of the relations with the Damilas in South India. The focus on this, and on the history of Buddhism in Sri Lanka, turns the narrative away from events in North India, which now have less bearing on events in Sri Lanka.

The conflict between the Sihala and Damila rulers continues for a while since they are chiefs of principalities with quick turnovers. The next major event is Duṭṭhagāmaṇi's defence of the kingdom against Elāra, the Damila. Duṭṭhagāmaṇi destroys the Damila principalities, re-establishing the royal line and patronage to the Saṅgha. He is from a collateral line and his antecedents are not glorified, as one would expect of a hero, although his ousting of Elāra takes on epic proportions. Was it such a devastating campaign, or was the author trying to divert attention from the crisis in the Saṅgha? The record of patronage, although somewhat diminished in disturbed times, is still maintained with the history of structures and their patrons extending over five chapters.

The opposition to Elāra was political, aggravated by his not being a patron of the Saṅgha, thereby contributing to its decline. This seems to be suggested in the startlingly non-Buddhist statement that Duṭṭhagāmaṇi's *karma* was not diminished because of the thousands that he had killed in the war against Elāra, since they were not Buddhists and therefore not human.[49] A similar

[48] *Mahāvaṃsa*, e.g. 26.11–14, 27.2ff., 28.6ff., 29.1–22, 30.42ff., 31.36ff.

[49] *Mahāvaṃsa*, 25,108–11; H.L. Seneviratne, *The Work of Kings*, 21ff.; also discussed in J. Dhirasekera, "Texts and Traditions – Warped and Distorted".

ambivalence regarding *ahiṃsā* occurs in a commentary, stating that the *yakkhas* are incapable of understanding the *dhamma* and are opposed to the Saṅgha, therefore violence against them is permissible.[50] Duṭṭhagāmaṇi has been described as an epic hero, even more so in this chronicle than the earlier one.[51]

The record begins to change with Vaṭṭagāmaṇi Abhaya, who expels the Nirgrantha/Jaina sects from their monasteries and establishes a new monastery, the Abhayagiri-vihāra.[52] This rivals the Mahāvihāra, which it supersedes when the later king Mahāsena turns hostile to the older monastery.[53] The monks of the Abhayagiri-vihāra separate themselves as the sect of the Abhayagirivādin but incorporate some elements of Mahāyāna practices, forming a powerful group, finally leading to a schism. Mahāsena not only shifted his patronage to the Abhayagiri but also confiscated the property of the Mahāvihāra, leaving it bereft of power. A rebellion against Mahāsena persuades him to patronize the Mahāvihāra once again, which gradually emerges successful from the conflict with the other monasteries. The Saṅgha seems to have been heavily into politics, and may have only seemingly distanced itself from secular power.[54] The Aśoka of the Chronicles was depicted as the firm promoter of the Theravāda sect, unlike the Aśoka of his own edicts who was willing to accommodate all sects.

There is logic to the structure of the *Mahāvaṃsa* and the narratives revolve around distinctive themes. It is a politically charged chronicle: the author, although a monk, was a member of the royal family and therefore close to court politics; but above all the narrative had to show the superiority of the Theravāda sect and its triumph in competition with others. It was written at a time when the Mahāvihāra, having known distress, saw its fortunes improving. The attitude to the audience had also changed from the century before, when the *Dīpavaṃsa* was written. The *Dīpavaṃsa* was addressing an audience with which it had some empathy, whereas

[50] R.A.L.H. Gunawardana, "The Kinsmen of the Buddha: Myth as Political Charter in the Ancient and Medieval Kingdoms of Sri Lanka".

[51] W. Geiger, *The Dīpavaṃsa and Mahāvaṃsa*, 19ff.

[52] *Mahāvaṃsa*, 33.80.

[53] *Mahāvaṃsa*, 37.3ff.

[54] S. Kiribamune, "The State and Sangha in Pre-modern Sri Lanka", 47–76.

the *Mahāvaṃsa* strikes a more polemical note. The conflict of the sects made a validation from history more urgent and the issue became one of who controlled the institutions. The re-establishment of the Mahāvihāra is projected as heralding the re-establishment of the kingdom of Laṅkā on a firmer footing than before. This is reflected in the *Mahāvaṃsa*, but more so in the *Cūlavaṃsa*.

4. Subsequent to the *Mahāvaṃsa*

From the mid-first millennium AD new texts were written, updating the history of the Theravāda Saṅgha in particular. Complementing the chronicles were the many commentaries on the earlier texts, both Canonical and non-Canonical. The commentaries were not just glosses but were partially historical writing, since they incorporated current explanations of narratives from the past. The commentaries were in turn commented upon. Pāli continued to be used, partly because the original texts were in it, and partly because it gave access to a wider audience than Sanskrit. Possibly, Sanskrit was too closely associated with brahmanical and Mahāyāna scholarship, from both of which the Theravādins were distanced.

Buddhaghosa, who came to Sri Lanka in about the fifth century, was perhaps the most important exegete, with his annotated commentaries and translated texts, resulting in an extraordinarily large scholarly output,[55] the best-known being the *Visuddhimagga*, the *Samantapāsādikā*, and the *Sumaṅgalavilāsinī*.[56] His work initiates a renaissance of the Pāli Canon, indirectly giving authority to the perspective of the Theravāda.

Buddhaghosa makes a point of listing his sources. These included popular literature as well as scholarly texts. He referred

[55] B.C. Law, *Buddhaghosa*. Buddhaghosa is associated with the authorship of, among other texts, the *Jñānodaya, Visuddhimagga*, the *Samantapāsādikā* on the *Vinaya Piṭaka,* the *Sumaṅgalavilāsinī* on the *Dīgha-nikāya*, *Papañcasūdanī* on the *Majjhima-nikāya*; the *Sāratthappakāsinī* on the *Saṃyutta-nikāya*, the *Manorathapūraṇī* on the *Aṅguttara-nikāya*, commentaries on the *Abhidhamma Piṭaka,* and the *Kathāvatthu*.

[56] H.C. Warren and Dharmanand Kosambi (eds), *Visuddhimagga of Buddhaghosa*.

to, but had little use for, the core narratives of the *Mahābhārata* and the *Rāmāyaṇa,* which he called the Bhārata-yuddha and the Sītā-haraṇa.[57] Narratives relating to the origin of the Śākyas and to rulers such as Pasenadi of Kosala and Ajātasattu of Magadha were included.[58] His coverage of Indian history remains restricted to the middle Ganges plain and up to the Aśokan period—the time frame and geography of the earlier texts. Although it is thought that he came from South India, he refers to the Andhras and Damilas as *milakkhas/mlecchas* (beyond the social pale), and as speaking a different language, thus indicating a bias in favour of Sanskrit.[59] Interestingly, he places Sihala in the same category, and this may have been an additional reason for translating Sihala texts into Pāli. For the texts from Sri Lanka he mentions using *bhānakas*—monks who transmitted the Canon orally.

Other important commentaries included those of Buddhadatta, a close contemporary of Buddhaghosa, whose *Madhuratha-vilāsinī* was a commentary on the *Buddhavaṃsa*.[60] The style is similar to that of Buddhaghosa, and the major questions posed to the text are "by whom was it spoken, where, when, for who's sake and for the sake of what?"[61]

Other commentaries were on the Chronicles, the major one on the *Mahāvaṃsa* being the twelfth-century *Vaṃsatthappakāsini*—literally, throwing light on the *vaṃsa.* It carries some additions, which are likely to have come from the original Sihala *Mahāvaṃsa Aṭṭhakathā*.[62] Myths of origin, similar to those of the texts, are also narrated in inscriptions. References are made to both Hīnayāna and Mahāyāna schools of Buddhism. The *Vaṃsatthappakāsini* not only fills out the details but presents what one historian has called a Buddhist imperial world vision.[63] This may be a

[57] *Sumaṅgalavilāsinī*, vol. I, 84; volumes II and III appeared in 1931 and 1932.

[58] *Sumaṅgalavilāsinī*, vol. I, 134, 258–60.

[59] *Sumaṅgalavilāsinī*, vol. I, 255.

[60] K.L. Hazra, *Studies on Pali Commentaries*, 89ff.

[61] *Madhuratha-vilāsinī* (trans.); I.B. Horner, *The Clarifier of the Sweet Meaning.*

[62] *Vamsatthappakāsini*, lvi–lvii.

[63] J.S. Walters, "Buddhist History", 99–152.

somewhat exaggerated phrase, but there is in this account a sense of triumphalism colouring the success of the Theravāda. Since this commentary is much later, it can take the liberty of selecting what it regards as the most appropriate from earlier sources and also refute statements that might have questioned the correctness of the *Mahāvaṃsa* version.

Various monks and scholars continued to maintain the chronicles after the writing of the *Mahāvaṃsa*, with commentaries to follow, but not all of these have survived. In the twelfth century, traditions were collated and what came to be called the *Cūlavaṃsa* was compiled as a sequel to the *Mahāvaṃsa*. A further addition to this was made in the fourteenth century, and then again in the eighteenth century, and ultimately the narrative was brought up to 1815, after which the kingdom was annexed by the British.[64] The continuation of the tradition is significant. There was recognition of the importance of having an authoritative history related to the Saṅgha, and the need therefore to update the chronicle.

The thirteenth century saw the composition of the *Dāṭhavaṃsa* and the *Thūpavaṃsa*, among other histories, where the focus was on the history of objects and relics, such as the Tooth of the Buddha. The relic, like all relics, became the idiom of a special symbol, in this case kingship, and was fought over by claimants. There seems to have been a spurt of interest in historical writing at this time, perhaps because of further sectarian conflict referred to in the texts and the need to renew legitimizing the Theravāda.

The tradition of maintaining the chronicle was regarded as important and necessary, even though during this period other texts with a flavour of history—such as biographies of kings and royal succession—were also written. Two texts on these subjects, both of a later period, have been described as secular histories: the *Rājaratnākara* and the *Rājāvalī*. There was by now a routine practice of consulting earlier texts in order to write the past afresh. The philosophical tradition was familiar to both brahmanical and Buddhist scholars, and this enhanced the force of the debate. Hermeneutics and exegeses were a continuing intellectual exercise. Buddhaghosa's work on the *Abhidhamma* strengthened the

64 L.S. Perera, "The Pali Chronicles of Ceylon", 31–2.

theological base of the Theravāda. This probably was his intention, for he barely mentions other theories, such as those current in the Abhayagiri monastery. The Mahāvihāra was in the process of rebuilding its base and the writings of Buddhaghosa were an asset.

5. Chronicles from Elsewhere

The writing of chronicles was not limited to Sri Lankan Buddhism, although I have taken these as an example. From the late first millennium AD, chronicles recorded the arrival and establishment of Buddhism in various regions, and history was a part of this story. The Tibetan Lama Tāranātha, in his much-quoted sixteenth-century *History of Buddhism in India*, intersperses the reigns of kings with Buddhist teachers, with prominence given to Aśoka. He refers to three periods when the Buddhists were persecuted but the doctrine survived. These were the reigns of Puṣyamitra Śuṅga (second century BC), the time of Turuṣkas in Kashmir (? The Hūṇas of the fifth century AD), and the burning of the Nalanda Library by *tirthikas* (non-Buddhists) in the monastery. For him, the Third Council was the one held in Kashmir and associated with Kaniṣka.

He refers to the many sources that he consulted when writing the book, particularly the sections on the kings of eastern India. Long accounts from various texts included the *Buddhapurāṅa* of Indradatta, and the works of *paṇḍita* Kṣembhadra of Magadha and *paṇḍita* Bhaṭāghāṭi.[65]

Others from western Tibet and the adjoining Himalayan region tend to be brief, the exception being the Chronicles pertaining to Ladakh, which draw on a range of sources.[66] The structure and function of these Chronicles is similar to those from Sri Lanka, though of course the context is different. The pattern of the narrative is familiar, as is the intention. The first section sets out the

[65] Tāranātha, *History of Buddhism in India*, folio 139-A, 350. See also pp. 121, 137, 141. Peter Skilling kindly drew my attention to this passage.

[66] A.H. Francke, *Antiquities of Indian Tibet*; L. Petech, *A Study of the Chronicles of Ladakh*; R. Thapar, "Antecedents, Religious Sanctions and Political Legitimation in the Ladakh Chronicles", in *Cultural Pasts*, 173–92.

myths describing primitive conditions, delving into the Northern Buddhist tradition and the Tibetan Chronicles. The second refers to the coming of Buddhism and introduces data from Tibetan sources and from the history of the other neighbour, Kashmir. Wherever Buddhism was present, connections needed to be established. Campaigns and treaties were required in many directions. The third section focuses on events concerning Ladakh, and where royal patronage is as important as political events. The data began to be collected in the second millennium by monks in the more established monasteries.

The equivalent of Aśoka was the seventh-century king Songtsen Gampo in Tibet, and the sixteenth-century Senge Namgyal in Ladakh, both of whom were patrons of Buddhism. The history of the state seems to merge with the history of the religion. Buddhism in Tibet and Ladakh was not the alternative belief system but the established religion, as was the case in Sri Lanka. This may account for the greater emphasis on chronicles rather than biographies.

6. Buddhist Monastic Chronicles: Tradition as History

The Buddhist chronicle tradition is more recognizably historical than the Puranic. There is generally a systematic narrative within a chronological framework and a clear purpose, namely, upholding the Saṅgha. The Chronicles enhanced the prestige of the Saṅgha, helped by being hinged on the historical person of the Buddha. This was not necessarily based on historical accuracy, but was strengthened by suggesting that it was historical. The monastic chronicle is in effect the chronicle of sectarian activities and the literature incorporates narratives of the patrons of the Saṅgha who were frequently persons in power. Political authority gives an edge to such patrons, for even where wealthy citizens made donations, often as handsome grants, they did not bring the aura of royal authority. This is evident from a comparison between the Chronicles and votive inscriptions recording donations to the Saṅgha during the period under discussion.[67] The interplay

[67] L.S. Perera, *The Institutions of Ancient Ceylon from Inscriptions*, vol. I.

between religion and political power is evident. The scholarly monks who were the authors of the Chronicles assumed a courtly milieu as their context. Versions of sectarian conflict heightened the context of time and heresy. The institutional foundation of the Chronicles added to their sense of specificity.

The projection of Aśoka as the patron par excellence uses history for sectarian purposes. The Chronicles seem to suggest that the establishing of Theravāda in Sri Lanka stems from various decisions taken by Aśoka: residing over the Council at Pāṭaliputra, sending Mahinda as a missionary, and his close relationship with Devānaṃpiya Tissa. Yet Aśoka has little to say on such connections. Barring the hint that the Schism Edict may have followed from the Council, it is noticeable that Aśoka refers to Taṃbapani/Tāmraparṇi—possibly Sri Lanka—rather in passing and more as a limit of his southern frontier.[68] There is no indication in his edicts of any special relationship with Sri Lanka, not even in his more retrospective Pillar Edicts. It would seem that Māhanāma exaggerated the contours of the relationship, for obvious historical reasons. One may object to the exaggeration, but one has to recognize the centrality of the resort to history.

The Chronicles and the commentaries on them are essentially the history of the Theravāda in Sri Lanka.[69] That a more wide-ranging history is also reflected can be observed in the historical process of change, of chiefdoms mutating into kingdoms, and these into early and late state systems, although the change is not described in these terms.[70] The narrative goes back briefly to origins in northern India. The organization of the early Saṅgha in India used the *gaṇa-saṅgha* system of chiefdoms as its model. The Saṅgha as described in the Chronicles points to a different context, one in which the state and kingship are central. Buddhism arrives when this change has just occurred in Sri Lanka. The paradox is that now the success of Buddhism is projected as requiring an endorsement from the state and royal authority.

The Chronicles depict a difference between societies of the

[68] J. Bloch, *Les Inscriptions d'Asoka*, 93, 130.

[69] H. Bechert, "Theravāda Buddhist Saṅgha: Some General Observations on Historical and Political Factors in its Development", 761–78.

[70] R.A.L.H. Gunawardana, *Periodisation in Sri Lankan History*.

pre-Buddhist and Buddhist times. Earlier, the record shows conflict between the existing population and migrant settlers, the latter being resented as encroachers. The migrants are said to be of a higher social status, and from them emerge the ruling families of later times. Territorially, the existing population, generally not a peasantry, can live only within the limits of the forests and come to be identified with the *mleccha*—those outside the social pale. Physical boundaries often defined social boundaries, and even the *vihāra* has its *sīmā* (boundaries). Kingship is accompanied by the appropriation of Mauryan symbols of power, perhaps to reiterate the change. The politics are those of rival chiefdoms and kingdoms, until the kingdom at Anurādhapura comes to dominate politics.

The monks, originally housed in rock-cut cells, move into monasteries in the vicinity of settlements and of the capital. The king, as patron, gifted buildings to the Saṅgha. Among these are included large water reservoirs, constructed under royal patronage, changing the resource base of the region to wet rice cultivation. This encourages land being granted to monasteries and eventually results in what has been called monastic landlordism.[71] Such grants meant a judicial and financial immunity from royal officials, which immunity buttressed a status already equivalent to the landowning nobility and higher bureaucracy. Given this, monastic participation in politics would have been expected. That Mahāsena confiscated the property of the Mahāvihāra was part of the crisis.[72]

Maintaining property was recognized as one category of the monk's work, apart from meditation and recitation, and some *bhikṣus/bhikkhus* had also to work in a managerial capacity, even performing other jobs. These duties were classified at some length, with comments on supervisory tasks. If rosters had to be kept, records would be the next step.[73]

The extensive enshrining and worshipping of relics in various parts of the subcontinent led to monuments and structures

[71] H.H. Gerth and C.W. Mills (eds), *From Max Weber*, 332ff.; Max Weber, *Economy and Society*, vol. II, 586ff.; R.A.L.H. Gunawardana, *Robe and Plough, Monasticism and Economic Interest in Early Medieval Sri Lanka.*

[72] *Mahāvaṃsa*, 37.8–9, 36ff.

[73] J. Silk, *Managing Monks*, 22ff., 98ff., 160ff.

attracting a large lay following. This was seen as a catchment of support for the royal patron, which consolidated the authority of the state and of the sect it patronized.

Manipulation of succession is partially an indication of changed relations between the central state and its dependencies. This is also reflected in splinter groups of the Saṅgha getting access to patronage, as in the rise of the Abhayagiri faction. Such segmentation requires an acceleration of claims to legitimacy, and therefore a greater inclusion of political factions in the narrative.

These changes are also reflected in the titles given to rulers. *Gāmaṇi* refers to an important person, a chief or headman or leader, and not necessarily a king.[74] Duṭṭhagāmaṇi is clearly the former at the start, and only later does he become a regular king or *mahārāja*. The use of the title *mahārāja* in the *Mahāvaṃsa* was either restricted to monks addressing the king or used for those highly respected. This may be a reflection of its wider use at the time. That both Vijaya and Devānaṃpiya Tissa are called *mahārāja* does not make them equal in terms of royal status, since the status implicit in the title was not unchanging over time.

The sacral power of the Saṅgha is symbolized in the *bhikkhu*, the renunciate monk. The notion of divinity is absent. The *bhikkhu* who collects alms from the settlement is not the ultimate renunciate, for he is basically changing one order of life for another. Joining the order of monks or nuns remains a social role since both the monk and the monastery are dependent on society.[75] The sacred cannot be manipulated for political ends, but the *mahāthera* as head of the monastery had a relationship with the king that required a balance of the two.

The writing of chronicles indicates that despite Buddhism being established in some regions, a historical tradition was necessary to buttress it, a need heightened by not only non-Buddhist neighbours but also the competition between the various Buddhist sects. Underlining the history of the religion was not enough. The authority of a particular sect had to be justified, even drawing on

[74] T. Hettiarachchy, *History of Kingship in Ceylon upto the Fourth Century* AD.

[75] R. Thapar, "Renunciation: The Making of a Counter-culture?", in *Cultural Pasts*, 876–913.

secular governance. Furthermore, kingship had come to be recognized as the sole legitimate political institution: hence the attempt to record king lists from Devānaṃpiya Tissa of the third century BC to Mahāsena of the fourth century AD. As in the case of the *Purāṇas*, so too with the Ceylon Chronicles, this was the crucial period when the historical tradition had to be formalized and prised out of floating oral traditions. The form taken by the various categories of texts could differ, but their underlying similarity as projects towards establishing a historical tradition is visible.

The Buddhist Saṅgha, now also playing a political role, needed to establish its status as the pre-eminent religious institution. One way of doing this was by endorsing kingship. A historical tradition was needed to explain the economic power of the monasteries, to indicate when and how and for which pious purposes the Saṅgha obtained an endowment or a grant. To prevent the image of the Saṅgha becoming that of just another avaricious institution, the morality and piety of its actions, which brought the Saṅgha wealth, had to be emphasized or even exaggerated, going back to earlier times. The doctrine had been subject to numerous controversies, the major ones being sorted out at the various Councils, the lesser ones continuing at a less obvious level and giving way to yet newer ones. Sectarian differences and loyalties required a record of the patriarchs and Elders of the Saṅgha, the Theras, whose particular interpretations of the doctrines were to be followed. This intensifies the rivalry among the sectarian Saṅghas—as narrated for instance in that between the Mahāvihāra and the Abhayagiri-vihāra. From the mid-first millennium the Theravāda at the Mahāvihāra gained ascendancy, lauding the Theravāda interpretation of the doctrine and its version of Buddhism in Sri Lanka. These chronicles are statements from the Mahāvihāra–Theravāda perspective. Had anything similar survived from the Abhayagiri monastery, the context would have been even sharper and the Mahāvihāra version contested. This suggests the process of how a hegemonic religious institution can consolidate its authority by deploying historical narrative to its advantage. The process has been recognized in other institutions in modern times, but is rarely used in analysing similar institutions of the early past. The question that needs to be addressed is whether the history of a religious institution as a disguised defence of political power is not in effect also a project of writing history.[76]

The proselytizing mission of Buddhism is said to have become active after the Third Council at Pāṭaliputra. Records of these missions were presumably kept. By the fifth century AD, with Buddhism having centres in Central and South East Asia, increasing sectarian rivalries sought sanction from their own attempts at constructing historical traditions, as is evident from the literature of Northern Buddhism. Introducing Buddhism to new areas, both within the subcontinent and elsewhere, meant having to accommodate local rituals, belief systems, and ideas, an accommodation requiring concessions on both sides.

Historicity was subjected to the niceties of the *kāvya* or poetic style, where literary embellishment could override precision in factual narration. Moral lessons were also to be drawn from the past, particularly from the action of kings. Patronage ranked high in the list of meritorious actions. There is an attempt to provide a historical framework by referring to ruling kings, providing in addition a chronological cross-reference.[77] Such histories were probably taken from various traditions, some no longer available, and given a Buddhist gloss. The centrality of Aśoka is a striking contrast to his being a mere name in a king-list in Puranic sources. After Aśoka the history of the middle Ganges plain recedes and other areas such as South India and later Kaliṅga are more frequently mentioned.

The importance of kingship perhaps also draws on the idea that the Buddha could either have become a *cakkavatti* or a *bodhisattva*; the duality is that of conquest or renunciation. However, this duality is not as sharp as is sometimes suggested in modern writing. It is as well to keep in mind that the *cakkavatti* was a conqueror but not given to violence. The practise of law, justice, and righteous rule made a worthy king. This was not the *kṣatriya* ethic of conquest by the *digvijayin*. The *bodhisattva* ideal allows the king

[76] Rukun Advani has pointed to a comparison with the study of the Sikh Khalsa as analysed by H. Oberoi, *The Construction of Religious Boundaries*, as one among other such works on this theme.

[77] *Mahāvaṃsa*, xli.

to become a source of both political and religious power, and the two form an interface.

A moot question is whether *dhamma* is to be read as religion or in a broader context as social ethics. The *cakkavatti*, as promoter and protector of the *dhamma*, is not merely a factor in the well-being of the Saṅgha. He is also concerned with *rājadhamma* laying emphasis on the nature of governance. Although there is a seeming contradiction in conquest and renunciation, nevertheless acting righteously is what determines each. Thus the ideal political state was one governed by *dhamma*. The rituals of kingship can be brahmanical but the ethic has to be Buddhist.[78] Kings from history who were quoted as close to the ideal are Bimbisāra and Pasenadi. Neither of these were Buddhists and Pasenadi is known to have performed brahmanical rituals, but both are thought to have ruled according to the *dhamma*.[79] However, the problem is that the social articulation of the ethic differs. In theory, the Buddhist ethic does not admit of divine intervention or of inequality in a society, whereas the brahmanical ethic gets its sanction from the intervention of deity and the inequalities of *varṇa*.

The close relationship between the king and the Saṅgha, as supposedly practised by Aśoka, is consciously emulated by Devānaṃpiya Tissa and later by Parakkambāhu/Parākramabāhu I.[80] There is a correlation with Damila power and patronage, for each time the Damilas are defeated the Saṅgha revives. In conditions of adversity where the king was required to consolidate power, the monastic networks could be a support—provided there was harmony among the sects and between them and the king. Where sectarian conflicts prevailed, political factionalism was also prevalent, as with Mahāvihāra and Abhayagiri. Where sects other than Buddhists were also present, such as the Jainas/Nirgranthas and the Ājīvikas,[81] there could be further tension.

The need to maintain a historical record becomes necessary

[78] R. Lingat, *Royautes Bouddhiques*, 63ff.

[79] T. Ling, *The Buddha*; R. Heine-Geldern, *Concept of State and Kingship in Southeast Asia*.

[80] T. Hettiarachchy, *History of Kingship in Ceylon upto the Fourth Century* AD, 166ff.

[81] *Mahāvaṃsa*, 10.96–102.

when rival sectarian conflicts threaten those that are established, or when new ones become powerful. The Damila political threat to the Mahāvihāra coincided with the Canon being given a more permanent written form. The history of the Mahāvihāra becomes particularly necessary when the Abhayagiri sect becomes a successful competitor, and more so when it supersedes, however briefly, the earlier institution. Establishing the rights of rival monasteries also encouraged the keeping of historical records and claiming ancient ancestry. The Abhayagiri schism traces itself back to the Vajjiputtas at the Council of Vaiśāli in an obvious attempt to give itself an ancestry as old, or older, than the Theravāda.

The Mahāvihāra attacked the new doctrines.[82] Why Vaṭṭagāmaṇi supported the Abhayagiri schism has a complex political answer. Built on an earlier Jaina/Nirgrantha site which Vaṭṭagāmaṇi wished to destroy, the initial move may have been only against the Nirgranthas and associated sects. But when he recognized the political potential of a new monastic focus, he may have decided to patronize a new sect, and it was this potential that needled the Mahāvihāra—or this is how the latter seems to have viewed it.

When the Mahāvihāra regains its position, its history becomes imperative afresh. The *Dīpavaṃsa* is insufficient. The *Mahāvaṃsa* has a more definitive agenda and sharpens the focus of the conflict, and, above all, of its pre-eminence. This is maintained in subsequent histories, which cover every aspect of the support for the Theravāda—royal patronage, other monasteries, relics, and *stūpas*.

It was a time of many debates on the interpretation of the doctrine, with contests between the sects supporting either the Hīnayāna or the Mahāyāna schools. The expansion of the latter sects extended the horizon of the debates. It was thought that there was some Mahāyāna teaching in Sri Lanka.[83] If the Abhayagiri and Jetavana monasteries were also centres of important traditions, and had their versions survived in the same way as those

[82] W.M.K. Wijetunga, "The Spread of Heterodox Buddhist Doctrines in Early Ceylon", 14–28.

[83] J.C. Holt, *Buddha in the Crown: Avalokitesvara in the Buddhist Tradition of Sri Lanka*.

of the Mahāvihāra, a comparative study would have been useful to understanding the rivalry. Mention of the Theravāda comes fairly late in the texts and may more often have been subsumed in references to the Mahāvihāra.

It was therefore required that the history of the Mahāvihāra should explicitly restate the monastery as the legitimate and recognized Saṅgha, and that the history of Sri Lanka up to that point be co-opted into the history of the Mahāvihāra monastery. The requirement of history could also result from political conflict where the authors of the tradition supported one party against the other.[84] Thus the Saṅgha supported Duṭṭhagāmaṇi against Elāra, arguing that the former was defending Buddhism. Was the conflict deliberately posed in these terms? In taking over the Duṭṭhagāmaṇi epic, was the author converting it conveniently into a story supporting the Saṅgha? The opposition was fierce at times, and is reminiscent of other heresies and inquisitions when books were burnt and monks banished. The king, Mahāsena, also destroyed brahmanical shrines, and the connection with South India was part of the politics of this region—given the presence of the Damilas. It was not just a conflict over religious belief, because even the two Buddhist sects were fiercely opposed. Mahāsena becomes king after a fairly long period of quick turnovers among rulers and disturbed conditions resulting from usurpers and rebels, both Sihala and Damila.

The *Dīpavaṃsa* and the *Mahāvaṃsa* were written subsequent to two crises in Theravāda Buddhism. The first was when the Damilas from South India began to rule intermittently and were not patrons of the Mahāvihāra. Yet the *Dīpavaṃsa* is not as hostile to them as the later Chronicle, which makes much of Duṭṭhagāmaṇi defeating the Damilas. The second crisis had greater gravity when in the conflict between the Mahāvihāra and the Abhayagiri-vihāra the king almost extinguished the Mahāvihāra. The Chronicles date to when the Mahāvihāra was rejuvenated and its success in doing so was strengthened by legitimacy from history.

Royal favour virtually controls the fortunes of the Mahāvihāra. This is somewhat surprising as the votive inscriptions from

[84] E.g., *Cūlavaṃsa*, 37.53–90.

various places suggest a substantial and continuous lay following. The Chronicles were focusing on events in the capital Anurādhapura. The schisms in the Saṅgha were not restricted to controversies over the teachings or the regulations for monks and extended into court politics. The resort to narratives of a believed history were intended as indicating the truth of the doctrine, illustrating once again the role of history in the projection of what we today call ideology.

Chronicles were, thus, a significant form taken by the Buddhist historical tradition. Ideas of a historical past were embedded in the Canon. It was now less a question of adjusting regulations listed in the Canon and more of making a new bid for the authority of the Saṅgha. The Chronicle became the form for this and was a category of text external to the Canon. This was not necessarily the pattern in every region where Buddhism was present. In northwestern India, for instance, there appears to have been a greater investment in biographies and biographical fragments contributing to the historical tradition.

11

Buddhist Biographies

1. Early Biographies

Moving away from the history of the Saṅgha and from monastic chronicles, another kind of text came to be used to narrate the Buddhist view of the past through biographies of the Buddha, or personalized narratives underlining his ideas. Partial biographies included those of persons important to the history of Buddhism, predictably the emperor Aśoka. The biographical genre required the subject to be presented in a historical form for the narrative to be viable. Inevitably, therefore, the earliest biographies evoked the canonical tradition. However, whereas in the Pāli Buddhist tradition biographies are few, with narratives on the Saṅgha and monasteries being frequent, biographies seem to have been more popular in the Northern tradition. A possible reason may have been that the Saṅgha in north-western India did not have as close a relationship with royalty as did the Mahāvihāra, nor as fierce a rivalry with other Buddhist sects competing for status.

The writing of such biographies comes into its own at the turn of the Christian era and the early centuries AD. The biography was not necessarily a life history from birth to death, for often, only the salient events were narrated. Nor was the biography always devoid of hagiography, particularly in the case of the Buddha.

The *Buddhavaṃsa* narrates the succession of the previous twenty-four Buddhas and provides a prelude to Gautama,[1] taking the narrative back to *asankhya* (uncountable) *kappas* (eons)

[1] R. Morris (ed.), *The Buddhavaṃsa and the Cariya-piṭaka.*

and underlining the impermanence of time.[2] Utopian beginnings are exaggerated, while the chronicle of Gautama becomes more realistic. This was doubtless intended both as ancestry and as contrast. It traces the evolution of a *bodhisattva* to Buddhahood, thus claiming to cover a span of history from remote antiquity, to less remote history, and eventually to recent history. These time divisions become axiomatic to representing the past history of the Buddhas.

Reference to the Buddha to come, the Buddha Maitreya/Metteya, was a logical continuation of the *Buddhavaṃsa* and the increasing visibility of Maitreya as the future Buddha. Mentioned somewhat in passing in the *Dīgha-nikāya*, he comes into his own by the early Christian era. The projection of a future Buddha had several reasons: schisms, splits, and the persecutions of sects which, in desperation, have to believe in the impending arrival of a saviour; the ambience of the times, which required every religion to have such a figure—St John of the Revelations among Christians, Saoshyant among Zoroastrians, Kalkin among Vaiṣṇavas; and the downswing in the cycle of time which brings the fear of a cataclysm before the upswing begins.[3] A collection of texts, the *Anāgatavaṃsa*, presents a history of the future where Metteya plays a central role. His utopia will bring ample wealth and no labour. Desire, hunger, and old age will disappear and men and women will live to an extraordinary age. His dispensation will last for 101,000 years. Calculating in millennia could favour a forward projection of history.[4]

A seeming link to the idea of a future Buddha was the discussion on the decline of the *saddharma* (the good law), conforming to the general decline of the human condition.[5] In this case, the deterioration will be of the Saṅgha, and of its monks who will stop observing the precepts, and foreign kings who will attack Buddhists. A distinction is made, however, between the immutability

[2] *The Minor Anthologies of the Pali Canon*, vol. III.

[3] R. Thapar, "Millenarianism and Religion in Early India", in *Cultural Pasts*, 946–61.

[4] S. Collins, *Selfless Persons: Imagery and Thought in Thervāda Buddhism*, 355.

[5] E. Lamotte, *History of Indian Buddhism*, 191ff.

of the teaching and the existence of the Saṅgha. The first cannot disappear but the second can be evanescent. Attempts were made to calculate precisely when this would happen, but the date kept shifting—from 500 years after the *mahāparinirvāṇa* to 1500 years. The early termination is linked in some texts to the admission of women into the Order. Tibetan sources refer to a longer time span of 2000 to 3000 years. Buddhaghosa extends it to 5000 years and some Chinese commentaries take it to 12,000 years.

The *Nidāna-kathā* is also a narration of the lineage of the Buddhas, not in terms of family and descent but as a succession of Buddhas.[6] The life of Gautama is reiterated from the Canon but punctuated with miraculous events at crucial points. Hints of divinity shift the focus from his teaching to his person. The narratives are stylistically different from the brief biographies in earlier texts. The Buddhas appear with regularity, although not quite like *avatāras* since they do not take diverse forms.

Early elements of the Buddha biography are recorded in conversational form, and in ballad style in the *Sutta-nipāta* of the *Khuddaka-nikāya*.[7] Parallel to this are the *Jātakas*, which mix narratives supposedly of the past with a Buddhist moral, the narrative serving as argument.[8] They are reminiscent of some revised versions of epic stories which illustrate a moral point, except that the *Jātaka* stories do so invariably. The opening sentence of many stories attempts a historical flavour via references to a place, a time, and a ruler. The *Jātakas* range from fables emphasizing the importance of *nīti* (ethics) and politics, to tales, anecdotes, sayings, and pious legends with a moral, and are told in the form of narratives, ballads, and small epics. Those with an *itihāsa* connection are possibly drawn from a wider oral tradition and correspond to the stereotypes in such narratives, as for example the theme of exile, used to great effect in the *Vessantara Jātaka*.[9] Exile can be a motif in a narrative, or it can be part of a historical perspective encapsulating the settlement and colonization of a new area. Story

[6] T.W. Rhys Davids, *Buddhist Birth Stories*.

[7] D. Anderson and H. Smith (eds), *The Suttanipāta*, Pabbaja-sutta 3.1; Padhana-sutta 3.2; Nalaka-sutta 3.11.

[8] M. Winternitz, *History of Indian Literature*, vol. II, 113ff.

[9] *Vessantara Jātaka*, no. 547, in *The Jātaka*, ed. E.B. Cowell; see also nos. 461, 523, 539, and 544.

lines were borrowed indiscriminately across traditions but given a sectarian twist.

The *Kathāvatthu* of the *Abhidhamma Piṭaka* relates events in the history of Buddhism,[10] but is not accepted by all Buddhist sects. It takes the form of a clarification of the doctrine through a catechism which also touches on episodes of the Buddha's life.[11] References are also made in a systematic way to the various sects and their interpretations of the doctrine. The Theravāda claims that this text was compiled by Tissa Moggaliputta for use in the Third Council at Pāṭaliputra, but some other sects disagree. Even if this contention is correct, the text was probably augmented each time there was a new controversy. Thus, at one level, the historical material was built into the Canon through the sheer necessity of maintaining a record of disputations and controversies. The present version of the *Kathāvatthu* dates to the early centuries AD.

Biographies of the Buddha are also part of the collections relating to the Sarvāstivāda sect. According to Theravāda history, this sect had split off at the Council at Pāṭaliputra and was influential in Mathura, Kashmir, and Gandhāra. The texts that ensued are often written in Hybrid Sanskrit. Earlier forms are likely to have been written in the regional Gāndhārī Prākrit, which survive in fragments. The Sanskrit Canon is more fully available in Tibetan and Chinese translations used by the missions to these areas.[12] Some major non-Canonical works, such as the *Buddhacarita*, *Mahāvastu*, *Lalitavistara*, and *Divyāvadāna*, were also written in Sanskrit or Hybrid Sanskrit. In a comparison of the Pāli and Sanskrit Canon there is corroboration in some and divergence at other points. This acts as a useful means of correlating statements from one source to another.

Biography hints at a tendency to individualism and this may be ascribed to the initial growth of Buddhism at urban centres.[13] In the early phase the ideal Buddhist was the *arhant*—he who

[10] M. Winternitz, *History of Indian Literature*, vol. II, 169ff.; *Kathāvatthu*, vols I and II; Shwe Zan Aung and C. Rhys Davids (trans.), *Points of Controversy, The Kathāvatthu*.

[11] Shwe Zan Aung and C. Rhys Davids (trans.), *Points of Controversy*, e.g., 1.3.2ff., 1.5.15, 1.1.243, 2.3.20, 2.7–11, 3.1.1–16, 18.5.1–5, 21.4.1–5.

[12] M. Winternitz, *History of Indian Literature*, vol. II, 227ff.

[13] E. Conze, *A Short History of Buddhism*.

is free from desire and consequently from rebirth. Later, the *bodhisattva* emerged as the role-model in trying to help others towards *nirvāṇa*. The focus then moves to the *siddha* who acquires powers over the cosmos. Each of these phases produces its own Canonical literature, although there is a flow from one to the other. The biography of the Buddha was encouraged by the fact that the Buddha was a historical person. The two central events—his enlightenment and his death—become pivotal. His ashes and small bones, venerated as relics, perhaps encouraged the continuity of presence, annulling time. Later, when the Buddha was viewed as a transcendental being and not merely as a historical person, this view changed. The degree to which the Buddha was projected as human became controversial and the worship of his bodily relics became central to ritual. The physical body is also important in demarcating the thirty-two auspicious marks of the man who is destined to be either a Buddha or a *cakravartin* (universal monarch).

The concern with the history of Buddhism and the biography of the Buddha was not, as we have seen, confined to Canonical literature. Towards the turn of the Christian era non-Canonical writing developed around these themes. Thus the *avadānas*—celebrating great and glorious religious deeds—relate stories of the Buddha or of *bodhisattvas* or of important persons, and present them as part of the past. The *Buddhāvadāna* is among the earliest narrating the glory of the historical Buddha; of the *paccekabuddhas,* who have become enlightened but do not proclaim the doctrine; and of the important Theras and Therīs (monks and nuns).[14] The *avadānas* have a clearly defined format. They begin with an adoration of a previous Buddha by a past devotee, with the former then prophesying the rebirth of the devotee and the discovery of the Buddha by the devotee. Patrons of the Buddhist Saṅgha are the protagonists in the new versions of the past. The *avadānas* had elements of biography but were distinct from the *caritas* (biographies).

2. The *Buddhacarita*

The most impressive biography of the Buddha was undoubtedly the *Buddhacarita* of Aśvaghoṣa, dated to the first century AD or

[14] M. Winternitz, *History of Indian Literature*, vol. II, 158ff.

soon after.[15] It has on occasion been described as hagiography; nevertheless it remains a valuable demonstration of how biography was used as a form of history. As late as the seventh–eighth centuries, Chinese Buddhist monks visiting India referred to the popularity of the *Buddhacarita* as still read or sung in recitation.[16] Of the seventeen chapters of the text, only the first thirteen are authenticated as the work of Aśvaghoṣa, the latter four being attributed to a later author. The original *Buddhacarita* covered the life of the Buddha, but the existing Sanskrit text stops soon after the enlightenment—the later chapters exist in a Chinese translation. The former are characterized by high quality Sanskrit courtly poetry. Some ideas parallel narratives in the Vālmīki *Rāmāyaṇa* and the *Jātakas*, since any serious literary person would have been familiar by this time with the Vālmīki text.[17] That the Śākyas and the lineage of Rāma were said to be of the Sūryavaṃśa may have strengthened the connection,

The question has been asked whether the *Buddhacarita* was written both as a fine biography of the Buddha and also as a defence of Buddhism against brahmanical attacks.[18] As we have seen, recent views have argued for the late books of the *Mahābhārata* being in part responses to the competitive popularity of Buddhism, making Rāma and Yudhiṣṭhira symbols of *dharma*. Could the *Buddhacarita* have also been partially a response to this debate?

Aśvaghoṣa's knowledge of the Śānti *parvan* of the *Mahābhārata* is evident from his discussion on kingship and ethics—a matter of primary concern to the *rājadharma* section of the Śānti *parvan* and to the Buddhist understanding of kingship, all of the ongoing debate. This had doubtless been fuelled by Aśoka endorsing a social ethic akin to the Buddhist as his way of governance. Aśvaghoṣa's depiction of Māra, the evil one, taunting the Buddha on the eve of his enlightenment—urging him to follow his *svadharma,* his

[15] *The Buddhacarita or the Acts of the Buddha*; *Life of the Buddha by Ashvaghosha*; A. Hiltebeitel, "Aśvaghoṣa's *Buddhacarita*: The First Known Close and Careful Reading of the Brahmanical Sanskrit Epics", 229–86.

[16] E.g., I Tsing, quoted in S. Beal, *The Romantic Legend of Sakya Buddha*, 256ff.

[17] *Buddhacarita*, 1.43, 6.36, 8.8, 8.81, 9.9.

[18] *Life of the Buddha by Ashvaghosha*, xixff.; *Aśvaghoṣa's Buddhacarita, or Acts of the Buddha*, Introduction by E.H. Johnston (trans.).

varṇa duty as a *kṣatriya* and be a king and a warrior rather than a renunciate—suggests parallels with the dialogue in the *Bhagavad-Gītā*. The equating of Māra with Kṛṣṇa is telling![19]

The high point in the *Buddhacarita* is the Buddha's enlightenment towards which the action moves. Conversions are described as the *digvijaya* of the Buddha, invoking a simile from heroic literature. This is underlined by frequent comparisons with epic heroes such as Yayāti, Janaka, Bhīṣma, Mandhātṛ, Purūravas, and Śantanu, depending on the context. The discourse relates to *kṣatriyas* and it is the earlier heroes of the Sūryavaṃśa who are the role-models. The Buddha's *kṣatriya* antecedents are heavily underlined, prior to his being chronologically associated with the kings of early dynasties. This suggests some shift in emphasis.

The Buddha's upbringing follows that of a royal prince of contemporary times. In this the author shows little historical awareness that the Śākya clan would have functioned differently, a difference that would have been evident on a careful reading of the *Sutta Piṭaka*. Some persons familiar from other Buddhist texts are introduced, such as Bimbisāra trying to dissuade Gautama from asceticism. The kernel of belief in this text lay in devotion to the Buddha and this, as has been noticed, was parallel to the worship of the Puranic deities in the form of *bhakti*—devotion to and sharing in the grace of the deity, and to that extent differs from the Pāli Canon. But the insistence on the historicity of the Buddha remains central, perhaps also hinting at a dialogue between the Buddhist authors and the emergent Puranic tradition, despite the latter reviling the Buddha.[20]

That a pattern developed for the Buddha biography is evident from a still later Tibetan biography.[21] Here the origin myth goes back to timeless time, followed by the story of Mahāsammata and the subsequent genealogy and origin of the Śākyas. The life of the Buddha coincides chronologically with the kingdoms of Kosala, Magadha, Avanti, Kauśāmbī, and the confederacy of the

[19] A. Hiltebeitel, "Aśvaghoṣa's *Buddhacarita*: The First Known Close and Careful Reading of the Brahmanical Sanskrit Epics", 276.

[20] R. Thapar, "The *Purāṇas*: Heresy and the *Vaṃśānucarita*", 28–49.

[21] *Life of the Buddha and the Early History of the Order*.

Vṛjjis. The campaign of Magadha against the Vṛjjis is described, as also various conspiracies among the kingdoms. The Buddha is honoured as a *cakravartin* on his death. The Saṅgha declines with the passing away of the leading disciples, although this is sought to be corrected by the monk Kāśyapa. The founding of another sect that settled in Kashmir is narrated, paralleling those described for Sri Lanka and Gandhāra. The account continues with schisms and sects. It is also said that 137 years after the death of the Buddha the rulers of Magadha, Nanda and Mahāpadma, convened an assembly to discuss problems facing the doctrine.[22] Although the Council of Pāṭaliputra is not mentioned, a schism in the reign of Dhammasoka, 160 years after the death of the Buddha, is referred to. This chronology differs from that of the Ceylon Chronicles, but the *mahāparinirvāṇa* again predates the Nanda dynasty.

The biographies in general have certain common features. The earlier genealogies have no regnal years but are similar in style to the descent lists of the the *Purāṇas*. The Śākyas mark a turning point, as the societies where the Buddha preaches are already mutating into kingship and a state system.[23] The emphasis on the conversion of kings and their participation in the affairs of the Saṅgha, such as calling the Councils, marks the difference. It is significant that the clans of the Vṛjji confederacy play a lesser role in this activity, although in the Canon the Buddha states that the Saṅgha should function in a manner similar to that of the assemblies of the clans.

3. The *Mahāvastu* and the *Lalitavistara*

The translation into Chinese of many stories on the life of the Buddha appears under a generic title in the early centuries AD.[24]

[22] These dates allow little time between the Councils and do not refer to the reigns of Candragupta and Bindusāra that are mentioned in the Pāli Chronicles.

[23] R. Thapar, *From Lineage to State*, 147–8.

[24] *Fo-pen-hsing-chi-ching*, viff. Confucian and Taoist influences on Chinese translations of Buddhist texts have been noticed: H. Nakamura, "The Influence of Confucian Ethics on the Chinese Translation of Buddhist Sutras", 156–70; E. Lamotte, *History of Indian Buddhism*, 177, 654–5.

The *Abhiniṣkramaṇa Sūtra*, taken to China, relates the accepted narrative of the Buddha's life, but with a few changes in name and minor activities. The author was said to have been a Buddhist monk from Gandhāra who realized the necessity of a biography in his mission to China in order to acquaint the new converts with the life and teaching of the Buddha. This was obviously an easier way to start than to plunge into the Canon. It might explain in part the many biographies in the Northern Tradition. The colophon of the text claims that the stories of the Buddha's biography had various titles in India and lists these as the *Mahāvastu* and the *Lalitavistara*, among others.

The *rājavaṃśa* (succession of rulers) begins in remote times and traces many generations of *cakravartins* and ultimately describes the rise of the Ikṣvāku lineage to which the Śākyas belonged. The earlier ancestral figure is called Sammata. The smaller *cakravartins* are associated with establishing various cities. The origin of the Śākya clan carries the usual symbolism of parents in exile. Political power and its relations with the Buddha are deliberately brought in when we are told that the king of Magadha, Bimbisāra, anxious that he should be the most powerful ruler, was put out when he heard the prophecy that the Buddha would be a world conqueror. However, when the Buddha comes to the capital to preach, Bimbisāra states that the boon he wanted was that he be taught by the Buddha. Once again political power is humbled before the Buddha. Since these texts were about the Buddha and not the history of the local Saṅgha, political power was predictably subordinate. The attempt is to include history and chronology in the biography.

The *Mahāvastu* of the Mahāsaṅghika sect is dated to about the third century AD.[25] Although in essence a compendium of legends about the Buddha, it is nevertheless seen as a popular biography of a historical person. The present text incorporates earlier material and is composed partly in Hybrid Sanskrit and partly in Prākrit.[26] Some legends are evocative of the Pāli *Vinaya*, others draw on

[25] *Mahāvastu*, ed. E. Senart, 3 vols; *The Mahāvastu*, trans. J.J. Jones.

[26] *Mahāvastu*, trans. J.J. Jones, vol. I, x–xiff; B.C. Law, *A Study of the Mahāvastu*.

the *Nidāna-kathā*, and some parallel parts of the *Divyāvadāna*, although their sectarian origins differ. The genealogies of *kṣatriyas* start with an account of creation, followed by the lineages, focus on the descent of the Śākyas.

The biography is based on the *Nidāna-kathā*, but its style is more ornate and the story is replete with miracles. It begins with narratives of the previous Buddhas, followed by those about Gautama Buddha. The *rājavaṃśa* (succession of rulers) relates the genesis of the world and repeats in effect the story of the Mahāsammata as given in the Canon.[27] The Śākyas are traced back to Ikṣvāku, who in turn is traced to the Mahāsammata, and not to Manu as in the *Purāṇas*. The *rājavaṃsa* elaborates on the account of creation and the initial state of bliss as given in the *Dīgha-nikāya*.[28] The Mahāsammata when selected and authorized to rule was compensated with a wage of one-sixth of the produce (*saḍbhāga*), now a regular tax collected by the king. Because he was deserving of this he was a *rājā*, and as a *kṣatriya* he had to protect the people. The election is a concession to his sovereignty. Subsequent to this came the genealogy of the successor kings.

The origin of the Śākyas and the Koliyas, is in essentials the same story as the earlier one. The young Koliya men have to be trained to the ways of the Śākyas, thus pointing to the superiority of the latter. The Koliyas owe their importance to the Buddha's mother, being of their clan. The life of the Buddha covers his birth, renunciation, enlightenment, teaching, disciples, the multiple conversions of various categories of people to his doctrine, and his eventual passing away. Interspersed with this are a large number of stories in the style of the *Jātakas*, each with a moral or a reference to an earlier incarnation of the Buddha as a human or an animal or bird.

Two strands are intertwined. One is Gautama working his way towards appearing on earth as a Buddha, for which he had to prepare himself through almost infinite time. The other is the usual concern that his status on earth derives from the authority of being born in an appropriate lineage. Both strands have been

[27] *Dīgha-nikāya*, 3.84ff.; *Mahāvastu*, I.338–48.
[28] *Mahāvastu*, I.338–52ff.

teased out at some length. The narrative incorporates three themes. The first is that of the origins of society and rulership, which is the antecedent for the actions of the Buddha; yet, occasionally, it has the imprint of times later than that of the Pāli Canon. The second is the ancestry of the Buddha being traced back to the Mahāsammata and not to Ikṣvāku. The Buddha is a *kṣatriya* and has the right to claim authority over society, which authority he prefers to claim not as a king but as a renunciate. The Śākya genealogy underlines the correct status of the authority. Having established his antecedents and the general formulations supporting his mission, the third section highlights his life and activities.

The Buddha's correlation with political authority is stated more directly in the conversion of Bimbisāra. Whereas in the Pāli texts Bimbisāra is said to have met the Buddha and perhaps even tried to dissuade him from renunciation, here the relationship is reversed and Bimbisāra is said not only to be anxious to meet the Buddha, but on meeting him is converted.[29] Bimbisāra is also anxious for the approval of the Buddha. When he visits the Buddha he is accompanied not only by his court, all in their richest array, but also by the townsmen, guild members, merchants, and professionals, almost as if the approval was the validation of his being king. The doctrine becomes more important than the historical significance of the conversion of Bimbisāra; although by implication it is suggested that the conversion was not just of the king but of all his subjects as well.

The life of the Buddha is also narrated in the *Lalitavistara*, starting with his descent from the Tuṣita heaven, and the complexities of choosing his family are discussed.[30] The sequence of events is again based on the *Nidāna-kathā.* The heavy emphasis on his divinity and miraculous birth is a change from the Pāli Canon and reflects the sectarian bias of the author.

Buddhas are not born in low-caste families, such as those of the *caṇḍāla* or *pukkusa*. Only *brāhmaṇa* and *kṣatriya* families are appropriate, and the choice between these would depend on which was the more respected status at the time. The choice of Śuddhodana and the Śākyas is determined by their pure descent as

[29] *Mahāvastu*, 3.437; *Mahāvagga*, 1.22.

[30] *Lalitavistara*, ed. S. Lefmann; *Lalitavistara*, ed. R. Mitra.

well as their many virtues. Mention is made of various kingdoms that were powerful, with royal families that could qualify to be associated with the Buddha's birth—Magadha, Kosala, Kauśāmbī, Avanti, Mathura, Mithila, Hastināpura under the Pāṇḍavas, and Vaiśāli as the centre of the Vṛjji confederacy, a reasonably accurate list from a perspective of half a millennium later. All these are dismissed as having blemishes of various kinds. They were ruled either by illegitimate kings, such as the Pāṇḍavas who claimed to be sons of gods, or others who were of impure descent, or who were tyrants. Sixteen kingdoms are referred to and this number could be from the Pāli Canon. This was a reference to a history of five centuries ago as they no longer existed as independent states.

The writing of these biographies was a counterpart to changes in the doctrine of Mahāyāna Buddhism. Whereas it was claimed that their texts had incorporated the words of the Buddha, at the same time the historical Buddha began to be less insistently etched. The Buddha was projected as the embodiment of *dharma* and some even argued against his *nirvāṇa*, maintaining that he was virtually immortal. Biographies were sliding into hagiography.

4. The *Divyāvadāna*

A different kind of composition narrating biographical episodes seeks to recall the activities of a past king and patron of the Saṅgha—the emperor Aśoka. The possibility of a Sanskrit Buddhist text veering towards a historical tradition lay in sections of the *Divyāvadāna*.[31] These sections—biographical vignettes of Aśoka Maurya, his son Kunāla, and younger brother Vīṭāśoka—are the *Aśokāvadāna*, the *Kunalāvadāna*, and the *Vītāśokāvadāna*. Also included was the early material from the *Avadāna-śataka*, a collection of stories that link past lives with the present through rebirth.[32] The borrowings are mainly from non-Canonical texts but also with some later parts of the Canon. The literary style

[31] *Divyāvadāna*, ed. E.B. Cowell and R.A. Neill; *Divyāvadāna*, ed. P.L. Vaidya, chs 29, 27, 28 / C. 348–434. The *avadāna* narrates a person's religious deeds illustrating his devotion and the working of his *karma*.

[32] M. Winternitz, *History of Indian Literature*, vol. II, 279ff.; G.M. Bongard-Levin, "The Historicity of the Ancient Indian *Avadānas*", 123–51.

mixes simple Sanskrit prose with ornate Sanskrit poetry. The final composition is of about the third century AD but drew on earlier compositions, oral and written.

The *Aśokāvadāna* is one of the oldest sections of the larger text and is believed to have had as its nucleus the *Aśokarājā-sūtra*, a biography of the emperor Aśoka first composed at Pāṭaliputra.[33] This then had many versions—the *Aśoka-sūtra* at Kauśāmbī, the *Aśokāvadāna* at Mathura, the *Avadānakalpalatā* in Kashmir, and the *Ayu-wang-zhuan* in Chinese. There are also later references in Tibetan and Sanskrit.[34] It is thought that it was possibly first recorded as a versified oral tradition in Magadha. The Sanskrit prose form probably took shape in Mathura, where the Buddhist moralistic dialectic may have been introduced into simple stories about the king. By the time it reached Kashmir it had doubtless taken on the sanctity of an ancient tradition. The geographical movement was from Pāṭaliputra via Kauśāmbī and Mathura to Kashmir and Gandhāra.

The *Aśokāvadāna* is believed to have been composed by a monk of the Mathura region. It chronicles segments of the Mauryan dynasty, focusing on the Aśokan legends and of his son Kunāla, into which is woven the history of the Elders of the Buddhist Saṅgha in northern India from the time of the Buddha. Although the perspective of the Councils and the succession of teachers is assumed, the intertwining of the Saṅgha with political authority while being present is not so evident as, for example, in the *Mahāvaṃsa*. The focus here is on Aśoka as the ideal king from a Buddhist perspective and therefore amenable to the Saṅgha. So successful was his projection as a *cakravartin* responding to the Saṅgha and the *dharma* that the sixth-century Chinese emperor Liang Wudi modelled himself on the Aśoka of the *avadānas*, as did the empress Wu Zetian in the seventh century.[35] Closer home there were attempts to fit Kaniṣka, the Kuṣāṇa ruler, into the mould of Aśoka, with fragmentary references to his building *stūpas* and calling a Council in Kashmir to clarify the doctrine.[36]

[33] J. Przyluski, *La Legende de l'Empereur Asoka*, 66–7, 100ff.

[34] See also J. Brarvig and F. Liland, *Traces of Gandharan Buddhism,* 59ff.

[35] M. Deeg, "From the Iron-wheel to Bodhisattvahood: Aśoka in Buddhist Culture and Memory", 109–44.

[36] J.M. Rosenfield, *The Dynastic Arts of the Kushans*, 31ff.

But the narratives remained a collection of episodes rather than a connected history—as in the Ceylon Chronicles.

This is of course a striking contrast also to the brahmanical tradition, where Aśoka is ignored and the title *devānaṃpiya* becomes virtually a term of contempt. In the Northern Buddhist tradition Aśoka is said to have convened a Council attended by hundreds of monks and presided over by Yaśas, interestingly not Moggaliputta Tissa.[37] Themes significant to its deliberations were the determining of the doctrine, the recording of the succession of the Elders, and the link with political authority underlying royal patronage. The locally powerful sect legitimized itself through claiming these connections. That decisions may not have been accurately recorded or that the lists of succession were contradictory at some points did not matter. They were referred to and linked to political history for an authoritative endorsement. The tradition of holding a Fourth Council in Kashmir was in part an endorsement of Buddhism arriving in new territory, and an assertion of defining the doctrine independent of the Theravāda.

The treatment of the Mauryan dynasty is from the perspective of the Saṅgha. Legends abound, some similar to the southern tradition and some not. In a previous birth Aśoka as a child is said to have placed a handful of earth in the Buddha's begging bowl and asked to be a ruler of the earth.[38] This has been compared with the southern tradition, in which he gives a bowlful of honey as alms.[39] His *karma* acts as a causal factor. People do not eat the earth, but this echoes the Buddhist story of genesis in which they did once eat the earth—in an age when there were no kings. Is this therefore an annulling of the present and an assumption that kingless times were better? In the telling of this story it is significant that the Buddha alone can convert the bowlful of earth into a kingdom and grant the child's wish.

In the *Aśokāvadāna,* Aśoka is described as the son of Bindusāra and a *brāhmaṇa* woman from Campā in the east.[40] In his youth Aśoka is said to have subdued the region of Taxila in the

[37] K. Upreti, *India as Reflected in the Divyāvadāna*, 114ff.

[38] J. Strong, *The Legend of King Aśoka*, 63, 287, 292.

[39] P. Mus, *Barabudur: Esquisse d'une Histoire du Bouddhisme fondee sur la Critique Archaeologique des texts,* vol. II, 289.

[40] J. Przyluski, *La Legende de l'Empereur Asoka*, 106ff.

north-west and the Khasa peoples in the mountains. The start of his administrative career was in Taxila, rather than in Ujjain, as stated in the *Mahāvaṃsa*. Many of the episodes of his earlier life are set in Taxila, as is the central episode in the life of his son, Kunāla. The geography changes from Vidiśā to Taxila with the change of sect and the location. Aśoka undergoes the usual transformation from wicked to righteous ruler. Another story, also in the Ceylon Chronicles, narrates his visit to all the places sacred to Buddhism. The pilgrimage is linked to the overnight construction of 84,000 *stūpas* to receive the relics of the Buddha. This sets out a sacred geography of the spread of Buddhism, apart from indicating what was thought to be the area of Aśoka's control.

The story of Aśoka making the young and attractive Tiṣyarakṣitā his Chief Queen, which brought about his unhappiness, is told in the Pāli Chronicles and also narrated here. She is accused of trying to destroy the *bodhi*-tree, feeling that it had priority over her in Aśoka's attention. She orders the blinding of Kunāla, her stepson, who rejected her advances. This episode links Kunāla to the Northern tradition, and possibly that is why it is not included in the Ceylon Chronicles. On being told of the blinding of Kunāla, his father Aśoka is inconsolable and orders that Tiṣyarakṣitā be put to death. The story has the popular stereotypes of stepmothers and an ageing man unable to control a young wife who eventually causes him sorrow.

In another story Aśoka, as an expression of faith, donates his realm to the Saṅgha. The ministers request his grandson to intervene, which he does: he buys back the realm with large sums from the treasury. In similar vein we are told that Aśoka, towards the end of his life, was unable to make donations to the Saṅgha as he had given everything away.[41] When a monk comes asking for alms, all that Aśoka can give him is half an *āmalaka*, a myrobalan fruit. This is reminiscent of the *Vessantara Jātaka*.

The composition of the *Aśokāvadāna* coincided with the

[41] *Aśokāvadāna*, ch. 29, C. 431; J. Przyluski, *La Legende de l'Empereur Asoka*, 296. Curiously there are no inscriptions recording donations from Aśoka to the Buddhist Saṅgha. There is one inscription requiring that the donations of his queen be recorded, but the recipients are not mentioned.

period of the transition of Buddhism from a local sect to a well-established and widely-spread religion. From a following in the Ganges plain and Central India, Northern Buddhism expanded into north-western India and Central and East Asia. A tradition had therefore to be created to preserve salient events in the history of the religion, hence the narrative of the Councils and the Elders. If these events could be linked to powerful political personalities, the tradition would be taken more seriously and would receive added patronage. So the Mauryas, and particularly Aśoka, came in very handy. The Mauryas were known to be patrons of the "heterodox" sects, what with the Jainas claiming Candragupta and Samprati, the Ājīvikas claiming Bindusāra and Daśaratha, and Aśoka who was a Buddhist. In the Northern tradition Aśoka is projected not just as an imperial patron but also as being near-subservient to the Saṅgha. This is a different treatment from that of the Pāli Chronicles, where he is more assertive in giving direction to the doctrine. Neither of these depictions is endorsed in the Aśoka of his own edicts.

It is striking but perhaps not surprising that the Buddhist tradition tends to ignore Aśoka's definition of the *dhamma*, where the emphasis is on social ethics and the need for the coexistence of all sects in the interests of social harmony—the statements that he makes in his Major Rock Edicts and Pillar Edicts. In those few edicts where he addresses the Saṅgha, his concern is with protecting the teachings, to the extent that he orders the expulsion of dissident monks and nuns. But as a contrast, in his edicts to his subjects his constant plea is that all sects—*pāsaṃḍas*—of whatever persuasion are to be given equal respect. *Brāhmaṇas* and *śramaṇas* are both to be honoured. This is foundational to his definition of *dhamma* and stems from his function as a statesman and emperor. What he addresses to the Saṅgha are more in the nature of directives, and in no way do they sugest his subordination to the Saṅgha. The Buddhist tradition therefore presents him in a different light from his own edicts. This historiographical representation partially explains why modern historians, barring a few, have also projected him as a Buddhist ruler essentially concerned with the propagation of Buddhism, rather than exploring his particular definition and use of the concept of *dhamma*.

Buddhism was spreading into new areas both in the North and in the South. The Śakas, Yavanas, and Kuṣāṇas arrived as a result of invasions, migrations, and commercial activities and settled in the north-west. Those among them who showed an interest in Buddhism, as many of the new elite did, required a history of the Buddhist tradition, as also biographies of the exemplars of the *dhamma-rājās*, such as Aśoka. The processes of assimilation, incorporation, and co-option were now fairly common both among the ruling groups and those whom they ruled. Buddhism, not being a rigidly ecclesiastical religion, lent itself to inducting local flavours. The tradition could also be used to strengthen the faithful against what was viewed as the persecution of Buddhism by the Śuṅga dynasty further east, and some hostility from local rulers.[42]

Various religious groups—such as Buddhist sects, Vaiṣṇava Bhāgavata cults which focused on Viṣṇu and his incarnations, and some Śaiva cults—attracted the attention of the new arrivals, ruling families, and others. It was easier to accommodate the latter within these religions than among the orthodox beliefs and practices of Brahmanism. As a concession to local sensitivity, it was maintained that the Buddha had actually visited Mathura and Kashmir and predicted the coming of Buddhism to these lands, an idea which is the mirror image of the Buddha having visited Sri Lanka. In the earlier tradition the Buddha was accompanied by his disciple Ānanda; in the later tradition, the Thera Upagupta accompanies Aśoka.[43] The insistence on the earlier visits of the Buddha would also have helped to create a sense of community, vital to the functioning of the Saṅgha, and confirmed by the claim to a common history.

The Mauryan dynasty, and especially Aśoka, is made to play a particularly important role in the history of the Saṅgha and the succession of the Elders. The list of Elders is not identical in the northern and southern traditions, but this is of less consequence. What matters is the listing of succession and the chronological

[42] *Aśokāvadāna*, ch. 29, C. 434, in the *Divyāvadāna*; J. Przyluski, *La Legende de l'Empereur Asoka*, 162.

[43] J. Przyluski, *La Legende de l'Empereur Asoka*, 3–5ff.

parallel with the rulers. Fictitious genealogies of teachers, for example, are known from as early as the *Upaniṣads*, where the actuality is less significant than the notion of legitimate succession. What matters is the acceptance of even a marginally accurate succession.

The Northern tradition is addressed to both monks and lay followers. The biographies of the Elders are used to instruct the monks, and the texts are aimed at exalting the monasteries and the associated teachings. This was necessary where sects competed, not only for royal patronage, but also for patronage from highly placed officials, rich merchants, and traders on the routes from the Ganges valley to north-western India, and beyond to Central and West Asia. These trading activities also introduced ideas prevalent in one area to another. An awareness of Greco-Bactrian, Zoroastrian, and Manichaean religion and practices become pertinent to the Northern Buddhist tradition, as for example in the delineation of the Buddha Maitreya. The concentration in the north-west may also be explained by the claim that Puṣyamitra Śuṅga was hostile to Buddhist establishments in the middle Ganges plain,[44] and is accused of massacring many monks at Sāketa and other monasteries, stopping only because of popular opposition. The Thera Yaśas escaped miraculously and continued his work elsewhere. But even apart from this, some sections of the doctrine took new forms through the imprint of local beliefs, a process that was not specific to time and place.

The notion of prophecy, common to the Puranic tradition as well, led to the prediction that, a hundred years after the death of the Buddha, Aśoka would rule and propagate the Buddhist *dhamma*.[45] The event had already happened, therefore prediction was a ploy to enhance the claim of the texts. Persecution seems to have encouraged the prediction of Buddhism disappearing a thousand years after the death of the Buddha, attributed to the Buddha in some recensions of the *Aśokāvadāna*. However, it is

[44] *Aśokāvadāna*, ch. 29, C. 434, in the *Divyāvadāna*; J. Przyluski, *La Legende de l'Empereur Asoka*, 99.

[45] In the Ceylon Chronicles, Aśoka is said to come to the throne 218 years after the *mahāparinirvāṇa*.

said that there will be a gradual return to the *Dharma*, which in its final phase will witness the coming of Maitreya. This millenarian aspect reverses the disappearance of the religion.

The *Aśokāvadāna* carries some ideas on the notion of the *cakravartin*. Aśoka is the *caturbhāga-cakravartin* and the *bala-cakravartin*, the universal monarch who rules the four continents and is willing to use force (*bala*) if necessary. Was this a concession to the underlying fear of kingship and the possibility of the king using force?[46] This is later expanded into a theory of four categories of *cakravartins*: the one with the golden wheel rules four continents, the one with the silver rules three, the one with the copper rules two, and he with the iron wheel rules a single continent—the home continent of Jambudvīpa. The scheme has a corresponding change from rule through persuasion to rule through force, although force is subservient to *dharma*.[47] Not only does Aśoka remain the epitome of the royal patron, little attempt is made to give the same publicity to other patrons. This is a comment on how the history of the Saṅgha was viewed and a contrast to the Pāli Chronicle.

It is curious that, given the number of Aśokan edicts in north-western India in Prākrit, Greek, and Aramaic—all languages with scripts in use—these inscriptions are not referred to. Were they, however, read as sources for information on events such as pilgrimages (*dhammayāttā*), visiting the bodhi-tree (*ayāya saṃbodhi*), or even the reference to displaying relics? This would have confirmed the depiction of Aśoka as a universal monarch, the righteous king of righteousness—*rājā cakkavatti dhammiko-dhammarājā.*

The succession of Elders is an example of sectarian needs creating a history. The *Majjhima-nikāya* states that there was to be no head of the Saṅgha. Yet the succession lists are carefully maintained by each sect, even to the extent of preserving a variant list where there are small differences. Thus, the Pāli Chronicles preserve a list which is different from that of the Northern

[46] H. Kern and B. Nanjio (ed.), *Saddharmapuṇḍarīka Sūtra*, 6, 20, 263, quoted in J. Strong, *The Legend of King Aśoka*, 54–6.

[47] J. Strong, *The Legend of King Aśoka*, 55.

tradition. The list of teachers represents those in authority in the Saṅgha of a particular region, and correlates the chronology of change in the doctrine by links with particular Elders, assuming that the Elders were present.

Biographies become far less prominent after the mid-first millennium AD, when the decline of Buddhism begins to be noticed in the subcontinent, the degree varying from region to region. The religion was being shaped by internal dissensions, the assimilation of local cults, and the continuity of the urban economy and culture on which it was largely dependent. The area where it remained important was eastern India, probably because of the trade with South East Asia, which kept the financial networks in a healthy condition, and where the patronage from royalty and merchants was forthcoming. Eastern Indian Buddhism had close connections with Tibet and Buddhism there. Texts on Tibetan Buddhism included sections on the biography of the Buddha.

5. Buddhist Historical Traditions

As a contrast to Sri Lanka, Buddhist texts from Gandhāra are not presented in a systematically historical manner. Despite the region having hosted monasteries, the relative absence of chronicles is striking. One reason may have been that it was an area where people were frequently reshuffled through migrations and invasions, with the continuity of politico-religious relations being broken. Being at the crossroads of trade, substantial wealth was generated, but it was dispersed over distant places. Patronage came from the *gahapati* and the *seṭṭhi* (the householder and the merchant), the spectacular patronage from royalty being somewhat less forthcoming. Northern Buddhism was into intensive proselytizing in Central Asia and further into China, competing with Manichaeanism, Zoroastrianism, and Nestorian Christianity for a start. Closer home, the popularity of Puranic Hinduism was increasing with the worship of Śiva and the *avatāras* of Viṣṇu. Puranic deities were open to mutation into syncretic cults. Buddhism was therefore anxious to attribute miraculous powers to the Buddha. In Sri Lanka the mission is presented as immediately successful and the status it attained was reinforced by linking the

Saṅgha to a royal patron, who in turn was a patron to the Sihala royalty. The monasteries of Kashmir and Gandhāra did not maintain records parallel to those of Sri Lanka, nor is the Kuṣāṇa king Kaniṣka projected as a latter-day Aśoka.

The dynasties that ruled were generally not of local families and traced themselves back to distant places. The patronage of the two dominant powers, the Kuṣāṇas and the Sassanians, was not exclusively to the Saṅgha, for many other religions sought and received patronage. The Buddhism of the north-west also had to contend with an array of deities and semi-divine beings, some of whom coloured its self-perceptions—and of its role in the region. There was no gnawing rivalry for patronage with dissenting Buddhist sects, an absence that would have reduced the urgency of keeping records and maintaining a history. The reciprocal closeness of the Saṅgha to political authority, as in Sri Lanka, or for that matter later in Tibet and Ladakh, all of which maintained chronicles, was not apparent in the north-west. The monastery in Sri Lanka did go into decline but only in competition with another monastery, and finally revived.

The biographical form was effective in areas new to conversion. Life stories can be enriched with myth and fantasy more easily then chronicles, even if the latter are not free of such enrichment. Using the *carita* form was an indirect way of suggesting historicity, not so much of the Buddha which was established, but of events related to the Saṅgha. The focus is on the Buddha and the long line of preceding ones becomes an attempt to give antiquity and legitimacy to the teaching. The biographical form isolated the individual and could place him in a different context from his original one. Written 500 years after the Buddha, and depicting the Śākya oligarchy in the form of a contemporary kingdom, the earlier form would have been better observed had the *Nikāyas* been read from a historical perspective.

Buddhist historical perspectives reveal a variety of characteristic features. Although the Buddha emphasized the need to be sure of the reliability of the information that is quoted in terms of its coming from impeccable sources, nevertheless events could be over-dramatized to make a point, as in the description of the activities of Aśoka in relation to the Saṅgha. The *Mahāvaṃsa* sets him in the context of events and politics of the Mauryan period. He is significant not only for his patronage of Buddhism but also for the claim that his son preached the message of the Buddha in Sri Lanka, making it the formal religion in the island. In the northern tradition his other son, Kunāla, does not play this role. Only after he is blinded does he turn to Buddhist teaching, and there is no conversion of others. The *Mahāvaṃsa* depicts Aśoka as part of a historical unfolding of events concerning the past of Buddhism, and indirectly of the monastery of the Mahāvihāra; in the *Aśokāvadāna* the focus is on the activities of Aśoka as a Buddhist king, but not linked to any specific monastery.

Interests have to be subordinated to the welfare of the Saṅgha and its primacy. However, the Saṅgha is not above criticism. Although this is put forward in a mild manner—except where it relates to a rival sect when it can be vituperative—there is the awareness that even the Saṅgha can make mistakes. Most texts are polemics of their own sect against others regarded almost as heresies. Historicity becomes essential to religions such as Buddhism and Jainism because of their strong sectarian loyalties. Debates on these teachings and their elaboration give direction to the evolution of the sects. The institutionalization of the sects as monastic centres also needed to be recorded. Historicity is underlined by linking this history with known persons from the past. To prove the historicity of the Buddha himself, his life had to be fitted into a historical chronology with an established context, as indeed also the narrative of expanding Buddhism and its various missions. This was done by linking both to historical persons, even when the nature of the link was uncertain. Material from the oral tradition where the *itihāsa-purāṇa* tradition provided names and narratives of the *kṣatriya* ancestors was included.

The Buddha's death becomes the pivot of a chronological system, which again suggests a historical possibility, particularly where chronological disparities are not too great. Sectarian conflicts were carefully recorded. Groups in opposition, although claiming to derive their views from the same doctrine, have to explain, where possible, their differences. The writing of explanatory commentaries at frequent intervals acted as a further means of both preserving the record, adding new material, and reformulating the narrative in accordance with current perspectives. It also encouraged some reflection on the past, as in the commentaries of Buddhaghosa.

The Buddha stated that as long as the monastery followed the same procedures as the *gaṇa-saṅghas* there would be no divisive tendencies. However, the *gaṇa-saṅghas* in the post-Canonical texts are societies of the past and the attempt was to present the Buddha in a contemporary setting, even though alluding to the past. The first schism conceded by the Saṅgha happened at the Council at Vaiśāli, with the monks of the Vṛjji *gaṇa-saṅgha* demanding changes in monastic practices. Given the free range of ideas associated with the period of the Buddha, it would not have been surprising that dissidence would be common in any order of *śramaṇas.* Subsequent to this the patronage is almost exclusively from kingdoms. Kings such as Bimbisāra and Pasenadi are depicted in conversation with the Buddha.

The concern with the politics of the *kṣatriyas* is different from the *Purāṇas*. For all its philosophical heterodoxy, the Buddhist tradition focuses more on kingship, and on the power and moral authority of the ideal king visualized as the *dharmarājā* and the *cakkavatti*, and in approving of the king as patron of the Saṅgha, resulting in a complex interplay between the Saṅgha and the king. The Saṅgha was a community of renunciants and therefore outside the jurisdiction of state and society; nevertheless, it had to maintain some equation with the state. The claim to royal patronage was also a claim to state protection, as indeed a claim to status, all of which is knitted into the pattern of its historical tradition.

Patronage of a substantial kind also came from the *gahapati* (householder) and the *seṭṭhi* (trader). There was a consciousness of breaking away from orthodox belief and practice in the opposition to sacrificial ritual, and this meant altering ritual and the intention of religion. In areas where Buddhism prevailed, the earlier sacrificial rituals and prestations were gradually replaced by the institution of the Saṅgha which required *dāna* (gift-giving) to the Saṅgha and alms to *bhikkhus.* In this both royal patronage on a grand scale, as well as the routine patronage of daily alms rounds made a significant difference.

The Saṅgha required patronage from the community to maintain monasteries. Initially, a gift from a wealthy merchant or a *rājā* was sufficient. But when the Saṅgha grew to be a powerful institution the patronage had to be greater and required the largesse of kings. The transition to association with royalty, as demonstrated in the Chronicles, was not unexpected. The narrative begins with legends of heroes and the society associated with them, and the legends give way to the presumed history of kings. From this perspective the earliest society of indigenous forest-dwellers has to be conquered or destroyed, since such people cannot support a Saṅgha. Settlers, preferably cultivators, are necessary to provide the required resources. It thus becomes the historical fate of all those categorized as *rākṣasas* and *yakkhas* to be eventually overcome by the people of the settlement, symbolized by Vijaya or any other adventurer.

The authorship of the tradition was largely in the hands of monks and was intended in the main for monks and lay followers—"to arouse the serene joy and emotion of the pious", as the Chronicle states. The discourse was among the converted but with an eye on disabling those ideologies to which it was opposed. Even if the authors were many, the purpose was single. Authentication lay, among other things, in mentioning the sources consulted. Notions of the remote past drew upon creation and origin myths, some parallel to the Puranic tradition. There was a large fund from which the themes and symbols were borrowed by many groups with varying ideologies. The narratives were altered to suit these ideologies.

At another level, the understanding of historical explanations of the past was helped by the foundational thinking of the Buddhist doctrine. The focus was on dependent origination—*pratīta-samutpāda*—of all phenomena. This was the natural law of causality which the Buddha recognized and used in explaining his doctrine. Because it is a law of nature it does not even require the presence of any supernatural being. The chain of cause and effect through actions is also an explanation of the how and the why of past events. Actions are presented in the context of ethical norms, and this is an underlying argument even if the writing is formulaic. Change is expected given the impermanence that prevails, but this is not discussed in relation to the past. There is an awareness of the *śāsana* (doctrine) of the Saṅgha declining, as predicted after 500 years. But a distinction is made between *śāsana* and *dharma* where the latter will continue as long as there are *arhants*. Whereas this reflects the downswing of the time-cycle, it also carries the eschatology of the return of the utopia with the coming of Maitreya.

Whether in chronicles or biographies, the balance between the Saṅgha and political authority can be uneven. There are occasions when the Saṅgha legitimizes the king, and others when the king does not recognize the legitimacy of the Saṅgha. Those sympathetic to Buddhism, such as Aśoka, are given a high social status, a status denied them in the *Purāṇas*. A son of Aśoka is involved with the spread of the doctrine in Sri Lanka. The Councils are invariably associated with kings, largely for prestige, but also for chronology, even if uncertain, and for an assertion of additional authority. Royal patronage is not one-sided; the sectarian network, being a beneficiary of patronage, provides an agency that cultivates support for the king. Should the ideology be that of fostering universality and cutting across social and other distinctions, this would be additionally useful in governing a society of diverse groups.

A new element introduced through Mahāyāna Buddhism was the concept of the *bodhisattva*, not merely as a figure of the past but one concerned with attaining perfection in the future. Perfection comes close to hinting at some elements of deity. The lives of *bodhisattvas*, however formulaic, encouraged the idea of the biographies of the Buddha and of the great patrons. The teaching moves from an oral tradition to the literate, from hearing and reciting to reading and writing. The updating of texts becomes an important activity. Because the early texts are also preserved in a written form from a certain point onwards, changes required a new text. Thus, although the *Dīpavaṃsa* and the *Mahāvaṃsa* cover much the same ground, the details and intentions can differ. The audience was both monks and lay people, and those associated with the royal court. Where the original text could not be changed except marginally, changes were recorded in the commentaries, including new versions of earlier themes. This had to do not only with written texts being more closed, as against the openness of most oral traditions, but with commentaries explaining the past.

These were signs of a literate society. Of the categories of texts discussed, the chronicle form is essentially that of an institution through which the history of Buddhism is related. It is therefore partial to the institution. History, in this case, involves the initial demarcation of territory through the visits of the Buddha to sanctify the area. The Saṅgha requires its own authentication, hence the history of the Councils and the succession of Elders and of missions and the interface with kings. Pre-Buddhist populations have to be kept separate and are dismissed as primitive. The arrival of the mission is therefore a time-marker and the history of the region changes. The establishment of the doctrine entails acquiring property and involves records of buildings and structures. The Saṅgha was the fixed point of the community of monks, nuns, and lay-followers: *bhikkhus, bhikkhunīs, upāsakas*, and *upāsikās*. The history of the Saṅgha claimed to be the history of this community. This was a departure from other contemporary forms of recording, reciting, and writing the past.

Biographies emerge as a new genre, reiterating the fact that the founder of Buddhism was a historical figure and biography evokes history. The biography links up with origin myths and genealogies, which are incorporated, and sometimes modified or embellished. What is new is the focus on the individual, not altogether unexpected in an ideology where liberation from rebirth focuses on the actions of the individual. Both categories of texts are central to creating the identity of a community, and the identity draws from the way in which its history is presented, even if the medium is the chronicle of the monastery or the biography of the Buddha.

In some ways, the period around the sixth century AD is a turning point. In Sri Lanka it sees the revival of the authority of the Mahāvihāra monastery, in Gandhāra it prepares itself for the challenge from other religions—which ultimately it loses for a variety of reasons. In the context of northern India and of historical traditions, there were to be new genres, some responding to the Buddhist traditions.

Biographies of the Buddha tended to become hagiographical.

But the genre as a form of historical writing came to be adopted by royal courts wishing to provide majesty and legitimacy to the ruler, and to make virtually official statements about matters that may have been in doubt. These biographies, known as *caritas*, knitted together *kāvya* and facets of *itihāsa.* Although similar in intent, they were different in content from those of the Buddha.

PART V

The Historical Tradition Externalized

12

Historical Biographies

The *Harṣacarita* and the *Rāmacarita*

1. Biography and History

Biography, in order to be considered part of a historical tradition, has to show awareness of that tradition even while narrating events in the life of a person. He may be both witnessing and recording events. He selects the events that he regards as worthy of transmission to a contemporary audience and to posterity. What permits such biography to be included as an articulation of historical consciousness is not merely that several such works relate to the activities of those in authority, but that the structure within which the biography is composed hinges on the historical tradition which is used to legitimize the subject.[1] The biographer is a committed witness. He chooses the actions of a particular person, indicates their cause and purpose, and locates them at a point in time and space. When it is the biography of a contemporary, the biographer and his patron choose what they want transmitted. The biographical span is linear.

Both genealogies and epic narratives provide commencement to the idea of biography. It could be argued that the *Mahābhārata* is a compilation of biographical fragments written by a grandfather on his sons and grandsons! The historical biography differs from

[1] A. Momigliano, "History and Biography", 153–84; idem, *The Development of Greek Biography*.

the epic in that its subject is historically known and not merely presumed to have existed and has an element of historicity. When the past is necessary to the present, it can be appropriated—as in genealogies and brief histories of the dynasty. Fantasy may be permitted in both epic and biography, but the degree of fantasy has perforce to be controlled in the latter. Biography finds expression in literature in the form of the *carita*, and occasionally also in summary form in inscriptions, both of which are relatively new genres but significant as later versions of the *itihāsa-purāṇa* tradition.

The *carita* as a *kāvya* has a literary form with an aesthetic appeal and differs in content from the *kāvya* as its intention is to attempt an authentic portrayal of the subject as viewed by the biographer, who also has a historical purpose in writing it. However, these texts were not intended as critical historical writing, but as literature, except that they related to the exercise of power and claimed that they were delineating events from the past and the present as they actually happened.

The prominence of the royal biography marks a change from the succession of lineages to that of kings, a shift from the importance of the collective lineage to the individual. The biography by a contemporary, a known person with appropriate credentials, is in essentials largely authentic, else it would be criticized as false. As a document it is recording the present but with the knowledge that it will be read in the future.

This new genre differs from earlier ones. The author is unambiguously identified, and his credentials have to be of the best so that his claim to authenticity can be sustained. The autobiographical section explains who the author is and his qualification to write the biography, as also implicitly why it had to be written. Some bias is to be expected since the biographer is writing on his patron. The narrative need not cover the life-span of the subject, but focus on crucial events. When these have been satisfactorily narrated and the intention achieved, the biography can close. These are not birth-to-death life histories.

In interweaving the biographical with the historical, the time period of the events can be short but the context is a longer historical time-span. When biographical writing becomes more common towards the end of the first millennium AD, the earlier biographies are treated as precedents. In some narratives memory is important, both personal and public, and the author attempts to capture it.

The various contexts of the biographies were similar. The author was either a court poet or a senior official, and of an upper caste. The audience was the royal court and those constituting the literate elite formally educated in Sanskrit. The patron was the king, who was also the subject of the biography—and to that extent the biography was in part eulogy. This was the continuation and elaboration of a tradition, the nuances of which had to be known to be comprehended. The occasion was a celebratory moment and the outcome of critical events around which the biography is written, observing a chronology. Snippets of history pertain to the royal family, to political and marital alliances, and the crisis. The biography was often written when authority and legitimacy had to be emphasized and the mutation to courtly life established, with some allusions to the past. Problematic events are sometimes smoothened out by the intervention of a deity, but the deity is a façade, its function being to endorse royal ambition. This is almost invariably so in biographies where the rule of primogeniture is broken. The action is justified as having been ordered by a deity, or at the wish of the dying father, or by showing the elder brother to be incompetent.[2]

2. Writing Biographies in the Context of the *Itihāsa-Purāṇa*

In the period subsequent to the seventh century AD, the more relevant segments of the *itihāsa-purāṇa* tradition were not discontinued but given new forms, being incorporated in new genres of texts. However, the future tense of the prophetic form, used in recounting dynasties in the *Purāṇas*, gives way to the present tense of contemporary times in the biographies. The significance of these genres has to be seen in a changed historical situation. They centre on the king's relations with his subordinate chiefs and functionaries, a complement or a counterpoint to the inscriptions that provide yet another official version of the more important aspects of a reign.

[2] V.S. Pathak, *Historians of Ancient India*, 69–71.

There was also something of a bifurcation in the *itihāsa-purāṇa* tradition because the *Purāṇas* became texts associated with religious sectarian worship, whereas the more historical concerns came to be expressed in other kinds of literature. Dynastic lists peter out in the *Purāṇas* after the Gupta dynasty, or approximately the mid-first millennium AD. They were now incorporated into royal biographies, and even more so in epigraphic documents, and later in chronicles. The tradition of using the past as a reference point for the present becomes significant to these new genres. Mention is made of the *ākhyāyikās*, said to be based on actual happenings, and these were linked to the *ākhyāna*, *itihāsa*, and *purāṇa*, of the historical tradition.

The term *carita*—literally "moving", "doing", "going"—refers to the activities of a person. The protagonists were kings and occasionally ministers. The narrative is not boxed into a series of larger or smaller stories, as often happens in the *kathā*, but stands on its own in a linear form. The *caritas*, in describing the origin myths of the dynasty, often linked them to heroes from the Puranic genealogies or deities. The early history and antecedents of both the subject and the author involve justifying those actions which deviate from accepted norms. Such explanations often derive from the remembered tradition of the past and of earlier rulers.

Among the concerns of the *itihāsa-purāṇa* tradition was the political legitimacy of lineage and dynasty. Political power was open to all castes, although theoretically confined to the *kṣatriya,* which, although it contradicted the normative codes, accompanied the growth of kingdoms as state systems. Genealogies were resorted to even as statements of caste. Status could be acquired through marriage alliances, using at times the ceremony of a *svayamvara,* evoking past practices. The symbolism of the *digvijaya*, or conquest of the four quarters, could be a symbolic claim to political power and not necessarily a statement of actual conquest; hence the frequency of formulaic descriptions of such conquests, and the inclusion sometimes of names of clan territories from the ancient past. These features associated with the earlier tradition, although transformed in meaning, were carried over into the courtly culture of the later monarchies. Where dynasties claim to be of the Sūryavaṃśa or the Candravaṃśa lineages and latch themselves onto the relevant descent list from the *Purāṇas*, there the record of these links becomes even more central to the present, although there is a tacit admission that the past was different.

The eulogistic component of the *caritas* was symptomatic of courtly literature, comparable to similar literature from other parts of the medieval world.[3] There was a selected core of information on contemporary events around which was woven a framework of eulogy. This was composed in elegant courtly language, replete with linguistic virtuosity and sophisticated allusions to classical learning. It was the formal picture of the ideal king according to existing canons. To an extent, the subject of the biography was an exemplar. This was particularly important where dynasties came from newly established families anxious that they be respected. Vices and virtues were exemplified for moral instruction, as they had been in the *Aśokāvadāna*. There were also some supposedly divine utterances and predictions to support the actions of people in high places. The desire to link the accepted past to the present may well have been motivated by the fear of alienation from this past.

The writing of the *carita* was in part an attempt to link the new dynasty with earlier dynasties. Desirable antecedents often had to include references to a local culture in the process of acquiring social elevation. The Puranic tradition remained an initial reference point for this. Where the authors of the biographies were also Bhṛgu *brāhmaṇas*, this would have provided a familiar approach to the subject.[4] The proliferation of royal courts through the increase in the number of small and new kingdoms meant that kings vied with each other for the services of the better court-poets. This often resulted in the biography including embellishments in the style of court poetry, which happily subordinated historical authenticity to a well-turned phrase. The biography therefore became, as it often did in other parts of the contemporary world, a form of legitimizing a dynasty and publicizing the activities of

[3] R.W. Southern, "Aspects of the European Tradition of Historical Writing", 1970, 20, 173–96; 1971, 21, 159–79; 1972, 22, 159–80; 1973, 23, 243–63; W.J. Brandt, *The Shape of Medieval History*.

[4] V.S. Pathak, *Historians of Ancient India*, 12, 34, 52.

a king. At the same time, it articulated and validated the culture of the royal court, which had now become significantly different from pre-Gupta times.[5] The earlier courts had been less formal, less anxious to follow uniform patterns of court culture, and were characterized by an openness of language and style.

Among the many other reasons for the interest in royal biographies may have been the growth of varieties of *bhakti* sects and teaching, where the actions of the individual were central to the assessment of his/her life, and therefore to the condition of the future life. The endorsement of the ideas of *karma* and *samsāra*, actions conditioning rebirth, which by now were widespread, could well have encouraged the assessment of individual actions.

3. The Evolution of the Biographical Form

The germ of the *carita* tradition was perhaps the *dāna-stuti* hymns of the *Ṛg Veda,* with their praise of individual heroes and seminal connection to the longer hero-lauds of the epics. The early inscriptions eulogizing rulers were probably effective in encouraging the biographical form. Thus, Khāravela in the first century BC, ruling in Kaliṅga, in eastern India, provides a chronological résumé of his reign.[6] From western India, Gotami Balasiri, queen-mother to the Sātavāhana ruler Siri Sātakaṇi Gotamiputa, refers to the achievements of her son in a miniature *carita*, the inscription containing elements which were later characteristic of historical biography.[7] He prevented the mixing of the four *varṇas*, a phrase which was to become a fairly common qualifier, but which remained largely rhetorical for it was not adhered to in practice. The only noticeably missing reference is to an appropriate marriage alliance.[8]

Parallel to the inscriptions, and described as *pratimāgṛhas* (image houses), are a few sculptures carrying the names of kings who had died, such as those of the Sātavāhanas, and some others

[5] Daud Ali, *Courtly Culture and Political Life in Early Medieval India*.

[6] Hathigumpha Inscription of Khāravela, *Ep. Ind.*, 20, 71ff.

[7] Nasik Cave Inscription of Gotami Balasiri, *Ep. Ind.*, 8, no. 2, 59ff.

[8] Kṣatrapa inscriptions refer to a marriage alliance which apparently led to Rudradāman being lenient in his campaign against the Sātavāhanas.

at Naneghat, and of the Kuṣāṇas at Maṭ near Mathura.[9] These appear not to be portraits but representations. The *Pratimānāṭaka,* a play by Bhāsa, refers to statues of dead kings but this is not evidence enough of their being portraits. A couple of panels at the *stūpa* at Kanaganahalli carry label inscriptions that read "*rāyā asoko*", but these again are representations of Aśoka Maurya and not portraits.[10] Portraiture was not popular, despite descriptions in plays of kings painting portraits of their beloveds. Portraits on coins introduced by the Indo-Bactrian Greeks were bypassed by the Guptas, who preferred to depict an action instead. Hero-stones set up as memorials to dead heroes represent the hero symbolically but do not claim to be portraits.[11] It is almost as if the portrait resemblance was unimportant as long as its presence was indicated by a representation. There may possibly have been a belief that portraits were inauspicious.

Biographical writing as a form is likely to have been influenced by the treatment of the lives of kings and Elders in Buddhist and Jaina texts. The traditions were not segregated, even if observed as distinct. Aśvaghoṣa's *Buddhacarita* was an innovation despite the poetic embellishments enveloping the historical person. The authors of the biographies would have read the *Buddhacarita,* which was likely to have been influential as literature, even among the *brāhmaṇa* literati.

Statements about individual rulers in early inscriptions were minimal but they were based on historical information. Comparisons were made with the heroes of the epics, now relegated to the remote past. These early inscriptions were generally statements on the specific achievements of the king but they did not generally carry detailed references to the genealogical antecedents of the ruler. This was a marked feature of the later period, where the genealogy and ancestry, even if partially fictitious, become a statement of status. Nevertheless, there is enough even in the

[9] A.M. Shastri, *The Sātavāhanas and the Western Kṣatrapas*; J.M. Rosenfield, *The Dynastic Arts of the Kushans*; H. Bakker, "Monuments to the Dead"; P. Granoff, "Worship as Commemoration . . .", 181–202.

[10] R. Thapar, "Rāyā Asoko from Kanaganahalli: Some Thoughts", 249–62.

[11] S. Settar and G.D. Sontheimer (eds), *Memorial Stones*; R. Thapar, "Death and the Hero", in *Cultural Pasts*, 680–95.

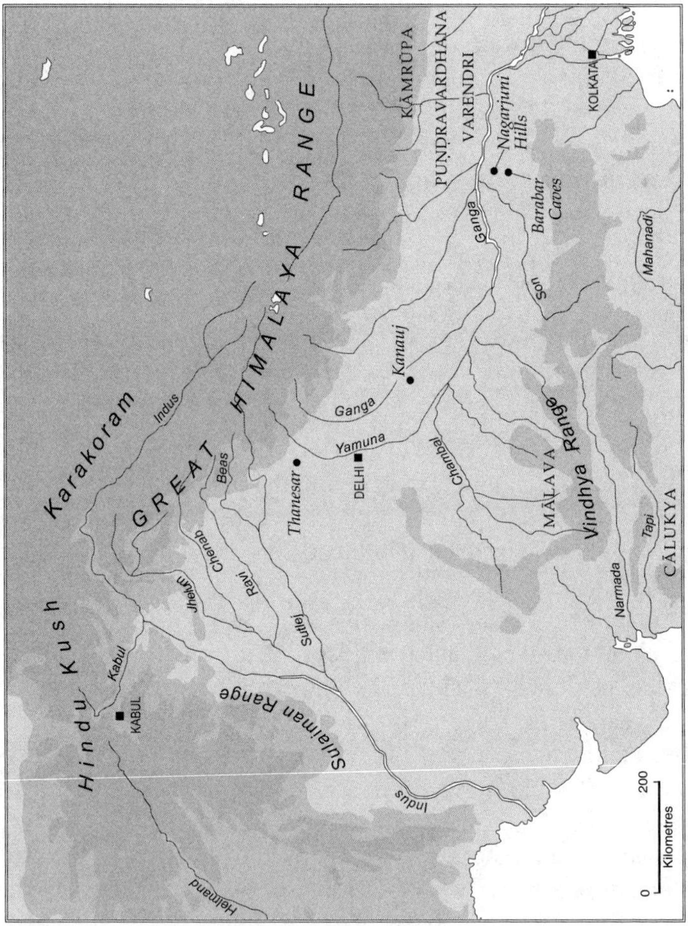

Map 5: Locations of the More Important Places, Clans, and Dynasties

earlier inscriptions, and in the narrative poems on the heroes of the Buddhists, Jainas, and Bhāgavatas, to provide a curtain-raiser for the historical biography.

The two examples of *caritas* that I have chosen are Bāṇabhaṭṭa's *Harṣacarita* and Sandhyākaranandin's *Rāmacarita*.

THE *HARṢACARITA* OF BĀṆABHAṬṬA

1. Bāṇabhaṭṭa

The first major royal biography was the *Harṣacarita*, a biography of king Harṣavardhana written by Bāṇabhaṭṭa in the seventh century AD.[12] One view dates it to *c.* 620, which is now generally accepted, although others have argued for a slightly later date.[13] The two most quoted works of Bāṇa are somewhat different in character: the *Harṣacarita* is a biography of the early part of the life of Harṣavardhana, and the *Kādambarī* is fiction and poetic fantasy of a high order. Harṣa eventually ruled from Kānyakubja, more often referred to as Kanauj, in the western Ganges plain.

The *Harṣacarita* has the characteristic features of a *carita*. It begins with invocatory verses to Śiva and Pārvatī, presumably the deities worshipped by the author, and probably also by the subject of the biography. It includes mention of previous poets of renown such as Vyāsa, Hāla, Pravarasena, Bhāsa, Kālidāsa, Guṇāḍhya—writing in Sanskrit and in Prākrit. Bāṇa is stating his literary ancestry before recounting his lineal descent. His was a literary family with a father-in-law who was a poet and a son who, it is thought, completed Bāṇa's unfinished work of fiction, the *Kādambarī*.

In the first two chapters (*ucchvāsas*) Bāṇa, in accordance with convention, traces his descent back to deities and sages. The goddess Sarasvatī was cursed by the *ṛṣi* Durvāsas to spend time

[12] Bāṇabhaṭṭa, *Harṣacarita*, ed. K.P. Parab; *The Harshacarita of Bāṇabhaṭṭa*, ed. P.V. Kane (hereafter Kane); E.B. Cowell and F.W. Thomas (trans.), *The Harṣacarita of Bāṇa* (hereafter Cowell and Thomas). References to the Kane edition are to chapter numbers followed by page numbers.

[13] D. Devahuti, *Harsha: A Political Study*, 3, 11; Shankar Goyal, *History and Historiography of the Age of Harṣa*, 61ff.; S.R. Goyal, *Harṣa and Buddhism*, 143ff.

on earth. She settles in a forest on the banks of the river Śona and by accident meets Dadhīca, a Bhṛgu, and bears him a son. This releases her from the curse and she returns to the celestial world. Gods and humans mingle, as is characteristic in mythology, and the gods behave like humans. The story echoes that of Purūravas and Urvaśī from the *Vedas*. The boy left behind grows up with a foster mother, also a Bhṛgu, and her son, Vatsa, but later chooses to become an ascetic. From Vatsa there descended the Vātsyāyanas. Among them and much later were born the lineage of Bāṇa. This is the effective part of the genealogy. The association with the Bhṛgus is important to him as a writer of *itihāsa*.

It has been asked why Bāṇa gave priority to information on his own life in the initial chapters rather than beginning with the biography of the king, as in other *carita* texts. Was he assuming that his status as a Vātsyāyana *brāhmaṇa* should have precedence as it was higher than that of Harṣa, said to be a *vaiśya*? Or, had there been some doubt about his choice as a biographer, a doubt that is perhaps hinted at by the unconventional company that he kept? Establishing the credentials of the author was crucial to the authenticity of the biography and the legitimation of the subject.

There follows a description of the *agrahāra* (a *brāhmaṇa* settlement on a royal donation of land) of Prītikūṭa on the banks of the Śona, where his family resided, and which predictably Bāṇa claims as the place where Sarasvatī stayed for a brief while. In describing the activities of the village he makes particular mention of the reading of the *Vāyu Purāṇa* and adds that it was also recited by a bard. This seems to suggest literacy on the part of some, with a continuing oral rendition by bards.

Bāṇa's parents having died in his youth, he was free to discover the world and draw around him a range of unorthodox companions. These are listed by name and occupation and not by caste, perhaps because most of their occupations were of the lower castes, with the exception of a few poets and singers. With such a range, their genealogies have to be dispensed with. Bāṇa makes no secret of his earlier bohemian life and rather unconventional ways, which, when he reformed them, won him royal favour.

Harṣa's invitation to Bāṇa comes in a roundabout way through a kinsman who is said to have a *sūdra* mother. Bāṇa hesitates as he is critical of those who serve at the court, arguing that they become sycophants and lose their independence. But eventually he decides to go. Bāṇa's family obviously has some connections with the court, else he would not have been sent for, particularly as the initial comment of the king about him is not exactly complimentary. He also makes a point of mentioning that the person whom he regards as his teacher was much revered at the Maukhari court, where Harṣa's sister had been married.

After three days of travel he arrives at the *skandhāvāra* (military camp) of Harṣa. This is a huge spectacle, with crowds of people, many sectarian groups, many kings from elsewhere, and large numbers of animals, including horses with *caṇḍāla* grooms. In effect, this was a mobile royal court together with a civilian population accompanying the army (and probably thereby reducing its military effectiveness). Such camps are associated with kings on the move, inspecting local administration, controlling feudatories and other intermediaries, and fighting campaigns.

There follows an elaborate and highly eulogistic description of Harṣa, more appropriate from a royal retainer than from a critic of the royal court. Harṣa is compared to the heroes of the *Mahābhārata*, and only the heroic qualities seem to count. Other associations—such as Yudhiṣṭhira wishing to renounce kingship and Arjuna being loath to do battle—are not mentioned. The king is described as being calm of mind like the Buddha, carrying out the duties of the *varṇāśramadharma* as directed in the *Dharmaśāstra* of Manu and bearing the *daṇḍa* (rod) like Yama, the god of death: all these were qualities expected of a ruler, and doubtless Harṣa was assured of such a description when he chose Bāṇa as his biographer.

The king finally invites Bāṇa to write the biography. After some months at court, Bāṇa returns to his village with its ambience of an ideal *agrahāra*—as described by Bāṇa. That Bāṇa was in the king's favour is made much of by his kinsmen. They request Bāṇa to recite his composition, which they compare to a second *Mahābhārata*. It is also said that the recitation will purify their Bhṛgu *vaṃśa*, though we are not told how. The emphasis on his being a Bhṛgu *brāhmaṇa* was doubtless an additional credential. That the biography of the king would be written in the third person is expected. But curiously Bāṇa writes on his own early life in the third person as well. Is this an attempt to distance himself in order to suggest the greater authenticity of the narrative?

The biography does not cover Harṣa's entire reign but only his early years until his acquisition of sovereignty over Kanauj. The remaining years it is said were completed in a rather summary fashion by Bāṇa's son, Bhūṣana Bhaṭṭa. However, the earlier part is the major portion of the text, and whether it was originally intended to end where it does remains a matter of controversy. If the *Harṣacarita* was written as a narrative leading up to Harṣa's accession and elevated title, then in its day perhaps the narrative would not have been regarded as incomplete. Since Bāṇa does not refer to the king being the author of three plays, they were presumably written after the events described in the biography.

The format of a *carita* is said to consist of five stages: an introduction to the subject of the biography, a description of his activities, the aspirations of the person, followed by efforts to achieve these aspirations, and the eventual success.[14] This format may not always be adhered to, but here it is. The narrative requiring eventual success limits biographies to those who have succeeded, and to the point where the success is registered. Bāṇa addresses three aspects of Harṣa's life: his ancestry and the establishment of the dynasty, his claim to the throne, and his aspiration to rule from Kanauj—which would give him sovereignty over a substantial kingdom.

2. The Biography of the King

The text begins with the king's ancestry. The home base of the family was Sthāṇvīśvara, modern Thanesar north of Delhi. The land around it was extremely fertile, with buffaloes stained by rolling in saffron! Cultivation using the water-wheel yielded a rich harvest. The ultimate in well-being is asserted via comparison with conditions in the earliest and utopian Kṛta age.

Harṣa was the sole ruler to give prominence to the short-lived Puṣyabhūti/ Puṣpabhūti dynasty and ruled from 606 to 647. Other

[14] Ibid., 47.

kingdoms competing for high status were the Later Guptas, the Maukharis, the Maitrakas of Valabhī, and some further afield in Gauḍa and Kāmarūpa in eastern India. The founding ancestor of Harṣa's family was Puṣpabhūti, who is the focus of the third chapter. The ceremony of legitimation of this early ancestor is described.[15] A Śaiva ascetic, Bhairavācārya, performs the *mahākālahṛdaya* rite at a deserted temple in the cremation ground. He is assisted by three disciples—Ṭīṭibha, Pātālasvāmi, and a Drāviḍa called Karṇatāla—and by Puṣpabhūti. Whilst Bhairavācārya is seated on a corpse during the ritual, a being arises from the earth, the Nāga Śrikaṇṭha, who claims to be the lord of the region. The description of the Nāga conforms to the conventional description of *rākṣasas* and forest-dwellers. The king uses a magic sword, presented to him earlier, to vanquish the Nāga, but does not kill him as he notices him wearing a sacred thread. The sword then turns into a radiant woman, the goddess of good fortune, Śrī, who offers him a boon. He asks for the success of Bhairavācārya's rite. Pleased with his magnanimity, she prophesies that he will be ancestor to a line of heroic kings, of whom the foremost will, predictably, be the *cakravartin* Harṣa. Bhairavācārya, having successfully performed the rite and become a Vidyādhara as he had wished, flies into the sky and the goddess re-enters the earth. The Vidyādharas are linked to magical powers and have an ancient and respected ancestry. The rite was non-Vedic, the power and legitimacy coming from the goddess. The only obvious concession made to Brahmanism is the reference to the sacred thread. Yet in a Tantric ritual the identity of caste would probably have been broken.

Thanesar was a centre of the Pāśupata Śaiva cult which, like Tantric rituals, also involved worship of the goddess. Śiva worship was now popular among court circles in northern India after the Gupta period, where earlier Vaiṣṇava Bhāgavatism had been on the rise. In the immediate post-Gupta period, Śaivism and Buddhism seem to have been the contenders for royal patronage. As a legitimation rite, the ritual differs from the Vedic sacrificial rituals required of *kṣatriyas*. This deviation may have been because the family is said to be *vaiśya* in some sources, their lower origin

[15] Kane, 3.45; Cowell and Thomas, 3.111ff.

denying them *kṣatriya* rites in theory.[16] The ritual was a concession to local worship, bringing in a larger loyalty which helped clear the path to kingship. It has been suggested that it may symbolize the defeat of the Nāgas of Śūrasena by an ancestor of Harṣa.[17] Another possibility could be that the area was given as a grant to a *brāhmaṇa* in an earlier period who may then have associated himself with the culture of the forest-dwellers, emerging as the Nāga but with a sacred thread. Such situations were not unknown in the origins of principalities eventually evolving into small kingdoms. The dynastic descent from Puṣpabhūti is given but names are not mentioned. This is surpising since Harṣa in his inscriptions names his immediate ancestors.

The scene then shifts to Harṣa's childhood. The valour of his father, Prabhākaravardhana, is described in resounding phrases which become part of the conventional rhetoric of a king's conquests. He was "a lion to the Hūṇa deer, a burning fever to the king of the Indus land, a troubler of the sleep of Gujarat, a bilious plague to that scent elephant the lord of Gandhāra, a looter to the lawlessness of the Lāṭas, and an axe to the creeper of Mālwa's glory."[18] Despite the hyperbole, these were not permanent conquests since his sons were soon to be involved in campaigns against some of those named. We know from inscriptions that his father dropped the simple title of *mahārāja* to use the more grandiose *paramabhaṭṭāraka-mahārāja-adhirāja*. The title marked a change of status and the royal biography was also meant to underline the change. Yet it is in this chapter that Bāṇa gives a list of those ancient *kṣatriyas* who, because of acts of misdemeanour, came to grief. This suggests that whatever the act of legitimation might have achieved, reference to the ancient *kṣatriya* tradition had still to be recalled from time to time.

Prabhākaravardhana had three children. The eldest son was Rājyavardhana and the younger was Harṣa. Rājyaśrī was their

[16] T. Watters, *On Yuan Chwang's Travels in India*, vol. I, 344–5; *Āryamañjuśrīmūlakalpa*, ed. T.N. Ganapati Sastri; K.P. Jayaswal (ed. and trans.), *An Imperial History of India*, 28.

[17] D. Devahuti, *Harsha: A Political Study*, 67–8; Cowell and F.W. Thomas, 3.124.

[18] Kane, 4.56; Cowell and Thomas, 4.132ff.

sister. Much is made of Harṣa's birth and the auspicious signs that accompanied it, as also the drunken festivities. Bhaṇḍi, the mother's brother's son, was appointed to serve the princes. Later, the two sons of the Mālava king are also appointed as companions, an indication of their subordinate status. The marriage of Rājyaśrī to Grahavarman, the Maukhari ruler of Kanauj, is agreed upon. This was either marrying into a peer group family, or better, one that was a rung higher.

The fifth chapter mentions renewed attacks by the Hūṇas. Rājyavardhana, accompanied by his younger brother, was sent to hold them back. Meanwhile, their father fell ill and Harṣa had to hurriedly return to the capital. As he was leaving the camp, there were two ill omens—the cry of a crow and the appearance of a naked Jaina monk! The father's condition was clearly serious and various rites were being performed, most of them non-Vedic, such as a Drāviḍa who prayed to a *vetāla* with the offering of a skull. The doctor attending on him was called Rasāyaṇa, normally meaning "alchemy". Strangely, the elder son was not sent for, perhaps because he was conducting the campaign. With the king's condition deteriorating, the queen decided to become a *satī*. Bāṇa does not criticize this action, although he opposed the idea in his other work, the *Kādambarī*.

The father on his deathbed lists the principles by which his son should govern: acquiring territory, maintaining the treasury, controlling intermediaries or feudatories, upholding royalty even if burdensome, protecting subjects, bearing arms, controlling self-indulgence, and exterminating enemies. These aspects are partly in consonance with the earlier *saptāṅga* theory—the seven constitiuents of the state discussed by Kauṭilya. But the new feature is the presence of *sāmantas*, creating a layer of intermediaries between king and subject, and the protection of the subject being now at one remove. The command to control self-indulgence was a critique presumably of royal extravagance.

It is implied that the father seemed to prefer Harṣa as his successor, but Harṣa did not wish to supersede his elder brother. The death of their father, their mother becoming a *satī*, overwhelms both brothers with grief. Rājyavardhana was not altogether averse to Harṣa succeeding to the throne; his interest in Buddhism may have been a reason for his diffidence, it being suggested that he may have contemplated joining a Buddhist order. Prabhākaravardhana being a worshipper of Sūrya may not have approved of his elder son's inclination towards Buddhism. Nor does Bāṇa mention that Rājyavardhana did rule for a brief period—as stated in Harṣa's inscriptions.[19] There is a hint that Harṣa was the more ambitious, and that there may have been some rivalry over the succession. Clearly, the eventual succession of the younger brother had to be justified in the biography. The pace of the narrative picks up halfway through the book. Descriptions become briefer and conversations are reported. Rājyavardhana expresses his distaste for kingship and preference for a hermitage, reminiscent of Yudhiṣṭhira in the *Mahābhārata*. Harṣa wonders if his brother is testing him by these remarks. Harṣa it is said was averse to breaking the rule of primogeniture.

Further bad news informs them of the killing of their sister Rājyaśrī's husband, the Maukhari ruler of Kanauj. The assassin is the ruler of Mālava, and thus a feudatory of Thanesar. Rājyaśrī had been imprisoned but escaped and was now somewhere in the Vindhyan forest. It is curious that she did not return to Thanesar, instead of seeking refuge in the Vindhyas. There is also the threat of an impending attack on Thanesar by the Mālava ruler. Rājyavardhana insists that a rebellious feudatory has to be punished for, as he puts it, a frog cannot slap a cobra, or a calf take the tiger captive, or a hind clutch the lion's mane. Rājyavardhana leaves to defend the kingdom but is treacherously killed by Śaśāṅka, the king of Gauḍa in eastern India. Their hostility was political, but it could also have had a religious undertone since Śaśāṅka, according to Buddhist sources, was anti-Buddhist. Linked to the events leading to Rājyavardhana's death is a lengthy digression on twenty-eight earlier kings, some of whom are historically known, who, moving away from the path of *dharma*, were killed in various ways by disgruntled officers, courtiers and others.[20] Some of the names are also referred to in the dynastic lists of the

[19] V.S. Pathak, *Historians of Ancient India*, 55.

[20] Kane, 6.105–6; Cowell and Thomas, 6.221–4. These include the assassination of the Mauryan Bṛhadratha by the Śuṅga Puṣyamitra, and the killing of the Śaka king by Candra Gupta II in order to rescue the queen, Devī, as narrated in Viśākhadatta's play, *Devīcandragupta* (see Chapter 8).

Purāṇas, but Bāṇa's list does not follow a chronological order. His digression is either an indirect comment on the inherent inefficiency of Harṣa's brother to rule, or intended to warn Harṣa against court intrigue. The killing of Rājyavardhana is entangled in the politics of North India at that time.

By the seventh chapter Harṣa assumes kingship and is preparing a campaign against Gauḍa. There is a hint that he was in any case inclined to do both and was nudged towards it by Lakṣmī, the goddess of prosperity. This was yet another intervention of a deity, but a goddess. He declares that in addition to avenging the death of his brother and rescuing his sister, he wishes to conduct a *digvijaya.*[21] This would reflect a wish to at least retain the rhetoric of kingship, although the *digvijaya* no longer had the same resonance as in the *Vedas* and epics. This was both a statement of his claim to power, perhaps a necessary formality before he could assume the titles which his father had held, as well as a prelude to rituals of sovereignty in imitation of earlier times. Harṣa's aspiration to be a successful *digvijayin* is compared to the exploits of the ancient heroes of the *Mahābhārata.*[22] The figures that are given for the various wings of the army are of course highly exaggerated, as they generally were in the ancient world. A huge commissariat accompanied the military force; nevertheless, villages near where they camped were pillaged.[23] Both the inflated figures and the pillaging were aspects of the exercise of power.[24]

Harṣa's immediate concern being to find his sister, he sets out with his army. This becomes symbolic of a *digvijaya,* as he eventually ruled from Kanauj when he established his sovereignty. Kanauj was more strategically located, commanding a rich agrarian region and at the hub of trade, different from the more limited income which came to Thanesar. The *digvijaya* was not necessarily a military campaign but could be an assertion of control over designated territory. The preliminary gift-giving is reminiscent of rituals that demonstrate excessive wealth. In earlier times gifts were distributed after the *digvijaya*, but here the "campaign" follows

[21] Kane, 6.106 and 7.108–9; Cowell and Thomas, 6.223–4.

[22] Kane, 7.239; Cowell and Thomas, 7.114.

[23] Kane, 7.112; Cowell and Thomas, 7.235.

[24] R. Thapar, "The Role of the Army in the Exercise of Power in Early India", 25–38.

gift-giving. Was this because the campaign had become more symbolic? Bāṇa's account of the march and the setting up of camp, the *skandhāvāra*, includes passing mention of a disgruntled countryside with a few mutterings about the prevalent poverty. Some peasants even comment on the right of the king to rule. Was this linked in any way with the presence of Lokāyata thinkers in their midst who argued that the king is appointed by the will of the people, a sentiment also reflected in the earliest Buddhist texts?

At this point Bhāskaravarman, the king of Kāmarūpa (in Assam), also recently risen in status, requests a treaty with Harṣa, for he too is battling against their common enemy, the king of Gauḍa.[25] The alliance is accompanied by a large number of gifts for Harṣa. Among these the umbrella is singled out, presumably as an indication of his acceptance of Harṣa's sovereignty. The genealogy of Bhāskaravaraman is given but only the names of the earliest ancestors are listed. At one point mention is made of a *mahārājā* whose great-grandson was a *mahārājādhirāja,* pointing to the commonly occurring political mutation in these times. Judging by these titles both Harṣa and Bhāskaravarman were of the same status, but now Harṣa was recognized as superior. Both kings are said to be patrons of the Śaivas.

The king of Gauḍa, who had also started his career as a feudatory,[26] was anxious to establish an independent kingdom. His alliance with the ruler of Mālava was intended as a two-pronged movement against Kanauj, as was the alliance of Harṣa and Bhāskaravarman against Śaśāṅka. Bāṇa's references to Śaśāṅka are not complimentary, although he concedes the brilliance with which he gradually manoeuvred the forces of his allies and feudatories against Harṣa. Buddhist sources depict him as a persecutor of Buddhists.[27] Bhaṇḍi arrives at Harṣa's court, ashamed that he could not protect Rājyavardhana. Harṣa is asked to inspect the enormous booty taken from the campaign against Mālava, and this is then put under the control of overseers.[28] Campaigns are a ready source of

[25] Kane, 7.118; Cowell and Thomas, 7.246.

[26] Rohtasgadh Seal-matrix of the Mahāsāmanta Śaśānkadeva, *Corpus Inscriptionum Indicarim*, III.78, 283–4.

[27] *Āryamañjuśrīmūlakalpa*, 49, no. 33ff.; K.P. Jayaswal (ed. and trans.), *The Imperial History of India*, vv. 715–23.

[28] Kane, 7.122–3; Cowell and Thomas, 7.254.

wealth. Booty is differentiated from theft, considered legitimate, and distributed according to its own rules.[29]

The scene shifts again to a village in the heart of the Vindhyas, where Harṣa meets the young chiefs (described as *sāmantas*) of the Śabara and other forest tribes.[30] These areas are yet to be enveloped in sanskritic culture-ways and the description is therefore valuable in depicting the non-caste, tribal or clan-based societies still extensive in this region. The location was probably on the frontier of the kingdom of Harṣa or of the Maukharis. Who actually controls these forest is ambiguous since most of the inhabitants live by hunting. The state derives income from timber and elephants, both being under its control. The settlements consist of huts of bamboo and reed. Those who live there organize their own protection against thieves and predators. A rudimentary system of guards and village headmen was probably more a protection in theory than practice.[31]

Bāṇa's detailed description of these villages is a glimpse of the process by which kingdoms were extending their control over forested areas, converting forests to cultivable land. Forest-dwellers, earlier given to hunting, gathering, and shifting agriculture, were now being converted into settled peasants—in this case the Śabaras, the name occurring frequently in references to forest peoples. Pockets of the earlier pattern of life did, however, continue.

In the eighth chapter the king goes into the deeper part of the forest, rather like the epic heroes, in contrast to the villages on the edge. Rājyaśrī is still being sought. Sovereignty extends to the forest despite the forest being distanced from civilization. The chief of the forest tribe, designated as *aṭavika-sāmanta*, goes by the formulaic name for such persons, Vyāghraketu, invoking the tiger. The description bears the same features as that of all forest-dwellers from earlier literature—a dark body, flat nose, thick lips, heavy jaws, projecting cheek bones, and moving through the forest like a dense black cloud or a mass of black collyrium—all familiar from the description of the Niṣāda, Pulinda, Bhilla, and from the

[29] *Manu's Code of Law*, 7.96–7.

[30] Kane, 8.125; Cowell and Thomas, 8.259.

[31] Kane, 7.122–3; Cowell and Thomas, 7.255ff.

rākṣasas of the *Rāmāyaṇa*. Just as one thinks that there is now a greater acceptance of forest people, no longer called *rākṣasas*, there follows a string of expletives about them. But at least they are not violently killed, as in the past. The settlement (*grāma*) was gradually coming to terms with the forest (*araṇya*).

Harṣa makes enquiries about his sister and is directed to the hermitage of a Buddhist ascetic, Divākaramitra. He is said to be a *brāhmaṇa* who became a Buddhist—not uncommon at the time—and that he was a childhood friend of Grahavarman, the late husband of Rājyaśrī.[32] This turns out to be the habitat of persons with various religious affiliations, including Buddhists, Jainas, Bhāgavatas, Śaivas, Lokāyatas teaching materialism, alchemists, reciters of the *Purāṇas*, and grammarians,[33] so wide an intellectual range that one wonders what was specifically Buddhist about it. The persons collected here are a mirror image of Bāṇa's youthful companions. The repeated presence of the unorthodox Lokāyatas is an interesting facet of such hermitages. The place has an ambience which is in some ways reminiscent of the earlier *kutuhala-śālās*, the parks at the edge of cities where debates took place. However, the references are generally sympathetic to the Buddhists, though some humorous satire is irresistible, as in the statements that even the parrots were expounding Śākya *śāstras* (Buddhist texts), and that the tigers had given up eating meat! In essentials the hermitage has the ambience of gentle intellectual activity.

Harṣa's sister is eventually found—in the nick of time, as she is about to immolate herself. The text ends with the happy return home of brother and sister together with Divākaramitra, and finally the coronation of Harṣa. It has been argued that the sister is also to be seen as allegorical and represents the goddess Śrī, the goddess of Good Fortune.[34] The episode is therefore symbolic of the settling of good fortune on Harṣa, and to that extent completes the function of the biography. At a more mundane level the rescue of his sister was essential to his ambition as she strengthened his claim to sovereignty over Kanauj, earlier held by his brother-in-

[32] Kane, 8.126; Cowell and Thomas, 8.261–2.
[33] Kane, 8.128; Cowell and Thomas, 8.265ff.
[34] V.S. Pathak, *Historians of Ancient India*, 30–56.

law. The sovereignty was significant to the politics of northern India, as confirmed by subsequent dynasties that battled over the control of Kanauj. The succession would normally have gone to Grahavarman's brother, but he had died early. Kanauj had access not only to the Ganges river system but also to routes to Central and north-western India. With the decline of Mathura in the Gupta period, Kanauj came into focus.[35]

The attempt in the biography was therefore not to cover the entire life of the king, but to focus on the acquisition and establishing of sovereignty over Kanauj. The *Harṣacarita* is the prototype of the genre. While it draws on some elements of the continuing tradition, it does not depend on the *kṣatriya* legitimation which is characteristic of some later biographies. The reign of Harṣavardhana was close enough to the period when such legitimation was not required, and his personal involvement with Buddhism and Śaivism may not have encouraged him to perform Vedic rituals. That his sovereignty was acknowledged is suggested in the inscription of the Cālukya king Pulakeśin II, who defeated Harṣa's attempt to conquer south of the Narmada.[36] References to Harṣa's authority in the inscription are doubtless exaggerated in part by having to compliment Pulakeśin II for having restrained such a formidable foe. The inscription dates to AD 634, therefore the biography is likely to have been written before Harṣa's defeat.

3. Other Sources Complementing the Biography

Among the other texts of that time are the king's grants of land recorded in inscriptions.[37] Bāṇa provides a limited genealogy of Harṣa's ancestors, but this is fleshed out in the inscriptions. In these,

[35] Watters, *On Yuan Chwang's Travels in India*, vol. I, 340ff.; *Alberuni's India*, vol. I, 200–9; idem, vol. II, 316–20. *Brāhmaṇa* horse traders are referred to as making donations to temples at Kanauj: Peheva Inscription, *Ep. Ind.*, 1, 184–90.

[36] Aihole Inscription of Pulakesin II, *Ep. Ind.*, 6, 6, v.23.

[37] E.g., Madhuban Copper Plate, *Ep. Ind.*, 1, 67, 7, 155; Banskhera Plate of Harshavardhana, *Ep. Ind.*, 4, 208; Sonpat Copper Seal Inscription of Harshavardhana, *Corpus Inscriptionum Indicarum*, III, 52, 231.

the founding ancestor Puṣpabhūti is absent and is replaced by three previous kings: *mahārāja* Naravardhana, *mahārāja* Rājyavardhana I, and *mahārāja* Ādityavardhana, before the mention of Harṣa's father. The wives of each are also listed so that there is no ambiguity about the person referred to.[38] Both inscriptions are in the era started by Harṣa, calculated from AD 606, and refer to the past. The story of Puṣpabhūti as a founding ancestor may not have been considered appropriate to official genealogies of Harṣa's reign, when he had acquired the sovereignty linked to Kanauj, since the myth suggests an obscure origin.[39] Instead of countering the myth or creating an alternative, it may have been thought better just to ignore it. The intention here would be to claim that Harṣa's family always had status as substantial intermediaries and they improved on this, as suggested by their titles.

Whereas the earlier kings are referred to as *mahārājas*, Harṣa's father takes the title of *paramabhaṭṭāraka-mahārājādhirāja*, claiming to rule an independent polity. He is also described conventionally as protecting the *varṇāśramadharma*—the laws of caste. He is said to be a worshipper of Sūrya, as were his father and grandfather, although the earlier ancestor in Bāṇa's narrative performed Tantric rites. Bāṇa mentions Taraka, a Maga *brāhmaṇa* astrologer at the court who prophesies the greatness of Harṣa. The Maga *brāhmaṇas,* linked to sun-worship, came from western India and may well have had connections with sun cults even further west. The choice of religious sects as recipients of royal patronage varied within the same ruling family and even with the same king. The ancestors are associated with Śaivism and Tantra, Prabhākaravardhana with the worship of Sūrya, Rājyavardhana with Buddhism, and Harṣa with Buddhism and Śaivism. Some were personal preferences, others were tied to political considerations. There is inscriptional reference to Rājyavardhana II, Harṣa's elder brother.

An interesting coincidence is the reference in inscriptions to a

[38] Banskhera Plate, *Ep. Ind.*, 4, 208; Madhuban Copper Plate, *Ep. Ind.,* 1, 67; 7, 155.

[39] Clay seals of Nalanda, *Ep. Ind.*, 21, 72; Sonpat Copper Seal Inscription of Harsha, *Corpus Inscriptionum Indicarum,* III, 231.

senior official, Skandagupta, with the designation of *dūtaka*, and dating to 628 and 631.[40] He may have been identical with the official mentioned by Bāṇa as giving friendly advice of a political nature to the king. A large range of officers and feudatories are listed, and this hierarchy is reflected in the biography as well. Another *dūtaka* carries the grand scribal title of *mahākṣapaṭalādhikaranādhikṛta sāmanta-mahārāja*.[41] One of these inscriptions is more literary in content and may have been drafted by Harṣa who, judging by the plays attributed to him, may have cultivated a literary turn. What was finally engraved was presumably not the actual draft of the king, for it bears the occasional linguistic error.

Two of the plays attributed to Harṣa, the *Priyadarśikā* and the *Ratnāvalī*, are conventional romances which focus on Udayana, a king of earlier times made famous through a cycle of plays by Bhāsa. The third play, *Nāgānanda*, has a different mood. The hero sacrifices his life to save a snake deity and is restored to life by the goddess Gaurī, and he emerges as a *cakravartin*. Interestingly, he becomes a *cakravartin* not through conquest or the rule of law but through the favour of a deity: an innovation in the concept. This is a parallel to Harṣa's acquisition of sovereignty through the goddess Śrī. The play epitomizes *dāna* (gift-giving), and the Buddha's blessings are invoked. It could have been interpreted by some as empathizing with Buddhist ethics.[42]

Xuanzang, the Chinese Buddhist pilgrim travelling through India during Harṣa's reign, left a detailed itinerary with comments on what he saw.[43] He is as consistent in projecting Harṣa as a patron of Buddhism as are the inscriptions in giving him a Śaiva identity. Among many other events, Xuanzang and his biographer, Hwui Li, describe the vast quinquennial religious assemblies called by Harṣa at Kanauj and at Prayāga (modern Allahabad). At Kanauj

[40] Cowell and Thomas, 6.219; *Ep. Ind.*, 4, 208–11; ibid., 1.67ff.

[41] Shankar Goyal, "The Recently Discovered Kurukshetra-Varanasi Grant of Harsha: Year 23", 193–203.

[42] D. Devahuti, *Harsha: A Political Study*, 178–80; S.R. Goyal, *Harsha and Buddhism*.

[43] S. Beal, *Buddhist Records of the Western World*; T. Watters, *On Yuan Chwang's Travels in India*; S. Beal (trans.), *The Life of Hiuen-Tsiang by the Shaman Hwui Li*.

there were eighteen important kings in attendance, and many thousands of priests of various denominations. The assembly was held in the great enclosure where kings and nobles were wont to bestow charity.[44] There was a distribution from the royal treasury both to members of various religious sects and to those who were impoverished. This would be a spectacular manifestation of the shift from *yajña* (sacrifice) to *dāna* (gift-giving) as forms of legitimation.

Bāṇa's *Kādambarī* is as a work of fiction in some ways a counterpoint to the *Harṣacarita*. It has a complex structure of subnarratives within the main narrative.[45] The story occurs with some variations again in a part of Somadeva's *Kathāsaritasāgara* of the eleventh century, perhaps going back to Gunāḍhya's *Bṛhatkathā*. The story is located in the forests of the Vindhyas, the habitat of the Śabara tribes, and may reflect Bāṇa's experience of these forests when accompanying Harṣa. The *Kādambarī* acts as the structural opposite of the *Harṣacarita*—in that the royal biography is the text on the court and settled society (the *grāma*), whilst the *Kādambarī* is a fantasy based on the court poet's perception of the forest (the *araṇya*). There is a tendency to romanticize the forest in this work, which is somewhat ironic, given that some of these forests were being cut down to become the agrarian base of kingdoms.

Some of the families mentioned in the *Harṣacarita* are also known from their inscriptions, such as the Maukharis.[46] Bāṇa compares the joining of the two houses in marriage as that of the Sun and the Moon.[47] This could be an attempt to introduce accepted lineages, the solar and the lunar, or merely a poetic simile. The Maukharis claimed descent from the hundred sons of Aśvapati and the latter claimed links with the Kekeyas or Madras,[48] of *kṣatriya* status, although not the most exalted.

[44] S. Beal, *Buddhist Records of the Western World*, vol. 1, 233 ; S. Beal (trans.), *The Life of Hiuen-Tsiang by the Shaman Hwui Li*, vol. 5, 176–81.

[45] A.B. Keith, *A History of Sanskrit Literature,* 319ff.

[46] Haraha Inscription of Ishanavarman, *Ep. Ind.*, 14, 110; Asirgadh Copper Seal Inscription of Sarvavarman, *Corpus Inscriptionum Indicarum,* III, 219.

[47] Kane, 4.71; Cowell and Thomas, 4.161.

[48] F.E. Pargiter, *Ancient Indian Historical Tradition*, 109.

The Maukharis also initially take the simple title of *śri mahārāja*; and at about the same time as when Prabhākaravardhana moved to a more exalted title, the Maukhari king did likewise, subsequent to which they seem to have split into many small ruling families. One among these has left inscriptions in the Barabar and Nagarjuni hills which have a curious historical continuity. Located close together at the eastern end of the Vindhyas in south Bihar, both these hills have cave shrines and cells initially donated by the Mauryas. The Maukhari inscriptions are located at the entrance to each cave and record the placing of icons: of Kṛṣṇa in the Barabar hill cave, and of Śiva in the Nagarjuni hill cave. There is no reference to either of the earlier votive inscriptions, still visible, nor of the Ājīvika or other sects which would have been the earlier occupants. Nevetheless, the sites obviously remained sacred from past times and were re-used by the later sects of Vaiṣṇavas and Śaivas. Whether the earlier sects were forcibly expelled or their cells fell into disuse remains an open question. At some point an attempt was made to try and obliterate the name of the original donee, but not very successfully. The Maukhari kingdom extended to the region of Kālañjara in Bundelkhand.[49] Therefore, the search for Rājyaśrī in that direction by Harṣa would have been expected. These families were ex-feudatories of the Guptas, and therefore Harṣa was battling among equals—all the more reason for Bāṇa to elevate his status. They were rivals but linked by marriage alliances and defined by their ambitions of establishing substantial kingdoms.

The *Āryamañjuśrīmūlakalpa*, of a slightly later period, narrates the history essentially of eastern India over a few centuries. It refers to the *vaiśya* dynasty of Śrīkaṇṭha-Sthānvīśvara and describes it as a family of wealthy men who became ministers and then kings. If the reading of Soma as Śaśāṅka is correct (as it appears to be), then we are told that he was a *brāhmaṇa* extremely hostile to the Buddhists and Jainas, although he is also described as a hero.[50] Reference is made to Ra (Rājyavardhana?), who

[49] Barah Copper-Plate Inscriptions of Bhojadeva, *Ep. Ind.*, 19, 15ff.

[50] *Āryamañjuśrīmūlakalpa*; K.P. Jayaswal (ed. and trans.), *An Imperial History of India*, vv. 715–23.

was a *vaiśya* and a Buddhist and opposed to Soma, as was Ra's younger brother Ha (Harṣa?), the latter having attacked Soma at his capital at Puṇḍra. There is a hint that the two brothers made a joint attack. Other contemporary dynasties mentioned include the kings of Valabhī, the Later Guptas, the Maukharis, and so on. The east remains in a state of anarchy after Soma's death. The succession of rulers includes some *vaiśyas* who, on occasion, take on *kṣatriya* status. Among them a *śūdra* king of Gauḍa is said to have attacked the *dvijāti-gaṇa-sāmantas*, a group of upper-caste feudatories. Rulers referred to as Gopālas are said to be of low caste—*dāsajīvinaiḥ*—and hostile to the *brāhmaṇas*. The brevity of reference is tantalizing, given the social significance of the statements made. Uncertainty in eastern India continues until the reign of Gopālaka (Gopāla of the Pāla dynasty?), whose positive image includes the fact that he was a patron of the Buddhists as well as the Deva religion, i.e. Brahmanism.

Bāṇa's biography became an exemplar among *caritas* and the subject of commentaries. The *carita* form is discussed or referred to in major studies on literary criticism by Ānandavardhana, Bhoja, and Kṣemendra, from the tenth to the twelfth centuries. Authors who fancied themselves as writing to record the activities of kings either quote from Bāṇa or claim to be the "new Bāṇas".

B. THE *RĀMACARITA* OF SANDHYĀKARANANDIN

A biography of another kind, the *Rāmacarita*, was written by Sandhyākaranandin in the early twelfth century.[51] Different in content and form from the *Harṣacarita*, its context is the Pāla kingdom of eastern India, its focus on an event in the reign of the king Rāmapāla. The event is the political and military effort

[51] *The Rāmacaritam of Sandhyākaranandin, edited with Sanskrit Commentaries and English Translation*, by R.C. Majumdar, R. Basak, and N.B. Banerji; Haraprasad Sastri (ed.), *Rāmacarita by Sandhyākara Nandi,* ed. Haraprasad Sastri, Memoirs of the Asiatic Society of Bengal, 3.1–56; *Rāmacarita of Sandhyākaranandin*, Revised with English Translation and Notes, by R. Basak, Memoirs of the Asiatic Society of Bengal, 3.1; S. Brocquet, *La Geste de Rāma: poeme a double sens de Sandhyākaranandin.*

made by Rāmapāla to successfully recover the region of Varendrī, the heartland of Pāla power, which had been lost to the Kaivartas through the mismanagement of Rāmapāla's elder brother. The Kaivartas were the feudatories who as intermediaries had led a revolt against the Pālas. Composed in the reign of his successor, Madanapāla, the biography focuses on this event, but narrates Rāmapāla's life from his becoming king to his voluntary death. It is a literary *tour de force* because it can be read as a biography of Rāmapāla, as well as the story of Rāma from the *Rāmāyaṇa*. Narrating two distinctly different stories within the same text was rare, but it was also a known demonstration of linguistic erudition. Sandhyākaranandin states his familiarity with literary concepts such as *rasa*, *rūpaka*, *dhvani*, and *śleṣa*,[52] writing that involves equivocation, punning, and double meanings.

The two stories in the *Rāmacarita* focus on the recovery of Varendrī, referred to as *janakabhū*. In one reading it refers to the homeland of the Pālas, and in the other it is a synonym for Sītā—and by extension could refer to Bhū, the earth-goddess. The recovery of the territory/Sītā seems to be a variation on the theme of acquiring Śrī. The intermeshing of the two stories suggests that Rāmapāla is being compared with Nārāyaṇa/Viṣṇu.[53] The projection of the two hero figures in the context of monarchy, the complexities of patriliny and primogeniture, and the idea of royal divinity run parallel. Using the same text to provide a double meaning was a demonstration of skill, but also a somewhat trite literary exercise.

The text is inevitably complicated and a commentary was thought necessary to explain the sometimes unusual use of words and imagery. A commentary exists for the earlier part of the text (ch. 1 and ch. 2, vv. 1–35) written by Śīlacandra, and focuses on Rāmapāla, but the precise date of the commentary is not known. Was a bifurcation intended where the commentary conveyed the history whereas the text incorporated the poem? The name of the commentator and the opening invocation suggest that he might

52 A.B. Keith, *A History of Sanskrit Literature*, 137–9. The *Rāghavapāṇḍavīya*, for example, tells the stories of the *Rāmāyaṇa* and the *Mahābhārata* simultaneously. *Rāmacaritam of Sandhyākaranandin*, ed. R. Basak.

53 4.28; 5.6–8.

have been a Buddhist.[54] The Pālas were patrons of Buddhism as well, and the early king Dharmapāla is particularly remembered as such.

1. Sandhyākaranandin

The final chapter of the text is the *kavipraśasti* (in praise of the poet), which has an immodest assessment of the merits of the author, in part perhaps as an answer to his numerous critics.[55] He states that he comes from a family of scribes, his caste being *karana* (*kāyastha*). The story is also that of his homeland, his family home being in a village in Varendrī, in the smaller locality of Bṛhadvatu, which he describes as the *maṇḍala-cūḍāmaṇi*—the crest jewel of the principalities of Varendrī—and near the capital at Puṇḍhravardhana. The grant of land was probably to his father, a *sandhi-vigrahaka* (minister) during the reign of Rāmapāla. The author would have been familiar with the king's activities and the politics of the court at Puṇḍhravardhana. He refers to himself as the full moon to the forest of lilies of the Nandi family![56]

The author claims that, having written a version of the Rāma story, he is the Vālmīki of the Kali age,[57] a title earlier claimed by a learned *brāhmaṇa* serving the Pāla kings.[58] Sandhyākaranandin's claim appears to have been motivated by what he refers to as the pointless criticism of those hardly in a position to judge the biography, although admittedly such criticism helps to advertise it. The work was kept hidden until people of learning demanded that it be made public because it had their approval. It would seem that the criticism might have been political. Even if there is little direct reference to this, the text had a political value.[59] It was composed during the reign of Rāmapāla's son Madanapāla and inevitably carries another eulogy, although more limited, of his immediate patron. The author is therefore writing not about contemporary

[54] *The Rāmacaritam of Sandhyākaranandin, edited with Sanskrit Commentaries and English Translation*, Introduction, vi.

[55] 5.1–20.

[56] 5.4.

[57] 5.11: *kaliyuga rāmāyaṇam iha kavirapi kali kāla vālmīkiḥ.*

[58] Badal Pillar Inscription, *Ep. Ind.*, 2, 160–7, v. 24.

[59] 5.12–16.

events, as in some other biographies, but about a historical event relating to the previous king.

2. The Narrative

The reading of the Rāma story opens with salutations to Śiva, Sūrya, and the Ikṣvākus. The Pāla narrative is somewhat ambiguous since it harks back to a *samudra-kula*, or Ocean-family origin, but also has an association with Ikṣvāku and links to the Solar lineage. A *nāga* appears, but this time as the progenitor of the founder. Since the early and more powerful Pāla kings were recognized patrons of Buddhism, there is also a salutation to the images of Lokeśa and Tārā.[60] Another concession is made to the authority of Buddhist Elders when it is stated that one of them arranged a treaty between two warring parties, the Pālas and the Kalacuris of Central India.[61] This is also stated by the Lama Tāranātha writing at the end of the sixteenth century.[62] This might have been an instance of *kapālasandhi*, where peace comes through buying off the aggressor.[63] There is an interleaving of Pāla kings who profess one religion but are patrons of other religions as well, as is evident from their inscriptions.[64]

Other sources refer to Gopāla as the founder of the dynasty, and to his being elected to kingship with the blessings of the goddess Caṇḍi. This was to avoid a condition of *mātsyanyāya*, the anarchy that results from the absence of kingship. Was Caṇḍi an alternative for Śrī? The link with the goddess probably disguised Gopāla's possible low origin and his election to kingship. The biography does not refer to this; since the author claimed that the

[60] 3.7.

[61] If it can be argued, as I have done in Chapter 4, that the Cedis were the enemies of Kosala and are pilloried in Vālmīki's *Rāmāyaṇa* as *rākṣasas*, then this gives another layer of interpretation to the *Rāmacarita* being the story of both Rāmapāla and Rāma. The Kalacuris being Cedis would be seen as enemies, apart from the actual hostilities between the two.

[62] Tāranātha, *History of Buddhism in India*, ch. 28ff./257ff.

[63] *The Rāmacaritam of Sandhyākaranandin, edited with Sanskrit Commentaries and English Translation*, Introduction.

[64] The Bangarh Grant of Mahipala, *Ep. Ind.*, 14, 324; Belwa Plates, *Ep. Ind.*, 29.1ff.

Pālas were of high status,[65] his work conveniently leaves out the more obscure early rulers. The marriage of Dharmapāla with a Rāṣṭrakūṭa princess was both a political alliance and an acquisition of status.[66]

Events leading up to the loss of Varendrī are narrated briefly. This was a major crisis in an otherwise not uncommon situation where the Pāla hold was tenuous, with territory being lost and recovered.[67] Rāmapāla's eldest brother, Mahipāla, suspecting his two younger brothers of conspiring against him, imprisoned them, but then faced a revolt of his feudatories.[68] He lost the battle against them and fled from Varendrī, which was occupied by the Kaivartas under their victorious chief Divya/Divokka, succeeded later by Bhīma. The loss is explained as being due both to *durnaya* (wrong policy), and *yuddha-vyāsana* (obsession with war). Possibly, the ministers were disgruntled by the policies of the Pāla king. The revolt is described as a calamity, against the norms—*dharma-viplava*—and essentially a rebellion of feudatories.[69] It has been argued that this was not the sole revolt and that others also occurred in eastern India. [70] The death of Mahipāla and the accession of the younger brother, Rāmapāla, introduced the other theme common to biographies—the breaking of primogeniture and the need for a biography to justify it. Much is made of the imprisonment of Rāmapāla by his elder brother.[71]

Divya is described as a highly placed officer, a royal servitor, but constantly fraudulent.[72] The epithet used, *dasyu*, has led to varied readings. Some would argue that it means an enemy, others that he was a member of an oppressed section of society. The Kaivartas

[65] 1.4ff.

[66] Monghyr Copper-Plate Inscriptions, R. Mukherjee and S.H. Maity, *Corpus of Bengal Inscriptions*, 117, 122.

[67] Baghaura Narayana Image Inscription, *Ep. Ind.*, 17.353ff.

[68] The revolt is also referred to in inscriptions, e.g. Copper Plate Grant of Vaidyadeva, king of Kamarupa, *Ep. Ind.*, 2.347ff., vv. 13–14. Some verses of the inscription hint at knowing the *Rāmacarita,* v. 4.

[69] *Rāmacarita*, 1.24–31.

[70] R.C. Majumdar, "The Revolt of Divokka Against Mahipāla II and Other Revolts in Bengal", 125ff.

[71] *Rāmacarita*, 1.22–36.

[72] Ibid., 1.38.

were of a mixed caste and occupationally said to be fishermen.[73] Unfortunately, inscriptional references to Divya do not clarify his identity.[74] Rāmapāla's successful attempt at recovering the lost homeland involved a battle against Bhīma. In spite of their oppressive taxation, the Kaivartas had an inadequate army. Their auxiliary army hastily put together after the initial defeat drew on ill-equipped peasants and local people as an armed force riding buffaloes and using bows and arrows—*kāsara-vāhanaka-bala*.[75] This has led to a reading of the event as a peasant revolt—perhaps the first in Indian history.[76] If that is what it was, there is surprisingly no comment from the author on what must have been a most unusual confrontation. A more feasible reading is that it was of lesser feudatories led by the Kaivartas, making a bid to establish their own independent authority,[77] in which case it would not have been an unusual event.

Rāmapāla was able to organize a force through various alliances with neighbours and feudatories, and, by offering land and wealth in addition, won them over together with their armies.[78] The author includes a list and explains who they were. None were rulers of consequence and both the revolt and its quelling involved the politics of *sāmantas* rather than that of kings. The place names associated with them tend to be forested areas and administrative districts—*aṭavi, bhukti, maṇḍala*; and one person is described as *aṭavika-sāmanta-cūḍāmaṇi*—literally, the crest jewel

[73] A.M. Chowdhury, *Dynastic History of Bengal*, 105–7; N. Ray, *History of the Bengali People* (Ancient Period).

[74] Copper-Plate Grant of Bhojavarman, D.R. Bhandarkar, *Inscriptions of Bengal*, 3, 22.

[75] *Rāmacarita*, 2.42.

[76] R.S. Sharma, *Indian Feudalism*, 220ff. Curiously, the terms generally used for peasants, such as *kīnāśa*, or derivatives of *kṛṣi* such as *kṛṣivāla*, are not used and those in revolt are referred to as the Kaivarta, presumably a clan before they became a caste. One view reads an inscription as referring to them being feudatories of low caste and of a *dāsa* family which rose to ministerial status. But this view has been contested. Bhaturiya Inscription, *Ep. Ind.*, 33, 150–4. S.P. Lahiry, "Bhaturiya Inscription of Rājyapāla", *Indian Historical Quarterly*, 1955, 31, 215–31.

[77] K. Chakrabarti, "Brahmanical Hegemony and the Oppressed Social Groups: The Kaivarta 'Revolt' and After" (forthcoming).

[78] *Rāmacarita*, 1.43–5; 2.2–6.

of the forest feudatories. The circles of kings come into operation through alliances, his major ally being his maternal uncle. This section reads like a vignette of the peer group of a family, with one among them trying desperately to maintain a position superior to the intermediaries. The loss of Varendrī was a blow to the Pālas, and its recovery was crucial.

The battle against Bhīma was fierce and is described at length. Those that resisted were eventually won over by promises of wealth. Some of the wealth came readily from the plunder of Bhīma's *skandhāvāra* (camp) by the victorious army, the consequential act in virtually every campaign.[79] The recovery of Varendrī was sealed by establishing the city of Rāmāvatī, the description of which echoes that of Laṅkā in the *Rāmāyaṇa*.[80] Lengthy passages speak of the natural beauty and fertility of Varendrī. These seem more an exercise in poetry than as fulfilling the requirements of a biography. The earlier oppressive taxation—*krūra-kara-pīḍitā*—was replaced by a mild taxation. At various times Rāmapāla was involved in campaigns against the Gāhaḍvālas in Varanasi, the eastern Gaṅgas in Orissa, the Karṇāṭas from the Deccan, and the Colas from further south. The last is mentioned in Cola sources. An interesting aside in a play, *Candikauśika* by Ārya Kṣemeśvara, states that Rāmapāla destroyed the Karṇāṭas in the same way as Candragupta Maurya destroyed the Nandas. Would this reflect a reading of the *Mudrārākṣasa*?

Since Rāmapāla is said to have ruled righteously, it was inevitable that his reign would be characterized by an absence of drought, and with much rain ensuring plentiful crops. Deeply moved by the voluntary death by drowning of his maternal uncle, Rāmapāla follows suit.[81] Madanapāla, as the new patron of the author, receives a fulsome eulogy befitting the successor of Rāmapāla.[82] The later part of the text suggests troubles over succession and aggression from neighbouring powers, but asserts that the reign of Rāmapāla was a high point in Pala history.

[79] *Rāmacarita*, 2.29–34.
[80] 3.31ff.
[81] 4.9ff.
[82] 4.16–21.

The *Rāmacarita* focuses on a crucial moment in the history of the Pālas, when the later members of the dynasty, declining in power, lost their homeland. The centrality of this event to Pāla history is being underlined by the biographer-historian. Varendrī/ *varendra-maṇḍala* had been important for some centuries and was therefore a developed region, and more strategic than the territory to the south-east which was being gradually opened up to colonization. The latter process required organized labour and effort before the land could yield a revenue, which is why it may have been left to intermediaries. Whereas there are references to officers in Varendrī, there are more frequent references to *sāmantas* in the neighbourhood. The revolt was led by feudatories and not by poor peasants, although the latter may have been encouraged by the former in the possibility of discontinuing the revenue demands of the paramount power, which oppressive demands had eventually to be met by the peasants. The concentration of population in the area may have assisted in furthering the revolt. The successful recovery of this territory led to the re-establishment of Pāla status. But good government had to follow. His excursus, into the benefits that accrue to the king who follows the advice of ministers and scribes, is a point of some interest, given that the author himself was a scribe and the son of a minister. This is a rather different assessment of the court than was the initial opinion of Bāṇa. It also offers a glimpse of the complicated process of organizing the suppression of a revolt, a picture not often available.

If the evoking of Rāma was a compliment to Rāmapāla, it would have been offensive to the Kaivartas and their *sāmanta* allies, who were equated with the *rākṣasas*. Divya and Bhīma would be thought of as Rāvaṇa. It would seem that the author's intention was to show the Kaivartas in poor light in order to establish the superiority of the Pāla overlord, even when in dire circumstances and facing a revolt. The problems in organizing a counter-offensive are evident. The biography had not merely to justify the suppression of the rebellion but also to reassert the legitimacy of Pāla control over Varendrī. Rāmapāla was to be projected as the exemplar to other kings facing similar opposition. The revolt of intermediaries was not a rare occurrence in those times.

After his victory, Rāmapāla developed Varendrī economically and established the rule of law. Curiously, if Varendrī had once been under Pāla rule prior to the Kaivarta revolt, surely good government should have been familiar to its people. The parallel reading of the two themes was not just an exercise in literary gymnastics but had a historical and political function. The threads from the epic were drawn into the contemporary narrative. The recovery of Varendrī was historically crucial to the authority of the Pālas in eastern India. The politics of the turnover of ruling families destabilized kingdoms and the biography depicts a rather different scene from that of a powerful Pāla kingdom making a bid for empire. It competed with the Pratihāras and the Rāṣṭrakūṭas, who also had to deal with recalcitrant intermediaries.

3. Other Sources

Epigraphic records of the Pālas provide other details of the early Pāla rulers. In one of these, recording the bequest to a *mahā-sāmantādhipati* of four villages, the ancestor referred to was Dayita Viṣṇu, succeeded by his son Vapyata, who was in turn succeeded by his son Gopāla.[83] It is said of Gopāla that rulership was forced on him by the people (*prakṛti*), who wanted to end the condition of *mātsyanyāya* (anarchy) that prevailed.

Of his successor Dharmapāla, the claim was that he combined in himself the best of the ancient heroes, was installed as king of Kānyakubja/Kanauj (which was the focus of a struggle between the Pālas, the Rāṣṭrakūṭas and the Pratihāras, in the late first millenium AD), and was accepted by people such as the Bhoja, Matsya, Madra, Kuru, Yadu, Yavana, Avanti, Gandhāra, Kīra, and Pañcāla. These were peoples of the past, so the list is evoking earlier histories. Elsewhere, the Pālas are said to have been of the Solar line although there are assertions of their not being *kṣatriyas* at all.[84] Dharmapāla (as his name suggests) is described as a devout patron of Buddhism. He is credited with having called an assembly at Kanauj, doubtless emulating Harṣa as well as the

[83] Khalimpur Copper Plate, *Ep. Ind.*, 4.243–54.

[84] R.C. Majumdar, *History of Bengal,* vol. I, 101. If they were *kāyasthas*, then they may have thought it appropriate to have a *kāyastha* biographer.

earlier Buddhist memory of kings convoking religious assemblies. He also takes the exalted title of *parameśvara-paramabhaṭṭāraka-mahārājādhirāja*, which was perhaps necessary given the extensive hierarchy in the ranks of his feudatories and officers. Other inscriptions give a detailed pedigree which begins with Gopāla and continues to Mahipāla, also mentioning patrons of Buddhist or Puranic sects.[85] Later kings with the same name are sometimes differentiated by adding the suffix *deva* to their names, thus Gopāla-deva and Vigrahapāla-deva would refer to Gopāla II and Vigrahapāla II.[86] Some inscriptions have a Buddhist invocation and are therefore different in style from those with invocations to Śiva or Viṣṇu, even if the grant recorded is to a *brāhmaṇa*.

Dedicatory inscriptions on icons, many of which were Buddhist, were isued by Rāmapāla and Madanapāla. A retrospective inscription of the reign of Madanapāla records a grant of land to a *brāhmaṇa* who recited the *Mahābhārata* to the queen. It gives the descent list of the Pāla kings with a brief comment on each. There is little on the Kaivarta revolt, although Divya is mentioned. Had the revolt now become a matter of little consequence?[87] Another inscription refers to an earlier reverse suffered by a Pāla king who had to retreat to the southern territory of this kingdom, which became the base for Pāla administration, and the northern territory had to be reconquered.[88] The Pāla hold was tenuous, given loss and recovery more than once.

It is curious why there is no biography of Dharmapāla by a Buddhist author. The Tibetan work of the Lama Tāranātha refers to the Pāla dynasty as of the Sūryavaṃśa, which would make them *kṣatriyas*.[89] There are some cross-references to Harṣadeva, the eleventh-century king of Kashmir, as well as to contemporary

[85] Two Pala Plates from Belwa, *Ep. Ind.*, 29, Plate B, 9ff.; Bangarh Copperplate, *Ep. Ind.*, 14, 324; J. Bagchi, *The History and Culture of the Pālas of Bengal (circa 750–circa 1200)*, 22–6; Amgachi Inscription, *Ep. Ind.*, 15, 293–301.

[86] Belwa Plates, *Ep. Ind.*, 29, 1–9.

[87] S. Brocquet, *La Geste de Rāma: poeme a double sens de Sandhyākaranandin*, 45ff.; J. Bagchi, *The History and Culture of the Pālas of Bengal (circa 750–circa 1200)*, 22–6.

[88] The Baghaura Narayana Image Inscription, *Ep. Ind.*, 17, no. 4, 353.

[89] Tāranātha, *History of Buddhism in India*, trans. Lama Chimpa and A. Chattopadhyaya, chs 26–33, folio 123Aff.

kings of Tibet, and to Elders of the Buddhist Saṅgha. The Pāla kings are identified with the monasteries which they either constructed or restored. The section on Dharmapāla includes details of the teachers at various monasteries, which was again an attempt to correlate the history of the dynasty with that of the Saṅgha. A rather garbled version of the Kaivarta revolt is narrated. Both the Bhangala and the Turuṣka waged war and were subdued by Mahipāla and his maternal uncle Canaka. Perhaps by this time the term Turuṣka, originally referring to people from Central Asia, was sometimes being used for those seen as adverse or alien, and therefore in popular memory the Kaivartas were seen as Turuṣkas, i.e. those who are in opposition, which would have been a historically curious transposition of the name.

The writing of royal biographies was not just a fashion of the courts, it was a political necessity. Beginning with compositions in Sanskrit and occasionally Prākrit, such works were later written in the regional languages. The format was similar but the idiom was that of local politics. There were few such biographies from Buddhist authors. Harṣa was not a Buddhist—unlike Aśoka. The Jainas maintained biographical notes on their Elders and the succession of the major pontiffs.

The biographies summarized here conform to the format of the *carita* but their intentions vary. The *Harṣacarita* is in many ways the most intellectually provocative. It spans various contexts and questions some of the assumptions of a *carita*, making it thereby more of a historical document than just a literary form. It touches on facets that were significant to the formulation of the new genres that went into the making of the historical traditions from the seventh century onwards. The *Rāmacarita*, which ostensibly is an exercise in playing with language, actually has a perspective on a historical event of much consequence. Under the veneer of a eulogy on a king, there is much on the crucial relationship between the king and his feudatories and intermediaries, especially in a situation where the politics of opposition is made apparent. The new genres of biographies, inscriptional annals, and chronologies, legitimate in themselves as depicting a period of history, can perhaps be better understood if also viewed in the changing historical context from the mid-first millennium AD.

13

Biographies as Histories

1. Towards Historical Writing

The three new genres narrating the history of persons and events that became current in the post-Gupta period were biographies of kings, official inscriptions, and chronicles of region or dynasty. These were more recognizably historical than the earlier ones, barring the Buddhist. This transition dates to post-Gupta times and has some echoes from Sramanic historiography and Puranic sources. Sandhyākaranandin may not mention the sources he consulted, but as a man of learning it can be assumed that he would have read the *Āryamañjuśrīmūlakalpa*, among others. Despite ideological differences, there would have been some mutual interchange, at least among the literati.

To place this change towards historical writing in context, it might be helpful to take an overview of its background. Drawn from the biographies, such a survey would also be pertinent to the study of inscriptions and chronicles.[1] Although the three forms differ, they emerge from similar historical contexts and are closely tied to the mainstream culture of royal courts; and their authors come from a common cultural matrix. There is therefore some overlap in their content.

The genre of historical biography developed in the period from the seventh century AD. These *caritas* are initially the literature of the royal court and could emerge only when the court became hegemonic, governed by codes specific to its functioning.[2] The

[1] These will be discussed in the subsequent chapters.

[2] Daud Ali, *Courtly Culture and Political Life in Early Medieval India*.

focal point of administration remained the court, but now also emphasizing a different style of functioning from before. Forms of address, manners, and body language became social indicators and clues to levels of relationships. Some terms from earlier times continued, as for example *digvijaya*, but the connotation changes. Resort to past usage suggests continuity but the metaphors used may disguise the change. Sandhyākaranandin, in using the story of Rāma, draws attention to a symbol of ideal kingship extended to the actual king, and the association of deity with the king has a literary precedent in the *Rāmāyaṇa*.

Historical biography focusing on the king points to his centrality as one whose authority had to be reiterated. The narrative frequently centres on a key event, viewed as crucial to the king's authority, and on sequential events. *Caritas* were not intended as critical history but as making a statement about a particular king and his concerns. Although viewed essentially as literature, their being related to the exercise of power emphasized their claim to presenting contemporary events as they actually happened—but not excluding the past which was necessary to their presentation.

The focus in *carita* literature was on a person rather than a lineage or a pedigree, and the family replaced the clan. Individual achievement and abilities were more important to status than only to lineage. The contrast can be seen in the *vaṃśānucarita* of the *Purāṇa*, which had dismissed such rulers with the mere mention of a name in a king-list, but now the *caritas* expand on the activities of some. The choice is significant to the tradition and the times. The earlier dismissive attitude was partially because many rulers were patrons of non-brahmanical sects. In the new situation of competition, with relatively equal opportunities for those competing, the successful had to single out their patron for praise.

2. The Authors

These compositions are no longer anonymous, or of attributed authorship. The authors are named and their credibility established through a brief autobiographical sketch, which was a contrast to the attributed or unknown authorship of the epics and *Purāṇas*.

Appending an appropriate biography of the author was another means of legitimizing the subject of the biography. The author, as Bilhaṇa puts it, provides the nectar of immortality to the king's body of fame when the drum of eternal departure sounds.[3]

Some, such as Bāṇa, claim a Bhṛgu association, emphasizing the suggestion that the Bhṛgu *brāhmaṇas* were virtually the keepers of the *itihāsa-purāṇa* tradition, and therefore the preferred authors of such texts. The association of *kāyasthas* with the historical tradition is anticipated from texts and inscriptions composed by them by the end of the first millennium AD.

Juxtaposing authorial autobiography with the subject's biography reinforces the idea that the choice of the author was not arbitrary. If not actually a court poet or an officer of the court, he came from a family closely associated with the court. As a freelance intellectual from a rich *agrahāra,* Bāṇa did not need connections. Sandhyākaranandin came from a family of the upper bureaucracy, well established and anxious to demonstrate his learning as being comparable to that of any scholarly *brāhmaṇa*. This meant that authors tended to be *brāhmaṇa* or *kāyastha* members of the elite, whose concerns they reflected in the biographies. Pinpointing the credentials of the authors was important in a period when the *brāhmaṇa* caste itself was opening up to a variety of recruits, not all of whom were at home in brahmanical and Sanskritic learning.[4]

The choice of author also reflected the likely sources that he would consult, since few mention their sources. With Bāṇa, one can tell what these sources were from the text and the people with whom he kept company. Bāṇa explores various situations that give a richer flavour to his historical account. Sandhyākaranandin, even if he was not a *brāhmaṇa*, would have used court records and epigraphs, as well as the oral tradition of the court, leaving scope for divergent personal assessments.

The language is largely Sanskrit, which creates a degree of uniformity and links the courts, but contemporary with this are the

[3] *Vikramāṅkadevacarita*, 18.106.

[4] B.M. Morrison, *Political Centres and Culture Regions in Early Bengal*; K. Chakrabarti, *Religious Process: The Purāṇas and the Making of a Religious Tradition*.

emerging regional languages, creating almost a two-tier linguistic culture by the start of the second millennium AD. The use of Sanskrit as the official language at the royal courts was a godsend to educated *brāhmaṇas,* who migrated long distances in search of employment and introduced their characteristic culture into new areas at elite levels The migration was not limited to *brāhmaṇas*: scribes and professional administrators were in demand and *kāyasthas* also travelled.[5] Following soon after came the skilled builders and artisans to construct royal temples. This network of migrants created an elite Sanskrit culture. The use of Sanskrit has been described as "the Sanskrit cosmopolis", an endorsement of the hegemony of Sanskrit.[6] Implicit in this was super-regional use of Sanskrit through political channels, and with the language introducing cultural forms. This contrasts with the use of regional languages as the vernacular among those not part of the elite. In earlier centuries, Sanskrit changed from its limited use as a ritual language to a broader use by the literati, ultimately replacing Prākrit, as is evident from the early inscriptions.[7] The interface of Sanskrit with a local language would have been a reality since not all those claiming *brāhmaṇa* status were migrants, some being local recruits.

3. The Acquiring of Status

Highlighting the role of the king was only in part to establish his legitimacy and that of his family. He had to claim the appropriate caste and ancestry competing with obscure families acquiring power. Although political power was in practice open to any caste, there had developed an insistence on formally reiterating the order of caste society in accordance with the *Dharmaśāstras*. Thus, although in the seventh century Xuanzang writes that dynasties

[5] The earliest recorded case of a scribe travelling far is that of Capaḍa, a *kharoṣṭhī*-knowing scribe who was sent to Karnataka to engrave the edicts of Aśoka in *brāhmī,* and who could not resist signing some of them with his name in *kharoṣṭhī*. J. Bloch, *Les Inscriptions d'Asoka*, 151.

[6] S. Pollock, "The Sanskrit Cosmopolis, 300–1300 CE: Transculturation, Vernacularisation and the Question of Ideology", 197–249.

[7] See Chapter 7.

of various castes, including *śūdras*, were ruling, a claim to being *kṣatriya* became almost a requirement.

Alternatively, it can be argued that the claim was only made in texts emanating from the court and that the actual caste of the dynasty was known, suggesting an interesting dual perception of status. If the social origins of the dynasty were challenged, the official version could be produced to legitimate the claim, involving the harking back to what were believed to be past connections. Gradually, in this way, a new process of becoming *kṣatriya* evolved, giving a new meaning to the category. *Kṣatriyas* were no longer the ruling clans in a clan-based society, they were those that claimed royal descent from earlier heroes. The context now was kingdoms, not clans. This change had been emerging in the pre-Gupta period, but it now became established and the claim was significant to dynastic history.

The *Viṣṇu Purāṇa* makes a caustic statement reflecting the rise of a new *kṣatriya* order,[8] to the effect that those who have horses and chariots will become rulers and those without will be servitors. The *Purāṇas* had reiterated what they called another category of *kṣatriyas*,[9] claims that required shuffling caste statuses among the newly surfacing groups. The call to observe *varṇāśramadharma* became more insistent. Origin myths were linked to one of the two *kṣatriya* lineages—Sūrya or Candra *vaṃśa*—or an equally appropriate origin. Yet the variations in genealogical linkages suggest the use of presumed genealogies and pedigrees in balancing political factions. This could well result in contradictory affiliations for the same dynasty, but *kṣatriya* status remained central. This was governed by the point in time at which the origin myth gives way to a historically attested genealogy, marking a change in the political status of a dynasty.

Puṣyabhūti has to perform a Tantric ritual of seemingly Drāviḍa origin, somewhat curious for the founder of the principality of Thanesar in northern India, except that by now such rituals had probably become fairly widespread. Possibly astrology, alchemy,

[8] 6.1.35.

[9] F.E. Pargiter, *Dynasties of the Kali Age*, 53: . . . *utsādayitvā kṣatram tu kṣatram anyat kariṣyati* . . .

and rituals claiming to be based on magic were seen as more efficacious than the conventional Vedic ones. Were the *siddhas* holding out larger promises than the *śrotriya brāhmaṇas*?

Marriage into a family of high status was crucial, for such marriages would endorse claims to land, political power, and to further alliances. The *svayamvara* was acceptable to patriarchal norms because the assumption was that the woman was being gifted in marriage, even if the ritual had built into it the pretence that she was choosing. This ritual too underlines the role of the *kṣatriya* as the pre-eminent giver of gifts. Where the bride was of a higher status, it helped to cover up the social discrepancy by saying that she chose her husband, even if the choice was a subversion of caste rules. The early Pāla rulers of somewhat ambiguous status are not mentioned in the *Rāmacarita,* the list effectively starting with Dharmapāla, who takes royal titles, but the marriage alliance with the Rāṣṭrakūṭas is mentioned. Its political function is apparent from the statement that a cousin on the Rāṣṭrakūṭa side led the first attack on the Kaivartas.

The gifting of a daughter was considered righteous and suggested the gifting of Śrī/Fortune and Bhū/Earth. This was not a literal possession of land but symbolic of the Earth accepting the lord, recalling the story of Pṛthivī naming herself after Pṛthu. In the *Rāmacarita* the symbolism of the acquisition of Śrī is projected back to the *Rāmāyaṇa*, where Sītā represented both Śrī and Bhū, and where sovereignty is associated with the mother goddess.[10] Varendrī being finally acquired by Rāmapāla was the recovery of *janakabhū*, both Sītā and Śrī. This was probably also influenced by the pervasive belief that *śakti,* personifying the female principle or deity, was necessary to the fulfilment of any action. Further, male deities had acquired female consorts whose roles did not confine them to the wings but brought them centrestage. The centrality of Śrī and Bhū as deities was not characteristic of the Vedic pantheon. The mother goddess was increasingly a power to be reckoned with, the more so among those who came not from the courtly Sanskritic tradition but the more parochial folk tradition.

This had a bearing on two other issues, primogeniture and

[10] *Rāmacarita*, 1.13.

colateral succession; both are brought into royal biographies. In genealogical constructions, colateral lines could be suppressed—as in the case of the Sūryavaṃśa. Interregna can be glossed over and factions disguised. The successful contender temporarily terminates the prowling for power among competitors. This is not reflected in the Puranic dynastic lists. But biographies have to justify either the withholding or the transfer of power to colateral lines. Primogeniture and the succession of colaterals are interrelated, since the first often marginalizes the second. The politics of opposition hovers over many sentiments that are expressed about the relationship between the king and his kinsmen, even if it is not openly referred to. The intermediaries that lead the opposition tend to be described as lower castes, though not invariably. They could as well be the distanced kinsmen of the royal family.

The concern with primogeniture varies in the biographies. Although Bāṇa hints at Harṣa's political ambition, it is clear that his elder brother did rule briefly and died without an heir. Rāmapāla needed an indirect Vaiṣṇava association, though a favour from Śiva is also mentioned. Succession through the eldest male is common in patriarchal societies, although the degree of adherence will have varied. Where primogeniture is not observed, descent can fan out beyond control.

Legitimacy of succession in the biography is expressed through approval from various authorities, such as ministers in the case of Harṣa. The central role of the deity in legitimating succession is a later feature. In the *Harṣacarita*, the deity Śrī is a metaphor. Could this have been in part due to the prevalence of Buddhism at that time—even if by now Buddhism itself had conceded various roles to deities and *bodhisattvas*? According to Xuanzang, it was a *bodhisattva* who prompted Harṣa to accept kingship.[11] Public symbols for establishing recognition could also include starting an era and reckoning in regnal years within the era; and winning a bride who could be projected as a goddess. A variation on this was Harṣa rescuing his sister, which strengthened his claim to sovereignty.

Legitimation by ritual involved the performance of rites, but not

[11] T. Watters, *On Yuan Chwang's Travels in India*, 343ff.

as the invocation of the past. For the past was now invoked through genealogical links and heroic paradigms, but not invariably so. The handling of these new forms was, however, again the privilege of the *brāhmaṇas*. Dynasties were linked to the earlier genealogies of *kṣatriya* heroes through origin myths. The *vaṃśanucarita* section of the *Purāṇas* therefore becomes a charter for validating these links. Recourse to such a charter depended on the degree to which this kind of legitimacy was sought.

With increasing gifts of land to *brāhmaṇas*, there was a further diversification in *brāhmaṇa* activities. Some confined themselves to the performance of rituals, or to the perpetuation of learning in their *agrahāras*. Others took to more lucrative professions, such as participating in the horse trade with the north-western regions. Most, however, used their grants of settled land to become intermediaries collecting revenue from the local peasantry; or they colonized the large acreages granted to them in virgin lands. Since the lands were treated as heritable, they became ancestors to those that had emerged as ruling families in these areas. Such families could claim that they were *brahma-kṣatra*, *brāhmaṇas* by birth who took to professions associated with *kṣatriyas*.[12] Battle is seen as the metaphor for a sacrificial ritual. The mixed pedigree introducing the *brāhmaṇa* connection could be claimed as a higher *kṣatriya* status.

4. Gift-giving

The performance of Vedic sacrificial rituals as a mechanism of claiming status gradually became perfunctory,[13] giving way to the great gifts or *mahādānas*—gifts of gold and grants of land, made largely to *brāhmaṇas.* The preferred rituals now were the *hiraṇyagarbha* (the king emerging from a golden womb), and the *tulāpuruṣa* (the king weighed against precious metals), possibly because the latter incorporated more recent rites and not archaic. Bāṇa refers to a contention among the *ṛṣis* as to how the Vedic *mantras* should be recited (a contention that continues to this day),

[12] N.G. Majumdar, *Inscriptions of Bengal,* 44, fn. 3, and App. 192.

[13] D.C. Sircar, "Some Performers of Aśvamedha", 93ff.

which might also have encouraged the preference for new rituals. The visibility of the gift was enhanced when singled out, as was its political meaning, now enmeshed in status and diplomacy, and represented an indirect statement on the economy.

Gifts came as tribute, either directly from one ruler to another, as when Bhāskaravarman sought an alliance with Harṣa; or on special occasions, such as wedding gifts for Rājyaśrī; or in association with *digvijayas* and assemblies. Bāṇa describes the lavish gifts bestowed on the *brāhmaṇas*, kings, and nobles before Harṣa set out on his *digvijaya*.[14]

The changing forms of gift-giving point to historical change. Wealth as always was linked to status, but the nature of the wealth and the mechanism of the display had changed. Cattle and horses gave way to land, but gold was constant. (Given that gold was not easily available in India, the exaggerated descriptions were more likely fantasies of desire.) The major distribution of wealth was in the form of land grants. Land, whether virgin or cultivated, brought an income to the donee and was a loss of potential income to the donor.

The noticeable change from earlier times was that land, being immovable, was a permanent donation. Although initially only the revenue was granted to a specific person, it soon became heritable private property, and the foundation for the accumulation of wealth and authority by the grantee, who could use it to build political power. Land donated to the Saṅgha could never play this role, since it was neither private property nor heritable by a family. It could build the political strength of the Saṅgha, but only as a Buddhist institution. For *brāhmaṇa* grantees, by contrast, such land could be exploited for an immense political and economic potential, invaluable both personally and as a caste identity.

Gift-giving, tied into the hierarchy of rank and status, acknowledged lesser persons, and was thus on occasion the reverse of tribute. Bāṇa mentions a range of ranks—*rājā, mahārāja, bhūpāla, pārthiva, kṣitipāla, kumāra, lokapāla, nṛpati, narapati,* etc. *Sāmantas* and *mahāsāmantas* could be further elevated by the suffix *mahārāja*. Grandiose titles are reserved for the patron

[14] Kane, 7.108–9; Cowell and Thomas, 7.226–7.

who is, at a minimum, the *parameśvara-parama-bhaṭṭāraka-mahārājādhirāja.* Sometimes the victor provides such a title for the defeated king so that his own status is further enhanced, as was said of Pulakeśin II, who held back the powerful Harṣa.[15] These were among the codes and modalities of the royal court.

But perhaps the most interesting discussion of gift-giving is by Xuanzang and his biographers, suggesting a deliberate recalling of a past narrative—although this is not specifically said. It describes the quinquennial assemblies held by Harṣa, two of which were at Kanauj and Prayāga. The distribution of wealth from the royal treasury was such that finally Harṣa was left with just a worn-out coat given him by his sister. At Prayāga the gifts were redeemed by the kings present and given to the treasury, only to be distributed at a later point.[16] This is a Buddhist view of Harṣa and seems to draw on earlier texts depicting ideal rulers.

Harṣa being left with nothing but an old coat is a little too close to the story in the *Aśokāvadāna* of Aśoka being left with half an *āmalaka* fruit to give to a monk on his alms round. Xuanzang would have known the earlier story and its implications. He was evoking these from earlier Buddhist writing to point out the mutual interdependence of the Saṅgha and the king. The descriptions are neither factually precise nor perhaps meant to be. If the distribution was as narrated, the regular quinquennial depletion of the treasury would have created serious fiscal problems. Extraordinary displays of wealth and gift-giving carry hints of the earlier potlatch with its display, consumption, distribution, and destruction of wealth. This was the *dāna-stuti* being superseded by the *praśasti*, the coming into being of new ways of displaying wealth in a courtly culture.

There is a reminder also of the role of assemblies in the forging of the Buddhist doctrine, particularly when it is the Hīnayāna Buddhists at the Kanauj assembly opposed to the Mahāyāna Buddhists, with Harṣa ruling in favour of the latter. This recalls the decision of the Schism Edict of Aśoka, and the description in the Sri Lankan chronicles of his role at the Council of Pāṭaliputra supporting the Theravāda.

[15] The Aihole Inscription, *Ep. Ind.*, 6.6ff.

[16] *Si-yu-ki: Buddhist Records of the Western World*, 5, 233–4, 214ff.

At least two features drew on earlier forms but restructured them to suit the new form of kingship. The traditional *digvijaya* as part of the rhetoric of kingship was extended to skirmishes and raids, and could be poeticized to include campaigns. But conquest held meanings other than the obvious. War symbolizes collecting wealth through booty, or through the settling of conquered lands which later yield revenue. Booty captured in a campaign, and the ensuing pillage and plunder, are reviewed.[17] Bāṇa's references to poverty as well as the cynical remarks of peasants about the unpleasantness of the king's *digvijaya,* and even some reported questioning of the king as the upholder of *dharma*, point to a reversal of fulsome praise.[18]

Royal orders, including grants, could be issued from the *skandhāvāra*.[19] Constant feuding meant armies on the march with court being held in such military camps. The *Harṣacarita* depicts the camp as virtually a temporary capital, allowing the inspection of outlying regions and the administration of feudatories, which brought the king in touch with local persons and matters. Courtly culture now moves into new areas. Earlier forms were ostensibly evoked, but their meanings had changed and the new definitions were of greater import.

Marriage alliances were politically important, but with Harṣa the central position remained that of his sister—if Xuanzang is to be believed. He depicts brother and sister acting jointly in affairs of state, reminiscent of Buddhist origin myths.

5. The *Cakravartin*

Conquest alone does not make a universal monarch; the association of good fortune is through the goddess, Śrī. This, in theory had been exercised through claims to conquest and is now represented in the biographies as the favour of the deity. Śrī blesses his ancestor and is personified as Harṣa's sister Rājyaśrī. Viṣṇu, in his incarnation as Rāma, by implication bestows favour on Rāmapāla. Conquest, necessary to the brahmanical image of a *cakravartin*, is being replaced by *bhakti* and devotion to the deity.

[17] Kane, 7.122; Cowell and Thomas, 7.254.

[18] Cowell and Thomas, 7.207–9.

[19] E.g., the Bangarh Inscription, *Ep. Ind.*, 14.324ff.

Tantric sects were the substratum religion for many centuries, and their visibility begins to surface from the early first millennium AD. Since this belief was rooted in the populace and not imposed from above, its appropriation by the ruling caste is a concession to the practices of its subjects, and the creation of an identity not limited to the norms of the elite. Or alternatively the social origins of many ruling families being "obscure", such families would have elevated their cult observances into elite practices when they became ruling families. The Tantric rites of Harṣa's ancestor suggest this, whereas Harṣa performs the rites of gift-giving in forms that are Buddhist and Śaiva.

Ultimate power was with the *cakravartin,* the king who was above the need for alliances, supreme among competitors. In Buddhist and Jaina thought the *cakravartin* upheld the moral order, cutting across clan, caste, and other identities, and to that extent even undermining the *kṣatriya* ethic of earlier times. The *Bhagavad-Gītā* upholding the ethic of the warrior was not compatible with the social ethic of the Buddha. The latter did not require the backing of priests but required the goodwill of monks, since the king and the Saṅgha were in a relationship of mutual support.

The *cakravartin* of the post-Gupta period continued to be projected as a conqueror. The mention of his conquests in royal eulogies was often included in a formulaic way in the larger rhetoric of conquest. Cultural assimilation also led to the incorporation of territory, and this could pass for conquest. The epic hero may still have been a model and the terminology may not have changed substantially, but the hero was now a king with grandiose titles. Was the modification of his qualifications by bringing in the favour of the deity a subconscious influence of the Sramanic ideal of the *cakravartin*? The possibility of such influence is strengthened by some texts actually deploring a frequency of campaigns and pillaging.[20]

The stabilizing of the *varṇāśramadharma* is also expected from rulers. The form, at least, should be observed, even if the actual functioning of society was at some variance from it. Its support

[20] *Skanda Purāṇa*, 6.48.42–4, quoted in A.B.L. Awasthi, *History from the Puranas*, 153ff.

of social inequality was the reverse of the Sramanic social ethic. Caste society was introduced in areas where it did not exist. The granting of land to *brāhmaṇas* and utilization of the grantees as vanguards of state and society may have been a more effective means of changing the social mores in these regions than the attempt to consolidate through conquest, even if the rhetoric of conquest prevailed. Conquest required a large financial outlay whereas conversion to caste society, to whatever degree, was less expensive and had the advantage of being an easier way to subordinate labour.

The assertion of sovereignty is vague in some areas, as for example among the forest-dwellers. They are treated as distinctly different and inferior, but they have their own life-ways. The description of such people as *rākṣasas* underlines the point, the paradigm being provided by the *Rāmāyaṇa.* The analogy of Rāmapāla suppressing a revolt and Rāma destroying *rākṣasa* power would have been obvious. In Bāṇa's text, forest chiefs (*aṭavika-rājās*) are largely confined to the Vindhyan region, where even *aṭavika-sāmantas* ("forest feudatories") are mentioned, a category that goes back to earlier times.[21] This was an area being encroached upon by the monarchical state and caste society. Settlements encroaching into forests become a form of colonization and such colonization was justified as introducing a superior culture. The conversion of forest-dwellers into a peasantry becomes apparent in the description, as noted earlier, of the Vindhyan forest in the *Harṣacarita*. Deities and rituals of the forest-dwellers or even the local population were incorporated into Puranic cults, wherever acculturation was called for. The pulls of local belief at various levels resulted in the creation of amalgamated religious forms.

6. The Theory of *Maṇḍala*

The notion of the *cakravartin* as the paramount ruler became a more pertinent idea with increasing numbers of kingdoms and their interface, captured in the political theory of *maṇḍala*. Although referred to in earlier texts, the political economy of post-Gupta times provided a greater political reality for the theory

[21] *Corpus Inscriptionum Indicarum*, III, 7ff.

and of its practice on more occasions. The word had many meanings: a circle which demarcates an area from its surroundings, therefore a sanctified area, and by extension temples and *stūpas* seen as *maṇḍalas* in stone; a geometrical design involving a circle enclosing squares and triangles in infinite patterns, said to be conducive to meditation; an administrative analogy referring to a group of villages and subsequently to a larger area of territory, often an administrative unit which was administered by a *maṇḍaleśa* (officer in charge of the *maṇḍala*), one of the ranks in the hierarchy of intermediaries.[22]

As a formulation in political theory it referred to a circle of territories held by intermediaries or independent rulers and the relations between them. Each king desirous of victory (*vijigīṣu*) was ringed around by allies and enemies. Those on the outer fringe were viewed as potential enemies who had either to be wooed or conquered, as evident from Harṣa's relations with Bhāskaravarman and Śaśāṅka. The *sāmantas* could become the counterpoint to the power of the king—as happened with Rāmapāla. Politics was a competition for supremacy, with the balance shifting after each major campaign or with the politics of conciliation.

The theory has a pattern in delineating allies and enemies. At the centre of the *maṇḍala* (circle) was the *vijigīṣu*—the king desirous of conquering the four quarters.[23] Facing him are categories of enemies and friends: the *ari* (the enemy), then the *mitra* (the friend), and further out the *ari-mitra*, the *mitra-mitra*, and the *ari-mitra-mitra*. Behind him are the *pārṣṇi-grāha*—literally the heel-grabber; the *ākranda* or friend, the *pārṣṇi-grāha-sāra* (the friend of the heel-grabber), and the *ākrandā-sāra* (the friend of the friend). There were two negotiators: the *mādhyama*, close to both the king desirous of victory and to his enemy; and the *udāsina*, the one who was at a distance from all these and therefore neutral. The categories are described in greater detail.

The alliances and the conquests of the *vijigīṣu* kept the system going. Relationships were seen in a circular framework. At the same time, there were bilateral relationships between the *vijigīṣu*

22 B.N.S. Yadav, *Society and Culture in Northern India in the Twelfth Century*; D.N. Jha (ed.), *The Feudal Order*, 78ff.

23 *Arthaśāstra*, 6.2.13–23.

and his adversary from within the circle. Policies were determined by alliances, wars, simulations of war, neutrality, bribes, the creation of factions among the enemy, dependence, or simultaneous moves towards war and peace. Some of these are ostensibly non-violent, control being exercised through a mix of coercion and concession. This was a contrast to the style both of biographies and inscriptions, where the resort to violence is often represented as a quick solution.

The *digvijaya* could consist of campaigns or even of raids and pillage, but also merely a ceremonial procession.[24] It was synonymous with the acquisition of new resources: through booty, revenue from colonized lands, and the use of prisoners of war used as labour. Civil and military functions could overlap and successful military activities would enhance prestige in administrative function. War brought wealth, quite apart from the revenue that came from taxes and judicial fines.[25] The notion of *digvijaya* was therefore important, even if actual conquest was absent. The perspective was from a particular region, the view being from the inside out as it were—from the kingdom looking at the wider world.

The monopoly of the paramount state over the various wings of the army, projected from earlier sources, had by now given way to a considerably decentralized functioning, since feudatories were required to maintain troops for their overlord. The soldiers of the suzerain would run amok if they had won a victory, as in the *Rāmacarita* when describing the destruction of the Kaivarta camp by the soldiers of Rāmapāla.[26] The peasantry appears to have changed from being without weapons, as in Mauryan times, to having access to some weapons. But judging by the description of the resistance faced by Rāmapāla in the battle for Varendrī, weapons could be as simple as bows and arrows. Those using them were often peasants and locals, hastily mobilized by *sāmantas* against the Pāla army, rather than soldiers trained for combat. The theory seemingly encouraged violence, but also advocated a balancing of relations to avoid unnecessary campaigns.

[24] *Ep. Ind.*, 5, 223 (note 5), 6, 51 (note 5).
[25] *Nāradasmṛti*, 1.48–50.
[26] *Rāmacarita*, 2.29.

7. The King's Power

The theoretical role of *cakravartins* and *maṇḍalas* receives a different focus when seen in terms of the actual working of the royal function in the context of *dharma*. Discussion on its meaning varies somewhat and it is not consistent even within a single source.[27] This throws open the connotation of *dharma*. It is therefore suggested that perhaps the opinions of the *dvija*—the twice-born upper castes—should be final,[28] endorsing the king's dependence on advisors.[29] But this was unacceptable to those of the view that the king's authority has precedence over *dharma*.[30] This issue also hinges on the ultimate source of law where the *dharma* of the king incorporates *ācāra*—the custom and usage of his people.

The king, in the earlier texts, is subject to banishment and even assassination, sometimes by his subjects, if he has behaved unethically, and sometimes by those qualified to do so.[31] Mention is made in the *Harṣacarita* of kings in the past who were removed or assassinated.[32] The sacrality of kingship seems less effective than its temporal power.

The presence of intermediaries of many categories, from *aṭavika-rājās* (forest chiefs) to *sāmantas* and *maṇḍaleśvaras* (land-owning intermediaries and tributary allies), was more proximately experienced in the countryside than the distant control by the king. The intermediaries acted as an integrative network to support the policy of the state, or to oppose it. The cultivator had a closer link with the intermediary than with the king. The Kaivarta revolt was not the sole example of the weakening control of the king, with *sāmantas* declaring independence. Where such revolts succeeded, they would not have been described as revolts but as the succession of a new family. The hierarchy in titles indicates

[27] *The Laws of Manu*, 7.203, 8.41.

[28] *Āpastamba Dharmasūtra*, 1.7.20.6–7.

[29] *The Laws of Manu*, 7.54; *Mahābhārata*, 12.87.7.

[30] *Arthaśāstra*, 3.1.39.

[31] *Saccamkira Jātaka*, no. 73, *Padakusulamānava Jātaka*, no. 432, in *The Jātaka*; *Mahābhārata*, 13.85.35.

[32] Cowell and Thomas, 6.222–4; Kane, 6.105–6.

a shift in power from *sāmanta* to *sāmanta-rājā*, *mahārāja*, and eventually *mahārājādhirāja*. The rise of the Maukhari family ruling in Kanauj is an example of this process.[33]

The chiefs of clans, when conquered by a kingdom, acquired a feudatory status. The ambitions of the upper bureaucracy were not met by access to power through administration, the same family holding high office over four or five generations,[34] made possible by the absence of a system of recruitment. Lateral personal relations perhaps became more immediate than lineage links in this office. Such groups were either local persons of status or incoming migrant *brāhmaṇas* and *kāyasthas* familiar with administrative functions and keeping records.

Despite the fact that the *sāmanta-mahārājas* could be powerful and overthrow dynasties, the biographies suggest a distance between overlord and intermediaries. Yet underlying each example is a subtle interplay of power in what were relationships of mutual dependence. This is more evident in the two later texts, by which time it would seem that the politics of the relationship had become more apparent. Rāmapāla could not negotiate with the Kaivartas, the revolt had to be put down.

8. The New Codes

Among the more influential and much commented upon texts was the *Nāradasmṛti*, generally dated to the mid-first millennium AD or slightly later.[35] Its substantial concern is with legal procedure, by now a necessary part of administration in many more places than before, given the growth of kingdoms. It builds on the knowledge of earlier texts. It is at times vehement in support of the priority of the decisions of the king, although it concedes the importance of other institutions of society. The loss of *dharma* in the Kaliyuga made legal procedures necessary. The more likely reason was that the king had now to deal with the practices of

[33] Clay Seals of Nalanda, *Ep. Ind.*, 21, 72ff.; Haraha Inscription of Isanavarman, ibid., 14, 110ff.; *Corpus Inscriptionum Indicarum*, vol. III, 219ff.

[34] Badal Pillar Inscription, *Ep. Ind.*, 2, 160–7.

[35] *The Nāradasmṛti*, vols I and II.

diverse groups, each claiming a different legality for its activities. This may be the reason why the *Nāradasmṛti* reiterates the importance of documents and witnesses.[36]

The *Nītisāra* of Kāmandaka, a text on polity, draws on the late recension of the *Arthaśāstra* and reflects an awareness of change. For instance, in speaking of the requirements of good governance it includes *bhakti* which, when adapted to a political idiom, refers to the relations between king and intermediary as expressed in some inscriptions. Both *sāmantas* and *aṭavikas* are mentioned but the weightage is different in the earlier and later text.[37] Since *sāmantas* as intermediaries was a development of Gupta times, the *Arthaśāstra* has little to say on them, but it comes down heavily on the *aṭavikas,* their guerrilla tactics being destructive. In the *Nītisāra* the *sāmantas* are powerful but the *aṭavikas* tend to be treated as marginal.

The *Nāradasmṛti* and the *Nītisāra* are not sources of history nor written by a historian but they reflect the change in the relationship between law and the king, as well as agencies of authority different from what they were earlier. They demonstrate one of the arguments asserted, namely that authors looked at earlier texts and, without saying so, updated their own to contemporary conditions. In this they parallel the writing of history in new genres of texts, such as the biography, which also record political change.

For the *Nāradasmṛti*, legal proceedings come under the purview of the *kula* (organizations of merchants and leading citizens), *gaṇa* (organized groups), *adhikṛta* (chief officer or judge), and *nṛpa* (king), in ascending order.[38] The four feet of *vyavahāra* (legal procedure) are said to be *dharma*, the law, custom, and the king, and each overrules its predecessor. (The *Arthaśāstra* supports the king as the final authority in law.[39]) Thus, *rājaśāsana*, or the royal order, is final. At another place it gently contradicts the classical *Dharmaśāstras* and says that custom prevails over the *Dharmaśāstra*.[40] This seems to have been a concession to the

[36] *Nāradasmṛti*, 1.3.
[37] *Nītisāra of Kāmandaka*, 14.29, 15.23.
[38] Ibid., 1.7.
[39] *Arthaśāstra*, 3.1.38.
[40] *Nāradasmṛti*, 1.10–11.

practices of local communities being currently brought into the court culture, newly established in certain areas. The position of the king was now hedged by new factors. If the law was under the control of the king, his right to rule would have to resort to precedent and history—among other forms of legitimation.

However, the same section of the *Nāradasmṛti* also refers to the king's relations with a variety of corporate bodies—the *nigama*, *śreṇi*, *pūga*, and *vrata*—whose conventions had perhaps to be accepted. This would tend to dilute the king's absolute powers. An attempt is therefore made to curb such bodies by stating that activities inimical to the interests of the king and his subjects are not permitted. Thus, they are prohibited from carrying arms, feuding, and forming large confederacies. Evidently, such activities did take place and are referred to in passing in some inscriptions. The Kaivarta revolt is better known, being central to a royal biography. The prohibition could only be effective if the king was an astute ruler. As a final touch, it is said that actions contrary to the *śāstras* should not be permitted. This could have involved interpreting afresh the texts relating to past precedents.

That the king protects the *varṇāśramadharma* is repeated, and the king is expected not to act against the accepted norms.[41] Castes should honour their established functions, for if they do not the strong will roast the weak like fish on a skewer.[42] Despite this insistence, new castes are established, as for example the *kāyastha*, a powerful component of the upper bureaucracy irrespective of its ambiguous origin as given in the *Dharmaśāstras*. The *brāhmaṇas* too break the restrictions on their prescribed occupations to become civil and military administrators and traders. Caste could be used as a focus to bind groups into social categories convenient for state functioning, and could be bonded afresh if need be. Few castes have an actual history of continuity from early times.

A section of the text deals with the rules governing the king's handling of the *pāṣaṇḍas* (heretical sects), or those said to preach fraudulent doctrines. The *pāṣaṇḍas* are generally regarded with contempt by *brāhmaṇa* authors. Their inclusion here may point to

[41] Ibid., 18.5–9.
[42] Ibid., 18.14–16.

a more vocal contestation with brahmanical views by other groups. Both *jātis* and religious sects multiplied among conservative and heretical communities. The consciousness of sectarian identity, encouraged by Puranic and Sramanic religion, is more evident, and this brings with it competition among the sects. The range of sectarian views reflected in the hermitage of Divākaramitra, as listed in the *Harṣacarita*, included many such *pāṣaṇḍas*. It should also not be forgotten that for Xuanzang as a good Buddhist, and for the Jainas, the heretics were the *brāhmaṇas*.

The power of the king lies in his edict, for he can change the earlier decisions of kings with which he would have been familiar from court records. A statement often repeated in such texts is that the king's revenue comes from his claim to the *saḍbhāga*—or one-sixth of the produce—to which he is entitled in return for protecting the subjects. What emerges from this is that despite the rhetoric of conquest and dominance, kingship was a system in which the king had to negotiate control over a variety of groups rather than assert unilateral authority. It is interesting that the *Nāradasmṛti* does not endorse conquest as the sole stamp of a superior king.

The acculturation to Sanskritic culture was not limited to language but included associated mores, beliefs, and institutions. The degree of accommodation between local and Sanskritic culture varied. The post-Gupta state did not uproot local authority but preferred to work through it.

9. Revenue and Grants

A decline in urban activity and commerce was a brief interlude before it picked up again. The similarity of the economic pattern over a large area accelerated the commercial economy in terms of more routes and exchange centres. The latter would be places where agrarian produce would be exchanged for artisanal goods and the use of the standard currency of *drammas* and *gadhaiyas* often of billon, a debased metal.[43]

Stratification would have had to recognize those that controlled economic enterprise and those that laboured for it. The former

[43] J. Deyell, *Living Without Silver*, 111.

were the intermediaries, the landowners, with their rights, obligations, and dues in accordance with the grant, as well as wealthy merchants less closely linked to the court. Those who laboured were the cultivators, both peasants and others, paying taxes to the intermediary of the state, and the artisans that produced the goods traded by the merchants.

More detailed information on the changing economy and state structure comes from inscriptions and relates largely to grants. *Agrahāras*, as the name suggests, were villages and land assigned to *brāhmaṇas* for their maintenance. The grantor, generally the king, sometimes a queen or a member of the royal family, or a *sāmanta* or a high official, had the right to choose who would get what kind of grant. Members of the *agrahāras* therefore could perform a dual function: they were the managers of religious and educational institutions, and they were also a community of landholders. Since the *agrahāra* could incorporate various occupational groups, the rights and obligations of each had to be registered.

That the administration of an *agrahāra* was considerable is evident from the revenues and dues collected by the *brāhmaṇa* grantees. Doubtless some of the latter, as in the case of heavily endowed Buddhist monasteries, forsook their religious or educational profession and concentrated on the administration required by the grant. The extensive monastic establishments in eastern India, such as those at Nālanda, Vikramaśīlā, and Paharpura, to mention just a few, had an enviable income from large numbers of villages—a quantitative leap compared to earlier times. This would have required administrative expertise to carry out the functions of monastic landlordism. The royal order incorporating the grant was inscribed or written as a charter and maintained by specified officials, the *kārṇikas*, with one copy being kept by the administration and the other by the grantee. Where the grants were to a large body of people, they could be inscribed on stone in a public place such as a temple. Grants to individuals and families were more often engraved on copper-plates, which became legal documents of possession, to be consulted when required.

The *agrahāras* and *maṭhas* (colleges for *brāhmaṇas*) in some instances, became a network of political support in return for royal patronage, parallel in some ways to the Buddhist Saṅgha. When the religious sectarian identity among these institutions changed or became pronounced, the king may have had to adjust to the change. This may account for the switch from Jainism and Buddhism to Śaivism and Vaiṣṇavism among various dynasties. Conversion could have been a matter of personal conviction, but could also have been conditioned by extraneous reasons of political support.

A Pāla inscription records the setting up of a temple and monastery of the Śaiva Pāśupata sect in eastern India.[44] Another mentions *brāhmaṇas* coming from Lāṭa in western India and establishing a Vaiṣṇava temple which was supported by grants of villages in the Puṇḍravardhana *bhukti* in eastern India.[45] A South Indian Śaiva performs the ritual for the ancestor of Harṣa and other Tantrics are mentioned as Drāvidas.[46] This movement of Tantric ritualists from Andhra to Thanesar has some parallels in reverse—*brāhmaṇas* going from Kashmir to Karnataka. Regional custom and practice must surely have travelled with them. Perhaps the notion of the Sanskrit cosmopolis needs modification to accommodate the more subtle *deśī* regional contribution to the *mārga* mainstream.

The charisma of the renunciate, constituting his moral authority—which was earlier derived from the power of renunciation and vows of celibacy—was now being replaced by the strength of sectarian institutions based on wealth and proximity to the state. Religious identities could have a political edge. Extensive endowments to temples, including land, required committees of administrators appointed by the authorities of the temples, and most were *brāhmaṇas*. This was a parallel to Buddhist and Jaina monks as managers of monastic endowments and establishments. Given their sources of wealth, royal temples became architecturally elaborate since they were also statements of power. Rituals for the king and the deity were either parallel or overlapping.

Other than royalty, patrons of consequence were intermediaries and feudatories, the upper bureaucracy, and merchants and traders.[47] Among the latter, land on occasion was first purchased and

[44] E. Hultzsch, "Bhagalpur Plate of Narayanapāla", 304ff.
[45] Khalimpur Plates, *Ep. Ind.*, 4, 243–54.
[46] Cowell and Thomas, 5.169; Kane, 5.76.
[47] Inscriptions at Ittagi, *Ep. Ind.*, 13, no. 4.37ff.

then donated. Similarly, money was invested and the interest was used in maintaining the institution, an activity expanding from earlier beginnings. Some of the most prosperous temples are located at centres of exchange and trade, and along routes linking these centres, a situation not too different from the location of Buddhist monasteries.

Villages are sometimes mentioned as having councils where their headmen, merchants, and officials, occasionally together with the *sāmanta* and higher-level *adhikārīs* (officers), met to consider matters relating to administration, maintenance, revenue, irrigation, and disputes.[48] Sometimes a caste changed from a low status to respectability, as with the Kaivartas. In the earlier period they were rated low, associated with boatmen, fishermen, or else forest-dwellers such as the Niṣāda or even the *dāsas*,[49] or were described as a mixed caste—*sankīrṇa jāti,* or as *antyajas*. Yet in Pāla times they had status and were ranked as a *sat-śūdra* or clean *śūdra* caste, in the hierarchy of various *śūdra* non-brāhmaṇa castes.[50] Others holding high office, such as scribes (*karaṇas*), are described as being of mixed *brāhmaṇa* and *śūdra* origin, the perennial problem of the *varṇāśramadharma*—conceding high status to those earlier said to be of low origin.[51] These were the agencies through which a limited upward social mobility was possible over a few generations.

The biographies suggest that there were areas of either no or little governance, with autonomy left relatively undisturbed. The Śabaras in the *Harṣacarita* are forest-dwellers well away from state administration. The departure of Harṣa leaves them to their own resources. The Kaivartas were feudatories, but their rise to power and functioning suggest recent chiefdoms rather than long-standing dissatisfied feudatories in a well-controlled kingdom. Rāmapāla introduced agriculture, cattle-breeding, and trade after he conquered Varendrī.[52] This is generally said of areas

[48] Miraj Inscription, *Ep. Ind.*, 19, 37–9.

[49] R. Fick, *Social Conditions in North-eastern India during the Buddha's Time,* 302; *The Laws of Manu*, 10.34.

[50] V.N. Jha, "Varṇasaṃkara in the Dharmasūtras: Theory and Practice", 273–88; R.C. Majumdar, *History of Bengal*, I, 567ff.

[51] Tippera Copper-plate, *Ep. Ind.*, 15, 301–15.

[52] *Rāmacarita*, 2.28.

newly opened up, but here it would probably have been the extending and intensifying economic resources. The Kaivartas are referred to as *nāyaka* and occasionally *rājā*, but not *sāmanta* or *mahārāja*. The election of Gopāla, the first Pāla king, to kingship suggests a frontier area where kingship was still new.

10. The King as Deity

From the brahmanical perspective the *cakravartin* could be a manifestation of deity, which doubtless encouraged kings to claim they were *avatāras*. Where the king was transgressing a norm, this claim attempted to explain away the transgression. Claiming incarnation as a political manoeuvre suggests that the appeal to divinity had multiple utility. Part of the reason for this claim could go back to the possible Bhṛgu redaction of the epics. If the epics were converted into texts of Vaiṣṇava Bhagavatism by a protagonist in each being projected as an incarnation of Viṣṇu, then the intercession of Viṣṇu and Śiva in the actions of later kings would be an extension of their earlier effort. The king as the incarnation of a deity both drew from and added to the prominence of the deity, familiar to the Puranic religion. The shift from divine attributes to divine incarnation made a qualitative difference to the notion of causality in the historical presentation of a particular reign. The idiom changes between the early and later authors of the *carita* literature, in which some play of imagination is permitted.

The king as an incarnation of Viṣṇu had many familiar resonances. The symbol of Viṣṇu was the *cakra* (wheel), suggesting the *cakravartin*; the *vijigīṣu* is the hub of the wheel in the circle of the *maṇḍala*; in the concept of the *trimūrti* (trinity of gods), Viṣṇu is the one who preserves and sustains, a function also required of the king. The intervention of Śiva incarnate is less frequent, but Viṣṇu being incarnated is a familiar idea.

Divinity in the epics and in these biographies is significantly different, for when a king is said to be an incarnation, he is not made into an icon of worship—as were the epic incarnations Rāma and Kṛṣṇa. The earlier incarnations were an afterthought, whereas in the biographies the kings were contemporary with the authors and were historically established persons. The function of incarnation was therefore different in the biographies.

What adds a further dimension to invoking deity is that the biographies were liberated from being knitted into or added on to ritual texts; nor did they become such texts. Although deities are invoked, the priority of this genre is political. This may explain the more flexible treatment of divinity. A god is rustled up whenever required, or else introduced indirectly, as in the *Rāmacarita*.The king as patron and the court poet as author gave a different turn to the earlier patron–priest/bard relationship.

Curiously, references to earlier *cakravartins* are not to actual rulers who held sway over vast territories—such as those of the Maurya, Kuṣāṇa, or Gupta dynasties—but to the heroes of still earlier times who would at most have only been *rājās* of small territories. The obvious parallel is to the contrary, namely, the invoking of Aśoka in the Buddhist tradition. Mauryan and Kuṣāna kings would probably have been excluded because they were patrons of the heterodox, but the Guptas who patronized Puranic Hinduism could have been invoked.

The use of incarnations and divine intervention also had to do with the greater political accommodation of the Puranic religion, as compared to the earlier Vedic Brahmanism. The former availed itself of some aspects of Brahmanism, partly for purposes of legitimation, but was essentially different. It incorporated the new *bhakti* or devotional forms of worship, though Bhagavatism and the Śākta and Śaiva cults, as well as subsuming aspects of Sramanism. Among the significant changes was the focus on the individual seeking liberation from rebirth. Whereas previously one's *karma*—the effect of one's actions in a former life on the present—was crucial, now there was through *bhakti* the mediation of the deity as well. Reliance on the deity could take the form of the grace of the deity and a sharing in this grace.

In references to the king's access to divinity, the question of whether the deity is controlling human action or acting according to human ambition is not made clear. The significance of the deity also raises the question of whether the divinity claimed by the king, demarcating or separating him from others, was in fact conducive to reducing his actual power. Those who claimed that a particular king was a reincarnation of a deity were controlling the claim since their claim was what gave it authenticity. But the claim, having once been accepted, would provide the necessary legitimacy to the king in any confrontations with others. The divinization of the king therefore isolated him. His access to power took on a dual dimension. The isolation was increased by surrounding him with retainers rather than kinsmen. With kinsmen there are norms of expected behaviour devolving from the relationship. With retainers, the relationship has to be negotiated on the basis of expectancy and expediency. This did not entirely preclude using kinsmen, as Rāmapāla did in the initial foray against the Kaivartas.

The politics of associating a deity with an action or of making the king an incarnation of deity is demonstrated in some other biographies, as for example in Bilhaṇa's biography of the Cālukya king Vikramāditya VI, the *Vikramāṅkadevacarita*, written in the late eleventh century. The central act on the part of the king which had to be justified in the biography was his getting rid of his elder brother and usurping the throne. This we are told was done on the instructions of Śiva, who appeared to the king and complained that the elder brother was evil and incompetent. In a subsequent biography of Vikramāditya VI written by his son, the king is said to have been an incarnation of Viṣṇu, perhaps in competition with the contemporary Hoysala king—also said to be an incarnation of Viṣṇu! As for the elder brother, the inscriptions he issued suggest that he was a patron of the Jainas and may possibly have been a Jaina himself. Given the intense rivalry between Śaivas and Jainas in the peninsula in those times, the biographies and inscriptions seem to point to a confrontation between religious sects vying for power, supporting various contenders for the throne whose confrontations were not for political office alone. These are not flurries of religiosity but carefully thought-out political manoeuvres using the idea of divine incarnation. Despite the biographer's attempt to hide this conflict, it becomes visible to the discerning reader.

Where there was uncertainty of political authority, there the resort to a deity helped in maintaining the rhetoric of power. Identification with a deity, for which the compulsion was both personal and political, was, in addition to patronage, also a mechanism for strengthening particular religious sects; or it could have been an attempt to subordinate other religious groups; or else to balance political and religious authority. As an incarnation, the king would be of immediate consequence to the ranking of religious sects in the hierarchy of privilege and power. Where the association was with religious sects already in positions of dominance, there the status of the king would be strengthened. Deity and religious sect could also be used to challenge the power of a particular family. All this added to the instrumental significance of biography.

A partial comparison may be possible here with the thesis of the king's two bodies as propounded for medieval European kingship,[53] in which it is argued that there is a Body Natural and a Body Politic, but the need to unify the two is constantly emphasized. The Body Politic is sometimes seen as descended from Grace. Kingship becomes in part a mediary between the Christian Church and the secular state, where the latter comes increasingly to be represented by the Law. The hierarchical apparatus of the Roman Catholic Church became the prototype of an absolute monarchy based on the use of mystical ideas. But gradually the state becomes more polity-centred. The absence of a properly regulated church in the Puranic context gives a different complexion to king and deity. Nevertheless, even if a universal church was absent, there was a degree of institutionalization in most religious sects of this period, which allows of a relationship between the sect and the state, although the nature of this relationship differed from that of the Christian Church.

11. Politics of Sects and Factions

Religious factionalism was obviously of political importance. Even if it is not referred to openly in the biographies, it marks a further historical change from earlier times. In the *Harṣacarita* it is significant that Harṣa takes the Buddhist ascetic Divākaramitra back with him. Buddhist groups were also proximate in the Pāla kingdom. If religious factionalism was involved in the ambiguity of succession, stemming in part from Rājyavardhana being a Buddhist, then the presence of these heterodoxies and their potential in the politics of the time have to be acknowledged.

[53] E.H. Kantorowicz, *The King's Two Bodies*.

Judging by the description of the Kaivartas, it would seem that the dissension between them and Rāmapāla and his immediate predecessors was due to economic and social disparities, common among overlords and those who labour. It may also have had a sectarian dimension. Buddhist and Tantric sects were popular in eastern India at this time, to the extent that the local variant of Buddhism, Vajrayāna, had a strong Tantric component; and the biography refers to an important Buddhist monastery.[54] It is unlikely that the *aṭavīyasāmantāḥ* (forest chiefs) and the *vyālāḥ* who confiscated the *agrahāra* land of the *brāhmaṇas* and are listed among the rebels, were conventional worshippers of Śiva and Viṣṇu. Rāmapāla being referred to as the incarnation of Viṣṇu may not have been compatible with the popular sects.[55]

The induction of deity into the political activities of the king contributed to what appears to have been the parallel authorities of court and temple. Both were statements of power. However, patronage could be distributed when the same king supported diverse sects; or else it could be conditioned by social needs, as when royalty built temples to Puranic deities whereas the wealthy merchants were patrons of the Jainas.

There are inscriptions in which royal donors establish temples to a variety of sects—Śaiva, Vaiṣṇava, Buddhist, Jaina.[56] There are also single sites where royal patrons made donations to a temple over decades. Such statements on grants read as a history of the site, and information on the past becomes available to those who want it. Many grants are made by officials, ministers, merchants, and landowners going back to an earlier period, suggesting that particular sects were well endowed with patronage.

The biographies need also to be viewed from the perspective of the religious polemics of the period. Had the patronage to the Buddhists or in other cases to the Jainas been augmented each time, then the predominant institutions legitimizing the monarchy would have been the Buddhist or the Jaina Saṅghas and the biographies would have read differently. This was avoided by the

[54] *Rāmacarita*, 3.7.

[55] Ibid., 5.7–8.

[56] Sikarpur Taluk Inscriptions of Somesvara III, *Epigraphia Carnatica,* 7, Sk 100.

succession of the younger brothers and the intervention of Śiva and Viṣṇu.

Affiliation with a religious sect becomes part of the signature even of the more localized hero. The heroic ethos is elaborated in the clusters of hero-stones in various parts of the subcontinent, becoming more common in this period.[57] These commemorate death on the battlefield, or in protecting the village from human predators, or its cattle from raiders. They are a reflection of the heroic qualities associated with a local leader or sometimes a potential *rājā*. This may have been the counterpoint to the notion of the earlier *aśvamedha* and similar rituals. Specific incidents of heroic action distinct from great conquests are commonly linked to the lesser persons of the hero-stones. For the hero there is no *karma*, no rebirth, only an eternity in heaven. His sectarian affiliation depicted on the stone was doubtless a matter of personal belief, but given the social identity of religious sects, linkages relating to the affiliations of villages or overlords cannot be ignored.

Yet the theory of *karma* is not the sole causal explanation in the biographies for there is also the interplay of one's *karma* with the *varṇāśramadharma*, the need to observe the social code of one's caste. The biography was aware of the norms and kept as close as possible to them. Discrepancies entered where this could not be done. Individual action was also in part influenced by the point in the cycle of time in which the person lived. Thus, in the Kaliyuga the ability to conform to the social code becomes more difficult as the code is disregarded by most. There is an inevitable social decline implicit in the time cycle. But the individual can opt out of it by pursuing his own liberation from rebirth, his *mokṣa*.

12. Time Concepts

Notions of time continued to be multiple, used simultaneously in the same society, but varying with different functions. The span of cosmological time remained the cyclic *mahāyuga* (the great

[57] Romila Thapar, "Death and the Hero", in *Cultural Pasts*, 680–97; S. Settar and G.D. Sontheimer, *Memorial Stones*.

overarching age) as described in the *Purāṇas* with the vast figures of its cosmological frame. Cosmological time was still viewed as the geometry of space, infinite and not subject to calibration; or rather, even the measurement becomes a fantasy. Cyclic time is essentially metaphorical, and by now the decline of *dharma* through the ages becomes far more central than the measurement of time, which remains a mathematical figment. The *mahāyuga* is so immense that its return can only be thought of as an idea. It is beyond measurement. References were to the current Kaliyuga but largely in association with the decline of *dharma*, rather than as time-reckoning. The notion of social and moral decline in the Kaliyuga is predictable as a theory where, in a declining cycle of time, this would be an inevitable description.

As against the immeasurable *mahāyuga*, manageable timespans were common, such as the sequence of generations, where each was an approximate unit of reckoning, or the short span of an event as covered in the biographies and set in the time and space of routine events and daily actions. These were calculated more frequently in linear time. Linear time therefore continues to record human action. The biography picks the single person, magnifies his actions, and provides him with a dynastic history. This is not a history determined by cosmic cyclic time which is too distant, but it can be viewed as a minuscule arc of time within the cosmic cycle. However, its treatment of time is linear. It is pragmatic time relating to eras, generations, and events of significance within reach of contemporary dynasties.

The narrative of the biography was in chronological order. Occasionally, a later event may be brought forward to explain the narrative in greater depth. Thus, possibly Bhāskaravarman's alliance with Harṣa was subsequent to the latter ruling from Kanauj. Familiar eras were used,[58] except when a reigning king wished to proclaim his status by departing from these and commencing a new era with a major event of his reign, thus also providing, on

[58] Such as the *samvats* of Vikrama 58 BC, Śaka AD 78, Kalacuri/Cedi AD 248–9, Gupta AD 320, Harṣa AD 606, Laukika 3076 BC, and Kaliyuga 3102 BC, etc. Some discrepancies of upto a year occur in a few of the reckonings, often relating to current or expired years, and the precise date of the commencement. Generally however a correct equivalent calculation is possible.

occasion, evidence of regnal years. The more prestigious of such eras, which included the Harṣa era of AD 606, continued in use for a few centuries.[59]

Cyclic time is not emphasized in the biographies, in part because their concern is with historical and contemporary events. The Kaliyuga prophesies the current period as one of decline.[60] The biography assumes the reverse, a movement up towards the golden age of the king's reign, and the successful outcome of the central event. This was the return of rightfulness and stability, where social codes were observed and economic prosperity widely experienced. The evils of the Kali age begin to fade and the millenarian fantasy also becomes somewhat irrelevant.

The continuing references in the *Purāṇas* to the world turned upside down are surprising, since from the Guptas onwards there was an assertion of the brahmanical presence in court circles; for, even when lower-caste families rose to the status of dynasties, they claimed the correct *kṣatriya* status and sought the assistance of the *brāhmaṇas* to establish this status. Admittedly, however, together with the new *kṣatriya* castes of *rājaputra*, *sāmanta*, *rauta*, *ranaka*, and so on, were the lesser but powerful castes of the *kāyasthas*, *gāvuṇḍas*, *heggdes*, and suchlike. The behaviour of the overly powerful and arrogant *kāyasthas* in Kashmir, for example, is described as that of upstarts.[61] The fears linked to the Kaliyuga in the *Purāṇas* registers the awareness of a change from the past.

13. Literacy

Literacy in an oral society, it has been argued, can have an enabling effect, with a dependence on the literate for interpretation,

[59] *Alberuni's India,* vol. II, 5.

[60] The Kaliyuga is referred to in the Aihole Inscription of Pulakeśin II, the Cālukya king, and its date has been calculated to 3102 BC: *Ep. Ind.*, 6, 1ff. It remains debatable as to whether it reflects the conditions prevalent in northern India after the turn of the Christian era, when the norms of the *Dharmaśāstras* were being flouted in the growing social change and the induction of foreign elites from the north-west of the subcontinent and Central Asia: B.N.S. Yadav, "The Accounts of the Kali Age and the Social Transition from Antiquity to the Middle Ages", 31–63; R.S. Sharma, *Early Medieval Indian Society*, 44–76.

[61] *Rājataraṅgiṇī*, 4.621–9, 8.131.

identification, and order.[62] The *itihāsa-purāṇa* tradition not only takes form in new genres of texts but uses new sources. There are references to the *akṣapaṭalādhikṛta* (officer in-charge of legal documents) in inscriptions of the Gupta period, and to a keeper of state documents in Chinese accounts of travel in India.[63] Xuanzang refers to official annals but provides no details. Such keepers of records may have originated earlier.[64]

The spread of literacy was doubtless assisted by the multiple places of learning associated with grants of land. But the emergence of elites is not dependent only on what has been called the feudalization of the agrarian economy. Urbanization also created wealthy elites through the activity of agrarian market centres and the revival of trade in cities within the subcontinent as well as with other parts of Asia.[65] Elites of mixed origins and cultures inhabited urban centres at the turn of the Christian era social codes were flexible, as when wealthy *brāhmaṇas* drew a substantial income, from trading in horses.[66]

The literate at the court are presumed to have been largely *brāhmaṇas*, but members of other castes participated in administrative functions requiring literacy. There is a historical distinction between *brāhmaṇas* learned in the *Vedas*, emphasizing ritual and *mantra*, and those who used literacy for more general purposes. At the other end of the spectrum from ritual texts were the *Pañcatantra* and the *Hitopadeśa*, both written by *brāhmaṇas*. The Bhṛgu *brāhmaṇas*, for example, may not have abandoned ritual, but their control over the *itihāsa* literature shows a perceptive understanding of the importance of capturing the past and reflecting a particular version of it in a literate form. Recognition of the historical functions of a strongly literate tradition may initially have come from observing these in Buddhist and Jaina institutions. Castes such as the *kāyasthas*, who functioned as scribes and record-keepers of

[62] M. Finley, *Politics in the Ancient World,* 30ff.

[63] Copper-Plate Inscription of Śīlāditya VII, in J.F. Fleet, *Corpus Inscriptionum Indicarum,* III, 171–91; T. Watters, *On Yuan Chwang's Travels in India*, 1, 154.

[64] Such as the *karana* of the Mauryan period: J. Bloch, *Les Inscriptions d'Asoka,* 96, 134; *Arthaśāstra*, 2.7.17–36.

[65] B.D. Chattopadhyaya, *The Making of Early Medieval India.*

[66] Peheva Inscription, *Ep. Ind.*, 1, 184–90.

the administration (though ranked lower than *brāhmaṇa*), were on occasion highly respected as royal biographers and composers of lengthy inscriptions.[67] The articulation of the past was viewed as important to the political representation of both past and present. It is also interesting that the term *itihāsa* occurs with greater frequency in this period, in both texts and inscriptions.

The increase in *agrahāras* resulted in larger numbers of educated *brāhmaṇas*. This was not unconnected with the impressive articulation of learning and literature in Sanskrit during this period, as also with a *brāhmaṇa* diaspora in distant places, both in the subcontinent and beyond, competing with the diaspora of Buddhist scholars, monks, and traders. In the subcontinent this migration coincided with the multiplication of courts seeking *brāhmaṇa* retainers as court poets and chroniclers. The *carita* literature was part of the formal education of those who claimed to be learned, and those who described themselves as the "new Bāṇas".[68] Creative literature in Sanskrit during this period was closely tied to life at the court but had a habitat in the *maṭhas* and *ghaṭikās* often attached to temples, and more so in the *agrahāras,* as indeed also in the Jaina monasteries of Karnataka and Gujarat, and the Buddhist monasteries in eastern India. Monastic establishments of whatever denomination were repositories of earlier texts, and many monks or students spent their days making fresh copies of these texts, and scholars writing commentaries on them.

The premium on literary creativity is expressed in the pride which kings took in being regarded as literary figures. Of the three major rulers of the seventh century in the subcontinent, two—Harṣa, and Mahendravarman the Pallava king—are credited with being playwrights of high quality. Even if Harṣa was not the author of the plays attributed to him, it is significant that he wished to be seen as such, as indeed a few centuries later the Cālukya king Someśvara III wished to be remembered as a scholar.

This also tended to encourage the creation of cultural idioms which were recognized across large regions and acted as bonds

[67] Rewa Stone Inscription of the time of Karna: Cedi *samvat* 800, *Ep. Ind.*, 24, no. 13, 101ff.; Kalanjara Inscription of VS 1147, *Ep. Ind.*, 31, no. 22, 163ff.; *Yājñavalkya*, 1.322; *Viṣṇu Dharma Sūtra,* 7.3.

[68] A.K. Warder, *Indian Historiography*, 116–17. Sakalavidyācakravartin's *Gadyakarṇāmṛta* was composed in the thirteenth century.

between those who subscribed to a sanskritized, mainstream culture—what was referred to as *mārga*, as opposed to *deśī* or the localized observances.[69] That the distinction is made in theoretical works points to its recognition. A change in cultural ways is signalled by the use, however haltingly, of Sanskrit, and by the transition to a semblance of *varṇa* society adopting social norms traced to the *Dharmaśāstras,* even if adhered to more in theory than in practice.[70]

Similarities in narratives and symbols begin to be noticed, and gradually become a kind of cultural shorthand. This cultural capital came to be invested in local communities which witnessed a manipulation of language, caste, and deity. Models are imitated and the act of imitation spurs a dialogue between the *mārga* and the *deśī*, where elements of each are intertwined, although the former may underplay the presence of the latter. One of the consequences of this was bilingualism in the court and administration, which is reflected in bilingual inscriptions, as well as in the composition of texts in the regional languages that draw on models from literature in Sanskrit. From the early second millennium AD categories of *itihāsa* texts begin to be composed in the regional languages. The historical moment at which the regional language becomes significant would mark a change among those involved in maintaining the historical tradition.

Literacy among non-*brāhmaṇa* castes such as the *kāyasthas* points to some flexibility as to who could be taught Sanskrit. Engravers of epigraphs mention their names alongside that of the author. This was in part a legal requirement, but also had to do with recognizing the importance of script to learning. That these

[69] The terms are used largely in works on music, aesthetics, and literature, but were extended to a wider context of types of cultures. As such, they are useful in demarcating the mainstream Sanskritic culture—*mārga*, from what is referred to variously as the local, regional, or vernacular culture—*deśī*.

[70] This was a process of "sanskritization" and not of "aryanization", Aryan being a language label and not having a distinct racial or ethnic connotation. At best it can be used for the introduction of a Sanskritized language and the culture ways that went with it. I am using the term in a different sense from the more accepted term "Sanskritization", introduced by M.N. Srinivas, where the reference is more to caste behaviour in which lower castes attempt to adopt the lifestyle of upper castes.

engravers appear to have been of lower castes would point to the availability of a minimum literacy at levels other than those in the upper castes, although the range of the literate lower castes would have been confined to certain occupations.

Respect for the written document was not merely the result of conforming to the requirements of legal procedures. Texts were maintained, preserved, and copied when necessary. The importance of the text is also demonstrated by the large number of *ṭīkās* (commentaries) written at this time. The earlier original text was valued as an articulation from the past, as also the need for updating or explaining it without tampering with it. By their very nature, commentaries are conscious of a historical relationship between an earlier text and contemporary views. However, questions concerning the historicity of the events and persons, although occasionally considered, are not central to these commentaries. The implicit evolution of concepts receives greater recognition. The commentaries may also have been encouraged by the proximity of scholarship from heterodox sources, since the commentarial tradition was established earlier in Buddhist scholarship, of which, as we have seen, it was a significant component, especially in narrating earlier history.

14. *Caritas* and History

Itihāsa-purāṇa was recognized by now as a branch of knowledge and *itihāsa* is mentioned as deserving attention.[71] The interpretation of the past was in the hands of those who were educated in the *agrahāras,* or linked to the royal court, or directly involved in the administration of the kingdom. Other keepers of the past are less visible in the records of the elite, but are present elsewhere. By the end of the first millennium AD, scholasticism in the subcontinent went beyond the tradition of Vedic learning and included much else, such as the Puranic and the Tantric, not to mention the diversity of philosophical schools and the impressive advances in mathematics, medicine, and astronomy. A transition had taken place where, in many areas, there had been a change from "heterodoxy"—the dominance of Buddhist and

[71] Two Eastern Ganga Copper Plates, *Ep. Ind.*, 26, no. 5, 62ff., ll. 9–10.

Jaina institutions—to the emergence of brahmanical institutions, but in part modelled on the heterodox. An example of this was the adaptation of the idea of the Buddhist monastery to the Śaiva *maṭha*. Brahmanical learning would not have been averse to the unacknowledged appropriation of aspects of these historiographies. This encouraged explorations in other ways of thinking, such as in creative literature, philosophy, and aesthetics, and, not least, new ways of recording the past.

The imprint of brahmanical learning influenced other contenders for the status of intellectuals. Foremost among these were the *kāyasthas*. Even as a functional group, they had come to be associated with extensive learning. It would be expected that their perspective would be much more tied to ground realities, given that it grew out of the nitty-gritty of routine administration and proximity to political authority. It is interesting that Sandhyākaranandin does not flinch at describing the rebellious intermediaries causing the Pālas to lose Varendrī. Admittedly, at one level a detailed description of the revolt, and the cajoling of the feudatories required to counter it, strengthens the claim that Rāmapāla was politically more astute than his brothers, and capable of organizing the suppression of the revolt. But that this was made the central event of the biography may have had more to do with the social and intellectual outlook of the author, reflecting his perception of the power of the state. The implicit argument is that intermediaries and feudatories at any level are not to be trusted and have to be almost beguiled into loyalty. Was he demarcating cateogires of grantees? Even scribes who were recipients of grants of land, because they were primarily the administrators, probably had a greater loyalty to the dynasty.

This is in some ways a contrast to the description of officialdom in the *Harṣacarita*, where Bāṇa describes it in unflattering terms, as consisting of people virtually bereft of self-respect and constantly fawning on their superiors.[72] Four centuries later, such groups had found a niche and a superior status. Chronicles from the court were almost by definition hagiographical: exaltation of

[72] Kane, 2.23ff., 7.118ff.; Cowell and Thomas, 7.248ff., 2.60–2.

the ruler is characteristic of most. Chinese annals describing the reception of the Chinese ambassador at the court of Harṣa and the message of goodwill sent by Harṣa to the Chinese ruler, or the report of the mission of Wang-hsuan-ts'e in India against the usurper of Harṣa's throne, use a phraseology which is far from a historically accurate reflection of the relations between Harṣa and the T'ang ruler.[73] Its intention is to flatter the latter.

The *vaṃśa* lists in the *Purāṇas* had been discontinued. The material on contemporary dynasties was incorporated into the new historical narratives and royal inscriptions. The court poet as an employee of the king changed the relationship between political authority and its legitimizer. The bard had not been an employee. Although there continued to be a mutual dependence between the poet and the ruler, the balance had tilted in favour of the latter, particularly where the court poet was also a functionary. In kingdoms where the bard continued to keep the genealogy—possibly in the smaller courts which could not maintain a court poet—he remained the legitimizer of the ruling family. He was more integrated in such a society, for it was not imprinted fully with courtly culture. Still regarded as inviolable and respected because of his function as legitimator of the ruler, he had a different relation with chiefs, *rājās*, and even kings. The formal status of the bard, the *sūta*, and the *māgadha* was by now unambiguously low.[74] Nevertheless, the bard was permitted to dissent, and pass judgement on his patron. He had the freedom to criticize the king, as is recorded for Mewar in the fourteenth century.[75] To that extent the bard had a floating status, respected because of his occupation but conditioned by his actual relationship with the court. Ideas spread faster through oral communication, although they remained in a more limited region, whereas literacy tended to nourish a relatively closed group, even if it had a much wider lateral spread.

The maintaining of a court poet and the writing of a biography became something of a status symbol. When the kingdom

[73] D. Devahuti, *Harsha*, 244ff.
[74] *Nāradasmṛti*, 12.113–16.
[75] V.N. Zeigler, "Marwari Historical Chronicles", 219ff.

was economically sound and the royal family reasonably secure, it could move from the local bard to the court poet. The latter, familiar with the *itihāsa-purāṇa* tradition and *kāvya* literature, picked up the family history perhaps from the bard, consulted the oral and the literate traditions including the inscriptions, and wove these strands into a *carita,* withholding or disguising that which he thought more prudent not to mention openly. Biographies and chronicles were a merging of records, memory, and intentions. Common elements structured the form and made it distinctive as an authorized version of an activity of a king.

It may well be asked if this changed form of the *itihāsa-purāṇa* tradition can still be considered a continuation of the earlier tradition. There was nostalgia for the past, continuity from the past, and the claim that the past as well as the present were being described as having actually happened. Legitimacy of status and action, and royal antecedents, drew on this tradition as sources of information on the past. What did change, and most obviously so, was the form of the record. It was no longer attached to another text. As in the Buddhist and Jaina historical tradition, the *itihāsa-purāṇa* was given recognition in new and independent forms specific to the discourse on *itihāsa.* Consequently, what was also quite new was that the authorship differed from earlier times, priests and monks being replaced by courtiers and administrators. A large part of the narration now pertained to the present, although it was treated as historical by the next generation. Characteristic of the *carita* was that it narrated the story of an individual and not a community, clan, or lineage. It endorsed individual action, giving a direction to events. Inevitably the individual rises above the office he holds.

Kingship had also to relate to institutions. In the Buddhist tradition the relationship of the king to the Saṅgha is unambiguous. History mobilizes support for the king, who models himself on exemplars. The Puranic tradition is ambiguous in identifying an institution. In an indirect way, the *sāmantas* as recipients of grants of land formed an institution to which the king had to relate, as is evident in the *Rāmacarita*. *Brāhmaṇas* holding grants of land also legitimized kings, although in a less direct way.

Genealogies are memories of social relationships. They are

renewed and change over time. Texts emanating from courtly literature remain largely unchanged. New perspectives cannot be accommodated by an interpolation into an existing composition. It requires a new text. "Fixation in writing once achieved, primarily had a preserving effect upon the oral tradition because it put an end to the involuntary shiftings of the remembrances and drew limits to the arbitrary creation of new stories."[76] The possibility of transmuting the past decreases; the past now becomes that which is set apart and can be enquired into. The heroic past and the post-heroic past do have continuity, but the external forms can be very different. Nevertheless, the biography is not entirely an official document since it incorporates the perspective of the author. To that extent, it may disagree even marginally with the more recognized official documents, namely the inscriptions issued by king and court. The *caritas* were a recitation of the present but with an awareness of the past through a narrative that largely kept to the order in which events happened.[77] The author creates a flexible link between the past and the present. The reliability of sources depends on whether the account is accepted or dismissed by contemporaries. Other authors are seldom quoted.

The centrality of the individual in the context of the socio-religious ethic was perhaps more sharply etched in Buddhist and Jaina writing. It was pursued in the *bhakti* teaching of Puranic Hinduism and in the focus on the self in Tantric practice. Notions of the king's *dharma* drew from the ideals of the *cakravartin*, although defined differently in the Buddhist and brahmanical tradition. The sense of history is apparent in placing the king in the context of a dynasty with a past, in references to the acts of earlier rulers with a comment on these. An assessment of the role of kingship meant referring to past occasions when kings faced situations that were either problematic or celebratory. The play on divinity is new and shows a political use of deity which can be either subtle or obvious. Whether kings should see themselves as constituted of divinity is debatable and this provides multiple

[76] F. Jacoby quoted in J. Goody (ed.), *Literacy in Traditional Societies*, 2ff.

[77] Cf. B. Guenée, *Historie et Culture Historique dans l'Occident Medievale*, 20ff.

ideas. Despite the hype about the power of kingship, its actual fragility is recognized.

This new understanding of the function of historical traditions can be seen further in the royal inscriptions issued by most dynasties, which treated them as official documents, and in *vaṃśāvalīs* validating rulers and their activities.

14

Inscriptions as Official Histories—and the Voice of the Bard

1. Inscriptions as Annals

Inscriptions of all periods, being tangible remains from the past, were initially treated as archaeological objects. They were read only for information on dynasties and chronologies, the argument being that they were more reliable than texts for this purpose—as most are. When first read for socio-economic data, it was realized that the post-Gupta inscriptions were documents recording grants as property transactions, and reflected a significant change in the economic structure of kingdoms. This gradually led to reading them as texts. Even more recently, they have been viewed as representing courtly culture, including their role as annals,[1] and inevitably therefore with a context of state power.

As a text, an inscription is also conditioned by its form, the material on which it is inscribed, its function, its authorship and audience, and whether it encapsulates power or not. That they should be read as distinctive categories of *praśasti, śāsana, dāna*,

[1] R.S. Sharma, *Early Medieval Indian Society*; Daud Ali, "Royal Eulogy as World History: Rethinking Copper-plate Inscriptions in Cola India", 165–229; D. Ali, *Courtly Culture and Political Life in Early Medieval India*.

rather than a single category, is moot. That virtually every dynasty was in its inscriptions following a generally accepted format marks these texts as distinct. The format becomes a dialogue, both within the political office of a dynasty and one that is inter-dynastic. The titles assumed by rulers need not be taken literally as they were part of the rhetoric of these relations.

Inscriptions, as we have seen, are historically significant independent records. Pre-Gupta inscriptions tended to be diverse and scattered, pertaining largely to the activities of individual rulers in summary form. Few were concerned with a more systematic record of dynastic rule. From about the sixth century AD, their numbers increase and they become official statements recording events thought to be significant. Many delineate royal grants of land to religious and other beneficiaries. Although some record ritual occasions, this information is not embedded in ritual texts but remains an independent statement, whether private or official. Issued by a variety of people for various purposes, priority is given to the larger number of the *rājakīyam* (official royal inscriptions). Others in positions of authority—such as ministers, wealthy merchants, householders, and members of religious sects—also had their statements engraved. This they did for a variety of reasons, but most frequently in votive inscriptions recording donations for various religious purposes. Additionally, post-Gupta inscriptions embody an awareness of historical traditions.

There are fewer inscriptions on pillars than earlier. When Firuz Shah Tughluq and others wished to incorporate tangible elements of past history into their buildings, they had to shift early period pillars to their new constructions or engrave their inscriptions at existing sites.[2] Reassembling and relocating these entailed an incorporation of the past into the new record. There were no extensive discourses on ethics after the Aśokan edicts, but occasionally a short statement on *dharma* was included. Reinscribing earlier pillars was easier as there was enough space on them and the very act was a statement of incorporation.

Manuals for the writing of inscriptions, among other administrative matters, such as the *Lekhapañcāśika* or the *Lokaprakāśa*,

[2] B. Flood, *Objects of Translation*, 227–59.

provide a format and give examples. The scribe who wrote the document was referred to in early inscriptions as the *lipikāra* or *lekhaka,* and later was often a *brāhmaṇa* or a *kāyastha*, proficient in scribal work and bureaucratic functioning. The written document was then given to an engraver, described either as a *śilpin* (craftsman), or an *ayaskāra* (ironsmith), or a *hemakāra* (goldsmith). Mistakes in engraving individual letters were corrected where possible.

The *Arthaśāstra* refers to many categories of inscriptions and the variations within each, which include a command, a communication, an authorization, recording a gift, and statements of a universal nature.[3] One of the indications of the more extensive use of royal inscriptions is that they include categories, such as *śāsanam* (instructions), *jayapatram* (legal decisions), *ajñapatram* (orders), and *prajñāpanam* (proclamations).[4] The *śāsana* was meant for future kings as well, and therefore had a historical purpose which required that it be kept in royal custody. Some inscriptions carried the royal seal or an autograph, which not only authenticated them but made them viable for future reference. As noted earlier (in chapter 2), the information provided often included the genealogy of the person issuing the statement, its purpose, and a precise date.

The language of these inscriptions is mostly Sanskrit. In the pre-Gupta period, as we have seen, inscriptions were initially in Prākrit and subsequently in Sanskrit. In post-Gupta times, Sanskrit was used extensively. But by the second millennium AD in northern India inscriptions showed traces of the regional language. These changes were linked to the marking of social differences. Whereas Prākrit was inclusive and cut across caste and community identities, Sanskrit tended to reify the upper-caste identity. Cosmopolitan Sanskrit, or what has been called a public political language transcending political boundaries and affiliations,[5] was the reverse of the local regional language. Its uniformity lay in its

[3] *Arthaśāstra*, 2.10.1–5, 23–4, 38.

[4] *Yājñavalkyasmṛti*, 1.317–19; *Dharmakośa*, 1.1.349.

[5] S. Pollock, "The Sanskrit Cosmopolis, 300–1300 CE: Transculturation, Vernacularisation, and the Question of Ideology", 197–249.

use by administrators, selective religious sects, philosophers, and litterateurs. Prākrit had reflected regional variations, but now the regional languages registered these differences. The adoption of Sanskrit had elements of a formulaic code familiar to the courtly and urban elite, and was therefore distanced from the popular language.

Inscriptions do not circulate like books, but most, being public, enable the circulation of their contents. Some were engraved on the walls of temples, making them political statements with religious authority, echoing the earlier latching of historical narrative onto ritual texts. There may also have been the correct assumption that the temple, built of superior material, would survive longer, providing greater longevity to the inscriptions. Not only authorship but also intent is here different from the votive inscriptions at Buddhist sites at the turn of the Christian era. The latter recorded both individual and group donations which had contributed to financing the monument. They became community records: such inscriptions are only occasionally associated with temples.[6]

The construction of a royal temple marked a distinct phase in the evolution of the kingdom and symbolized the claim to independence and power. The change is marked by the fact that the temple could have evolved from a local cult shrine associated with the place of origin of the royal family, and graduated to a more elaborate structure. The *garbha-gṛha* (womb-house), which housed the icon, grew with the addition of *maṇḍapas* (pavilions) and antechambers, courtyards, and *vimānas* (towers), all embellished with sculpture for a large complex. The eminence of the religious structure helped enhance its assertion of authority.

Inscriptions were also engraved on rock surfaces in the vicinity of a fort or town, evoking a more direct political authority. Other inscriptions recording grants were engraved on *tāmrapatras/tāmrapaṭṭas*, copper plates held together with a ring and possibly embossed with the royal seal. These were kept as legal documents with the family to which the grant had been made. The seal sometimes has a skeletal list of the rulers of the dynasty. The ring

[6] The obvious example is the silk-weavers' guild at Mandasor. A.L. Basham, "The Mandasor Inscription of the Silk Weavers", 93–106.

suggests the format of a *grantha* (manuscript), the pages of which were held together by being threaded through one or two holes. These copper-plate inscriptions were intended as texts, the metal providing longevity. Kalhaṇa mentions grants and copper-plate charters of previous times being consulted for information on past happenings.[7] Scribes of the post-Gupta period could probably read the box-headed *brāhmī* and its later forms, but Aśokan *brāhmī* and *kharoṣṭhī* may by now have become obscure. Seals increase in frequency when inscriptions as legal documents have to be protected from forgery.

The emblem of the Candella rulers, for example, was often inscribed on the royal seal or on the copper-plate of the grant. The emblem was that of the *gaja-lakṣmī*, representing the goddess Lakṣmī, standing or occasionally seated, being libated by an elephant on either side. This image had earlier appeared on some coins of the *gaṇa-rājyas* (chiefdoms) and lesser kingdoms around the Christian era, and was later adopted by various ruling families. Lakṣmī emerged as the goddess of prosperity and good fortune (and the consort of Viṣṇu), although in origin she may have had a different function.

Forgeries (*kūṭa-śāsana*) were known, and though infrequent were punishable by death.[8] As always, the author and the purpose of the forgery are of historical interest.[9] The forgery was less of the dynastic data—although an occasional royal seal is tampered with to change the succession; more often, it was an attempt to appropriate the rights stated in the grant, especially grants of land. Harṣa issued an inscription accompanied by what he states is his signature, revoking such a forgery.[10] Occasionally, there are altered documents, which are of course different from the replacement copies necessary when the original is damaged.[11] Where the forgeries were dated back to past times, there must have been records

[7] *Rājataraṅgiṇī*, I.15.

[8] *The Laws of Manu*, 9.232.

[9] R. Salomon, "The Fine Art of Forgery".

[10] Madhuban Plates, *Ep. Ind.*, VII, 155–60.

[11] Paithan Plates of Govinda III, ibid., III, 103–10; Nidhanpur Copper Plates of Bhaskaravarman, ibid., XII, 65–79; Kurud Plates of Narendra, ibid., XXXI, 263–6; *Rājataraṅgiṇī*, 6.14–41.

available to the forger with which to make plausible copies. Some later kings are known to have engraved their statement on an earlier record, presumably to acquire credibility—Samudra Gupta's inscription on an Aśokan pillar is well known. A few become palimpsests, but the old engraving remains visible.

Formulae for royal inscriptions evolve from those issued in the post-Mauryan period. As a new style they carry a *praśasti* (eulogy), initially only of the king but soon including his dynasty. Such inscriptions are often referred to as *praśastis*. The *praśasti* was not intended as a precise statement about the king, but was a signifier and therefore not always taken literally. It extended its reach to earlier rulers as well. The titles may be hyperbolic, but the events were not necessarily fantasy. The point at which the titles change to those more grand is a significant political moment. The text of the inscription begins with a benediction in symbol or in words, and suggests the religious affiliation of the author, as for example *siddham, omsvasti, śrī om namaḥ śivāya, namo bhagavate vāsudevāya*, and so on. In later inscriptions the benediction could be quite detailed.

Because the copper-plate was a legal document, it had to carry an updated version of dynastic history, mentioning the more important kings. The format of the *praśasti*, generally but not invariably, traced ancestry back to deities such as Brahmā and Candra, and *ṛṣis* such as Marīca, Kaśyapa, Atri, and Manu. Subsequently, descent was traced through either the Sūryavaṃśa or the Candravaṃśa or a similar lineage of status, such as the Agnikula, with a reference to the better known of its heroes. The latter provide connections to the lineages listed in the *Purāṇas*. The *praśastis* could be exaggerated descriptions of previous rulers. This was a claim to superiority among a crowd of feudatories who followed the same rules in their own statements, the exaggerations having to be decoded.

The place from where the order was issued is mentioned, such as the royal court or the *skandhāvāra* (military camp). This was a way of establishing the credentials of the person issuing the inscription. Some *praśastis* read almost like a continuation of the descent lists in the *Purāṇas,* linking them to the embedded historical tradition as well as being a claim to respectability. As against *caritas*, they were not restricted to one major figure and central event. The underlying concern was to tap the past for credibility and ensure future recognition. Ancestral links are sought with *kṣatriya* descent groups and not with dynasties, probably because the dynasties were of *śūdra* and *brāhmaṇa* caste.

The purpose of the inscription is then stated, often the gifting of revenue from land. The gift is generally treated by the grantee as heritable, so ownership of the land from which the revenue comes is assumed. The land bestowed could be a small area, or one or several villages. Initially, donations were made to Buddhist monasteries, and this continued in a small way. With a change in the religious affiliations of kings, the donees were overwhelmingly *brāhmaṇas*—either individuals or a group. This resulted in a substantial colonization of new areas. The *brāhmaṇas* were inducted either as intermediaries in areas already settled, or they colonized forest land that had been the preserve of forest-dwellers. There were varying degrees of assimilation, and therefore change on both sides could be consensual, but could equally result in conflicting situations.

Inscriptions recording grants are in effect recording the shift from *yajña* to *dāna*—from the sacrificial ritual to the gift—as methods of legitimating the donor as the patron and the donee as the legitimizer. Such inscriptions, where they include information on the *vaṃśa* (lineage) of the donor, indicate his authority. *Dāna* is not just an expression of generosity, it incorporates the exchange of authority and status between patron and legitimizer. In some ways it is a continuation of the idea of gift exchange implicit in the *yajña*. However, unlike in the first millennium BC when the wealth was movable—cattle and gold—the wealth provided in this period has permanence in the shape of heritable land. This becomes the basis of tangible power for a category of *brāhmaṇas* who were the recipients of grants of land.

In detailing the grant, the qualifications and credentials of the donee, the terms and conditions of the gift—involving entitlement to revenue, tax exemptions, judicial rights, and its location—had all to be stated. Witnesses to the gift, who could be royal officials or members of the local administration and the community, had to be listed. The tendency to render this portion of such inscriptions into the regional language grew with the increasing use of these languages in local administration. This was particularly so where the regional language was different from Sanskrit. The formulaic portion, the *praśasti*, continued to be in Sanskrit. The use of two languages, each representing a different function, was an innovation. To preclude revocation of the grant by future rulers, a phrase going back to Aśoka was used: "that it was to last as long as the moon and the sun endure".

That these grants were of consequence is borne out by the punishment enunciated for those who revoked them. One seeks to deter potential revokers with sufferings in hell for 66,000 years, another threatens rebirth as a dog a hundred times, or finally as a *caṇḍāla* or a snake in the desert. Not even digging thousands of wells, performing a hundred *aśvamedhas*, and gifting a million cows will suffice as expiation.[12] Another curses the revoker with rebirth as a germ in excreta, to be followed by rotting with his ancestors.[13] Yet grants were revoked despite these dire possibilities.[14]

In choosing particular grantees, the royal patron and his advisors were well aware of the politics of religious sectarian factions. Patronage was a form of exercising some control over these, apart from being an obvious mechanism of drawing benefactions from them. Vedic specialists claimed they could alter or divert the ill effects of astrological happenings. Perhaps those in power played with this notion, even if not fully succumbing to it. There was a search for a coherent universe and astrology claimed to provide one.

The part of the *praśasti* linked with the *vaṃśānucarita* used the link as a charter for claims to lineage and descent. It was a significant step in crystallizing historical consciousness as part of the Puranic tradition. The personal legitimacy of the ruling family and the king's right to grant land were enhanced via the genealogical link. Coercing new communities to accepting new dynastic rule or converting clan societies into subservient peasants required legitimation. *Brāhmaṇa* grantees settled on gifted land

[12] Four Candella Copper Plate Inscriptions, *Ep. Ind.*, XX, no. 14, 125.
[13] Damodarpur Copper Plate Inscriptions, Plate 1, ibid., XV, 129–32.
[14] Barah Copper Plate of Bhojadeva, ibid., XIX, no. 2, 17–18.

with the full support of royalty, introduced brahmanical traditions, and fostered the acceptance of kingship. Such people could grow into *sāmantas*, the intermediaries and feudatories who aspired to independent power. Once the *brāhmaṇa* became the agency of the state, a self-conscious utilization of the past conditioned by the needs of the present brought about an enhanced sense of history as an asset. Other aspirants to authority, such as the *kāyasthas*, also became aware of this. These categories issued their own inscriptions stating the history of their authority.

A rise in status was marked by the *praśasti* being composed by a court poet, for whom it was an occasion to show his literary accomplishments; or else by an officer of the upper bureaucracy, such as an *amātya, senāpati*, or *akṣapaṭalādhikārin* or *sāmanta* at the court. The authors were generally *brāhmaṇas* and *kāyasthas*, frequently attached to or close to court circles. The audience was not limited to members of the court (as with the *caritas*) but extended to those who read or heard the contents of the inscription.

There was now the realization that if the past was to be put to work for the present, it would have to be ordered into a usable pattern. An earlier example of this lay in organizing the past in Buddhist and Jaina texts: the advantage of referring to precedents was being recognized. In a sense, the Mauryan rulers had released the court from Vedic ritual since they were patrons of the heterodox. This was reflected in the construction of pre-Mauryan and Mauryan history, particularly in Buddhist texts, such as the *Mahāvaṃsa* and the *Pariśiṣṭaparvan*.

The past had been reformulated in the *vaṃśānucarita* section of the *Purāṇas*, which in turn had been formatted as sectarian texts, a format faintly familiar from Sramanic literature. The new institutional base of the Vedic and Puranic sects lay in the *agrahāras* and temples, and later the *maṭhas*, and *ghaṭikas* analogous with Buddhist *vihāras*. The competition with Buddhist and Jaina sects was in part articulated by different notions of kingship and social ethics. Buddhism maintained that the ruler was elected by the people and was untouched by deity. The social ethic pointed to the irrelevance of *varṇa* by emphasizing a universally applicable social ethic, denying the inequality central to caste. The Puranic sects furthered the difference from the Sramanic by their support of deities and even of theism—both Vaiṣṇava and Śaiva—over those arguing that deity was dispensable.

Consciousness of chronology was another aspect of the change. The event referred to in an inscription is dated in some detail, mentioning the *tithi* (lunar day), the *pakṣa* (lunar fortnight), the *māsa* (month), the season, and the *samvat* (era). To this can be added the occasional mention of constellations, equinoxes, or solstices. Earlier inscriptions tend to be dated in the regnal year of the king, such as those of the Mauryas, Śuṅgas, and Sātavāhanas. Those of the Śakas, Indo-Bactrian Greeks, Kṣatrapas, and Kuṣāṇas use the regnal years as well as an era, such as the Śaka era of AD 78. This era gave way in many areas to the Vikrama era of 58–7 BC. The origins of both remain controversial.

The advantage of using an era was demonstrated in Buddhist and Jaina texts. Each used an era, based on the date of the death of Mahāvīra (527 BC) and the Buddha (486/3 BC). This may have been reinforced by Hellenistic usage as well. But, above all, inscriptional records required precise dating using an era. From the early first millennium, a series of eras were instituted largely by kings commemorating events and persons in their respective dynasties: the Kalacuri-Cedi era of AD 248–9, the Gupta era of AD 319–20, the Harṣa era of AD 606–7, the Bhāṭika era of 624, the Newari era of 879, and the Lakṣmaṇasena era of AD 1179, to mention just a few. Despite these more localized eras the Vikrama and Śaka eras remained widespread.

The Cālukya king Pulakeśin II's Aihole inscription of AD 634 uses both the Śaka era, calculated in linear time, as also the Kaliyuga era from cyclic time. This gives a date of 3102 BC for the start of the Kaliyuga, thought to be the invention of a later period and used in calculations relating to astronomy.[15] The synchronization of the two systems of time measurement is useful for correlations. Prior to this, Āryabhaṭṭa the astronomer, writing in about AD 499, had calculated the start of the Kaliyuga to the same date. References to dating in the Kaliyuga era are rare in inscriptions because cyclic time is not their preferred chronological system.

[15] Aihole Inscription of Pulakeśin II, ibid., VI, 11–12.

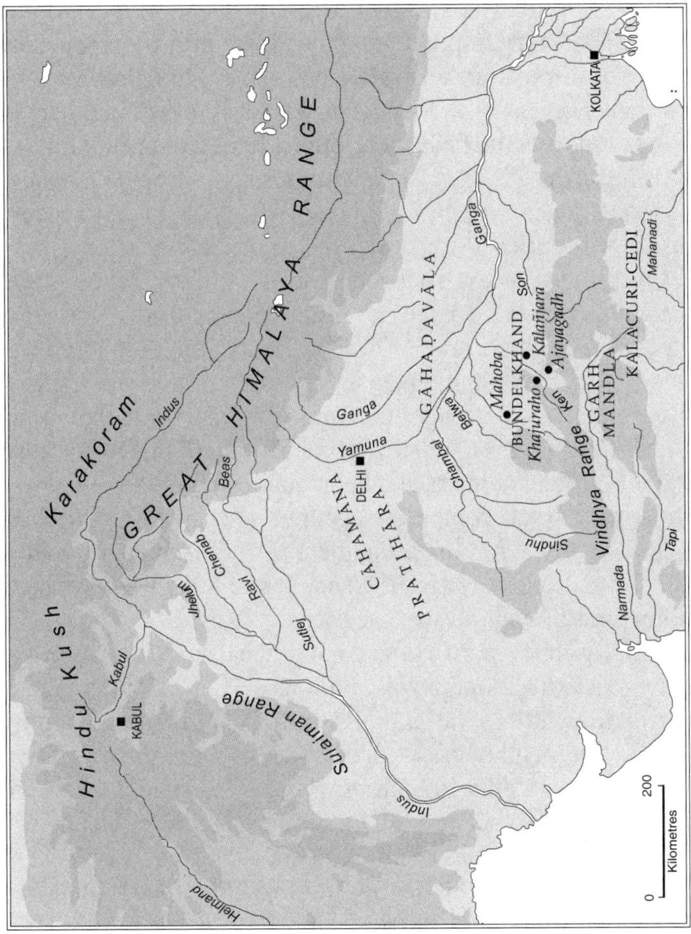

Map 6: Locations of the More Important Places, Clans, and Dynasties

2. Early Candella Inscriptions as Annals

With this background, I would like to demonstrate the use of inscriptions as annals by considering the inscriptions of the Candella dynasty. I have chosen the Candellas at random: they were one among the many dynasties of the post-Gupta period and not of extraordinary importance. Their inscriptions demonstrate how a pattern of history was followed in many kingdoms, and in inscriptions not nearly as long and impressive as some others of the period, such as the Cola inscriptions from South India. If we limit the inscriptions to those that consciously provide a history of the dynasty, they suggest a recognition of the need to record history. I would like to illustrate this as aspects of what I have earlier referred to as externalized history.

The Candellas ruled from the ninth century to the thirteenth century AD in Central India.[16] The heartland of their kingdom was bounded by the river Yamuna to the north, the valleys of the Ken and Betwa to the west, that of the Tons in the east, and their sway extended south almost to the Narmada. The area came to be called Jejjākabhukti/Jejākabhukti, and later Bundelkhand. The kingdom was relatively small compared to others of that time. The locations and locational references in the inscriptions help to broadly track the areas controlled by the Candellas, although geographical identifications are not always precise.

The inscriptions record a process of gradual state formation and the emergence of a kingdom in what was earlier a frontier area at the peripheries of the Pratihāra, Rāṣṭrakūṭa, and Pāla kingdoms. The proximate neighbours of the Candellas were the Pratihāras and the Kalacuri-Cedis, in both of whose state systems the Candellas were initially *sāmantas*. Later, they had to contend with the Cāhamānas/Cauhānas and the Gāhaḍavālas to the north-west, and even briefly with the fleeting raids of Mahmud of Ghazni. The Candella family may have originally come from the area of Mahobā, but their first important centre was Kharjūravāhaka/

[16] N.S. Bose, *History of the Candellas*; S.K. Mitra, *The Early Rulers of Khajuraho*; R.K. Dikshit, *Candellas of Jejakabhukti*; K.K. Shah, *Ancient Bundelkhand*.

Khajuraho, subsequent to which they established forts at Kālañjara and Ajaygadh.

The genealogy of the dynasty, gathered from epigraphs, is as outlined below.[17] (The dates are approximate because they are calculated on the chronology of the inscriptions.)

Nannuka
|
Vākpati
|
Jayaśakti, followed by his brother,
Vijayaśakti
|
Rāhila
|
Harṣa, married Kañcukā
|
Yaśovarman (925), married Puppā
|
Dhaṅga (950–1003)
Gaṇḍa (1003–1018)
Vidyādhara (1018–1022)
Vijayapāla, married Bhuvanadevī
(1022–1051)

Devavarman (1051)	Kīrtivarman (1070–1098)
Sallakṣanavarman (1100)	Pṛthvīvarman (1125)
Jayavarman (1117)	
Madanavarman, (1129–1163) married Vālhanadevī, Lakhamādevī, Cāndeladevī	
Yaśovarman II (1165)	
Paramardi (1165–1202)	
Trailokyavarman (1205–1241/47)	
Vīravarman, married Kalyāṇadevī (1247–86)	
Bhojavarman (1286–1289)	
Hammīravarman (1289–1308)	

[17] Based on S.K. Mitra, *The Early Rulers of Khajuraho*, Appendix II.

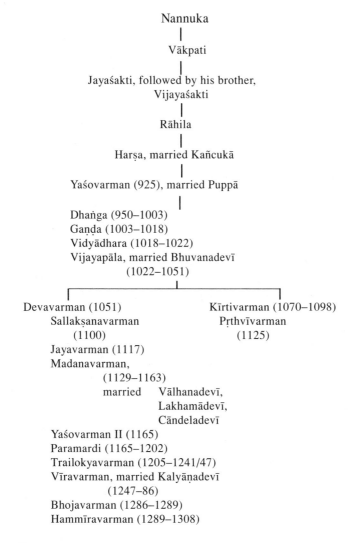

The Candella as a clan is mentioned in inscriptions on *pāliyas* and *govardhana-dhvajas*, hero-stones memorializing dead heroes of various clans. But it is uncertain whether this was prior to their attaining royal status, or from lesser branches of the clan at a later period.[18]

The inscriptions point to a process of state formation, following a pattern common to many kingdoms of the late first millennium AD.[19] Starting with the status of *sāmanta*, there is a mutation into an early kingdom through proclaiming an autonomous status. From this there evolves a full-fledged kingdom, with inscriptions as the record of the official version of events important to the history of the kingdom. These records begin to decrease with the last few rulers and usually indicate the kingdom's decline.

The earliest Candella inscription, of what was to become the royal family, is that of Harṣa/Harṣadeva.[20] This is a fragmentary inscription found near the temple of Vāmana at Khajuraho. The text begins with a description of the creation of the universe, and then refers to an ancestor of the Candellas. Another early ancestor, Vākpati, had two sons, Jejjāka and Vijjāka, mentioned in later inscriptions as Jayaśakti and Vijayaśakti, the later names being an attempt at "sanskritization". Harṣadeva not only conquered territory, he also assisted the Pratihāra *nṛpati,* king, probably his overlord, to regain his lost throne.[21] The statement indicates that the Candellas, who were erstwhile subordinate to the Pratihāras, were now aspiring to an independent status, and the kingdom was taking shape. Later dynastic inscriptions suggest that Harṣa was probably the one who broke away from being a feudatory.

An inscription of his successor, Yaśovarman, dated to the Vikrama *saṃvat* 1011 or AD 953, declares the establishment of the kingdom and gives its history.[22] It was engraved at the Lakṣmaṇa temple, dedicated to Viṣṇu, at Khajuraho. The inscription in good Sanskrit verse records the building of the temple by Yaśovarman, but the record dates to the reign of his son, Dhaṅga. There is

[18] B.D. Chattopadhyaya, *The Making of Early Medieval India*, 85.

[19] H. Kulke (ed.), *The State in India, 1000–1700 CE*, Introduction.

[20] Inscriptions from Khajuraho, no. 1., *Ep. Ind.*, I, 121–2.

[21] Stone Inscription of Harshadeva, *Ep. Ind.*, I, 121ff.

[22] Stone Inscription of Yasovarman, ibid., 122ff.

mention of a Pratihāra ruler, which could by now suggest an alliance. This inscription is an early historical record of Candella history and is qualitatively superior to the previous ones.

The inscription begins with an invocation to Viṣṇu as Vaikuṇṭha, perhaps chosen because of his association with the destruction of enemies, the *asuras*, or because of the influential Pañcarātra sect of Vaiṣṇavas. It refers in passing to the primary and secondary creation, which constituted two of the five facets of the *Viṣṇu Purāṇa,* continues with a mention of various Vaiṣṇava *avatāras* and myths, echoing, not unexpectedly, the same source. Having indicated this as the reference, the history begins with the birth of the Creator, from whom sprang the sages. Among them Atri begat the sage Candrātreya, the founding ancestor of the Candella family. This would give them *brāhmaṇa* status, but the name Candra + Ātreya also links them with the Candravaṃśa, the Lunar lineage of *kṣatriyas* described in the *Viṣṇu Purāṇa*.

An early *brahma-kṣatra* status moved to *kṣatriya*; this was a not uncommon procedure among Rajput royal families, where the former would be a transitional status.[23] Widely current in Rajput origin myths, its relative openness allowed flexibility for manoeuvre in caste society.[24] It also hints at the ancestral figure having possibly been a *brāhmaṇa* grantee whose family gradually established overlordship in an area.[25] The genealogy of the family is given with appropriate laudatory padding and some description of each successor. Ascendant genealogies such as this are common in inscriptions and were regarded as historical, even if they were subjected to some telescoping or the suppression of collaterals, not unusual in genealogies. The names that are retained are those viewed as historically significant.

Rajput clans had a recognized hierarchy. Those of the Agnikula, the Fire Family, were four, of which the Cāhamānas were one, and the ancestor of each of these four was said to have emerged from the sacrificial fire of a sage. Of lesser status were the remaining

[23] B.D. Chattopadhyaya, *The Making of Early Medieval India*, 71.

[24] D.C. Sircar, *Problems of Kuṣāṇa and Rajput History*, 6–11.

[25] As, for example, in the Khoh Copper-plate Inscription, *Corpus Inscriptionum Indicarum*, III, 93ff., 100ff.

ones, descended from human ancestors, such as the Kalacuris, who linked themselves to the ancestral hero Yayāti of the Candravaṃśa. The Candellas, being of lower status, had to invent an origin myth incorporating deities, sages, and ancient heroes with names that could provide an etymology for the name Candella. A tribal Gond origin is hinted at by bards and has been thought plausible by some scholars. This may account for the origin myth, with its insistent link to the *Viṣṇu Purāṇa* and correct status.

An early ancestor was the *nṛpa* Nannuka, who is not given royal titles but is described as "a touchstone to test the worth of the gold of the regal order", and is associated with the conquest both of territory and of princesses. Elsewhere, he is referred to as a *kṣitipā* (a chief), one who excelled the heroes of old such as Pṛthu and Kakutstha. Nannuka's son was Vākpati, who made the Vindhyan region his playground and sported with the Kirāta women—perhaps the women of the forest-dwellers. This could point to encroachments into the Vindhyan forests becoming an important part of Jejākabhukti.

His sons were Jayaśakti and Vijayaśakti. The latter, the younger of the two, had a son Rāhila, who succeeded and was the father of Harṣa. Legitimation rituals are not referred to, but an allusion to them comes from the elaborate metaphor of battle as a sacrificial ritual. In a later inscription Rāhila is described as *nṛpati* (the lord of men),[26] but is not given the royal titles of an independent ruler. This is further underlined in his being described as a skilled archer and compared to Arjuna of the *Mahābhārata*. He is also said to be a touchstone in assessing the worth of the *kṣatriya* order, thus staking a claim early on of the family being *kṣatriya*. The *brāhmaṇa* origin is being added to implicitly by claiming the correct status for royalty. His base was the region around Mahobā, the area continually associated with the Candellas, but he was presumably still in some kind of a subordinate status to the Pratihāras.[27]

The next king, Harṣa, was the father of Yaśovarman and the grandfather of Dhaṅga, the king issuing the inscription. Harṣa is

[26] Stone Inscription of Dhangadeva, *Ep. Ind.*, I, 137ff., 142, v. 21.

[27] The Barah Copper-plate of Bhojadeva of AD 836 claims that the Kālañjara-maṇḍala, later to become the core of Candella territory, was under the Pratihāras: ibid., XIX, no. 2, 15ff.

said to have married Kaṅcukā, the Rajput Cāhamāna princess, it being specifically mentioned that both were of equal caste status (*savarṇa,* v. 21). Kañcukā was the mother of Yaśovarman. The Candellas could now insist on their *kṣatriya* status. The Cāhamānas were a recognized Rajput family of high status, and the marriage would have assisted the upward mobility of the Candella family. This would make them *kṣatriyas,* moving on from being *brahma-kṣatra*, so that somewhere along the line the Candellas chose to ignore their earlier claim to *brāhmaṇa* origins.

With Yaśovarman, the Candellas come into their own. He is described as a sword cutting down the creeper of the Gauḍas, quelling the forces of the Khasas, capturing the treasure of the Kosalas, annihilating the warriors of Kāśmīra, emasculating the Mithilas, coming as the god of death to the Mālavas, the bringer of distress on the Cedis, a destructive storm to the Kurus, a scorching fire to the Gurjaras, and superior even to the heroes of the *Mahābhārata*. This is an echo of Bāṇa's description of the father of Harṣavardhana in his *Harṣacarita,* a model for these later authors. Yaśovarman's campaign against the powerful Cedis, to whom the Candellas were previously subordinate, is singled out for detailed mention and has a ring of authenticity distinct from the hyperbolic verses referring to other conquests. Yaśovarman established himself over the Kālañjara region, possibly taken from the Cedis. Kālañjara became a core area of the Candella domain and great pride was attached to the title of *kālañjarādhipati* (Lord of Kālañjara), taken by subsequent Candella rulers. The Kālañjara mountain is described as so high that it impedes the progress of the sun at midday (in fact it is only 2000 ft high). Elsewhere there is mention of a Candella princess being given in marriage to the Cedi royal family, which doubtless clinched the alliance. Marriages were crucial to diplomacy and politics, especially in the quick succession of alternating friendship and enmity. Yaśovarman's wife was Puppā/Puṣpā, the mother of Dhaṅga, but we are not told her family connections.

The inscription goes on to record that Yaśovarman built a temple to Viṣṇu and installed therein a special image of the deity. The building of a grand temple signified sovereignty and was a statement of pre-eminence. The image is said to be old and much travelled and had a history of being passed from person to person. Its provenance was the Himalaya. Yaśovarman received it from Devapāla, the son of Herambapāla, whose father had obtained it from Sāhi, the *rājā* of Kīra, perhaps in the north-western mountains, in exchange for a force of elephants and horses; he in turn had got it from the lord of Bhoṭa (a part of Tibet), who had found it at Kailāsa in the Himalaya. The introduction of a special image obtained with some difficulty from a distant area is not unconnected with the legitimation of power. Installing an icon of Viṣṇu and housing it in a splendid temple would have been part of the ritual of kingship and appreciated by the Vaiṣṇava Pañcarātra sect. This was in lieu of the Vedic sacrificial rituals of kingship, referred to obliquely and in passing. Viṣṇu appears to have replaced the earlier local family deity, Maniya Deo, as part of the effort to be acculturated to the mainstream culture. Maniya Deo, or Maniya Devi, according to some, was said to be the special deity of the Candellas. It was also associated with the Gonds, and continues to be worshipped at Mahobā. The temple at Khajuraho and the icon of Viṣṇu are symbols of the demarcation being made by a dynasty of consequence which had moved on from its less exalted origins.

We are told that Yaśovarman was succeeded by his son Dhaṅga, *c.* 950–1003. Popular belief that he had brought the Kaliyuga to an end, even if prematurely, was a great compliment since it was meant to convey that *dharma* had returned. Given the description of *dharma* as standing on one leg in the Kaliyuga, according to Manu, this was doubtless meant as a formal endorsement of the *varṇāśramadharma* and Puranic sectarian religion.

The inscription concludes with the name of its author, the poet Mādhava, perhaps the court chronicler and son of Dedda, said to be learned in grammar. The text was written by Jaddha from Gauḍa, who knows the Sanskrit language and is familiar with the work of the *karaṇika* (scribe). Jaddha seems to have come from a family either resident in the east or recently migrated from there. The date in the Vikrama era is given as 1011 (AD 953). The name of the engraver who is described as an artisan cannot be read. It would seem that the persons involved in composing, writing, and engraving the text were not fully confident of their handling of

Sanskrit, and therefore make a special point of mentioning their qualification to do this, a qualification essential to appointment at the court. *Brāhmaṇas* from Gauḍa also had a reputation for scholarship. The reference to Gauḍa may suggest that the scribe was a *kāyastha*, since other *kāyasthas* from Gauḍa are mentioned in Candella inscriptions and they would have been the official record-keepers. Inviting *kāyasthas* as professional scribes was another indicator of an established kingdom.

That such records were conserved is clear from a later inscription issued by Dhaṅga in 1059/AD 1001,[28] and which was renewed by a subsequent king, Jayavarmadeva, a century later, in AD 1117. The list of earlier kings appears to have been copied from the previous inscription, but interestingly omitting Jayaśakti, an indirect reference to a break in primogeniture. Dhaṅga's donations read like those of a well-established king. He had a magnificent Śiva temple erected, designed by an architect with the non-Sanskritic name of Chicha, and he provided residences and grants to *brāhmaṇas* apart from endowments to the temples. He is compared in passing to Viṣṇu-Kṛṣṇa. Some of the statements about his conquests read more like wishes rather than fulfilment and interestingly include references to eastern India, the peninsula and even Siṇhala (modern Sri Lanka). A more factual indicator is the much later inscription of Kīrtivarman stating that in terms of armed strength Dhaṅga had equalled the mighty Hammavīra, most likely Sabuktigin, the Turkish Ghaznavid ruler making forays into northern India at this time.

Dhaṅgadeva is referred to as *kālañjarādhipati* and the son of the *paramabhaṭṭāraka mahārājādhirāja parameśvara.* Yaśovarmadeva and his father in turn are also given full royal titles, reiterating status. Part of the inscription was damaged and was therefore rewritten in the reign of Jayavarman by the *kāyastha* Jayapāla of the Gauḍa region in AD 1117. Clearly, the maintenance of historical records had priority.

Dhaṅga died by entering the Ganges when he was more than a hundred years old. His inscription was completed by Yaśodhara,

[28] Stone Inscription of Dhangadeva, renewed by Jayavarmadeva, *Ep. Ind.*, I, 137.

a *dharmādhikārin* (senior minister of justice), who was also the priest of the royal household. It was composed by the poet Rāma the son of Balabhadra and grandson of Nandana, who was of the Śabara-Sāvara family from Tarkārikā. Śabara is used sometimes of *brāhmaṇa* families but also of some forest clans. If it was the latter, then clearly the family had been assimilated into the culture of the court and this particular Śabara family may well have been of *brāhmaṇa* extraction—if it was linked to a land grant. The inscription was written by the *kāyastha* Yaśaḥpāla and engraved by Siṁha.

Kālañjara becomes central to Candella power, and is also seen as such in the Turkish chronicles recording the attacks of the Ghaznavids on various north Indian kingdoms. Forts as *durgas* (capitals) were important symbols of sovereignty, included as one of the seven limbs of statehood in Kauṭilya's *saptāṅga* theory. *Kālañjarādhipati* therefore becomes a regular title for the Candella kings. Issuing inscriptions from forts also points to a particular kind of political authority and how it was viewed. This would suggest that the power of the later Candellas was somewhat on the edge.

3. The Later Candellas

Later inscriptions refer to the next three rulers, Gaṇḍa, Vidyādhara, and Vijayapāla. Given the age at which Dhaṅga died, these successors are likely to have been elderly, with short reigns. Gaṇḍa kept the kingdom intact. Vidyādhara was given grandiose titles and is said to have caused the downfall of the Pratihāra king, thus negating any suggestion of a status subordinate to the Pratihāras. The other enemy now was Mahmud of Ghazni. A battle between them was apparently bypassed in 1019 and the siege of Kālañjara by Mahmud in 1022 may have been lifted after an exchange of gifts. Inscriptions eulogize Vidyādhara's defence of his realm. The name Vidyādhara was associated earlier with the Meghavāhana lineage, who were Cedis, hinting possibly at a Cedi connection, perhaps on the maternal side.

The competition for power in Central India was now between the Candellas, Paramāras, Cāhamānas, Kalacuri-Cedis, and

Pratihāras. Juxtaposing their inscriptions is like filling the blanks in a jigsaw puzzle to obtain a more complete picture. What is mentioned and what is omitted in the inscriptions of each dynasty is of interest. The Cāhamānas claim to have overrun Jejākabhukti, but there is no hint of this in the Candella inscriptions. Was one exaggerating a victory or the other effacing defeat? With the frequent raids of Mahmud of Ghazni into northern India in the early eleventh century, Turkish and Persian sources refer to local rulers, among whom Vidyādhara was important. Vidyādhara attacked the king of Kanauj who was an ally of the Ghaznavids.[29] However, Candella inscriptions make only a passing reference to the new antagonist, focusing still on neighbouring kingdoms and their constant vacillations on the axis of power.

Vidyādhara's son, Vijayapāla, is known from the inscriptions of his sons and successors, Devavarman and Kīrtivarman who are complimentary about their father. Two grants of Devavarman have survived, both being of a village each to two *brāhmaṇas*. In the second grant, given to secure merit for himself and his ancestors, he mentions his father and grandfather.[30] The recipient, said to be well-versed in the *Vedas* and the *itihāsa-purāṇa,* migrated from Kumbhaṭi-bhaṭṭagrama, described as a place of brahmanical learning. The king is mentioned with royal titles and the grant dates to AD 1051.

Little else is known about Devavarman, but his younger brother Kīrtivarman succeeded him and initiated a colateral line, the second in the Candella dynasty. He has left many inscriptions, apart from those issued at this time by ministers and wealthy merchants. There might however have been a conflict over succession. Despite Devavarman's inscriptions referring to him as *kālañjarādhipati*, and his meditating at the feet of Vijayapāla, not all Candella inscriptions mention him in the list of succession: Kīrtivarman is often the successor to Vijaypāla.[31]

[29] Candella Inscriptions from Mahoba, *Ep. Ind.*, I, 217ff., 220, v. 22.

[30] *Indian Antiquary*, 1887, XVI, 201.

[31] Mau Stone Inscription of Madanavarman, *Ep. Ind.*, I, 198, v. 7; F. Kielhorn, "Deogarh Rock Inscription of Kirtivarman", *Indian Antiquary*, 1889, XVIII, 237–9.

The successors however were unable to keep the power intact. Typical of the quick turnover of centrality in the *maṇḍala* theory, subordinates and overlords changed positions within a century. The Kalacuri-Cedis were again in the ascendant and threatening the Candellas. One inscription, although it gives Devavarman royal titles, also describes him as *mahāsāmanta-rāja-putra*, which suggests a decline or an ambiguity in status.[32] The Kalacuris are more than a threat and the fragility of Candella power is evident.[33] The news had spread at least as far south as the Deccan, for Bilhaṇa, in the *Vikramāṅkadevacarita*, states that the Kalacuri king spells death to the lord of the Kālañjara fort.[34] The inscriptions are effusive in praising Kīrtivarman for stemming the power of the Cedis. However, there is a different take on events, also emanating from court circles, suggesting an alternative to the official version.

In the *Prabodhacandrodaya* of Kṛṣṇa Miśra, a contemporary play performed at the court, one of the generals, Gopāla, defeats the Cedis and restores the power of the Candella king.[35] A feudatory comes to the aid of the king as Gopāla is the *sakala-sāmanta-cakra-cūḍāmaṇi,* the crest-jewel of the circle of *sāmantas*, a phrase frequently used of important feudatories. A later inscription looking back at this period associates Kīrtivarman with *nutana-rājya-sṛṣṭau*, rejuvenating the kingdom, presumably defending it from the Cedis.[36] *Prabodhacandrodaya* was staged at the court and one wonders how its virulent satire on Jaina and Buddhist monks was taken by the Jaina members of the court, or whether this satire, seemingly religious, might not have had a factional edge involving court politics given the many claims to various people having come to the aid of the king. The satire on the heterodox includes the Cārvākas, the philosophers of materialism.

Kīrtivarman was succeeded by his son Sallakṣanavarman, who, in later inscriptions is described as using the booty from successful campaigns against the Mālavas and Cedis, to ensure the welfare of

[32] Charkari Plate of Devavarma, *Ep. Ind.*, 20, 127, lines 9–10.

[33] Inscription from Mahoba, ibid., I, 222, v. 22.

[34] 18.93.

[35] *Prabodhacandrodaya*, iv.

[36] Ibid., I, 217; Rock Inscription of Vīravarman, ibid., 327, v. 3.

his subjects. His son Jayavarman ordered the rewriting of Dhaṅga's inscription which had been damaged, for dynastic annals had to be conserved. Another switch to a colateral line was Jayavarman being succeeded by Pṛthvīvarman.[37] Jayavarman is said to have taken to renunciation, implying a voluntary abdication, which need not have been voluntary.

The inscriptions of Madanavarman (*c.* 1125–63), the son of Pṛthvīvarman, are often located in forts.[38] This hints at the court being somewhat beleaguered, and is known to be in conflict with the Cedis, the Gāhaḍavālas, the Mālavas and the Caulukyas/Solaṅkis of Gujarat. In one inscription certain names are omitted from the genealogy, and one wonders if this was an attempt to change the list of succession.[39] The date is Maṅgala Caitra vadi 5, Visuvasaṁkrānti in Vikrama Samvat 1192 = 24 March AD 1136.

In the time of Madanavarman (*c.* 1125–63) three grants were made to *brāhmaṇas*, not all of whom were ritual specialists. Two were exchanging their land from a previous donation to the present location, a complex transaction carried out at the orders of the queen and endorsed by her husband. One family came from the *bhaṭṭāgrahāra* of Pāṭaliputra to the east of Jejākabhukti.[40] The grant was authorized at the assembly of the village where the land was granted, and the assembly was to include a cross-section of those living there, the *brāhmaṇas*, officials including *dūtas* and scribes, cultivators, *mahattaras* (headmen), and then those of the lowest castes, the *medas* and *caṇḍālas.* The order was written by the *dharmalekhin* Sūḍha of the Vāstavya family (elsewhere referred to as *kāyasthas*), and was engraved by a *ritikāra* or brazier *vijñānin*, Uheno. The order is addressed to the officers and to the village assembly, which is a departure from earlier inscriptions. This suggests a greater participation of local bodies and communities. The king's authority may not have been so effective, despite the formulaic eulogy.

[37] Mau Stone Inscription, ibid., 198, v. 12.

[38] Ibid., 195.

[39] Three Candella Charters, ibid., XXXII, 121, vv. 2–4.

[40] The *bhaṭṭāgrahāra* was generally a village or a cluster of villages. It was a settlement of learned *brāhmaṇas* as a rent-free holding and acquired by their ancestors through an initial royal grant.

Madanavarman had a long reign, his inscriptions dating from AD 1129 to 1163. Their locations suggest that the Candella territories were intact. That he was particular about alliances is evident from his naming his three queens with their respective ranking. He was also particular about the highlights of dynastic history and states that Dhaṅga, after defeating the Pratihāra ruler of Kannauj, attained *sāmrājyam* (sovereignty).[41] He mentions other important events from the past. A later inscription states that Yaśovarman II came to the throne after Madanavarman and before Paramardideva but had a short reign.[42]

The grandson of Madanavarman, Paramardideva/Paramardivarman, ruling from AD 1165 to 1202, took the full gamut of royal titles: *paramabhaṭṭāraka-mahārājādhirāja-parameśvara-paramamaheśvara-śri-kālañjarādhipati-śrimanmat-paramardideva*. But no mention is made of his somewhat unhappy confrontation with the Cāhamāna king, Pṛthvīrāja. The latter's encroachments into Candella territory are referred to in Cāhamāna inscriptions,[43] but little is said about this in Candella records. It would seem from other sources that Paramardideva had recovered his territory by 1201, but was then attacked by Turkish armies under Qutb-ud-din, soon after which he died.

The inscriptions of Paramardideva's successor, Trailokyavarman (*c.* AD 1205–41), suggest that a change of fortune had set. He takes the predictable royal titles but there is a political uncertainty about the content of the inscriptions, which are also far fewer. Trailokyavarman made one grant of two villages to the son of a *brāhmaṇa rauta* killed in battle against the Turuṣkas (Turks).[44] The Turks were on the doorstep of the Candellas and the confrontation may have occurred in the last years of Paramardivarman. In an inscription of his successor, Trailokyavarman is compared rather poetically to Viṣṇu. Whereas the deity in his boar incarnation is said to have lifted the earth out of the sea, Trailokyavarman is said to have lifted the earth out of the sea of Turuṣkas, a reference to the campaigns of the Sultans of Delhi.[45] Mention of a confrontation

[41] *Ep. Ind.*, I, 197, v. 3.
[42] Ibid., 212.
[43] *Archaeological Survey Reports*, X, 2000 (rpt), 98–9; ibid., XXI, 171–4.
[44] Garra Plates, ibid., XVI, 272ff.
[45] Ajayagadh Rock Inscription of Vīravarman, ibid., I, 327, v. 7.

with the Turks is a contrast to the silence about hostilities against the Cāhamānas although the records of the latter make much of it. Curiously the Turks are just another enemy at this stage. There is no hint that they were recognized as a new presence, and the implications of this for northern India.

Grants were issued by Trailokyavarman from his camp on Friday 22 April and 6 May 1205, in peripheral areas of the kingdom to the family of *brāhmaṇa rautas,* the last of whom was killed in battle against the Turks.[46] The *brāhmaṇa rauta* is now part of the typology of *brāhmaṇas*.

Vīravarmadeva, his successor, made a grant to a non-brāhmaṇa *rauta* for valour in a battle in AD 1254, probably against the Cāhamānas.[47] The genealogical section of this inscription telescopes the earlier rulers and then mentions the names of his father, grandfather and great-grandfather. This change in the genealogical style seems common to the descendents of Pṛthvīvarman. Vīravarman faced opposition from a confederacy of intermediaries in AD 1273, as mentioned in a series of brief inscriptions commemorating the warriors who fought for one of these *rājās.*

Inscriptions issued during the reign of Vīravarman's successor Bhojavarman (1286–9) were issued by his ministers from Ajaygadh and its environs. The power base appears to have made a significant shift from Khajuraho to Kālañjara and Ajaygadh.[48] Problems with the forest-dwelling clans are mentioned going back to the reign of his grandfather, Trailokyavarman. The officer in charge of the Ajayagadh fort was responsible for the subjugation of the Śabaras, Pulindas and Bhillas – the generic terms used for forest tribes.[49] The trouble now may have been caused by fresh Candella encroachments into forest areas perhaps occasioned by a need to clear land and settle cultivators, to increase revenue.

The last of the Candella kings was Hammīravarman (*c.* AD 1289–1309). Inscriptions of this period in the name of Śrimad Hammīravarmadeva as *kālañjarādhipati* have raised the question of the relationship of Hammīravarman to Bhojavarman, both as kin

[46] Garra Plates of Trailokyavarman, ibid., XVI, 272ff., 275, vv. 9–11.

[47] Charkhari Plate of Vīravarmadeva, ibid., XX, 132ff.

[48] Ajayagadh Stone Inscription, ibid., XXVIII, 98–107.

[49] Rock Inscription of the Time of Bhojavarman, ibid., I, 334ff., vv. 18–22.

and politically.[50] The former does not take royal titles in these inscriptions despite mentioning that he meditated at the feet of Vīravarman, which was the usual formula for successors. He may therefore have been the governor of the fort. He describes himself as *paramabhaṭṭāraka-sāhi-rājavali* . . . He also gives the title of *sāhi* to his predecessors three generations up, the approximate date for when the Turks started threatening the Candella kingdom. This new title indicates a more insistent political presence of the Turks. The name Hammīra, fashionable in quite a few Rajput families, is in itself a sanskritized form of the Turkish title *amir*. There appears to be no stigma attached to taking the title of an enemy: it seems to refer merely to status in a new dispensation. The absence of the more grandiloquent titles points to a reduced status. Interestingly, the inscription was written by the *brāhmaṇa* Rāmapāla, doubtless working in some official capacity.

The firmness of the Candella genealogy now wavered and started later than in the early records. Hammīravarman's reign sees an increase in the number of *satī* memorial inscriptions from 1304.[51] One of them states, "*samvat* 1366 (AD 1309) of the village of Baliakhera in the time of Alayadina Sultana who is ruling." This was the Sultan Allah-ud-din, confirmed by Persian chronicles as well. Two others probably refer to the wives of his feudatories. In a grant of a village to two *brāhmaṇas*, he again takes the title *sāhi*. This seems rather ironic since he was unable to withstand the attack of the Turks. The termination of the inscriptions marks the effective termination of this dynasty. That memories, traditions, and possibly even claims to Candella descent continued is apparent from the bardic epics.

There seem to have been some claimants to minor branches of the family ruling at Kālañjara and Mahobā. These feature in the later composition of the bards. The *rājā* of Kālañjara was killed in battle against Sher Shah in 1545, and at about the same time the daughter of the Candella *rājā* of Mahobā married into the Gond ruling family at Garh Mandla. The Candellas were either

[50] Charkhari Plates, ibid., XX, 134–6.

[51] Ibid., XX, 134; Mahoba Plates of Parmardideva, ibid., XVI, 10–11.

so reduced in status that they were willing to marry into a tribal Gond family, or the Gonds had so improved their status that they could marry into a *kṣatriya* family; or else there was some truth in the tradition that the Candellas were in origin a Gond clan and therefore the marriage was acceptable.

Reading the inscriptions sequentially thus provides an effective narrative of the history of the Candella rulers.

4. Inscriptions of Administrators and Intermediaries

The writing of history in the form of inscriptions was not limited to dynasties. The recognition of history as a stamp of authority meant that people of wealth and status maintained family histories. The completeness of such histories depended on whether the family wanted such a record. They vary, therefore, from those that are issued by the same family—their information extending to almost the entire period of the dynasty—to others that are single lengthy inscriptions, containing data on the family.

Inscriptions in Jejākabhukti intended as a form of historical writing were composed by those associated with governance and political authority, apart from those by kings. Although these inscriptions are fewer and not so fulsome, the intention is the same. Among them some were issued by powerful families of ministers and administrators, *brāhmaṇa* and *kāyastha*; some by *śreṣṭhins* (wealthy merchants) associated with the court who were often members of the Jaina community; and some by the *sāmantas* serving the Candellas. These were all groups that had access to literacy, economic resources, and the makings of an upper-caste identity. Their records begin in the middle period of Candella rule, when it was doing well, and continue even to when the kingdom was in decline, but such groups continued to prosper. It is also striking that their records from an earlier period are re-engraved when they are damaged, as in the case of an inscription at a Jaina temple.

Pre-eminent among *brāhmaṇa* administrators was the family of Gadādhara, serving the Candella kings since the reign of

Dhaṅga.[52] The inscription is issued during the reign of Madanavarman and therefore covers a large span of Candella rule. The format parallels that of royal inscriptions, with some differences. The family came from Gauḍa, which gave them a high status. It claims descent from Aṅgirasas (the *brāhmaṇas* associated with the Bhṛgus and the historical tradition) and later with Gautama Akṣapāda, linked with the philosophical school of Nyāya. The more immediate ancestor was Prabhāsa. The family members were ministers to the Candella kings with whom their genealogy is correlated with reigning kings.

Statements of the royal inscriptions are generally confirmed.[53] The acts of piety of Gadādhara and his brothers are mentioned and credit is also taken by the ministerial family for the eminence of the Candellas. The ministerial succession lists generations with a concern for accurate history.

Another inscription mentions one Puruṣottama as the *mantrimukhya* (chief minister) of Paramardideva. He succeeded his father in office, as recorded in an inscription in 1195.[54] Once again, the genealogy of the dynasty is correlated with that of the minister's family, although this time it is telescoped and relatively brief. The royal genealogy is traced back to Atri and Candrātreya and then jumps to Madanavarman, Yaśovarman II and Paramardideva. The genealogy of the ministerial family claims to belong to the well-known *brāhmaṇa* Vasiṣṭha *gotra.* The inscription interestingly was composed by Devadhara, a son of Gadādhara, who was the *sāndhivigrahika* of Paramardideva. It was written by another of his sons, Dharmadeva. In one grant the land already granted to a Buddhist monastery is excluded.[55] This is the only passing mention of a grant to a Buddhist institution.

Among other powerful families of administrators the Vāstavya *kāyastha* caste of scribes were also marking their presence. Given the demand for literate officers at the many royal courts, there was not only mobility but competition among those who could function

[52] Mau Stone Inscription of Madanavarman, *Ep. Ind.*, I, 197ff., vv. 17–45.

[53] Ibid., XXXII, 118.

[54] Batesvar Stone Inscription, ibid., I, 207ff.

[55] F. Kielhorn, "Ichchhawar Plates of Parmardideva", 205ff.; *Ep. Ind.*, XVI, 9; ibid., X, 44ff.; ibid., XX, 128.

as administrators. Their ambiguous caste status in brahmanical social codes may have encouraged them when acquiring office to insist on recording their origins and history as an assertion of identity. This may have been partly conditioned by the many branches of the *kāyastha* caste that had become powerful in the administration of contemporary kingdoms.

Such inscriptions carry a reference to a past which almost anticipates their present status.[56] The authority of the *kāyasthas* increased with the decline in royal power. Therefore, their inscriptions tend to belong to the late period of Candella rule. An early reference to the Vāstavya *kāyasthas* comes in an inscription of Kīrtivarman in the eleventh century.[57] Ancestry moves from deity to mythical beings to humans, a pattern resembling the royal inscriptions and the Puranic *vaṃśānucarita*, reflecting a recognition of the historical tradition.

About a century later, an inscription links the name Vāstavya to a town or a cluster of thirty-six settlements,[58] indicating that they were a caste of urban professionals. The omission of deity and sage would suggest a confidence in their established status as administrators.

An inscription in the Kalacuri-Cedi kingdom dating to 1249 provides an origin myth of the *kāyasthas*.[59] It is said that a learned sage Kācara was born from Śiva and embellished the town of Kulāñcā. A *śūdra* propitiated him on the Gaṅgā and the sage granted him a boon that his son would be the founder of the *kāyastha* caste, so called because of the innumerable merits of his *kāyā* (body). Despite his *śūdra* origin, the author elsewhere in the inscription makes a claim to being twice-born. Providing the genealogy of the ministers signifies a change in political functioning and is a comment on royal power, with the ministers becoming more important than before. The fact of *kāyasthas* being ministers meant that they were now more than just a professional caste. Power is shared to some extent, even if in theory it is held

[56] K.K. Shah, "Self-Legitimation and Social Primacy: A Case Study of Some Kāyastha Inscriptions from Central India", 857–66.

[57] Ajaygadh Rock Inscription, *Ep. Ind.*, XXX, no. 17, 87ff.

[58] Rock Inscription of Bhojavarman, ibid., I, 330.

[59] Rewah Stone Inscription of the Time of Karṇa, ibid., XXIV, 101ff.

by the king and his family, as suggested by parallel genealogies of the ruling family and ministers.

Nevertheless the genealogies indicate differences. The *brāhmaṇa* Gadādhara establishes his credentials as a man of learning by claiming descent from a well-known philosopher, as well as his knowledge of texts on polity and theories on good government. The reference was to a family which had controlled ministerial offices over at least five generations, and so doubtless formed an authoritative faction at court. The *kāyasthas* claim almost secular origins in later inscriptions, but mention the help they gave to the kings in times of trouble. This is a different kind of historical connection with the dynasty.

Others with access to wealth and standing also maintained historical records and updated them. Inscriptions were conserved as historical and administrative documents. Earlier inscriptions were read for reference, as is evident from an inscription of an important dignitary at the Jaina temple at Khajuraho.[60] It records the donation of gardens by a Jaina merchant, Pāhilla, who is said to have been held in honour by Dhaṅga. These donations point to Khajuraho being not only a royal centre but also the focus of wealthy merchants. The proximity to the royal temples points to their patrons being persons of consequence. Among them, the Grahapati family is particularly generous. The original inscription recording the grant and dated to 955, was re-engraved in a subsequent century from an earlier copy which had doubtless been kept as a legal document—an instance of historical documentation exemplified through the medium of inscriptions.

Another history of a merchant family is recorded in an inscription of AD 1001 at a temple donated by the Grahapati family, whose parentage and kinsmen are mentioned.[61] The history of this merchant family surfaces again during the reign of Madanavarman in 1147, when the illustrious Panidhara of the Grahapati family is described as a *śreṣṭhin*.[62] Whereas earlier the family was linked

[60] Inscription from a Jaina temple, ibid., I, 136.

[61] Stone inscription of Kokkala, ibid., 147ff.

[62] Three Inscriptions from Images in the Jaina Temples at Khajuraho, ibid., I, 152ff.

to the building of a Śaiva temple, now the donation is to images in a Jaina temple, wealthy merchants frequently being patrons of the Jainas.

Inscriptional records of *sāmantas* were to be expected. There are grants by one of Trailokyavarman's feudatories, dating to AD 1240. The *mahāraṇaka* Kumārapāladeva refers to the king as the overlord who is given the same titles as the earlier Kalacuri-Cedi overlord.[63] Elaborate titles are not just extravaganza but claims to victories over specific enemies. The erstwhile feudatories of the Cedis, when integrated into the Candella domain, incorporate elements of Cedi titles into the lengthy compound title that they now give to their Candella overlord. These include, apart from the others, *vāmadevapādānudhyāta* and *tṛkaliṅgādhipati*. The latter is rhetorical since the Candellas did not conquer Kaliṅga, but the message to the person reading the grant would clearly state that it reflected Candella overlordship over the Cedis, particularly if the grant was in erstwhile Cedi territory. The feudatory in question appears to have been a minister under the Cedis who had transferred his loyalty to the Candella king. His title is hereditary as his father was the *mahāraṇaka* Harirāja.

Another inscription records the mortgage of a village pledged by a Śaiva guru to a *brāhmaṇa raṇaka*.[64] The execution of the deed is witnessed by seven persons listed in an official capacity. There is also a quotation from Dandin's *Kāvyadarśa*, doubtless to make the point that the composer of the epigraph was a literary man. The village was located in what was erstwhile Kalacuri-Cedi territory and the Cedi era is used, although the overlord mentioned is Trailokyavarman, an indication that this was contested territory. The excessive use of royal titles is in imitation of the Cedi style but includes, strangely enough, *kānyakubjādhipati,* normally the title of the Pratihāras of Kānyakubja/Kanauj. The same style is continued in inscriptions recording grants made by *mahāraṇakas* (feudatory lords). The *mahāraṇakas* provide their own genealogies, with only a mention of the Candella king.

[63] F. Kielhorn, "Four Rewa Copper Plate Inscriptions", *Indian Antiquary*, XVII, 224–36.

[64] Rewa Plates, *Corpus Inscriptionum Indicarum,* IV, 37ff.

These major inscriptions constitute the records of a history of the Candella dynasty and some influential families of that time. The earliest inscriptions on stone are largely statements of kings and are located at or close to the temples of the reigning kings at Khajuraho. The information they carry incorporates their version of Candella history. Khajuraho marks the establishment of the Candella kingdom. From the reign of Madanavarman, inscriptions are more frequently linked to the fort at Kālañjara, which seems to have superseded Khajuraho in political importance, as also the fort at Ajaygadh. That both were forts points to the more threatened existence of the later kings.

The inscriptions of Kīrtivarman were issued from various places other than Khajuraho, and even when in camp. The place from where the order was issued would also have a meaning. Focal points of administration and control seem to have gradually become more extensive and there is considerable activity among ministers, *śreṣṭhins*, and *kāyasthas.* Patterns of patronage to various religious sects are also statements of wealth, authority, and status.

Brāhmaṇa donees coming from *bhaṭṭāgrahāras* in Pāṭaliputra and further east migrated from Magadha and Gauḍa attracted by both designations of *ṭhakkura* and *rauta* as well as the gift of land. For those making the gift the intention was to be included in the cultural circuit of the Sanskritized elite. This was defined in the more powerful kingdoms as the culture of the court and the *agrahāras*, the *mārga* culture differentiated from the *deśi*. The poor quality of the language of some inscriptions betrays the inaccessibility of Sanskritic culture to all those seeking it. These compositions suggest that some *kāyasthas* and *śreṣṭhins* moved from fairly humble beginnings to exalted positions. The claim to being skilled allows some to take the epithet of *vijñānin*—not just skilled but knowledgeable. Both *brāhmaṇas* and *kṣatriyas* have the designations *rauta* and *ṭhakkura*. In one case the grandfather was a *dīkṣitar* and the family appear to have moved from priestly functions to administrative office. As recipients of office and holders of grants of land, *brāhmaṇas*, *kāyasthas*, and *śreṣṭhins* were moving into a cultural circle which attempted to diffuse a Sanskritic culture but not invariably with impressive results.

5. The Voice of the Bard

Inscriptions are the texts of official history, representing the view of royalty or of other people of status and authority. There is, however, another perspective on such persons, particularly the rulers, which differs from the official. It is not as consistently available as the inscriptions, but where it is present it forms a counterpart to the formal view. This is the bardic tradition, to which I have referred earlier (chapter 2) as constituting a third substratum tradition for much of Indian history, and it continues to this day, though now fading out. In its later manifestation in the second millennium AD, it is often literature from the subaltern or subordinate perspective—the view of those who occasionally might have participated in court activities or fancied themselves doing so, but essentially were at a distance. Its initial oral compositions were worked over by literate authors and this changed their intention and function.

Some well-established families, such as those of the *sāmantas*, maintained bards who kept a record of their genealogies and property rights. This was another mark of status and remained so until a few decades ago.[65] When the *sāmanta* became a *mahārāja*, the bard could also move up in status but was overshadowed by the scribe and the *brāhmaṇa rājaguru* who authored the inscriptions and the chronicles, which were regarded as the more impressive historical documents, either shorn of the paraphernalia of forms of legitimation or else given an alternative source of legitimacy. Where the bardic narrative is a different one, it is often serving an alternative claim to authority and status. The alternative claims may be from co-lateral lineages of the royal family, or may be rival claims. In bardic epics, royal families are not too far away from their actual origins.

[65] Families of the dominant castes were patrons of the *pāṇḍās*, priests-cum-genealogists residing in places of pilgrimage—such as Pushkar, Hardwar, Mattan—who were visited by members of these families on special occasions, such as a marriage, the birth of a son, or the death of an elder, or whenever a special rite had to be performed. The *pāṇḍās* performed the rituals and updated the records. On their annual brief visits to the families they served, the *pāṇḍās* received hospitality and again updated the records.

Because of the accessibility of the bards to the public, these compositions were likely to have been familiar to people outside the court. This is suggested by the reappearance of bardic epics composed on a range of rulers from the second millennium AD, whom we know of from inscriptions and sometimes chronicles. The perspective of the bard provides a different representation and its juxtaposition with inscriptions adds to the diversity in historical awareness. Calling it the voice of the bard, which makes it the voice of the other, is therefore to underline the contrasting form of the two historical traditions.

Epic poems have a long life as recitations of oral poetry before they are recorded in written form. This gives them a structure and content. Small incidents and lesser people ignored in the official version are filled out in lengthy descriptions. This is in part a facility of the oral form. The epic claims historicity but is not too concerned with ensuring it, and therefore it frequently lapses. Its importance lies in providing a perspective, sometimes even an alternative one, arising from popular perceptions of events and persons. Of the three categories of texts that represent historical writing in this period, epics have some affinity with the *vaṃśāvalīs*, but remain distinct as they do not reflect the vision of the court—as do the chronicles.

The poems of the bards focused on local heroes. They reflect the perceptions of groups of a lower status, those from whom the king had demarcated himself in the inscriptions. They were the protectors of the local people. Popular perception saw the local heroes as the defenders of the state, probably because the bards with whom this tradition lay had greater access to these families than to those of the ministers and royalty.

Material on the Candella dynasty is included marginally in the well-known epic poem on the Cāhamāna Rajputs, the *Pṛthvīrāja-rāsau* of Chand Bardai. There is a debate as to whether the segment referred to as the *Mahobā-khaṇḍa* was originally a part of the *Pṛthvīrāja-rāsau* or whether it began as an independent composition, the *Parmāl-rāsau*, and was later incorporated into the *Pṛthvīrāja-rāsau*.[66] The date is also uncertain. The epic in its

[66] M.V. Pandia and S.S. Das (eds), *The Pṛthvīrāja Rāsau of Chand Bardai*;

present form is thought to be of the sixteenth or seventeenth century, although it refers back to events four centuries earlier, when it may have been composed in its original form. Written in support of the Cāhamānas, it touches on their conflict with later Candella kings and, not unexpectedly, differs from the official history of the Candellas as given in their inscriptions. This conflict becomes part of the *Pṛthvīrāja-rāsau*, as indeed of other bardic compositions of the area, such as the *Ālhā Rāso* of Jagnaik Rao.

Parts of the oral epic were rendered into Sanskrit and, with additional narratives, formed a section of the *Bhaviṣya Purāṇa.* Inducting it into the Puranic tradition would have given it greater credibility for a general audience. Reincarnating the *Mahābhārata* heroes into folk heroes was an appropriation of the established epic to give status to a new one, thought to be politically and socially significant, and to link it to the old, seen as a precursor.[67] The local epic of heroes linked to Āhir and Banaphar origins drew on the *Mahābhārata* to claim Sanskritic sanction, and the *Bhaviṣya Purāṇa* legitimized the sanction by incorporating the local epic. The *Bhaviṣya Purāṇa* then projects it primarily as a conflict between the Cāhamānas and the Candellas. A small part of this history thus finds its way into a ritual text, although the larger part was free of this connection. The oral version remained independent.

The *Mahobā-khaṇḍa* relates the history of three dynasties—the Goda, Gahirawar, and Candel—of which the last is the main one. Could the reference to these three be to the Gonds, Gāhaḍavālas, and Candellas, suggesting that the original rulers were Gond and that the Gāhaḍavāla and Candella were later but connected? The narrative begins with the story of the founder of the dynasty, Candravarman. The Cāhamānas/Cauhānas are given a higher status since they are said to be among the Agnikula, the four preeminent clans whose ancestors arose out of the sacrificial fire of a sage.[68] The Candellas are not of the same rank. The origin of the

---

S.S. Das (ed.), *Parmāl Rāsau,* 2507–615; S.K. Mitra, *The Early Rulers of Khajuraho*, 14ff.

[67] A. Hiltebeitel, *Rethinking India's Oral and Classical Epics*, 123–8.

[68] J. Tod, *Annals and Antiquities of Rajasthan*, vol. I, 112–13.

Candellas in this source involves a *brāhmaṇa* ancestry but hardly a respectable one. The Tomara Rajput king Ānaṅgapāla, to whom the bard is said to be reciting the story, is puzzled over how a *kṣatriya* can be born of a *brāhmaṇa*, and that too of a widow, which would normally have made him low caste. However, the association of *brāhmaṇas* with *kṣatriya* functions was not new and the category of *brahma-kṣatra* may have taken care of such anomalies.

The story goes that Hemarāja, the *purohita* to Indrajit Gahirwar, has a beautiful daughter, Hemavatī, who is unfortunately widowed at the early age of 16 because of Indra's curse. On a hot summer night, when she goes to bathe in a pool, she is seen by the Moon-god (Candra) who, impassioned, spends the night with her. She, not knowing who he is but fearful of the consequences, threatens to curse him. Whereupon the Moon-god predicts that a son will be born to her, Candravarman or Candra-brahma, who will be a king. He will go to Khajjūrapura where he will perform *yajñas* and give gifts in charity, he will reign in Mahobā and build tanks, temples, and a fort at Kālañjara; and furthermore he will be a *kṣatriya* of the highest order. That the Moon-god had to predict his high status suggests the lowness of his actual status. The qualifications of being accepted as a *kṣatriya* seem to have changed. They have less to do with birth and more with performing sacrifices, and with building tanks, temples, and forts.

Hemavatī comes to Kālañjara, where she stays with the family of the village headman and gives birth to a son. His status is conceded by his not being born in the forest but in the home of a functionary. This is emphasized by the Moon-god holding a festival in his honour, by Bṛhaspati writing his horoscope, and by the *apsarās* celebrating his birth. Candravarman is blessed by a variety of gods. His father gives him a touchstone—a pragmatic understanding of the need for wealth in order to establish a kingdom! He accumulates wealth through using the touchstone and occupies Kālañjara, conquers the neighbouring area, and founds a ruling family. (The frequency of conquest in the establishing of power would suggest that acculturation often tended to be confrontational as the new status would have to be accepted by erstwhile peer groups.) He makes a gift of a hundred crores of gold coins to *brāhmaṇas* and *ṛṣis*: this would have silenced aspersions on his origin. He establishes a kingdom largely at the expense of the Gahirwars, who flee to Kāśī (suggesting that the author may have intended them to be identified with the Gāhaḍavālas). Candravarman then comes to Khajuraho, invokes Viśvakarman, with whose help eighty-five temples are constructed, each with a pool and a garden, and he gifts vast amounts to *brāhmaṇas*. He builds a new capital at Mahobā, thus fulfilling the prophecy of his father. The story suggests the manner in which an ambitious son of a court appointee could start founding a small kingdom.

We then come to the central focus which involves the Cāhamāna king Pṛthvīrāja and the Candella king Paramardideva, known in this poem as Parmāl. Pṛthvīrāja abducts the princess of Sameta. On his way home some of his wounded soldiers take refuge in Parmāl's garden but are killed by Parmāl's guards. Therefore, Pṛthvīrāja takes revenge by killing the valiant Malkhan, who was defending the territory of the Candellas, and moves on to lay siege to Mahobā. Parmāl, largely at the instigation of his queen Mālandevī, requests a truce which is granted. The queen had wanted time to send for the local heroes, Ālhā and his brother Ūdal. In these narratives the queens play a more central role than in the courtly literature.

The story of Ālhā and Ūdal, which is at the core of the epic, introduces another dimension where the perspective is yet more localized. The two brothers were Banaphar Rajputs, therefore of a lower standing than the Candellas, and held the territory of Kālañjara. In this account, it has no links with the Kalacuri-Cedis, perhaps because the link, having been tenuous, was no longer remembered. Intrigue involving some kinsmen of Parmāl led to the brothers having to leave Mahobā and Kālañjara and take refuge with the Gāhaḍavāla ruler Jayacanda in Kanauj. The Candella queen recognized the worth of the brothers, and sent the Candella bard Jagnaik to Kanauj to persuade them to return. Ālhā argued that the Candellas were ungrateful, listing the many battles he had fought for them but with no recognition in return. But eventually the brothers were persuaded by their mother to return to Mahobā.

The Candellas, from this account, had a bard at court to record their history in addition to their issuing inscriptions, and he also carried messages to other courts, as was expected of bards.

A prolonged battle was then fought and Pṛthvīrāja eventually captured Mahobā. Parmāl's army of 100,000 led by his son Brahmānand and by one of his Pathan generals, Talhan Khan, was routed. Ūdal and Brahmānand were killed and Ālhā retired to the forest with his guru Gorakhanātha, a peripatetic teacher of the highly popular Nātha cult of northern India. Mahobā and Kālañjara were sacked, Parmāl was captured but eventually rescued by Indal, the son of Ālhā, only to die later in Kālañjara. Pṛthvīrāja appointed Pajjan Rai as the *thānāpati* (officer in charge) of Mahobā, but the son of Parmāl, Samarjit, with the help of Jayacanda, retook Mahobā and installed himself as king. These events are not mentioned in the official inscriptions possibly because it would have been too embarrassing, or else they were contested. Chand Bardai was a spokesman for the Cāhamānas and would therefore have depicted Paramardideva in poor light.

Connections with local tribes such as the Gonds are implied in this text, which places the Candellas at a lower social level than the Cāhamānas. Perhaps the later hostility between the two kingdoms accounted for this. Chand Bardai states that the Candellas worshipped Maniya Devī, a Gond cult deity installed at their capital. In the Puranic version she is linked to the goddess Śāradā. This would suggest the upgrading of the family's deity from an original clan deity to one that could now be worshipped as a royal deity. This was legitimation from below, where the benefit to the Candellas would be a large catchment area of the cult which would now support the dynasty. It also registered the continuity of the family deity, although in a changed form.

The bardic tradition was not necessarily consistent in its view of the same events. Each bard was loyal to his patron, so versions differed. Thus, a different version from the above comes in the *Ālhā-khaṇḍa,* composed as part of an oral tradition and written from the perspective of the Candellas. It is a counterpoint to Chand Bardai and is attributed to Jagnaik, the bard of the Candellas, also said to be Parmāl's sister's son. The various versions of the epic were sought to be collated a few centuries later, and this is what is generally referred to as the epic.[69]

It was unusual for a Rajput of the ruling caste to take on the profession of a bard. Here it seems acceptable because of their initial lower-caste rank. Their own loyal supporters, such as the hero Ālhā, had an Āhir connection which is still lower and which is commented upon and made an issue of in the poem. Ālhā and Ūdal as Banaphar Rajputs are the heroes but are not recognized as full-fledged *kṣatriyas*. It is their heroism that establishes them as warriors rather than their birth. The *Ālhā-khaṇḍa* is staking the claim of those of lesser caste status not only to be heroes but to be greater heroes than the higher-caste Rajputs. The social tensions glossed over in the official version are much clearer in the version of the bards, even if there are discrepancies of chronology and event. The area covered in the epic was broadly that of the Candella kingdom and the events concern the last few rulers. Was the bardic composition intended as an alternative to the inscriptions?

The version in the *Ālhā-khaṇḍa* differs from both the official Candella history as well as that of Chand Bardai and only some minimal events are similar. Many events take place before the major one of the battle between Parmāl and Pṛthvīrāja. Parmāl sends the bard Jagnaik to persuade Ālhā to return, which he does eventually. (Thus the author of the poem also participates in the events, a situation not dissimilar from that of Vyāsa and Vālmīki in the earlier epics.) In this version Ālhā is the hero, defeating Pṛthvīrāja and forcing him back to Delhi while Parmāl reigns from Mahobā. Much of the poem is taken up with narratives involving local families, marriages, and the collecting of revenue on behalf of the overlord, as well as other stock-in-trade folk legends. Marriages and battles seem to go hand-in-hand since the stake in the first is control over women which determines caste ranking,

[69] W. Waterfield, *The Lay of Alha*. The text was collected from variant versions by a number of bards, and this compilation dates to the nineteenth century. One may therefore expect interpolations and recognize that the text is not close to the period it describes. It is looking at the history of a few centuries ago. The translation is from Bundeli Hindi.

kinship rights and status. Despite the grandeur of Khajuraho the bard sees the decline of Candella power whittled down to the location of Mahobā, from where they originated. Descriptions of events become a comment on the behaviour of the elite.

The hero frequently calls upon Maniya Devī for help. She is now addressed by a properly Sanskritic name, as the goddess Śāradā, but retains a skull as a drinking vessel. The transition from an aniconic cult deity to a Puranic-type goddess follows a recognizable pattern.

The *Parimāl-rāsau* and the *Ālhā-khaṇḍa* are narratives of the decline of the Candellas. This possibly accounts in part for royalty being seen as more accessible, but at the same time dependent on local heroes, for it is the Banaphar Rajputs and not the high-ranking *kṣatriyas* who are the heroes. These divergences of perspective, when seen in the broader context of the similarity of the general pattern in such compositions, would suggest that their authors were aware that they were reconstructing a past which had undergone change, that their reconstructions differed from the others, and that they understood the meaning of the alternative patterns.

The epics provide the subaltern history which may or may not coincide with the events narrated in the official dynastic history. They have to be assessed as complementing the latter or even providing counterparts. History constructed on the basis of inscriptions goes back to earlier inscriptions for information or for cross-checking data. Epic compositions are dependent on memory and poets can only cross-check with each other's compositions.

The authenticity of the bardic version is weakened by the distance in time. Even if the claim is that the original epic was composed at a time contemporary with the events, interpolations of later times introduced changes, and this was easier in the oral tradition. Changing the contents of an engraving on stone and copper required the forging of a new inscription.

The epic of the bard reflected the perspective of those who were creating, remembering, and reconstructing the past from a different social perspective, that of lower-status clans and intermediaries who were wooed by royalty but who had their own priorities. The audience was the local community. A discrepancy would doubtless lead to each accepting its own version, although it is likely that some concession might have been made to the official version.

6. Inscriptions as Annals

Inscriptions, when taken as annals, require an enquiry not only into authorship and intention but also into whether they constitute historical writing. Do they present a narrative of events and persons in sequential order, and is this narrative broadly corroborated in other sources? Are the complexities of the state and changes in this reflected when referring to the past? Does the explanation for the cause of an event provide a viable understanding of the event?

There has been much discussion on varieties of states in the post-Gupta period, the most extensive of these being whether these were feudal states. Some have argued for a period of Indian feudalism, whereas others have suggested degrees of change alternative to a feudal form. This has raised issues of how Rajput states, in particular, came into being through processes of what have been called integrated polities.[70] Others have suggested state systems which attempt to balance political and ritual authorities, with the former declining in areas distant from the centre of power. This idea draws on an argument that *brāhmaṇa* bureaucrats were essentially functioning as ritual specialists, an argument difficult to sustain. The inscriptions make it evident that their ritual functions were often largely only in name, if at all, when they and their descendants became administrators and landed intermediaries, and began founding kingdoms. Where the grandfather was a *dīkṣitar*, his grandsons were *rautas* and *ṭhakkuras*.

Of the earlier theories concerning the state, the *saptāṅga* is referred to in passing in the inscriptions.[71] Although the constituents remain the same as in the kingdoms of the pre-Gupta period, each plays a more complex role and the interface varies. The *svāmi* (king) is now the focus of power, although his authority may have become more precarious—hence the taking of exaggerated titles. *Rāṣtra* (territory) is more precisely defined, in part because the competition over it has more contenders. The *amātya* (administrators) drew on specially appointed officers but also on intermediaries and feudatories who participated in the upper

[70] H. Kulke (ed.), *The State in India, 1000–1700*; B.D. Chattopadhyaya, *The Making of Early Modern India.*

[71] Mau Stone Inscription of Madanavarman, *Ep. Ind.*, I, 198, v. 8.

bureaucracy. This, in part, made alliances somewhat uncertain. Replenishing the *kośa* (treasury) meant an extension of agriculture and commerce, and therefore clearing more land and safeguarding routes. A frequency of campaigns as an additional source of revenue, bringing booty to the victor, may have contributed to economic improvement to a greater degree than has been noticed so far. However, frequent campaigns also consumed revenue. This frequency led to more activity in the military camps, with the *durga* being either a city or a fort. The capital city became increasingly the focus of ritual and courtly culture, with the fort becoming the retreat in troubled times.

In some ways the theory of *maṇḍala* becomes more relevant in the period after the eighth century AD, with the continual rise and decline of intermediaries aspiring to royal power. The theory visualizes alliances as a series of circles in a situation of ambitious small kingdoms. The pattern need not be literally applicable, but represent a justification for hostility, especially when asserting independence could resort to the theory. In Candella history the tilting, as reflected in the inscriptions, was with the Pratihāras and the Cedis, whereas in the bardic epics it was with the Cahāmānas and the Gāhaḍavālas, before the Turks entered the scene. The centrality of the king emerges from the titles which he takes and which are also given on occasion to previous kings of the dynasty—if it is thought that they were significant. This is usually accompanied, as we saw, by the claim to being of the *kṣatriya varṇa*.

The audience for the inscriptions was extensive: the royal court and persons from other contemporary courts, officials concerned with the administration involved in the royal statement, religious sects being assisted in the case of a grant, and the local community in the area of the grant—defined at least in theory as including everyone from the highest official to the *caṇḍāla*. The formation of a state involves all levels of a society since it breaks existing systems and creates new ones. The consciousness of the past legitimizing the present was therefore not to be dismissed. The encapsulation of history was either publicly displayed on a monument, such as a temple wall, or else as a copper-plate when it was kept with a family, but was recorded in the court and was doubtless discussed. In the case of the former it could be read by, or to, the many who visited the temple as public space, thereby reiterating history as narrated in the inscription. This would be consulted by later authors and would also feed into the popular perceptions of the bards. The inheritors of the property given in the copper-plate charter would recall the history of the grantor and their own history on reading the inscription. The official past was public knowledge and remained so over the generations, even when the dynasty had become a memory. It was open to the comments of the elite—the *sāmantas, śreṣṭhins, kāyasthas, brāhmaṇas*—who were participating in the process.

The king's centrality is encapsulated in the *praśasti* and filled out with the dynastic genealogy suggesting that they were giving recognition to Puranic history which is projected as hegemonic.[72] What was hegemonic was the *vaṃśānucarita* section, perhaps not intrinsic to the *Purāṇa* anyway, and relevant to the *praśasti*.

Legitimacy for the dynasty required, among other things, that it be linked to the genealogical origins preferably as given in the *vaṃśānucarita*, or from any other equally acceptable source, such as the Agnikula. Genealogies could be fabricated if required, linking the dynasty to an appropriate descent group. Those that provided such links would be duly recompensed, perhaps with a grant of land. Gifts could be preceded by sacrificial rituals claiming a history from earliest times. Other forms of recompense, such as the *mahādānas* (high-value gifts), are also mentioned, but grants of land would be preferred, for obvious reasons. The Candella inscriptions have fewer references to *mahādānas* as compared to land grants.

Inscriptions increase after Yaśovarman, coinciding with their taking the normal royal titles but also that of *kālañjarādhipati,* which becomes a marker of Candella power. They also take fancy royal titles which are a contrast to the simple earlier ones of *rājā, nṛpa, bhūpati, kṣitipati, mahipati, kṣitidharatilakaḥ,* the mark of the supporter of the earth, *nṛpakulatilakaḥ,* the mark of the family of kings, and so on. The more fancy titles become rhetorical when the later and lesser kings insist on using them. Taking grandiose

[72] Daud Ali, "Royal Eulogy as World History: Rethinking Copper-plate Inscriptions in Cola India", 165–225.

titles signals the centrality of the historical self-perception of the rulers, and it coincides with another statement of status, that of building royal temples.

The territorial base of the kingdom was the area of Khajuraho, hence the cluster of temples. The emphasis is on a centralized control emanating from an area where power was concentrated. When this begins to weaken there is more than one area associated with the focus of governance, hence the issuing of inscriptions from Kālañjara and Ajaygadh.

The officials more frequently mentioned in the inscriptions were the senior ministers such as the *mantrīmukhya* and the *saciva*, some of whom made their own grants. The Vāstavya *kāyasthas* were not indigenous to Jejākabhukti and had migrated from eastern India, suggesting a caste network of professionals proficient in administration across northern India. This would encourage some uniformity in format and style of the inscriptions as records of history, and the relevance of the history recorded.

The ideology for sustaining a monarchy was provided by brahmanical support. Some *brāhmaṇas* were locals, others were invited to settle, constituting many new categories. A few continued to be *śrotriya* (learned *brāhmaṇas*). More frequent mention is made of *brāhmaṇa rautas* and *ṭhakkuras*, whose concerns were primarily political and administrative. Ritual specialists were called to divert the ill effects of an eclipse or other such untoward happenings, or perform the ceremonial rites.They received grants of land from the king but did not necessarily serve him in any official capacity at the court.They propagated the virtues of kingship, especially in areas where it was new.

They would be agents for the spread of brahmanic culture but not averse to incorporating non-brahmanic cultures if this enhanced their authority and prestige, assisted by the mutation of forest-dwelling clans into castes and the introduction of agrarian economies. *Brāhmaṇa* settlements generally loyal to the king could curb the hostile ambitions of new competitors for power.

Of the *varṇa* categories, that of *kṣatriya* was largely limited to the royal family and was underlined when a clan assumed kingship. In terms of exercising administrative authority, the *kāyastha* caste was visible, and as a caste almost more so than even the *kṣatriya*.

The *vaiśya varṇa* seems to have been subsumed in references to the *śresṭhin.* Occupational groups come under the rubric of *śūdras,* more often identified as *jātis*, with their own hierarchies. The lowest unchanging level is that of the *caṇḍāla*. Despite the statements that the king is protecting the *varṇaśrama-dharma* and preventing the mixing of castes, it would seem that actually the system of *varṇa* was not necessarily being observed as required by the normative texts.

Inscriptions from the period of decline of Candella power indicate that factions at the court probably played a large and effective role in the kingdom. This would be expected in a situation where such factions would be the potential for new states and ruling families. It is curious that in the interface between religious sectarianism and political factionalism, as depicted in the *Prabodhacandrodaya*, there is little concern with the potentially overwhelming faction waiting at the threshold of the kingdom, that of the Turks and Afghans and their local allies.

Initially the substratum cult was that of Śākta-Śaktī and Tantrism together with varieties of shamanism. Adapting elements of the mythology and ritual practices of those at the lower end of the social stratification became a mechanism of control. The peasants in service relationships to the *brāhmaṇas* could be kept subordinated through caste codes and religious ideology. Taxation imposed on peasants was oppressive, referred to as *karapīḍā*, the pain of tax.[73] Turning clansmen into *śūdras* converted them into a tied peasantry technically not enslaved but in effect unfree.

Social history from inscriptions is more pointed than in the normative texts. The difference is perhaps striking in the specification of witnesses to a grant,[74] who are not listed by *varṇa* but more generally by occupation, suggesting that the formality of the *varṇa* listing was dropped on such occasions. The earlier inscriptions mention the king addressing the village assembly and use the term, *samajñapayati*, he orders them all. Later, mention is made of three inclusive categories, the revenue collectors, the village headman and the rest. In the twelfth century the list is more

[73] E.g. references to *karapīḍa*, *Viṣṇu Purāṇa*, 6.1.38.

[74] K.K. Shah, "Social Structure in Candella Grants", 28–34.

detailed and includes *kuṭumbins*, *kāyasthas*, and *mahattaras*. Still later the list includes those at the lowest social position, the *medas* and *caṇḍālas*. The change takes two hundred years but does point to an administrative difference in the specific listing of various professions and castes and the need to do so.

Demarcation between caste society and the forest-dwellers can be strident. There is a continued use of generic names for the latter—Śabara, Pulinda, and Bhilla. There is no longer the partially romantic, partially realistic description of the Śabaras, as in the *Harṣacarita,* with a sneaking admiration for the son of the chief who knows every leaf in the forest. Now, four centuries later, they are expendable since only the state has rights over the forest. They resist the encroachment of the state, therefore their subjugation is necessary. Their suppression assists the process of cultural incorporation. They have their own hierarchy though, and the Gonds are superior in the Vindhyan region.

Forts and temples were the main location of royal inscriptions. Given that a number of trade routes traversed the kingdom it is possible that forts also served as sanctuaries for travelling merchants fearful of being set upon by brigands. In lean periods, the state itself may have indulged in some degree of indirect brigandage. The use of the term *viśiṣa* (eminence) in relation to the administration of forts again underlines their importance. Forts would have housed the core of the armies maintained by such dynasties, which, even if not as large as the Turkish chroniclers or the bards would have us believe, were nevertheless sizeable.

Candella rule witnessed a shift in cult centres and in the forms of the monuments that marked them, both of which are reflected in the inscriptions. The earlier inscriptions cluster around Khajuraho although there are a few from Mahobā. Yet Mahobā was the more fertile tract, with extensive agricultural activity using a number of reservoirs and lakes.[75] This may have been one reason why the declining Candella power survived in this area. A sizeable number of inscriptions are grants of arable land and villages, and describe the measuring of land and the placing of boundary markers, so

[75] K.K. Shah, "Economic Revolution in Early Medieval Bundelkhand", 167–74.

essential to efficient revenue collection.[76] The *brāhmaṇa* grantees, instrumental in agricultural expansion, authored texts on technical expertise such as the *Kṛṣiparāśara*. The focus is on rice cultivation and mention is also made of the cultivation of sugarcane, cotton, hemp, and to the working of mines for metals. The presence of a substantial Jaina community would point to active commerce. However, the Candellas do not issue their own coins until the reign of Kīrtivarman. Prior to this, the *gadhaiya* coins commonly used in northern India were in circulation. Candella coins tended to imitate those of the Kalacuris, suggesting that commerce was directed to and from that area.

Royal temples were symbolic of the closeness of royalty to divinity and also to economic wealth that sustained such patronage. A historical trajectory can also be traced through the evolution of temple-building, from the simple structures meant for housing an image to the multiplex buildings and courtyards which expanded historically in keeping with the prosperity of the patron. Temple-building coincided with the taking of royal titles and the composition of lengthy inscriptions on the history of the dynasty. Yet the earliest cult centres would have had links with people of lesser social status associated with the popular Śākta shrines. The Caunsaṭh-Yoginī temple at Khajuraho was one among others in the neighbouring areas. It dates to the ninth century AD and consists of a platform lined with small shrines, with the main shrine located off-centre at the back.[77] Most *yoginī* temples are circular. Cell-like shrines along the inner circumference hint perhaps at the Buddhist *vihāra* form.[78]

One of the origin myths of the Candellas, as we have seen refers to the founder constructing shrines at Khajuraho. The bardic tradition associates them with the worship of Maniya Devī or Maniya-deo, located originally at Manyagarh, the original home

[76] N.S. Bose, *History of the Candellas*, 137ff.; S.K. Mitra, *The Early Rulers of Khajuraho*, 179ff.

[77] Krishna Deva, "The Temples of Khajuraho in Central India", 4–43; O.C. Gangoli, *et al.*, *The Art of the Candellas*; D. Desai, *Erotic Sculpture of India, A Socio-Cultural Study*.

[78] E. Zannas, *Khajuraho*, 88ff.

of the Candellas and important to the Gonds.[79] The cultic origins therefore could have been tribal and Śākta. Śākta cults with associations to the Śaiva Kaula and Kapālika sects remained a substratum expression in the area. This is present in the erotic sculpture at some temples in Khajuraho, as well as references in the *Prabodhacandrodaya*. The continuity of the cults would indicate that they had a popular following, and this provided a support base for patrons. While still a feudatory, Harṣa helped to reinstate his overlord at Kanauj, following which he built a temple to Mātaṅgeśvara. The Śākta-Śaktī concern with power other than political was in any case a useful link for a reigning king, who also claimed that he was being favoured by the goddess Śrī.

Given this background the temple to Viṣṇu built by Yaśovarman is a distinct point of departure. It demarcates the royal family and the court from those who adhered only to the earlier cult centres. It is an indication of the appropriation of Vaiṣṇavism and Sanskritic culture on the part of the elite, and it is a statement of power: the family now had the resources to build such a temple. The Viṣṇu temple is one of the markers of independent statehood. The inscription was composed by the *kavi* Mādhava who was evidently familiar with Sanskrit literary texts. Specific mention is made of the image coming from the Himalayan regions, having passed through the hands of various rulers. Icons were captured or gifted as expressions of power. The coming of the image of Viṣṇu symbolizes the coming of kingship, and if need be with divinity. For the prevailing Bhagavatism the icon of Viṣṇu spoke of divinity and sovereignty. This was an additional source of power that claimed to go beyond sacrificial rituals and genealogical connection.

Royal temples were built, imitating those in other kingdoms, and claiming equality. The earlier *sthapatis* and builders would have been brought in from existing temple centres, some still based at sites linked to the post-Gupta temples of the region, and others being invited from major temple centres of contemporary dynasties. *Sthapatis* and *śilpins*, architects and master craftsmen, were another impressively mobile profession, judging by the spread

[79] V.A. Smith, "The History and Coinage of the Chandel (Chandella) Dynasty of Bundelkhand", 114–48.

of styles traversing many kingdoms. The evolution of a style would partly draw on their earlier experience of having worked in neighbouring kingdoms, on their observation of architectural history in the region, on the forms desired by individual patrons and on the rules as described in the texts on temple construction. Temple architecture evolved historically, and the architects not only knew this history but used its language. Images which carry the name of the sculptor, such as the *rūpakāra* Rāma or Lakkhan or Devarāja, were the ones made by the then better-known craftsmen who might have used this as a method of publicizing their craftsmanship. Sculptors and builders would tend to disperse when a dynasty declined, at which point they searched for new patrons. Stylistic elements travelled from place to place, as part of this dispersal, apart from the dominance of certain stylistic forms. But the period of magnificence was brief, lasting a century and a half. From the reign of Madanavarman, there seems to have been a greater outlay of wealth on constructing forts than temples.

Khajuraho sees the peak of artistic and religious patronage in the tenth and eleventh centuries with its cluster of temples, Vaiṣṇava, Śaiva, and Jaina. Subsequently the centre moves to Kālañjara and includes Ajaygadh. Not much effort is made to convert these forts into royal capitals with impressive palaces and temples. As against this, there are many more tanks being constructed around Mahobā. Clearly, this was a time of political uncertainties and threats from neighbours and feudatories. In the later period, more inscriptions were issued from the forts than from places in the plains, barring copper-plate grants.

Inscriptions narrate a history of the Candella kingdom. There is evidence on its politics, on the economy that sustained it, on caste statuses, and on religious sects with an implicit indication of how they changed. The sequence of the inscriptions is in chronological order and there is a firm sense of linear time. Evidence for statements pertaining to the past was possible because there were court records of earlier rulers and events. The history is limited to that of the Candella dynasty and does not go back to previous times. This is probably because Jejākabhukti was not an independent kingdom earlier. There is a consciousness of the need to conserve documents and where necessary to copy documents that may be damaged in order that they may be conserved. Earlier inscriptions are the sources of historical information and their format becomes the precedent for later inscriptions. Causality in explanation lies in the theory that political power is determined by the play and ambition of surrounding kingdoms and by intermediaries, and that this contributes to the rise and fall of kingdoms.

The intention of the inscription was to legitimize the dynasty through various ways: ancestral claims to lineage; marriage alliances; the activities of the court; recording the major events associated with the rulers; registering grants and explaining why they were made, and to whom, and when. The intention was to document and record information on which to base claims and continuities, and to make such information available for the use of future rulers. As annals, inscriptions expressed history in a form recognizable in the knowledge systems of the time—which today may not be so clearly recognizable.

15

Vaṃśāvalīs

Chronicles of Place and Person—The *Rājataraṅgiṇī*

1. The Chronicle

The *vaṃśāvalī* as a genre was the chronicle of a state, region, or kingdom. It recorded various changes at the tipping point, as it were, of the small kingdom being converted into a more powerful larger one. As I have suggested in the previous chapter, these changes included the mutation of clan societies into caste societies when the kingdom was established, the extension of the peasant economy to support the kingdom, and recognition of the mutual acculturation of Puranic and local religion. The change was manifested most clearly in the establishing of a court culture and administration in the kingdom, requiring literacy for maintaining records. Its most visible form lay in royal temples as symbols of power. The records covered local events, but their form reflected the processes of change that were taking place in other regions as well.

The initial form of the *vaṃśāvalīs*, as fragments of information, probably began from the latter part of the first millennium AD, but their more definitive forms took shape a few centuries later. Found in many parts of the subcontinent, they vary from brief and somewhat cryptic dynastic lists to lengthy poems treated as *kāvyas,* narrating events in sequential order. They draw on a number of sources since they had to adjust the descent lists of dynasties and create a linear history.

Shuffling events into a single chronology can also be problematic. For the earlier entries, some concession may be made to what they assume is history. When the sources become more reliable, as for instance when inscriptions are consulted, this is less of a problem. The distinction between the *vaṃśāvalī* and the other genres of the time that have been discussed in previous chapters is that its scope is not limited to a single king, as in the *carita,* or to a single dynasty, as in its inscriptions. The chronicle incorporates the history of a region from its beginnings to the present. The sources consulted therefore vary. Some could have their information "edited" from time to time. Early genealogies would have been subjected to telescoping or padding—eliminating some names, adding others—without too much attention to historicity. Nevertheless, the *vaṃśāvalī* was written from the perspective of a point in time, and this would have left a mark on the narrative. Such chronicles focused on the region and referred to the history of neighbouring areas only where it impinged on the history being recorded: other areas would have had their own chronicles.

Vaṃśāvalīs draw on both the *itihāsa-purāṇa* and the local tradition, focusing on the court or the temple or even, on occasion, the caste. In some places they are referred to by different names, such as *pīdhiyāvalī* (the line of generations); *prabandha* and *rāso* in Gujarat and Rajasthan; *buruñjis* among the Ahoms of Assam; *Mādalā Pañjī* in Orissa. The keeping of court records is advocated by Kauṭilya and others from earlier centuries, and although these have not survived, except for inscriptions, some fragmentary records may have been available to those writing chronicles.

Since the time of William Jones, it has been repeatedly said that there was only one text from early India that could be regarded as historical writing: the *Rājataraṅgiṇī*, a history of Kashmir written by Kalhaṇa in 1148–9.[1] Yet even this statement was doubted by

[1] *Kalhaṇa's Rājataraṅgiṇī, Chronicle of the Kings of Kashmir*, Sanskrit Text with Critical Notes, ed. M.A. Stein; *Rājataraṅgiṇī*, ed. and trans. M.A. Stein; U.N. Ghoshal, "Dynastic Chronicles of Kashmir"; H.C.Ray, *Dynastic History of Northern India*, vol. 1, 107–84.

some. Aurel Stein, who worked extensively on the text, argued that it was intended for didactic religion and not history, a statemnent that shows little familiarity with the religion of India, or with the genre of chronicles as historical writing. The choice of what is included in a chronicle draws on a historiographic tradition, however muted it may seem. Kalhaṇa describes it as a *kāvya*,[2] but this should not be read as a disclaimer of its being history. The literary form is that of a *kāvya*, as was so with many literary compositions, especially in Sanskrit, but its contents are intended as history. The persons and events he describes are those that he believed existed and occurred in the past. This is different from other contemporary *kāvyas* that are clealy fictional. It is also different from the *caritas* and the *praśasti* inscriptions, but is closer to the *vaṃśāvalī* with its larger canvas and its more expansive historical perspective.

The uniqueness of this text has been attributed to what some see as a kind of demarcation of Kashmir, suggesting a sense of nationalism at that time;[3] there was also contact with other people who had a stronger sense of history, such as in the Chinese and Islamic traditions. However, there is little evidence of the Sanskrit literati's familiarity with Chinese historical texts, or with texts in Arabic, Persian, and Turkish. The persistence of Buddhism in the region, with its recognizable sense of history, as well as the proximity of Ladakh and Tibet with an incipient tradition of chronicles, could well have made an impact on scholarship in Kashmir. To this one may add that although the *Rājataraṅgiṇī* is of a remarkable quality in historical writing, the genre as such was not unique to Kashmir and was known to other courts. What may have made a difference is that Kashmir from the ninth to the twelfth century was a significant centre of scholarship in grammar, aesthetics, and philosophy—in the work of Ananadavardhana, Abhinavagupta, and others—and this ambience would have affected the work of a sensitive scholar such as Kalhaṇa.

This intellectual vibrancy is attested to by Al-Biruni, the Central Asian scholar who spent time in India in the eleventh century. He

[2] 1.4–5, 1.23.

[3] A.L. Basham, "The Kashmir Chronicle", 57–65.

makes particular reference to what he calls the Hindu sciences flourishing in Kashmir and Banaras, and thinks that the inroads of Mahmud of Ghazni led scholars to flee to these two places.[4] But the high point of the intellectual articulation of Kashmiri scholars was before the arrival of Mahmud.

Kalhaṇa's deep interest in the past of Kashmir seems to have arisen from his observation of recent politics, combined with what a scholar of that time would have read. There was doubtless an imprint of the *itihāsa-purāṇa* tradition through the reading of various *Purāṇas*. For someone curious about the past of Kashmir, there also had to be a familiarity with Buddhist historiography, reflected in the history of the Saṅgha and the narratives of kings who were patrons of Buddhism, such as the *Aśokāvadāna*. This would be expected in an area where once Buddhism had been an important ideological component of the culture.

I shall not discuss the *Rājataraṅgiṇī* in detail since so much has already been written on it as a history. I would like to draw attention to the chronicles or *vaṃśāvalīs*, of which genre the *Rājataraṅgiṇī* is one, and without doubt the most impressive. A comparison with less-known ones, such as the *vaṃśāvalī* of Chamba, might provide some insights into the relation of *vaṃśāvalīs* with the *itihāsa-purāṇa* tradition. As a genre, it is found in various parts of the subcontinent, although those of the hill states tended to be discussed in earlier writings on the subject.[5]

Vaṃśāvalī is a path of succession, and the succession is of kings. It is not the path of a single line of kings, which is not possible because the narrative generally starts in the remote past. The history of various dynasties is being narrated, and these have to be aligned to provide continuity. The integrating of more than a couple of chronicles in some cases also creates problems. Other information fills out the details of the path.

The corpus of inscriptions of a dynasty recorded past events and persons, but the chronicles fleshed these out with information on other facets. The pattern of the inscriptions and that of

[4] *Alberuni's India*, vol. I, 22, 45.

[5] E.T. Atkinson, *Himalayan Gazetteer* (1881–4); J. Ph. Vogel, *Antiquities of the Chamba State*; S.P. Sen, *Sources for the History of India*.

the chronicles suggests a continuity and development in historical thinking. The *vaṃśāvalī* was different in form and content from what preceded it and which remained parallel—namely, historical biographies and inscriptions. Nevertheless, there are similarities with these that are incorporated into the chronicles. The unit was, relatively speaking, the small state and not large imperial systems. Where there was limited data on early dynasties and if the turnover of dynasties as in later times was fairly frequent, then the author of the chronicle had to find ways to make the narrative read preferably as seamless.

2. The Author

The *Rājataraṅgiṇī* forms a useful starting point for looking at the format of the *vaṃśāvalī*. Stein edited the text, which appears to have been put together by Ramakantha in 1648–86. Although it was distributed later among various members of the family of Pandit Sivarama, who interestingly treated it as a patrimony, it nevertheless survived.[6] Manuscript copies were available in the nineteenth century in Calcutta and Lucknow.[7] The manuscripts as we have them now and the variations have been discussed elsewhere.[8]

Kalhaṇa is described in the colophon as the son of Caṇpaka, a minister at the court of the previous king. The king was deposed and killed in 1101. Caṇpaka was at the court for many years but may not have had an official position. The successor dynasty may not have continued the services of families who had served the previous king. What the court had experienced in the actions of recent kings was not attractive to a discerning scholar. Kalhaṇa thus was familiar with court circles, even if not serving at the court himself. This distancing probably enabled him to make independent judgements on various rulers. In this, one is reminded of Bāṇa's perspective on the court: it may explain the intellectual

[6] The genealogical records of present-day dominant castes, maintained by *pāṇḍas* at pilgrimage centres, are similarly viewed as property, hence the hesitation to show them to those who are not clients.

[7] *Kalhaṇa's Rājataraṅgiṇī*, ch. 3, 42–55.

[8] M. Witzel, "On Indian Historical Writing", 1–57.

quality of both texts. It has been suggested that the *Rājataraṅgiṇī* was in part a response to the events linked to the change of dynasty and the removal of Kalhaṇa's father from office, but the nature of the narrative suggests a wider interest in the history of the region. He is critical of earlier rulers but more circumspect about the current dynasty, whose reigns are addressed in the last book, which is half the length of the whole text.[9]

Unlike the historical biographies, in this text there is no brief biography of the author. Kalhaṇa's birthplace was the ancient Buddhist centre at Parihāsapura. He began to write his chronicle in the Laukika era 4224, i.e. AD 1148/9, and completed it the following year. His intention was to write a *kāvya*, a long poem in *śānta rasa*, a mood evoking peace, but what resulted was somewhat different owing to the turbulence at the court.

3. The *Rājataraṅgiṇī*

The chronicle begins with invocatory verses to Śiva. Even though he was a Śaiva *brāhmaṇa*, Kalhaṇa does not omit narrating the earlier Śaiva persecution of Buddhist monks and the destruction of Buddhist monasteries. Possibly he and his family were eclectic, as would seem from his uncle having saved the Buddha image from Parihāsapura when the eleventh-century king Harṣa was plundering temples and religious centres.[10] The name Kalhaṇa has been explained as an Apabhraṃśa form of the Sanskrit *kalyāṇa*; if this is so, it is curious that he did not sanskritize his name.

Kalhaṇa was not writing to pamper any particular patron. His work appears to be an exercise in intellectual curiosity about the past of Kashmir, the kingdom where he lived and the court at which his father had served. He is also concerned with understanding the inexplicable behaviour of kings just prior to the current dynasty. Hence his criticism of the actions of kings who were his close contemporaries. His narrative is peppered with severe judgements on various groups who exploited Kashmir. There is symmetry between the historian and the court, for if the dynasty

[9] Ibid., Book 8.
[10] *Rājataraṅgiṇī*, 7.1097–8.

is being legitimized by the historian, the king has to recognize the delicate relationship between ruler and historian—lest the latter use it to the disadvantage of the former. With the decline of Vedic rituals of legitimation, grants to *brāhmaṇas* were on occasion an acknowledgement of their facility in providing status in various ways, as occasionally by constructing genealogies. This reduced the dependence on actual kinship and instead relied more on using the historical tradition to establish legitimacy. The author with links to the court could emerge as an authoritative figure.

There has been some discussion on whether the *Rājataraṅgiṇī* should be viewed as a *kāvya* or as history; or, is such a distinction tenable only for modern historical writing?[11] Early societies tended not to make a sharp differentiation between the two and there can be overlaps in descriptions of events and persons. Even if it is called a *kāvya,* it is not romantic fiction. Kalhaṇa is aware of representing the past "as it was", as *itihāsa*. This was characteristic of the *vaṃśāvalī*, and it could take the form of a *kāvya*. Kalhaṇa granted the right of the poet to represent the past which the poet evokes and sees as *divya dṛṣṭi* (divine insight).[12] But the poet must also be impartial in narrating what happened.[13] A Buddhist strand lay in his underlining the impermanence of event and person because he believed this encourages the mind to be at peace—*śānta rasa*. His narrative incorporates rulers such as Aśoka and Kaniṣka, and even the evil Mihirakula. These persons figure in Mahāyāna Buddhist texts but not in the *Purāṇas*, barring Aśoka who is just a name in a list of kings.

The text is *itihāsa* in *kāvya* form, narrating the history of Kashmir and incorporating into the narration legends, chronology based on written records, and details of events closer to the author's time. It has many poetic passages but there is little of *rasa*, *dhvani*, and varying metres. It is written in Sanskrit, and his handling of the language makes it evident that he was a man of considerable learning. Kalhaṇa maintains that a poet in a sense resurrects the past, and a good *kāvya* must on that account be an impartial narration

[11] See, for example, the discussion in W. Slaje, "In the Guise of Poetry—Kalhaṇa Reconsidered", 207–44.

[12] *Rājataraṅgiṇī*, 1.4–5.

[13] Ibid., 1.7.

of events, free from love and hatred. It must incorporate information from as many sources as possible. It must bring together the fragments and give a connected account. Echoing Bilhaṇa, he writes that the poet can bestow immortality on kings who would otherwise not be remembered.[14] He uses the term *bhūtārtha*, which is not just "the past" but "the meaning of the past", and "that which has really happened", and this makes a significant difference to the narration of the past.

Kalhaṇa claims that his narrative has been arranged in accordance with the time and succession of kings, and can be read or heard.[15] He further claims that he is correcting the chronology of his predecessors and giving a connected account of the past by partly filling in gaps and removing fictitious genealogies.[16] This of course is an area where the reliability of the source becomes crucial, and Kalhaṇa, even though generally careful, may not have been so on every occasion.

His attitude to history was also conditioned by his belief in *karma,* the consequence of individual actions. But to this he added that the *karma* of the king was intertwined with that of his people, a ready explanation for good or bad kings. The narrative is straightforward and takes an independent position—all the more striking in an age when eulogies were a common idiom. Belief in the supernatural is, however, conceded when he attributes events to the power of Fate, divine retribution, magic, the decline of *dharma* in the Kaliyuga, and *karma*. However, this does not prevent him from explaining the intricacies of factions at the court or the importance of fiscal and political policies.

4. The Sources

Unlike many other chronicles, Kalhaṇa takes care to mention the sources that he has consulted, apart from his reading as a scholar. The work shows a familiarity not only with the epics and *Purāṇas*, which would be expected, but with more historically-oriented writing, such as the historical biographies written by Bāṇa and

[14] Ibid., 1.3–4, 45–6.
[15] Ibid., 1.21–4.
[16] Ibid., 1.8–18.

more recently by Bilhaṇa. The influence of the *Harṣacarita* is noticeable.[17] The discussion on his sources is not only of interest to the writing of the chronicle, it also indicates the lively interest in the past of various scholars and keepers of records. This appears to have been, not unexpectedly, normal to the activities of royal courts. Kalhaṇa's description of the sources provides further evidence for the existence of such texts.

As sources for the *Rājataraṅgiṇī* he consulted eleven works on the *rājakathā* (narrative of rulers).[18] He read the *prabandha* or chronicle of Suvrata, a collation and summary of fragmentary chronicles, and thought it lacked learning. Writing the biography of a contemporary king, he feels, requires less skill than writing a chronicle. Other sources include the important local *Purāṇa* called the *Nīlamata Purāṇa*, with its minimal historical data, and Kṣemendra's *Nṛpāvalī*, or list of kings, which he dismisses as incorrect. Various local inscriptions, especially the *śāsanas* (orders) for establishing temples and monasteries, which were generally grants of land and often included *praśastipaṭṭas* (the history of the dynasty in summary form), and coin legends were consulted, as were segments of the oral tradition preserved in popular legends and other historical narratives. Among them, the *Chavillākara* had information about Aśoka and his successors;[19] the *Pārthivāvalī* of Helarāja mentioned other kings, as did the text of Padmamihira.

The *Nīlamata Purāṇa* was an important source being the specific *Purāṇa* for Kashmir.[20] It had been named after Nīla, whose identity is a little ambiguous, either as an early king or a Nāga. It was probably composed around the late first millennium AD and was well known by the twelfth century (although dated to as early as the sixth or seventh centuries AD).[21] Since it does not conform to all the themes required of an ideal *Purāṇa* it is perhaps better categorized as an *upapurāṇa* or sub-Purāṇa.[22] It has some

[17] *Kalhaṇa's Rājataraṅgiṇī*, vol. I, Introduction, 11.

[18] *Rājataraṅgiṇī*, 1.9–15.

[19] Ibid., 1.17–19.

[20] Ved Kumari, *The Nīlamata Purāṇa*.

[21] G. Buhler, "Report on a Tour in Search of Sanskrit Manuscripts in Kashmir", 38ff.

[22] Krishna Mohan, *Early Medieval History of Kashmir*.

information on ideas of time and of the descent of various lineages similar to those of the major *Purāṇas,* reflecting a familiarity with the *manvantaras* (reckoning in enormous time spans), the *yugas*, as also the *vaṃśānucarita* section with genealogies of earlier rulers. Kalhaṇa quotes from these but some names in the genealogies were by now missing in their more recent recensions, suggesting that there had been a "telescoping" of this section by eliminating a few names. All the names are unlikely to have been authentic, so the deletion of some would have resulted from a variety of reasons, not least simple forgetfulness in memorizing a list. In starting with the *Nīlamata Purāṇa* Kalhaṇa is locating Puranic history well into the past, and prior to the kind of history that follows. History for him is not an extension of the *Purāṇa*, although this has been suggested.[23]

Other categories of texts used as sources were the *sthala-purāṇas* and the *māhātmyas.* These purported to narrate the believed histories of specific sacred places and their topographies and were enveloped in the mythology of the location, its deities and its associations. Of these the *Vitasta-māhātmya* was the most relevant for Kalhaṇa. This relates to the Jhelum river, the mainstream in every sense of the Kashmir valley. The *māhātmyas* attempt to put together the legends of temples and places of pilgrimage and the rituals to be performed at each place. They often subsume what is believed to be local history. A fair amount of geographical information is included through the descriptions of the places. Such texts were written on birchbark, which requires that they be copied more than once, and the rewriting could have introduced changes.

The *Nīlamata Purāṇa* is thought to have borrowed from the *Brahmāṇḍa* and *Viṣṇudharmottara Purāṇas* whereas borrowing from the *Mahābhārata* is more subtle. It has been argued that it has three frame stories in imitation of the two of the *Mahābhārata*,[24] each frame representing a cultural tradition. It starts with a question that Vaiśampāyana is said to have asked Janamejaya at the *yajña*

[23] R. Inden, "Imperial Purāṇas: Kashmir as Vaiṣṇava Center of the Words", 29–99.

[24] Masato Fuji, "On the Textual Formation of the Nīlamata Purāṇa", 55–82.

with which the epic opens, and the question was why the kings of Kashmir did not participate in the war at Kurukṣetra. This is the first frame linking the text to the epic and could well have been added on at some point. It reflects the wish to associate the history of Kashmir with events of the *Mahābhārata*.

The second frame, which is more regional, is the imagined conversation between the first mythical king of Kashmir, Gonanda I, and the *ṛṣi* Bṛhadāśva. This introduces aspects of the early history of Kashmir which have parallels with the epic. The third is the local frame of the conversation between the imagined king Nīla, the lord of the Nāgas, explaining the rituals and customs of the first inhabitants to the *brāhmaṇa* Candradeva. The first frame is a claim to wide cultural links and depth in time, the second incorporates most of the text, and the third focuses on events linked to the Nāgas who are said to be the indigenous inhabitants—in a sense constituting the prehistory. This perhaps suggests that the current religions were brought in by later settlers such as the *brāhmaṇas*.

The mythological history of Kashmir is related through the legend that the area was once a great lake and devastated by the presence of a demon. Eventually the demon, through a ruse, was made to drink dry the waters of the lake and the valley emerged. This story is also told in the account of Xuanzang. It is a stereotypical story which occurs in the origin myths of many Himalayan kingdoms.[25] The mention of various places leads to the narration of their *māhātmyas*. A list of people who inhabited Kashmir at various times is given, and this includes the Nāgas who were predominant and the Piśācas associated with the north-west of India. Many of the names are known from other sources, such as the Abhisāras, Gāndhāras, Śakas, Khasas, and Madras—interestingly, all people of the North. The term *nāga* is also used for tutelary deities residing in the springs and pools of the valley, each of which had a small shrine or temple, described in some detail in the text.[26]

[25] N. Allen, "And the Lake Drained Away", 435–51; H.H. Wilson, *The Hindu History of Kashmir*, 8–9, mentions later historians of Sultanate times referring to the breaching of the Baramullah Pass to allow the lake to be drained.

[26] *Rājataraṅgiṇī*, 1.29ff.

A number of well-known stories relating to religious events, as given in the major *Purāṇas*, are repeated here. Buddha is included as an *avatāra* of Viṣṇu. Although also known from other areas, in Kashmir this might suggest that there was still a presence of Buddhism. Some texts speak of the *Śaivaśāstras* having been written to stem the spread of Buddhism and expose the Buddha as fraudulent.[27] In the tenth century a *vihāra* was burnt and what remained of it was used for building a temple to Śiva.[28] The ostensible reason for burning the *vihāra* was to trap a rebellious feudatory, but the revocation by the king of the grant of thirty-six villages to the *vihāra* and their being granted to others, suggests that the motive was the suppression of Buddhism. Kashmir was one of the important centres of Northern Buddhism, from where Buddhist monks and scholars went to Central Asia and China in the early centuries AD. The competition with the Śaivas was fierce since, among other things, they saw the Buddhists as rivals for royal patronage.

Reference is made to many groups of *brāhmaṇas.* Those concerned with historical traditions are two: the *kathāvid* who recites or reads the *Purāṇas* at various ceremonies, and the *itihāsavid* who is knowledgeable about the past. The latter category is an additional qualification to the usual ones associated with *brāhmaṇas*, although the Bhṛgu-Aṅgirasas were already associated with *itihāsa*. Referring specifically to an *itihāsa*-knowing *brāhmaṇa* makes *itihāsa* more central to the construction of knowledge about the past.

3. The Development of the *Rājataraṅgiṇī*

The *Rājataraṅgiṇī* consists of eight books of unequal length and divides seemingly into three sections, suggestive of the pattern of the *vaṃśānucarita* (the section on succession) in the *Viṣṇu Purāṇa*. This may be a natural division based on themes.[29] The first part

[27] Ved Kumari, *The Nīlamata Purāṇa*, 177.

[28] T. Funayama, "Remarks on Religious Predominance in Kashmir: Hindu or Buddhist", 367–76; *Rājataraṅginī,* 6.171–3.

[29] A.L. Basham, "Kalhana and his Chronicle", 57–65.

covers origin myths and early inhabitants. The second moves towards kings of vaguely defined early dynasties. The third and most substantial section is the narrative of established dynasties.

The origin myths of Book One continue into Book Two with its references to scattered kings and dynasties. The draining of the lake prior to the settlement of the area coincided in time with the first six Manus and was ready for settlement during the time of the seventh Manu.[30] This links the local narrative with the meta-narrative in the *Viṣṇu Purāṇa.* The earlier text was taken as a source for the beginnings of history, and in the *itihāsa-purāṇa* tradition, history began with the narrative as given in the *Purāṇas.* (Significantly there are no references to Aryans as the founders of history!) The draining of the lake was necessary to forming a nucleus for the region. The implicit symbolism is that of the receding of water to provide land for settlement, as in the story of Manu and the Flood from the *Purāṇas*. It helps establish territorial boundaries which were more firmly defined by subsequent events.

The names of fifty-two rulers approximately contemporary with the early lineages listed in the *Purāṇas* are said to be lost.[31] The chronology is then synchronized with the calculation of the Kaliyuga, as given in the *Bṛhatsaṃhitā*, a post-Gupta text on astronomy.[32]

The earliest people were the Nāgas associated with the Vidyādharas, an association that is more frequent in the Sramanic texts. The kings of the first book often borrow names from the *Nīlamata Purāṇa*, which links them with the major *Purāṇas*. The earliest king, Gonanda I, is said to be related to Jarāsandha of the *Mahābhārata*, and therefore involved in the battles with Kṛṣṇa. The choice of relationship was with someone who was opposed to the Yādavas, and therefore to Kṛṣṇa, and was virtually murdered in the epic. His son Gonanda II was a mere child when the *Mahābhārata* war took place and therefore could not participate

[30] *Rājataraṅgiṇī*, 1.25–8.
[31] Ibid., 1.44ff.
[32] Ibid., 1.56.

in it. This answers the question why the kings of Kashmir were not present on the battlefield at Kurukṣetra. Participation in the war was a matter of status but also suggested links with the *kṣatriya rājās* of the genealogies of the *Purāṇas*. The fifty-two lost generations appropriately belong to this period, a grey area in historical events.

A further list of kings includes Lava, the first to grant an *agrahāra*, and Kuśa, the latter succeeding the former, but these two are not connected with the *Rāmāyaṇa*. Rather, the early times involve many *siddhas* (holy men), and Śaiva ascetics, common to other chronicles as well. The former would have been attuned to the local religion, the latter probably less so although their opposition was to the Buddhists. The opposition is sometimes disguised in stories of misbehaviour against royalty.[33] An example of this was a Buddhist monk seducing, through magical power, the wife of king Nara. The predictable punishment is the burning down of many *vihāras*, with their grants being revoked and given instead to *brāhmaṇas*. These Śaiva–Buddhist confrontations are referred to often, and, with royalty generally supporting the former, some decline in Buddhism was inevitable and the decline has to be explained. This contrasts with earlier times, when both were recipients of royal patronage.

Aśoka receives more attention than he gets in other brahmanical works, where he is merely a name in a king-list. Here he is the first historically known king in the narrative. Kalhaṇa cites a specific source, the *Chavillākara*, now unavailable, as providing information on the king. Such information was also available from the Buddhist texts of the Northern Tradition, such as the *Aśokāvadāna*. Kalhaṇa states that *Aśoka* embraced the doctrine of the Jina, i.e. became a Buddhist, founded the city of Śrīnagara, and built many *stūpas*. He is said to have brought Buddhism to Kashmir.[34] He is treated as a king of Kashmir with no mention of the rest of his empire, except that he is called a *bhūpati* (lord of the earth). He obtained a son, Jalauka (not mentioned in any other source) through propitiating Śiva, and this son was instrumental in

[33] Ibid., 1.199–200.
[34] Ibid., 1.101ff.

attacking the *mlecchas*—presumably the Hellenistic Greeks that threatened the kingdom. Unlike his father, Jalauka was not a patron of the Buddhists. He settled new lands, introduced the practice of caste in social functioning, and created a kingdom with a state administration comparable to that of Yudhiṣṭhira (who by now was being held up as the paragon of a dharmic king). The process described by Kalhaṇa seems fairly accurate. Subsequent to this, the Kuṣāṇa kings are listed but described as *turuṣkas* (Turks), the label doubtless pointing only to their Central Asian origin. Some of the names in the list are known from other sources but their order here is confused. This is the period when Buddhism was prevalent but conflict with the *brāhmaṇas* is apparent.

The competition between Buddhists and *brāhmaṇas* soon descends into the persecution of the Buddhists, with their monasteries being burnt, their grants revoked, and on occasion their monks killed. The Hūṇa/Hun king Mihirakula was especially vicious and is described as *bhūpāla vetāla* (demon king).[35] Kalhaṇa is contemptuous of the *brāhmaṇas* of Gandhāra who accepted grants from such a despicable king. He is surprised that the subjects did not rise in revolt and kill him and asserts that he was probably protected by the gods.[36] The Hūṇas are followed by a series of kings that came from elsewhere. Among them was a Meghavāhana brought from Gandhāra, at the request of the *prajā* (subjects), and the *saciva* (ministers), which was an unusual procedure.

Book Three opens with the narrative of Meghavāhana's rule and ends with that of Balāditya. Meghavāhana is a non-brahmanical figure given to Buddhist and Jaina ethics, such as forbidding animal sacrifice. He is said to have conquered Laṅkā, the sea having parted, allowing the army to cross over.[37] He and his queen are donors of many *vihāras* for monks, but also many *agrahāras*. The listing of some of the *vihāras* is reminiscent of Buddhist chronicles listing monasteries. Further on in the narrative the removal of a king is signalled by his abdication in order to become an ascetic, a theme that crops up from time to time in various narratives.[38]

[35] Ibid., 1.292ff.
[36] Ibid., 1.289, 307–16, 324.
[37] Ibid., 3.71, 7.1137–8.
[38] Ibid., 2.143–4, 151–3, 162.

The wish to become an ascetic may have been a euphemism for being forced to abdicate.

Book Four introduces dynastic history in a more systematic way, constituting a distinctive second section of the text. It begins with the Kārkoṭa dynasty, which was responsible for consolidating the kingdom of Kashmir in the seventh century. The origin of the Kārkoṭas is linked to the Nāga Kārkoṭa, said to be a deity but also a kinsman of the ruling family. Since this was a dynasty of the seventh century AD, Chinese annals also provide incidental references to corroborate the text, the T'ang rulers being interested in northern India. They mention that the Kārkoṭa king Candrāpīḍa requested assistance against the Arabs in AD 713, a time when the Arabs were attempting a conquest of Sindh. The chronology seems to tally. Northern India at this time experienced at its frontiers the proximity of the Chinese, the rise of Tibetan power, the presence of the Arabs, and the threat of Turkish rule in Afghanistan. This is not reflected even in a history as perceptive as that of Kalhaṇa, which may be a comment on the visibility of the threat.

Lalitāditya Muktāpīḍa, the most accomplished king of this dynasty, carried out expeditions, moving round the earth like the sun.[39] Claims to conquest echo the *praśasti* inscription of Samudra Gupta, which may have become a model for the writing of *praśastis*. Victories in distant places, such as against the almost mythical Uttarakurus or against Prāgjyotiṣa in Assam may be an exaggeration, but his campaigns against the Dards in the northwest of Kashmir and the Bhoṭas or Tibetans to the east are more plausible. The spectacular campaign against the Central Asian Turkish tribes, the Tukhāra, is also alluded to by Al-Biruni.[40] Kashmir had close relations with them and they are remembered as having been patrons of Buddhism.[41] The story is told of a Tukhāra who used a magic charm to part the waters of the river so that the army could cross over. When asked for the charm he was willing to exchange it for an icon of the Buddha from Magadha.[42] Lalitāditya was not a major patron of Buddhism as is evident from

[39] Ibid., 4.126ff.

[40] *Alberuni's India*, vol. I, 302.

[41] This would of course have been prior to their conversion to Islam.

[42] *Rājataraṅgiṇī*, 4.259.

his having built the magnificent Mārtaṇḍa temple to the sun-god Sūrya. *Brāhmaṇas* had been invited to settle in Kashmir and they had come in large numbers, some from Gandhāra and some from *āryadeśa*—Central India, Kanauj, and Gauḍa.[43]

Another narrative states that an icon of Viṣṇu in a temple was suspended by two magnets, one above it and one below it, a notion known to more than one author, and may reflect the popularity of magnetic material at this time.[44] This presumes that the icon was made of metal, possibly iron, although bronze was frequently used in Kashmir for icons.[45] On another occasion, when a piece of waste land was dug at his orders, two ancient temples were found with images, and engraved on the pedestals were the words "Rāma" and "Lakṣmaṇa". The story suggests wishful thinking. Similarly, water wells up when Lalitāditya pierces the surface of the desert with his lance. These are symbolic of the good king deriving from recognized stereotypes.

Lalitāditya's grandson Jayāpīḍa set out to conquer Kanauj, and Kalhaṇa speaks of him as moving in the *maṇḍala* of kings just as the sun moves in a *maṇḍala* of clouds.

The third section of the *Rājataraṅgiṇī*, consisting of Books Five to Eight, covers the history of Kashmir over the 300 years prior to Kalhaṇa. This part is more focused, the narrative becoming more historical, perhaps in part due to epigraphic records. The turbulence of politics probably demanded a more precise account of events. Avantivarman, ruling in the mid-ninth century (AD 855–83) built the town of Avantipura. He is best remembered for permitting the engineer Suyya to redirect the course of the Jhelum by an upstream dam with strategically located dykes. This resulted in controlling the river for irrigation and an amazing increase in agricultural production, with a dramatic reduction in the price of rice.[46]

[43] Ibid., 1.313, 341–3.

[44] For modern readers this statement is similar to that of al-Qazwini, who maintains that the *liṅgam* at Somanātha, made of iron, was suspended by a magnet, to the amazement of Mahmud of Ghazni and his entourage, who were anxious to destroy it. R. Thapar, *Somanatha: The Many Voices of a History*, 55.

[45] *Rājataraṅgiṇī*, 4.185.

[46] Ibid., 5.68–117.

Śaṅkaravarman, who succeeded Avantivarman, campaigned in the plains of the Punjab and more repeatedly against the Hindu Shāhiya dynasty which had established itself in Kabul after the decline of the Turkish Shāhiyas. Kashmir in the ninth century was involved in the politics not only of the Punjab but also of Gandhāra and Central Asia. Despite the agricultural prosperity of the earlier time, there now seems to have been a fiscal crisis which is reflected in various ways. The peasants came under an oppressive administration which Kalhaṇa attributes to the appointment of unscrupulous *kāyastha* officers. This was intensified by forced labour in the form of *kara-begara* (porterage corvée), carrying loads where there was an absence of roads, and the demand of high taxes.[47] Not content with this, the king began plundering temples, a form of acquiring wealth which was resorted to by other Hindu rulers of Kashmir as well.

Kalhaṇa mentions the rise of the Tantrins and their rivals the Ekāṅgas. Both were military groups serving as royal bodyguards but with a base in land holdings. Each supported opposing factions at the court especially when a succession was being contested, and made demands on the one who succeeded. In the tenth century the intrigue involving these two groups increased, which finally led the king to call for help from the land-owning intermediaries, the Ḍāmaras, to re-establish the authority of the ruler. They were disliked by the *kāyasthas* and the *brāhmaṇas* at the court who saw them as rivals, and were finally brought under control in the eleventh century.

Kalhaṇa argues that the amassing of wealth by these groups and their associates and by the king was a disaster,[48] as it followed from famines dislocating people. Storing food in excess of a year's consumption, or more than that produced by the tillage of the fields, was to be prohibited. Surplus food encouraged accumulation which led to wealth and in turn to rebellion.[49]

Much historical detail follows, till we reach the queen Diddā, wife of Kṣemagupta, who emerged as the *eminence grise* during

[47] D.D. Kosambi, "Origins of Feudalism in Kashmir", 31–2, 108–20; *Rājataraṅgiṇī*, 5.51–2.

[48] *Rājataraṅgiṇī*, 5.270–5.

[49] Ibid., 4.347–8.

the reigns of a few short-lived kings and eventually in AD 980 assumed the rulership herself for a period of twenty-three years. This was an extraordinary event, unforeseen in the *śāstras,* but quite logical in terms of the contemporary politics of Kashmir as described by Kalhaṇa. It brought her family, from Lohara, into the contest for kingship. Among other things she restored old and ruined temples, whereas her husband Kṣemagupta had burnt down a Buddhist monastery, and had used the remains and those from decaying temples to build a new temple to Śiva.[50] On her death in 1003 the throne passed to the family of Lohara with the accession of Diddā's nephew, Saṁgrāmarāja, who was her brother's son. This was in effect a change in the patriline. He was called upon to assist the Hindu Shāhiya king against Mahmud of Ghazni, referred to by Kalhaṇa as Hammīra, the king of the Turuṣkas. With the defeat of the Hindu Shāhiyas, princes from their family took refuge in Kashmir.

Kalhaṇa repeatedly blames the *kāyasthas* for maladministration, and regards them with contempt for being oppressive, and for looting temples and the treasury. Harṣa, who seized the throne and ruled from 1089 to 1101, is also called a Turuṣka because he looted temples in an attempt to overcome a fiscal crisis. Catastrophic conditions caused by floods and famine resulted in a devastating rise in prices. The king instituted a special category of officers, the *devotpatananāyaka*, the officer for the uprooting of the deities, and they plundered the temples,[51] keeping the wealth for the king and themselves, despite the extreme distress of the people, Kalhaṇa attributes Harṣa's weakness to his lack of policies, his poor ability to implement orders, his exploitation of his people and his lack of morality.

Book Eight records the Lohara dynasty of the twelfth century. The personalities of the time were close contemporaries so there are virtually blow-by-blow accounts of court politics where some descriptions read like pen-portraits of people. The intrigues, faction fighting, and violence continue, and some of this is attributed to the scheming *brāhmaṇas* and *kāyasthas* at the court. There

[50] Ibid., 6.171ff., 307, 8.2380.
[51] Ibid., 8.1095.

is additionally a pendulum swing between collaterals. Kalhaṇa praises the king Uccala, whose benefactions took care of some of the distress of the subjects.[52]

In Kalhaṇa's world deities do not come to the aid of kings, rituals do not bestow divinity but only status, and caste observances are not observed by royalty—queens were sometimes from the lowest castes, the passion of the king overcoming social codes. Rules of marriage are not observed, with kings marrying indiscriminately. Was this necessitated by the manoeuvring of the intermediaries or by a weakness in patriarchy?

The role of ministers, as given in theoretical texts referring to polity of the post-Gupta period, seems divorced from the reality presented by Kalhaṇa, where they are part of the faction-fighting and dissensions in the administration of the kingdom. His father having been a minister either to Harṣa or to the later kings, Kalhaṇa would have had fuller information on their activities. This is reflected in the details of their reigns. Although the planets were malignant at his birth, argues Kalhaṇa, Harṣa's dependence on ministers and his aversion to confrontations accounted for many of his problems.[53] Resort to the supernatural, and to fate occasionally mentioned in earlier sections of the text, now tend to fade. There is greater discussion of the politics of those involved in governance.

5. The Chronicle as History

The *vaṃśāvalī*, although it is a succession of kings, is also conducive to constructing the history of a region, which is a characteristic attempt of the genre. It is written at a point when the identity of the region has been understood, even if not defined, and therefore events tend to lead up to this identity. The geography and topography help in the definition. The construction of the region includes pointers of change, which become apparent from about the late first millennium AD: the establishing of the state in the newly emerging kingdoms; forms of political economy different

52 Ibid., 8.107ff.

53 Ibid., 7.1715–16.

from the earlier ones; the acculturation of the region to caste and Puranic religion; the coming of literacy and the interface between mainstream culture and local culture, the *mārga* and the *deśī*; and new styles of architecture and sculpture.

Space having been contoured, there remained the problem of time, and this was more complex. The sources used were not always meticulous about time and often the contradiction between *yugas* (ages) and *samvats* (eras) required some manipulation of the succession, whether genealogical or dynastic. There was always the temptation of telescoping, removing some names, and padding by adding names when constructing genealogies. Editing of this kind was common to the form, which is seldom tightly structured, since its function is not limited to chronology. The concern with status was often more central.

The format of the *Rājataraṅgiṇī* follows that of most *vaṃśāvalīs*. The narrative begins with an origin myth relating to the region. Connections are made with the early *kṣatriya* heroes of the *Purāṇas* to provide a link with the main Puranic tradition. The narrative then moves to listing early kings that are believed to be local, with indications of a Sramanic presence. This gradually gives way to dynasties, with descriptions of greater detail for more recent dynasties. Independent statehood is claimed by the taking of royal titles, but the more effective indicators are conquests, such as those of Lalitāditya and Avantivarman (which seem like *digvijayas*), or making marriage alliances with families of established status, or building a magnificant temple which becomes a statement of power.[54] The focus of the narratives is usually on the king and this gets sharper in contemporary times when the politics of opposition also becomes more apparent. Kalhaṇa criticizes the oppression of subjects by kings.[55]

Women intervening in the policies of kings is deplored, particularly when kings were susceptible to their beauty to the extent of one king making a woman of the lowest Domb caste his queen.[56] Yet he does give space to queens such as Yaśovatī, Sugandhā,

[54] Ibid., 4.183–207, 5.44, 7.299.
[55] Ibid., 1.188, 7.1091–1115, 5.165–77.
[56] Ibid., 5.387–9.

Sūryamatī, and of course much more to Diddā. Some bestowed status on the royal family, others reduced the status. Politics was not entirely a male preserve and even concubines had some say in matters of state, especially when they involved questions of regency and of collateral lines succeeding to the throne.[57] Kalhaṇa seems to suggest that the competition for the throne largely resulted from the ambitions of women involved in this struggle.

Kalhaṇa's social conservatism is apparent from his discussion of high and low castes. The *brāhmaṇas* seem to divide easily into three categories: the *sāmanta-dvija*, the *brāhmaṇa* intermediary generally of the family of the recipient of an *agrahāra*; the *purohita pāriṣadyas*, the *brāhmaṇas* who ran the temple corporations; and the *paṇḍits* or scholars who could be dedicated to learning or could be ministers, high officials, and even military commanders, and play politics at the highest levels, organizing opposition to the king.[58] The *purohita pariṣads* were corporations of those who were the *brāhmaṇa* administrators of the temple and its property, and of places of pilgrimage which brought in a sizeable income. They had common ownership of the properties, the fees, and the endowments of these places. They were therefore extremely rich, powerful, and politically influential.[59] This allowed them to confront kings and ministers, often threatening to fast to death, an effective threat in a society that believed that causing the death of a *brāhmaṇa* was a heinous sin.[60]

Kalhaṇa takes the granting of *agrahāras* back to the earliest dynasties, presumably because he could not visualize a situation when they did not exist. The *brāhmaṇas* from Gandhāra he categorizes as the lowest because they accepted *agrahāras* even from Mihirakula.[61] The propitiation of *brāhmaṇas* was necessary because it was thought that they could cause the destruction of the king by magical means and through witchcraft, and also by expressing opposition to the king.[62] Kalhaṇa describes the use of the fast as an instrument of threat to the king, as it was also used

[57] D. Rangachari, *Invisible Women, Visible Histories*, 83–191.

[58] *Rājataraṅgiṇī*, 5.461–6, 7.12–13, 177, 675, 8.1071.

[59] Ibid., 2.132, 5.465–6, 8.900.

[60] Ibid., 8.898–900, 2224.

[61] Ibid., 1.307.

[62] Ibid., 1.272; 4.122–5.

in other regions. Opposition by the *brāhmaṇas* takes the form of *prāyopaveśa*, a voluntary fast that would cause havoc should the *brāhmaṇa* die. There is a hint of blackmail in this form of opposition since it is not accompanied by a lengthy and appropriate preparation. Such a fast was attempted against Diddā but failed because she bribed the *brāhmaṇas*.[63] In the next reign both *brāhmaṇas* and the *pāriṣadyas* fasted against Bhikṣācāra.[64]

Kalhaṇa's description of the functioning of the king in a world of Ḍāmaras and other political groups, and particularly the *purohita pariṣad,* provides little evidence to justify the theory that there was a separation of political and ritual power, and that ritual power was predominant in the peripheries of the kingdom and political power in the centre; or that the relations between ritual and power are best understood by seeing them through the heavy emphasis on symbolism and the practice of ritual.[65] The *brāhmaṇas* of the *pariṣads* and the *agrahāras* drew an income primarily from the land they controlled, and much less from their control over ritual. Land made them so wealthy that they became a target for the Ḍāmaras. Their power was based on their intervention in politics, not as ritual specialists but as landowners: hence their being called *sāmanta-dvijas*.

Kalhaṇa, being himself a *brāhmaṇa*, nevertheless holds these *brāhmaṇas* in contempt, both for accepting the patronage of sub-standard kings and for making this their claim to power.[66] At the popular level the respect and fear of the *brāhmaṇa* arose as much from his status as from his wealth as a landowner, and the power this brought, as also from the fear of the curse of the *brāhmaṇa.* Brahmanical sects were competing for royal patronage on the one hand, but were incorporating popular local practice into their beliefs and practices to acquire wider support. One of the manifestations of this was the assimilation of Tantric belief and practice into the conventional practices of the sects.[67]

[63] Ibid., 6.335–40.

[64] Ibid., 8.768–75.

[65] B. Stein, "The Segmentary State in South Indian History", 3–51; R. Inden, "Hierarchies of Kings in Medieval India", 99–125.

[66] K. Mohan, *Early Medieval History of Kashmir*, 217.

[67] A. Sanderson, "Religion and the State: Śaiva Officiants in the Territory of the King's Brahmanical Chaplain", 229–300.

The confrontation of religious sects and their involvement in the politics of the kingdom is also laid bare in another text of the late ninth century, the play *Āgama-ḍambara* by Bhaṭṭa Jayanta, with which Kalhaṇa is likely to have been familiar.[68] The play dates to the reign of Śaṅkaravarman. Jayanta was known for his commentaries on Nyāya philosophy and discussions on the centrality of logic. This may have encouraged the satire of the play.

The leading character in the play, Saṅkarṣaṇa, is hostile to the Buddhists, Jainas, and Cārvākas, as well as to the Śaiva Nīlāmbaras. The presence of the Cārvākas as materialists is interesting since they hardly figure in most brahmanical texts. Not only is the relationship of these sects extremely problematic, but there is the additional role of the Vaiṣṇava Bhāgavatas, also patronized at the time by the queen and some members of the court. This is not unusual, since factions in the royal courts each supported different sectarian views. The debate in the play takes strongly opposing positions. Finally, a way is suggested that allows the validity of variant views, provided none supports overthrowing the social order. But this is the crux of the matter, since the *varṇa* ordering of society was at issue, among other things.

Kalhaṇa observes a social distance with the lower castes. Even when praising the hydraulic engineering of Suyya, he mentions Suyya being a *śūdra.*[69] His intention seems to have been to emphasize Suyya's innate intelligence, which led him to such an unusual solution and eventually a high position. Elsewhere he states that a king took a Śvapāka woman as his wife—which led to the rise in status of the low-caste Śvapākas. He asks what could have happened to the gods that they permitted her to enter the temple, adding that the *brāhmaṇas* who allowed this were committing a sin.[70] He refers to some categories of people as impure, such as a queen that came from the Domb community, and the Gāndhāras, the Khasas from the mountains, the Bhauṭṭa from Tibet, and the Dārada.[71] The Dārada of the trans-Himalayan region are said to speak an unfamiliar tongue, which makes them alien.[72]

[68] Bhaṭṭa Jayanta, *Much Ado About Religion.*

[69] *Rājataraṅgiṇī*, 5.73–4, 80–91, 110–12.

[70] Ibid., 5.387–94.

[71] Ibid., 1.312–17.

[72] *Rājataraṅgiṇī*, 8.2762–4. Recent work on the Dardic language points to it

According to Kalhaṇa the contestation for power began to include a wider range of people from about the eighth century AD. There was of course the traditional fear of princes overthrowing their father, a caution first articulated in the *Arthaśāstra*, which compares princes to crabs who eat their parents.[73] Kalhaṇa lists a variety of reasons which may cause disaffection between father and son. In these the roles of wives and stepmothers are as significant as that of ministers, brothers, and evil-minded persons.[74]

Kalhaṇa states that the contenders for power over a period of time were the Ḍāmaras, a term peculiar to Kashmir, but as a socio-economic entity found in many regions at this time. They were wealthy and powerful landowners anxious to control royal power and ready to revoke grants to temples and appropriate them.[75] Some began as ordinary householders but increased their power by either setting up strongholds on their land or taking over those of others. Since many of these were in the fertile portions of the valley, their success was guaranteed. Their resort to lawlessness led to their being disliked both by officials and *brāhmaṇas*. Their rise in social status is probably indicated by their marrying wives from among the local aristocracy and giving their daughters to the royal family.[76] During the reign of Avantivarman they appropriated the villages donated to a temple, and on another occasion they defeated the Tantrins whilst assisting Cakravarman to regain the throne; later they assassinated the king.[77] Conflict with the reigning kings continued, including a rising of the Ḍāmaras against Jayasimha and confrontations with Harṣa in the eleventh century. They were subdued finally by Uccala, who followed this act by magnanimous donations, which makes one wonder whether Kalhaṇa is implying that the king seized the lands of the Ḍāmaras.[78] Clearly, those who had the potential to oppress were also the ones who had the power to revolt.

---

being among the early Indo-Aryan languages, but it seemed unfamiliar at that time to speakers of another Indo-Aryan language.

[73] *Arthaśāstra*, 1.17.4–5.

[74] *Rājataraṅgiṇī*, 7.678.

[75] Ibid., 5.48ff., 7.494ff.

[76] *Kalhaṇa's Rājataraṅgiṇī*, vol. II, 304ff., Note G-IV.348.

[77] *Rājataraṅgiṇī*, 5.51–2, 306, 406–13.

[78] Ibid., 7.154, 576–9, 1227–8, 8.991, 1157, 3129ff.

Revolts against the king by the Ḍāmaras and by other intermediaries are clearly of serious concern to Kalhaṇa, who sees them almost as an ongoing confrontation of the previous couple of centuries.[79] This is not an unusual condition in the political structures of North Indian kingdoms of this period and needs greater attention than it has received. Not only was there wealth to recruit private armies, the Ḍāmaras were also well armed.[80] Kalhaṇa calls them *dasyus* who destroyed whatever they could.[81] The same term was used for the Kaivartas, who rebelled against the Pāla king. As makers and breakers of royalty who intervened in the flow of political authority, keeping track of them in a historical narrative would have been problematic.

The repeated intervention of the Ekāṅgas, Tantrins, and Ḍāmaras in high-level politics, and the determination with which they tried to control the royal court, is a striking aspect in Kalhaṇa's account. The idea of *maṇḍala* in the politics of the hill states remains somewhat tangential, perhaps because intermediaries were less deeply grounded in territories from where they could aspire to create their own kingdoms. In Kashmir the intention was to intervene in the politics of the court and gain power through that process, by tring to overthrow the ruling family. That seems to have been the pattern by which the first Lohara dynasty came to power.

If Kalhaṇa protested against the power of the Ḍāmaras and described them as the scourge of the land, he was also hostile to the *kāyasthas*, who used literacy and administrative positions to build their strength in the hierarchy of power. As with the *brāhmaṇas, kāyasthas* were invited to Kashmir and many families came from the Ganges plain in search of employment. The land which had earlier been plundered by Ḍāmaras was now being severely punished by the administration of the *kāyasthas*—whom Kalhaṇa refers to as a plague on the people,[82] and are the ones who manipulate kings and policies. The king Śaṅkaravarman, whom Kalhaṇa

[79] Ibid., 5.395ff., 447, 6.354, 7.223, 404ff.
[80] Ibid., 8.709.
[81] Ibid., 8.991, 1157.
[82] Ibid., 5.439.

describes as "the foremost among fools", is said to have oppressed his subjects and plundered temples because he had fallen into the hands of *kāyasthas*.[83] Harṣa tormented his subjects through the fines and taxes imposed by the *kāyasthas*.[84] Again, it is Uccala who ridicules the *kāyasthas*, and especially the most powerful among them, Sadda, who was in control of the treasury and was accused of intrigue against the king.[85] Sadda is said to be the son of a lower-caste load-carrier, and obviously Kalhaṇa is not taken in by any subsequent origin myths of the *kāyasthas*.

Kalhaṇa was writing of a time that had seen disturbed conditions. His history therefore becomes a record of events as viewed by a member of the ruling elite whose family had been close to court circles, but who himself seems to have distanced himself from the powerful factions, his opposition to these being evident. This in part accounts for a change in historical explanation. From the Kārkoṭa dynasty onwards, his narrative reads as a relatively down-to-earth history of Kashmir, even critical at times, in which political factors are balanced with a variety of other fairly rational explanations. It is also intended to underline the importance of *rājanīti* (political concerns) in arguing that a strong king is necessary to protect the subjects and stating by implication that few such had ruled Kashmir in his time.

Resort to the supernatural and the mystical is not absent in his explanations of the course of events but occurs with rather more frequency in the earlier books.[86] The last book sees a fading out of such explanations and politics is discussed in terms of the personalities involved and their ambitions: the king; the feudatories, the Ḍāmaras, the politics of the *brāhmaṇas* and *kāyasthas*; and the economic conditions of the peasant at the receiving end of oppression by all these.

This is not to say, however, that his work is so strongly historical in the modern sense as to negate the occasional intervention of Fate.[87] The term which he uses for Fate, *vidhātṛ*, could also imply

[83] Ibid., 5.180–1.

[84] Ibid., 7.1226.

[85] Ibid., 8.258, 276ff., 298–308, 443.

[86] Ibid., 1.165, 179–81, 259, 333, 2.17–55, 4.101–5, 6.185.

[87] Ibid., 7.67, 916–17, 1187, 8.1811, 2999.

the Creator, and therefore divinity. Inevitably, there is a belief in divine retribution. A certain moralistic element runs through the narrative as well, but surfaces only occasionally. Thus he says, "In order to enjoy pleasures, which on account of the preceding evil deeds yield no enjoyment, the wicked destroy the virtuous as the young camels destroy the *ketaka* tree in order to get at its thorns."[88] Yet overall his is an independent position which he defends with arguments.

Kalhaṇa's purpose is to establish places and times of kings as against fluctuating and conflicting tradition; to set out the actions of those that govern; to please and entertain his readers by descriptions of the past; to give his readers food for thought on the impermanence of things, thereby encouraging resignation.[89] The latter suggests an attitude inspired by Buddhist thinking: it is interesting that, in spite of the disappearance of Buddhism, its imprint on the minds of the thoughtful remained. The profession of a historian was not seen as a distinct and separate profession. The historian was regarded as a *kavi* (poet). The *Rājataraṅgiṇī* is therefore treated as a *mahākāvya* by later writers, even if its style is far less ornate and embellished as compared to other *mahākāvyas*. Some brahmanical norms are conceded. The king's *karma* can affect historical events and is linked to the *karma* of his people; thus, good kings arise because of the merits of the people and meritorious action lies in the observance of brahmanical norms.[90]

Woven into this is the theory of the four *yugas* and the progressive decay of all things. The turmoil of more recent times was almost expected. A hint of the world turned upside down in the Kaliyuga hovers in the background of factions and feudatory revolts. Yet the events recorded are dated not in the Kaliyuga but in the more commonly used Laukika era.

That Kashmir had been intellectually vibrant over the couple of centuries before Kalhaṇa is evident from the quality of thought and writing of authors based there. A likely reason is that there had been for a while a migration of the learned to Kashmir. A

[88] Ibid., trans. M.A. Stein, 4.113.
[89] A.L. Basham, "Kalhana and his Chronicle".
[90] *Rājataraṅgiṇī*, 1.158, 161, 324.

tradition of learning seems to have been established through the presence and work of many scholars. Not that their writings would have necessarily lent themselves to the genre of *vaṃśāvalīs*, but at least they created an ambience of intellectual curiosity of the kind which is evident in the chronicle.

The tradition of writing chronicles continued in Kashmir with those of Jonarāja, Śrīvara, Prajyabhaṭṭa, Śuka, and Dāmodara Paṇḍita, among others. Jonarāja continued his account of the period subsequent to Kalhaṇa's text, from Jayasimha to the reign of the Sultan Zayn-al-'Ābidin. It has been plausibly argued that Śrīvara's "Jaina Rājataraṅgiṇī" is a reference to Zayn, and its contents would support this proposition.[91] But these were not of the quality of Kalhaṇa's work, neither in their writing nor in their understanding of the past.

[91] W. Slaje, "A Note on the Genesis and Character of Śrīvara's So-Called *Jaina-Rājataraṅgiṇī*", 379–88.

16

The Chamba *Vaṃśāvalī*

1. The Area

The less-known *vaṃśāvalī* from Chamba is another example of the chronicles of this period. Although of the same genre, it is a contrast to the *Rājataraṅgiṇī* in language and quality of thought. Chamba in the western Himalaya was a small hill state comprising the upper reaches of the Ravi river and touching the Chenab river. Apart from the succession of rulers and events, other significant processes of change are implicit in the *vaṃśāvalī,* such as the formation of the kingdom, the emergence of intermediaries, the transition to a caste society, and the coming of Puranic Hinduism. States that were neighbours of Kashmir, and had relationships with the kingdoms in the vicinity, vacillated from independence to occasional subservience. They attempted to maintain *vaṃśāvalīs*; that of Chamba is the most coherent.

The earlier focus of the text was the settlement at Brahmaur in the upper reaches of the Ravi. This area, though seemingly isolated, was connected by routes in various directions—to Kishtwar, Jammu, and Kangra with access to the plains of Kashmir and Punjab, and others via the Manimahesha lake and Trilokanath to Lahul and Kulu.[1] The passes were connected with the higher

[1] J.Ph. Vogel, *Antiquities of Chamba State*, vol. I; B.Ch. Chhabra, *Antiquities of Chamba State*, vol. II, is substantially devoted to the inscriptions from the area starting in the fourteenth century AD. Earlier sources of various kinds are discussed in volume I. See also *Chamba District Gazetteer*, 1963; A. Cunningham, *ASIR* 1872–3, vol. V; V.C. Ohri (ed.), *History and Culture of the Chamba State*; M. Sharma, "State Formation and Cultural Complex in Western Himalaya: Chamba, Genealogy and Epigraphs 700–1650 CE", 387–432.

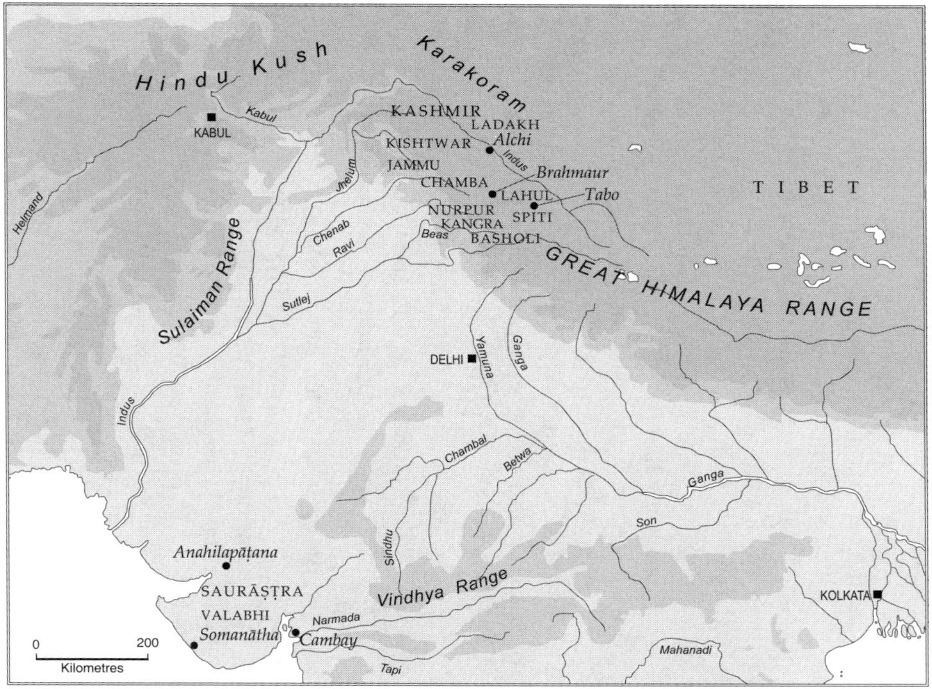

Map 7: Locations of the More Important Places, Clans, and Dynasties (chps. 16 and 17)

Himalaya and to infrequently used routes along the ranges. Brahmaur came to be called Gaderan—the habitat of the Gaddi shepherds known to various parts of the western Himalaya. Pastoralists practising transhumance would in summer have moved up to the Manimahesha Pass linking the Ravi valley with the Beas valley. At the turn of the first millennium AD, when the state was established, the location of the capital moved down to a lower elevation on the plateau of Chamba. The proximity of Chamba to Kashmir resulted in historical connections, sometimes close, but also with occasional brief periods of the subordination of Chamba. A paucity of coins suggests that trade remained an exchange of goods in the more remote valleys. The larger markets handling both agricultural produce and goods from more distant areas, would have been in Chamba and at entry points to the plains. Referred to in the inscriptions as Cāmpā or Campaka, the town of Chamba, after which the kingdom was named, was located on a fertile plateau above the junction of the Ravi and Saho rivers. The valleys branching off were generally held by *rāṇās*, intermediaries who were under the suzerainty of the king of Chamba.

2. The Narrative Before the Coming of the State

The Chamba *vaṃśāvalī* lists the succession of rulers of Chamba coming down to the seventeenth century, closing with the war between Chamba and Nurpur (to the south) in 1642. It appears to be incomplete and therefore may have carried the story further in time, but that part is unavailable.

The work is not just a genealogical roll, as it has been called by earlier scholars, since it considers other features that affect kingship. It may not be an exact chronicle, but it does record a historical process. Its authorship is unknown. The final version, as we have it, comes from the family of the *rājaguru* of the kingdom of Chamba. It is unclear whether it was composed afresh in the seventeenth century, or whether the data was collected from various sources (such as other brief chronicles and inscriptions) and put together at this time. The text itself suggests the latter, since no court poet would have claimed it as his *kāvya*. The intention of the genealogy was probably to present a seamless descent from the beginning, although it unwittingly shows breaks at various points. Chronicles claim to be historically accurate, but such a claim cannot be taken literally—there are usually contradictions with other sources. The intention of putting together a chronicle at a particular point, or updating and re-editing an existing one, usually has a political purpose. The significance of the chronicle is that it is one perspective of the past; and, in this case, the version offered is not seriously contradicted by other views.

Composed in Sanskrit, the *vaṃśāvalī* consists of 120 *ślokas* (verses), but the quality of the language is poor and suggests a composition of the period when Sanskrit was declining in this region. It claims, among its sources, the *Bhāgavata* and *Skanda Purāṇas,* both late. The *Bhāgavata Purāṇa* drew on earlies ones, such as the *Viṣṇu Purāṇa,* hence the repetition of some of the descent lists. The early part of the narrative is drawn from these and contains much that is mythological. *Purāṇas* were, as we have seen, read and recited, and known to those regarded as learned, and their genealogical sections were important as skeletal structures for chronology. Inscriptions of various kinds, issued by most rulers, were doubtless additional sources on the past within the work.

It has been argued that the author must have relied on inscriptions for data on the rulers of Chamba, particularly from about the eleventh century onwards, since the order of succession is largely common to both. The language often tends to be ungrammatical. Another possibility is that there was a version in the local Chambiyali language, referred to as the *bansauli*. An Urdu version, probably composed for the Mughal court, has also been mentioned, but would have been very late. Another Sanskrit copy, said to have been in the family of the *rājaguru* of the Chamba royal family, was destroyed in a fire.[2] Unlike Kalhaṇa, the author of this chronicle is not named. He was evidently a *brāhmaṇa* belonging to Chamba and attached to the court, since other than the lists of kings and dynasties there is some information on grants made for pious acts, miracles, and the efficacy of austerities.

The *vaṃśāvalī* was in part a document for the court and the royal

[2] J.Ph. Vogel, *Antiquities of Chamba State*, vol. I, 78ff.

family, and in part a history on how Chamba came to be what it is. Its more recent authorship, if it had more than a single author, would have remained in the family of the *rājaguru*, passed on from generation to generation for updating, the text being treated as a part of the patrimony.

The Chamba *vaṃśāvalī* can be seen as consisting of three sections (although the author of the text does not make this division). The three observe the format of the *vaṃśānucarita* of the *Purāṇa*. The first discusses origin myths and descent from the gods as claimed for royal lineages. The second has a rather garbled account of earlier rulers, borrowing from the *kṣatriya* descent lists of the *Purāṇas*, although the selection of names is somewhat arbitrary, such as Ikṣvāku, Pṛthu, Mandhātṛ, Trasadasyu, Sagara, Raghu, Daśaratha, Rāma, Kuśa, Atithi; and the Puranic forms of expressing succession, such as *ātmaja* (born from), or *tastut* (from), are also used. The third section provides the evidence for the establishing of the kingdom and the dynasty/dynasties that ruled. Initially the more important kings are listed, but subsequently it mentions virtually all. Genealogies play an important role in reflecting the politics of the present in terms of whom the authors select and whom they leave out. They draw on the past for providing a prologue, even if it has to be constructed afresh, and they thereby invest in the future.

The text begins with an invocation of the Guru—*om śrī gurve namaḥ* and praise of the Creator, Nārāyaṇa. The rulers of Chamba are said to be of the Sūryavaṃśa or the Ādityavaṃśā, the Solar lineage of the *Purāṇas*. The text states that "the garland of Sūryavaṃśa is wound round the neck of Nārāyaṇa." Descent therefore is traced from Nārāyaṇa via Brahmā, Kaśyapa, and various *ṛṣis* to Manu. Stories from the Vedic corpus are included to give the document a stamp of learning. From Manu it moves to his eldest son Ikṣvāku, and draws in familiar characters ending up with Daśaratha, Rāma, and Kuśa. The descent then follows Rāma's son Kuśa and includes a curious list of names—Atithi (literally, a guest), Niṣadha, Nala, and eventually Hiraṇyanābha.

Hiraṇyanābha's descendant revived the Sūryavaṃśa which had gone into decline although we are not told why. All this it would seem was before the Mahābhārata war, since a later member of the line is said to have been killed by Abhimanyu at the "batle of the Bharatas". Other descendenats include the later Ikṣvākus, such as Śākya, Śuddodhana, Lāṅgala, and so on until the list comes to the childless Sumitra.

The attempt in this section is to make two connections with the mainstream *mārga* tradition: one is a link with the succession lists in the *Purāṇas*; the other is the appropriation of the *Mahābhārata* tradition by associating one of the earlier local *kṣatriyas* with participating in the war, a technique known to other areas and other times as well. Furthermore, this introduction seeks to provide the region with a history dating to the earliest period of the historical tradition.

After a break of many years, according to the narrative, there comes the *rājā* Marū, who is a *yogasiddha* (one proficient in yoga), who marries the daughter of a king and fathers a number of sons. This suggests a new line, should an earlier one have existed. He settles one son in the village of Kalāpa and the rest in various other places in the Himalayas, and proceeds with his eldest son to Kashmir, where his son is anointed ruler of Varmapura/?Brahmapura/ Brahmaur. Subsequent to this, Marū wanders away. He appears to have been a minor chief in a subordinate political relationship with Kashmir.

His initial association in the locality was with sects of a transregional kind, such as the *yogīs*, who had a sizeable following in the western Himalayas. Such sects often invoked local practices, or those associated with non-brahmana belief, but also had affiliations to wider and older sectarian groups linked to Śaiva and Śākta cults. The local tradition is now added to the Puranic source. Marū's association with *yogīs* and his eventual disappearance suggest a break in the succession, or a cover-up for Marū having been superseded by a new contender for power. Adventurers often tie up with wandering religious teachers, for they can help in providing popular support.

Marū's son, Jayastambha, through whom the succession devolves, was brought up in Kashmir, an indication that the family were subordinate intermediaries in the kingdom of Kashmir, or else that an aspirant from Kashmir was sent to this area. A later descendant, Ajayavarman, also a *yogī*, does *tapasya* at Brahmaur, which results in the magical appearance of *liṅgas.* This leads him to renunciation. He anoints his son Meruvarman as *rājā*, for the good of the state (*rājyasiddhaye*), but the paternal link is ambiguous.

Meruvarman's act of sanskritization in establishing his credentials was to ask his Kashmiri guru to install metal images of Narasiṃha, Ganeśa, and Nandi, at Brahmaur, inscribing the latter with his *rājaśāsanam* (royal commands).[3] Prior to this there appear to have been wooden temples for a number of deities, such as Lakṣaṇādevī and Śaktidevī, all significantly *devīs* (goddesses), as was customary in many rural areas, especially in the uplands. Devī worship seems to have prevailed in the area, onto which was imposed the worship of Śiva. This would mark the entry of Puranic sects. The temples too conformed to the local pent-roof style of three-storeys.[4] The sculptor of the metal images refers to himself as Gugga, a non-Sanskritic name. The switch from wooden to stone temples was in imitation of mainstream architecture in Kashmir and the plains.

The suffix *varman* is perhaps a claim to *kṣatriya* caste. Later inscriptions of intermediaries suggest that Meruvarman raised the status of the family. He is described as belonging to the Āditya-vaṃśa—the Solar line—and the *moṣūṇa gotra*. The inscriptions are composed in faulty Sanskrit and have been dated palaeographically to about the eighth century AD, on the basis of which Meruvarman has also been dated to the same century, although this may be a little too early since he is separated from Jayastambha by ten generations.

His grandson, Lakṣmīvarman, suffered two misfortunes: one was a pestilence in which large numbers died and the other an attack by the neighbouring Kīra tribes in which he himself was killed. It is not certain whether the Kīras were from Ladakh and Tibet, as would seem likely, or from the Kīragrāma. This provides a break, ending the second section. This more legendary part of the chronicle gives way to a narrative with some precision. We are now introduced to the origin myth of the dynasty, with which the future kings of Chamba are associated.

[3] Some of these images can still be seen at Brahmaur.

[4] H. Goetz, *The Early Wooden Temples of Chamba*.

The widowed queen of Lakṣmīvarman, being pregnant, was rescued by the ministers and went into hiding in the mountains, where she gave birth to a son and was taken care of by the *brāhmaṇa purohita* of the family. She placed her son in a cave (*guha*), where they lived for a while. The ministers were secretly informed about the birth of an heir. The family priest took the queen and her son to a neighbouring state, where for some time they lived incognito with the *mlecchas* (tribal people and low castes) until they were recognized. Then the *rājā* of nearby Sukheta received them with hospitality and honour. The young boy, when of age, married the *rājā's* daughter and was given the village of Pangi, eventually to become a part of the Chamba kingdom. Assistance with wealth and an army helped him destroy the Kīras and get back his inherited status.

He ruled as Mūṣaṇavarman, establishing the possibly new dynasty of the Mūṣaka-vaṃśa, thereby also indicating the independence of the family from the overlordship of Kashmir, but claiming links with the earlier ruler, Meruvarman. The name Mūṣūṇa/Moṣūṇa, although it goes back as a *gotra* name to the time of Meruvarman, has to be explained, and this explanation is associated with the birth of Mūṣaṇavarman.

The story of his birth is curious because it is stereotypical of many origin myths in the subcontinent during the late first millennium AD. *Guha*, meaning a cave or something hidden, is frequently associated with those beyond the social pale, the people of the forest. Tribal connections hover in the background of all variants of the story. This perhaps reflects a break in descent and the coming to power of another family. The popular explanation for the name, but not given in the chronicle, is that whilst in the cave as a child he was guarded by mice (*mūṣaka*).[5] Strangely, the more obvious connection of the *mūṣaka* as the vehicle of Ganeśa is not made despite Ganeśa being one of the deities whose image was set up at Brahmaur. That this marks the use of a dynastic name for the ruling family suggests acknowledged kingship. This echoes the pattern of the Puranic *vaṃśānucarita*, where in the third section, with its lists of dynasties, legitimacy was perceived as coming through political power rather than genealogical links.

[5] J.Ph. Vogel, *Antiquities of Chamba State*, vol. I, 96ff.

An inscription of one of the king's feudatories refers to him as being of the *moṣūṇādityavaṃśa*. That the myth was reintroduced at a later point in time was doubtless for it to be a time-marker and to highlight the activities of Mūṣaṇavarman.[6]

Mūṣaka as a dynastic name is also known from the history of the Guhila Rajputs of Mewar;[7] further away, the Mūṣaka-vaṃśa refers to a ruling family in Kerala. The *Mūṣakavaṃśa-kāvya* relating to the Ay dynasty ruling in the Eli region of Malabar was composed by Atula, who was attached to the Cera court, in the eleventh century.[8] As the name of a people, *mūṣaka/mūṣika* occurs frequently in the *Purāṇas*. If Meruvarman's *gotra* was linked to this name, he need not have been a local person.

In each case the story involved a widowed but pregnant *kṣatriya* queen fleeing from enemies, protected by a *brāhmaṇa*, giving birth to a son in a cave. Added to this was an association involving a mouse with some underlying importance. Eventually, the young boy is brought up among tribal peoples, with whose aid the throne is regained.[9] What is curious is not the occurrence of the word as a name in various distant regions, but the similarities in the myths of origin. Was this story consciously carried by bards and *brāhmaṇas* to various parts of the subcontinent, making it common to many origin myths?

Interestingly, the root **mūṣ* can also be used for the word *mūṣaka,* to mean a thief or a plunderer. Was this a memory of how local people viewed the intrusion of a new family claiming

[6] Vogel has suggested that *mauṣaṇa* could perhaps be read as *pauṣaṇa*, linking it to Puṣān. The *pa* and *ma* are similar in the script. But he recognized that there was a grammatical problem in this reading: J.Ph. Vogel, *Antiquities of Chamba State*, vol. I, 97–8, 164, 197, 141ff. They are unlikely to have had a solar *gotra* and a solar *vaṃśa*.

[7] *Ep. Ind.*, 39, 191ff.

[8] Ganapati Rao, "Extracts from the Mushika-vaṃśam", 87–113; M.G.S. Narayanan, "*Mūṣakavaṃśa-kāvya* of Atula", 301–10; S. Aiyer, "An Unidentified Territory of South India", 161–75; G. Warriar, "Studies in the Mūṣaka-vaṃśa", 7, 2, 118–31 and 8, 1, 9–36; N.P. Unis, *A History of Mūṣikavaṃśa*. A name similar to *mūṣaka* also occurs in Strabo, quoting Onesicritus, who describes the Musikenoi near the Indus delta: *Geography of Strabo*, 15.1.21.

[9] R. Thapar, "The Mouse in the Ancestry", in idem, *Cultural Pasts*, 797–806.

greater rights, and appropriating a larger share in a society earlier characterized by economic reciprocity? Was this action viewed as theft? The establishment of the state sharpens the divide between those who produce and those who appropriate. The existing order appears to have been disrupted and control over land obtained through violent means. The mouse in the ancestral myth may have been invented to provide a socially acceptable explanation of the word when its meaning of plunder or theft became embarrassing.

Possibly Meruvarman was the adventurer who was given or took the *gotra* name. The mouse could have been the totem of his clan. Mūṣaṇavarman need not have been of the same lineage but sought a connection with the earlier line. The popular story would then have grown around him.[10] The later inscriptions of Āsaṭa refer not to the *gotra* but to *mauṣaṇa-kulaika-tikkaḥ*, which gives a slightly different identity. Reference is also made to *mūṣaṇa vaṃśa bhūṣaṇa maṇi*. Elsewhere, *moṣaṇa* occurs as a name and is differentiated from Ādityavaṃśa, *moṣaṇāmnaya ādityavaṃśa*.[11] There is a change from *gotra* to *vaṃśa* to *kula* to a name.

3. The State Emerges

According to the Chamba *vaṃśāvalī*, five generations after Mūṣaṇavarman came Sāhilavarman making a strong imprint of kingship. He and his successors were exalted by their royal titles—*paramabhaṭṭāraka mahārājādhirāja parameśvara*. Associated with this is the epithet *deva*, which has been translated as "divine", or, "of divine descent", but could be the term used for the king. This is an indication of a pronounced change of status. The chronicle now corroborates other sources. He is said to have defeated the *kṣatriyas*, presumably the feudatories, and founded the town of

[10] V.C. Ohri has made a similar suggestion, but on other grounds: *Sculpture of the Western Himalayas: History and Stylistic Development*.

[11] Thundhu Copper-plate Inscription of Āsaṭa, in J.Ph. Vogel, *Antiquities of Chamba State*, vol. I, 147; Chamba Copper-plate of Anandavarman, in ibid., vol. II, 41; Sungal Copper-plate of Vidagdha, in ibid., vol. I, 164; Kulait Copper-plate, in ibid., 184.

Campā which he settled as the capital, adorning it with temples. As a location it was an improvement on Brahmaur since it was centrally situated in a wider valley at a lower elevation and controlled access to other valleys and to the plains further away. A royal capital would be the seat of the court and of the administration, both of which presupposed some agrarian and commercial expansion. The shift to a broader valley provided more land for cultivation and for making grants. The state of Chamba was taking shape. The guardian deity of the town was the goddess Campāvatī, who had killed the Mahiṣāsura. Other temples, such as those to Candreśvara and Kurmeśvara, were also built at Campā.

The larger state of Chamba incorporated the smaller earlier one of Brahmaur. The vagueness of the earlier succession gives way to a well-formed idea of a dynasty. The narrative is now directed towards a presumed history with indicators of change—the shift to Chamba, the administration of a state, the centrality of caste norms, the presence of Vaiṣṇava temples, the marked status of the king as superior to the feudatories, his genealogical claims which carry the imprint of mythical times. The grants of land to *brāhmaṇas* increases from this time, indicating a stable state.

Sāhilavarman is closely associated with the *yogīs* and was himself accomplished in yoga since both he and his wife performed the required austerities. Eighty-four *siddhas*, the conventional number, are said to have appeared and there is some mention of their being from the south—*dakṣine yogasiddhe*. The marker of eighty-four *siddhas* comes first with Marū, again when the kingdom is taking shape, and then again with Sāhilavarman when it is established. The number eighty-four was because it was considered auspicious and the blessing of the *siddhas* is a different kind of legitimacy from that bestowed by *brāhmaṇas*. They granted him a boon of ten sons. The *yogī* Carpaṭi/Carpaṭa, the most renowned among them, became his perceptor and the king established a sanctuary for him. Carpaṭa was known to the Nātha cult which was a mix of esoteric Buddhism, Yogic Śaivism, and other ideas. This was a channel through which notions of magic and the supernatural entered the more conservative forms of religion. Such groups were generally linked to low-caste priests and practised rituals of birth, illness, and death.[12] They had small shrines to begin with, but when their popularity increased, so did the donations. It was doubtless at this point that the *brāhmaṇas* muscled in and there were some mutual adjustments.

Whereas the *liṅgas* conveyed the benediction of Śiva, the *yogīs* introduced a concession to popular culture which did not necessarily conform to the Sanskritic. That the succession had to go through sons born as a boon could be a hint of a break. Nevertheless, the Sanskritic mainstream was given appropriate emphasis. Sāhilavarman sought validation by building a temple to Viṣṇu. This required a special image to be sculpted from stone, only obtainable in the Vindhyas. He sent his nine sons to the plains, asking them to bring an unsullied, flawless, white stone from the Vindhyas. The stone they brought was unacceptable to the guru, who said that it had a frog inside, as indeed upon examination this was so. The sons were sent out again, but while returning with a fresh stone they were set upon by brigands and slain. The king then sent his last but eldest son, Yugākāra, who killed the brigands and returned with the stone. This stone was appropriate and was used for the image of Viṣṇu in the main temple of the Lakṣmī Nārāyaṇa complex, which the king constructed in Chamba. Sāhilavarman installed his son Yugākāra as king. He himself joined the *yogīs* and became an ascetic. Did he abdicate or was the throne usurped? Events had come round full circle with the return of the *yogīs* and their being joined by the king.

The inducting of Carpaṭa is not incidental. It has to do with the state bringing together the various communities of the region into a new identity. Carpaṭa is well known and mentioned in Buddhist and Śākta sources as influential. The participation of Carpaṭa suggests the continuation of some earlier practices and beliefs. The Nātha cult to which these groups broadly subscribed drew together the subalterns and the lower caste groups, although eventually they had patrons among the elite.

[12] M. Sharma, "Contested Claims: Land, Ritual and the Jogis of Charpaṭnath", 488–510; D.G. White, *The Alchemical Body: Siddha Traditions in Medieval India*, 81–4, 92–3.

Two elements in the story about the stone are important. One is the establishment of Vaisnavism as the pre-eminent religious base of a kingdom which would enable the newly risen monarchy to reach out to wider geographical networks and alliances—hence the stone from the Vindhyas—and to draw on a vast catchment area of Vaiṣṇavas. The coming of Vaiṣṇava Bhagavatism coincided with the expansion of the state of Chamba and, as elsewhere too, it helped to integrate social groups even if it sought the patronage of the elite. Its form of integration was to bring people into the sectarian fold as a way of entering the mainstream. The network of *siddhas,* although more flexible in assimilating beliefs, was initially distanced from the mainstream. This changed when it entered elite practices. The boon of ten sons given by the *siddhas* was in a sense nullified by the demands of the Viṣṇu image, leaving the single son and successor to bring it home. Vaisnavism would also enable the court circles to draw on a range of mythology which, although ostensibly religious, was also an endorsement of social hierarchy and the recognition of an appropriate placement in society. This would tie in with using the *Bhāgavata Purāṇa* as a source.

At another level the story legitimizes the succession of Yugākāra, who may not have been the eldest son and may have run into problems with rival claimants. The other competitors were conveniently dispatched in the story of the brigands. These events may also reflect a tension between the *siddhas* and the Puranic religion now being adopted by the royal court, and providing validation to a new polity far removed from a clan society. The *siddhas* and *yogīs* represent the first stage of acculturation between local religious practice and that which came from the plains. *Brāhmaṇas* were invited to settle by being given grants of land, which assisted the process of acculturation.

This was also the period when in the trans-Himalaya, in Ladakh and Zanskar and closer to Chamba, many Buddhist monasteries were being established, such as at Alchi and Tabo, and Buddhist texts translated into Tibetan. Some of this was under the direction of scholars such as Rin chen bzang po, in the late tenth and early eleventh century. Routes linking these areas, not only to Tibet but to Central Asian trade as well, would have affected the economy of the region. Traders from the plains and lower valleys would have been anxious to use and maintain these routes. Problems with the Kīras were not unconnected with these concerns.

Other sources state that, a couple of generations after Yugākāra, Chamba was attacked by Kashmir and the reigning king replaced by his son. This inaugurated intermittent periods of the subordination of Chamba to Kashmir. But these are not mentioned in the Chamba *vaṃśāvalī*. It continues with a succession of kings, some of whom issued inscriptions. Mention is made in the *Rājataraṅgiṇī* of a rājā of Chamba, Āsaṭa, who together with others came to a conclave in Kashmir in the late eleventh century.[13] The Kashmir chronicle does not refer to the Chamba rulers as *sāmantas.* A few successors after Yugākāra saw Vijayavarman on the throne and battling with the old enemies of Chamba, the Kīras, as also Kashmir. A new factor is referred to as the Mudgalas, which has been interpreted as the Mughals; but this seems to be a mistake since the Mughals came later, and it probably refers to an earlier group of people.

Among the successors was Bhoṭavarman, a curious name since Bhoṭa was the term used for people from Tibet. There is no indication of a break in the lineage or conquest and the name may reflect some connections with Lahul and areas of Tibetan culture. A Tibetan inscription near Brahmaur of uncertain date, but possibly of this period, refers to Markulai. This could have been the well-known Tibetan monastery of Mar-skul.[14] Bhoṭavarman's inscription of 1396 is bilingual, in Sanskrit and Chambiyali, with mistakes in both languages.[15]

The more important among the later kings, which brings the text to the sixteenth century, is Pratāpasiṃhavarman, said to be the equal of Yudhiṣṭhira in this Kali age. He encouraged the suffix of "siṃha/singh" rather than "varman". No reason is given for this being gradually taken up by later rulers. It could have been an attempt to imitate the Rajput style of the plains as an assertion of status without the myth of an Agnikula origin. It would have

[13] *Rājataraṅgiṇī*, 7.588; 7.218.

[14] Brahmor Rock Inscription, in J.Ph. Vogel, *Antiquities of Chamba State*, vol. I, 252ff.

[15] Mhesa Plate of Bhotavarman, B.Ch. Chhabra, *Antiquities of Chamba State*, vol. II, 23.

widened the circle of marriage alliances now central to the politics of hill and plain. Or it could have been an attempt to play politics with the new powers of the Sultanate and the Mughals, in association with the Rajputs. The later ruler, Pṛthvīsiṃha, in accordance with the Rajput pattern, was given a *mansab* of 1000 by the Mughals.

Pratāpasiṃhavarman is associated in the *vaṃśāvalī* with restoring temples, particularly the Lakṣmī-Nārāyaṇa temple. But before he could do so there was the problem of acquiring the necessary finances. He consulted his ministers on how he could obtain the required resources without creating further burdens for his subjects—*prajāpīḍanam vinā*. It could be that the tax was already so high that it would have been difficult to increase it. The chronicle maintains that, one night, Viṣṇu appeared to him in a dream and assured him that finances for the restoration would be provided for by the deity. On waking, the king was wondering how this could happen, when a body of peasants brought him some pieces of copper and reported the discovery of a copper mine. With the wealth from the mine he is said to have restored all the temples.

The significance of the story becomes evident from the next statement, that it was during his rule that the state of Chamba expanded its borders through conquest, and this expansion must have consumed a large part of the treasury. He defeated the neighbouring king of Nagar-kot, and returned home with much booty as well as the revenue from the fertile valley and the lands of the *sāmantas*.

Pratāpasiṃha's great-grandson was Janārdana who battled with the *rājā* Jagatsiṃha of Nurpur. Jagatsiṃha was the councillor and representative of the lord of the Yavanas—*yavanādhīśa*—a reference to the Sultans and later to the Mughals. One might have expected a disjuncture with the presence of the Yavanas but the chronicle runs on without a break. The enemy remains the kingdom of Nurpur.

Jagatsiṃha of Nurpur treacherously killed Janārdana, burnt his land, carried off his wealth, and deprived his son of the kingdom. Janārdana's young son was Pṛthvīsiṃha, who took refuge in the neighbouring mountains of Mandi and Kola. After some years,

Pṛthvīsiṃha, together with some feudatory chiefs who were his allies, battled successfully against the army of Nurpur and regained Chamba. He overpowered the *rājā* of Basholi as well, thus clearing his access to the plains. He then set off to settle scores with the representative of the Yavana. At this point the *vaṃśāvalī* breaks off, remaining incomplete.

4. The Chronicle

The Chamba *vaṃśāvalī* was the chronicle of a relatively unimportant state, but its importance is as an illustration of the kind of record maintained in such states. It covers a longer span of time than most other lesser ones. The focus is on Chamba, and occasionally on the powerful state of Kashmir. Lesser neighbours come into prominence when Chamba begins to decline. The chronology of the rulers is largely preserved, but this did not preclude some shuffling.

There is much that is stated somewhat obliquely, and which becomes a code that would have been familiar to those who read it or heard it recited. It might be useful to read beyond the obvious, but without importing too much speculation. It is therefore conceived of differently from the more realistic and relatively precise narrative and explanation given by Kalhaṇa in the *Rājataraṅgiṇī*. Nevertheless, there is a recognizable pattern.

The imprint of the *itihāsa-purāṇa* tradition is evident, as is the fact that the narrative records historical change. The need to keep a chronicle may also have resulted from the influence of monastic chronicles maintained in the Buddhist monasteries a little further afield. As with the *Rājataraṅgiṇī*, the proximity of Buddhism would have been a factor in encouraging a consciousness of recording history. The Kashmir chronicle may well have been an inspiration to lesser kingdoms, even if the result was not of the same quality.

The descent of the family is traced to one of the two main *vaṃśas* of the *Purāṇas*. The earlier names assumed to be chronological give way to genealogy as part of dynastic succession in the later part of the chronicle. The origin myth of the founder of the dynasty suggests someone who might have been an adventurer from elsewhere or a local chief asserting himself above others. These activities give way to a move towards the norms of a state and the structure of a kingdom. Succession is not a continuous flow but attempts are made to cover up the disjunctures. The narrative refers to a series of rulers and is similar to the *praśasti* in inscriptions, where the reference is to the ruling family and not just to a single ruler.

The kingdom has to expand its territory, especially with an increase in grants of land. There is more space given to campaigns in the latter part. This was not merely because of an interest in military ambitions but also because campaigns, if successful, were a source of revenue through the booty they brought and the use of prisoners of war as labour. Territorial expansion meant placing intermediaries in a hierarchy. The right of overlordship is clear from the titles used, as for example in the inscriptions commemorating these intermediaries.

The centrality of caste in the royal family was asserted, among other ways, through matrimonial alliances. Women were the crux, and this was recognized through the insistence on controlling them, even if this was not publicly conceded. Women remained the substratum, even where the manipulation of alliances often depended on their placement in political chess. The extension of caste into new areas was through the conversion of forest-dwellers and pastoralists into peasants. The clan was a relatively vertical, narrow society drawing on kin relations. Caste was more horizontally structured, with multiple identities which spread and made connections across a wide area. Grants of land to *brāhmaṇas* either introduced caste into a new area or else reiterated it where it already existed. The expansion of trade saw artisan groups also being given *jāti* identities.

The ideological validation of the state as it matured drew on Vaiṣṇava acculturation as seen in the Lakṣmī-Nārāyaṇa temple that adjoined the royal palace. The acculturation is visually reflected in architecture and icons. The link with the past was important for creating a new identity in the region by bringing together a variety of groups. The obvious way was to give them all a shared history. So although the history is of the elite it can also resonate with the others.

5. The Narrative from Inscriptions

The narrative on the rulers thins out in the latter part but there is a large amount of evidence from inscriptions. Some were the inscriptions of the *rāṇās*, the feudatories. Another category of inscriptions with a different purpose is what have been called the "fountain stone inscriptions".[16] These are attempts to catch streams of water and pass them through an opening in a stone slab which is placed at right angles to the flow of the water; it is engraved and sometimes decorated with low-relief sculpture. The fountain inscriptions are largely those of *sāmantas* and members of the elite, some of whom are *brāhmaṇas*, and reference is often made to the ruling king. They date from the eleventh to the thirteenth centuries and the dates are generally precise. Some carry short genealogies, almost in imitation of the royal *praśastis* (eulogies). The inscriptions frequently state that the fountain stones were erected to provide merit for one's parents and *sansāra-bhaya-bhitaira-varuṇna-devaḥ-sthāpitaḥ* (to ensure freedom from rebirth).[17] The quality of the Sanskrit varies from poor to reasonable.

The fountain stones may have been attempts at controlling water channels, crucial to the distribution of water in the hills, concurrent with the need for irrigation when cultivated areas expanded. Their association in popular tradition was with the Nāgas. The decoration and sculptured icons of deities tend to be more like folk art, and different from even the early images at Brahmaur and its neighbourhood. If these were attempts at recording the presence of the *rāṇās* and families of that status, then clearly they were neither extremely wealthy nor perhaps as highly sanskritized as some feudatories in other kingdoms, particularly of the plains.

Some of these and other inscriptions may have been sources for the *vaṃśāvalī*. The earliest royal inscriptions, written in indifferent Sanskrit, cluster around Brahmaur. They are inscribed on the pedestals of images and are associated with Meruvarman, as stated in the *vaṃśāvalī*.[18] In a couple of inscriptions he is described

[16] J.Ph. Vogel, *Antiquities of Chamba State*, vol. I, 209–46.

[17] Bharara Fountain Inscription, in J.Ph. Vogel, *Antiquities of Chamba State*, vol. I, 237; Siya Dudhar Fountain Inscription, in ibid., 242.

[18] Ibid., 136ff.

as belonging to the Ādityavaṃśa, which would be a synonym for Sūryavaṃśa, and to the *moṣūṇa-gotra.* This pre-dates the story about Mūṣaṇavarman. These are all brief records, suggesting that Sanskritic culture was being initiated. The genealogies are short, with no fancy linguistic frills, possibly again suggesting a relative newness to political power. Some inscriptions are of the local feudatories—the *rāṇās*, the *rājanakas*, and the *mahaśrisāmantas*. Clearly, Meruvarman was rising on the backs of the *sāmantas*.

Another larger category was the grants of land and villages, generally to *brāhmaṇas*, and more frequently recorded on copper-plates. In a copper-plate inscription Yugākāra describes himself as *dvija-guru-bhakta-paramabhaṭṭāraka-mahārājādhirāja-parameśvara,* leaving no doubt about his status.[19] The language remains incorrect inspite of the grant being conveyed by an *akṣapaṭalika*, inscribed by the *kāyastha* Jasa and signed by the king. Migrations from the plains of *kāyasthas* and *brāhmaṇas* had begun.

Two inscriptions from the reign of Somavarman, who claims to be a son of Sāhilavarman, suggest that Yugākāra may have had to contend with rival claimants for the throne,[20] also suggested in the story of the ten sons and the icon. Somavarman is not mentioned in the *vaṃśāvalī*, yet one of his inscriptions is issued from Campaka jointly with Āsaṭa, who in the *vaṃśāvalī* is five generations down from Yugākāra, probably an attempt to extend the genealogy or to deliberately omit Somavarman. He is described in the inscription as belonging to the Mūṣaṇavaṃśa. Specific mention is made of his being an upholder of the four *varṇas, deva-dvija-guru-puja . . . paripālit-cāturvarṇya-vyavastha* . . . a clear signal that the idea of caste stratification was familiar. This statement becomes a standard formula.

The eulogy on Sāhilavarman echoes the *Harṣacarita* in saying that he was a rain cloud extinguishing the fire of the Kīras and that he impaired the fame of Paraśurāma. He is also described as attacking the Turuṣkas, which may well have been hyperbole since the Turks were still distant from the Chamba valley—unless the reference is to Turkish mercenaries employed in neighbouring kingdoms.

[19] Brahmor Copper Plate Inscription, in ibid., 159ff.

[20] Kulait and Chamba Copper Plates, in ibid., 182ff., 187ff.

The king grants seventeen acres of land in areas previously occupied by what appear to have been feudatories, to a *brāhmaṇa*. The grant is made on the same terms and conditions as of the previous occupancy relating to extent of pasture lands, fallow lands, orchards, gardens, resting places and rights to enter and leave. Earlier records were consulted. The assertion of the king's right over the land would point to a substantial change in his relations with *rājās* and *rāṇās* and that he was sufficiently confident of his authority to make such a grant.

Another inscription endorses a large network of administration with a long list of officials and others concerned with the grant, referred to as constituting the eighteen *prakṛtis* (elements) of the state. It is unclear whether such a large body of officials was actually involved or present at court when the grant was made, or for that matter whether this list was imitating a convention borrowed from the style of land grant inscriptions from elsewhere—a style which might have been introduced by knowledgeable *brāhmaṇas* migrating from the plains to the hill states, since it was they who were the recipients of the grants. The designations are familiar from inscriptions outside Chamba and, as has been pointed out, it is unlikely that there would have been an officer in charge of a camel corps and an elephant wing of the army in such terrain.

An inscription from the reign of Āsaṭa issued from Campaka carries much the same information, except that there is a change of occupancy. A reference to the record-keeper—the *kāyastha* who wrote it—and the king from whom the grant was received.[21] It would seem from these inscriptions that the king was claiming ownership over certain lands, which would have been a departure from the previous system, most likely associated with clan ownership. Possibly, these lands were previously allotted by the king to functionaries, perhaps on a temporary basis, and now were reallotted permanently to *brāhmaṇas*. The original occupants may well have continued to pay the revenue and the dues to the grantee rather than to the king. Thus, what were being transferred were the rights of the king over these lands to the grantees. The gradual process by which the elements of the state come to be established and recognized is a change more evident from the inscriptions

[21] Thundhu Copper Plate Inscription, in ibid., 197ff.

than from the chronicle. This recognition appears to have taken place during the reign of Sāhilavarman and the *vaṃśāvalī* reflects it in another idiom.

Salavāhana, a name referred to in an inscription, is missing in the *vaṃśāvalī*. Clearly, the author of the *vaṃśāvalī* is indulging in some editing, and for obvious reasons. The *Vikramāṅkadevacarita* and the *Rājataraṅgiṇī* mention the king of Kashmir defeating Salavāhana of Campa and installing another king in his place.[22] Kalhaṇa says Āsaṭa visited Kashmir in about 1088, together with seven other chiefs of the western Himalaya.[23] He was recognized as superior to the others and is not referred to as a *sāmanta*. His sister being married into the Kashmir royal family, was an event registering a step up for the royal house of Chamba. She was to be the mother of the infamous Harṣa of Kashmir. As kinsmen, the royal house of Chamba assisted Harṣa against his enemies, and also used the confusion to incorporate the neighbouring areas of Curah and Pangi into the state of Chamba.

There is a profusion of land grants from the fourteenth century, when it seems that the kingdom of Chamba was well established.[24] The inscriptions, however, suggest a hesitant sanskritization of language. Most inscriptions intermingle terms in Sanskrit with the local language Chambiyali, the latter being referred to as *bhāṣā* in the epigraphs. This doubtless made it easier for local functionaries to follow the orders of the grant.

One inscription of the fifteenth century is clearly spurious since it claims to be early but uses a number of Persian terms which do not enter the Chamba vocabulary until late in the sixteenth century. The script also changes from western Gupta *brāhmī* to Kashmiri *śāradā*, to *ṭākari*, and eventually to *nāgari*.

6. The Literati

Some mention is made of *kāyasthas*, but they are not as prominent as in Kashmir. Some *paṇḍitas* who are writers of grants have a poor knowledge of Sanskrit, which could only occasionally have

[22] *Vikramāṅkadeva-carita*, 18.38; *Rājataraṅgiṇī*, 7.218.
[23] *Rājataraṅgiṇī*, 7.588.
[24] B.Ch. Chhabra, *Antiquities of Chamba State*, vol. II.

been the fault of the engraver. Local recruits to the *brāhmaṇa varṇa* may not have had the required training in Sanskrit, although the quality improves over time. The designation of *paṇḍita* seems to have been used for *brāhmaṇa* functionaries at the court. The distinction between the migrant *brāhmaṇa* who came from well-established *agrahāras*, and those who were locally inducted into brahmanhood, is perhaps indicated by their names. Thus, among the early grants there are some made to Manikaśarman of the Kaśyapa *gotra* or to Bhīmaśarman. As a contrast there are grants made, for example, to Badu Legha and to Cipu, son of Rāsi son of Jin, said to be of the Bharadvāja *gotra*.

The term *badu* was the Chambiyali for *brāhmaṇa*. In a slightly later inscription a grant is made to two *brāhmaṇas*, Gaṅgādhara and Gayadhara, who are said to be the sons of Legha.[25] Perhaps this was a deliberate Sanskritization by the sons of Badu Legha.

A grant by Pratāpasiṃhavarman in 1575 to Rāmapatiśarman of the Bharadvāja *gotra* was made as *gurudakṣiṇā* (a fee for the teacher), since Rāmapati was then *rājaguru*.[26] A *paṇḍita*, Rāmapati is mentioned as the writer of another grant of this time, so perhaps it was the *rājaguru* himself, except that once again his knowledge of Sanskrit is poor. The *rājaguru* connection goes further, in that the Chamba plate recording the first donation remained in the family of *paṇḍita* Mohan Lal, the *rājaguru* of Chamba in recent times. Interestingly, a copy of this grant was also found, doubtless intended for the royal record-office.

Pratāpasiṃhavarman made a grant of rent free land whilst on pilgrimage at Haridvāra and this was recorded at Chamba. The recipient was Badu Ratana, the son of Badu Amno and grandson of Badu Gayadhara. An inscription of about 1481 describes Gayadhara as the son of Legha and the grandson of Sarmi and an inscription of about 1522 refers to Badu Amno. We have therefore a descent list of this family of *badus*. Being recipients of land in virtually each generation, the inheritance had to be maintained as a historical record. Inscriptional data also refers to the family

[25] Saṅgrāmavarman's Grant to Badhu Legha, in B.Ch. Chhabra, *Antiquities of Chamba State*, vol. II, 34; Chamba Plate of Anandavarman, in ibid., 41.

[26] Chamba Plate of Pratāpasiṃhavarman, in B.Ch. Chhabra, *Antiquities of Chamba State*, vol. II, 57ff.

of the *rājaguru* Rāmapatiśarman/*paṇḍita* Rāmapati as coming from Gauḍa and being well endowed with grants.[27] They are not referred to as *badus*, and they use their proper Sanskrit names.

The largest number of grants was made by Bālabhadravarman, whose known dates are 1589–1642. Evidently he succeeded his grandfather when quite young. His penchant for making grants is reflected in the *vaṃśāvalī*, which refers to him, somewhat cryptically as a veritable Balikarṇa, presumably a reference to the mythical rulers Bali and Karṇa remembered for their phenomenal generosity.

That the historical tradition of a state was largely confined to the events of that state seems to explain why there is so little interest in events in other parts of northern India. The Mughals, after defeating Rajputs, Turks, and Afghans, had established their power, and even Kashmir had had Turuṣka rulers and had now become the summer resort of the imperial Mughals. Their proximity is mentioned only in passing. The imprint is apparent from the use of the occasional term which comes from the new administration. A grant to the Lakṣmī Nārāyaṇa temple is recorded in the presence of the *koṭvāla bahādara*, a Persian designation which was used in Chamba in 1592.[28]

Differentiation between the *brāhmaṇas* from Gauḍa and the local *brāhmaṇas* may have had to do with a differentiation in function, possibly leading to some tension. From this period on it is possible to spot the local *brāhmaṇa* when his *āla* or clan is named.[29] Most of these grants were written by Rāmapati, but gradually others are mentioned and then his son Lakṣmīkānt takes over the work. Apart from Gauḍa there is also mention of another grantee who was a Drāviḍa *brāhmaṇa* from the south. Presumably, he too would have found his way to a Himalayan state via the performance of rites at a place of pilgrimage. This degree of mobility would also have allowed stories of royal origin to be borrowed.

[27] Ibid., 75ff.

[28] Lakṣmī Nārāyaṇa Temple Plate, in ibid., 83.

[29] Lakṣmī Nārāyaṇa Temple Plate of Bālabhadra, in ibid., 120; Chamba Plate of Bālabhadra, in ibid., 121. One is reminded of the construction of the name Pañcāla in the *Mahābhārata*.

The number of grants became dramatically small after the reign of Bālabhadravarman. His son Janārdana was involved for twelve years in campaigns against Nurpur and was eventually killed. Had Bālabhadravarman exhausted the revenue from good arable land by his extensive grants to *brāhmaṇas*? Insistence on royal titles did not hide the reduced circumstances of the Chamba *rājās*.

The three categories of inscriptions point to distinct historical changes. Inscriptions on image pedestals are largely the records of lesser rulers and intermediaries in the initial period of contact with mainstream culture. The fountain inscriptions record the continuing presence of intermediaries and their interests. The tone changes with the grants, and once these are established and linked to the founding of the Mūṣaka dynasty there seem to be virtually no other inscriptions. This would suggest that, inspite of being a small state, the ruling family of Chamba kept a firm control over its feudatories, or at any rate that is the impression it wished to convey through the inscriptions. It would seem that the *rājagurus* and the family *purohitas* made sure that the grants came their way and appear to have been largely dependent on the royal family for their lands, of which they had a substantial amount.

The records of events and decisions are fairly full. They provide evidence of a changing history and a consciousness of a historical past. The records from Chamba carry an air of informality, doubtless deriving from it not being a powerful state. Relationships were more casual and informal than in Kashmir or Gujarat. The evidence of the *vaṃśāvalī* coincides at some points with that of the inscriptions; at other places it differs. The chronicle, when it came to the establishing of the Chamba state, seems to have taken as its source the statements in the official records. It became therefore the official history of Chamba.

The compiling of the text in the seventeenth century was not accidental. The kingdom was well established. It had connections with other states in the hills and plains. But there were also areas with which there were hostilities and it was necessary to show strength as well as a long and dominant presence in the area. The *vaṃśāvalī* and the inscriptions ensured this presence. The insistence on continuity is such that the age-old hostility against Nurpur is given more space than that against the Yavanas. There is a quiet acceptance of the Yavanas and the adaption to their ways.

Both the *Rājataraṅgiṇī* and the Chamba *vaṃśāvalī* are not altogether free of inaccuracies. The methods we use today to check these inaccuracies were not available to the authors. What is of interest is the explanation that can be given for accuracy and inaccuracy.

The addition of *siṃha* to the name, imitating Rajput usage, marks a change. This is often explained as expressing a wish to be associated with the Rajputs in opposing the Mughals. It could equally well be an attempt to enhance their own status by associating with Rajputs who had matrimonial alliances with Mughal royalty, and thereby formed an exclusive community. Chamba's hostility towards Nurpur may have also been fuelled by the wish to oust other competitors, since Nurpur had good relations with the Mughals.

The central points in the narrative are the initial settlement and the link to the descent groups of the *kṣatriyas*; the relocation of the core of the state, the succession of kings as members of dynasties, the king's claim to status and to being above the feudatories by granting land to *brāhmaṇas* to construct a support structure, by using deities for validation, and by converting a relatively egalitarian society into a society stratified by caste inequality. Unlike the *Rājataraṅgiṇī*, the Chamba chronicle makes no comment on these changes. The multiple articulations of local culture resisting a preferred uniformity can perhaps be seen in the provincializing of Puranic Hinduism.

Chronicles, as I have tried to show, may not be based on a modern type of critical enquiry; nevertheless they reflect a consciousness of history. This takes the form of narrating perceptions of the past in a manner that observes the conventions of existing historical traditions, in this case the Puranic tradition. The narrative is sequential. It also attempts to explain events. It is an approximation, therefore, of historical writing.

17

The *Prabandha-cintāmaṇi*

1. Constituents of the Jaina Historical Tradition

An alternative tradition in the writing of chronicles, different from the *Rājataraṅgiṇī* or the Chamba *vaṃśāvalī*, was that of the Jaina *prabandhas* (chronicles), of which the *Prabandha-cintāmaṇi*, written by Merutuṅga at the start of the fourteenth century, is one.[1] Merutuṅga is not of the same intellectual calibre as his predecessor Hemacandra, but his *Prabandha-cintāmaṇi* is all the same a fine example of the Jaina historical tradition. This genre becomes important in the late first and early second millennium AD with the writing of a number of biographies and chronicles pertaining to kings as well as to Elders of the Jaina Saṅgha. It has similarities with the alternative history of the Buddhist traditions. J.G. Buhler and H. Jacobi, working on Buddhist and Jaina texts, disagreed long back with the notion that there was an absence of historical writing in India, citing Buddhist and Jaina chronicles as examples of such writing. Although primarily in the form of a literary text, the *Prabandha-cintāmaṇi* recorded social and dynastic history.

Among the categories of texts constituting the Jaina historical tradition, the foremost were the *prabandhas* (chronicles) and the *caritas* (biographies). The *Dvyāśraya-kāvya* of Hemacandra,

[1] Merutuṅga, *Prabandha-cintāmaṇi*; *Prabandha-cintāmaṇi of Merutuṅga Ācārya* (The Wishing-stone of Narratives), trans. C.H. Tawney.

dating to the twelfth century, with a substantial historical content, narrated in part the history of Gujarat under the Caulukya kings, although its primary function was as a grammar. Merutuṅga, writing later, could expand on this. The history was continued further in other texts treated as sequels, such as Rājaśekhara's *Prabandhakośa*, written in 1349 to update the narrative of the *Prabandhacintāmaṇi* of 1306.

The *caritas,* sometimes also referred to as the *Purāṇas* but dissimilar to the brahmanical *Purāṇas*, were biographies of great men. The pre-eminent text was the many-volumed *Triṣaṣṭiśalākāpuruṣacarita*, composed by Hemacandra in the twelfth century. These were biographies of sixty-three important persons, some of whom were heroes of olden times, often mythological; and some were the better-known historical rulers.

There were also biographies of individual rulers, among which was Hemacandra's *Dvyāśraya-kāvya,* the *Hammīramahākāvya* of Nayacandrasūri, and the *Vastupāla-Tejaḥpāla praśasti* of Jayasiṁha. *Caritas* and *prabandhas* are sectarian writings meant to edify an audience, but historical situations lie at their core.

The seat of authority in the Saṅgha was known as the *paṭṭa*, hence the importance of the *paṭṭāvalīs*, *guruvāvalīs*, and *sthavirāvalīs* providing the succession lists of the Elders, where *āvalī* was a lineage. These claimed to be a continuous succession from the time of Mahāvīra and were larger in number among the Śvetāmbara Jainas. There is a gradual shift from succession lists to the history of the institution. Since the manuscripts were repeatedly copied in the monasteries, their colophons provided evidence of this activity.

Many texts had colophons giving essential information about the author and the text. But the Jaina texts are somewhat unique in the length of their colophons and the range of information they provide; the name and background of the author and of the patron, the ruling king, the associated officers, the name of the copier, the date of the text, and whatever else seemed appropriate. The information was necessary as a record of who wanted the text copied and for what pious act. To some degree, the colophons are comparable to the *praśastis* in the copper-plate grants. Given the extraordinary literary activity in Jaina communities, these colophons are like brief summaries of the historical context of the book.

The other category of text common to virtually every part of the subcontinent was of course the epigraph. Inscriptions of this period of the history of Gujarat are found as usual on stone slabs, pillars, copper-plate charters, and on the pedestals of images, largely Jaina. Their contents are contemporary records, but among the more important ones there are references to dynastic history. There is a fair degree of corroboration between epigraphs and texts. They are issued as usual by kings, ministers, and *sāmantas* of various categories.

Secular texts—such as grammars, lexicons, works on logic, and mathematics, astronomy, and medicine as well as manuals of administration—all contributed to lively intellectual activity. Later writers referred back to earlier ones in their discussions. The language gradually changed from Ardha-Māgadhi and Prākrit to Sanskrit.

2. The Background to the Texts

There are many similarities in the Buddhist and Jaina traditions. Both grow out of the need to record the teachings and activities of historical figures, Mahāvīra and the Buddha. Mahāvīra is dated to approximately the sixth-fifth centuries BC, just prior to the Buddha. The generally accepted date for the death of Mahāvīra is 527 BC, although this date too, as that of the Buddha, has been re-examined in recent years and subjected to a range of fifty or so years. Nevertheless, within the Jaina chronological tradition there is by and large an adherence to a single date. Mahāvīra taught in the same geographical area as the Buddha—the middle Ganges plain. The Jaina tradition therefore focused on what it viewed as the history of the spread and establishment of his teaching, his biographies being written in later centuries.[2]

As with the Buddhist tradition, there was a questioning of

[2] For a general survey of Jaina teaching and texts, see P.S. Jaini, *The Jaina Path of Purification*; P. Dundas, *The Jains*; S. Stevenson, *The Heart of Jainism*; J.P. Jain, *The Jain Sources of the History of Ancient India*.

brahmanical beliefs such as those related to the Vedic deities. Deities have little or no place in early Jaina texts, nor the efficacy of Vedic rituals, the power of the divine being unacceptable. There was also a difference in defining the social ethic. Observing the *varṇāśramadharma,* with its caste-bound duties and obligations was not central to the ethic, since it was argued that the social ethic was universally applicable and involved the behaviour of one human being towards another irrespective of caste and sect. A distinction was maintained in Jaina thought between the ethic for the lay follower and that for the renunciate. The former was in some ways less rigorous and made some concession to local custom.

The Jaina historical tradition also had a distinctive gloss which tended to contradict or at least differ from the narrative in the brahmanical tradition. Jaina authors maintained that they were writing to dispel the untruths of other, primarily brahmanical, versions.[3] Two of the major brahmanical *Purāṇas* are hostile to the Jainas and predict that there will be some kings who will patronize the *pāṣaṇḍas* (false heterodox sects), and that people will attack *brāhmaṇas* and their rituals.[4] It is said that Viṣṇu created a man with deluded ideas (*mahāmoha*) to teach false doctrines, and those who converted to the heterodox sects were *rākṣasas*.

The early Jaina corpus is associated with centres linked to the region of Mathura. Among the texts are the *Kalpasūtra* and the *Ācārāṅgasūtra*, which include biographical references to Mahāvīra. He came from a *gaṇa-saṅgha* background and belonged to a clan which was part of a confederacy of clans based in Vaiśāli. Clan societies were in conflict with emerging kingship in Magadha, a conflict referred to in other texts as well. Nevertheless, the kings are claimed as patrons of the new ideologies and kinship links suggested.[5] Such connections may well have been an afterthought since the texts date to a few centuries later than the events.

[3] *Paumacariyam*, 2.117.

[4] *Bhāgavata Purāṇa*, 5.6.9–11; *Śiva Purāṇa,* 2.5.4.1–24, quoted in P.S. Jaini, "Jaina Purāṇas: A Puranic Counter-tradition", in W. Doniger (ed.), *Puranic Perenesis*, 207ff.

[5] S. Ohira, *A Study of the Bhagvatīsūtra: A Chronological Analysis*; J.P. Jain, *The Jaina Sources of the History of Ancient India*, 16ff.

Mahāvīra was familiar with the teachings of a number of sects that took non-orthodox positions. In composing some of these records an attempt was made to give them greater authenticity by locating them at a particular historical place and time. As in the case of the Buddhists, the first converts to his teaching are said to be *brāhmaṇas,* which may have provided the necessary status for the teaching.

Similar to the Buddhist tradition, the impetus to a historical perspective was given by the nature of the society from which Jainism grew. This required a list of teachers and statements on the teaching, some of which were part of the Canon. With the spread of the teaching came variants in observation and practice, resulting in dissident groups and schisms and diverse viewpoints. There was a need to sort out the disparities or recognize the differences and this took the form of a number of Councils. The Canon was first put together at Pāṭaliputra, recording the teachings and history to that point. These were reconstituted, or reiterated if need be, at Mathura in about the fourth century AD, and yet again a couple of centuries later at Valabhī in western India. By now the split into the two major schools—the Śvetāmbaras (white-clad monks) and Digambaras (sky-clad, i.e. naked monks)—was established.

The differences between the two sects were reiterated whenever the opportunity arose, especially when Jainism became prominent in some areas in the later first millennium AD. Jainas from Mathura tended to move to western India when patronage in northern India declined. A record of these changes was thought necessary even if each group maintained its own, not always in agreement with the other. In a sense, such records were the precursors of the *prabandhas* (chronicles) written by Jaina authors in later times, often bearing on the secular activities of rulers though not devoid of religious content.

The assertion of the Jaina perspective on early texts from the brahmanical tradition took the form, for example, of new versions of the *Rāmāyaṇa* and *Mahābhārata*. In the case of the former, this was the *Paumacariyam* of Vimalasūri; and of the latter, Jinasena's *Harivaṃśa-purāṇa.* Among the texts incorporating historical traditions were the *caritas*, *prabandhas*, and *paṭṭāvalīs*. These recorded the succession of the Elders of the Order but also dated the reigns of kings, occasionally including members of merchant families where they were patrons. Collectively, this provides both narrative and chronology, recalling passages from the Buddhist Theravāda tradition. Similar information was included in the colophons to these texts. The focus was naturally on personalities and events connected with the Jaina religion.

By the early second millennium AD in Gujarat, the influence of Jaina personalities was largely due to their being statesmen, ministers, generals, and wealthy merchants. Their political connections and dominant position in society required that their activities be recorded, even if the record was ostensibly concerned with religious activities. A fair amount can be read between the lines. Fortunately, we also have inscriptions issued by kings referred to in the chronicles, or in their reign, and these act as corroborative records.

In the turn to history, some persons from the past recur often. Śreṇika, also known as Bimbisāra of Magadha, becomes a historical marker in Jaina texts and the claim to authenticity is sometimes made by stating that the narration of events in a particular text took place in the presence of, or was told to, Śreṇika. The Mauryas receive attention, the claim being that the founder of the dynasty, Candragupta Maurya, became a Jaina towards the end of his life—as supposedly did his great-grandson, Samprati. Aśoka from the same family having been appropriated by the Buddhists, the Jainas may have thought of claiming the patronage of the other two, who were treated as major Jaina patrons.[6] This appropriation reflects the historical time when there was considerable interest in Sramanic teaching. The choice of Candragupta almost inevitably brought his *brāhmaṇa* minister Cāṇakya/Kauṭilya into the picture, since by all accounts the young king was the protégé of the *brāhmaṇa*.

Historical writing was not restricted to royal activities. When monasteries became powerful institutions, as they did with the patronage of kings and merchants, the succession of monks holding office had to be recorded. This "lineage" of monastic Elders took the form of lists of succession. Where the monk was

[6] E.g. *Bhadrabāhu cāṇakya candragupta kathānaka evam rājā kalkivarṇan.*

important, there was a biography as well.[7] Jaina monks performed rituals for their lay supporters and also recorded events relating to those important in the community.[8]

The need to maintain records also arose from the broader ideological background of those sects and communities that were opposed to brahmanical views, of which there were quite a few. The opposition took various forms: the denial of deity and sacrificial rites; the non-acceptance of an immortal soul, *ātman*, and its rebirth, different from the continuity of consciousness or the self; and a refusal to concede that society was governed by immutable rules deriving from divine sanction, such as those of *varṇāśramadharma*.

The category of *nāstikas,* among which such groups were included, ranged across a spectrum of non-orthodox thought, some at one extreme in pursuing a life of hedonism, others insisting on virtually altruistic social ethics. The concern with the centrality of the human condition, and of the origin of the institutions of society lying in human needs, was common to all such sects. This tended to encourage turning to the past to understand the reason for the existence of institutions and to view them as continuous from previous time to now.

3. Some Notions about Earlier Times

The shape of the Jaina universe was like an hourglass, with heaven located at the top, the earth in the middle, and many hells below it. The earth was a circular island, at the centre of which lay Jambudvīpa, surrounded by six concentric rings that were also islands separated by oceans. In the middle of Jambudvīpa was Mount Meru which, given its pivotal position, was inhabited by gods. The area around it was divided by mountains into seven continents, the southernmost being Bhāratavarṣa. This has mountains as a boundary and the two rivers Sindhu and Gaṅgā flow through it. The *janapadas* within the area is where the civilized live, whilst the barbarians inhabit the peripheries. Distances are

[7] P. Granoff, "Religious Biography and Clan History among Śvetāmbara Jains in Northern India", 195–211.

[8] The system prevails to this day among Hindu *pāṇḍā* priests.

vast and virtually immeasurable, although they are said to be measured by ropes (as was also the case in the administration of cultivated land for purposes of assessing tax).

The time cycle is a perpetually slow-turning wheel divided into six segments. The upward movement of the wheel is towards happiness and the downward is the reverse. Humans were born in pairs in remote antiquity and the continuity of society was through their procreation, an idea somewhat parallel to that of sibling incest in Buddhist origin myths. The initial extremely long life of humans decreases over time. The number of wish-fulfilling trees also declines dramatically, which then leads to the need for humans to labour. The *tīrthaṅkaras,* literally the ford-makers, come to teach the doctrine, although they come after long intervals,[9] suggesting the larger spans of cyclic time. This is a contrast to the firmly linear shorter time-frame time of the Jaina chronicles.

Historical concerns begin with discussions on what there was in the remote past and how different it was. The history of the universe begins with Ṛṣabha, who pronounced the earliest teaching. All mankind was a single caste—*manuṣyajātirekaiva*—and divisions arose because of livelihood and conflict. Ṛṣabha, seeing the disorder in society, decided to discipline it by instituting occupational groups which were given the names of castes—*kṣatriya*, *vaiśya* and *śūdra*.[10] His son was Bharata, known for propagating non-violence.[11] He created the *brāhmaṇas*, who initially lived up to Jaina ideals and kept away from violence. Currently, *brāhmaṇas* who sacrificed animals were apostates.[12] This was viewed as radical thinking, similar to that of the Buddhists; therefore the Jaina *śramaṇas* are also treated with contempt in brahmanical texts. Setting eyes on a Jaina monk was regarded as an ill omen!

Some of the names claimed as historical are common to other traditions as well. Apart from the initial twenty-four *tīrthaṅkaras*, two heroes from the epic tradition, Rāma and Kṛṣṇa, were popular

[9] J. Cort, "Genesis of Jaina History", 469–506.

[10] Jinasena, *Ādipurāṇa,* 16.179.

[11] Ibid., 38.8–32.

[12] Jinasena, *Ādipurāṇa*, 38.45, quoted in P.S. Jaini, *The Jaina Path of Purification*, 288.

and their stories are often retold. Perhaps Vaiṣṇava Bhagavatism was a competitor and therefore there was an attempt to present a Jaina perspective on the two epics, projected as true to what actually happened. These two heroes were part of the sixty-three *śalākāpuruṣas* (persons of renown), some of whom were known and others imagined, whose hagiographies were recorded. These became seminal to some of the biographies of rulers in the early second millennium AD.

Ultimately, the list of *tīrthaṅkaras* comes to Mahāvīra, who is clearly historical. The associating of teachers with royalty, which was frequent in this tradition, makes him a contemporary of king Śreṇika. The biography of Mahāvīra was written in later centuries, often together with the other *tīrthaṅkaras* who were teachers of the doctrine. Mahāvīra was sometimes given a kinship link to Bimbisāra, comparable to the attempt to link the Mauryas to the Śākyas. By the mid-first millennium the narratives had a larger component of the historical, as in the *Kālakācārya Kathānaka* and the *Vasudevahiṇḍi*. Dynasties of the Śakas, Śuṅgas, Guptas, and Pratihāras were referred to. Hemacandra, for instance, sought to correlate the succession of kings with that of Elders. Where the *paṭṭāvalīs* pertained to religious authority, the *rājāvalīs* listed secular authority. The ninth-century *Ādipurāṇa* of Jinasena attempted a reformulation of the Jaina tradition, probably urged by his being the religious preceptor of the Rāṣṭrakūṭa king Amoghavarṣa I.

The names of the Elders and of important monks of the various sects and institutions—the *senas*, *saṅghas*, and *gacchas*—and the correct succession to office are recorded and where possible correlated with reigning kings, which was chronologically useful.

The hagiographies of teachers may have encouraged the idea of biographies of rulers. A number of contemporary rulers are mentioned in connection with the narratives, including Bhoja Paramāra of Mālava against whom the Caulukyas campaigned, Jayacanda of Varanasi and Kanauj, Pṛthvīrāja Cāhamāna/Cauhāna, the Candella ruler Parmardideva, and in passing Lakṣmaṇasena of Gauḍa and Hammīra.

Discussions on kingship touched on perceptions of the past. The *Ādipurāṇa* maintains that kingship was not imposed on human society by the gods, although there is some uncertainty about the authority of the human king in terms of what he controls. He too is ideally subject to the Jaina ethic.[13] Superiority, however, lies in renunciation and the path of the monk. There is less emphasis on military campaigns, even for purposes of protection, although campaigns were not disbanded. Protection could also be ensured by accumulating wealth in order to distribute it in *dāna* (charitable gift-giving). The exemplar would probably have been Aśoka from the Northern Buddhist tradition. Protection is also required from the *brāhmaṇas* who delude people and whose wealth should be taxed. This reverses what is said about *śramaṇas* in the brahmanical *Purāṇas*. The centrality of *ahiṃsā* as a primary commitment in the social ethic distinguishes the Śramaṇa religions from Brahmanism, even if the practice of politics did not necessarily lead to an abjuring of violence by army commanders who were sometimes Jainas.

The *Nītivyākāmṛta* of Somadevasūri, a Digambara Jaina monk from the South, also discusses attitudes towards kingship.[14] The text initially invokes not a deity but his guru. As advice to princes, he was following the *Arthaśāstra* of Kauṭilya, although his Jaina commitment to rationalism and logic as necessary to kingship is apparent.[15] He distanced himself from the more materialist Lokāyata-Cārvāka view which he thought was too close to hedonism, and as such not close enough to morality.[16] Somadeva expresses admiration for Kauṭilya, who enabled Candragupta Maurya to establish a state for the welfare of all. Possibly this example was chosen because by now Candragupta was said to have become a Jaina. The ethos of Kauṭilya would hardly have been appropriate for a good Jaina monk.[17]

Ahiṃsā allowed the smooth working of society presumably because it disallowed violence as a solution to conflict. Somadeva saw society as having moved historically from *rāṣṭra* to *deśa* to *viṣaya* to *janapada*, from a society drawing wealth from agro-pastoral activities to increasing this wealth by other economies.[18]

[13] Chapter 42.

[14] Somadevasūri, *Nītivyākāmṛta*.

[15] 5.49–56.

[16] 5.33, 1.41.

[17] 10.4.

[18] 19.1–4.

Among these he mentions the extensive use of metal, the high production of goods, the organization of guilds, accumulated wealth, and the maintenance of irrigation. The authority to rule involves ensuring that there were no caste preferences before the law and all subjects were protected. Protection from the powerful and the establishment of a just authority requires the existence of the state.

The state was for him of considerable importance, ensuring the co-existence of all beings and the punishment for criminals. He argues that ignorance is the worst possible condition and that knowledge is primary in all public matters. In case of disputes the king is the arbiter and can refer a matter to the *sabhā* (a council). If accused, a king has also to submit to judgement.[19] He doubts the veracity of the king being a deity, as stated in some brahmanical texts. Following Kauṭilya he refers to the six expedients of the state, which in his list are wars, treaties, invasions, surrender, apathy, and duplicity. To kill an unarmed fallen foe was the equivalent of killing a *brāhmaṇa*.[20] This was an unlikely comparison coming from a Jaina, but perhaps by now the analogy had become shorthand for the worst conceivable act. Kingship is a matter of ruling ethically for when the strong devour the weak anarchy sets in. It is better to have a foolish king than to not have one—an opinion Kauṭilya would not have endorsed. *Brāhmaṇas*, *kṣatriyas*, and kinsmen should never be given a place of authority as they all misappropriate state funds.[21]

4. The Jaina Tradition in Gujarat

Merutuṅga's work on the Caulukyas (or Solaṅkis, as they are also called) draws on the immense scholarship of the earlier Jaina scholar, Hemacandra, who wrote in the twelfth century and was widely quoted. His scholarship was phenomenal, bringing together various strands of grammatical and philosophical thinking as well as the Jaina historical tradition. In what is seen as a *tour de force*, the *Dvyāśraya-kāvya*, a work on grammatical forms, incorporated in the Prākrit section a biography of the contemporary king,

[19] 27.1–38.
[20] 28.15, 28.37–44, 30.88, 112.
[21] 5.53, 9.8, 1.3, 18.21.

Kumārapāla, and similarly in the Sanskrit section a brief survey of the Caulukya dynasty to which the king belonged.[22]

The chronology in this section is generally correct. There are many vignettes on the persons who ruled and their association with others. References to Caulukya campaigns and victories are selective and defeats are passed over. Bhīma, who may have fled when Mahmud of Ghazni desecrated the temple at Somanātha, is not mentioned, but it is said that Bhīma pursued Mahmud on a later occasion. However, opposition to the kingdom is recorded—from the forest-dwellers labelled jointly as Bhillas, from lower-caste groups such as Ābhīras and Jāṅgalas, as well as from the *mleccha* here spoken of as the Turuṣka/Turks, Yavanas, Śakas and Hūṇas.

The more massive work of Hemacandra was the *Triṣaṣṭiśalākā-puruṣa,* the narratives on sixty-three great men, and its appendix, the *Pariśiṣṭaparvan,* also known as the *Sthavirāvalī.*[23] This, according to some, was written for the edification of his royal patron Kumārapāla, a king who was the subject of many works from Jaina authors since they held that he was gradually converted to Jainism by Hemacandra, who was his minister.[24]

Hemacandra, who inspired Merutuṅga, was born in Kathiawar to a *vania*, a merchant caste of Jainas, in 1088 and was brought up from childhood by a Jaina monk, which ensured his access to scholarship.[25] He lived mainly in Aṇahilapāṭana, the capital of the Caulukya kingdom, and his first royal patron was the ruler Jayasiṁha Siddharāja. He continued to be active into the reign of the successor king, Kumārapāla, whom he is said to have converted to Jainism. Hemacandra died in 1173, whilst Kumārapāla was reigning.

The *Triṣaṣṭiśalākāpuruṣa-carita* encompasses a perspective that seems to sweep in popular stories about people from the past. The

[22] *Hemacandra's Dvyāśraya-mahākāvyam.*

[23] *Triṣaṣṭiśalākāpuruṣacarita.*

[24] Jayasiṁha, *Kumārapāla-bhupāla-carita,* Jinamandana, *Kumārapāla-prabandha,* Śrisomatilakasūri, *Kumārapāla-deva-caritam,* Somaprabhācārya, *Kumārapāla-prabandha-pratibodha*, all of a slightly later period. Jinavijayamuni, *Kumārapāla-caritra-saṁgraha*, vol. 41, is a collation of some texts.

[25] G. Buhler, *Life of the Jaina Monk Hemacandra.*

sixty-three biographies are made up of the following categories of persons, important to Jainism:

24 *tīrthaṅkaras,* ford-makers, or teachers
12 *cakravartins*, great men, who rule vast territories
9 *vāsudevas*, who are righteous and opposed to the following
9 *prati-vāsudevas*, whom they are destined to destroy
9 *baladevas,* non-violent laymen

When a person is labelled as one among these, the characteristics of the narrative are almost predictable. Curiously, both Baladeva and Vāsudeva are personal names of members of the Vṛṣṇi clan and involved in the events narrated in the Jaina *Harivaṃśa*, which includes Jaina versions of some of the stories in the *Mahābhārata*.

The text inevitably draws upon the tradition of Jaina Elders from the past but also takes in characters from the epics. Starting with the story of Ṛṣabha, it moves on to the heroes of the brahmanical *Purāṇas*, such as Bharata and Sagara of the Lunar lineage, interleaving them with stories of Jaina *tīrthaṅkaras.* Echoing the *Mahābhārata,* the life of Kṛṣṇa is narrated with a focus on his enmity with Jarāsandha, the ruler of Magadha. This is given far greater prominence than the story of the Pāṇḍavas. Kṛṣṇa is of course not an *avatāra* of Viṣṇu in this version, and descriptions are given of his rather worldly interests culminating in his death. The choice of Rāma and Kṛṣṇa was obviously because of the widely known epics. But it may also have been that, because they had been deified in the later redaction of the epics and become the literature of Bhagavatism, the Jaina versions were a response questioning this conversion. Jainas believed that the *brāhmaṇas* had falsified the narratives and were therefore *kuśāstra-vādins*, as stated in the *Paumacariyam.*[26] The epic stories precede the biography of Mahāvīra, suggesting that they may have been thought to have occurred prior to the rise of Magadha at the time of Śreṇika. Many other lives are narrated in the text.

From the perspective of Jaina historical traditions the more precise text of a concise history is the *Sthavirāvalī-carita* or

[26] P.S. Jaini, "Mahābhārata Motifs in the Jaina Padma Purāṇa", 108–15.

the *Pariśiṣṭaparvan* of Hemacandra, the appendix to the *Triṣaṣṭi-śalākāpuruṣa*.[27] It draws from a variety of Jaina sources, such as *Vasudevahiṇḍi* in Prākrit, the narratives of the *Kathānaka* and other literature, as well as from commentaries on earlier writing referred to variously as *sūtras*, *cūrṇis*, *niruktas*, and *ṭīkās*. The primary themes are the biography of Mahāvīra, the history of the kings of Magadha in the main, and of Jaina *munis* and the Jaina Saṅgha.

The status of Mahāvīra is established through his upper-caste birth, the marginal intervention of deities at this event, and the first converts being *brāhmaṇas*. Both Buddhist and Jaina traditions use Magadha as their initial context, and this links the new teachings to the emergence of kingship. The narrative of Nanda rule continuing to the Mauryas is given in some detail, as also Cāṇakya organizing the usurpation of the Nanda throne by Candragupta. This was also the period of the spread of the Śramaṇa religions. The sending of Jaina missions is linked to the reign of Samprati, the grandson of Aśoka, and suggests parallels with the Buddhist missions said to have been sent by Aśoka. The central date is that of the death of Mahāvīra, taken as the equivalent of 527 BC, but the narratives are said to be later, dating from the time of Bhadrabāhu, which is given as 170 years after Mahāvīra. Candragupta is said to have renounced the throne and travelled to South India with Bhadrabāhu, the Jaina teacher. This date would be half a century earlier than the date for Candragupta calculated on the basis of other sources. The text concludes with the period prior to that of the Caulukyas.

The *Pariśiṣṭaparvan* has narratives about various early rulers of Magadha, doubtless to reinforce the date of Mahāvīra. These are the sections referred to as Pāṭaliputra-parvan, Nandarājyalābha, Cāṇakya Candragupta-kathā, Aśokaśrikunāla-kathā and Samprati-rājā-carita.[28] The narratives reflect the perceptions of the polity of Magadha of early times as envisaged in twelfth-century Gujarat.

[27] *Sthavirāvalī/Pariśiṣṭaparvan of Hemachandra*; R.C. Fynes (trans.), *The Lives of the Jaina Elders*; *Bhadrabāhu cāṇakya candragupta kathānaka evam rājā kalkivarṇan*; P. Granoff (ed.), *The Clever Adulteress and Other Stories: A Treasury of Jaina Literature*, 189–207.

[28] 6.231–52, 8.1–10, 194–469, 9.14–54, 11.23–127.

Śreṇika is described as visiting Mahāvīra to hear his teaching (as he did with the Buddha in the Buddhist tradition) and this was doubtless intended to give added stature to Mahāvīra. There is also a historical continuity of events. Whereas Śreṇika is associated with the earlier capital of Rājagṛha, the Nanda king is linked to ruling from the recently founded Pāṭaliputra, which was to become the imperial capital of the Mauryas. Unlike other accounts of the city, it is described here as a temple centre of the Jainas—despite their having had no temples at that time. After seven Nanda rulers, the *brāhmaṇa* Cāṇakya reversed their fortunes and the throne was taken by his protégé Candragupta Maurya.

There are many stories of Cāṇakya's tactics to ensure this, as in Viśākhadatta's *Mudrārākṣasa.*[29] In the Jaina tradition Cāṇakya is said to be a Jaina, but because he is a *brāhmaṇa* he is unscrupulous in his actions—a Jaina view of the *brāhmaṇas.* The villainous *brāhmaṇa* is not a surprising image, given that Jainism arose partially in opposition to brahmanical thinking. The curious story about the birth of the next Mauryan ruler, Bindusāra, was part of a play on his name, but the story about Aśoka and his son Kunāla seems to have been borrowed from the Northern Buddhist traditions. Samprati, who is not claimed by the Buddhists, is here described as a patron of the Jainas, and is also responsible for dispatching Jaina missions to South India.

That the Buddhists and the Jainas selected and allotted to themselves the Mauryan rulers would suggest that the Mauryas did patronize the heterodox sects rather than the *brāhmaṇas*. They are prominent in the writings of the heterodox authors, whereas their names are barely mentioned in brahmanical texts—another indication of ideological concerns influencing the perception of the past.

The early history of Magadha was important in both Jaina and Buddhist traditions, this being the area and the approximate period of their original teachings and first propagation. It was after its history in Magadha that Jaina teaching was organized canonically and spread to Mathura, western India, and the South. It recalls a time when Buddhist and Jaina sects had political patronage, and

[29] See chapter 8.

to that extent it was their "golden age". Magadha was projected as an early utopia. Heterodoxy lay in describing the *Vedas* as untrue and the ritual of sacrifice as false posturing, based on the slaughtering of animals.[30] There is an attempt to look historically at the reasons for the emergence of heterodoxy, but not necessarily in any depth.

Narratives are basic to explaining the teaching and often popular stories are reformulated to suit the ethics of Jainism as in the story of Rāma taken from Vālmīki's *Rāmāyaṇa* and changed according to Jaina ideas. Sermons and dogma become less direct when interwoven with stories. The ambience in these stories is often that of merchant society, substantial patrons of the Jaina Saṅgha.

5. Merutuṅga's *Prabandha-cintāmaṇi*: Sources and Audience

The *Prabandha-cintāmaṇi* by Merutuṅga, written in 1306, is a history of Gujarat narrating the reigns of kings of the Cāvaḍā and Caulukya dynasties in the main, ending with the Vaghelas, and with marginal references to other associated dynasties such as the Pratihāras, Candellas, and Parmāras. It focuses on the previous five centuries but is aware of earlier histories. To that extent it is a chronicle of the region. Written from a Jaina ideological perspective, its intention differs from the *Rājataraṅgiṇī* and the Chamba *vaṃśāvalī*.

Merutuṅga's scholarship is not of the same high quality as Hemacandra's. Nevertheless, he obviously took the trouble to consult widely in putting together his account of the dynasties that ruled in Gujarat, focusing on the Caulukyas. He says many have written on the same subject and expressed diverse views; he has selected what appeared to him as the most likely past. This suggests a range of sources and an awareness of inconsistencies. He is more centrally concerned with providing dynastic history, although not altogether shorn of some added events and emphases.[31]

[30] 4.19–35.

[31] A.K. Majumdar, *Caulukyas of Gujarat*, provides a survey of this history.

Sources that he is likely to have consulted on the Cāvaḍās, for instance, would have included the bardic version of the dynastic histories, the *Ratnamālā* of Kṛṣṇakavi composed in the thirteenth century,[32] and for others Someśvara's *Kīrtikaumudi*. The chronology of dynastic history incorporated a series of stories in each reign, pertinent to kingship and to the Jaina social ethic. History, therefore, is also an illustration of good kingship and the superiority of Jaina teaching. Hemacandra is evoked, particularly in what was believed to be his great achievement—converting Kumārapāla. Such a major conversion would be a prime subject for history.

Merutuṅga's sources would therefore have been earlier Jaina texts of a historical nature. Particularly important for reconstructing chronology was the availability of colophons from a variety of texts from the eleventh century, with their invaluable information. For example, the titles given to kings could be indications of their power as perceived from local usage, or the visualization of the author. Thus in the earlier books Jayasiṁha is referred to merely as ruling, whereas later colophons give him elaborate royal titles.[33] Merutuṅga states that he was assisted by Guṇacandra, who wrote the first manuscript copy of the *Prabandha-cintāmaṇi*.

As in most kingdoms, inscriptions were a valuable source of information and defined a particular format of court record, such as the *praśasti,* which observed a historical pattern in differentiating between the present and the past. These could be used as sources for historical statements should the authors choose. If the inscriptions are read seriatim, they provide an outline of dynastic events.

This is also reflected in the format of the text which is somewhat different from most chronicles. The narratives are smaller individual *prabandhas* named after the main person of the story and arranged chronologically. These are then strung together in chronological order, and the succession of rulers and their

[32] G.C. Choudhury, *Political History of Northern India from Jaina Sources, c. 650* AD *to 1300* AD, 200–307. A.K. Forbes, when writing the history of Gujarat which he called the *Rāsmālā*, depended heavily on these bardic sources.

[33] G.C. Choudhury, *Political History of Northern India from Jaina Sources*, 48–9.

activities read as a single text. Many *prabandhas* begin with the phrase *kadācit* (once upon a time). Predictions in the course of a story sometimes act as introductions to a theme and provide a play on time where a future refers back to the past. The Sanskrit of the narratives is relatively simple, with less of an overlay of literary embellishments common to many authors at the time.

Merutuṅga was a Jaina of high standing and moved in court circles. The audience for his writing was both members of the court and the Jaina community outside the court. His wish to reach out to the wider audience in celebrating Jaina achievements of the time might account for the more accessible language, which makes it rather different from the *Rājataraṅgiṇī*.

The chronicle would have been read by courtiers of more than one generation, wishing to be acquainted with the history of Gujarat, perhaps to draw lessons from the past. It would also have been read by monks, who would then deliver sermons to lay followers and others that were interested, on the great events and personalities of the past linking their lives to the Jaina ethic. These narratives are about many kings, but those that were partial to Jainism are specially commented upon and their actions treated as exemplary. In this second capacity the text would be transmitted both by reading and oral renderings.

6. The Narrative

The *Prabandha-cintāmaṇi* gives more importance to the Caulukya dynasty, which coincided with the high point of activity by Jainas in various offices of governance, and was linked to patronage. This history is therefore informed and detailed, even if accompanied by a fair amount of story-telling.

A list of Caulukya kings is provided: Mūlarāja I; Cāmuṇḍarāja; Vallabharāja followed by his brother; Durlabharāja; Bhīmadeva, who was the nephew of another brother; Karṇa; Jayasiṁha Siddharāja; Kumārapāla, a nephew of Jayasiṁha and great-grandson of the brother of Karṇa; Ajayapāla; Mūlarāja II; Bhīma II; Tribhuvanapāla; Arjuna; Saraṅgadeva; Karṇa. Regnal years are given for the Cāvaḍās and the Caulukyas, and are dated in the Vikrama *saṃvat*.

The focus is on the two leading rulers of consequence, Jayasiṁha Siddharāja and Kumārapāla. The rulers up to Kumārapāla are the same as in the Vadnagar *praśasti* inscription issued during the reign of Kumārapāla.[34] The *praśasti* was composed by Nāgara *brāhmaṇas* aspiring to high status. In this they were successful, which may in part account for the *praśasti*.

Caulukya rule begins in approximately AD 996, when the Cāvaḍās were replaced. In the thirteenth century, during the reign of Bhīma II, *c.* 1178–1239, the Vaghela chief was helping Bhīma II retain his position, indicating that the decline had begun. Soon the Vaghelas became the effective rulers. In 1299 Ulugh Khan annexed Gujarat and the axis of power began to shift in the direction of what was eventually to emerge as the Sultanate of Gujarat. This was when Merutuṅga was researching and writing the *Prabandha-cintāmaṇi*. The kingdom of Gujarat was most often in conflict with the Paramāras to its east, the Cāhamānas/Cauhānas of Nadol to the north, the rulers of Konkan to its south, and those referred to as the *mlecchas*—most likely the Arabs, Turks, and Afghans settling in north-western India.

Since this text is not closely tied to the *itihāsa-purāṇa* tradition, the history it narrates is somewhat different. There is less on origin myths, although these are not altogether excluded. There is also little on claiming ancestry with ancient lineages and descent groups of the early Puranic and epic heroes. It moves fairly quickly into narratives of kings and dynasties. Why this is so could in part be explained by the difference between Jaina ideas of the past and those of the brahmanical tradition, and perhaps partly because the Jaina tradition drew on a patronage not confined to the royal court but extended to include urban and merchant communities. Inevitably, it would have had a wider audience.

The text begins with an invocation not of any deity, but of Ṛṣabha and later of Mahāvīra. The opening passage is a simple statement naming the author and those who helped him write the book, which he speaks of as being as pleasing as the *Mahābhārata*, its concerns being the life and activities of persons of recent times. It would seem that he sees the epic as a series of biographies which

[34] *Ep. Ind.*, 1, 293.

would be feasible up to a point. He then narrates the stories of Vikramāditya and Sālivāhana, thus appropriating, but in a limited way, ancient heroes for the start of his chronicle, his choice being determined by his claim that they both became Jainas.

The historical narrative is initiated by the statement on the founding of the city of Aṇahilvād/Aṇahilapāṭana in the equivalent of AD 746, although another source dates it to 765. This is associated with Vanarāja, a local adventurer who rebelled against and killed the revenue collector sent from Kanauj, possibly an official of the Pratihāra administration. Such an event seems to have been common enough at that time. There is a passing suggestion of his having links with the Haihaya clan of the Yadus, associated sometimes with western Indian dynasties.[35] He established himself as an independent ruler founding the Cāpotkaṭa dynasty, also known as Cāvaḍā. There follows a list of rulers each with specific regnal years and with dates in the Vikrama era—an attempt at chronological precision.

According to the chronicle, the last member of the dynasty was assassinated by his sister's son, who then began to rule as Mūlarāja I and founded the dynasty of the Caulukyas in AD 941. The relationship may have been coincidental, but in communities observing cross-cousin marriage (if these were such communities), the sister's son would be acceptable as the successor in the absence of a son. The origin myth describes the Caulukyas as belonging to the Somavaṃśa, the Lunar lineage. Their name is said to derive from the *culuka* (cupped hands) of Brahmā, from which the hero arose, and is similar to the myth of the Cālukyas of the Deccan. Possibly there were some lineage links that cut across these families of the western region. Some have read *culuka* to mean a jar rather than cupped hands, which would make them born out of a jar. This would link them further afield with many jar-born heroes and dynastic families, not least the Kauravas of the *Mahābhārata.* There seems to have been a need for these claims, perhaps in competition with those of other families in western India. Variants of the name come in other sources, including Solaṅki, but gradually Caulukya became standard.

[35] G.C. Choudhury, *Political History of Northern India from Jaina Sources*, 202.

Mūlarāja seems to have battled on all fronts against the rulers of Mālava, Saurashtra, and Kaccha. The capital remained at Aṇahilapāṭana as it did for the duration of the dynasty. He is remembered here as having exempted the tax on peasants when there was a drought, but to have collected the share in later years when the harvest was good. The categories of intermediaries and the range of administrative positions are more clearly differentiated in the inscriptional references than in the Chronicle. Locally important people were not only the landed elite and the upper bureaucracy, for included in this category were wealthy bankers and merchants associated with the former and with the court.[36]

The regnal years assigned by Merutuṅga to the Caulukya kings are generally reasonable. Once again, collateral lines weave through the succession. Three short-term rulers follow, until the nephew of the third rules as Bhīma I in AD 1022 and reigns until 1064. Campaigns against the Paramāras of Malava and of lesser places, the Cāhamānas of Nadol, and the Ābhīra-raṇaka, are almost perennial, with mention also being made of campaigns against Sindh.

In referring to campaigns, curiously neither Hemacandra nor Merutuṅga make any particular mention of Mahmud of Ghazni's raid on the temple at Somanātha. Perhaps it was not worth mentioning, however much it was exaggerated in Turkish and Persian chronicles. Yet the Caulukyas were Śaiva kings and Somanātha was an important temple. Some less important Jaina sources make a casual reference to places plundered by the Turks, and Somanātha is included in the list.

Bhīma's successor Karṇa is associated with attacks on the Bhillas, the forest tribes of western India, who would have been at the receiving end of aggression from a state encroaching into forest areas. Encroachment involved clearing the forest to obtain cultivable land, which when settled by peasants would enhance the state revenue. During the reign of his successor the Bhillas are said to have blocked the road and had to be removed by force, suggesting hostility between them. Karṇa built a temple in Bhilla country, doubtless to control the area and help in its acculturation.

A marriage alliance with the daughter of the king of Konkan

[36] V.M. Jha, "Feudal Elements in the Caulukya State: An Attempt at Relocation", in D.N. Jha (ed.), *The Feudal Order*, 211–48.

(south along the west coast) probably extended trading networks. Karṇa was a patron of the poet Bilhaṇa during the latter's sojourn in Gujarat, where the king's romances were the subject of his poems.[37]

Karṇa was succeeded by one of the two celebrities of the dynasty, Jayasiṁha Siddharāja (1094–1144). There was much court intrigue before his coronation since he was of a collateral line. There is an interesting reference to various tax remissions and to the Queen-Mother abolishing the pilgrim tax at Somanātha, which had brought in a sizeable income of 72 lakhs.[38] It was clearly economically viable for a state to encourage a temple to become a place of pilgrimage, and no doubt some of the income would have been diverted to private hands. The king began an era, the Siṁha *samvat*, and used it in a few inscriptions, but it did not become the regular era and remained a claim to status.

Merutuṅga reports on the debate held at the court between the Digambaras and Śvetāmbaras presided over by Siddharāja. The Śvetāmbara monk Śrideva is described as "a lion to controversial elephants". He wins the debate and is granted twelve villages by the king. The arguments were recorded by a court officer. The debate was about how food is to be eaten by monks, the wearing of clothes, and whether women can be liberated from rebirth. The more liberal Śvetāmbara position was upheld and the Digambaras were ousted. This echoes the holding of the Buddhist Councils to clarify doctrine and the role of Aśoka in the calling of one of these in the Buddhist tradition. Hemacandra assembled the representatives of the sects and also persuaded the Queen-Mother to support the Śvetāmbara.[39] A reference such as this to the past was important to the authority of the Śvetāmbara sect in Gujarat. This then allowed it later to spearhead the defence of the Jaina religion against the Śaivas.

Merutuṅga then describes how Hemacandra, the grammarian, scholar, and literary figure at the court, was invited to write a grammatical work for the king. This was the *Dvyāśraya-kāvya*, or the

[37] See chapter 13.

[38] 3.93ff.

[39] 3.156.

Siddhahemacandra. The *praśasti* of the patron included a brief history of the dynasty to date, listing conquests and succession. The king was goaded into arranging for this in competition with his enemy, king Bhoja of Mālava, who is said to have authored a book on etymology. This was literally a war over words. Grammatical works were sent for from Kashmir for consultation, since literary activity at this time was at a height in the northern kingdom. There was a need for proclaiming the quality of literary and grammatical works, particularly as it would seem that the rival court of Bhoja prided itself on such achievements. It is said that three hundred copyists were employed and copies sent to various places. The linguistic facility of Hemacandra is constantly applauded. Like Agastya who drank up the ocean, Hemacandra drank up the ocean of language.[40] The *brāhmaṇas* when speaking about the past quote the *Purāṇas*; so Jaina historical traditions provide this other perspective.

Many anecdotes punctuate the history of kings. They often focus on merchants whose activities were respected in the society of Jainas.[41] Merchants generated wealth and this may in part explain the unusual emphasis given by Hemacandra and Merutuṅga to the restoration of dilapidated temples, said to be a merit-producing activity. These were not temples that had been desecrated: they had fallen into disrepair. This is a significant statement, because it was a period when some temples were desecrated by rulers, both local and Turkish. The narratives are interspersed with descriptions of local geography and references to constructing tanks and other good works. Aṇahilapāṭana was a wealthy city boasting of Jaina scholars and well-read *brāhmaṇas*. The text refers to discussions on a variety of subjects.

Then comes the reign of the celebrated Kumārapāla (1144–74). He is also mentioned in Persian historical writing of a later period. Merutuṅga could draw upon several general works, although many biographies came to be written later.[42] He seems to have

40 *Prabandha-cintāmaṇi of Merutuṅga Ācārya*, 129.

41 3.110–11.

42 Among these was Jayasiṃhasūri's *Kumārapāla-carita*. Jinavijayamuni, *Kumārapāla-caritra-saṁgraha*, vol. 41.

consulted the inscriptions issued during Kumārapāla's reign, since some information is the same in both.

Kumārapāla was a nephew of Siddharāja and was kept away from the throne not only because he was from a collateral line, although Siddharāja had no son, but perhaps because he was the great-grandson of a courtesan.[43] Siddharāja disapproved of him as a successor but the ministers, including Hemacandra, supported and protected him. Hemacandra therefore continued to receive favours when Kumārapāla became king in his middle age.

Merutuṅga refers to the various campaigns of Kumārapāla with details of who led them and anecdotes associated with them. The campaign against Mallikārjuna of the Konkan is made much of. He does not explain why, but doubtless it had to do with controlling the ports along the western coast tying in with the Arab trade in Gujarat. Kumārapāla is described as *śrīrājya-cūḍamaṇi,* the crest-jewel of the realm of the goddess Śrī/Good Fortune, which marks a change of status and makes greater claims than those made by previous rulers.[44]

Kumārapāla is also described as a Jaina *arhat* (enlightened one), and the claim is made that he became a Jaina with Hemacandra as his preceptor. The incident that is said to have clinched his conversion is narrated at length. Hemacandra persuades Kumārapāla to restore the temple to Śiva at Somanātha.[45] This had fallen into disrepair through lack of maintenance and weathering from sea spray. After two years the renovated temple was ready and its consecration ritual was performed by the Śaiva chief-priest Bhāva Bṛhaspati, who is given hardly any prominence in this account. Hemacandra accompanies the king and performs the rituals, somewhat to the surprise of the court as he is a Jaina and not a Śaiva. Kumārapāla takes him into the sanctum of the temple and asks him to demonstrate the superiority of Jainism over Saivism. Hemacandra requests the god Śiva to manifest himself and the god obliges. Kumārapāla, quite overcome by this miracle, enquires of the god the value of various teachings and Śiva pronounces that what Hemacandra teaches is the best. The converted king takes the

[43] 4.126.
[44] Vadnagar Prasasti, *Ep. Ind.*, 1, 296, v. 14.
[45] R. Thapar, *Somanatha: The Many Voices of History*, 113ff.

vow of abstinence from flesh and alcohol, forbids animal slaughter in temples for fourteen years, and builds Jaina temples.[46]

Merutuṅga's version has a strong political motif. The religious opposition of the Śaivas and Jainas to each other included competition for royal patronage. It is unlikely that Śiva would have approved of Jaina teaching being superior to all others. There was disagreement among Jainas and Śaivas about the religion of Kumārapāla. Given that there had been opposition to his becoming king, it is possible that he courted the heretics as a way of keeping control over the Śaiva factions at court. At another level the story is also a putting down of Śiva, a deity for whom the Jainas had hardly any devotion. The brahmanical *Dharmāraṇya Mahātmya* makes light of this event by describing Kumārapāla as a *pākhaṇḍa* Jaina (a false Jaina) who ascended the throne with the help of Hemacandra.[47]

Bhāva Bṛhaspati, in a long inscription, claims that it was he who persuaded the king to renovate the temple, and makes no mention of Hemacandra.[48] Interestingly the inscription issued by the Nāgara *brāhmaṇas* in AD 1151 has no hint of Kumārapāla being a patron of any other religious sect but the Śaiva. This is contradicted by another inscription of AD 1184, where the Jaina temple is stated to have been built by *mahārājādhirāja śrī* Kumārapāla after his being enlightened as a Jaina by his preceptor Hemasūri.[49] This would suggest that he may have become a Jaina in the latter part of his reign but also that the narrative of Hemacandra was well known in Jaina circles.

The description dates to a century and a half after the event, with a changed historical context and some decline in patronage to Jainism. Is this an attempt to suggest that there can be an elision from Śaiva to Jaina belief? Acclaim from the deity of the rival was the best form of acquiring presence. This was also the threshold time of the coming of Islam, and the Jainas had to work out their equation with the new religion. The virtual invisibility of Islam in these records is in itself a comment on how it was viewed.

[46] 4.140ff.; *Prabandha-cintāmaṇi of Merutuṅga Ācārya*, 126–30.

[47] J.E. Cort, "Who is King?" 96.

[48] R. Thapar, *Somanatha: The Many Voices of History*, 81ff., 113ff.

[49] Jalor Stone Inscription of Samarasiṃhadeva, Samvat 1242, *Ep. Ind.*, 11, 54ff.

The narratives of Kumārapāla's conversion to Jainism and his enthusiasm parallel once again the stories of Aśoka's conversion to Buddhism and his patronage under the guidance of Upagupta, as described in Buddhist texts. They also evoke what might have been thought to be Candragupta's relationship to his preceptor, Bhadrabāhu. Kumārapāla is said to have built 14,140 Jaina temples, which echoes the statement about the 84,000 *stūpas* constructed by Aśoka. Hemacandra is said to have written his major works at the request of Kumārapāla, and in part to enlighten him. Possibly, Merutuṅga was aware of the representation of Aśoka in the *Aśokāvadāna* of the Northern Buddhist tradition. Hemacandra died at 84, having desired it to be so. Is this a way of saying that he observed the rite of *sallekhanā*, the Jaina method of a controlled fast leading to death? Mahāvīra is said to have foretold the reign of Kumārapāla and his conversion to Jainism. This can only be taken as the author's attempt to provide the ultimate unquestionable endorsement for a Jaina readership and community.

That the court was not as dominated by Jainism as Merutuṅga suggests is apparent from inscriptional evidence. A major epigraph of Kumārapāla composed by the court poet Śripāla in AD 1151, praises the Nāgara *brāhmaṇas*.[50] It was copied and added to in AD 1632 by yet another Nāgara *brāhmaṇa* long after the Caulukyas had ceased to rule.

Kumārapāla was succeeded by his nephew Ajayapāla, the descent again moving to a collateral line (1173–6). He destroyed the temples of the previous rulers (*pūrvaja prāsādān*), and dismissed or had killed those who had worked for Kumārapāla.[51] As an ardent Śaiva he is depicted as hostile to the Jainas, a hostility perhaps again rooted in a faction fight at the time of his succession. He was involved in the usual campaigns against the Cāhamānas and the Guhilas. Aggressive relations with Mālava continued even into the next reign, despite his having to defend the kingdom against the *mlecchas*. There is no comment on the latter as a significant enemy, the traditional enemies still being around.[52] Ajayapāla was murdered; the succession therefore went to his minor son, whose

[50] Vadnagar Prasasti, *Ep. Ind.*, 1, 293.
[51] 4.175.
[52] 4.179ff.

mother took on the Turkish armies and defeated them. This is also mentioned in some Turkish chronicles.

In the declining years of the Caulukya dynasty the kingdom was torn by *sāmantas* feuding amongst themselves and others in revolt against the king. Centre-stage is now taken by the two brothers Vastupāla and Tejaḥpāla, who became ministers and eventually virtually ruled the kingdom. Coming from a family of high office, their fortunes accumulated and they made substantial donations towards building temples and institutions. This is visible in the finest Jaina temples of the time being built through their patronage. Merutuṅga wrote a *prabandha* on their activities.

An interesting episode relates to the perception of the new political power, the Turks, referred to as *mlecchas*. The guru of the *mlecchas* is an Islamic scholar, an *ālima,* who was leaving for Mecca from a port in Gujarat. Some advised the king to capture him en route, but Tejaḥpāla advised to the contrary. This safe conduct led to amity between Tejaḥpāla and the Suratrāna/Sultan.[53] The presence of the Turk at this point does not mark any particular disjuncture in this area.

Merutuṅga gives no explanation for Caulukya decline. It is once again the *sāmantas*, *raṇakas*, and *maṇḍalikas* competing for power that are foremost in political events. The successful one, Arṇorāja, had been made a *sāmanta* by Kumārapāla and given the village of Vyāghrapalli, which provided the name of the subsequent dynasty—Vaghela. There was a marginal kinship connection with Kumārapāla. Associated with them was the upper bureaucracy, and it is not surprising that ministers become the virtual rulers in periods of decline. The king's dependence on the two brothers continued. This is reflected even in texts that provide examples of how to draft administrative documents.[54]

The Chronicle briefly moves away from Gujarat and there are anecdotes about kings and peoples from neighbouring areas, such as Pṛthvīrāja the Cāhamāna holding back the *mleccha*. Some fanciful stories are told about earlier scholars such as Varahamihira, Bhartṛhari, and Nāgarjuna. There is further mention of the contestation between the Śvetāmbara and Digambara sects, and

[53] 4.191.

[54] *Lekhapaddhati*.

between the Śvetāmbaras and what remained of the Buddhists in the area.[55]

7. The Jaina Chronicle

The three chronicles, discussed in this and the two previous chapters, differ in many ways. The *Rājataraṅgiṇī* is an intellectually sophisticated narrative describing the evolution of the kingdom of Kashmir. Kalhaṇa is particular about stating his sources and assessing their reliability. His span of interests includes threats from neighbours, the politics of feudatories, fashions at the court, hydraulic engineering, and fiscal problems that led to the oppression of peasants and to the plundering of temples by kings and their officers. Its historical perspective is undeniable and was recognized a couple of centuries ago. The Chamba *vaṃśāvalī* is the history of a small kingdom, the narrative just about rising above minimal information. An interesting aspect is the transition from deriving legitimacy from local *Siddhas* and Nātha *yogīs* to the mainstream Bhāgavata sect, demarcating sources of legitimacy from a local tradition to one with a much wider reach. The *Prabandha-cintāmaṇi* of Merutuṅga, a text of the Sramanic tradition, shows a clear sense of the historical, but with a Jaina ideological focus. The conversion of the king Kumārapāla to Jainism by his minister, Hemacandra, is therefore highlighted, but in the context of an account of three dynasties that ruled in Gujarat.

Merutuṅga's text was read as a source by later Jaina authors. Their writings were either a continuation of the chronicle or, more often, took the form of biographies of prominent rulers and Jaina monks and Elders. Jaina chronicles parallel in many ways the *Rājataraṅgiṇī* with its focus on the politics of the court and its factions. The factions are represented as either sympathetic or hostile to Jainism. There is less said on the political interventions of the intermediaries.

The chronicle inevitably concerns itself with the concept of the state and the king's relationship with society. The seven constituents of the state are repeated as defined in the *Arthaśāstra* of Kauṭilya. Familiarity with the *itihāsa-purāṇa* tradition is required

[55] 5.201–18.

of any author who is writing about the past and this familiarity is demonstrated in Merutuṅga's chronicle. But there is more to it than just this tradition which is subordinated to the alternative Sramanic tradition. There is also the association of the *cakravartin* which by now was common to all traditions but interpreted differently. The Buddhist and the Jaina concept is subtle and more complex involving both the ethics of law and governance as well, with less emphasis on military conquest as in the brahmanical tradition. This is up to a point ironic since kings partial to Jainism fought battles, and respected Jainas were included among the better-known military commanders.

Within the Jaina tradition asceticism even temporarily is often a prelude to kingship as a source of strength. The incidence of kings renouncing the throne may have been influenced by this ethic, although in more practical terms it may have been forced on such kings by their successors. An ideal king was to be powerful in conquest, extending protection to all, creating wealth, and combining this with being the patron of Jainism and its ethic.[56] The aspiration to conquest in some ways reverses the commitment to *ahiṃsā* but presumably if it benefits the religion it is acceptable.

Rivalry between Jainas and Śaivas becomes apparent from the *Prabandha-cintāmaṇi*. The two reigns that symbolize the power and prosperity of the Caulukyas—those of Jayasiṁha Siddharāja and Kumārapāla—are the ones in which royal patronage was extended to both religions. Was the patronage due entirely to the religious inclinations of the two kings, as the Chronicle would have it, or did the politics behind the patronage wish to draw on the wealth of the Jaina community? Kings were a source of patronage even if the recipients were from diverse and competing sects. Kings therefore had to defend *dharma*, even when its definition varied, as between the Jainas and the Saivas. The continuity of administrators may have eased the contentions. The political aspect of patronage is implicit in the support that it brought to the king. Patronage to the Jainas implied good relations with the wealthy commercial community and Kumārapāla's reign coincides with a high point in commerce.

[56] *Triṣaṣṭiśalākāpuruṣacarita*, 6.309.

Jainism did not endorse deities controlling human action hence divinity in the concept of kingship would be distant.[57] But on occasion the deity could be introduced to emphasize a point as in the story of Śiva endorsing the *dharma* of Hemacandra. The ideal king was to model himself on the ideal layman observing the Jaina ethic and not dependent on divine sanction. The ultimate attainment lay in renunciation.

The *Prabandha-cintāmaṇi* is a sequential narrative and carries the continuity of a history. It observes the chronologies of the dynasties in linear fashion and relates them to the era of the Vikrama *saṃvat*. This was a prevalent era and probably more easily followed than the one based on the death of Mahāvīra. The narrative recalls major events associated with the reign of each king. Apart from this, the ideological concern is to depict the Jaina interest in the best possible way and to claim royalty as patrons. This patronage was so special that even Śiva, the deity of one of the competitors for patronage, approved of it. It is a narrative of past times but comes up to the contemporary period.

A large number of Jaina sources and detailed data on the court and associated interests came to be written about in these times, and were presumably discussed by the literati. A study of these post-fourteenth-century texts might illumine some of the reasons given for events and decisions. It may be possible to categorize authors on the basis of the explanations that they offer. Sources can be contradictory about events. The Turkish sources speak of Qutb-ud-din Aibek plundering Gujarat, but the Gujarat sources are silent. Were they avoiding a reference to what was considered an embarrassment, or were the Turkish chroniclers exaggerating their claims? The *Prabandha-cintāmaṇi* was treated as reliable by chroniclers of the Sultanate and by later scholars such as Abu'l Fazl in Mughal times, who cite and even occasionally quote its representation of the past of Gujarat. This introduces another dimension into the historiography of the period and could be a source of insightful comparative study.

[57] J.E. Cort, "Who is King?", 85ff.

18

Therefore

Looking Back and Looking Forward

1. Locating History

The purpose of this book has been not just to ascertain whether or not there was a sense of history in early India. More than that, it has been to search for the forms this might have taken, and how it might have been defined. My concern has been with how authors from the early past saw the past before them.[1] I have tried to refine what is meant by a sense of history in the context of early societies and locate its articulation in varied Indian texts from early India, at various times during the period *c.* 1000 BC to *c.* AD 1300.

In doing this I was not attempting to broaden the current definition of history in order to accommodate forms of writing prevalent in early India. Such forms existed in many societies of the ancient world and have been seen as expressions of historical consciousness. I have argued that what is included as history in the present day is no longer limited to what it was in the nineteenth century, and many more forms are now seen as being potentially

[1] To argue that Indian historians of modern times have shown a sense of history, and that too in conformity with how history is defined in modern times, is irrelevant to the sense of history in early India. In discussing this, A. Sharma, *Hinduism and its Sense of History*, does not differentiate between the pre-modern and the modern.

or actually historical. In relation to pre-modern times, in particular, this has largely been an outcome of writing the history of societies and cultures outside Europe, and of questioning some of the generalizations about the pasts of the non-European world made during the colonial period. The earlier definition of what constitutes history evolved from a narrower focus of European understandings of its own past—within which the Judaeo-Christian tradition provided a limited perspective, although this has been considerably enlarged in recent times.

Two commanding debates in the last couple of centuries have discussed evolution and its parallel, history, both as explanations of the past. Initially, a narrative of events had sufficed as history, but, when seen as a possible way of organizing knowledge, historical events had to be verified and causal explanations sought. A teleological perspective strengthened its evolutionary direction. The Enlightenment emphasized the notion of progress, and Marx and Weber sought laws governing historical forms. Thereafter the focus was on how and why there was historical change, which in turn introduced the idea of legitimate methods of narrating the historical past. History as we know it had arrived. But it is as well to keep in mind that this was not what was understood by "history" in earlier times. This book has been an attempt to view history in such a time.

Even within European historiographical perspectives, there has been a recognition of changes in what constitutes a historical tradition. Greco-Roman narrative history gave way to the Christian concern with seeing God's will and the authority of the Church as determining factors, followed by the more secular approaches of the Enlightenment, which in turn have recently been questioned. In reconstructing Islamic and Chinese historiography there was little attempt, initially, to consider the worldview of the authors of the texts apart from the information they provided. The shift today from political history to social history has moved the narrower definition of history—as the narration of events concerning rulers—to the broader definition of history—as representing those in authority alongside other segments of society. This shift draws on a wider range of sources and assumes that, directly or indirectly, these shaped, and were shaped by, social contours.

Mine is not an attempt to legitimize any or every claim to an indigenous reading of Indian history. The status of history in a text has now to meet the requirements of the discipline as it is practised in current times: the evidence has to be checked for reliability, and causality in explanation has to be based on logical analysis with as objective a generalization as possible. Few pre-modern "histories" meet these contemporary requirements. But that should not stop us from investigating how authors of that world understood their past, and, more importantly, why they understood it the way they did. Whether we think their interpretation conformed to historicity or not is a substantial but subsequent question.

I have therefore read ancient texts not primarily for the information they provide on person and event—such readings being already extensive in the modern writing of early Indian history. I have instead also tried to read them from the specific focus of how they understand past societies and the actions of persons believed to have been historical: in sum, the past looking at its own past.

This is possible now that we have a new understanding of historical change in early India arising from the research of the past half century. I have argued for the possibility of seeing it, at one level, as the change from the predominance of clan-based societies to that of kingdoms, where records with a historical potential would differ from one to the other. The change in most situations was a mutation rather than a disjuncture.

I have also suggested that this difference is partially linked to an aspect of what I have called embedded history and externalized history. The former is that which is presumed to be historical by the authors and their audiences, and where the narrative is embedded in ritual texts. This is followed by a gradual reduction in the need to embed narratives in ritual texts, and to recording them in new genres specifically recognized as pertaining to the past, as well as recording the past as seen from the perspective of those in authority. These new narratives articulate both the past and the present as independent statements, released from having to be embedded. Such texts constitute externalized history and date to the post-Gupta period. This history assumes the demise of most clan societies, which were replaced by kingdoms, requiring more recognizably historical records. The authorship of these records now lay with Buddhist and Jaina monks, scholarly *brāhmaṇas*, *kāyastha* scribes, and the occasional bard.

I have also argued for three kinds of historical traditions—as determined by the authors, by the audiences to whom they are addressed, and by the agenda of the text. The predominant tradition was the *itihāsa-purāṇa*, attributed to *brāhmaṇa* authors writing about those that ruled.[2] A rather different, and in some ways more realistic, perspective on the latter comes from the compositions of the bards. Their early compositions are thought to have been overwritten by *brāhmaṇa* authors, making it difficult to retrieve the original, although it was not entirely obliterated. We have a flavour of what some might have been from the bardic epics that have survived in later times from the second millennium AD. A counterpoint to this is the third tradition, the Sramanic, where those that ruled are tied into the history of the teaching of the Buddhist and Jaina Saṅghas, the central institution in each case. Although some narratives drew on common sources, this created a largely alternative reading to the *itihāsa-purāṇa* tradition. These relationships, however, are more implicit than visible. The Sramanic tradition emerged from a more urban context and concerned itself with the evolution of the sect and its patrons. What is put together as the past in the three traditions inevitably differs from each other in various ways.

Given these differences, the meaning of "a sense of history" cannot be reduced to a brief definition. The texts reflect gradations in the perception of what might be historical. I have tried to trace the gradual recognition of historical consciousness, and its formulations as representations of the past, in a variety of genres. These, it seems to me, reflect three phases: historical consciousness, or showing an awareness of the difference between a fantasized past and one that has elements of what was believed to have actually happened; historical traditions, which are more consciously constructed representations of the past and where the purpose of the construction is evident; and historical writing,

[2] J.L. Fitzgerald uses a felicitous phrase—"the genre of *purāṇa* (and its crucial sibling *itihāsa*)": see idem, "History and Primordium in Ancient Indian Historical Writing: *Itihāsa* and *Purāṇa* in the *Mahābhārata* and Beyond" (forthcoming).

which claims to be a narrative of a person or an event backed by a claim to historicity. An overview of the genres considered should make these differentiations apparent.

2. The Genres—I

The seminal genre, as in many literatures of the ancient world, consists of compositions in praise of heroes. Reflecting a consciousness of referring to the past, and of preserving some activities of the present, these are genres illustrated by verses praising the generosity of a hero after a successful raid, as in the *dāna-stutis*, and by passages praising those *rājās* who hosted public sacrificial rituals—these being implicit strategies of legitimation and declarations of identity. The subject of both was the *rājā,* to be remembered because of his activities. Embedding them in ritual texts was the method of ensuring that they would be remembered.

The epics, the *Mahābhārata* and the *Rāmāyaṇa,* draw on the idea of the *dāna-stutis* but extend it and deviate. They are not stating the present position as much as looking back on the past and recalling the societies of past times. These were clan societies, as is evident from the *Mahābhārata*, and they were mutating into kingdoms, which is equally evident from the *Ramāyaṇa*. Conflict is over status, wealth, and control over territory. The identity of the hero lies in his lineage, recorded as genealogy, and through patterns of descent and alliances.

The epics are free-standing compositions but, at the same time, pinned to the idea of ritual. The initial recitations of each epic take place on ritual occasions. The interpolations in the *Mahābhārata* are not casual additions because they change the purpose of the text. Although the *Mahābhārata* is called an *itihāsa*, its claims to history are still restricted to a consciousness of history without any defining articulation. This contrasts strongly with the Jaina version of the *Rāmāyaṇa*, the *Paumacariyam*, which states unequivocally that it is narrating what actually happened, which is not identical with the Vālmīki *Rāmāyaṇa*, and claims historicity. The *Rāmāyaṇa* in its original form takes the interface between clan societies and kingdoms a step further. It projects an antagonism between them, and at one level perhaps fantasizes the former into demons, a fantasy powerfully challenged by the Jaina version. The Vālmīki poem encapsulates the triumph of the kingdom.

The social melange of the epics is organized into clearer identities in what I have called the genealogical mode of representing the past. The *vaṃśānucarita* section of the *Viṣṇu Purāṇa* is an attempt at ordering the past in a pattern that is not conventionally historical but is suggestive of a historical perspective. The remote past is seen as the shadowy period of the Manus, terminated by the Flood as a time-marker,[3] which separates it from the lineages of the *kṣatriya* descent groups. These, observing diverse patterns, are slotted broadly into the Sūryavaṃśa or the Candravaṃśa. Most from the latter group perish in the Kurukṣetra battle, which becomes another time-marker, others fade out. The dynasties, distinct from the clans, emerge subsequent to this. Many of these are historically attested in inscriptions and other texts.

This appears to be a move towards creating a historical tradition. Was it due entirely to the emergence of kingdoms? Kingship demands distinctive legitimation, yet the early dynasties did not latch onto the *kṣatriya* lineages—as did the post-Gupta dynasties who frequently called themselves *kṣatriya*. The administration of kingdoms demands the keeping of records, including mention of who ruled. Gift-giving was no longer of movable wealth on the hoof, but began to include land, which involved the transfer of property, and this again required recording.

Genealogies are useful to the beginnings of historical records and provide a historical grid. They are flexible and can be stretched and padded with names, or clipped, pruned, and telescoped. In emphasizing succession they encouraged a chronological ordering that was linear in form. This hints at the beginnings of a historical turn. Was this idea of history, spurred by socio-economic change, also influenced by the alternative history maintained in the Śramaṇa tradition of the Buddhists and Jainas? When the *Purāṇas* began to be composed the Śramaṇas had sects, ran

[3] The symbolism of the Flood was immense and varied as has been pointed out by many, as for example A.K. Coomaraswamy, "The Flood in Hindu Tradition", 398-407.

missions, were property-holders, and had been patronized by royalty and by the wealthy. They were compiling histories of the teaching and its institution, the Saṅgha. The epics having already been appropriated to Bhagavatism, the authors of the *Purāṇas* may have observed the advantages of creating a reasonably credible past, or even many pasts, for those in authority. Additionally, it could give identity to the emergent Puranic religion, and to its sects aspiring to royal patronage, and thereby to acquiring property.

The move towards envisaging a historical tradition can be seen in other nascent forms, as in early inscriptions from the third century BC to the sixth AD. These are a mix of royal statements and those associated with support for sectarian religion. It was no longer necessary to embed information in a ritual text. Statements from the state or from established institutions carried enough authority and, if properly recorded, could last in perpetuity. These were some of the elements of what was to form the core of the historical tradition in post-Gupta times.

The early inscriptions recorded the actions of kings, and of other categories of people such as donors to religious institutions, and were also intended to inform future generations. Some refer to the past directly, as in the records spanning eight hundred years of repairs to an embankment. Others do so inferentially, as for example through venerating the relics of the dead. Invoking the historical past was also a form of validating present action. This continued to be so even when the inscriptions could no longer be read, as in the case of those who inscribed their statements on a pillar originally set up by Aśoka Maurya.

A more extensive recognition of the importance of historical consciousness is demonstrated in plays using historical themes. Viśākhadatta's *Mudrārākṣasa* is a long view back over many centuries to a prime historical moment—that of the transfer of power from the Nandas to the Mauryas. The play represents history through depicting an event but with the dramatist's licence to imaginatively configure the reconstruction. The author presents the historical role of Cāṇakya—as a political economist, as a practising politician, and as a theorist drawing on rational arguments. The familiarity with what were to become the legends about Cāṇakya in the Sramanic tradition suggests that the latter was being read by a wider audience of the literati than we have assumed.

In describing the past as it was believed to have happened, these texts point to the evolution of the *itihāsa-purāṇa* tradition. The bardic tradition was at its elbow, as it were, and could not be entirely ignored. But apart from this, the other category of writing that underlined the significance of history was the Sramanic tradition.

3. Genres—II

I have referred to the Sramanic historical traditions as the alternative to the embedded brahmanical tradition, because in them the choice of persons and events from the past are different, as are the concerns. The Buddhist tradition is perhaps a more distinct alternative with a more pronounced sense of history. The authority in this tradition is the teaching of the Buddha incorporated and propagated through the Saṅgha. Patrons do not create history by their own actions so much as through the Saṅgha.

The writing of history therefore presumes that there be a record of the organization of the Saṅgha. This is given in the Pāli Canon, moving from an orally remembered account to texts recording it as determined by the various Councils, whose history has also to be recorded. Included in this is the presence of dissenting sects. It is the Councils that give legitimacy to the particular sects that emerge, debating the veracity of what the Buddha is said to have taught and explaining why deviations, even if recognized as such, have to be accommodated. The authority of the Saṅgha in each case is backed by political authority—Ajātaśatru, Aśoka, Kaniṣka. The association with the term *śāsana*—teaching, instruction, order—is both telling and pertinent. The history of a major monastery, the Mahāvihāra, encapsulates the relationship between the king and the Saṅgha.[4] In the case of Aśoka, the manner in which both Hīnayāna and Mahāyāna Buddhism appropriate the king as

[4] The *Mahāvaṃsa*, for instance, suggests some parallels of purpose with the third-century AD *History of the Church* by Eusebius.

patron becomes apparent in their writings. Whereas Aśoka's policy of *dhamma*, as defined in his edicts, is not merely the propagation of Buddhism, but rather an attempt to persuade people to observe an ethic conducive to social well being, the Buddhist tradition projects him as a patron of the Saṅgha, concerned almost solely with the advancement of Buddhism.

Apart from the various sectarian splits a major division was that of Hīnayāna and Mahāyāna Buddhism, the latter often referred to as Northern Buddhism. Unlike the texts from the Sri Lankan Theravāda, history in the Northern tradition is often articulated as biographies of the Buddha and of important patrons and Elders. Where teaching was hemmed in by competing religious sects and the Saṅgha was not politically powerful, it may have been thought that the more effective way of using history to establish the authority of Buddhism was through such biographies. The concept of the exemplar would carry weight. There was therefore a temptation to turn biography into hagiography, further emphasized by the increasing importance of the concept of the *bodhisattva*. The prediction of the decline of the teaching introduces chiliastic notions that also require some delineation of a past that differs from the present.

These texts claim to be historical and would have been noticed even if not referred to, and up to a point perhaps the format was imitated in the *itihāsa-purāṇa* tradition that followed. It was doubtless noticed that claiming a history enhanced one's authority, whether personal or institutional. Sects of the Puranic religions imitated the Sramanic institutions in setting up their *maṭhas* and *ghaṭikās*, and would seem to have become more aware of the use of history.

Hovering in the background, and possibly more influential to the understanding of history than we have conceded, was the powerful debate, *vādavidya*, between the Buddhists and the Naiyāyikās—those of the Nyāya school of philosophy.[5] This continued from the second century BC to the sixth AD, and was

[5] B. Matilal, *The Character of Logic in India*; S. Sarukkai, *Indian Philosophy and the Philosophy of Science*, 1ff., 209ff.; R. King, *Indian Philosophy*, 198–229.

subsequently picked up again. Beginning with Nāgarjuna and continuing with Dinnaga and Dharmakīrti, Buddhist philosphers argued with Naiyāyikās on the centrality and role of logic in debate. This involved questions on the importance of evidence, perception, causality, and inference. The procedures of the debate were also set out, moving from statement to evidence to example. Historical examples are not necessarily quoted in the debate, but the implications of the discussion would have affected scholarship and been of interest to those narrating the past and the present.

4. The Genres—III

The genres of the post-Gupta period were new and different from the earlier ones. They consisted in the main of *caritas* (historical biographies), inscriptions that were effectively dynastic annals, and *vaṃśāvalīs* (chronicles). In their forms and in what they record they move from historical traditions to the nuclei of historical writing.

In the changing polity and society of the time, political control was extended in various ways. New territory with a settled population was conquered and incorporated in the earlier manner, but additionally, sparsely populated frontier zones could be colonized and forest-dwellers assimilated by converting them into peasants and introducing caste as a mechanism of control. This involved adjusting the new rules of kinship, cultural patterns, and customary law that came with this assimilation. The insistent emphasis on observing the *varṇāśramadharma* in newly-created kingdoms could have been an attempt to gloss over deviations. Hierarchy replaced egalitarian forms, with frequent references to *kṣatriya* status and demarcated from the *śūdra*. Hence the Puranic prophecy that new *kṣatriyas* would be created and these would require validation of their status. Divinizing the king was thought of as one solution. The other was bestowing *kṣatriya* status on him. However, neither was sufficient as these changes merely isolated him or became so common as not to be taken too seriously.

Up to a point, events shape the narrative and there can be an attempt to ascertain what happened.[6] History was to be represented

[6] G.M. Spiegel, *The Past as Text*, 99ff.

and not analysed. Legends were not discontinued and sources were implied rather than discussed, with some exceptions. Changes in society required to be melded, preferably with some point of identity. It could be argued that the new genres were attempting to do this by providing a past that was more credible than it had been earlier, and by recoding and recording the events of the present for use in the construction of such a past, and for the future.

The intention of the *carita* (biography) was to locate a person of significance in moments of consequence and allow glimpses of that person and those moments. This was done through the many layers that converged: from formulaic treatment and some possible familiarity with the Sramanic biographical forms, from the innovation of the genre as court literature, and from the historicity of the person. The biography became a document of contemporary polity but introduced some elements of past history, whether remote or recent. The contemporary polity could be the establishing of sovereignty, as in the *Harṣacarita*, or battling against competitors and/or rebellious subordinates, as in the *Rāmacarita*. Dynastic history is included as a way not only of providing a context, but also giving validity to royal actions. In the two biographies discussed here, political and historical concerns drive the narrative even if it is presented in *kāvya* form. These concerns were pervasive in establishing kingship but become more visible in texts such as these.

Inscriptions ceased to be fragmentary statements from the court, or brief records. They included elaborate official statements, often issued by the king or on his behalf, and when read sequentially over a number of reigns they constitute the annals of the kingdom. The initial section carries a benediction invoking the deity, followed by a brief history of the dynasty, ruler by ruler, culminating with the contemporary one. Titles are given, conquests listed, and alliances mentioned. References are made to problems with neighbours, with aliens, with the forest tribes, and suchlike. This is the *praśasti* (eulogy), in which history is the source of the dynasty's legitimacy, maintained as a record. Subsequent to this comes the purpose of the inscription, which also on occasion carries some historical information apart from the immediate royal order. Further validation requires mentioning the authorship of the text and the precise date and era. Ministerial families or those of wealthy merchants, declaring their status, also issued inscriptions which included statements on the history of the family. Votive inscriptions, longer than earlier ones, carried the family history of the donor, even if briefly.

By way of contrast, and at the end of the discussion of Candella inscriptions, I have included the bardic epic of the hero Ālhā, which narrates events in the declining years of Candella rule and provides a view of the rule from a subaltern or subordinate perspective. It is not a eulogy and presents person and event in a more realistic setting, but within the formulaic structure of a bardic composition, which has its own perspective. It is not the story of the victor, or one who claims to be so, as in the other genres of this time, and the view is from lesser but perhaps more independent participants. It may initially have been composed in times contemporary with the persons it refers to, but much of it has later additions—memories of succeeding generations—as is usual with oral transmissions. So essentially what we have is a later view of an earlier period, and a particular view claiming to be historical but not directing us to specific sources.

Some royal courts encouraged the keeping of a *vaṃśāvalī*. This could be written as a text recording history at a point in time by a single person, as with Kalhaṇa and the *Rājataraṅgiṇī*, and Merutuṅga with the *Prabandha-cintāmaṇi*. Or, it could be kept as a court record and updated from time to time by successive authors, as is likely with the Chamba *vaṃśāvalī*. The chronicle had a wider assessment of the past and reflected a broad span of opinion, leaving the main ideological intention to the author—where there was a single one.

Following the pattern of the *vaṃśānucarita*, chronicles seem to follow three phases. There is first a statement on the origins of the region. This can be mythical and replete with fantasy. The second phase suggests links with the heroes of the lineages, often through some association with an event from the *Mahābhārata,* or refers to local heroes of a distant past. The most substantial part of the chronicle is the third phase, that of the establishing of the kingdom and its dynastic history, highlighting those that are remembered as persons of consequence. The narration may be hesitant and uncertain to begin with, but there is always a point when it becomes confident, coinciding with more certain historical sources.

The three chronicles that I have discussed differ in many ways. The *Rājataraṅginī* is an intellectually sophisticated historical narrative describing the evolution of the kingdom of Kashmir. Kalhaṇa is particular about stating his sources and even assesses their reliability. His analysis of dynastic history is remarkable for the span of interests he includes, such as threatening neighbours, the politics of feudatories, political and religious factions at the court, hydraulic engineering, and fiscal problems that led to the oppression of peasants and to the plundering of temples by kings and their officers. The logic of actions and politics emanates from political concerns but pervades a wide social range. Its historical perspective is undeniable and was recognized a couple of centuries ago.

The Chamba *vaṃśāvalī* is the history of a small kingdom, the narrative just about rising above minimal information. An interesting aspect is the transition of deriving legitimacy from the local *siddhas* and Nātha *yogīs* to the better recognized mainstream Śaiva and Bhāgavata sects. This seems to demarcate the sources of legitimacy required in the earlier phase from those needed when the kingdom is established.

The *Prabandha-cintāmaṇi* of Merutuṅga, coming essentially from the Sramanic tradition, shows a clear sense of the historical, but with a Jaina ideological focus. The narrative covers the activities of the kings of three dynasties of Gujarat, but stays for longer on Kumārapāla, whom the author claims was converted to Jainism by his minister, Hemacandra. The conversion has to be highlighted.

Of all the genres discussed here, each follows from and yet in some ways marks a departure from the previous one. This reflects the degree to which the awareness of history—whether consciously or subconsciously—increases. Where the degree of history changes, its record will also change in form, and in language if need be.

Some of these texts are referred to as *kāvyas* (literary compositions, generally a poem), since the distinction between *kāvya* and *itihāsa* was not strictly defined nor observed. *Kāvya* could also refer to the literary form irrespective of the contents, which allows for an overlap in nomenclature. Literary and historical writing is often close in form, with time, place, and person being important to both. That these texts were referred to as *kāvyas* does not mean that their historical orientation was not recognized.

The genres discussed pertain largely to social groups constituting the elite or those in their proximity. They do not reflect the entire society. Unfortunately, the larger part of society has not left us texts that inform us about how they looked at the past; or, we have yet to discover ways of prising out that information from existing texts.

5. Authorship and Audience

The change in genre assumes changes in authorship and audience. It is possible that the initial compositions of the hero-lauds and the epics, were by bards and poets attached to the clans, but were worked over by *brāhmaṇas* with a literary bent. The audiences for both would have been gatherings of clan members and others. The Vālmīki *Rāmāyaṇa* in its original shorter form probably had just the one author, who collated the legends and knit them into a single story. The text would later incorporate additions. Public recitations would again have been common, as also some smaller gatherings such as in the royal courts, starting with those of the early kingdoms and continuing into later times.

The authors of the *Purāṇas* were *brāhmaṇas* who collated the material from various sources. For the *vaṃśānucarita* section, the data would have come from the Vedic corpus and from oral sources such as the genealogies of the bards. These texts were recited and read in *agrahāras*, in temples, at places of pilgrimage, and at various ritual gatherings. That their recitations were in demand is evident from the category of professionals referred to as the *paurāṇikas.*

The Buddhist texts were largely composed by learned monks and written as the history of the teaching and of the Saṅgha, intended both for the discipline of monks and for the edification of the lay community. The purpose of the texts is evident and the intention single-minded. They were copied and kept in the monasteries so as to be easily consulted.

Inscriptions, both early and late, being statements associated with rulers, involved the court and administration. Their authors therefore could be court officials or court poets and they rendered the orders of the king in appropriate language. Some carried *brāhmaṇa* names and others towards the later period identified themselves as *kāyasthas*. The latter were recruited especially as administrators and scribes in addition to *brāhmaṇas* employed in this capacity. The inscriptions were composed by persons of the upper castes at the court, but the actual engraving was done by those of lower-caste status.

Inscriptions were intended to be read by, or read to, the public, so the audience rippled out from the court circles to the populace. This was a narrower audience than that for the epic of Ālhā, which was doubtless known from village to village in the region. The bard in this case was said to be a kinsman of one of the queens, but this did not necessarily make him a *kṣatriya*.

It was again in the context of the court and the literati that plays were performed and the royal biographies read. This demanded a combination of fine poetry and scholarship, evident in the plays, the *caritas*, and the chronicles discussed: the *Rājataraṅgiṇī* is a history that is relatively secular whereas the *Prabandha-cintāmaṇi*, also relatively secular in concept, does succumb to the power of Jaina belief. The Chamba *vaṃśāvalī* is largely just a record of events. It claims to be written by the *rājaguru*, or a succession of them, but the language suggests a person not so literate in Sanskrit and possibly from a family of locally recruited *brāhmaṇas*.

Given the variety of genres and authors, the language also changed. Sanskrit—Vedic and Classical—was used in the texts of the *itihāsa-purāṇa* tradition. Pāli, Prākrit, and Sanskrit were the languages of the various Sramanic writings, some of which were subsequently translated into Tibetan, Chinese, and other languages, in which we have them today. Inscriptions were initially written in Prākrit, followed by Sanskrit, but by the late first millennium AD they began to use the emerging regional languages. These latter languages were also used in the epics of the bards in the second millennium AD.

6. Why is there a Turn to the Historical?

The need for the historical in early India becomes critical at two points in the evolution of authority. The first is when authority is being initially established and often amidst competition from rival groups, which therefore requires a statement on claims to incorporate believed history; and the second is when there has been a crisis and the authority has almost disappeared but has either been salvaged or has become the narrative of the successor.

At the simplest level, the turn to the historical is intended to record the present and implicitly compare it to the past, and to record something that would be available to the future. In time, the record comes to represent the past and has to be conserved. This could mean having to select what of the past should be conserved. But it is not just any past, it must have a meaning for the present. In the process of pruning, the requirements may change. Is the record meticulously preserved? Or is it adjusted in accordance with contemporary needs? Preserved records recall the past but have to be seen from the perspective of the various points in time when they were recalled—and that perspective differs from the one of our times.

The past needs to be recalled for a variety of purposes, not least because it establishes the identity of those in power. This can be done by making connections, as also by providing exemplars. This is made evident from the narratives chosen and examples quoted in the *Mahābhārata* and the *Purāṇas* and in the biographies. This was important to the understanding of *itihāsa*.[7] Connections with persons of significance and participation in important events of the past bestow legitimacy. Latching on to the lineages of the Solar and Lunar lines of the *Purāṇas* in the post-Gupta period was part of the search for legitimacy from the past. It was important therefore to conserve the *vaṃśānucarita* section of these texts. The question of whether or not the ancestors of a family had participated in the

[7] M. Tokunaga, "Vedic Exegesis and Epic Poetry: A Note on *atrāpy udāharanti*", in P. Koskikallio (ed.), *Parallels and Comparisons*, 21–30. Examples were an essential component of *itihāsa*: *atrāpy udāharantīmam itihāsam purātanam* is the phrase repeated so often. Quoted in J. Fitzgerald, "History and Primordium in Ancient Indian Historical Writing: *Itihāsa* and *Purāṇa* in the *Mahābhārata* and Beyond" (forthcoming).

battle at Kurukṣetra was part of drawing on the past and may not have been intended literally. The aspect of the past that is recalled is relevant to why it is needed in the present.

Legitimation also requires someone with credibility to do the legitimizing. This can be indirect, as when a connection is made to a narrative in an earlier text, but nevertheless needs an endorsement from those who are the authors and controllers of the tradition—bards, priests, monks, court poets, court officials. The credibility of the person who controls the data is essential.

Association with divinity was resorted to in some traditions, but not generally in the Sramanic. Divinity is malleable and the gods play along with local politics. This is very distant from the sternness of history having to follow the will of God. Divinity as a causal factor occurs in three ways: the king may be imbued with elements of deity, or may be in communication with deity, or may be an incarnation. Endorsement from local cult figures and ascetics was also drawn upon. Renunciation plays a role in narratives, but perhaps not always in a literal sense. When a king is said to have renounced the throne to become an ascetic, one wonders if this is a polite way of stating that he was forced to abdicate, or that usurpation was being recorded under the pretence of continuity. In each case the form had to be relevant to the audience for which the claim was intended.

What is being validated are the qualifications of the persons or the institution seeking authority and status. This could be the authority to be the *rājā* of a clan, or to rule a kingdom, or to constitute a Saṅgha. It becomes particularly necessary in a society where political power is relatively open but the assertion of power requires conventional trappings—either acculturation to Sanskritic culture or the observance of Sramanic values. What is being recalled varies according to the record of their activities and the requirements of the present. It can be the actions of heroes, clans, battles, and emerging kingship—as in the epics and *Purāṇas*. For later times it was the creation of kingdoms and the acquiring of sovereignty.

Concepts of time also become part of this process, especially in the interface of cyclic and linear time. The cyclic time of cosmology plays on imagined numbers, some drawn from astronomy and some invented. The sequencing presents various mathematical patterns. The figures have some links with the cosmology of ancient societies with which there was dialogue, the Mesopotamian and the Hellenistic. Cycles of time had captured the imagination of the ancient world. The patterns seem to represent an image of how human interaction with time was perceived rather than an exact measurement of time. It was probably also meant to place human activities in remote or recent time. It constituted a vision of the universe in its immeasurable size, contrasted with the smallness of the human. The contradiction in this construction as pertaining to history is that the length of each age is so unreal that the repetitions of the cycle remain a grand but historically meaningless concept. Therefore the end of one *yuga* and the start of the next is not precisely defined, as with the more than one occasion on which the Kaliyuga is said to start.

However, the two forms, cyclic and linear, were not projected as dichotomous. They were separated by function. Thus, the cycle did not close at the point where it began but continued into the next cycle, and, doing this over four cycles, created a spiral or a helix. A spiral when stretched becomes a wavy line, and if sufficiently stretched can almost become a straight line. The working out of the *yuga* cosmology coincides with observing linear time in historical records. This is characteristic of both the *itihāsa-purāṇa* and the Sramanic traditions. It is almost as if the cycles of time were thought to belong to another dimension of reckoning, from which history was generally but not invariably insulated. Or else a distinction was being made between fantasy and the credible.

In the interface of cyclic and linear there is a potential of more than just two concepts of time. The intersection is very occasionally directly stated, as in the inscription of Pulakeśin II, where the calculation of both the Vikrama *samvat* and the Kaliyuga are given.[8] More frequently it is implied, as in the *vaṃśānucarita* which, constructed in linear time, is located in the *Purāṇa*—which otherwise endorses cyclic time. This could therefore be seen as a linear fraction of the cosmic cyclic arc.

The more exact measurement of time by which human activity could be approximately dated was calculated in linear time. This was a coming together of various linear forms of calculation:

[8] Aihole Inscription, *Ep. Ind.*, 6, 1ff.

genealogies, regnal years, a fixed chronological point for reckoning such as the *parinirvāṇa*, and the much more precisely calculated use of eras drawing on both astronomy and history. The last two of these forms were used extensively in the Sramanic tradition and in inscriptions and historical genres of the *itihāsa-purāṇa* tradition. Linearity tends to give a sharper and more manageable sense of time.

How then do all these texts relate to history? They are essentially narrations of how the past, recent or remote, was visualized. This may, however, on occasion require a description of the present as well, in part to point up the difference. They locate and interconnect persons and events in space and in a chronological sequence of time, although this latter in the earlier texts need not be calculated as numerical dates.

The use of what is thought to be historical surfaces in situations of crisis. The battle at Kurukṣetra brought to an end the *kṣatriya* clans, so this had to be recorded and explained. The *vaṃśānucarita* section of the *Viṣṇu Purāṇa* is an attempt to order and define the past more precisely by stating the importance of the lineages in earliest times and registering the change to kingdoms in more recent times. The Sramanic tradition presents a different past for different reasons. It is not a continuation of the first two and is therefore not referred to. It has its own history.

Each authority seeks validation from the past. The lineages as recorded in the *Purāṇa* are validating a segment of the past. But they are also providing for dynasties to acquire status should they wish to latch themselves onto these lineages as part of their ancestral claims, even if it means manipulating history. The sanction of the past imbues it with credibility.

A commonly believed history confirms an identity, since the construction of history is also stating identities. This is an evident message of the Sramanic tradition. It began as an alternative tradition and consolidated its position by insisting on a history of sequential events. This had to be adjusted to the many dissident groups that evolved, each with their authority, which created innumerable situations of crises. These were doubtless changes that were observed, discussed, and debated by all concerned, apart from the Sramaṇa groups. If there is a difference between one historical tradition and another, as with the *itihāsa-purāṇa* and the Sramanic, then, although the one does not refer to the other, it could well have internalized some aspects of it, as I have tried to argue. A juxtaposition of the two becomes necessary to ascertain the dialogue. The employment of the past to create an identity seems to be reflected in the new genres that emerged in the post-Gupta period.

The ordering of the past as history becomes all the more necessary when there is a crisis of acculturation with new groups having to be adjusted in existing society, but with the probability that new identities will have to be forged. There is therefore a need to be inclusive in periods of historical change. The justification for setting aside social codes, or reiterating other codes, often comes from a reading of the past, as for instance in the form of examples. Given the range of non-conformity in those times, it might have been useful to keep the past a trifle vague so that innovations could be more easily accommodated.

The centrality of explanation in the historical narrative varied from text to text. The Buddhist tradition introduces a degree of causality, which is not surprising given that causality is significant to Buddhist thinking. The crisis of dissidence may have intensified the need for explaining it, and the explanation could extend to other matters as well. Personal characteristics play a role in the actions of the protagonists. In the *itihāsa-purāṇa* tradition, explanation is not reflected in the narration of the change from lineage to dynasty in the *Purāṇa*, but in the biographies and the chronicles explanations are sometimes given for historical change, for the ambition of rulers, and for times of crises—although the simplest is to ascribe decline to the inevitability of the Kaliyuga.

Despite the length of this book, I am aware that my discussion touches only the surface of these texts. Ideally, a study such as this requires examining the various recensions (sometimes in more than one language), ascertaining their authenticity, and analysing them for historical content. This would also demonstrate the process by which the text was composed or compiled, as has been done for a few.[9] Such studies would help us understand the

[9] *The Gopālarājāvaṃśāvalī*; M. Witzel, "On Indian Historical Writing", 2, 1–57.

projection of history in early India, would take a few lifetimes, and depend on an extensive range of expertise. Hopefully some may think it worthwhile.

But somewhere a beginning has to be made towards thinking about the idea of history in early India, and that is what this book has attempted. I have tried to argue that there is what might be called a historiographical trajectory, although not altogether smooth, in the texts to which I have referred. This points to a concern with a historical past, even if this past is constructed in ways different from what we conventionally regard as historical. I have argued that a sense of history and historical consciousness existed, that there were historical traditions emerging from diverse historiographies, and that these occasionally took the form of historical writing.

Bibliography

Primary Sources

Agni Purāṇa, Poona, 1900.

Aitareya Āraṇyaka, A.B. Keith (ed. and trans.), Oxford, 1909.

Aitareya Brāhmaṇa, A.B. Keith (trans.), Delhi, 1971 (rpnt).

Alberuni's India, E.P. Sachau (ed. and trans.), vols I & II, Delhi, 1964 (rpnt).

Aṅguttara Nikāya, R. Morris and E. Hardy (eds), London, 1885–1900.

Antiquities of Chamba, vol. I, J. Ph. Vogel, vol. II, B. Ch. Chhabra (ed.), Calcutta, 1911, Delhi, 1957.

Āpastamba Dharmasūtra, G. Bühler (trans.), Delhi, 1975 (rpnt).

Āpastamba Dharmasūtra, P. Olivelle (trans.), New York, 1999.

Āpastamba Śrauta Sūtra, R. Garbe, Calcutta, 1882–1902.

Āryamañjuśrīmūlakalpa, T.N. Ganapati Sastri (ed.), Trivandrum Sanskrit Series, Trivandrum, 1925.

Āryamañjuśrīmūlakalpa, K.P. Jayaswal (ed. and trans.), *An Imperial History of India,* Lahore, 1934.

Arrian, *Anabasis Alexandri, Books V to VII, Indica*, P.A. Brunt (trans.), *History of Alexander, and Indica*, vol. II, Cambridge (Mass.), 1983.

Arrian's Indica, J.W. McCrindle (trans.), *Ancient India as Described by Megasthenes and Arrian*, London, 1877.

Arthaśāstra, R.P. Kangle (ed.), Bombay, 1965.

Aṣṭādhyāyī of Pāṇini (2 vols), S.C. Vasu (ed. and trans.), Delhi, 1969 (rpnt).

Āśvalāyana Gṛihyasūtra, H. Oldenberg (ed. and trans.), *The Gṛihya-sūtras*, 2 vols, Delhi, 1964 (rpnt).

Āśvalāyana Śrautasūtra, K. Mylius (ed.), Wichtrach, 1994.

Atharvaveda, W.D. Whitney (trans.), Delhi, 1971 (rpnt).

Bāṇabhaṭṭa's Harṣacarita, K.P. Parab (ed.), Bombay, 1925.

Baudhāyana Dharmasūtra, P. Olivelle (trans.), New York, 1999.

Baudhāyana Śrauta Sūtra, W. Caland (ed.), New Delhi, 1982 (rpnt).
Bhadrabāhu cāṇakya candragupta kathānaka evam rājā kalkivarṇan, R.R. Jain (ed.), Varanasi, 1982.
Bhāgavata Purāṇa, V.L. Pansikar (ed.), Bombay, 1920.
Bhāgavata Purāṇa, J.L. Shastri (ed.), New Delhi, 1976/1986 (rpnts).
Bhaviṣya Purāṇa, Kśemarāja Srīkṛṣṇadāsa (ed.), Bombay, 1897.
Bilhaṇa's Vikramāṅkadevacarita, S.C. Banerji and A.K. Gupta (trans.), Calcutta, 1965.
Book of Kindred Sayings: Saṃyutta-nikāya, The, vol. II, C.A.S. Rhys Davids (trans.), London, 1972 (rpnt.). Also see below, *Saṃyutta-nikāya.*
Book of the Discipline, The (*Vinaya Piṭaka*), 6 vols, I.B. Horner (trans.), London, 1938–66. Also see below, *Vinaya Piṭaka.*
Bṛhad-devatā, A.A. Macdonell (ed. and trans.), *Bṛhad-devatā Attributed to Śaunaka*, Cambridge (Mass.), 1904.
Bṛhad-devatā, M. Tokunaga (ed. and trans.), Kyoto, 1997.
Brahmāṇḍa Purāṇa, K. Srikrishnadas (ed.), Bombay, 1913.
Brahmāṇḍa Purāṇa, G.V. Tagare (trans. and annotated), Delhi, 1983.
Buddhacarita: Life of the Buddha by Ashvaghosha, P. Olivelle (trans.), New York, 2008.
Buddhacarita, or the Acts of the Buddha, The, E.H. Johnston (ed. and trans.), Delhi, 1972 (rpnt).
Buddhaghosācārya Papañcasudāni (Majjhimanikāya-aṭṭakathā), J.H. Woods, D. Kosambi, and I.B. Horner (eds), London, 1922–38.
Caurapañcāśikā, S.N. Tadpatrikar (ed.), Poona, 1946.
Collection of the Middle Length Sayings, The, 3 vols, I.B. Horner (trans.), London, 1954–9.
Corpus of Bengal Inscriptions, R. Mukherjee and S. Maity (eds), Calcutta, 1967.
Corpus Inscriptionum Indicarum
I: E. Hultzsch (ed.), London, 1888–1925.
III: J.F. Fleet (ed.), Varanasi, 1970.
III: (revised edn), B.C. Chhabra and G.S. Gai (ed.), Delhi, 1981.
IV: V.V. Mirashi (ed.), Ootacamund, 1955.
V: V.V. Mirashi (ed.), Ootacamund, 1963.
Corpus of Sharda Inscriptions from Kashmir, B.K. Kaul (ed.), Delhi, 1982.
Cūlavamsa, W. Geiger (trans.), London, 1973.
Devī-Bhāgavata Purāṇa, Swami Vijnananda (ed.), Allahabad, 1921.
Dharmakośa, Laxmanshastri Joshi (ed.), Satara, 1937–53.
Dialogues of the Buddha, The, T.W. Rhys Davids and J.E. Carpenter (eds), London, 1890–1911.

Dialogues of the Buddha, The, 3 vols, T.W. Rhys Davids and C.A.F. Rhys Davids (trans.), London, 1899–1921.

Dīgha-nikāya, B.J. Kashyap (gen. ed.), Patna, 1958.

Dīpavaṃsa, The, H. Oldenberg (ed. and trans.), London, 1879.

Divyāvadāna, E.B. Cowell and R.A. Neill (eds), Cambridge, 1886.

Divyāvadāna, P.L. Vaidya (ed.), Darbhanga, 1959.

Dravidian Etymological Dictionary, T. Burrow and M.B. Emeneau (eds), Oxford, 1961.

Epigraphia Indica, New Delhi.

Epigraphia Zeylanica, Colombo.

Fo-pen-hsing-chi-ching, S. Beal (trans.), *The Romantic Legend of Sakya Buddha*, London, 1875.

Gautama Dharmasūtra, P. Olivelle (trans.), New York, 1999.

Geography of Strabo, The, H.L. Jones (trans.), London, 1966 (rpnt).

Gopālarājavaṃśāvalī, The, D. Vajrācārya and K.P. Malla (ed. and trans.), Wiesbaden, 1985.

Gopatha Brāhmaṇa, R. Mitra and H. Vidyabhushan (eds), Calcutta, 1872.

Harṣa-carita of Bāṇa, The, E.B. Cowell and F.W. Thomas (trans.), London, 1929.

Harshacarita of Bāṇabhaṭṭa, The, P.V. Kane (ed.), Delhi, 1965 (2nd edn).

Hemacandra's Dvyāśraya-mahākāvyam, A.V. Kathavaṭe (ed.), Delhi, 1996.

Hemacandra's Kumārapāla-carita, S.P. Pandit and P.L. Vaidya (eds), Poona, 1936.

Hesiod's Theogony: Works and Days, D. Wender (trans.), Harmondsworth, 1973.

Hymns of the Ṛgveda, R.T.H. Griffith (trans.), Varanasi, 1963 (4th edn).

Inscriptions of Bengal, N.G. Majumdar (ed.), Rajshahi, 1929.

Jaiminīya Brāhmaṇa, H.W. Bodewitz (ed.), Leiden, 1973.

Jaiminīya Upaniṣad Brāhmaṇa, H. Oertel (trans.), New Haven, 1894.

Jātaka, The, E.B. Cowell (ed.), London, 1969 (9th edn).

Jinavijayamuni, *Kumārapāla-caritra-saṁgraha*, vol. 41, Bombay, 1956.

Jinaprabhāsūri, *Vividhatīrthakalpa*, Jinavijayamuni (ed.), Bombay, 1934.

Jinasena, *Ādipurāṇa*, Pannālāl Jaina (ed.), Calcutta, 1963–5.

Kalhaṇa's Rājataraṅgiṇī, Chronicle of the Kings of Kashmir, Sanskrit Text with Critical Notes, M.A. Stein (ed.), Bombay, 1892/1979 (rpnt).

Kāmandaka, *Nītisāra*, T.N. Ganapati Sastri (ed.), Trivandrum, 1912. See also below, *Nītisāra*.

Kāṭhaka Saṃhitā, V. Schroeder (ed.), Leipzig, 1900–11.
Kathāvatthu, A.C. Taylor (ed.), vols I and II, London, 1894–7/1979 (rpnt).
Kātyāyana Śrauta Sūtra, V. Sarma (ed.), Banares, 1933–7.
Kauṣītaki Brāhmaṇa, E.B. Cowell (ed.), Calcutta, 1861; A.B. Keith (trans.), Delhi, 1971 (rpnt).
Kumārapāla-prabandha-pratibodha: see below, Somaprabhācārya.
Kunāla Jātaka, W.B. Bollee (ed. and trans.), London, 1970.
La Geste de Rāma: Poeme a double sens de Sandhyākaranandin, S. Brocquet (ed.), Pondicherry, 2010.
Lalitavistara, S. Lefmann (ed.), Halle, 1902–8.
Lalitavistara, R. Mitra (ed.), Calcutta, 1877–81.
Lāṭyāyana Śrauta Sūtra (3 vols), H.G. Ranade (ed. and trans.), New Delhi, 1998.
Lekhapaddhati, P. Prasad (ed. and trans.), Delhi, 2007.
Law Code of Viṣṇu, The: A Critical Edition and Annotated Translation of the Vaiṣṇava-Dharmaśāstra, P. Olivelle (trans.), Cambridge, Mass., 2009.
Life of Hiuen-Tsiang by the Shaman Hwui Li, The, S. Beal (ed. and trans.), London, 1911.
Life of the Buddha and the Early History of the Order, The, W.W. Rockhill (trans.), Varanasi, 1972 (rpnt).
Mahābhārata, *The*, 19 vols, V.S. Sukthankar, S.K. Belvalkar, and P.L.Vaidya, *et al.* (eds), Critical Edition, Poona, 1933–66.
Mahābhārata, *The*, vols 1, 2, 3, 4, 5, J.A.B. van Buitenen (trans.), Chicago, 1973.
Mahābhārata, *The*, vols 11, 12, J.L. Fitzgerald (trans.), Chicago, 2004.
Mahāvaṃsa, W. Geiger (trans.), London, 1912/1964 (rpnt).
Mahāvastu, J.J. Jones (trans.), London, 1973 (rpnt).
Mahāvastu, 3 vols, E. Senart (ed.), Paris, 1987–97.
Maitrāyaṇī Saṃhitā, V. Schroeder (ed.), Leipzig, 1881–6.
Majjhima-nikāya, *The*, 3 vols, V. Trenckner and R. Chalmers (eds), London, 1888–96.
Manu's Code of Law, P. Olivelle (ed. and trans.), New Delhi, 2006.
Matsya Purāṇa, H.N. Apte (ed.), Poona, 1907.
Megasthenes' Indica, J.W. McCrindle (trans.), *Ancient India as Described by Megasthenes and Arrian*, London, 1877.
Merutuṅga, *Prabandha-cintāmaṇi,* ed. Jinavijayamuni, 1933, Santiniketan.
Milinda-pañho, V. Trenckner (ed.), London, 1880; T.W. Rhys Davids

(trans.), *The Questions of King Milinda*, New York, 1963 (rpnt.). Also see below, Rhys Davids, T.W.

Minor Anthologies of the Pali Canon, The, I.B. Horner (trans.), vol. III, London, 1975.

Mudrārākṣasa of Viśākhadatta, M.R. Kale (ed.), Delhi, 1976.

Mudrārākṣasa or The Signet Ring, K.H. Dhruva (ed.), Poona, 1930 (3rd edn).

Mudrārākṣasa of Viśākhadatta, C.R. Devadhar and V.M. Bedekar (eds), Bombay, 1948.

Nāradasmṛti, The, R.W. Lariviere (ed. and trans.), vols I and II, Philadelphia, 1989.

Nighantu tathā Nirukta, Laksman Svarup (ed.), Delhi, 1967.

Nirukta of Yāska, B. Bhattacharya (ed.), *Yāska's Nirukta,* Calcutta, 1958.

Nītisāra of Kāmandaka, Trivandrum Sanskrit Series, no. XIV, Trivandrum, 1912. See also above, Kāmandaka.

Padma Purāṇa, V.N. Mandlik (trans.), Poona, 1893–4.

Pañcaviṃśa Brāhmaṇa, W. Caland (trans.), Calcutta, 1982 (rpnt).

Pariśiṣṭaparvan, H. Jacobi (ed.), Calcutta, 1932 (2nd edn).

Parmāl Rāso, S.S. Das (ed.), Benaras 1919.

Patañjali's Vyākaraṇa-Mahābhāṣya, S.D. Joshi (trans. and ed), Poona, 1968.

Paumacariyam, vols I and II, H. Jacobi (ed.), *Ācārya Vimalasūri's Paumacariyam*, Varanasi, 1962.

Plato: *Timaeus*, R.G. Bury (trans.), London, 1952.

Pliny: *Natural History*, H. Rackham (trans.), Ann Arbor, 2004 (rpnt).

Points of Controversy: The Kathāvatthu, Shwe Zan Aung and C. Rhys Davids (trans.), London, 1915.

Prabandha-cintāmaṇi of Merutuṅga Ācārya, The (The Wishing-stone of Narratives), C.H. Tawney (trans.), Calcutta, 1899/1907 (rpnt).

Prabodhacandrodaya, V.L. Pansikar (ed.), Bombay, 1924.

Rājataraṅgiṇī, M.A. Stein (ed. and trans.), *Kalhaṇa's Rājataraṅgiṇī, or, A Chronicle of the Kings of Kaśmir*, Delhi, 1960/1979 (rpnt).

Rāmacarita by Sandhyākara Nandi, Haraprasad Sastri (ed.), Memoirs of the Asiatic Society of Bengal, 3, 1–56, Calcutta, 1910.

Rāmacarita of Sandhyākaranandin, Revised with English Translation and Notes, Memoirs of the Asiatic Society of Bengal, R. Basak (ed.), Calcutta, 1969.

Rāmacaritam of Sandhyākaranandin, The, *Edited with Sanskrit Commentaries and English Translation*, R.C. Majumdar, R. Basak, and N.B. Banerji (eds), Rajashahi, 1939.

Ramāyaṇa of Vālmīki, The: An Epic of Ancient India, Critical Edition, vols I–VI and VII forthcoming, R.P. Goldman (gen. ed.), Princeton, 1984–2008. See also below, *Vālmīki Ramāyaṇa.*

Ṛgveda, M. Müller (ed.), London, 1890.

Rhinoceros Horn and Other Early Buddhist Poems (Sutta-nipāta), The, K.R. Norman (trans.), Oxford, 1996.

Rig-Veda, Der (German), K.F. Geldner (trans.), Cambridge, Massachusetts, 1951.

Saddharmapuṇḍarīka Sūtra, H. Kern and B. Nanjio (eds), St Petersburg, 1912.

Samantapāsādikā: Buddhaghoṣa's Commentary on the Vinaya Piṭaka, J. Takakusu and M. Nagai (eds), London, 1924.

Saṃyutta-nikāya, L. Freer (ed.), London 1984–1904; C.A.S. Rhys Davids (trans.), *The Book of Kindred Sayings*, 1972 (rpnt.), London. Also see above, *Book of Kindred Sayings.*

Śāṅkhāyana Gṛihyasūtra, H. Oldenberg (ed. and trans.), *The Grihya-sūtras*, 2 vols, Delhi, 1964 (rpnt).

Śāṅkhāyana Śrautasūtra, A. Hillebrandt (ed.), Calcutta, 1886–9.

Śatapatha Brāhmaṇa, J. Eggeling (trans.), Delhi, 1972 (rpnt).

Śiva Purāṇa, A. Kunst and J.L. Shastri (ed.), Delhi, 1970.

Si-yu-ki: Buddhist Records of the Western World, S. Beal (ed. and trans.), Delhi, 1969 (rpnt).

Skanda Purāṇa, G.V. Tagare and J.L. Shastri (trans. and annotated), Delhi, 1993.

Somadevasūri, *Nītivyākāmṛta*, R. Malaviya (ed.), Varanasi, 1972.

Somaprabhācārya, *Kumārapāla-prabandha-pratibodha*, N.V. Vaidya (ed.), Poona, 1956.

Śriviṣṇupurāṇa, Gorakhpur, 1970.

Sthavirāvalī / Pariśiṣṭaparvan of Hemachandra, H. Jacobi (ed.), Calcutta, 1932 (2nd edn).

Sumaṇgalavilāsinī, T.W. Rhys Davids and J.E. Carpenter (eds), London, 1886.

Sutta-nipāta, The, D. Andersen, and H. Smith (ed. and trans.), London, 1913.

Taittirīya Brāhmaṇa, R. Mitra (ed.), Calcutta, 1855–70.

Taittirīya Saṃhitā (2 vols), A.B. Keith (trans.), Delhi, 1967 (rpnt).

Tāranātha, *History of Buddhism in India*, D. Chattopadhyaya (ed.), L. Chimpa and A. Chattopadhyaya (trans.), Simla, 1972; rpnt. Calcutta, 1980.

Triṣaṣṭiśalākāpuruṣacarita, H.M. Johnson (trans.), B. Bhattacharyya (ed.), 1931, Baroda.

Upaniṣads, in S. Radhakrishnan (ed.), *The Thirteen Principal Upaniṣads*, London, 1953.

Vājasaneyī Saṃhitā, A. Weber (ed.), London, 1852.

Vālmīki Rāmāyaṇa, The, 7 vols, Critical Edition, G.H. Bhatt and U.P. Shah (gen. eds), Baroda, 1960–75. See also above, *Rāmāyaṇa of Vālmīki.*

Vaṃsatthappakāsinī / Mahāvaṃsa Ṭīkā, G.P. Malalasekera (ed.), London, 1933.

Varāhamihira's Bṛhatsaṃhitā, M.R Bhat and R.S. Sastri (trans. and ed.), 2 vols, Bangalore, 1947.

Vāyu Purāṇa, R. Mitra (ed.), Calcutta, 1880.

Vikramāṅkadevacarita, The, by Vidyāpati Bilhaṇa, G. Buhler (ed.), Bombay, 1875.

Vinaya Piṭaka, 6 vols, I.B. Horner (trans.), *Book of the Discipline, The*, London, 1938–66. Also see above, *Book of the Discipline.*

Vinaya Piṭakam, 5 vols, H. Oldenberg (ed.), London, 1879–83.

Vinaya Texts, T.W. Rhys Davids and H. Oldenberg, Oxford, 1881–5.

Vishnu Purāṇa, The, H.H. Wilson (trans. and ed.), London, 1840.

Viṣṇu Purāṇa, parts I-III, M.M. Pathak (ed.), Gorakhpur/Vadodara, 1967/1997.

Viṣṇu Purāṇa, part IV, Gorakhpur, 1970.

Yājñavalkyasmṛti, M.N. Dutt and K. Joshī (eds), Delhi, 2005.

Secondary Sources

Abrams, M., 1971, *Natural Supernaturalism,* New York.

Adikaram, E.W., 1946, *Early History of Buddhism in Ceylon*, Migoda.

Agashe, S., forthcoming, *The Geography of the Ramayana.*

Agrawala, V.S., 1950, "Catalogue of the Mathura Museum", *Journal of the Uttar Pradesh Historical Society,* 23, 36ff.

———, 1963, *Matsya Purāṇa: A Study,* Varanasi.

———, 1966, "Original Purāṇa Saṃhitā", *Purāṇa*, 8, 2, 232–45.

Ahmad, A., 1992, *In Theory: Classes, Nations, Literatures,* London.

———, 1992, "Orientalism and After", *EPW*, XLVI, 98–116.

Aiyer, S., 1922, "An Unidentified Territory of South India", *JRAS*, 2, 161–75.

Ali, D., 2000, "Royal Eulogy as World History: Rethinking Copper-plate Inscriptions in Cola India", in R. Inden, *et al.* (eds), *Querying the Medieval: Texts and the History of Practices in South Asia*, Delhi.

———, 2004, *Courtly Culture and Political Life in Early Medieval India*, Cambridge.

Allaby, M. (ed.), 1985, *The Oxford Dictionary of Natural History*, Oxford.

Allen, N., 1997, "And the Lake Drained Away", in A.W. Macdonald (ed.), *Mandala and Landscape*, Delhi.

Alsdorf, L., 1964, "The Ākhyāna Theory Reconsidered", *JOI (Baroda)*, 13, 3, 197ff.

Anderson, P., 1979, *Lineages of the Absolutist State*, London.

Antoine, R., 1975, *Rama and the Bards: Epic Memory in the Ramayana*, Calcutta.

Apte, Vaman Shivaram, 1957–9, *The Practical Sanskrit–English Dictionary*, Poona.

Aquil, R. and P. Chatterjee (eds), 2008, *History in the Vernacular*, Delhi.

Asher, C.B., 1997, "Appropriating the Past: Jahangir"s Pillars", *Islamic Culture*, 71, 4, 8ff.

Atkinson, E.T., 1972 (rpnt), *Himalayan Gazetteer, 1881–84*, Delhi.

Avineri, S. (ed.), 1969, *Karl Marx on Colonialism and Modernisation*, New York.

Awasthi, A.B.L., 1975, *History from the Puranas*, Lucknow.

Bagchi, J., 1993, *The History and Culture of the Pālas of Bengal (c. 750 – c. 1200)*, Delhi.

Bailey, G., 1997, "Intertextuality in the Purāṇas: A Neglected Element in the Study of Sanskrit Literature", in M. Brockington and P. Shreiner (eds), *Composing a Tradition: Concepts, Techniques and Relations*, Zagreb.

———, and M. Brockington, 2000, *Epic Threads*, New Delhi.

Bailey, H.W., 1959, "Iranian *Arya* and *Daha*", *Transactions of the Philological Society*, 58, 71–115.

Bajpai, K.D., 1977, "Development of Jaina Art in Madhya Pradesh", *JIH*, December, LV, 89ff.

Bakhtin, M.M, 1986, *The Dialogic Imagination*, New Jersey.

Bakker, H.T. (ed.), 2004, *The Vākaṭaka Heritage: Indian Culture at the Crossroads*, Groningen.

———, 2005, "Monuments to the Dead", in D. Handa and R.K. Sharma (eds), *Revealing the Past*, Delhi.

Balslev, N.A., 1983, *A Study of Time in Indian Philosophy*, Wiesbaden.

Barth, A., 1907, "The Inscription on the Piprahwa Vase", *Ind. Ant.*, XXXVI, 117–24.

Basham, A.L., 1961, "The Kashmir Chronicle", in C.H. Philips (ed.), *Historians of India, Pakistan and Ceylon,* London.

———, 1964, *Studies in Indian History and Culture*, Calcutta.

———, 1983, "The Mandasor Inscription of the Silk Weavers", in B.L. Smith (ed.), *Essays on Gupta Culture*, Delhi.

———, 1990, *The Origins and Development of Classical Hinduism,* Delhi.

Beal, S., 1907, *The Romantic Legend of Sakya Buddha*, London.

Bechert, H., 1969–70, "Thervāda Buddhist Sangha: Some General Observations on Historical and Political Factors in its Development", *JAS*, 29, 761–78.

———, 1977, *William Geiger: His Life and Works,* Colombo.

——— (ed.), 1991, *The Dating of the Historical Buddha*, vols I–II, Goettingen.

Bentley, J., 1799, "Remarks on the Principal Eras and Dates of the Ancient Hindus", *Asiatic Researches,* 5, 315–93.

———, 1809, "On the Hindu System of Astronomy", *Asiatic Researches,* 8, 195–244.

Bhandarkar, D.R., 1911, "Foreign Elements in the Hindu Population", *Ind. Ant.,* 40, 24ff.

Bhargava, P.L., 1952/1956, *India in the Vedic Age*, Bombay/Lucknow.

Bhatnagar, V.S. (trans.), 1991, *Padmanābha's Kanhadade Prabandha: India's Greatest Patriotic Saga of Medieval Times*, Delhi.

Bhatt, G.H., 1959–60, "On Vālmīki", *JOI (Baroda)*, 9, 1–4.

Biardeau, M., 1968, "Etude de Mythologique Hindoue", *BEFEO*, 54, 19–45.

———, 1968, "Some More Considerations About Textual Criticism", *Purāṇa*, 10, 2, 115–23.

———, 1981, "The Salvation of the King in the Mahābhārata", *Contributions*, 15, 1 and 2, 75–97.

Bloch, J., 1950/1955, *Les Inscriptions d'Asoka,* Paris.

Bohanan, L., 1952, "A Genealogical Charter", *AJIAI*, 22, 301–15.

Bonazzoli, G., 1980, "Puranic Parampara", *Purāṇa*, 22, 1, 33–60.

———, 1981, "Places of Puranic Recitation according to the Purāṇas", *Purāṇa*, 23, 1, 48–60.

———, 1983, "Composition, Transmission and Recitation of the Purāṇas", *Purāṇa*, 25, 2, 254–80.

———, 1983, "Remarks on the Nature of the Purāṇas", *Purāṇa*, 25, 1, 77–113.

Bongard-Levin, G.M., 1971, "The Historicity of the Ancient Indian *Avadānas*", in G.M. Bongard-Levin (ed.), *Studies in Ancient India and Central Asia*, Calcutta.

Bose, N.S., 1956, *History of the Candellas of Jejakabhukti*, Calcutta.

Bowra, C.M., 1957, *Heroic Poetry*, London.

Brandt, W.J., 1966, *The Shape of Medieval History*, New Haven.

Brarvig, J. and F. Liland, 2010, *Traces of Gandharan Buddhism,* Oslo.

Brockington, J., 1976, "Religious Attitudes in Vālmīki's *Rāmāyaṇa*", *JRAS*, 2, 108–30.

———, 1984, *Righteous Rāma*, Delhi.

———, 1991, "Issues Involved in the Shift from Oral to Written Transmission of the Epics: A Workshop Report", in J. Brockington and P. Schreiner (eds), *Composing a Tradition: Concepts, Techniques and Relationships*, Zagreb.

———, 1998, *The Sanskrit Epics,* New Delhi.

———, 2002, "Jārasandha of Magadha, Mbh. 2.15–22", in M. Brockington (ed.), *Stages and Transitions*, Zagreb.

Brocquet, S., 2010, *La Geste de Rāma: poeme a double sens de Sandhyākaranandin,* Pondicherry.

Brodbeck, S.P., 2009, *The Mahābhārata Patriline,* Ashgate.

Brough, J., 1953, *The Early Brahmanical System of Gotra and Pravara*, Cambridge.

Buhler, G., 1877, "Report on a Tour in Search of Sanskrit MSS in Kashmir", *JBBRAS*, 38ff. (extra number).

———, 1892, "New Jaina Inscriptions from Mathura", *Ep. Ind.,* I, Calcutta.

———, 1892, "Further Jaina Inscriptions from Mathura", *Ep. Ind.,* II, Calcutta.

———, 1936, *Life of the Jaina Monk Hemacandra*, M. Patel (trans.), Santiniketan.

Bulcke, C., 1950, *Rāmakathā*, Allahabad.

———, 1952–3, "The Genesis of the Bālakāṇḍa", *JOI (Baroda)*, 2, 327–31.

———, 1958–9, "About Materials for the Biography of Vālmīki, Author of the First Rāmāyaṇa", *JOI (Baroda)*, 8, 3–19, 121–31, 346–8.

Burgess, J. and B. Indraji, 1976 (rpnt), *Inscriptions from the Cave Temples of Western India*, *ASWI*, 10, 1881, Delhi.

Burke, P., 1969, *The Renaissance Sense of the Past*, London.

Burrow, T., 1965, *The Sanskrit Language*, London.

Burstein, S.M. (ed. and trans.), 1978, *The Babylonica of Berossus*, Malibu.

Caland, W. (ed.), 1919, *Das Jaiminīya Brāhmaṇa*, Amsterdam.

Carr, E.H., 1986, *What is History?*, Basingstoke.

Chadwick, N.K., 1952, *Poetry and Prophecy*, Cambridge.

Chakrabarti, D.K., 1988, *A History of Indian Archaeology from the Beginning to 1947*, Delhi.

Chakrabarti, K., 2001, *Religious Process: The Purāṇas and the Making of a Religious Tradition*, Delhi.

———, forthcoming, "Brahmanical Hegemony and the Oppressed Social Groups: The Kaivarta 'Revolt' and After".

Chakravarti, U., 1988, *The Social Dimensions of Early Buddhism,* Delhi.

———, 1989, "Whatever Happened to the Vedic Dāsī?", in K. Sangari and S. Vaid (eds), *Recasting Women*, Delhi.

Chamba, 1996, *Gazetteer of the Chamba State*, New Delhi.

Champakalakshmi R. and S. Gopal (eds), 1996, *Tradition, Dissent and Ideology*, Delhi.

Chanana, D.R., 1963, *The Spread of Agriculture in Northern India*, New Delhi.

Chandra, K.R., 1970, *A Critical Study of Paumacariyam*, Vaishali.

Chatterjee, P., 1993, *The Nation and Its Fragments*: *Colonial and Post-colonial Histories*, New Jersey.

Chattopadhyaya, B.D., 1994, *The Making of Early Medieval India*, Delhi.

——— (ed.), 2002, *D.D. Kosambi: Combined Methods in Indology and Other Writings*, Delhi.

Chaudhuri, S.B., 1955, *Ethnic Settlements in Ancient India: A Study of the Puranic Lists of the Peoples of Bharatavarsa*, Calcutta.

Chaudhury, R.K., 1964, *Vratyas in Ancient India*, Varanasi.

Chhabra, B. and G.S. Gai (eds), 1981, *Corpus Inscriptionum Indicarum*, vol. III. See also above, *Corpus Inscriptionum Indicarum.*

Choudhury, G.C., 1954, *Political History of Northern India from Jaina Sources, c. 650 AD to 1300 AD*, Amritsar.

Chowdhury, A.M., 1967, *Dynastic History of Bengal*, Dacca.

Church, C.D., 1974, "The Myth of the Four Yugas in the Sanskrit Puranas", *Purāṇa*, 16, 1, 5–25.

Cohn, B., 1987, *An Anthropologist among the Historians and Other Essays*, Delhi.

Colie, R.L., 1973, *The Resources of Kind: Genre-Theory in the Renaissance*, Berkeley.

Collingwood, R.G., 1946, *The Idea of History,* Oxford.

Collins, S., 1982, *Selfless Persons: Imagery and Thought in Thervāda Buddhism,* London.

———, 1992, "Notes on Some Oral Aspects of Pāli Literature", *IIJ,* 35, 2–3, 121–36.

Conze, E., 1980, *A Short History of Buddhism*, London.

Coomaraswamy, A.K., *c.* 1940s (unpublished), "The Flood in Hindu Tradition", in R. Lipsey (ed.), *Coomaraswamy, Selected Papers 2*, Princeton, 1977.
Cornford, F.M., 1907, *Thucydides Mythhistoricus*, London.
Cort, J.E., 1995, "Genesis of Jaina History", *JIP*, 23, 469–506.
———, 1998, "Who is King?", in J.E. Cort (ed.), *Open Boundaries*, New York.
Coulson, M., 2006 (rpnt), *Rākṣasa's Ring* (trans.), New York.
Cousins, L.S., 1983, *Buddhist Studies,* London.
———, 1996, "The Dating of the Historical Buddha: A Review Article", *JRAS*, Series 3, 6, 1, 57–63.
Cumont, F., 1910, *The Mysteries of Mithra*, Chicago.
Cunningham, A., 1872–3 / 2000 (rpnt), *ASR*, "Report for the Year 1872–3", V, 145–75.
———, 1874–5 and 1876–7 / 2000 (rpnt), *ASR*, "Tours in Bundelkhand and Malwa", X, 98–9.
———, 1883–4 and 1884–5 / 2000 (rpnt), *ASR*, "A Tour in Bundelkhand and Rewa 1883–84", XXI, 171–4.
Dani, A.H., 1963, *Indian Palaeography*, Oxford.
Das Gupta, S.B., 1946, *Obscure Religious Cults*, Calcutta.
Davis, S., 1799, "On the Indian Cycle of Sixty Years", *Asiatic Researches*, 5, 289ff.
de Certeau, M., 1988, *The Writing of History*, New York.
de Gobineau, J.A. Comte, 1853–5, *Essai sur l'inegalite des races humaines*, Paris.
de Jong, J.W., 1968, *Buddha's Word in China*, Canberra.
———, 1975, "Recent Russian Publications on the Indian Epic", *The Adyar Library Bulletin*, 39, 1–42.
———, 1976, *A Brief History of Buddhist Studies in Europe and America*, Varanasi.
de la Vallee Poussin, L., 1976, *The Buddhist Councils*, Calcutta.
de Silva, K.M. (ed.), 1970, *History of Ceylon*, Colombo.
de Souza, J.P. and C.M. Kulkarni (eds), 1972, *Historiography in Indian Languages*, Delhi.
Deeg, M., 2009, "From the Iron-wheel to Bodhisattvahood: Aśoka in Buddhist Culture and Memory", in P. Olivelle (ed.), *Aśoka in History and Historical Memory*, Delhi.
Dehejia, V., 1997, *Discourse in Early Buddhist Art*, Delhi.
den Boer, W., 1968, "Greco-Roman Historiography in its Relation to Biblical and Modern Thinking", *HT*, 7, 60–75.

Desai, D., 1975, *Erotic Sculpture of India: A Socio-Cultural Study*, New Delhi.

Deshpande, C.R., 1978, *Transmission of the Mahabharata Tradition*, Simla.

Deshpande, M.M., 1978, "Genesis of Ṛgvedic Retroflexion: A Historical and Sociolinguistic Investigation", in M.M. Deshpande and P.E. Hook (eds), *Aryan and Non-Aryan in India*, Ann Arbor.

Deshpande, P., 2007, *Creative Pasts: Historical Memory and Identity in Western India 1700–1960*, Delhi.

Deva, K., 1959, "The Temples of Khajuraho in Central India", *Ancient India*, 15, 4–43.

Devahuti, D., 1998, *Harsha: A Political Study*, Delhi.

Devasthali, G.V., 1948, *Introduction to the Study of the Mudraraksasa*, Bombay.

Deyell, J., 1990, *Living Without Silver*, Delhi.

Dhirasekera, J., 1979, "Texts and Traditions—Warped and Distorted", in *Narada Felicitation Volume*, Colombo.

Dikshit, R.K., 1977, *Candellas of Jejakabhukti*, New Delhi.

Dikshitar, V.R.R., 1933, *Some Aspects of the Vāyu Purāṇa,* Madras.

———, 1950, "The Age of Viṣṇu Purāṇa", *IHQ*, 13, 46–50.

Dimock, E.C. and P.C. Gupta (eds), 1965, *The Mahārāṣṭra Purāṇa*, Honolulu.

Dirks, N.B., 1987, *The Hollow Crown*, Cambridge.

———, 2001, *Castes of Mind: Colonialism and the Making of Modern India*, Princeton.

du Perron, M. Anquetil, 1786, *Recherches Historiques et Geographiques sur l'Inde*, vol. II, Berlin.

Dumezil, G., 1986, *The Plight of a Sorcerer*, Berkeley.

Dumville, D., 1977, "Kingship, Genealogies and Regnal Lists", in P.H. Sawyer and I.N. Woods (eds), *Early Medieval Kingship*, Leeds.

Dundas, P., 1992, *The Jains*, London.

Earle, T. (ed.), 1991, *Chiefdoms: Power, Economy and Ideology*, Cambridge.

Eggermont, P.H.L., 1956, *The Chronology of the Reign of Aśoka Moriya*, Leiden.

Eliade, M., 1957, "Time and Eternity in Indian Thought", in J. Campbell (ed.), *Man and Time*, Bollingen Series XXX.3, New York.

———, 1959, *Cosmos and History: The Myth of the Eternal Return*, New York.

Eliot, H.M. and J. Dowson, 1996 (rpnt), *History of India as Told by Its Own Historians*, vol. 1, Delhi.

Embree, A., 1962, *Charles Grant and the Evangelicals*, London.
Erdosy, G. (ed.), 1995, *The Indo-Aryans of Ancient South Asia: Language, Material Culture, Ethnicity*, Berlin.
———, 1988, *Urbanisation in Early Historical India*, Oxford.
Errington, S., 1979, "Style in the Meaning of the Past", *JAS*, 38, 2, 231–44.
Evans-Pritchard, E., 1940, *The Nuer*, Oxford.
Falk, H., 2006, *Aśokan Sites and Artifacts*, Mainz.
Fausboll, V., 1871, *The Dasaratha-Jātaka, being the Buddhist Story of King Rama,* Copenhagen.
Fick, R., 1974 (rpnt), *Social Conditions in North-eastern India during the Buddha's Time,* Varanasi.
Filliozat, P., 1982, "The Afterdeath Destiny of the Hero According to the Mahābhārata", in S. Settar and G.D. Sontheimer (eds), *Memorial Stones*, Dharwar.
Finley, M., 1983, *Politics in the Ancient World,* Cambridge.
Finnegan, R., 1977, *Oral Poetry*, Cambridge.
Fitzgerald, J.L., 1991, "India's Fifth Veda: The Mahābhārata's Presentation of Itself", in A. Sharma (ed.), *Essays on the Mahābhārata*, Leiden.
———, 2010, "No Contest between Memory and Invention", in D. Konstan and K.A. Raaflaub (eds), *Epic and History*, Chichester.
———, 2012, "History and Primordium in Ancient Indian Historical Writing: *Itihāsa* and *Purāṇa* in the *Mahābhārata* and Beyond", in K.A. Raaflaub (ed.), *Thinking, Recording and Writing History in the Ancient World*, Oxford.
Fleet, J.F., 1879, "The Cālukya-Vikrama Varsha, or Era of the Western Cālukya King Vikramāditya VI", *Ind. Ant.*, 8, 187ff.
———, 1911, "The Kaliyuga Era of BC 3102", *JRAS*, 43, 2, 479–96.
Flood, F.B., 2003, "Pillars, Palimpsests and Princely Practices", *Res*, 43, 95–116.
———, 2009, *Objects of Translation*, Princeton.
Forbes, A.K., 1973 (rpnt), *Ras Mala*, Delhi.
Fortes, M., 1953, "The Structure of Unilineal Descent Groups", *American Anthropologist*, 55, 17–41.
Francke, A.H., 1972 (rpnt), *Antiquities of Indian Tibet*, New Delhi.
Freud, S., 1968 (rpnt), "Constructions in Analysis", in idem, *The Complete Psychological Works of Sigmund Freud* (The Standard Edition, 24 vols), vol. 23, 255–70.
Frye, Northrop, 1957, *Anatomy of Criticism*, New Jersey.
Fuji, M., 1994, "On the Textual Formation of the Nīlamata Purāṇa", in Y. Ikari (ed.), *A Study of the Nīlamata*, Kyoto.

Funayama, T., 1994, "Remarks on Religious Predominance in Kashmir: Hindu or Buddhist", in Y. Ikari (ed.), *A Study of the Nīlamata*, Kyoto.

Furedi, F., 1992, *Mythical Past, Elusive Future*, London.

Fussman, G., 1989, "The Māṭ *Devakula*: A New Approach to its Understanding", in D. Srinivasan (ed.), *Mathura*, New Delhi.

Fynes, R.C. (trans.), 1998, *The Lives of the Jaina Elders*, Oxford.

Gai, G.S., 1968–9, "Three Inscriptions of Rāma-Gupta", *JOI*, XVIII, 247–51.

Gangoli, O.C., *et al.*, 1957, *The Art of the Candellas*, Calcutta.

Gaur, R.C., 1974, "The Legend of Purūravas and Urvaśī: An Interpretation", *JRAS*, 106, 2.

Geiger, W., 1908, *The Dīpavamsa and Mahāvamsa*, Colombo.

Gerth, H.H. and C. Wright Mills (eds), 1961, *From Max Weber*, London.

Ghose, N.N., 1965 (2nd edn), *Indo-Aryan Literature and Culture,* Varanasi.

Ghoshal, U.N., 1942, "The Dynastic Chronicles of Kashmir", *IHQ*, Calcutta, XIX, 1–4, 27–38.

———, 1944, *Beginnings of Indian Historiography and Other Essays*, Calcutta.

———, 1965, *Studies in Indian History and Culture*, Delhi.

Ghurye, K.G., 1950, *Preservation of Learned Tradition in India*, Bombay.

Goetz, H., 1955, *The Early Wooden Temples of Chamba*, Leiden.

Gokhale, B.G., 1979, "On Buddhist Historiography", in A.K. Narain (ed.), *Studies in Pali and Buddhism,* Delhi.

Goldman, R.P., 1969, "Mortal Man and Immortal Woman", *JOI (Baroda)*, 18, 4, 273–303.

———, 1976, "Vālmīki and the Bhṛgu Connection", *JAOS*, 96, 1, 69ff.

———, 1977, *Gods, Priests and Warriors: The Bhṛgus of the Mahābhārata*, New York.

Gombrich, R., 1985, "The Vessantara Jātaka, the Rāmāyaṇa and the Dasaratha Jātaka", *JAOS*, 105, 427–37.

———, 1989, "Recovering the Buddha's Message", in T. Skorupski (ed.), *The Buddhist Forum*, vol. I, London.

Gonda, J., 1975, "Gifts and Giving in the Rigveda", *Selected Studies*, vol. IV, Leiden.

———, 1975, *Vedic Literature*, Wiesbaden.

——— (ed.), 1973, *History of Indian Literature*, vol. III, Wiesbaden.

Gonzales-Reiman, L., 2002, *The Mahābhārata and the Yugas*, New York.

———, 2006, "The Divinity of Rāma in the Rāmāyaṇa of Vālmīki", *JIP*, 34, 203–20.
———, 2009, "Cosmic Cycles, Cosmology and Cosmography", in K.A. Jacobsen (ed.), *Brill's Encyclopaedia of Hinduism*, vol. I, Leiden.
Goody, J. (ed.), 1968, *Literacy in Traditional Societies,* Cambridge.
——— and I. Watt, 1963, "The Consequences of Literacy", *CSSH*, 5, 304–45.
Gopal, Sarvepalli (ed.), 1990, *Anatomy of a Confrontation,* Delhi.
Gough, K., 1961, *Matrilineal Kinship,* Berkeley.
Goyal, S., 1992, *History and Historiography of the Age of Harṣa*, Jodhpur.
———, 2007, "The Recently Discovered Kurukshetra–Varanasi Grant of Harṣa: Year 23", *EW*, 57, 1–4, 193–203.
———, 2009, *Probings in Indian History*, Jodhpur.
Goyal, S.R., 1967, *A History of the Imperial Guptas*, Allahabad.
———, 1986, *Harṣa and Buddhism*, Meerut.
Granoff, P., 1989, "Religious Biography and Clan History among Śvetāmbara Jains in Northern India", *EW*, 39, 1–4, 195–211.
———, 1992, "Worship as Commemoration", *BEI*, 10, 181–202.
Grassman, H., 1976 (rpnt), *Worterbuch zum Rigveda*, vol. II, Wiesbaden.
Gregory, C.A., 1982, *Gifts and Commodities*, London.
Guenée, B., 1980, *Historie et Culture Historique dans l'Occident Medievale*, Paris.
Guha, R., 1988, *An Indian Historiography of India*, Calcutta.
———, 2002, *History at the Limit of World History*, New York.
Guha, S., 2004, "Speaking Historically: The Changing Voices of Historical Narratives in Western India 1400–1900", *AHR*, 109, 4, 1084–1103.
Gunawardana, R.A.L.H., 1976, "The Analysis of Pre-colonial Social Formations in Asia in the Writings of Karl Marx", *IHR*, 11, 2, 365–88.
———, 1976, "The Kinsmen of the Buddha: Myth and Political Charter in the Ancient and Medieval Kingdoms in Sri Lanka", *SLJH*, II, 1, 53–62.
———, 1979, *Robe and Plough*: *Monasticism and Economic Interest in Early Medieval Sri Lanka,* Tucson.
———, 1988/1990, "Subtile Silks of Ferrous Firmness", *SLJH*, XIV, 1 and 2, 1–59.
———, 2008, *Periodisation in Sri Lankan History,* Colombo.
Gupta, A.S., 1964, "Purāṇa, Itihāsa and Ākhyāna", *Purāṇa*, VI, 2, 451ff.
Halbfass, W., 1988, *India and Europe*, Albany.

Hardy, F., 1993, "Information and Transformation—Two Faces of the Purāṇas", in W. Doniger (ed.), *Purana Perrenis*, New York.

Havale, S., 1946, *The Pradhans of the Upper Narbada Valley,* Bombay.

Hazra, R.C., 1940/1975 (rpnt), *Studies in the Puranic Records of Hindu Rites and Customs*, Dacca /Delhi.

———, 1955, "The Aśvamedha, the Common Source of Origin of the Purāṇa Pañca-lakṣana and the Mahābhārata", *ABORI*, 36, 190–203.

———, 1958, *Studies in the Upa-Puranas,* Calcutta.

Heehs, P., 2003, "Shades of Orientalism: Paradoxes and Problems in Indian Historiography", *HT*, 42, 2, 169–95.

Heesterman, J.C., 1957, *The Ancient Indian Royal Consecration*, The Hague.

———, 1985, *The Inner Conflict of Tradition: Essays on Indian Ritual, Kingship and Society*, Chicago.

Hegel, G.W.F, 1857/1958, *Lectures on the Philosophy of History,* J. Sibree (trans.), London/New York.

Hein, N., 1986, "Epic *Sarvabhūtahite Rataḥ*: A By-word of Non-Bhārgava Editors", *ABORI,* 67, 17–35.

Heine-Geldern, R., 1942, "Conceptions of State and Kingship in South East Asia", *FEQ*, 2, 1, 15–30.

Held, G., 1935, *The Mahabharata: An Ethnological Study*, London.

Henige, D.P., 1974, *The Chronology of Oral Tradition*, Oxford.

———, 1974, *Oral Tradition and History*, Oxford.

———, 1982, *Oral Historiography*, London.

Hettiarachchy, T., 1972, *History of Kingship in Ceylon upto the Fourth Century AD,* Colombo.

Hiltebeitel, A., 1976, *The Ritual of Battle*, Ithaca.

———, 1997, *Rethinking India's Oral and Classical Epics,* Chicago.

———, 2001, *Rethinking the Mahābhārata*, Chicago/Delhi.

———, 2005, "Buddhism and the Mahabharata", in F. Squarcini (ed.), *Boundaries, Dynamics and Construction of Traditions in South Asia*, Firenze.

———, 2006, "Aśvaghoṣa's *Buddhacarita:* The First Known Close and Careful Reading of the Brahmanical Sanskrit Epics", *JIP,* 34, 229–86.

Hindess, B. and P.Q. Hirst, 1975, *Pre-Capitalist Modes of Production*, London.

Hobsbawm, E.J., 1972, "The Social Function of the Past: Some Questions", *P and P*, 55, 3–18.

Hoffner, H.A., 1980, "History and Historians of the Ancient Near East: The Hittites", *Orientalia*, 49, 283–332.

Holt, J.C., 1991, *Buddha in the Crown: Avalokiteśvara in the Buddhist Tradition of Sri Lanka*, New York.

Hopkins, E.W., 1887, *The Social and Military Position of the Ruling Caste in Ancient India as Represented in the Sanskrit Epic*, *JAOS*, 13, 57ff.

———, 1920, *The Great Epic of India*, New Haven.

Horsch, P., 1966, *Die Vedische Gāthā und Śloka Literateur*, Bern.

Huang, C.C., 2007, "The Defining Characteristics of Chinese Historical Thinking", *HT*, 48, 180–8.

Huizinga, J., 1963, "A Definition of the Concept of History", in R. Klibansky and H.J. Paton (eds), *Philosophy and History*, New York.

Hultzsch, E., 1886, "Bhagalpur Plate of Narayanapāla", *Ind. Ant.*, 15, 304ff.

Huntington, C.W., Jr., 2007, "History, Traditions and Truth", *HR*, 46, 3, 187–227.

Imam, Abu, 1966, *Alexander Cunningham and the Beginnings of Indian Archaeology*, Dacca.

Inden, R., 1982, "Hierarchies of Kings in Medieval India", in T.N. Madan (ed.), *Way of Life: King, Householder, Renouncer: Essays in Honour of Louis Dumont,* New Delhi.

———, 1986, "Orientalist Construction of India", *MAS,* 20, 3, 401–46.

———, 1990, *Imagining India*, Oxford.

———, 2000, "Imperial Purāṇas: Kashmir as Vaiṣṇava Center of the Words", in R. Inden, *et al.* (eds), *Querying the Medieval*, Oxford.

Irwin, J., 1973, "Aśokan Pillars", *Burlington Magazine*, 115, 706–7.

Jacobi, H., 1976 (rpnt), *Das Rāmāyaṇa: Geschichte und Inhalt nebst Concordans der gedruckten Recensionen,* Bonn.

Jain, J.P., 2005, *The Jaina Sources of the History of Ancient India*, Delhi.

Jaini, P.S., 1979, *The Jaina Path of Purification*, Berkeley.

———, 1984, "Mahābhārata Motifs in the Jaina Padma Purāṇa", *BSOAS*, 47, 1, 108–15.

———, 1993, "Jaina Purāṇas: A Puranic Counter Tradition", in W. Doniger (ed.), *Purana Perennis*, New York.

Jayanta, B., 2005, *Much Ado About Religion*, New York.

Jayaswal, K.P., 1934, *An Imperial History of India*, Lahore.

Jeganathan, P., 1995, "Authorizing History: Ordering Land: The Conquest of Anuradhapura", in P. Jeganathan and Q. Ismail (eds), *Unmaking the Nation: The Politics of Identity and History in Modern Sri Lanka*, Colombo.

Jha, D.N. (ed.), 2000, *The Feudal Order*, New Delhi.

Jha, V.N., 1970, "Varṇasaṃkara in the Dharmasūtras: Theory and Practice", *JESHO*, 13, III, 273–88.

Johnson, M.D., 1969, *The Purpose of Biblical Genealogies*, Cambridge.

Jones, D.H., 1970, "Problems of African Chronology", *JAH*, 11, 161–76.

Jones, W., 1788 (delivered in 1786), "Third Anniversary Discourse", *Asiatic Researches*, 2, 415ff.

———, 1788, "On the Gods of Greece, Italy and India", *Asiatic Researches*, 1, 221–75.

———, 1794, "On the Chronology of the Hindus", *Asiatic Researches*, 2, 111–47.

———, 1799, "On the Mystical Poetry of the Persians and Hindus", *Asiatic Researches*, 5, 165–83.

Joshi, J.P., 1978, "Interlocking of Late Harappan Culture and PGW Culture in the Light of Recent Excavations", *Man and Environment*, 1, 100ff.

Joshi, M.C., 1979–80, "Ayodhya: Mythical and Real", *Puratattva*, 11, 107–9.

Justin, 1896, *Historiae Philippicae*, quoted in J.W. McCrindle (trans.), *The Invasion of India by Alexander the Great*, Westminster.

Kailasapathy, K., 1968, *Tamil Heroic Poetry*, Oxford.

Kane, P.V., 1935, "Gotra and Pravara in Vedic Literature", *JBBRAS* (n.s.), II, 1–17.

———, 1974 (2nd edn), *History of Dharmasastras*, vol. II, Poona.

Kantawala, S.G., 1964, *Cultural History from the Matsya Purana*, Baroda.

Kantorowicz, E.H., 1957, *The King's Two Bodies*, New Jersey.

Kantowsky, D., 1982, "Max Weber on India and Indian Interpretations of Weber", *Contributions*, 16 (n.s.), 141–74.

———, 1984, "Max Weber's Contributions", *Contributions*, 18 (n.s.), 307–17.

——— (ed.), 1986, *Recent Research on Max Weber's Studies on Hinduism*, Munich.

Kapoor, N. Sinha, 2005, "State Formation in Vidarbha: The Core of the Eastern Vākāṭakas", *IHR*, XXXII, 2, 13.

Karmakar, R.D., 1952, "The Pāriplava at the Aśvamedha", *ABORI*, 33, 26–40.

Kashikar, C.G., 1968, *A Survey of the Śrauta-sūtras*, Bombay.

Keith, A.B, 1925, *Religion and Philosophy of the Vedas and Upanisads*, Cambridge, Mass.

———, 1928, *History of Sanskrit Literature*, Oxford.

———, 1971 (rpnt), *Ṛgveda Brahmanas*, Delhi.
Kejariwal, O.P., 1988, *The Asiatic Society of Bengal and the Discovery of India's Past*, Delhi.
Kennedy, V., 1831, *Researches into the Nature and Affinity of Ancient and Hindu Mythology*, London.
Kielhorn, F., 1888, "Four Rewah Copper-Plate Inscriptions", *Ind. Ant.*, XVII, 230–6.
———, 1896, "Ichchhavar Plates of Parmardideva", *Ind. Ant.*, XXV, 205–8.
King, R., 1999, *Indian Philosophy*, Edinburgh.
Kiparsky, P., 1976, "Oral Poetry: Some Linguistic and Typographical Considerations", in B.A. Stolz and R.S. Shanon (eds), *Oral Literature and the Formulae*, Ann Arbor.
Kiribamune, S., 1978, "The *Mahāvaṃsa*: A Study of the Ancient Historiography of Sri Lanka", in L. Prematilake, *et al.* (eds), *Senerath Paranavitana Commemoration Volume*, Leiden.
———, 1979, "The Dīpavaṃsa in Ancient Sri Lankan Historiography", *SLJH*, V, 1 and 2, 89–100.
———, 1993, "Buddhist Historiography: Sri Lankan Perception", in S.A.I. Tirmizi (ed.), *Cultural Interaction in South Asia: A Historical Perspective*, New Delhi.
———, 1995, "The State and Sangha in Pre-modern Sri Lanka", *Ethnic Studies Report,* XIII, 1, 47–76.
Kirk, G., 1965, *Homer and the Epic*, Cambridge.
Kosambi, D.D., 1956, *An Introduction to the Study of Indian History*, Bombay.
———, 1956–7, "Origins of Feudalism in Kashmir", *JBBRAS,* 31–2, 108–20.
———, 1962, *Myth and Reality*, Bombay.
———, 1964, "The Autochthonous Element in the *Mahābhārata*", *JAOS*, 84, 31–44.
———, 1965, *The Culture and Civilisation of Ancient India in Historical Outline*, London.
———, 1969, *Ancient India: A History of its Culture and Civilisation*, New York.
———, 2009, "Early Brahmins and Brahminism", in B.D. Chattopadhyaya (ed.), *D.D. Kosambi: Combined Methods in Indology and Other Writings*, Delhi.
———, 2009, "On the Origin of Brahmana Gotras", in B.D. Chattopadhyaya (ed.), *D.D. Kosambi: Combined Methods in Indology and Other Writings*, Delhi.

Koskikallio, P. (ed.), 2009, *Parallels and Comparisons,* Zagreb.
Krader, L., 1975, *The Asiatic Mode of Production*, Assen.
Kuiper, F.B.J., 1991, *Aryans in the R̥gveda*, Amsterdam.
Kulkarni, V.M., 1960–1, "Origin and Development of the Rama Story in Jaina Literature", *JOI (Baroda)*, IX, 2, 189–204.
———, 1990, *The Story of Rama in Jaina Literature*, Ahmedabad.
Kulke, H., 1979, "Geshicteschreibung und Geshictesbild in Hinduistechen Mittelalter", *Saeculum*, 30, 100–13.
——— (ed.), 1995, *The State in India, 1000–1700*, Delhi.
———, 2001, "Historiography in Early Medieval India", in G. Berkemer, *et al.* (eds), *Explorations in the History of South Asia: In Honour of Dietmar Rothermund,* Delhi, 71–83.
———, 2001, *Kings and Cults: State Formation and Legitimation in India and South Asia*, Delhi.
Kumari, V., 1968, *The Nīlamata Purāṇa*, Jammu.
Lad, G., 1983, *Mahābhārata and Archaeological Evidence,* Poona.
Lahiry, S.P., 1955, "Bhaturiya Inscription of Rājyapāla", *IHQ,* 31, 215–31.
Lal, B.B., 1954–5, "Excavation at Hastinapur and Other Explorations in the Upper Ganga and Sutlej Basins", *Ancient India*, 10 and 11, 4ff.
———, 1978–9, "Was Ayodhya a Mythical City?", *Puratattva*, 10, 45–9.
———, 1981, "The Two Indian Epics vis-à-vis Archaeology", *Antiquity*, LV, 27–34.
———, 1988, "Historicity of the Mahabharata and the Ramayana: What has Archaeology to Say in the Matter", paper presented at the International Seminar on New Archaeology and India, Indian Council of Historical Research, New Delhi.
Lal, V., 2003, *The History of History: Politics and Scholarship in Modern India*, Delhi.
Lambert, W.G. and A.R. Millard, 1969, *Atra-hasis,* Oxford.
Lamotte, E., 1958, *Histoire du Bouddhisme Indien*; Sara Webb-Boin (trans.), 1988, *History of Indian Buddhism*, Louvain.
Lassen, C., 1858–74, *Indische Alterthumskunde*, vol. I, Leipzig.
Law, B.C., 1930, *A Study of the Mahāvastu*, Calcutta.
———, 1941, *A Manual of Buddhist Historical Tradition*, Calcutta.
———, 1946, *Buddhaghoṣa*, *JBBRAS*, Monograph 1, Bombay.
Leach, E., 1990, "Aryan Invasions over Four Millennia", in E. Ohnuki-Tierney (ed.), *Culture Through Time*, Stanford.
Leelashantakumari, S., 1986, *History of the Agraharas: Karnataka, 400–1300*, Madras.

Lefeber, R., 1990, "The Minister Cāṇakya, from the *Pariśiṣṭaparvan* of Hemacandra", in P. Granoff (ed.), *The Clever Adulteress and Other Stories: A Treasury of Jaina Literature*, Oakville.

LeGoff, J. and P. Nora (eds), 1985, *Constructing the Past*, Cambridge.

Levi, S., 1923, "Deux nouveaux traits de dramaturgie Indienne", *Journal Asiatique*, CCIII, 193–218.

Levitt, S.H., 1976, "A Note on the Compound *Pañcalakṣaṇa* in Amarasiṅha's *Nāmalingānuśasāna*", *Purāṇa*, 18, 1, 5–38.

Lewalski, B.K., 1985, *Milton's Paradise Lost and the Rhetoric of Literary Forms*, Princeton.

———, 1986, *Renaissance Genres: Essays in Theory, History and Interpretation*, Cambridge (Mass.).

Ling, T., 1973, *The Buddha*, London.

Lingat, R., 1989, *Royautes Bouddhiques*, Paris.

Lord, A.B., 1960, *The Singer of Tales*, Cambridge (Mass.).

Lorenzen, D.N., 1972, *The Kāpālikas and Kālāmukhas*, Delhi.

———, 1982, "Imperialism and the Historiography of Ancient India", in S.N. Mukherjee (ed.), *India—History and Thought: Essays in Honour of A.L. Basham*, Calcutta.

MacDonell, A.A., 1900, *History of Sanskrit Literature*, London.

—— and A.B. Keith, 1967 (rpnt), *The Vedic Index*, vols I and II, Delhi.

Mahadevam, I., 2003, *Early Tamil Epigraphy from the Earliest Times to the Sixth Century AD*, Cambridge (Mass.).

Majeed, J., 1992, *Ungoverned Imaginings*, Oxford.

Majumdar, R.C., 1935, "The Revolt of Divokka against Mahipāla II and Other Revolts in Bengal", *Dacca University Studies*, 1, 2, 125ff.

———, 1943, *History of Bengal*, vol. I, Dacca.

———, 1961, "Ideas of History in Sanskrit Literature", in C.H. Philips (ed.), *Historians of India, Pakistan, and Ceylon*, London, 13–28.

—— and A.S. Altekar (eds), 1946, *New History of the Indian People*, vol. VI, Lahore.

Malalasekera, G.P., 1958, *The Pali Literature of Ceylon*, Colombo.

———, 1960, *Dictionary of Pali Proper Names*, London.

Malamoud, C., 1996, *Cooking the World*, Delhi.

Malinar, A., 2007, *The Bhāgavad Gītā: Doctrines and Contexts*, Cambridge.

Marshall, J., 1915, "Excavations at Bhīṭa", *ASIAR 1911–12*, Calcutta, 44–60.

Marx, K., 1975 (rpnt), "The Future Results of British Rule in India", in *Karl Marx, Friedrich Engels: Collected Works*, vol. 12, 217–22.

Matilal, B.K., 1989, *Moral Dilemmas in the Mahabharata*, Shimla.
———, 1999, *The Character of Logic in India*, Delhi.
Mauss, M. (trans.), 1954, *The Gift*, London.
McCrindle, J.W., 1892, *The Invasion of India by Alexander the Great*, Westminster.
Mehendale, A., 1973, "The Puranas", in R.C. Majumdar (ed.), *The History and Culture of the Indian People, Vol. III: The Classical Age*, Bombay.
———, 1988, Review of "Yardi, M.R., 1986, *The Māhabhārata: Its Genesis and Growth*", *ABORI*, 69, 349–55.
Meisami, J.S., 1999, *Persian Historiography to the End of the Twelfth Century*, Edinburgh.
Mendis, G.C., 1996, *The Pali Chronicles of Ceylon*, Colombo.
Mill, J., 1817, *The History of British India,* London.
Miller, B. Stoler, 1971, *Phantasies of a Love Thief*, New York.
Minkowski, C.Z., 1989, "Janamejaya's Sattra and Ritual Structure", *JAOS*, 109, 3, 401–20.
———, 1991, "Snakes, Sattras and the Mahābhārata", in A. Sharma (ed.), *Essays on the Mahabharata*, Delhi.
Mitchiner, J.E., 1978, "The Evolution of the Manvantara Theory as Illustrated by the *Saptarṣi* Manvantara Traditions", *Purāṇa*, 20, 1, 7–37.
———, 1986, *The Yuga Purāṇa*, Calcutta.
Mitra, R.L., 1874, "Note on Palam Baoli Inscription of Delhi", *JASB*, 43, 1, 104–10.
Mitra, S.K., 1958, *The Early Rulers of Khajuraho*, Calcutta.
Mohan, K., 1981, *Early Medieval History of Kashmir*, New Delhi.
Momigliano, A., 1958, "The Place of Herodotus in the History of Historiography", *History*, 43, 1–13.
———, 1963, "Christianity and the Decline of the Roman Empire", in A. Momigliano (ed.), *The Conflict between Paganism and Christianity in the Fourth Century*, Oxford.
———, 1974, "Polybius and Posidonius", *Historicism Revisited*, MKN, Akademie van Wetenschappen, Aftd. Letterkunde, Nieuwe Reeks, Decl., 37, 3, 63–70.
———, 1975, *Alien Wisdom: The Limits of Hellenisation*, Cambridge.
———, 1978, "Greek Historiography", *HT*, 17, 1, 1–23.
———, 1981, "History and Biography", in M. Finley (ed.), *Legacy of the Greeks,* Oxford.
———, 1990, *The Classical Foundations of Modern Historiography*, Berkeley.

———, 1993 (revised edn), *The Development of Greek Biography*, Cambridge (Mass.).

Monier Williams, M., 1863, *Indian Epic Poetry*, London.

Morris, I., 1986, "The Use and Abuse of Homer", *Classical Antiquity*, 5, 1, 81–138.

Morris, R. (ed.), 1882, *The Buddhavaṃsa and the Cariya-piṭaka*, B.C. Law (trans.), 1938, London.

Morrison, B.M., 1970, *Political Centres and Culture Regions in Early Bengal,* Tucson.

Morton-Smith, R., 1973, *Dates and Dynasties in Earliest India*, Delhi.

Mughal, M.R., 1997, *Ancient Cholistan*, Lahore.

Mukherjee, S.N., 1968, *Sir William Jones: A Study in Eighteenth Century British Attitudes to India*, Cambridge.

Müller, M., 1859, *A History of Ancient Sanskrit Literature*, London.

———, 1868, *Chips from a German Workshop*, vol. I, London.

———, 1883, *India: What Can it Teach Us?*, London.

Munshi, S., 1988, "Max Weber on India: An Introductory Critique", *Contributions*, 22, 1, 1–30.

Murthy, S.S.N., 2003, "The Questionable Historicity of the Mahābhārata, *EJVS*, 10, 5, 1–15.

Murti, T.V.R., 1960, *The Central Philosophy of Buddhism*, London.

Mus, P., 1935, *Barabudur: Esquisse d'une Histoire du Bouddhisme fondee sur la Critique Archaeologique des texts,* 2 vols, Hanoi.

Nakamura, H., 1957, "The Influence of Confucian Ethics on the Chinese Translation of Buddhist Sutras", *Sino-Indian Studies*, 5, 3–4, 156–70.

———, 1989 (rpnt), *Indian Buddhism*, Delhi.

Nandy, A., 1995, "History's Forgotten Doubles", *HT*, 34, 2, 44–66.

Nanyaura Plate A of Dhaṅga, 1887, *Ind. Ant.*, XVI, 201–4.

Narayanan, M.G.S., 1969/1972, "Mūṣakavamśa-kāvya of Atula", *Proceedings of the All India Orientalist Congress,* Calcutta/Poona.

Nora, P., 1989, "Between Memory and History: Les Lieux de Memoire", *Representations*, 26, 7–24.

Norman, K.R., 1983, *Pali Literature*, Wiesbaden.

O'Leary, B., 1995, *The Asiatic Mode of Production*, London.

Oberoi, H., 1994, *The Construction of Religious Boundaries: Culture, Identity, and Diversity in the Sikh Tradition*, Chicago.

Obeyesekere, G., 1991, "Myth, History and Numerology in the Buddhist Chronicles", in H. Bechert (ed.), *The Dating of the Historical Buddha*, vol. I, Goettingen.

Ohira, S., 1994, *A Study of the Bhagvatīsutra: A Chronological Analysis*, Ahmedabad.

Ohri, V.C. (ed.), 1989, *History and Culture of the Chamba State*, New Delhi.

———, 1991, *Sculpture of the Western Himalayas: History and Stylistic Development*, Delhi.

Oliver, R.T., 1971, *Communication and Culture in Ancient India and China*, Syracuse.

Ong, W.J., 1982, *Orality and Literacy*, London.

Pai, M.G. and S.K. Manjeshwar, 1960, "The Word *Vṛṣala* in Mudāarākṣasa", in H.L. Hariyappa and M.M. Patkar (eds), *Professor P.K. Gode Commemoration Volume*, Poona.

Pande, G.C., 1974 (2nd edn), *Studies in the Origin of Buddhism*, Delhi.

Pandia, M.V. and S.S. Das (eds), 1904–13, *The Pṛthvīrāja Rāsau of Chand Bardai* (Nagari Pracharani Granthamala Series), nos 4–22, Benaras.

Pandit, R.S. (ed.), 1944, *Viśākhadatta's Mudrārākṣasa or The Signet Ring*, Bombay.

Pargiter, F.E., 1910, "Ancient Indian Genealogies and Chronology", *JRAS*, 1–56.

———, 1914, "Earliest Indian Traditional History", *JRAS*, s. 3, 265–95; 741–45.

———, 1922, *Ancient Indian Historical Tradition*, London.

———, 1975 (rpnt), *The Purana Text of the Dynasties of the Kali Age*, Delhi.

Parpola, A., 1994, *Deciphering the Indus Script*, Cambridge.

Parry, A. (ed.), 1971, *The Making of Homeric Verse: The Collected Papers of Milman Parry*, Oxford.

Patel, M., 1961, *Die Dānastutis des Rigveda*, B.H. Kapadia (trans.), *The Danastutis of the Rig Veda*, Vallabha Vidyanagar.

Pathak, V.S., 1966, *Ancient Historians of India*, Bombay.

Patil, D.R., 1946, *Cultural History from Vayu Purana*, Poona.

Patvardhan, M.V., 1964–5, "Pañcajana", *JBBRAS*, 39–40, 169–82.

Perera, L.S., 1961, "The Pali Chronicles of Ceylon", in C.H. Philips (ed.), *Historians of India, Pakistan and Ceylon*, London.

———, 2001, *The Institutions of Ancient Ceylon from Inscriptions, Vol. I: 3rd cent. BC to 830 AD*, Kandy.

Petech, L., 1939, *A Study of the Chronicles of Ladakh*, Calcutta.

Peters, E., 1960, "The Proliferation of Segments in the Lineage of the Bedouin of Cyrenaica", *JRAIGBI*, 90, 29–53.

Philips, C.H. (ed.), 1961, *Historians of India, Pakistan and Ceylon*, London.

Pingree, D., 1963, "Astronomy and Astrology in India and Iran", *Isis*, 54, 229–40.

———, 1990, "The Purāṇas and Jyotiḥśāstra: Astronomy", *JAOS*, 110, 2, 274–80.

Plutarch, 1919, *Life of Alexander*, London; selections in J.W. McCrindle (trans.), 1896, *The Invasion of India by Alexander the Great*, Westminster.

Poliokov, L., 1974, *The Aryan Myth,* New York.

Pollock, S., 1989, "Mīmāṃsā and the Problem of History in Traditional India", *JAOS*, 109, 4, 603–10.

———, 1993, "Rāmāyaṇa and Political Imagination in India", *JAS*, 52, 2, 261–97.

———, 1996, "The Sanskrit Cosmopolis, 300–1300 CE : Transculturation, Vernacularisation, and the Question of Ideology", in J.E.M. Houben (ed.), *Ideology and Status of Sanskrit: Contributions to the History of the Sanskrit Language*, New York.

———, 1998, "The Cosmopolitan Vernacular", *JAS*, 57, 1, 6–37.

———, 2007, *The Language of the Gods in the World of Men*, Delhi.

———, *et al.*, 2007, "Debate on *Textures of Time*", *HT*, 46, 364–426.

Pradhan, S.N., 1927, *Chronology of Ancient India*, Calcutta.

Prasad, P., 1990, *Sanskrit Inscriptions of Delhi Sultanate 1191–1526*, Delhi.

Press, G.A., 1977, "History of the Development of the Idea of History in Antiquity", *HT,* 16, 280–96.

Propp, V., 1968, *The Morphology of the Folktale* (trans.), Austin.

———, 1984, *Theory and History of Folklore* (trans.), Minneapolis.

Przyluski, J., 1923, *La Legende de l'Empereur Asoka*, Paris.

Pusalker, A.D. (ed.), 1952, *History and Culture of the Indian People, Vol. I: The Vedic Age*, Bombay.

———, 1958, *Studies in the Epics and Purāṇas*, Bombay.

Raaflaub, K.A., 2005, "Epic and History", in J.M. Foley (ed.), *A Companion to Ancient Epic*, Malden.

——— (ed.), 2012, *Thinking, Recording and Writing History in the Ancient World*, Oxford.

Raeside, I.M.P., 1992, "A Gujarati Bardic Poem: The Kanhadade Prabandha", in C. Shackle and R. Snell (eds), *The Indian Narrative: Perspectives and Patterns*, Wiesbaden.

Raghavan, V., 1948, *The Mudrārākṣasa of Mahādeva*, Tanjore.

Rahurkar, V.G., 1960, "Devāpi and Śantanu in the Ṛg Veda", in H.L. Hatiyappa, and M.M. Patkar (eds), *P.K. Gode Commemoration Volume*, pt III, Poona.

Rangachari, D., 2009, *Invisible Women, Visible Histories*, Delhi.
Rank, Otto, 1959, *The Myth of the Birth of the Hero*, New York.
Rao, G., 1920, "Extracts from the Mushika-vamsam", in *Travancore Archaeological Series*, II.1.10, 87–113.
Rao, V. Narayana, 1993, "Purāṇa as Brahminic Ideology", in W. Doniger (ed.), *Purana Perennis,* New York.
———, Sanjay Subrahmanyam, and David Shulman, 2000, *Textures of Time: Writing History in South India 1600–1800*, Delhi.
Rapson, E.J. (ed.), 1922, *The Cambridge History of India,* vol. I, Cambridge.
Rau, W., 1973, "The Meaning of *Pur* in Vedic Literature", *Abhandlungen der Marburger Gelehrten Geselleschaft*, III.I, Munich.
Ray, H.C., 1931–6, *Dynastic History of Northern India*, 2 vols, Calcutta.
Ray, N., 1994, *History of the Bengali People (Ancient Period),* Delhi.
Raychaudhuri, H.C., 1923, *Political History of Ancient India*, Calcutta.
Redfield, J., 1975, *Nature and Culture in the Iliad: The Tragedy of Hector*, Chicago.
Renan, E., 1890, "L'avenir de la Science", *Ouvres*, III, 728ff.
Renou, L., 1956, *Études Vediques et Paninéennes*, Paris.
———, 1965, *The Destiny of the Veda* (trans.), Delhi.
Rewa Grants of 1240–1, 1888, *Ind. Ant.*, XVII, 230–6.
Rhys Davids, T.W., 1963 (rpnt), *The Questions of King Milinda*, New York.
—— and C.A.F. Rhys Davids, 1973 (rpnt) *Buddhist Birth Stories*, Delhi.
Risley, H., 1908, *The People of India,* London.
Rocher, L., 1986, *The Purāṇas*, Wiesbaden.
Rosenfield, J.M., 1967, *The Dynastic Arts of the Kushans*, Berkeley.
Rosenthal, F., 1970, *Ibn Khaldun: The Muqaddimah,* Princeton.
Roth, G., 2004, "Ayodhyā and Ganga", in H.W. Bodewitz and Minoru Hara (eds), *Gedenkschrift J.W. de Jong*, Tokyo.
Roy, K., 1988, "Women and Men Donors at Sanchi: A Study in Inscriptional Evidence", in L.K. Tripathi (ed.), *Position and Status of Women in Ancient India*, Varanasi.
Roy, S.N., 1972, "Textual and Historical Analysis of the Puranic Chronology Relating to the Maurya Dynasty", *Purāṇa*, 14, 2, 94–106.
Ruesen, J., 2002, *Western Historical Thinking*, Oxford.
Rufus, Q.C., 1896, *History of Alexander the Great*; selections in J.W. McCrindle (trans.), *The Invasion of India by Alexander the Great,* Westminster.
Sahlins, M.D., 1961, "The Segmentary Lineage: An Organisation of Predatory Expansion", *American Anthropologist*, 63, 2, 332–45.

———, 1985, *Islands of History*, Chicago.
Said, E., 1978, *Orientalism*, London.
Salomon, R., 1998, *Indian Epigraphy*, Austin.
———, 2009, "The Fine Art of Forgery", in G. Colas and G. Gerschheimer (eds), *Écrire et Transmettre en Inde Classique*, Paris.
Sanderson, A., 2004, "Religion and the State: Śaiva Officiants in the Territory of the King's Brahmanical Chaplain", *IIJ*, 47, 229–300.
Sankalia, H.D., 1982, *Ramayana: Myth or Reality*, New Delhi.
Sarukkai, S., 2008, *Indian Philosophy and the Philosophy of Science*, New Delhi.
Sastri, H., 1942, "Nalanda and its Epigraphic Material", *MASI*, no. 66, 49–53.
Schopen, G., 1997, *Bones, Stones and Buddhist Monks*, Honolulu.
———, 2004, *Buddhist Monks and Business Matters*, Honolulu.
Schwab, R., 1950, *La Renaissance Orientale*, Paris.
Selvanayagam, I., 1992, "Aśoka and Arjuna as Counter-figures Standing on the Field of Dharma: A Historical-Hermeneutical Perspective", *HR*, 32, 1, 59–75.
Sen, K.C., 1923, *Keshab Chandra Sen's Lectures in India*, Calcutta.
Sen, N., 1966, "Comparative Studies in Oral Epic Poetry and the Vālmīki Rāmāyaṇa: A Report on the Bālakāṇḍa", *JAOS*, 86, 397–409.
Sen, S.P., 1970, *Sources for the History of India*, Calcutta.
Seneviratne, H.L., 1999, *The Work of Kings*, Chicago.
Seneviratne, S., 1984, "The Archaeology of the Megalithic—Black and Red Ware Complex in Sri Lanka", *Ancient Ceylon*, no. 5, 237–307.
———, 1996, "Peripheral Regions and Marginal Communities: Towards an Alternative Explanation of Early Iron Age Material and Social formations in Sri Lanka", in R. Champakalakshmi and S. Gopal (eds), *Tradition, Dissent and Ideology*, 266–70.
Settar, S. and G.D. Sontheimer (eds), 1982, *Memorial Stones*, Dharwar.
Shah, A.M., and R.G. Shroff, 1959, "The Vahivanca Barots of Gujarat: A Caste of Genealogists and Mythographers", in M. Singer (ed.), *Traditional India*, Chicago.
Shah, K.K., 1986, "Economic Revolution in Early Medieval Bundelkhand", *Punjab University Research Bulletin (Arts)*, 17, 2, 167–74.
———, 1987, "Social Structure in Candella Grants", *JESI*, 14, 28–34.
———, 1988, *Ancient Bundelkhand*, Delhi.
———, 1993, "Self-Legitimation and Social Primacy: A Case Study of Some Kayastha Inscriptions from Central India", *Proceedings of the Indian History Congress*, no. 54, Mysore, 857–66.
———, 2001, *The Problem of Identity: Women in Early Indian Inscriptions*, Delhi.

Shah, U.P. and M.A. Dhaky (eds), 1975, *Aspects of Jaina Art and Architecture,* Ahmedabad.

Sharma, A. (ed.), 1991 (rpnt)., *Essays on the Mahabharata*, Delhi.

———, 2003, *Hinduism and its Sense of History*, New Delhi.

Sharma, B.R., 1959, "The Pañca-janas in the Vedas", *JBBRAS* (n.s.), 31 and 32, 244–64.

Sharma, M., 2004, "State Formation and Cultural Complex in Western Himalaya: Chamba, Genealogy and Epigraphs 700–1650 CE", *IESHR*, 41, 387–432.

———, 2006, "Contested Claims: Land, Ritual and the Jogis of Charpaṭnath" (New Documents from Chamba), *IESHR*, 43,4, 488–510.

Sharma, R.S., 1965/1980, *Indian Feudalism*, Calcutta/Delhi.

———, 2001, *Early Medieval Indian Society*, Delhi.

Shastri, A.M., 1998, *The Sātavāhanas and the Western Kṣatrapas*, Nagpur.

Shende, N.J., 1943, "The Authorship of the Māhabhārata", *ABORI*, 24, 67–82.

———, 1943, "The Authorship of the Rāmāyaṇa", *JUB*, 12 (n.s.), 2, 19–24.

Shokoohy, M., 1988, "Haryana I: The Column of Firuz Shah and Other Islamic Inscriptions from the District of Hissar", *Corpus Inscriptionum Iranicum,* part IV: Persian Inscriptions down to the Early Safavid Period, vol. XLVII, India, State of Haryana, London.

Siegal, J., 1979, *Shadow and Sound: The Historical Thought of a Sumatran People*, Chicago.

Silk, J., 2008, "Incestuous Ancestors: The Family Origins of Gautama Siddhartha, Abraham and Sarah in Genesis 20.12", *HR*, 47, 4, 253–81.

Singh, K.S. (ed.), 1993, *The People of India*, Delhi.

Singh, M.R., 1972, *Geographical Data in the Early Puranas*, Calcutta.

Sircar, D.C., 1957, "Some Performers of Aśvamedha", in K.K. Pillai, *et al.* (eds), *Professor P.S. Pillai Commemoration Volume*, Madras.

———, 1965, *Indian Epigraphy*, Calcutta.

———, 1965 (2nd edn), *Select Inscriptions*, Calcutta.

——— (ed.), 1969, *The Bharata War and Puranic Genealogies*, Calcutta.

———, 1969, "Myth of the Great Bharata War", in D.C. Sircar (ed.), *The Bharata War and Puranic Genealogies*, Calcutta.

———, 1969, *Problems of Kushana and Rajput History*, Calcutta.

———, 1971 (rpnt), *Studies in the Geography of Ancient and Medieval India*, Delhi.

———, 1974, *Studies in Yugapurāṇa and Other Texts*, Delhi.

———, 1977, *Early Indian Epigraphical and Numismatic Studies*, Calcutta.

Slaje, W., 2005, "A Note on the Genesis and Character of Śrivara's So-Called *Jaina-Rājataraṅgiṇī*", *JAOS*, 125, 3, 379–88.

———, 2008, "In the Guise of Poetry—Kalhaṇa Reconsidered", in W. Slaje, (ed.), *Śāstrārambha: Inquiries into the Preamble in Sanskrit,* Wiesbaden.

Smith, B.L. (ed.), 1978, *Religion and the Legitimation of Power in Sri Lanka*, Chambersberg.

Smith, M.C., 1975, "The Mahābhārata's Core", *JOAS*, 95, 479–82.

Smith, V., 1902, "Andhra History and Coinage", *ZDMG*, 56, 649–75.

———, 1924, *The Early History of India*, Oxford.

Southern, R.W., 1970, "Aspects of the European Tradition of Historical Writing", *Transactions of the Royal Historical Society*, 20, 173–96; continued in 1971, 21, 159–79; 1972, 22, 159–80; 1973, 23, 243–63.

Spiegel, G.M., 1997, *The Past as Text*, Baltimore.

Speiser, E.A., 1964, *Genesis*, New York.

Srimali, K.M., 1987, *Agrarian Structure in Central India and the Northern Deccan (c.* AD *300–500), A Study of Vākāṭaka Inscriptions*, New Delhi.

Staal, J.F., 1961, *Nambudri Vedic Recitation*, The Hague.

———, 1989, "The Independence of Rationality from Literacy", *European Journal of Sociology*, 30, 301–10.

———, 2008, *Discovering the Vedas: Origins, Mantras, Rituals, Insights*, Delhi.

Stein, B., 1969, "Early Indian Historiography: A Conspiracy Hypothesis", *IESHR*, 6, 1, 41–60.

———, 1977, "The Segmentary State in South Indian History", in R.G. Fox (ed.), *Realm and Region in Traditional India*, New Delhi.

Stevenson, S., 1970 (rpnt), *The Heart of Jainism,* New Delhi.

Stolz, B.A. and R.S. Shanon (eds), 1976, *Oral Literature and the Formulae*, Ann Arbor.

Strong, J., 1983, *The Legend of King Aśoka*, New Jersey.

Sukthankar, V.S., 1936–7, "The Bhṛgus and the Bhārata: A Text-Historical Study", *ABORI*, 18, 1–76.

———, 1957, *On the Meaning of the Mahābhārata*, Bombay.

Sullivan, B.M., 1990, *Krishna Dvaipayana Vyasa and the Mahabharata: A New Interpretation*, Leiden.

———, 1999, *Seer of the Fifth Veda*, Delhi.

Sumitra Bai, B.N. and R.J. Zydenbos, 1991, "The Jaina Mahābhārata", in A. Sharma (ed.), *Essays on the Mahabharata*, Delhi.

Sutton, N., 1997, "Aśoka and Yudhiṣṭhira: A Historical Setting for the Tensions in the Mahābhārata", *Religion*, 27, 4, 331–41.

Tessitori, L.P., 1914, 1919, 1920, "A Scheme for the Bardic and Historical Survey of Rajputana", *JASB* (n.s.), 10, 373–86; 15, 5–79; 16, 251–79.

———, 1917, "Bardic and Historical Survey of Rajputana: A Descriptive Catalogue of Bardic and Historical Manuscripts", in L.P. Tessitori (ed.) *Bibliotheca Indica: A Collection of Oriental Works*, Calcutta.

Thapar, R., 1978, *Exile and the Kingdom: Some Thoughts on the Rāmāyaṇa*, Bangalore.

———, 1978/2010 (2nd edn), *Ancient Indian Social History: Some Interpretations*, New Delhi.

———, 1981, "Death and the Hero", in S.C. Humphreys and H. King (eds), *Mortality and Immortality: The Anthropology and Archaeology of Death,* London.

———, 1982, "The Ramayana: Theme and Variation", in S.N. Mukherjee (ed.), *India: History and Thought*, Calcutta.

———, 1983, "The Archaeological Background to the Agnicayana", in F. Staal (ed.), *Agni*, II, Berkeley; rpnt in R. Thapar, 2008, *The Aryan: Recasting Constructs*, Delhi.

———, 1984, "The Mouse in the Ancestry", in S.D. Joshi (ed.), *Amṛtadhāra*, Pune, 427–34.

———, 1986, "Society and Historical Consciousness: The Itihāsa-Purāṇa Tradition", in S. Bhattacharya and R. Thapar (eds), *Situating Indian History*, Delhi.

———, 1989, "Epic and History: Tradition, Dissent and Politics in India", *P and P*, 125, 3–26.

———, 1990, "A Historical Perspective on the Story of Rama", in Sarvepalli Gopal (ed.), *Anatomy of a Confrontation*, New Delhi.

———, 1991, "Genealogical Patterns as Perceptions of the Past", *Studies in History*, January–June, 7, 1, 1–36.

———, 1997 (2nd edn), *Aśoka and the Decline of the Mauryas*, Delhi.

———, 2000, *Cultural Pasts*, Delhi.

———, 2000 (2nd edn), *From Lineage to State*, Delhi.

———, 2000 (2nd edn), *Interpreting Early India*, Delhi.

———, 2000, "The *Ṛgveda*: Encapsulating Social Change", in K.N. Pannikar, *et al.* (eds), *The Making of History*, Delhi.

———, 2000, "Sacrifice, Surplus and the Soul", The Foerster Lecture, Berkeley, in idem, *Cultural Pasts*, Delhi.

———, 2000, "Origin Myths and the Early Indian Historical Tradition", in idem, *Cultural Pasts,* 754–80.

———, 2000, *Time as a Metaphor of History*, Delhi.

———, 2001, "Perceiving the Forest: Early India", *Studies in History,* 17, 1, 1–16.

———, 2002, "The Role of the Army in the Exercise of Power in Early India", in A. Chaniotis and P. Ducrey (eds), *Army and Power in the Ancient World*, Stuttgart.

———, 2004, *Somanatha: The Many Voices of a History*, Delhi.

———, 2008, "Rāyā Asoko from Kanaganhalli: Some Thoughts", in *Airāvati*, Chennai, 249–62.

———, 2008/2011 (rpnt), *The Aryan: Recasting Constructs*, Gurgaon/ Delhi.

———, 2009, "The *Purāṇas*: Heresy and the *Vaṃśānucarita*", in I. Banerjee-Dube and S. Dube (eds), *Ancient to Modern: Religion, Power and Community in India,* Delhi.

———, 2009, "Variants as Historical Statements: The Rama-katha in Early India", in H.L. Seneviratne (ed.), *The Anthropologist and the Native: Essays for Gananath Obeyesekere*, Florence.

———, 2011, "Inscriptions as Historical Writing in Early India: Third Century BC to Sixth Century AD", in A. Feldherr and G. Hardy (eds), *The Oxford History of Historical Writing*, vol. I, Oxford.

———, 2011, "Was there Historical Writing in Early India?", in C. Talbot (ed.), *Knowing India*, Delhi.

Thompson, S., 1955–8, *Motif-Index of Folk Literature,* Bloomington.

Thomson, G., 1949, *Studies in Ancient Greek Society*, London.

Thorner, D., 1966, "Marx on India and the Asiatic Mode of Production", *Contributions*, X, 9, 33ff.

Tod, J., 1829/1960 (rpnt), *Annals and Antiquities of Rajasthan*, vol. I, London.

Tokunaga, M., 1993, "Structure of the *Rājadharma* Section in the *Yajñavalkya-smṛti*", *MFL*, Kyoto University, no. 32, Kyoto.

———, 2009, "Vedic Exegesis and Epic Poetry: A Note on *atrāpy udāharanti*", in P. Koskikallio (ed.), *Parallels and Comparisons*, Zagreb.

Trautmann, T., 1969, "Length of Generation and Reign in Ancient India", *JAOS*, 89, 3, 564–77.

———, 1971, *Kauṭilya and the Arthaśāstra*, Leiden.

———, 1981, *Dravidian Kinship,* Cambridge.

———, 1997, *Aryans and British India*, Berkeley.

Turnour, G., 1836, *An Epitome of the History of Ceylon Compiled from*

Native Annals; and the First Twenty Chapters of the Mahawanso, Cotta.

Unis, N.P., 1980, *A History of Mūṣikavamśa*, Trivandrum.

Upreti, K., 1995, *India as Reflected in the Divyāvadāna*, Delhi.

Utgikar, N.B., 1929, "Some Points of Contact between the Mahābhārata and the Jātakas", *JBBRAS* (n.s.), 4, 115–34.

Vaidya, C.V., 1906/1972 (rev. edn), *The Riddle of the Ramayana*, Poona/ Delhi.

Vajrācārya, D. and K.P. Malla (ed. and trans.), 1985, *The Gopālarājavaṃśāvalī*, Wiesbaden. Also see above, *Gopālarājavaṃśāvalī, The.*

Vansina, J., 1965, *The Oral Tradition*, London.

———, 1985, *Oral Tradition as History*, London.

Vassilkov, Y., 1995, "The Mahābhārata's Typological Definition Reconsidered", *IIJ*, 38, 249–56.

———, 2002, "Indian Practice of Pilgrimage and the Growth of the Mahabharata", in M. Brockington (ed.), *Stages and Transitions*, Zagreb.

Veyne, P., 1984, *Writing History*, Middletown.

———, 1988, *Did the Greeks Believe in their Myths?* Chicago.

Vogel, J. Ph., 1911, *Antiquities of Chamba State*, vol. I (ASI New Imperial Series), vol. 36, Calcutta.

von Fürer-Haimendorf, C., 1961, "The Historical Value of Indian Bardic Literature", in C.H. Philips (ed.), *Historians of India, Pakistan and Ceylon*, London.

Wagle, N.K., 2007, "Heroes in the Charitra-bhakhar, Povada and Akhyana of Seventeenth and Eighteenth Century Maharashtra", in H. Bruckner (ed.), *The Concept of Hero in Indian Culture*, Delhi.

Wagle, N.R., 1974, "A Study of Kinship Groups in the Ramayana of Valmiki", in G. Kurien (ed.), *The Family in India*, The Hague.

Waldman, M.R., 1980, *Towards a Theory of Historical Narrative*, Columbus.

Walters, J.S., 2000, "Buddhist History", in R. Inden, *et al.* (eds), *Querying the Medieval*, Oxford.

Wang, Q.E., 2007, "Is There a Chinese Mode of Historical Thinking? A Cross-Cultural Analysis", *HT*, 46, 201–9.

Warder, A.K., 1970, *Indian Buddhism*, Delhi.

———, 1972, *An Introduction to Indian Historiography*, Bombay.

———, 1974, *Indian Kavya Literature*, vol. II, Delhi.

Warren, H.C. and Dharmanand Kosambi (eds), 1950, *Visuddhimagga of Buddhaghosa*, Cambridge (Mass.).

Warriar, G., 1939, "Studies in the Mūṣaka-*vaṃśā*", *Rama Varma Research Institute Bulletin*, 7, 2, 118–31.

Waterfield, W., 1923/1990, *The Lay of Alha*, Gurgaon.

Watters, T., 1961/1973 (rpnt), *On Yuan Chwang's Travels in India*, vol. I, Delhi.

Weber, A., 1853, *Indische Literaturgesichte*, Berlin.

Weber, M., 1958, *The Religion of India: The Sociology of Hinduism and Buddhism*, Glencoe.

———, 1968 (rpnt), *Economy and Society*, vol. II, London.

Whaling, F., 1980, *The Rise of the Religious Significance of Rama*, Delhi.

White, D.G., 1996, *The Alchemical Body: Siddha Traditions in Medieval India*, Chicago.

Wijetunga, W.M.K., 1969–70, "The Spread of Heterodox Buddhist Doctrines in Early Ceylon", *The Ceylon Historical Journal*, 19, 14–28.

Wilford, F., 1799, "On the Chronology of the Hindus", *Asiatic Researches*, 5, 241–95.

———, 1809, "An Essay on the Sacred Isles in the West, with Other Essays Connected with that Work", *Asiatic Researches*, 8, 245ff.

Williams, B., 2002, *Truth and Truthfulness*, New Jersey.

Williams, J., 1973, "A Recent Aśokan Capital and the Gupta Attitude towards the Past", *Artibus Asiae*, 35, 225–40.

———, 1982, *The Art of Gupta India: Empire and Province*, New Jersey.

Wilson, H.H., 1828, *MacKenzie Collection: A Descriptive Catalogue*, 2 vols, Calcutta.

———, 1838, "Analysis of the Puranas", *JRAS*, V, 61ff.

———, 1960 (rpnt), *The Hindu History of Kashmir*, Calcutta.

Winternitz, M., 1977/1991 (rpnts), *History of Indian Literature*, 2 vols, Delhi.

Witzel, M., 1989, "Tracing the Vedic Dialects", in C. Caillat (ed.), *Dialectes dans les literatures Indo-Aryennes*, Paris.

———, 1990, "On Indian Historical Writing", *Journal of the Japanese Association for South Asian Studies*, 2, 1–57.

———, 1999, "Substrate Languages in Old Indo-Aryan (Rigvedic, Middle and Later Vedic)", *EJVS*, 5, 1, 1–67.

———, 2005, "The Vedas and the Epics: Some Comparative Notes on Persons, Lineages, Geography and Grammar", in P. Koskikallio (ed.), *Epics, Khilas and Puranas: Continuities and Ruptures*, Zagreb.

Woodward, F.W. and E.M. Hare (trans.), 1932, *The Book of Gradual Sayings*, London.

Wright, J.C., 1967, "Purūravas and Urvaśī", *BSOAS*, 30, 526–47.

Yadav, B.N.S., 1978, "The Accounts of the Kali Age and the Social Transition from Antiquity to the Middle Ages", *IHR*, 5, 1 and 2, 31–63.

———, 1973, *Society and Culture in Northern India in the Twelfth Century,* Allahabad.

Yajnik, M.N., 1930, *Genealogical Tables of the Solar and Lunar Dynasties*, Baroda.

Yamamoto, K., 2003, *The Oral Background of Persian Epics: Story-telling and Poetry,* Leiden.

Zaehner, R., 1961, *The Dawn and Twilight of Zoroastrianism*, New York.

Ziegler, N., 1976, "Marwari Historical Chronicles", *IESHR,* 13, 2, 219ff.

———, 1976, "The Seventeenth Century Chronicles of Marvara: A Study in the Evolution and Use of Oral Tradition in Western India", *History in Africa*, 3, 127–53.

Zurcher, E., 1959, *The Buddhist Conquest of China*, Leiden.

Index